JOHN TOMLINSON
COPYRIGHT 1994

San Francisco: The Ultimate Guide

RANDOLPH DELEHANTY

•

Drawings by WILLIAM WALTERS
Bird's-eye views by JOHN TOMLINSON

CHRONICLE BOOKS
SAN FRANCISCO

Printed in the United States of America.

Library of Congress Cataloging-in-Publication Data:
Delehanty, Randolph.
    San Francisco : the ultimate guide / by Randolph Delehanty.
        p.   cm.
    Includes bibliographical references and index.
    ISBN 0-8118-0443-7
    1. San Francisco (Calif.)—Guidebooks.   I. Title
    F869.S33D43   1995
    917.94'610453—dc20   94-17964
                                          CIP

Editing: Carey Charlesworth
Book design: Jill Jacobson
Cover design: Michael Schwab

Distributed in Canada by Raincoast Books,
8680 Cambie Street, Vancouver, B.C. V6P 6M9

10 9 8 7 6 5 4 3

Chronicle Books
85 Second Street
San Francisco, CA 94105

Web Site: www.chronbooks.com

for **PETER M. HIRSCH**
SAN FRANCISCAN

•

and for my grandmother
CARLOTA URRUELA DE LARRONDO
1894–1981
who opened my mind
to history

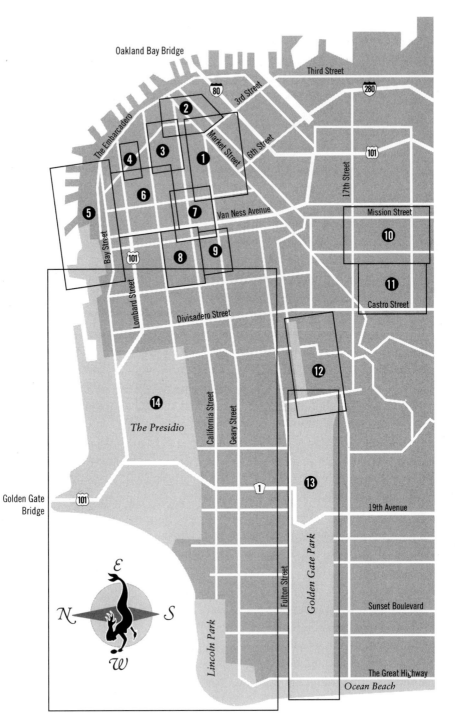

Key Map

Contents

Thanks and Acknowledgments

Many who visit San Francisco come back here to live. It happened to me. I first visited San Francisco with my parents in 1962 upon graduation from high school. I chose San Francisco as my home in 1970 and lived here until 1993. I never tire of her expressive people, her dramatic landforms, and her changing skies. My most heartfelt acknowledgment is to the city among whose people it was my good fortune to live and work during the best years of my early manhood. The French say that one always returns to one's first love, and perhaps that will be true for me.

My rewards have always come from readers, students, clients, editors, and friends—not mutually exclusive categories—who have asked me good questions and found ways to be supportive of my work. I am especially appreciative of the support my work has received from Mr. William M. Roth, The Foundation for San Francisco's Architectural Heritage, and Mr. and Mrs. Albert J. Moorman. The members, chair, and students of San Francisco State University's Humanities Department also have my thanks. The practical suggestions from many of my former students who walked these tours have been incorporated into this guide. For their generous help I wish to thank Mr. Chris Dichtel, Mr. Joseph Draper, Ms. Nina Haqiwara, Mr. Peter Hansell, Mr. William Kostura, Mrs. Anson Lucey, Mr. Brad Paul, Ms. Kit Yuen Quan, Ms. Jenifer Strickland, Ms. Shana Strum, and Mr. Philip Woollam. Mr. Peter M. Hirsch in particular, with his deep attachment to San Francisco, has my appreciation, and it is a pleasure to dedicate this revised edition to him.

I also wish to thank everyone at Chronicle Books who helped bring this ambitious revised edition to happy fruition, especially Mr. Jack Jensen, Mr. William LeBlond, Mr. Nion McEvoy, Ms. Judy Lewenthal, and everyone in the design department. I am forever in debt to the meticulous attentions of Ms. Carey Charlesworth, whose copyediting helped make this guide much better for the reader/walker.

Architect William Walters's drawings record with great precision, I think, the architectural character of San Francisco. He took time out from his busy practice designing buildings that are both modern and respectful of their local context to do the drawings for this book. The fine bird's-eye views of the Financial District, Chinatown, Nob Hill, and Russian Hill were field-compiled and hand-drawn by John Tomlinson and show San Francisco in 1994.

The changes and errors that are inevitable in a book such as this should be called to my attention in care of Chronicle Books, 85 Second Street, San Francisco 94105. I thank in advance all who help me improve subsequent editions of this guide to make it as practical and accurate as possible.

Enjoy!

Latitude
37°48' North
Longitude
122°24' West

San Francisco by the Numbers

San Francisco is something of an optical illusion: it looms larger culturally than it does physically. Its land area is only 46.38 square miles, or 29,056 acres. Elevation ranges from sea level to 938 feet at Mt. Davidson. The mean annual temperature is 56.4°F; the mean temperature of the coldest month, January, is 50°F and that of the warmest month, September, is 61.5°F. The average annual rainfall is a scant 19.33 inches.

The City of San Francisco was incorporated on April 15, 1850, and the present city limits were set in 1856 and remain unchanged. The current city charter has been in effect since 1932. San Francisco is California's only combined city and county. Municipal government is by a mayor and eleven-member Board of Supervisors (aldermen) elected at large.

The U.S. Census counted 723,959 San Franciscans in 1990, a surprising increase of 6.6 percent since 1980 (most old American cities are losing population). The city's population density is a very high 24.7 persons per acre, one of the three or four densest cities in the United States. This accounts for its intensely urban "feel." Incomes are high here. In 1980 the median household income was $26,591; by 1990 it had risen to $33,414. In 1990, 35 percent of the adult residents had college degrees, making this one of the most highly educated cities in the nation. Because jobs are created here faster than housing, San Francisco is one of the most expensive places to live in the United States. Two-thirds of San Franciscans are renters; one-third own their own homes. The liberal/conservative split in the city normally pits the eastside renters against the westside home owners.

According to the Census, in 1990 the population was 47 percent white, 29 percent Asian or Pacific Islander, 14 percent Latino, and 11 percent African American. The fastest growing group is Asian and Pacific Islanders (principally Filipino), which expanded by 43 percent in ten years. The Latino population grew by 8 percent. All other groups declined with the white population shrinking by 1.8 percent and the African American share falling by 8.5 percent. The soundest estimate of the gay and lesbian population is that it comprises 17 percent of the total population, or between 110,000 and 120,000 persons. Two-thirds are gay men and one-third lesbians. Highly educated and politically energized gays and lesbians are estimated to make up from 20 to 25 percent of the city's voters. In 1988, voter registration was 65.5 percent Democratic, 17.9 percent Republican, and 13.9 percent

Independent. The political temper of the city is reflected in the little-known fact that in 1988 Jesse Jackson beat Michael Dukakis here by 62,617 to 55,311 votes. A survey of church membership in 1983 found that only 35 percent of San Franciscans identified with a major religious denomination and that 64 percent were unchurched. This is key to the city's modern character. The largest denomination was the Roman Catholic, claiming 21 percent of the total population. Baptists were second with 3.2 percent, and American Baptists added another 1 percent; Episcopalians were third with 1.4 percent; African Methodists were 1.2 percent; and Jews were 1.2 percent. No other denomination reached 1 percent. The surprise in the survey was the small representation of Asian religions, a problematic finding. The public school population in 1994 was 26 percent Chinese American, 20.4 percent Latino, 18.1 percent African American, 7.6 percent Filipino American, 1.1 percent Korean American, 1 percent Japanese American, .7 percent Native American Indian, and 11.8 percent "other nonwhite." There are relatively many people of mixed racial descent in San Francisco, but we do not know exactly how many. Half of San Francisco's Chinese Americans, for example, marry people not of Chinese descent.

The population of the nine-county San Francisco Bay Area in 1990 was 6,023,577. The estimated gross regional product of the Bay Area was $112 billion in 1985, making this the fifth largest market in the United States.

Using This Guide

Welcome, traveler, to the beautiful and hospitable city of St. Francis. Nature has favored us with an incomparable setting of water, mountains, hourly changing atmosphere, and a bracing climate. History has showered us with gold and silver, wheat and specialty crops from the vast Central Valley, and silicon chips today. Representatives of all the peoples of mankind have come to flourish here.

The chief object of this guide is to enable the traveler to employ his or her time and money to the best advantage. It breaks the city into neighborhoods or districts with practical suggestions on parking; transit; cafés, restaurants, and bars; and sometimes shopping, walks, or entertainment, at the beginning of each section. It is best to scan this first, especially for the optimal times to visit. Use this guide; do not let it use you. Read the chapters before your explorations and choose what you want to see.

What makes this guide distinctive is that it is *built from the inside out*. Most of the walks here are organized around the often-almost-hidden minimuseums and key historic and modern interiors open to the public that tell parts of San Francisco's rich history in bright bits and pieces. The best times to see these places are noted. With these interiors as starting points or goals, this guide plots the path that best reveals the social and architectural layers of each neighbor-hood or district.

Tours usually begin and end at points served by public transit, and often near parking garages. Budgeting garage fees into your travel plans makes for an easier trip. Using public transit and/or taxis solves the parking problem entirely and precludes worrying about your car. Public telephones at bars and restaurants and radio-dispatched taxis make it very easy to dart around San Francisco and see a lot, even in only one or two days. Some tours end at or include vantage points with panoramas of the city and its magnificent setting. Only atypical expense is noted; many of the sites most revealing of San Francisco are free. Many of the paths traced through the separate districts in this guide have continuations, and many tours link together either directly or through easy transit hops.

What is distinctive about the physical San Francisco—her streets, blocks, bay windows, colors, landscapes, and views—and what is distinctive about the many histories of the people of San Francisco are sought here. The goal is to read San Francisco's architecture and people the way a detective would read the scene of a crime, that is, to look not only at a place but through it to visualize the people whose lives it was and is. For you should take great care in San Francisco to be distracted by her people. (Not all that difficult.) They have created, and sustain, this most distinctive city.

$\mathscr{P}$*reliminaries*

BEST TIMES TO VISIT

Spring and Fall are generally considered the best seasons to visit San Francisco. The weather is fine and the main attractions are not crowded. Summer, when school is out, is the peak season and you should have advance reservations then, especially for motels. Summer is also San Francisco's foggiest time of the year, though the mist usually burns off by 10 A.M. It is generally much cooler here in the summer than most visitors expect. But fogs that quickly come and go are one of the special characteristics of this special spot on the planet.

Winter—December, January, and February—is the riskiest but perhaps most beautiful season to visit. Between (usually) quite brief rainstorms are days of sapphire blue skies with clouds that look like baroque paintings, only alive and moving. The rains also wake the vegetation, making San Francisco's winter the equivalent of spring. (We like to be unusual.) In December the grass-covered California hills turn emerald green in a twinkling; wild flowers blossom and carpet the hills. Temperatures are cool, 60°F or so, but rarely cold (below 40°F).

Because city hotel rates are often greatly reduced on weekends, and because rural attractions like the Napa Valley and the scenic coastal highway are least crowded on weekdays, you should stay in the city on weekends and see the countryside on weekdays. Sometimes rural hotels and inns have special midweek rates.

Weekly patterns are conventional: Friday is the busiest "going out" night, and Saturday the next busiest. The finest French restaurants are closed on Sundays. Museums are closed on Mondays and Tuesdays.

Note: *All phone numbers, unless otherwise noted, are for area code 415.*

Cable Car Powerhouse
Washington and Mason

Nob Hill

Union Street
north of Van Ness

Sacramento Street
*between Presidio Avenue
and Arguello Boulevard*

Hayes Street
*between Franklin and
Laguna streets*

Broadway
North Beach

Haight Street
far west end

Eleventh Street
*between Folsom and
Harrison, south of
Market*

Aquatic Park
*across from Ghirardelli
Square*

The traveler should work around the two daily rush hours: 8 to 10 A.M. and 4 to 6 P.M. If you can avoid it, there is no reason to be on the freeways during those hours when drivers are impatient with those not on automatic pilot. Buses are most civil between 10 A.M. and 2 or 3 P.M., when they become flooded with voluble schoolchildren. Normality returns about 4 P.M.; rush hour starts at 5 P.M.

The best way to experience San Francisco's many districts is with a stimulating coffee at a local café about 10 A.M.—San Francisco wakes up slowly. A morning and noon-time's walking around, lunch in a local restaurant after the rush at about 2 P.M., browsing in the shops on the local shopping strip in the afternoon, and then dinner in a different neighborhood entirely on the other side of town (via taxi, not automobile) is the best way to skip around compact San Francisco.

If you are here during the summer and want to ride the cable cars, as you will, do so early in the morning, say 8 A.M., then go off and do something else. This will save you long waits in lines in often unpleasant places. Don't fail to visit the **Cable Car Powerhouse** at Washington and Mason streets (there is no easy parking nearby).

Few San Francisco public attractions require advance reservations. In the Bay Area only **Alcatraz, Filoli,** and **Tao House** do, and soon probably Muir Woods. The currently hot restaurants also do, and you should phone well ahead of time in those cases, even in advance of your visit. Often, however, you can phone in your restaurant reservation in the morning for a table that evening. San Francisco is not a twenty-four-hour town. Her restaurants keep civil but not late hours. Many stop seating patrons about 10 or 10:30 P.M. But San Francisco is probably the best city in the nation for evening strolls or dawn jogging. Both are safe in San Francisco. The top of **Nob Hill** makes a fine and level evening constitutional, as does posh **Union Street** or elite upper **Sacramento Street**, where you can window-shop as well as people-watch. Hip **Hayes Street** is lively on Friday evenings. The view of the inky Bay

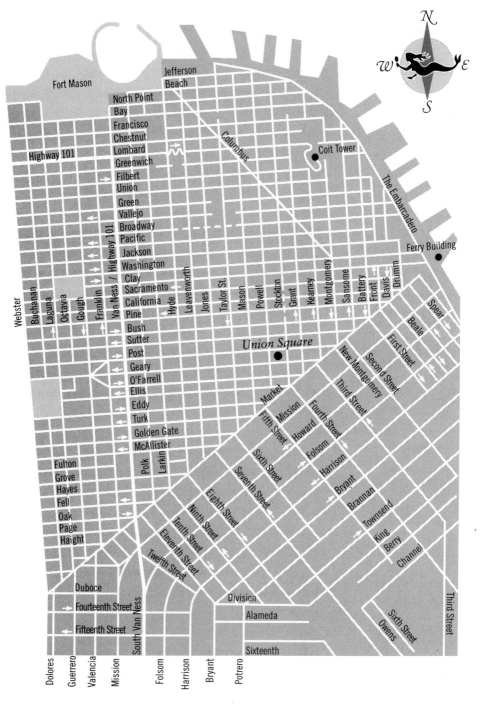

Core San Francisco

Visitor Information Center
*Hallidie Plaza, Market
and Powell Streets
Phone 391-2000 for
information. Recordings
in several languages
are also available:*
• *English, 391-2001*
• *French, 391-2003*
• *German, 391-2004*
• *Spanish, 391-2122*
• *Japanese, 391-2101*

**The San Francisco
Convention &
Visitors Bureau**
*P.O. Box 429097,
San Francisco
94142-9097*

**California State
Automobile Association**
*150 Van Ness Avenue,
at Hayes Street, just
north of Market Street,
San Francisco 94101.
Monday through Friday,
8:30 A.M. to 5 P.M.;
565-2012*

**Metropolitan Transportation
Commission**
*Metro Center,
101 Eighth Street,
Oakland 94607;
(510) 464-7700*

from Telegraph Hill is impressive at night. Fisherman's Wharf and Chinatown's Grant Avenue are alive with lights and tourists in the evenings. A few spots, such as North Beach's **Broadway,** the far west end of **Haight Street,** and **Eleventh Street,** attract nightclubbers from about 11 P.M. to bar-closing time at 2 A.M. **Aquatic Park** and the beach in front of the bleachers next to the Maritime Museum, might be the most beautiful place to stroll and sit at night, with the dark Bay edged with light spread out before you and the Japonesque profile of Mt. Tamalpais like an ink wash in the distance.

MAPS AND INFORMATION

San Francisco Visitors' Map, found at the **Visitor Information Center,** at Hallidie Plaza, near the Powell and Market cable car turntable. Take the escalator down to the plaza and look under the overpass. The Information Center provides this useful, free map that shows the downtown, the cable car lines, and the Forty-Nine-Mile Scenic Drive.

The San Francisco Book, an informative mini-magazine, is available for $2 from **The San Francisco Convention & Visitors Bureau.** Allow three weeks for delivery. It also publishes a separate *San Francisco Lodging Guide,* which is free.

The Muni Map, the Official San Francisco Street & Transit Map, is published by the city's public transit system and costs $1.50. You can buy it at the Visitor Information Center at Hallidie Plaza and at some bookstores. See page 27 for **Muni Passports**.

California State Automobile Association Maps are the best for drivers. If you are a AAA member, stop by the lobby-level office on Van Ness Avenue. Secure both the standard map of San Francisco and the San Francisco Tour Map. If you plan to visit the wine country, ask for the Sonoma and Napa County maps; if you plan to see Monterey, ask for the Tour Map of Monterey Peninsula. (Standard maps and Tour Maps are not the same thing.) These maps are available only to AAA members. Parking tickets can be paid here as well.

A **Regional Transit Guide/Map** is published by the Metropolitan Transportation Commission. This map shows the interconnecting transit systems of the entire Bay Area and gives phone numbers for all regional transit systems. At BART stations ask for the free *BART and Buses: A Guide to Public Transportation from BART.* It is useful for visiting the Oakland Museum or the University of California, Berkeley. The map and guide are usually available at the BART station at Market and Powell streets, next to the Visitor Information Center in Hallidie Plaza.

The National Park Service publishes a handsome free **Map of the Golden Gate National Park Association.** Try the excellent **Maritime Store** or **GGNPA headquarters** at Fort Mason. Very useful for the Presidio, Marin County, and Muir Woods National Monument. **Thomas Brothers Maps** publishes detailed street maps for all California counties. This is a fine general map store that also sells reproductions of historic views and maps of San Francisco. **Rand McNally Map Store** sells maps of the world, heavens, California, and San Francisco.

Maritime Store
Hyde Street Pier at Fisherman's Wharf
775-2665

GGNPA Headquarters
at Fort Mason, enter at the Franklin Street gate

Thomas Brothers Maps
550 Jackson Street, off Columbus Avenue in North Beach;
981-7520

Rand McNally Map Store
595 Market Street, at Second; 777-3131

CLIMATE AND CLOTHING

While palm trees do grow here, San Francisco is not semitropical; its average daytime temperature ranges between a low of 50.9°F and a high of 62.7°F. Temperatures seldom rise above 70°F or fall below 40°F. The San Francisco peninsula is on the shifting edge of the hard bright skies to the south and the somber gray skies to the north. The daily changes in temperature are usually only within about 10°F, yet the daily changes in atmospheric effects can be dramatic. The fogs have a transforming effect, turning the city and the Bay into a *grisaille* world. Spring is the best season for observing the fog's fantastic forms. Sometimes fog pours over Twin Peaks or the Marin County approach to the Golden Gate Bridge like a white, slow-motion waterfall. Other times, at night, the wind blows the fog around so that it looks like falling snow in July. In summer the fog usually burns off by 10 A.M. and returns with the chilling westerly wind about 3:30 P.M. Mark Twain quipped that the coldest winter he ever spent was a summer in San Francisco.

San Francisco enjoys the cleanest skies of any large American city. The constant westerly winds blow pollution across the Bay to Oakland and the South Bay. One can *see* in San Francisco, a phenomenon increasingly rare in cities. Sunsets are often memorable over the Pacific. At times the sea looks like burnished silver and the spacious cloud effects beggar description. The coloring when there are high clouds can be startling, bright pink and lemon yellow, for example.

The "layered look" of a sweater and jacket is the best way to adapt to variable temperatures. It is usually cool here late in the day. Men will find medium-weight suits the most practical; women will find a light dress or suit with a warm sweater or jacket most comfortable. Summer clothes are rarely useful here, except during the brief Indian summer in September. Dressing as if the city were a tropical cruise ship will signal to everyone that you are a tourist and that you will be shivering come late afternoon. If you dress for fall, you'll be comfortable year-round. Sensible walking shoes are recommended. Sunglasses are not an affectation in California; the light is quite strong here.

EXPENSES AND TIPPING

The San Francisco Convention & Visitors Bureau estimates that conventioneers spend about $160 a day, other travelers about $130. A savvy cabbie has estimated typical spending at about $200 a day per person, $400 a day for a couple. Of course, it can be done for much less.

Conventional tips are 15 percent for taxis and restaurants. Allow 20 percent for waiter service at bars. Bellhops expect $1 minimum, or 75¢ per bag. Desk clerks and elevator operators are not tipped, but doormen expect a minimum of $1 at arrival and a tip when summoning a taxi. Chambermaids should be tipped $2 per night; leave the money in an envelope marked "For the Maid."

FOREIGN EXCHANGE AND CASH

San Francisco Airport

The **Bank of America Foreign Exchange Office** at the airport has longer hours than downtown exchanges.

Downtown San Francisco

Major Financial District banks are generally open Monday to Friday, 10 A.M. to 3 P.M. **Bank of America Foreign Currency Services** is open Monday to Thursday, 9 A.M. to 4 P.M., until 6 P.M. on Friday, and 9 A.M. to 1 P.M. on Saturday. There is another Bank of America currency exchange with the same hours at the **Powell and Market** streets branch. **Macy's** at Union Square will exchange foreign currency for the amount of one's purchases only, at the Cashier's Office.

American Express

The office half a block east of Union Square has a currency exchange and an automatic teller; open Monday to Friday, 9 A.M. to 5 P.M.; Saturday, 10 A.M. to 5 P.M. The **Fisherman's Wharf** office in the Sheraton Hotel is open seven days a week, 10 A.M. to P.M.

Automatic Tellers Near Union Square

- **Bank of America** *400 block of Powell Street, near Post, half a block north of Union Square.*
- **Wells Fargo Bank** *2 Grant Avenue at Market Street.*
- **Citicorp Savings** *590 Market Street, on the north side, between Montgomery and Sansome streets.*

Bank of America Foreign Exchange Office
Central Terminal, International Building; 742-8079

Bank of America Foreign Currency Services
345 Montgomery Street at California; 622-2451

Powell and Market Streets branch, next to the cable car turntable and Visitor Information Center

Macy's Cashier's Office
Union Square; open all store hours, including Sundays; 397-4279

American Express: 237 Post Street Office
Between Stockton and Grant; 981-5533
• Fisherman's Wharf Office, Shearaton Hotel 2500 Mason Street, at North Point Street; 788-3025.

**San Francisco
International Airport**
Airport information;
876-7809

Bank of America
International Terminal
877-0264

**AT&T Communications
Center**
International Terminal,
upper level; 877-0269

SuperShuttle
558-8500

Airporter
673-2432

TRANSPORTATION

Airport to City

With three linked terminals in a horseshoe around a central parking structure, **San Francisco International Airport** serves many foreign airlines and is a regional hub for United Airlines. It is the fifth busiest airport in the United States and the seventh busiest in the world. The airport garage provides short-term, protected parking. The upper level of the loop roadway is for departures, the ground level for arrivals. The best times to arrive or depart are between 6 A.M. and 11 A.M. and 8 P.M. and 9 P.M. Peak congestion is between 12 and 3 P.M. A **free shuttle bus** circles the upper level.

SFO has all the usual airport services, plus often very imaginative art exhibits. In fact, because 1 percent of the cost of all public buildings must be spent on art, the airport has accumulated a large art collection. A Beniamino Bufano statue entitled *Peace* in the road median at the entrance to the airport is decorated with mosaic faces of all races. Clearing Customs and Immigration at the International Terminal takes from thirty minutes to an hour, sometimes longer at peak periods. The **Bank of America** branch has the longest hours for currency exchange, longer than anyplace downtown. The **AT&T Communications Center** is open from 10 A.M. to 8 P.M. with many services, including facsimile machines. Barber and shower facilities are available during business hours. Downtown San Francisco is a twenty-minute, fourteen-mile drive north on the Bayshore Freeway, Highway 101.

Taxi service from the airport to downtown is $24. Voluntary ride sharing for two or more persons to a maximum of three destinations is permitted. The flat fare of $24 should be divided among the passengers. **SuperShuttle**'s seven-passenger vans will take you to your door anywhere in the city for a reasonable fee; telephone for exact fare and reservations. The Yellow Pages in the phone book lists several other shuttle services. The **Airporter** bus leaves frequently for downtown and Fisherman's Wharf hotels; the fare is $9. The **SamTrans** 7B bus links the airport with the Transbay Terminal in San Francisco (for transfer to buses for the East Bay and north) but makes too many stops along the way. The BART subway does not serve the airport. (Welcome to America.)

Metropolitan Oakland International Airport

Equally convenient is this smaller airport, across the San Francisco-Oakland Bay Bridge. Outside rush hours, it is a twenty-five minute ride from downtown San Francisco. There is an AirBART shuttle to the BART subway system—the Coliseum station—but BART stops running at midnight.

TAXIS

The carless traveler should plan on spending money on taxis. While rates are high, the distances are generally short and so the costs remain reasonable. Taxi fare from the airport to downtown San Francisco is $24. In the city the rates are approximately $1.90 for the first mile and $1.50 for each additional mile. Public telephones and radio-dispatched taxis make it easy to dart around the city, even when time is limited, and especially when it's no small benefit to eliminate the parking problem altogether. Ask the driver to take slower, scenic streets. This will add only a little to the fare and show you the city's more attractive streets.

To the San Franciscan, one of the distinctive musics of the city is the sound of the taxi dispatcher sing-songing the paired names of San Francisco streets: "Larkin and Cal, Forty-Six and Wawona, Hyde and Filbert, Broadway and Diviz, Sutter and Polk, Sixteenth and Sanchez, Funston and Moraga." Each is a flash card of people and places.

Metropolitan Oakland International Airport
(510) 577-4000

Taxis:
De Soto
673-1414

Luxor
282-4141

Veteran's
552-1300

Yellow
626-2345

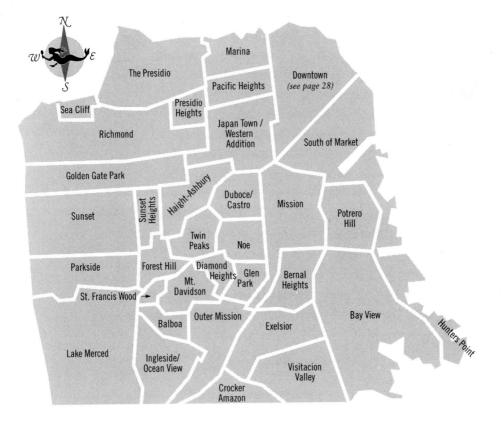

N
W   E
S

The Presidio

Marina

Pacific Heights

Downtown
(see page 28)

Sea Cliff

Presidio
Heights

Richmond

Japan Town /
Western
Addition

South of Market

Golden Gate Park

Haight-Ashbury

Sunset
Heights

Duboce/
Castro

Mission

Sunset

Potrero
Hill

Twin
Peaks

Noe

Parkside

Forest Hill

Diamond
Heights

Glen
Park

Bernal
Heights

Mt.
Davidson

St. Francis Wood →

Outer Mission

Bay View

Balboa

Exelsior

Hunters Point

Lake Merced

Ingleside/
Ocean View

Visitacion
Valley

Crocker
Amazon

Neighborhoods of San Francisco

Some Driving Tips

AUTOMOBILE

If you are driving up the coast from Los Angeles to San Francisco, turn off Highway 1 onto Highway 17 at Soquel (near Santa Cruz) and then take Interstate 280 up the center of the San Mateo Peninsula. The rolling, golden, oak-dotted hills here are a magnificently Californian landscape. The Junipero Serra Freeway, one of the last freeways designed by Caltrans District 4 Engineers, is one of the most beautiful freeways in California. Its soaring concrete overpasses on their sculpted pedestals make art out of roadbuilding.

Once over the city line, take the San Jose Avenue exit from I-280 and follow San Jose Avenue to palm-lined Dolores Street. San Jose Avenue follows El Camino Real, the King's Highway, which linked Baja and Alta California's presidios and missions, and which followed earlier Native American and animal trails. Bright, clean, residential Dolores Street, with its central strip of mature palms planted about 1910 and its roller-coaster profile, is a splendid entrance to San Francisco. Mission Dolores, at Dolores and Sixteenth streets, is an appropriate first stop.

Cable cars always have the right of way. Do not tailgate them. According to the California Traffic Code, *pedestrians always have the right of way, even when they are wrong.* You may make right-hand turns at red lights after slowing and yielding the right of way to pedestrians.

Parking

The Traffic Code requires that cars parked on grades block their wheels against the curb by "toeing" the front tire when headed downhill, or "heeling" it when parked uphill. You can be ticketed for unsafe parking. In addition, you should set the emergency brake and leave the car set in gear or in park. San Francisco has several different colored curbs each with its own restrictions:

White: Passenger loading zone, short stops permitted.
Green: Ten-minute parking limit.

Alcatraz Island, Angel Island *and* **Tiburon**
Pier 43½,
Fisherman's Wharf;
Phone 546-2896 or
546-2815 for fare and
reservations. Tickets can
also be charged by calling
546-2700

Larkspur *and* **Sausalito Golden Gate Ferry**
Behind the Ferry
Building, at the foot of
Market and California
Streets; For schedule
and fares, 332-6600
• **Guaymas** *435-6300*

Yellow: Half-hour loading zone for vehicles with commercial plates; parking allowed after 6 P.M.

Red: No stopping, standing, or parking. Includes bus zones.

Blue: Parking for the physically disabled with the appropriate placard or plate.

Towaway Zones You may be towed from any illegal spot. This is most frequent when some streets switch to no parking to provide extra lanes for morning and afternoon rush hours. Read the parking signs posted on each block for this restriction. S.F.P.D.'s towed vehicle information is at 553-1235.

FERRIES

San Francisco Bay and the Golden Gate are spectacular and well worth seeing from the water. Commuter ferries are least crowded and most enjoyable midday, between the morning and evening rush hours, roughly between 10 A.M. and 3 P.M. Refreshments are sold on most ferries. Always remember to ask when the last ferry departs.

• **Alcatraz Island** and **Angel Island** Advance tickets are recommended, especially in the summer. *(See Tour 16.)*

• **Larkspur** The Larkspur ferry is almost exclusively used by commuters and terminates at a space-frame terminal and a large parking lot. Larkspur Landing, the nearby shopping center, serves mostly local shoppers. It is a very scenic and tourist-free ride.

• **Sausalito** A half-hour ride to a scenic destination. *(See Tour 16.)*

• **Tiburon** The Tiburon ferry docks right next to **Guaymas,** a Californian Mexican restaurant with a modern, airy design. The town of Tiburon consists of a one-block-long upscale Main Street.

SAN FRANCISCO PUBLIC TRANSIT AND VISITOR PASSES

San Francisco has a smorgasbord of public transportation systems, of which cable cars are only the most famous. If you are normally a car-driving person, San Francisco's many lines, selectively used, let you see a city built on public transit. Drivers and operators know the system well and can guide you: they will call out stops if you request them to. And you can, if you want, really see a lot of the city inexpensively. **Muni Maps** can be bought at the Visitor Center at Hallidie Plaza and at many bookstores. The fare is $1; you will need exact fare since Muni drivers do not make change. The best thing is to buy a **Muni Passport**, which is valid on all lines including the cable cars. Muni Passports can be purchased at the Visitor Information Center at Hallidie Plaza at Powell and Market Streets, at the STBS booth on Stockton Street on the east side of Union Square, or at the City Hall information booth in the Civic Center. Special children's all-day passes are not available, but you may buy them adult passes. If you use the transit system to get around, it will be amply worth the expense. You can phone Muni to ask for assistance planning your route.

Muni Passports
One day ($6)
three days ($10)
seven days ($15)

For Muni information;
673-6864

Cable Cars

The best way to experience the cable cars, especially during the busy summer season and weekends, is to get up very early and travel much of the 4.4-mile system back and forth between 6 A.M., when the cables start up, and about 8:30 A.M., when the morning rush begins. When the **Powell-Mason** and **Powell-Hyde** lines are packed, it is often possible to ride the less-crowded **California Street** cable line.

Individual tickets for the cable cars cost $3 and are sold by machines that take $1 and $5 bills. These machines are at the ends of all the lines and at the California and Powell transfer point on Nob Hill. (There are no ticket machines at the Cable Car Powerhouse.) You can also pay your fare once you board; cable car conductors will make change (bus drivers do not).

Rainy, blustery days when you are all bundled up in a raincoat and hat are the best time to ride the cable cars. They return then to their old mix of local hill-dwellers and hardy visitors. It goes without saying that the cable cars are most enjoyable and historically evocative when not jam-packed with people. Vistas and sensations differ from different seats, so vary where you sit—on the outside, on the inside, in front, in back. It's hard to pick out where the cable car is most itself—perhaps climbing the seemingly per-

Fisherman's Wharf

North Point

Bay

Columbus

Lombard

North Beach

Coit Tower

Telegraph Hill

Union

Russian Hill

Powell/Hyde Line

Taylor

Powell/Mason Line

Powell

Stockton

Montgomery

The Embarcadero

Chinatown

Jackson

Washington

Cable Car Powerhouse

Ferry Building

Financial District

Van Ness / Highway 101

Nob Hill

Mason

California

Davis

California Line

Transfer Point

Union Square

Market Street

Tenderloin

Mission

Civic Center

N
E
S
W

·········	Cable Cars
··········	39 Coit Bus

Cable Car System

pendicular Hyde Street grades between Bay and Chestnut, or—the California car—stopped athwart Grant Avenue, when on a quiet, foggy night, if you squint your eyes a bit, Chinatown's glowing neon feels like a Dashiell Hammett mystery locale.

Cable Car Powerhouse

"*One of the principal developments of mechanical genius in San Francisco*," wrote C. P. Heininger in his guide to San Francisco in 1889, "*is the extensive and perfect system of cable street railways, of which the Clay street line was the pioneer. The system is unique, and a triumph of inventive genius and engineering skill, of which San Francisco has just cause to be proud.*" The surviving fragment of San Francisco's once-extensive cable line network is a living monument to nineteenth-century American mechanical and promotional genius.

Cable cars were first developed in San Francisco in the late 1870s. The plain brick **Powerhouse** on the border between Chinatown and Russian Hill, powers the four endless, or looped, cables that run under sixty-nine blocks of San Francisco's streets (California, Powell, Hyde, and Mason) propelling the three remaining cable car lines. There are twenty-six of the green, single-end cable cars on the Powell-Hyde and the Powell-Mason lines, and eleven of the larger red double-ended cable cars on the California Street cable line. Most of the Powell-Hyde and Powell-Mason cable cars date from 1887 to 1891; the California Street cable cars were built in 1906 through 1914, after the great earthquake and fire. Recently, the Muni built several new cars copying the old ones exactly. On all 4.4 miles of track, the maximum number of cars with passengers at one time is twenty-six. Today, the Powell-Mason and Powell-Hyde lines carry forty-one thousand passengers a day.

Like many inventions, the cable car has more than one "inventor." In both Europe and America, men were seeking better passenger transit systems for growing cities. **Andrew Smith Hallidie**, popularly considered the inventor of the cable car in 1873, is more accurately described as the first successful *developer* of a cable car line.

Cable Car Lines:
• *Powell-Mason*
• *Powell-Hyde, to Fisherman's Wharf*
• *California Street, serving Nob Hill;*
$3 Individual ticket

Cable Car Powerhouse
1201 Mason Street, northwest corner of Washington and Mason Streets

**The Clay Street
Hill Railroad**
*On Clay Street,
from Jones to Kearny*

Andrew Smith was born in London in 1836 and apprenticed as a mechanic. He adopted the surname Hallidie in honor of his uncle, Sir Andrew Hallidie, an English physician. With his father, a wire rope manufacturer, he came to California in 1852. He began designing wire-rope haulage systems for gold mines. In 1857 he established a small factory in North Beach to manufacture wire rope (cables that had manila hemp cores with steel wires wrapped around them). In 1867 he patented a system of gripping and ungripping ore buckets on an endless overhead cable. After 1869, he attempted to organize the financing to build a cable line up California Street on the east escarpment of Nob Hill. Construction costs seem to have been less on Clay Street two blocks north, however, and some Clay Street property owners were willing to invest in Hallidie's enterprise. **The Clay Street Hill Railroad** had its trial run on August 1, 1873. With Hallidie at the controls, the tiny car went down Clay from Jones to Kearny, and then back up. Hallidie formed the Traction Railway Company in 1875, hired the best legal talent, and attempted, with much success for a while, to patent all the important aspects of cable traction and to force other cable car lines to pay his company a royalty based on their mileage. At their peak, San Francisco had eight cable car lines operating over 112 miles of track, directly employing some 1,500 men.

The cable car brought the power of the stationary steam engine out onto the street, where it could be used to propel cars and passengers in a more hygienic and more dependable way than existing horse-car technology. (Cars pulled along tracks by horses polluted with animals' wastes, and they could not be used on steep hills.) Despite their expensive construction and high operating costs, cable car lines were the state-of-the-art for the six years between 1882 to 1888, peaking in 1889. They were rapidly made obsolete by the development of the superior, cheaper electric streetcar, which emerged in both Germany and America in the late 1880s.

Because there were no traffic signals, in 1882 the city required all cable cars to carry bells or gongs and to ring them as they crossed intersections. (Cable car bell-ringing has developed into a local art form. Every summer a bell-ringing contest at Union Square pits conductors and gripmen against each other for a prize. Each contestant has one minute to impress the judges with rhythm, flair, and musicality. Contact the Convention & Visitors Bureau for the date of the contest.)

Cable car systems have many drawbacks. They are costly to construct with expensive underground conduit in addition to tracks; they are mechanically complex and prone to breakdowns; and they are expensive to operate because they require two-man crews. Also, cable cars cannot pass one another on the same track; lost time cannot be made up; and one stoppage anywhere on a line shuts down the entire line. As if all this were not enough, cable car systems are prodigious energy wasters. Some 4 percent of the energy generated is used to move the cars and their passengers, and some 60 to 80 percent is used moving the cable.

Increasingly after 1893, cable car lines were replaced with more efficient electric streetcars. After the earthquake in 1906, traction companies replaced cable with electricity where they could, keeping cable operations only on the steepest slopes: Nob Hill, Russian Hill, Pacific Heights, and the Castro hill. **The Castro Street** cable line was converted to buses in 1941, and the scenic **Washington-Jackson** cable line in Pacific Heights was shut down in 1956, preceded by a brass band playing dirges. Today only Nob and Russian hills are served by cable lines.

Upon municipalization of many cable car lines after 1944, a cost-conscious city government announced plans to replace all the cable lines with buses. In 1947 a Citizen's Committee to Save the Cable Cars was formed by Frieda Klussman to raise public consciousness about the value of the unique cable car lines to the city. Eventually, a truncated system was preserved, and in 1964 the existing system was placed on the National Register of Historic Places, making this the nation's first moving landmark.

The entire cable car system was rebuilt in 1982 and 1984, mostly with federal public transportation grants plus local corporate and individual contributions. New tracks and underground conduit were constructed, and the Powerhouse and Car Barn were reconstructed.

Chin and Hensolt Engineers, Inc., with Ernest Born, consulting architect, rebuilt the fragile, red brick **Ferry & Cliff House Railways Powerhouse**, hastily built in 1909. They stabilized the four brick walls, scooped out the building's interior, built new foundations under the old brick walls and a new steel frame and concrete structure within the old four walls, then bonded the brick walls to the new, much stronger steel and concrete building. What you see is an entirely new, seismic-resistant building carefully tailored to fit within the old brick garment.

On entering the Powerhouse at its corner entrance, turn left and walk down the staircase to see the sheaves, the underground wheels playing out the four cables underneath the intersection at Washington and Mason streets. This unique viewing room was added in the reconstruction of 1984. Climb back upstairs to the viewing platform that lets you look down onto the great spinning wheels that power and regulate the cables, keeping them taut and smooth-running. The spinning white wheels power the looped cables. The electric engines themselves are quite compact and are mounted near the wheels. A few explanatory plaques mounted on the handrail explain the cables and their figure-eight loops.

For many years venerable **Car No. 8** of the Clay Street Hill Railroad was on display at the Powerhouse. It made the first trip with Hallidie at the controls in 1873. The relic survived because it was lent to Baltimore for an exhibition in 1905, and thus escaped the earthquake and fire of 1906. In 1907, when Baltimore suffered a great fire, the car was presumed lost. It was discovered in a Baltimore junkyard in 1939 and rescued.

The cables are kept moving at a speed of 9.5 miles per hour under the surface of the streets and make a throaty humming sound. Cables last from about 110 days on the Powell-Mason line to 300 days on the California Street line. To operate a cable car, the gripman in the center of the cable car operates a lever, or grip, that reaches through a slot in the street and grasps or lets go of the cable moving in its underground conduit. To stop a cable car, the grip lets go of the cable, then a second person applies the wheel brakes and track brakes, wooden blocks that scrape the rails. The grip and brakeman communicate through bell signals.

The interior of the great machinery room where the cables are propelled has an immensely strong, unadorned, gray-painted, steel I-beam-supported roof. It is like being under a bridge, not inside a building. The steel is this strong because the cable cars themselves are all stored at night on the upper level. The Powerhouse and Car Barn is on a slope with a one-story drop at the two ends of the lot, a most characteristic San Francisco hill lot, which permits vehicular access to more than one level of a building.

The California Street Cable Line

The **California Street Cable Railroad Company** was the third cable line in the city and was organized in 1876 by railroad millionaires **Leland Stanford** and **Mark Hopkins**, who wanted to build atop Nob Hill, and other local magnates. It was one of the most luxurious cable lines built, with the best equipment and largest cars. Its double-ended cars weigh six tons and carry thirty-four passengers. This "California" type car subsequently served as a model for the first electric street cars. The California cable line opened in 1878 and ran up wide California Street from the edge of the banking district at Kearny out to Fillmore Street in nineteen minutes. It served the Nob Hill palaces and opened up the Western Addition to Victorian house building. The California Street line does not have turntables since its cars are double-ended and need only a switchback at the ends of the tracks.

The Powell-Mason Cable Line

The Powell-Mason Cable Line was designed by engineer Howard C. Holmes, built by the **Ferries & Cliff House Railroad Company**, and put in service in 1888. This is the line for which the Powerhouse was built. Because the original lines went both east-west and north-south (only a fragment of the system survives), the cables feed out of the southeastern corner of the Powerhouse at Mason and Washington and circle the block to the east bounded by Mason, Powell, Washington, and Jackson streets. Navigating this block is called going "around the horn" in cable car lingo. Cars from the Powell-Mason line survived the fire of 1906 because they were stored outside the burned district in the cable car barn at Sacramento and Walnut. Some of the 1887-to-1891 vintage cars continue in use today.

The Powell-Hyde Cable Line

The present Powell-Hyde line was originally part of the **California Street Cable Railroad** and opened as an extension of that line in 1891. The Hyde line was built to link Russian Hill with downtown shipping via a crosstown cable line. The Hyde Street line also terminated a block from the Hyde Street Pier and the Sausalito and Tiburon Ferries. It was the last cable line built in San Francisco. Its 3.5 miles of track traverse the steepest slope, Hyde Street between Bay and Chestnut, with a 20.67 percent grade. It also enjoys the most spectacular panoramic views of the Golden Gate and mountainous Marin County.

HOTELS

San Francisco is justly famous for her hotels and has a complete spectrum of accommodations from the most luxurious to the spartan. In this she is unusual for an American city. You can come back to San Francisco many times and each time stay in an entirely different kind of hotel in a completely different part of the city. San Francisco has everything from commanding suites with panoramas of the Bay Area to cozy, plant-embowered bed and breakfasts, to budget places.

San Francisco Lodging Guide
San Francisco Convention & Visitors Bureau P.O. Box 429097, San Francisco 94142-9097; 391-2000

The average hotel rate in 1993 was about $153 for a standard double. The Fisherman's Wharf's midrise motels are the most popular; Nob Hill's hotels are the costliest. The older, mid-size downtown hotels along Post and Sutter streets, north of Union Square, are recommended for carless travelers and are the best value. Plan to garage your car if you stay downtown.

Today, business travelers constitute about half the hotel customers in San Francisco. On weekends, when corporate travelers are at home, many luxury hotels cut their rates to about half to lure weekenders. So always ask about weekend specials.

The 11 percent city hotel room tax on your final bill is the gentle "squeeze" San Francisco extracts for your enjoying yourself here. The money is used to help support the Convention & Visitors Bureau, Candlestick Park stadium, Yerba Buena Gardens and Moscone Convention Center, the Performing Arts Center, dance companies, theaters, musical performances in the parks, parades, museums, the symphony, and many of the things that make this a rewarding city to visit or live in. Some 120 arts and cultural organizations get part of their funding, and the important imprimatur of civic approval, from the Hotel Tax Fund.

For an overview of accomodations, write to The San Francisco Convention & Visitors Bureau, which publishes a free **San Francisco Lodging Guide**.

The Fairmont Hotel
950 Mason Street
San Francisco 94108;
772-5000

The Huntington Hotel,
1075 California Street,
San Francisco 94108;
474-5400

Mark Hopkins Inter-
Continental Hotel
999 California Street
San Francisco 94108;
392-3434

The Ritz-Carlton
600 Stockton Street
San Francisco 94108;
296-7465

The Stouffer Stanford Court
905 California Street,
San Francisco 94108;
989-3500

Hyatt-Regency
5 Embarcadero Center,
San Francisco 94111;
788-1234

Holiday Inn
750 Kearny Street,
San Francisco 94108;
433-6600

The Mandarin Oriental
222 Sansome Street
San Francisco 94104-
2792; 885-0999

Park Hyatt Hotel
333 Battery Street,
San Francisco 94111;
392-1234

Hotel Griffon
155 Steuart Street,
San Francisco 94105;
495-2100

Harbor Court Hotel
165 Steuart Street,
San Francisco 94105;
882-1300

Major Hotels

A brief listing of major hotels follows. Entries with *asterisks* are mentioned in the text in greater detail, for their place in the city's historical and architectural tapestry.

NOB HILL

- **The Fairmont Hotel and Tower** *
- **The Huntington Hotel** A hotel that prides itself on personal attention and remembering its guests.*
- **Mark Hopkins Inter-Continental Hotel** *
- **The Ritz-Carlton** The elegant adaptation of LeBrun and Sons' temple-fronted Metropolitan Life West Coast headquarters. Noted for its attentive service.
- **The Stouffer Stanford Court** A favorite with business travelers.*

THE FINANCIAL DISTRICT AND EMBARCADERO

- **Hyatt-Regency** Inside this 1973 design by John C. Portman Jr. and Associates is a seventeen-story interior space enlivened by light-studded glass elevators.
- **Holiday Inn Financial District** In Chinatown facing Portsmouth Square.
- **The Mandarin Oriental** The top eleven stories of Interstate Center at 345 California; twin towers in the sky with regional panoramas; glass "skybridges"; north views best. Opened 1987; expensive.*
- **Park Hyatt Hotel**
- **Hotel Griffon** A small, new luxury hotel near the foot of Market Street and The Embarcadero. **Roti**, a fine new restaurant with spit-roasted entrees, is located on the ground floor (phone 495-6500).
- **Harbor Court Hotel** A luxurious reworking of the 1924 Embarcadero YMCA, with a large pool and health club.

UNION SQUARE/DOWNTOWN

- **The Four Seasons-Clift Hotel** Hotelmen regard The Clift as one of the top hotels in the country. The elegant Redwood Lounge of 1935 was restored in 1977.
- **Grand San Francisco Hyatt***
- **Hotel Nikko**
- **The Pan-Pacific Hotel,***opened in 1988.
- **Parc Fifty-Five Hotel**
- **San Francisco Hilton & Towers** Recently expanded to a full block; now one of the largest hotels on the West Coast.
- **Sir Francis Drake Hotel** Designed by Weeks & Day in 1928; a good design from the stylish 1920s.*
- **The Westin St. Francis Hotel and Tower** An institution in San Francisco.*

SOUTH OF MARKET STREET/MOSCONE CONVENTION CENTER

- **San Francisco Marriott Hotel** This forty-story hotel with fifteen hundred rooms opened in 1989 a block from Moscone Convention Center. Designed by Tony Lumsden of the Los Angeles firm of DMJM, this busy, reflective-glass-topped behemoth is one of the city's most controversial new designs.*
- **ANA Hotel** A wall-like design that blocks the view corridor down important Kearny Street.
- **Sheraton-Palace Hotel** A splendid recent renovation has restored the luster of this grand San Francisco hotel and its famous Garden Court.*

JAPANTOWN

- **Miyako Hotel** A fourteen-story hotel in the east end of the 1968 Japan Center. Hotel suites have sunken tile baths and contemporary Japanese styling. The extraordinary **Elka** restaurant adjoins the hotel (phone 922-7788).
- **Best Western Miyako.**

The Four Seasons-Clift Hotel
495 Geary Street
San Francisco 94102;
775-4700

Grand San Francisco Hyatt
345 Stockton Street,
San Francisco 94108;
398-1234

Hotel Nikko
222 Mason Street,
San Francisco 94102;
394-1111

The Pan-Pacific Hotel
500 Post Street,
San Francisco 94102;
771-8600

Parc Fifty-Five Hotel
55 Cyril Magnin Street,
San Francisco 94102;
392-8000

San Francisco Hilton & Towers
333 O'Farrell Street,
San Francisco 94142;
771-1400

Sir Francis Drake Hotel
450 Powell Street,
San Francisco 94102;
392-7755

The Westin St. Francis Hotel and Tower
335 Powell Street,
San Francisco 94102;
397-7000

San Francisco Marriott Hotel
55 Fourth Street,
San Francisco 94103;
896-1600

ANA Hotel
50 Third Street,
San Francisco 94103;
974-6400

Sheraton-Palace Hotel
*2 New Montgomery
Street, San Francisco
94105; 392-8600*

Miyako Hotel
*1625 Post Street,
San Francisco 94115;
922-3200*

Best Western Miyako
*1800 Sutter Street,
San Francisco 94115;
921-4000*

The Bedford Hotel
*761 Post Street,
San Francisco 94109;
673-6040*

**Campton Place
Kempinski Hotel**
*340 Stockton Street,
San Francisco 94108;
781-5555*

The Cartwright Hotel
*524 Sutter Street,
San Francisco 94102;
421-2865*

Hotel Diva
*440 Geary Street,
San Francisco 94102;
885-0200*

Galleria Park Hotel
*191 Sutter Street,
San Francisco 94104;
781-3060*

Warwick Regis Hotel
*490 Geary Street,
San Francisco 94102;
928-7900*

Hotel Union Square
*114 Powell Street,
San Francisco 94102;
397-3000*

Boutique Hotels

The newest wave in hotels are so-called "boutique" hotels, many clustered near Union Square. These once-faded Edwardian hotels with good locations have been renovated into stylish lodgings with pampering service and blend the best of the old and new.

- **The Bedford Hotel** A good value.
- **Campton Place Kempinski Hotel** An expensive, well-appointed hotel with the **Campton Place Restaurant** (phone 955-5555).
- **The Cartwright Hotel** Filled with antiques and fresh flowers.
- **Hotel Diva**
- **Galleria Park Hotel** Located between the Financial District and Union Square, close to Chinatown.
- **Warwick Regis Hotel** Designed by Righetti & Headman in 1912, this fine Edwardian hotel was superbly transformed and has a restaurant and cocktail lounge.
- **Hotel Union Square**
- **The Hotel Vintage Court** The renowned **Masa's** restaurant is located here, 989-7154.
- **Inn at the Opera** Good for opera and symphony lovers; near now-hip Hayes Street.
- **The Inn at Union Square** The rejuvenation of a 1907 residential hotel designed by George A. Applegarth. The Swaine Adeney Brigg and Sons shop is on the ground floor.
- **Juliana Hotel** A delight. Near but not in Union Square and Chinatown.
- **Kensington Park** This is the fine 1924 Elks Club by Meyer and Johnson, with some decoration by Anthony Heinsbergen.

- **The Majestic Hotel** A posh 1902 hotel near Japantown; resplendantly restored and lavishly furnished with antiques. Stanley Eichelbaum's **Café Majestic** serves California cuisine with an emphasis on traditional San Francisco dishes (phone 776-6400).
- **Orchard Hotel**
- **Petite Auberge** A twenty-six-room "French-style inn" downtown.
- **Savoy Hotel**
- **Villa Florence Hotel** On the Powell Street cable car line near Union Square shopping.
- **The York Hotel** The sophisticated **Plush Room Cabaret** showcases fine entertainers in one of the city's most agreeable showrooms; call the hotel for information.

The Hotel Vintage Court,
650 Bush Street,
San Francisco 94108;
392-4666

Inn at the Opera
333 Fulton Street,
San Francisco 94102;
863-8400

The Inn at Union Square
440 Post Street,
San Francisco 94102;
397-3510

Juliana Hotel
590 Bush Street,
San Francisco 94108;
392-2540

Kensington Park
450 Post Street,
San Francisco 94102;
788-6400

The Majestic Hotel
1500 Sutter Street,
San Francisco 94109;
441-1100

Orchard Hotel
562 Sutter Street,
San Francisco 94102;
433-4434

Petite Auberge
863 Bush Street,
San Francisco 94108;
928-6000

Savoy Hotel
580 Geary Street,
San Francisco 94102;
441-2700

Villa Florence Hotel
225 Powell Street,
San Francisco 94102;
397-7700

The York Hotel
940 Sutter Street,
San Francisco 94109;
885-6800

1818 California Street
San Francisco 94109;
885-1818

El Drisco Hotel
2901 Pacific Avenue,
San Francisco 94115;
346-2880

Jackson Court
2198 Jackson Street,
San Francisco 94115;
929-7670

The Mansions Hotel
2220 Sacramento Street,
San Francisco 94115;
929-9444

The Monte Cristo Hotel
600 Presidio Avenue,
San Francisco 94115;
931-1875

The Queen Anne Hotel
1590 Sutter Street,
San Francisco 94109;
441-2828

Bed & Breakfast Inns/Small Historic Hotels

Many of San Francisco's bed-and-breakfast inns and small, revived historic hotels are in Victorian and Edwardian buildings and let you live, for a moment and at a price, in old San Francisco. They also bring you closer to San Francisco's congenial neighborhoods, for all are outside the downtown. Bed and breakfasts in San Francisco tend to be pricey but memorable. A few are covered as architectural sites elsewhere in this guide. This is a select list; the Yellow Pages lists more.

PACIFIC HEIGHTS

- **1818 California Street** The Lilienthal-Pratt house was built in 1876 and is a fine example of a San Francisco Italianate row house on a generous scale. Part of an outstanding cluster of Victorian landmarks.*

- **El Drisco Hotel** This Edwardian hotel is far from the hustle and bustle of the tourist zones and right in Pacific Heights, the poshest residential district in the city. Quiet; a good place for those who like to stroll in the evening. Serves meals. Expensive.

- **Jackson Court** An elegant old stone building of 1900, tastefully furnished with antiques in 1982; in a fine, quiet location.

- **The Mansions Hotel** A theatrically enlivened Queen Anne house of 1887 compatibly expanded in 1917. Now linked with a 1902 townhouse next door.

- **The Monte Cristo Hotel** An 1875 hotel with a colorful past, refurbished in 1980. Close to elite Presidio Heights.

- **The Queen Anne Hotel** A gabled and bay-windowed Queen Anne hotel with a corner turret, built in 1890 and restored in 1981.

UNION STREET AREA

- **Kavanaugh's Bed & Breakfast Inn** Two cozy cottages in a mews; restaurants and shopping around the corner.
- **The Sherman House** In tony Cow Hollow; built in 1876 with views of the Bay. A three-story Music Room was added in 1901. Restored in 1984 and furnished in antiques. Beautiful back garden. The restaurant here is a fine place for Sunday brunch. The surrounding blocks are rich in fine houses and great for walking. Expensive.
- **Union Street Inn** An Edwardian built in the 1900s and attractively adapted in 1979. Union Street's shops and restaurants are nearby.

NOB HILL

- **The Nob Hill Inn** This fine 1907 bay-windowed Edwardian building was luxuriously converted into a small hotel in 1982. Staying here, the traveler experiences the postfire building type so important to the real San Francisco, and also the tasteful period restorations that have been so characteristic of the city in the last twenty years.*

ALAMO SQUARE

- **Alamo Square Inn** An 1895 Queen Anne with a grand staircase furnished in Victorian and oriental decor.
- **The Chateau Tivoli** Designed by William H. Armitrage for lumber baron Daniel B. Jackson in 1892, this extravagant Queen Anne–style corner mansion is an ultimate San Francisco Victorian with a corner tower, bay windows, and every decorative trick known to nineteenth-century house design. The most wildly painted of the "painted ladies."
- **The Langtry** An 1894 Queen Anne house adapted as a hotel in 1986. A favorite with women travelers.

Kavanaugh's Bed & Breakfast Inn
4 Charlton Court,
San Francisco 94123;
921-9784

The Sherman House
2160 Green Street,
San Francisco 94123;
563-3600

Union Street Inn
2229 Union Street,
San Francisco 94123;
346-0424

The Nob Hill Inn
1000 Pine Street,
San Francisco 94109;
673-6080

Alamo Square Inn
719 Scott Street,
San Francisco 94117;
922-2055

The Chateau Tivoli
1057 Steiner Street,
San Francisco 94115;
776-5462

The Langtry
637 Steiner Street,
San Francisco 94117;
863-0538

The Red Victorian
1665 Haight Street,
San Francisco 94117;
864-1978

The Spencer House
1080 Haight Street,
San Francisco 94117;
626-9205

Stanyan Park Hotel
750 Stanyan Street,
San Francisco 94117;
751-1000

Victorian Inn on the Park
301 Lyon Street,
San Francisco 94117;
931-1830

Albion House Inn
135 Gough Street,
San Francisco 94102;
621-0896

Inn on Castro
321 Castro Street,
San Francisco 94111;
861-0321

24 Henry Street
near Castro and
Sixteenth, San Francisco
94114; 864-5686

The Willows Bed and
Breakfast
710 Fourteenth Street,
San Francisco 94114;
431-4770

Dolores Park Inn
3639-41 Seventeenth
Street, San Francisco
94114; 861-9335

The Inn San Francisco
943 South Van Ness
Avenue, San Francisco
94110; 641-0188

HAIGHT-ASHBURY/BUENA VISTA

- **The Red Victorian** Upstairs on Haight Street between Clayton and Belvedere; an Edwardian hotel revived with theme "hippie" rooms, such as the Peacock Suite.

- **The Spencer House** A very fine Queen Anne house of 1895, facing Buena Vista Park. Fine original interiors and tastefully decorated bedrooms; congenial and homey. Good for those who wish to jog or bicycle in nearby Golden Gate Park.*

- **Stanyan Park Hotel** A three-story, bay-windowed Edwardian hotel of 1904 attractively restored and improved in 1983. Good if you want to jog in Golden Gate Park early in the morning.*

- **Victorian Inn on the Park** A corner Queen Anne built in 1897 and opened as a hotel in 1982, at Golden Gate Park Panhandle.

THE CASTRO/UPPER MARKET

- **Albion House Inn** Post-earthquake hotel popular in the 1960s with musicians; now comfortably refurbished.

- **Inn on Castro** A bay-windowed Edwardian flats building typical of the city. Near, but not in, the lively Castro Street scene.

- **24 Henry Street** No breakfast; five rooms. An 1887 Victorian adapted as a guest house.

- **The Willows Bed and Breakfast** Near the Market and Church Muni Metro stop. A 1900s twelve-room inn, upstairs.

THE MISSION DISTRICT

- **Dolores Park Inn** A characteristic two-story Italianate house built in 1874.*

- **The Inn San Francisco** An 1872 mansion attractively adapted as a fifteen-room bed-and-breakfast inn.

NORTH BEACH

- **The Washington Square Inn** An intimate two-story, bay-windowed Edwardian hotel now tastefully furnished with antiques. Shared and private baths, some corner rooms. Perfectly located for sightseeing, dining, and for walking around at night.
- **San Remo Hotel** A few flat blocks from Fisherman's Wharf is this restored three-story, typical 1906 Edwardian hotel. Simple, comfortable, and reasonable, this is perhaps the most genuinely San Franciscan hotel near Fisherman's Wharf.

Small Downtown Hotels

Between penance and luxury there ought to be well-located, clean, inexpensive hotels. San Francisco has a good selection of these hotels as well.

- **The Andrews Hotel**
- **Atherton Hotel** Mixed gay and straight patronage; has a cozy lounge.
- **Beresford Arms Hotel**
- **Beresford Hotel** Small, comfortable rooms.
- **Canterbury Hotel & Whitehall Inn** Comfortably furnished and with a pub lounge.
- **Carlton Hotel**
- **The Gaylord Hotel**
- **Hotel Californian** Close to the Geary Street theaters.
- **King George Hotel** A favorite with European visitors. Excellent location for public transit.
- **Ramada Inn at Union Square** Reasonable rates.
- **Lombard Hotel**
- **Raphael Hotel** Many Californians stay here when they come to San Francisco.

The Washington Square Inn
1660 Stockton Street,
San Francisco 94133;
981-4220

San Remo Hotel
2237 Mason Street,
San Francisco 94133;
776-8688

The Andrews Hotel
624 Post Street,
San Francisco 94109;
563-6877

Atherton Hotel
685 Ellis Street,
San Francisco 94109;
474-5720

Beresford Arms Hotel
701 Post Street,
San Francisco, 94109;
673-2600

Beresford Hotel
635 Sutter Street,
San Francisco 94102;
673-9900

Canterbury Hotel & Whitehall Inn
750 Sutter Street,
San Francisco 94109;
474-6464

Carlton Hotel
1075 Sutter Street,
San Francisco 94109;
673-0242

The Gaylord Hotel
620 Jones Street,
San Francisco 94102;
673-8445

Hotel Californian
405 Taylor Street,
San Francisco 94102;
885-2500

King George Hotel
334 Mason Street,
San Francisco 94102;
781-5050

Ramada Inn at Union Square
345 Taylor Street,
San Francisco 94102;
673-2332

Lombard Hotel
1015 Geary Street,
San Francisco 94109;
673-5232

Raphael Hotel
386 Geary Street,
San Francisco 94102;
986-2000

Adelaide Inn
5 Isadora Duncan Court,
San Francisco 94102;
441-2261

Grant Plaza Hotel
465 Grant Avenue,
San Francisco 94108;
434-3883

Hotel Dakota
606 Post Street,
San Francisco 94109;
931-7475

Leland Hotel
1315 Polk Street,
San Francisco 94109;
441-5141

Obrero Hotel
1208 Stockton Street, '
San Francisco 94133;
989-3960

**Pension Hotel
San Francisco**
1668 Market Street,
San Francisco 94102;
864-1271

Budget Hotels

- **Adelaide Inn** Well located in an alley off Taylor. European students stretching their money stay here.

- **Grant Plaza Hotel** Located in Chinatown in a 1921 concrete building constructed for the Shanghai Low Company.

- **Hotel Dakota** For the budget-conscious traveler; close to Union Square.

- **Leland Hotel** On Polk Street at Bush.

- **Obrero Hotel** In Chinatown, upstairs. Well located for sightseeing, near North Beach. Simple rooms; shared baths.

- **Pension Hotel San Francisco** Near the Castro, well located for transit; the **Pensione Caffè** is downstairs.

MOTELS

The most popular listing of motels is the *AAA TourBook* for California and Nevada. The boldface type there is purchased and is not a quality distinction. The annual *Mobil Travel Guide* is another good listing. The following list of motels is not comprehensive.

FISHERMAN'S WHARF

The modern motels at Fisherman's Wharf are the favorites of families traveling during school vacations. They enjoy the highest occupancy rates in the city. Be sure to book ahead if you plan to stay here. All have parking.

- **Holiday Inn at Fisherman's Wharf** Two buildings; some rooms have views of the Bay. **Charley's Restaurant and Lounge** is located downstairs.
- **Howard Johnson's Motor Lodge and The Anchorage Shopping Center** A combination motel and shopping center with a small court. Well located.
- **Hyatt Fisherman's Wharf** Restaurant, pool, health club.
- **Ramada Hotel-Fisherman's Wharf** A 230-room motel with The Conch Pearl Restaurant and Pecan's Lounge.
- **Marriott-Fisherman's Wharf Hotel** Located here is **Wellington's Restaurant**, which also has a cocktail lounge.
- **Sheraton at Fisherman's Wharf** One of the newest motels, it has four small landscaped courts. **Shannon's Lounge** has entertainment Thursday through Saturday. American Express office is located here.
- **Travelodge Fisherman's Wharf Hotel**
- **Tuscan Inn at Fisherman's Wharf**
- **Wharf Inn**

Holiday Inn at Fisherman's Wharf
1300 Columbus Avenue, San Francisco 94133-1397; 771-9000

Howard Johnson's Motor Lodge and The Anchorage Shopping Center
580 Beach Street, San Francisco 94133; 775-3800

Hyatt Fisherman's Wharf
555 North Point Street, San Francisco 94133; 563-1234

Ramada Hotel-Fisherman's Wharf
590 Bay Street, San Francisco 94133; 885-4700

Marriott-Fisherman's Wharf Hotel
1250 Columbus Avenue, San Francisco 94133; 775-7555

Sheraton at Fisherman's Wharf
2500 Mason Street, San Francisco 94133; 362-5500

Travelodge Fisherman's Wharf Hotel
250 Beach Street, San Francisco 94133; 392-6700

Tuscan Inn at Fisherman's Wharf
425 North Point Street, San Francisco 94133; 561-1100

Wharf Inn
2601 Mason Street, San Francisco 94133; 673-7411

Bel Aire Travelodge
3201 Steiner Street,
San Francisco 94123;
(800) 578-7878

Motel Capri
2015 Greenwich Street,
San Francisco 94123;
346-4667

Lombard Motor Inn
1475 Lombard Street,
San Francisco 94123;
441-6000

Presidio Travelodge
2755 Lombard Street,
San Francisco 94123;
(800) 578-7878

**Rodeway Inn-Lombard
Street**
1450 Lombard Street,
San Francisco 94123;
673-0691

Star Motel
1727 Lombard Street,
San Francisco 94123;
346-8250

Surf Motel
2265 Lombard Street,
San Francisco 94123;
922-1950

**Travelodge Golden Gate
San Francisco**
2230 Lombard Street,
San Francisco 94123;
(800) 578-7878

Cathedral Hill Hotel
1101 Van Ness Avenue,
San Francisco 94109;
776-8200

Holiday Inn-Golden Gateway
1500 Van Ness Avenue,
San Francisco 94109;
441-4000

LOMBARD STREET

San Francisco's motel row is along Lombard Street, Highway 101, from Van Ness Avenue to the Golden Gate Bridge; more than thirty motels cluster here. As a blur of colored lights at night it is a very Californian street.

- **Bel Aire Travelodge** Off Lombard; quiet.
- **Motel Capri** A quiet, modern 1950s motel one block south of Lombard.
- **Lombard Motor Inn**
- **Presidio Travelodge**
- **Rodeway Inn-Lombard Street** Kitchens; pets accepted.
- **Star Motel** Simple, with a classic neon sign.
- **Surf Motel** Some kitchens.
- **Travelodge Golden Gate San Francisco**

VAN NESS AVENUE

Van Ness Avenue and Market Street are the widest streets in San Francisco. About a dozen motels cluster on Van Ness and almost as many along Market Street.

- **Cathedral Hill Hotel**
- **Holiday Inn-Golden Gateway** A stucco cereal box tower with excellent views east toward Nob Hill. Located near the end of the California Street cable car line.
- **Pacific Heights Inn** Kitchens; convenient to Union Street's shops and public transit.
- **Van Ness Motel** Basic; moderate rates.

CIVIC CENTER

- **The Phoenix Inn** A lowrise motel-with-a-pool painted post modern pink and aqua, with custom-designed bamboo furniture. Popular with rock musicians and hipsters.

CHINATOWN

- **Royal Pacific Motor Inn** A typical contemporary American motel with rooms you have slept in before (was it Newark, Delaware?). Its freestanding sign is so bad it's good.

SOUTH OF MARKET

San Francisco's budget motels are right off the freeway ramps in the South of Market district. This is the utilitarian, unfashionable side of town. Because San Francisco is so compact, you are still only a hop from all the major attractions.

- **Bay Bridge Inn**
- **Best Western-Civic Center Motor Inn** Not in the Civic Center.
- **Hojo Inn** At the Ninth Street exit off Highway 101.
- **Ramada Limited**

THE RICHMOND / OCEAN BEACH

- **Seal Rock Inn** At the end of Geary Street near the Cliff House, this "escape" motel is great for nature lovers; some rooms have a view of the ocean. Ocean Beach and rugged Land's End with its panorama of the Golden Gate are a short walk away.

Pacific Heights Inn
1555 Union Street,
San Francisco 94123;
776-3310

Van Ness Motel
2850 Van Ness Avenue,
San Francisco 94109;
776-3220

The Phoenix Inn
601 Eddy Street,
San Francisco 94109;
776-1380

Royal Pacific Motor Inn
661 Broadway,
San Francisco 94108;
781-6661

Bay Bridge Inn
966 Harrison Street,
San Francisco 94107;
397-0657

Best Western-Civic Center Motor Inn
364 Ninth Street,
San Francisco 94103;
621-2826

Hojo Inn
385 Ninth Street
San Francisco 94103;
431-5131

Ramada Limited
240 Seventh Street,
San Francisco 94103;
861-6469

Seal Rock Inn
545 Point Lobos Avenue,
San Francisco 94121;
752-8000

San Francisco International Hostel
Building 240,
Fort Mason,
San Francisco 94123;
771-7277

AYH-Hostel at Union Square
312 Mason Street,
San Francisco 94102;
788-5604

European Guest House
761 Minna Street,
San Francisco 94103;
861-6634

Inter-Club/Globe Hostel
10 Hallam Place,
San Francisco 94103;
431-0540

International Network Globetrotter's Inn
225 Ellis Street,
San Francisco 94102;
346-5786

American Youth Hostels
308 Mason Street,
between Geary and
O'Farrell Streets,
San Francisco 94102;
788-2525

HOSTELS

SAN FRANCISCO

- **San Francisco International Hostel** Near Aquatic Park and Fisherman's Wharf. Open for registration from 7 A.M. to 2 P.M. and from 4:30 P.M. to midnight. From the airport take SamTrans 7B bus to the TransBay Terminal in San Francisco. There take a Muni *northbound* 42 Downtown Loop "Gold Arrow" bus to Van Ness and Bay; follow the hostel signs.

- **AYH-Hostel at Union Square** American Youth Hostel membership required.

- **European Guest House** In the South of Market area, dormitory style, community kitchen, no curfew.

- **Inter-Club/Globe Hostel** Deep in the scruffy, trendy South of Market district, this hostel is popular with foreign student travelers; you need a foreign passport to stay here. **Brainwash**, a combination laundromat and cafe, is across Folsom Street.

- **International Network Globetrotter's Inn** in the Tenderloin near Union Square. Common kitchen, open twenty-four hours.

NORTH COAST

There are several hostels along the scenic, rugged coast near San Francisco. Some are in former lighthouses; the **Point Reyes Hostel** is in a former ranchhouse surrounded by fields, where there is splendid, hilly seacoast hiking. For a free list of California hostels and membership information send a S.A.S.E. to American Youth Hostels. Hostels are not limited to the young and are open to all ages. Members and nonmembers may stay here. A good way for single travelers to meet companion-explorers.

ALTERNATIVE LODGING

Residence Clubs

These clubs offer rooms with shared baths and meals and are useful for those planning longer stays and for job-hunters.

- **Baker Acres** Shared baths; meals optional; in Pacific Heights.
- **Kenmore Residential Club**
- **Monroe Residence Club** Shared baths; well located in an eastern-Pacific Heights apartment district.

Recreational Vehicles/Campgrounds

There are no campgrounds within the San Francisco city limits. **The San Francisco Recreational Vehicle Park,** off the Fourth Street exit of Interstate 80, across the street from the CalTrain Depot. Rail buffs should note that commuter trains operate from here to Stanford (Palo Alto) and down to San Jose.

Baker Acres
2201 Baker Street,
San Francisco 94115;
921-3088

Kenmore Residential Club
1570 Sutter Street,
San Francisco 94109;
776-5815

Monroe Residence Club
1870 Sacramento Street,
San Francisco 94109;
474-6200.

San Francisco Recreational Vehicle Park
250 King Street,
San Francisco 94107;
986-8730

Elka
1611 Post Street
San Francisco 94115;
922-7788

Postrio
545 Post Street,
San Francisco 94102;
776-7825

Masa's Restaurant
648 Bush Street,
San Francisco 94102;
989-7154

One Market
Market Street at the
corner of Steuart,
San Francisco 94105;
777-5577

Stars
150 Redwood Alley
San Francisco 94102;
861-7827

Lulu
816 Folsom Street,
San Francisco 94107;
495-5775

Zuni Cafe
1658 Market Street,
San Francisco 94102;
552-2522

RESTAURANTS, SALOONS, AND CLUBS

This book is only incidentally a guide to San Francisco's more than four thousand restaurants and numberless bars, far too many to discuss individually. Several restaurant guides are available to help you pick and choose among the multitude. The Yellow Pages also lists many of San Francisco's restaurants by cuisine. For particular districts check for "Restaurants, Cafes, and Bars" in the chapters' Preliminaries.

California—the Bay Area and Los Angeles' Westside in particular—seems to be making up for two hundred years of bad food by going through an accelerated evolutionary process of culinary development. The best general influence on contemporary San Francisco cooking is that of Asia, with its low-meat, steamed, and stir-fried foods. The fresh fruits and vegetables of California, especially custom-grown "organic" produce, make cooking here much more healthy. Today "California cuisine" has emerged as a health-conscious style of cooking and of food-as-art presentation.

Today's temples to gastronomy are San Francisco's newest attractions, and if you can afford it you should treat yourself to dinner at at least one great contemporary restaurant. Expensive but memorable, and highly recommended, are:

Elka, chef Elka Gilmore serves "definitive seafood" and other kinds of memorable dishes in an elegant, contemporary setting; located in Japantown. **Postrio**, a California cuisine restaurant in the Union Square area, has a posh modern interior. **Masa's Restaurant**, one of the best French restaurants in the nation. **One Market**, a new and superior restaurant. **Stars**, a half-block from City Hall in the block bounded by Van Ness, Polk, Golden Gate, and McAllister. This is Jeremiah Tower's fine restaurant and also a public stage for the glitterati. **Lulu**, located south of Market, has an airy, contemporary setting. **Zuni Cafe**, chef Judy Roberts prepares fine contemporary dishes and serves them in a relaxed southwestern setting.

The spirit of the Western saloon is alive and kicking in San Francisco, and always will be. In the Victorian city there was a saloon on virtually every corner. Historian A. M. Schlesinger wrote that in 1890 San Francisco had more saloons relative to its population than any other American city. Private sanctums, sophisticated *boîtes,* middle-class lounges, singles' bars, sports bars, working-class taverns, black joints, ethnic havens, gay rendezvous, punk bunkers, mixed places—San Francisco's bars have always been the city dweller's democratic "clubs." It is how Americans relax and compete at the same time. San Francisco bars are liveliest on Fridays and Saturdays after about 11:30 P.M.; all bars close at the early hour of 2 A.M.

Some New Clubs

South of Market, colloquially known as **SOMA,** is where you'll find the city's newest hot spots. In the daytime, **Eleventh Street** is a light industrial zone. By night it blossoms into an entertainment district, most active Friday and Saturday nights between 11 P.M. and 2 A.M. But the scene has moved on since Eleventh Street replaced North Beach's Broadway. To find the newest venues check the flyers taped to the utility poles near Eleventh and Folsom. In the 1990s many clubs float from location to location on different nights of the week. Cafes south of Market, cutting-edge record shops along Haight Street, and **A Different Light Bookstore** on Castro are places where small handbills for the latest clubs are distributed. Today the most advanced clubs are neither gay nor straight but a dynamic fusion of all possible human permutations. By the time a dance club is published in a guide the scene has probably moved on.

Crash Palace, a rock club, is located in the Western Addition. The terminally hip may want to check out **Komotion,** located in a garage in the Mission District. Punx cluster here, so you know how long this will last.

SOMA—South of Market
South of Market Street

Eleventh Street
between Folsom and Harrison streets

Crash Palace
628 Divisadero Street; 931-1914

Komotion
2779 Sixteenth Street; 648-4923

Ace Café
1539 Folsom Street;
621-4752

The DNA Lounge
375 Eleventh Street,
near Harrison;
626-1409

Hamburger Mary's
1582 Folsom Street,
near Twelfth; 626-9516

Paradise Lounge
1501 Folsom Street, at
Eleventh; 861-6906

Slim's Nightclub
333 Eleventh Street,
near Folsom; 621-3330

20 Tank Brewery
316 Eleventh Street,
between Folsom and
Harrison; 255-9455

Soma Caffè
1601 Howard Street,
at Twelfth; 861-5012

The Stud
399 Ninth Street, at
Harrison; 863-6623

SOUTH OF MARKET/ELEVENTH STREET

Ace Café, an artsy hangout/coffee house, open Monday to Friday; Saturday, Sunday brunch. (**Norfolk Alley**, between Folsom and Harrison, Eleventh and Twelfth, behind The Ace Café has some of the most artistic graffiti in town. But the spray can art is not as spontaneous as it looks; it's done from sketchbooks.) **The DNA Lounge**, a large, two-level rock club with Keith Haring art and a diverse selection of contemporary dance music; open after hours, without alcohol, until 4 A.M. **Hamburger Mary's**, funky; a survivor from the hippie days; inexpensive. **Paradise Lounge**, a bar and small lounges featuring local bands. **Slim's Nightclub**, Boz Scaggs' fine blues, r&b, jazz, and rock club; the best choice here. **20 Tank Brewery**, open from 11:30 A.M. to 1 A.M. Food and beer. **Soma Caffè** a relaxed and welcoming place. **The Stud**, alive, young, and gay since 1969; active dance bar even on weekday nights.

MUSEUMS

San Francisco has no truly encyclopedic museums of art or natural history, but does have spread out over the city many specialized museums, some of which are jewels. Several tours are built around these historical treasure houses. Asterisked entries are covered in greater detail in the appropriate chapter.

Art Museums

- **Ansel Adams Center/Friends of Photography Museum and Gallery** A fine-photography museum with changing exhibits and contemporary work; bookstore. Across the street from Moscone Convention Center.
- **Asian Art Museum/Avery Brundage Collection** See entry below for M. H. de Young Memorial Museum.
- **California Palace of the Legion of Honor** In Lincoln Park; the emphasis here is on French art. There is a large Rodin collection, including *The Shades*, across the parking lot from the museum. The superb **Achenbach Foundation for Graphic Arts** is located here as well. The black granite Japan-American Peace monument faces the Golden Gate Bridge near the museum.*
- **M. H. de Young Memorial Museum** This is the city's most diversified art museum. The Mr. & Mrs. John D. Rockefeller 3rd collection of American art, over a hundred fine works, was donated in 1979 and gives a good overview of American painting up to about 1900. The **Avery Brundage Collection** and **Asian Art Museum** adjoin the de Young.*
- **The Oakland Museum of California** An outstanding museum. *(See Tour 16.)*
- **San Francisco Museum of Modern Art** Swiss architect Mario Botta's superb new museum opened in 1995 and splendidly showcases this choice collection. There are strong holdings of the works of the French Fauves, German Expressionists, and Surrealists, and also American contemporary painting and photography. *(See Tour 15.)*

Ansel Adams Center/ Friends of Photography Museum and Gallery
250 Fourth Street, between Howard and Folsom Streets; 495-7000

California Palace of the Legion of Honor
Lincoln Park, near Thirty-Fourth Avenue and Clement Street; 750-3600

M. H. de Young Memorial Museum
Music Concourse, Golden Gate Park; 750-3600
• **The Avery Brundage Collection** *and* **Asian Art Museum**
668-8921

The Oakland Museum of California
1000 Oak Street, Oakland; (510)642-1207

San Francisco Museum of Modern Art
151 Third Street, in Yerba Buena Center, between Mission and Howard Streets; 357-4000

San Francisco Art Institute
800 Chestnut Street,
between Jones and
Leavenworth; 771-7020

Stanford University
Art Museum
Museum Way, Stanford
campus, Stanford;
723-4177

The University Art Museum
Bancroft Way between
Bowditch and College,
Berkeley; (510) 642-1207
• Pacific Film Archive
(510) 642-1412

African-American
Historical and Cultural
Society, *Fort Mason,*
Building C; 441-0640

Alcatraz Island
546-2628

Museum of the Money
of the American West,
Bank of California

Contemporary
Crafts Museum
900 North Point Street;
771-1919

Chinese Historical
Society of America
650 Commercial Street;
391-1188

Craft & Folk Art Museum
of San Francisco,
Fort Mason,
Building A, first floor;
775-0990

Haas-Lilienthal House
2007 Franklin Street,
441-3004

Jewish Museum
121 Steuart Street;
543-8880

- **San Francisco Art Institute** On Russian Hill. Shows in the Emmanuel Walter Gallery and student exhibitions. Not always open.*

- **Stanford University Art Museum** *Note:* due to damage from the earthquake of 1989, the museum has been closed, phone ahead to make sure that it is open. *(See Tour 16.)*

- **The University Art Museum** Eleven galleries; some Asian art; notable Hans Hofmann collection. The Museum also houses the agreeable theater of the **Pacific Film Archive**, which screens interesting films almost every evening. *(See Tour 16.)* *

Historical and House Museums

- **African-American Historical and Cultural Society** At Fort Mason.
- **Alcatraz Island** Schedules vary with the seasons. *
- **Museum of the Money of the American West** *(See Tour 2.)* *
- **Contemporary Crafts Museum** In Ghirardelli Square, has the ambiance of a store. *(See Tour 5.)*
- **Chinese Historical Society of America** *(See Tour 3.)*
- **Craft & Folk Art Museum of San Francisco** At Fort Mason, next to Greens Restaurant.
- **Haas-Lilienthal House** Open with guided tours. *(See Tour 8.)*
- **Jewish Museum** Near the foot of Mission Street.
- **Judah L. Magnes Museum, Western Jewish History Center** Near the Claremont Hotel. Jewish ritual artifacts from all ages and places; materials on the Jewish communities in California and the Western United States; changing art and history exhibits.
- **Joseph D. Randall Junior Museum** In Buena Vista Park area, for children.
- **Mission Dolores Museum** Open daily with seasonal hours *(See Tour 10.)*
- **Museum of the City of San Francisco** On the third floor of the Cannery at Leavenworth and Beach.
- **Museum of Russian Culture**, on Sutter Street between Divisadero and Broderick.
- **North Beach Museum** Upstairs over EurekaBank.
- **Octagon House** An 1861 octagonal house furnished by the Colonial Dames of America.
- **Old Mint Museum** "The Granite Lady" was built in 1874 and minted silver dollars and gold coins until 1937. In 1973 it opened as a U.S. Treasury Department museum with gold nuggets, coins, exhibits on minting, and Victoriana.
- **Pacific Heritage Museum** *(See Tour 2.)*
- **San Francisco Archives for the Performing Arts**
- **San Francisco Fire Department Museum** Antique equipment and memorabilia of the city's great fires.

Judah L. Magnes Museum, Western Jewish History Center,
2911 Russell Street, Berkeley; (510) 849-2710

Joseph D. Randall Junior Museum
199 Museum Way; 554-9600

Mission Dolores Museum
Dolores Street, near Sixteenth, behind the old mission; 621-8203

Museum of the City of San Francisco
2801 Leavenworth Street; 928-0289

Museum of Russian Culture
2450 Sutter Street; 921-4082

North Beach Museum
1435 Stockton Street

Octagon House
2645 Gough Street; 441-7512

Old Mint Museum
88 Mission Street; 744-6830

Pacific Heritage Museum
Bank of Canton of California, 608 Commercial Street, 362-4100

San Francisco Archives for the Performing Arts
399 Grove Street; 255-4800

San Francisco Fire Department Museum
665 Presidio Avenue; 861-8000

San Francisco History Room and Archives
Civic Center Public Library; 558-3949
City Guide Walks, 558-3981

San Francisco Presidio Museum/Refugee Cottages
Lincoln Boulevard and Funston Avenue; 556-0856

Society of California Pioneers, 957-1849

Sutro Library
480 Winston Drive; 731-4477

Telecommunications Museum, *140 New Montgomery Street,* 542-0182; *see Tour 2B*

Treasure Island Museum
Building 1; 395-5067

Wells Fargo Bank History Museum,
420 Montgomery Street, 396-2619; *see Tour 2A.*

Hyde Street Pier Historic Ships
at the foot of Hyde Street; 556-3002

S.S. Jeremiah O'Brien
Fort Mason, Pier 3 East; 441-3101

U.S.S. Pampanito
Pier 45; 929-0202

- **San Francisco History Room and Archives** Showcases San Franciscana. Also conducts free **City Guide Walks**; phone for information.
- **San Francisco Presidio Museum/Refugee Cottages** In the Presidio. *(See Tour 14.)*
- **Society of California Pioneers** Near City Hall, location under renovation. California history before 1869; has a good collection of Victorian silver and arti-facts.
- **Sutro Library** San Francisco photographs and other materials collected by Mayor Adolph Sutro; changing exhibits.
- **Telecommunications Museum** Off the lobby of the Pacific Telephone and Telegraph Company Headquarters.*(See Tour 2B.)**
- **Treasure Island Museum** Treasure Island. Navy, Marine Corps, Coast Guard museum; also relics of the 1939 Fair.
- **Wells Fargo Bank History Museum** *(See Tour 2A.)**

Maritime Museum and Historic Ships
- **Hyde Street Pier Historic Ships** near the turntable of the Powell-Hyde cable car line and Fisherman's Wharf.
- **S.S. Jeremiah O'Brien** National Liberty Ship Memorial.
- **U.S.S. Pampanito** Submarine at Fisherman's Wharf.
- **Balclutha** 1886 square-rigger, see Hyde Street Pier Historic Ships above.*

(See Tour 5 for all of the above.)

Scientific Museums and Zoo

- **California Academy of Sciences** in Golden Gate Park. Exhibits on natural history, an aquarium and a planetarium.*

- **Exploratorium** This science museum, behind the Palace of Fine Arts, has interactive exhibits on light and color, sound and music, motion, electricity, and other natural phenomena, with emphasis on human perception and how our senses work.

- **San Francisco Zoo** in the far southwestern corner of the city.

- **Lawrence Hall of Science** in the hills above the University of California campus in Berkeley. Activities in astronomy, computer science, and biology; also a planetarium.*

- **The Phoebe Apperson Hearst Museum of Anthropology** University of California, Berkeley. Changing exhibits from an outstanding anthropological collection. *(See Tour 16.)*

California Academy of Sciences *Music Concourse, Golden Gate Park:*
- *Aquarium, 750-7145*
- *Planetarium, 750-7141*

Exploratorium, *Marina Boulevard and Lyon; 561-0360*

San Francisco Zoo, *Sloat Boulevard and Forty-Sixth Avenue; 753-7061*

Lawrence Hall of Science *Centennial Drive in Berkeley; (510) 642-5132*

The Phoebe Apperson Hearst Museum of Anthropology, *Bancroft Way at College Avenue; (510) 643-7648*

Chevron's World of Oil Museum
555 Market Street;
894-7700

Guinness Museum of World Records
235 Jefferson Street;
771-9890

Musée Mechanique
1090 Point Lobos Avenue; 386-1170

Ripley's Believe It Or Not Museum
175 Jefferson Street;
771-6188

Tattoo Art Museum
841 Columbus Avenue;
775-4991

Wax Museum at Fisherman's Wharf
145 Jefferson Street;
885-4975

Miscellaneous Museums

- **Chevron's World of Oil Museum** Market Street between First and Second.

- **Guinness Museum of World Records** at Fisherman's Wharf.

- **Musée Mechanique** in the Cliff House.

- **Ripley's Believe It Or Not Museum** Jefferson Street near Taylor, at Fisherman's Wharf.

- **Tattoo Art Museum** on Columbus Avenue near Lombard Street.

- **Wax Museum at Fisherman's Wharf** Jefferson Street between Mason and Taylor.

TOUR ONE
Union Square/Yerba Buena Center

•

Tour 1A:

THE EMPORIUM OF THE WEST AND UNION SQUARE

Tour 1B:

SOUTH OF MARKET'S YERBA BUENA CENTER:
NEW ARTS FOCUS/MOSCONE CONVENTION CENTER

WILLIAM
WALTERS
© 1988

An art glass dome made by the United Art Glass Co.
in 1908 caps the *belle époque* rotunda of Bakewell and Brown's lost
City of Paris department store reconstructed within Johnson/Burgee's 1982
Neiman-Marcus at Stockton and Geary, at the southeast corner of Union Square.
The Latin motto is that of Paris: "It floats and never sinks."

What These Tours Cover
Preliminaries
Introduction: The Emporium of the West and Union Square, San Francisco's Civic Stage

San Francisco's Speciality Stores

1 Neiman-Marcus/City of Paris Rotunda

2 Frank Lloyd Wright's 140 Maiden Lane

3 Saks Fifth Avenue

4 Macy's California

5 Emporium-Capwell

6 Nordstrom/San Francisco Centre

7 Old Hale Brothers

Clubland

8 The Family Club

9 Tessie Wall's Townhouse

10 The Francisca Club

11 The Metropolitan Club

12 The Pan Pacific Hotel

13 The Olympic Club

14 The Bohemian Club

15 The Commonwealth Club of California

**TOUR 1A:
UNION SQUARE**

Preliminaries
Introduction: The South of Market, from
Skid Row to Arts Center

Continuation
    Outlets Further South

Map of Union Square

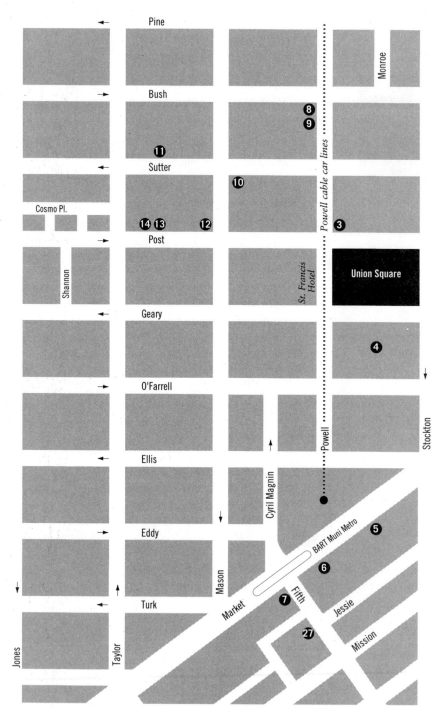

Map of Union Square

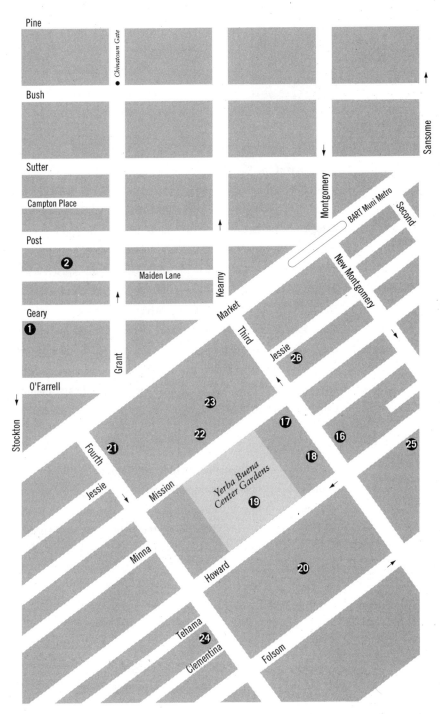

Preliminaries: Tour 1a

Sutter/Stockton Garage
*one block northeast of
Union Square, enter from
Bush Street headed east*

Downtown Center Garage
*at Mason/O'Farrell,
a block to the southeast
of Union Square*

Fifth and Mission

Moscone Center
*Third Street,
between Folsom and
Howard Streets*

Hearst Building Garage
*Third Street, between
Mission and Market
Streets*

**BEST TIMES TO
DO THIS TOUR**

About 10 A.M. to noon on weekdays is generally the least crowded time to shop, both at department stores and individual shops. Saturdays are the busiest times around Union Square. Some factory outlets are only open on Saturdays.

Parking

The glory of the Union Square shopping area is that it is a pedestrian zone. Garaging your car will cost about $13 for a full day from 10 A.M. to midnight. The twelve-level municipal **Sutter/Stockton Garage** one block northeast of Union Square is *the* garage; enter from Bush Street headed east. The private **Downtown Center Garage** at Mason/O'Farrell, a block to the southeast of Union Square, is well located for evening theater-going. The city garage underneath the Square itself, entered from Geary Street headed west, is central. Other garages are shown on the map. The massive **Fifth and Mission** city parking garage serves Nordstrom, The Emporium and the South of Market. **Moscone Center** has a large parking garage on Third Street, between Folsom and Howard streets. The **Hearst Building Garage** is at Third Street, between Mission and Market streets.

Transportation

The downtown is the nexus of public transportation routes in San Francisco, the ultimate goal implied when a route is heading "in." Throughout this guide transportation directions use Union Square as an origin and return point. Within the downtown, which is itself extensive, buses run toward most points of the compass and taxis are plentiful.

RESTAURANTS, CAFÉS, AND BARS

In the Union Square area, **Kuleto's** beautifully designed Art Deco restaurant with excellent Northern Italian cusine; weekend brunch. **Campton Place Bar and Restaurant**, stylish bar and restaurant serving American food, excellent breakfasts. The correct place to loiter, offers porthole glimpses of Union Square; expensive. **California Pizza Kitchen,** glitzy decor and good food at a fair price. **Ed's** The downtown worker's favorite hole-in-the-wall luncheonette. Good meatloaf sandwiches and chocolate milkshakes; inexpensive.

Around Clubland, **Postrio**, Wolfgang Puck and Anne and David Gingrass' artistic temple to contemporary gastronomy, designed by Pat Kuleto. Breakfast, lunch, and dinner; designer pizzas served at the bar; memorable; expensive. One of the places to be seen in San Francisco. **Fleur de Lys**, fine French cuisine well presented in a comfortable tentlike setting designed by Michael Taylor. Chef Hubert Keller's *haute cuisine* is superb; expensive. **Donatello** excellent Northern Italian cuisine nicely presented; no lunch; expensive. **Masa's Restaurant**, fine French *haute cuisine* well presented by chef Julian Seranno. Some consider this the best French restaurant in the country; no lunch, reservations essential far in advance; very expensive. **Trader Vic's**, opened in 1951, this is one of the city's famous spots, but culinary art has evolved considerably since then. Note: At the time of this publication, Trader Vic's was closed for renovation. Call for status. **La Quiche**, excellent quiche and crepes; inexpensive. **Mason Street Wine Bar**, piano music nightly. A wide selection of wine by the glass from California and Europe, nonalcoholic "wines," beers, Italian sodas, and juices. **Oz**, at the top of the Hotel St. Francis. The fastest exterior elevators in the city give a quick view of Union Square; acrophobes beware. **The Starlight Roof,** in the Sir Francis Drake Hotel, twenty-one stories above the intersection of Powell and Sutter. Sophisticated dancing nightly. The festive electric sign and revolving neon star atop the hotel are visible from Union Square and add the perfect touch of glamour and unreality to the downtown at night. **The Redwood Room**, located in the The Four Seasons Clift

Note: *See additional restaurant listings under South of Market, farther on in this Tour.*

Kuleto's
221 Powell Street, between Geary and O'Farrell; 397-7720

Campton Place Bar and Restaurant, *340 Stockton Street in Campton Place Hotel, a half-block northeast of Union Square; 955-5555*

California Pizza Kitchen
438 Geary Street, between Mason and Taylor; 563-8911

Ed's, *137 Kearny, between Geary and Post, next to Sherman-Clay; 989-7373*

Postrio, *545 Post Street, between Mason and Taylor; 776-7825*

Fleur de Lys, *777 Sutter Street, near Jones; 673-7779*

Donatello, *501 Post Street at Mason, in the Donatello Hotel; 441-7100*

Masa's Restaurant
648 Bush, between Powell and Stockton; 989-7154

Trader Vic's, *20 Cosmo Place, near Post and Taylor; 776-2232.*

La Quiche, *550 Taylor Street, between Post and Geary; 441-2711*

Mason Street Wine Bar
342 Mason Street, at Geary; 391-3454

Oz, *at the top of Hotel St. Francis, Powell and Geary;* 397-7000

The Starlight Roof, *in the Sir Francis Drake Hotel, 450 Powell;* 392-7755

The Redwood Room, *in the Four Season's Clift Hotel, 495 Geary Street, at Taylor;* 775-4700

STBS booth *Stockton Street near Geary;* 433-7827

Hotel St. Francis Theater Ticket Agency *Powell and Geary;* 362-3500

City Box Office *141 Kearny, at Sutter;* 392-4400

Downtown Center Box Office, *325 Mason, in Downtown Center;* 775-2021

ACT/American Conservatory Theater *in the* **Geary Theater** *415 Geary Street;* 749-2228

Curran Theater *445 Geary Street, between Mason and Taylor;* 474-3800

The Actors Theater of San Francisco *533 Sutter Street, near Powell;* 296-9179

Alcazar Theater *650 Geary Street, between Jones and Leavenworth;* 441-6655

Hotel, is one of San Francisco's most elegant public spaces. Designed by G.A. Lansburgh with Anthony Heinsbergen, a famous theater designer, this soft, luxurious Moderne room is the perfect place to experience the sophistication of traditional San Francisco.

Theater, music, and dance, especially experimental theater, are *alive* in San Francisco and Berkeley. This is a key sign of the cultural ferment in the Bay Area. Even the AIDS epidemic, which has hit the art world so brutally, has not dimmed this efflorescence. In fact, the epidemic has given an urgency to many artists in San Francisco. Today there are so many venues with so much going on that a small industry has developed in publishing free entertainment guides crammed with events. Of the many free papers, the **S.F. Weekly** is probably the hippest. **The San Francisco Bay Guardian** lists many events. The **B.A.R.** lists gay and lesbian entertainment, as does the progressive **San Francisco Bay Times**. The "pink section" of the **Sunday Examiner-Chronicle** is the best-known entertainment guide. You should take a chance and see something new while you are here. Check the entertainment suggestions at the beginning of the tours.

STBS booth, on the edge of Union Square itself in a small pavilion sells *half-price, cash-only, in-person unsold tickets* for day-of-performance events; also sells full-price tickets in advance as a BASS outlet. You can buy **Muni Passports** here, too, for public transit; open 11 A.M. to 6:30 P.M.; closed Sunday and Monday. Tickets can also be purchased at the **Hotel St. Francis Theater Ticket Agency**. **City Box Office** isopen Monday to Friday, 9:30 A.M. to 5 P.M., Saturday, 10 A.M. to 4 P.M.; and the **Downtown Center Box Office**, open Monday to Friday 12 noon to 4 P.M.

Union Square Theaters

Old theaters seem to hold in themselves something of all the emotions and pleasures that have saturated them over the years. A transporting piece of theater in a fine old theater has a satisfaction few things in life can equal. The ornate **Geary Theater** of 1909 and the **Curran Theater** of 1922 next door are two of the finest-for-their-purpose buildings in San Francisco. They, along with the **War Memorial Opera House** of 1932, make a night at the theater *feel* like a night at the theater.

            ACT/American Conservatory Theater, in the Geary Theater, is San Francisco's best known theatrical ensemble. Founded by William Ball and directed by him in San Francisco from 1967 to 1989. Stages about eight productions each season; also provides advanced training in acting. The **Geary Theater** opened in 1909 as the Columbia Theater and was designed by Bliss and Faville. Recently restored, it is built of reinforced concrete and finished inside with Utah Caen stone and Tennessee marble. Its façade is notable for its polychrome terra-cotta columns of fruits and garlands. The legends "Comedy" and "Tragedy" adorn opposite sides of the doorway. The elegant **Curran Theater** was built by Homer Curran and designed by Alfred Henry Jacobs in 1922. It is also of reinforced concrete with a fine ornamented façade, mansard roof, and fine marquee. Its metal sidewalk sign frames are notable. A great place to see a play. **The Actors Theater of San Francisco** is an intimate ninety-nine-seat theater presenting ensemble theater pieces. The **Alcazar Theater**, in the Tenderloin, was built in 1917 by the Shriners as an Islam Temple of the Shrine with a Moorish facade. It offers changing programs. Other Union Square theaters are **The Cable Car Theater**; the **Lorraine Hansberry Theater**, in the Sheehan Hotel, featuring the contemporary African American theater; **The Golden Gate Theater**; the **Marine's Memorial Theater**; the **Theater on the Square**; and the **Warfield Theater**, a favorite venue for big rock concerts.

Theaters Outside Union Square

Theater Artaud, in the Mission District presents new works that break the boundaries between dance, theater, music, and visual arts. **Asian American Dance Performances**, organized in 1974, presents modern pieces. **Asian American Theater Company**, in the Inner Richmond District, founded in 1973, often presents plays about the experiences of Asian Americans. **Climate Theater**, in the South

Cable Car Theater
430 Mason, near Geary, downstairs next to Regency III; 956-8497

Lorraine Hansberry Theater
620 Sutter Street, near Mason, in the Sheehan Hotel; 474-8800

Golden Gate Theater
42 Golden Gate Avenue, northwest corner of Taylor at Market; 474-3800

Marine's Memorial Theater
609 Sutter Street, at Mason; 771-6900

Theater on the Square
450 Post Street, near Mason; 433-9500

Warfield Theater
982 Market Street, northeast corner of Taylor; 775-7722

Theater Artaud
450 Florida Street, at Seventeenth Street; 621-7797

Asian American Dance Performances
225 Mississippi Street; 552-8980

Asian American Theater Company
403 Arguello Boulevard, at Geary; 751-2600

Climate Theater,
252 Ninth Street between Howard and Folsom; 626-9196

George Coates Performance Works
110 McAllister Street, near Leavenworth; 863-4130

Cowell Theater
Fort Mason Center, Marina Boulevard at Buchanan, Pier 2; 441-5706

Magic Theater
Building D; 776-8822

Footwork Studio
3221 Twenty-second Street at Mission; 824-5044.

Intersection for the Arts
446 Valencia Street, between Fifteenth and Sixteenth streets; 626-2787

Mission Cultural Center/Teatro Mision
2868 Mission Street, near Twenty-fifth; 821-1155

San Francisco Mime Troupe, *285-1717.*

New Conservatory Theater Center *, 25 Van Ness Avenue near Market, in the old Masonic Temple; 861-8972*

New Performance Gallery
3153 Seventeenth Street, at Shotwell Street; 863-9834

Phoenix Theater
301 Eighth Street, at Folsom; 621-4423

Theater Rhinoceros
2926 Sixteenth Street, near South Van Ness Avenue; 861-5079

Theater of Yugen
2840 Mariposa Street; 621-7978

of Market area, offers progressive theater with an emphasis on solo works. **George Coates Performance Works** in the Civic Center presents abstract theater pieces that fuse opera with drama and dazzling visual effects. **Cowell Theater,** in Fort Mason Center, is a multicultural theater in multicultural San Francisco. **Footwork Studio,** in the Mission District presents innovative dance with personal visions. **Intersection for the Arts,** also in the Mission District, offers new and experimental works, while the **Magic Theater** in Fort Mason Center is also dedicated to new plays. **San Francisco Mime Troupe**, performing in various venues including city parks in the summer, was founded in 1959 and is still radical after all these years—satiric political theater for the people. **Mission Cultural Center/Teatro Mision**, in the Mission District offers new Latino theater in both English and Spanish. **New Conservatory Theater Center** presents a range of live theater—from drama to musicals and is located near the Civic Center. **New Performance Gallery** in the Mission District features contemporary international dance, theater, and performance art. **Phoenix Theater,** in the south of Market area, focuses on contemporary theater by local and international playwrights. **Theater Rhinoceros**, in the Mission District, is an important venue for gay and lesbian theater. **Theater of Yugen,** offering various venues, specializes in Noh and Kyogen Japanese theater, but performs contemporary non-Japanese theater as well. The ensemble employs dance, masks, mime, and Asian and Western music—and performs in both English and Japanese.

Shopping

The culinary inclined will appreciate the **San Francisco Health Food Store,** open 9:15 A.M. to 5:30 P.M., selling extra-fancy California dried fruits, juices, and protein shakes so that you don't drop while you shop; for the less discerning, there is **Morrow's Nut House** and **The Candy Jar,** which makes its own chocolate truffles—the highest quality. **John Walker & Co.,** and **Wines and Spirits,** offer a fine selection of libations. **Malm Luggage,** carries all major lines, **Louis Vuitton, Gucci,** and **Mark Cross,** are located on Union Square as well. **Hermes,** much like the store in Paris, is downtown San Francisco's new classic. **Golden Gate Pen Shop** is the best place for fine writing instruments.

Jewelry

Among the places to find jewelry are **Tiffany & Co.; Cartier Jewelers; Shreve & Co.,** a historic Western silversmith that made out of Nevada silver many of the impossibly ornamented presentation pieces popular in the Victorian era; **J. M. Lang Antiques,** a treasure trove of antique jewelry, objects of art, silver, ivory, amber, and Russian Imperial things; **Robert F. Johnson, Inc.,** in The Phelan Building, coins and estate jewelry; **The Jewelry Center,** also in The Phelan Building, with many jewelry shops upstairs, designed by William Curlett in 1908, a white terra-cotta-clad flatiron building.

Note: *Those interested in silver should see the Victorian pieces at the Society of California Pioneers Museum, near the Civic Center; 861-5278.*

Note: *Also see outlet listings for the South of Market area, at the end of this chapter.*

San Francisco Health Food Store, *333 Sutter Street; 392-8477*

Morrow's Nut House *111 Geary Street; 362-7969*

The Candy Jar *210 Grant Street; 391-5508*

John Walker & Co., Wines and Spirits, *175 Sutter Street; 986-6836*

Malm Luggage, *222 Grant Avenue; 392-0417*

Louis Vuitton, *230 Post Street; 391-6200*

Gucci, *200 Stockton; 392-2808*

Mark Cross, *170 Post Street; 391-7770*

Hermes, *1 Union Square; 391-7200*

Golden Gate Pen Shop *278 Post Street; 781-4809*

Tiffany & Co. *350 Post Street; 781-7000*

Cartier Jewelers *231 Post Street; 397-3180*

Shreve & Co. *200 Post Street; 421-2600*

J. M. Lang Antiques *323 Sutter Street; 982-2213*

Robert F. Johnson, Inc.
The Jewelry Center
760 Market Street/
35 O'Farrell Street;
421-9710

Kris Kelly, *174 Geary Street; 986-8822*

Scheuer Linens
318 Stockton Street; 392-2813

Williams-Sonoma
150 Post Street; 362-6904

Britex Fabrics, *146 Geary Street; 392-2910*

Pierre Deux French Country Fabrics, *120 Maiden Lane; 296-9940*

Jessica McClintock Boutique, *353 Sutter Street; 397-0987*

Laura Ashley, *253 Post Street; 788-0190*

Obiko, *794 Sutter Street; 755-2882*

The Forgotten Woman, *550 Sutter Street; 788-1452*

Emporio Armani, *1 Grant Avenue; 677-9400*

Polo-Ralph Lauren Shop, *90 Post Street; 567-7656*

Banana Republic, *256 Grant Street; 788-3087*

Hound, *111 Sutter Street; 989-0429*

A. Sulka & Company, *255 Post Street; 989-0600*

Billyblue, *73 Geary; 781-2111*

Linen

Kris Kelly, fine linen and hand-embellished tablecloths and bed linen. **Scheuer Linens,** Stockton Street between Post and Sutter, has fine table linens, sheets, and towels; also French and Italian sheets.

Cookware

Williams-Sonoma, between Grant and Kearny, offers everything for the serious cook.

Fabric

Britex Fabrics, between Stockton and Grant, has four floors of fabrics from around the world; multi-lingual staff. **Pierre Deux French Country Fabrics,** on Maiden Lane between Stockton and Grant, carries fine French fabrics.

Clothing and Shoes

Jessica McClintock Boutique, between Stockton and Grant, sells beautiful clothes behind a postmodern facade that makes a theatrical contrast between plate glass and a stage-set stone wall. You will find **Laura Ashley** on Post Street between Stockton and Grant. **Obiko,** on Sutter Street near Jones, displays clothes as art—fine handwoven textiles and contemporary designs. **The Forgotten Woman,** on Sutter between Powell and Mason, offers high fashion for large sizes. **Emporio Armani,** at O'Farrell and Market, is located in an old bank designed by Bliss and Faville in 1919, modeled on the Pantheon. It has the Armani Express cafe as well. The **Polo-Ralph Lauren Shop** is on Post Street at Kearny, near the Crocker Galleria. **Banana Republic,** on Grant Street above Post, was founded in San Francisco. The **Hound,** gentlemen's clothiers, Sutter Street near Montgomery, is located in Schultz and Weaver's fine Hunter-Dulin Building of 1926. Socks, tweed jackets; one of the best men's stores in San Francisco. **A. Sulka & Company,** on Post Street near Stockton, is one of only four A. Sulka & Company shops in the world: shirts, ties, silk underwear. **Billyblue,** Geary near Grant, men's clothing. **Brooks Brothers,** Post Street at Grant. A large branch of this classic men's and women's clothing store. **Cable Car Clothiers-Robert Kirk Ltd.,** on Sutter Street near Grant is a San Francisco classic. Other clothing stores include **Bullock & Jones, Burberrys, Scotch House-Sweaters from Scotland, Ltd.,** located in the basement, **Eddie Bauer.** On Market Street at Powell, near the cable car turntable, find **The Gap** and **Urban Outfitters. The Gap for Kids** is found on Post Street at Kearney. **The Timberland Company** has their largest store here in San Francisco. **Kaplan's Surplus & Sporting Goods** is stocked in depth and is the ur-source for classic American work, athletic, military, and casual clothing. Also carries practical items a traveler might need in its camping department.

Tobacco and Pipes

Jim Mate Pipe and Tobacco Shop is on Geary Street between Taylor and Jones.

Bookshops

Tillman Bookshop, off Grant between Sutter and Post, is small and inviting, a booklover's paradise; offers a fine selection of books, particularly good for children's books. Also located in the Union Square area are **Borders Books and Music, B. Dalton Bookseller,**and **Doubleday Book Shop. A Clean Well-Lighted Place for Books,** on Van Ness Avenue at Golden Gate Avenue in the Opera Plaza, is one of the largest and best bookstores. **Argonaut Book Shop,** Sutter Street near Jones, features Californiana, Western Americana, plus a few African masks. **Eastern Newsstand,** in the Embarcadero Center, Sacramento Street between Davis and Drumm, is the best downtown newsstand; sells the *International Herald-Tribune* daily. **Jeremy Norman & Company,** on Market Street between Grant and Kearny, is a cozy den of rare books on subjects including medicine and life sciences. **John Scopazzi Books, Maps and Prints** sells antiquarian art, literature, maps. **Brick Row Book Shop,** on Post Street at Stockton, stocks English and American literature, first editions.

Brooks Brothers, *201 Post Street; 397-4500*

Cable Car Clothiers–Robert Kirk Ltd., *246 Sutter Street; 397-4740*

Bullock & Jones, *340 Post Street; 392-4243*

Burberrys, *225 Post Street; 392-2200*

Scotch House-Sweaters from Scotland, Ltd., *187 Post Street; 391-1264*

Eddie Bauer, *220 Post Street; 986-7600*

The Gap, *890 Market Street; 788-5909*

The Gap for Kids *100 Post Street; 421-4906*

Urban Outfitters *80 Powell; 989-1515*

The Timberland Company *100 Grant Avenue; 788-1690*

Kaplan's Surplus & Sporting Goods *1055 Market Street; 863-3486*

Jim Mate Pipe and Tobacco Shop *575 Geary; 775-6634*

Tillman Bookshop *8 Tillman Place; 392-4668*

Borders Books and Music *400 Post Street; 399-0522*

B. Dalton Bookseller, *200 Kearny Street; 956-2850*

Doubleday Book Shop
265 Sutter Street;
989-3420

A Clean Well-Lighted Place for Books
601 Van Ness Avenue;
441-6670

Argonaut Book Shop
786–792 Sutter Street;
474-9067

Eastern Newsstand
3 Embarcadero Center;
982-4425

Jeremy Norman & Company
720 Market Street, third floor; 781-6402

John Scopazzi Books, Maps and Prints
278 Post Street, suite 305; 362-5708

Brick Row Book Shop
278 Post Street, third floor; 398-0414

Virgin Records
2 Stockton Street

F.A.O. Schwartz Fifth Avenue
48 Stockton Street; 394-8700

The John Pence Gallery
750 Post Street; 441-1138.

John Berggruen Gallery
228 Grant Avenue; 781-4629

Erika Meyerovich Gallery
231 Grant Avenue; 421-9997

Stephen Wirtz Gallery
49 Geary Street, upstairs; 433-6879

Music

Virgin Records, located on Stockton Street at Market, is a vast "megastore" for music. A **Planet Hollywood** restaurant is located here as well.

Toys

F.A.O. Schwartz Fifth Avenue, Stockton Street at O'Farrell, has two floors of dazzling toys.

Art Galleries

Note: *The* **Gallery Guide** *available in a number of galleries lists the exhibitions in many of the city's galleries. The San Francisco Art Dealers Association's member galleries are open evenings on the first Thursday of each month. It is an interesting time to make the rounds.*

Some of the galleries in the Union Square area include **The John Pence Gallery,** on Post Street between Jones and Leavenworth; **John Berggruen Gallery** on Grant Avenue between Post and Sutter, upstairs with elevator; **Meyerovich Gallery** on Post between Grant and Stockton; **Stephen Wirtz Gallery,** Geary Street between Kearny and Grant; **Pasquale Ianetti** on Sutter Street near Powell carries original prints and drawings from the sixteenth century to the present; **Circle Gallery** on Maiden Lane off Stockton (originally V. C. Morris Store) has a superb Frank Lloyd Wright 1949 interior with gentle spiral ramp, some original Wright furniture, indifferent art. (See Tour 15 on *Great Interiors; see also the South of Market for Crown Point Press and Terrain Gallery.)*

Antiques

Ed Hardy, Inc. Antiques, at Showplace Square, is a great place for antiques and furniture. **Showplace Square,** near Kansas and Fourteenth and south of the South of Market, in a former brick warehouse district, has many to-the-trade antique dealers and some shops open to the public. *(See also Jackson Square in Tour 2A.)*

Asian Antiques

Orientations, on Maiden Lane off Stockton, has three compact levels of very fine Asian art; see the precious things in the basement vault. Other places to find Asian antiques are **Gump's, Far East Fine Arts, Inc.,** on Sutter Street near Powell, and **Wylie Wong Asian Art.** The latter two are by appointment.

Auctions

Butterfield & Butterfield Auctioneers, in Showplace Square area.

Stamps

The **Philatelic Unit** of the U.S. Postal Service is at the Rincon Post Office on Steuart Street near the foot of Mission Street. Open Monday to Friday, 10 A.M. to 1:30 P.M. and 2:30 to 4 P.M.

Pasquale Ianetti
522 Sutter Street;
433-2771

Circle Gallery
140 Maiden Lane;
989-2100

Ed Hardy, Inc., Antiques
188 Henry Adams Street;
626-6300

Orientations
34 Maiden Lane;
981-3972.

Gump's
135 Post Street;
982-1616

Far East Fine Arts, Inc.
518 Sutter Street,
third floor;
421-0932

Wylie Wong Asian Art
626-1014

Butterfield & Butterfield Auctioneers
220 San Bruno Avenue;
861-7500

Philatelic Unit
Rincon Center Post Office,
180 Steuart Street;
543-3340

Introduction:
Emporium of the West and Union Square

Fashion is, as Ambrose Bierce defined it, "A despot whom the wise ridicule and obey." In San Francisco, the seat of fashion is **Union Square.** San Francisco's Union Square area is one of the three best shopping districts in the nation, behind New York's and Chicago's, doing about $1 billion in sales. Great shops say something, and Union Square shops have a lot to say.

Because the entire district, with the exception of the new specialty department stores and parking garages, was designed during the peak of the streetcar era, and because people until recently would climb stairs or take elevators to second and upper floors, Union Square's shopping configuration is layered with uses; jewelers, furriers, hairdressers, tailors, and dressmakers, for example, are found over women's dress and shoe stores. To really savor Union Square, you must go upstairs inside buildings, to the second floor at least. Try the upstairs art and photography galleries in the **1907 Shreve Building** at Post and Grant.

The highrise boom of the 1970s doubled the amount of office space in the downtown and was followed by a boom in hotel building and the opening of three new upscale specialty stores in Union Square. **Saks Fifth Avenue** opened on the northwest corner of Union Square in 1981; **Neiman-Marcus** on the southeast corner in 1982; and in 1988 a spectacular new **Nordstrom** opened next to **The Emporium** on Market Street near the Powell Street cable car turntable. San Francisco's shopping district is like a fine old chassis fitted with a powerful new engine.

The recent history of Union Square is not surprising; with the revitalized city, rents have gone up to levels that only well-capitalized chain stores can afford. The individual, perfectionist shop is losing ground. On the positive side, these powerhouse specialty stores energize the luxury shopping district. Specialty store advertising draws shoppers past all the other shops and services surrounding Union Square. **Post, Grant,** and **Sutter** still offer individual, one-of-a-kind quality shops with fabrics, clothing, jewelry, fine books, and art. The second problem faced by merchants here is the collapse of policing by the city. The sidewalks and public spaces of San Francisco do not just happen; they must be maintained, cleaned, guarded, and nurtured. Shoppers and visitors—never mind the hard-working citizens of the city—are sensitive to the aesthetics of their surroundings; they do not *have* to spend their money here. Already most American downtowns are comatose, abandoned by the automobile-addicted middle class for policed, if sterile, shopping malls out on the highways. It is time for the government of San Francisco to spend more time protecting its still-lively retail core.

Union Square, San Francisco's Civic Stage

Union Square derives its name from pro-Union rallies held here in the 1860s on the eve of the Civil War. It is the center stage of the city's life, much more so than the misnamed Civic Center. Built into the west side of the center of Union Square is a little-noticed concrete platform/stage. The imposing façade of the Hotel St. Francis serves as its pleated back curtain. Here public receptions are staged and occasional protests erupt.

Of all the protests staged here, the memory of one always brings a smile. In August 1958, North Beach's beatniks, tired of being the objects of visitors' curiosity, marched—if that's the word—from North Beach across Union Square, into the major department stores and hotels. Called "The Squaresville Tour," a hundred beats in Bermuda shorts and beards, or black slacks and sandals, followed a bongo drum player and brandished signs that read: "Hi Squares! The citizens of North Beach are on tour!" After amazing the bourgeoisie, the beats fell back to Upper Grant Avenue.

Union Square itself, the park, is something of a vacuum. Its benches are mostly left to the poor who sit and watch the whirlpool of Fashion swirling by. The park is flooded at lunchtime with office workers eating their lunch and socializing. Designed for hard use and occasional large crowds, it is also the landscaped roof of a five-level underground parking structure built in 1942 and designed by Timothy Pfleuger. It was the first, and still the best, of several such garages under downtown parks. In its early days the Union Square garage offered valet parking, and shoppers could have their cars called for them, at nearby stores.

In the center of the park is the ninety-foot-tall Dewey Monument commemorating Admiral Dewey's victory over the Spanish navy at Manila Bay in 1898, during the Spanish-American War. This granite Corinthian column was designed by Newton Tharp, capped by a bronze of Victory bearing a trident and a wreath by sculptor Robert Aitken. The imperial monument was built by public subscription and dedicated in 1903 at the peak of the Edwardian Era. It did not topple in the 1906 earthquake.

Union Square and Geary Street together are the chief rift in the complex fault zones of San Francisco's social stratification. To the north is wealth and privacy, to the south and east are the poor; out Geary Street to the west is the middle class. In ten blocks, from California south downhill to Market, Mason Street slices through all the layers in the American class system from the uppercrust to the underclass.

The key players in the pageant of style here are the early morning wave of shoppers, particularly the wealthy matrons in chic suits wearing massive, sculpted jewelry. The famous white-gloved San Francisco old ladies are early shoppers, too. Both are in some quiet place by lunchtime when the second, younger wave of office-worker shoppers fills the sidewalks and floods the department stores. After school come bands of teenagers; after 5 P.M., more office workers do their shopping, perhaps staying downtown with a friend for dinner and a show.

Space for what became Union Square was reserved as one of only two new open spaces in Jasper O'Farrell's fateful city plan of 1847. Between Nob Hill and Market Street, Union Square became the focus for the elite Protestant churches and the principal Jewish synagogue. Calvary Presbyterian, the First Unitarian, and Trinity Episcopal churches faced the Square. Elite congregations occupied the sites of the Hotel St. Francis and Saks. Temple Emanu-El was a block up at 450 Sutter Street, and the First Congregational Church was, and is, a block west at Post and Mason. Elite private clubs also settled on the corners of the Square on Post Street, including the predecessors of the Pacific-Union Club and the Concordia and Argonaut clubs. The first Congregational Church, organized in San Francisco in 1849, moved to Post and Mason in 1870. It was the only one to stay; all the others migrated west with their congregations later in the nineteenth century to cluster along the axis of fashionable Van Ness Avenue and Franklin Street. *(see Tour 8.)*

Sutter Street leading west from the Square was a fashionable residential street in the Victorian period. Unlike Bush, Sutter had no alleys cutting up its prestige-block fronts. It had immediate access to all the services of the center of the city without crossing through any industrial zones or intervening slums. As happened everywhere in nineteenth-century cities, high-class retail pursued fashion and "invaded" aristocratic streets. In Manhattan it was Fifth Avenue that changed; in San Francisco, Sutter Street. As the rich were attracted to better, newer, and more fashionable houses further west in Pacific Heights, businesses occupied leased-out, adapted houses along Sutter.

The next big change was the construction of the Hotel St. Francis on the west side of the Square, in 1904–08. Developed by the Crocker family, and designed by Bliss & Faville, this great, modern hotel skyscraper shifted the nature of the Square from churches and clubs to commerce. As originally built, the hotel occupied only the Powell and Geary corner. It was later expanded to reach across the entire block front. (The compatible tower with its giant "cornice" and exterior elevators was added in 1972 and designed by William Pereira Associates.)

The Spring Valley Water Company, William Bourn's great monopoly, built the City of Paris department store across the Square in 1896, where Neiman-Marcus now stands. When rebuilt by Bakewell and Brown in 1908, that store introduced the new commercial Union Square's architectural treat: the great Rotunda. Here the city's fanciest Christmas tree delighted generations of San Francisco children being initiated into the "seasons" of shopping.

When the earthquake and fire destroyed the downtown in 1906, steel-frame buildings like the Hotel St. Francis and the City of Paris were rebuilt using the original frames. The lot owners who rebuilt Union Square called on the city's very best architects to design the new stores. If you look up, here—hard as that is with all the things to see at eye level—you will see a very handsome city, the city of the City Beautiful movement of the 1890s and early 1900s. Classical embellishments such as Corinthian pilasters, egg and dart moldings, sculpted brackets, and a whole dictionary of architectural decorations make this district a great ensemble of American Edwardian city design. Each architect did something interesting with the design of the upstairs windows. There are treasures for those who look carefully.

The façade of 311–19 Grant Avenue above Sutter, for example, is an instance of unnoticed genius. This, the **Abrahamsen Building**, whose architect is unknown, is a reinforced-concrete building that intelligently understands its fate. The composition of the windows of the top three stories floats forever separate above ground-floor shops whose facades are destined to change. It uses the Chicago window, a large window flanked by two narrow ones, in a pattern that rises to the level of art.

Another real sleeper is the **Bemiss Building** at 266–70 Sutter near Grant. This 1908, five-story building, whose architect also is unknown, was apparently designed using the largest standard-sized sheet of plate glass available. The windows are set in an almost skeletal façade. Here is one of the furthest developments in the efforts by San Francisco architects to get more natural light into their buildings.

Abrahamsen Building
311–19 Grant Avenue

Bemiss Building
266–70 Sutter

Neiman-Marcus/City of Paris Rotunda
150 Stockton Street, southeast corner of Geary; 362-3900
• Rotunda Restaurant
Phone 362-4777 for reservations
• Fresh Market Restaurant
Third floor; 362-3900

San Francisco's Specialty Stores

❶   Neiman-Marcus/City of Paris Rotunda, *1982, Johnson/Burgee*

On the prime southeast corner of Geary and Stockton, facing Union Square, is the harlequin-patterned, reddish Italian granite-clad **Neiman-Marcus** designed by Philip Johnson and John Burgee, which opened in 1983. Within its round glass and aluminum corner is the superb rotunda preserved from Bakewell and Brown's rebuilt **City of Paris** department store of 1908. Enter the rotunda and look up at the pale-colored art-glass dome depicting a sailing ship—the emblem of Paris, the city—and the motto *fluctuat nec mercitur,* "I float and do not sink." This four-story rotunda with its elaborate plaster decorations is one of the finest bits of *belle époque* design in the city—lavish, beautiful, festive. Its predominant colors are white and pale gold, a most sophisticated combination.

At the fourth level is the **Rotunda Restaurant**, from which piano music sometimes wafts. Some tables have a clear view of the Square across the street, and the booths are comfortable. It is open for lunch and tea and is expensive. Good but less pricy is the **Fresh Market Restaurant** on Neiman's third floor.

The interior of the new store is not much; there are some postmodern columns on the second level of the store at the entrances of the men's and women's areas, but that's about it. The skylit crystal display room on the top floor offers a view of the tops of the city's old and new buildings. Neiman-Marcus has one of the best large men's stores in San Francisco.

**Frank Lloyd Wright's
140 Maiden Lane**
*Circle Gallery
(V. C. Morris),
between Stockton
and Grant; 989-2100*

Saks Fifth Avenue
*384 Post Street,
at Powell; 986-4300*
• **The Restaurant at Saks**
986-4758

Macy's California
*170 O'Farrell, at
Stockton; 954-6000*

② Frank Lloyd Wright's 140 Maiden Lane, *1949,*
Frank Lloyd Wright

Halfway down Maiden Lane at number 140 is the outstanding V. C. Morris shop, now the Circle Gallery, which was designed by Frank Lloyd Wright in 1949, completely transforming a 1911 structure. This is one of the greatest architectural works in San Francisco. The facade and even the sidewalk were originally designed by Wright to work light into the architecture. Indirect lights are placed in the brickwork borders of the facade. White plastic lights with a key design border the bottom of the facade. Now cemented over, the three-quarters circle in the sidewalk in front of the entrance had lights under a thick slab of glass. The building was designed to lure the walker at night with its enticing lighting. Even when closed, the shop could be viewed by walking into the glass-roofed entrance vestibule and looking up. (The acceptably designed metal gate is a recent, unwelcome addition.) The original handsome Wrightian lettering is still visible, reading V. C. Morris. The red square tile placed in the lower left-hand corner of the facade bears Wright's signature.

Inside, a gently **curved ramp** rises weightlessly toward the skylighted ceiling. Some of Wright's original circle-motif walnut furniture survives among store fixtures. As a crystal and china shop, this was a perfect marriage of purpose and design. The round shapes of the dishes and glasses were repeated subtly in every detail of the building, from the semicircular entrance to the round stools to sit on and to the translucent ceiling with its circles.

③ Saks Fifth Avenue, *1981, Hellmuth, Obata & Kassabaum*
On the northwest corner of the Square, at Post and Powell, is the round-cornered **Saks Fifth Avenue** store of 1981 designed by Hellmuth, Obata & Kassabaum. For a contemporary department store, its exterior fits in relatively well with its context—it has windows and some modulation of its blank walls and is an appropriate color. Its top-floor curbed bay is occupied by **The Restaurant at Saks.** Some tables here look down on Union Square and across to the Hotel St. Francis. It is open for lunch and tea only. Saks has a disappointing central area crisscrossed by escalators going up five levels. A plain skylight caps the space. It is instructive to compare this space with the City of Paris rotunda: the Edwardians did it better. Saks has some of the best clothes shopping in the city for both men and women.

④ Macy's California, *1928, 1948, Lewis Hobart; 1968, brick façade on Geary Street*
Fronting on Geary, Stockton, and O'Farrell Streets, **Macy's California** is hardly ever looked at, which is understandable. It is an *ad hoc* building formed out of an old one, the O'Connor-Moffatt department store whose Gothic façade dating to 1928 and 1948 faces Stockton and O'Farrell streets, and the two intrusive 1968 brick-faced additions facing Geary Street and Union Square. The brick face does, however, have a useful public clock, an increasingly rare service.

Macy's California revitalized retailing in San Francisco in the 1970s, earning a reputation for an entertaining shopping environment. It does $200 million in sales a year and is strongest in fashion and home furnishings.

Macy's has expanded across Stockton Street into Macy's East, the blank-fronted former Liberty House store built in 1974. Men's clothing is downstairs and a futuristic electronics department occupies the entire top floor.

Emporium-Capwell
835 Market Street, foot of Powell; 764-2222

**Nordstrom/
San Francisco Centre**
865 Market Street, southeast corner of Fifth; valet parking at Fifth Street entrance; 243-8500

5 **Emporium-Capwell**, *1896, 1908, Albert Pissis and Joseph Moore*
Built in 1896, **The Emporium** on Market Street has a grand, classical façade, a spacious rotunda, but a lackluster interior. The introduction of the restaurant on a platform in the rotunda was a good idea poorly executed. The huge building was designed, for the Parrott Estate, by Albert Pissis and Joseph Moore. It was rebuilt with a steel frame behind its original sandstone and brick façade in 1908. The California Supreme Court once occupied the third floor. The Emporium has had a long tradition of rooftop rides for children at Christmas. Those looking for Levi jeans (from the San Francisco company) should check out the first floor of The Emporium, where a good selection is always in stock.

6 **Nordstrom/San Francisco Centre**, *1988, Whisler-Patri; Robinson, Mills & Williams and Stephen Guest, project designers*
Opened in 1988, Nordstrom's spectacular new store was designed by Whisler-Patri with Robinson, Mills & Williams and Stephen Guest as project designers. It occupies the top four levels of **San Francisco Centre**, a ten-level vertical shopping mall with some one hundred other shops. (The land it sits on has been owned by the public school system since 1858.) The stately gray granite façade relates to the great architectural row of which it is a part without parodying its neoclassical neighbors. The top of the building is stepped back to allow more sunlight into Hallidie Plaza across Market Street. The building's atrium is capped by a large glass-and-steel dome that opens when the weather is good. Three pairs of **curved escalators** designed by Mitsubishi, the first of their kind in the United States, link the first four levels of the complex (there are conventional escalators and elevators on the higher floors). It is a marble-floored palace of consumer delights.

Like older great department stores, San Francisco Centre is directly linked to BART, Muni Metro, and its neighbor, The Emporium. The complex's most dramatic feature is not visible to the public: two special sixty-foot-long elevators that lift sixty-thousand-pound trucks from the street to the upper floors to deliver merchandise.

Old Hale Brothers
901–19 Market Street,
southwest corner of Fifth

The Family Club
545 Powell Street
at Bush

Tessie Wall's Townhouse
535 Powell Street,
between Sutter and Bush

7 **Old Hale Brothers**, *1912, Reid Brothers*
Across Fifth Street from Nordstrom is the handsome classical block of the former **Hale Brothers Department Store**, designed in 1912 by the Reid Brothers. Between its giant columns are modified Chicago windows. It originally had a columned court on its roof open to the sky. The building has been adapted for stores, including a branch of Marshall's discount clothing, and offices upstairs.

Clubland

The blocks of Post and Sutter to the northwest of Union Square, where Nob Hill begins to rise steeply, are the heart of San Francisco's Clubland. There are more than a dozen elite private clubs in San Francisco, some of which have erected monumental, if discreet, buildings for their clubhouses. Most are in a modified Renaissance palazzo style. Some city clubs also own country retreats: golf links, farms, and redwood groves. Most of the city clubs provide dining rooms, bars, lounges, and libraries; some are organized around in-club theatricals. A quick tour of part of Union Square's Clubland begins at the corner of Powell and Bush at The Family Club.

8 **The Family Club**, *1909, C. A. Meussdorffer*
The Family Club, a men's club, dates from 1902. The club's motto is "Keep Young," and its emblem is the stork. Its purpose is fellowship and the staging of entertainments performed exclusively by its members. The club has a country refuge in Woodside, The Family Farm. The city clubhouse is an elegant building designed in 1909 by C. A. Meussdorffer in the Renaissance palazzo mode and fitted onto a steep Nob Hill corner lot with a dramatic wedge-shaped base. Here is a classical San Francisco hill lot whose steep grade encourages the design of a building with its services accessibly tucked underneath it. It's the *bases* of such buildings that make them uniquely San Franciscan. A row of handsome arched windows marches around the corner to provide a well-lighted interior. It is a jewel of understated Edwardian elite design.

9 **Tessie Wall's Townhouse**, *1911, C. A. Meussdorffer*
Immediately downhill from The Family Club is a Second Empire townhouse, built in 1911 and also designed by C. A. Meussdorffer. It is notable as the only surviving structure downtown built as a single-family residence. It was later bought by Frank Daroux, a gambler and the Republican boss of the Tenderloin's vice activity, for his bride Tessie Wall, a prominent madam. Tessie is credited with the immortal line that she would rather be a lamppost on Powell Street than own all of San Mateo County. But despite the centrally located real estate, Tessie shot Frank stone cold dead.

⑩ The Francisca Club, *1919, Edward E. Young*
The Francisca Club, on another prime corner, is a women's club housed in a sedate three-story Federal palazzo. It was designed by E. E. Young in 1919 and is built of fine red brick accented by white trim. Its domestic front door, painted in gleaming white enamel with white-shiny brass, is one of the most beautiful in the city, an icon of Anglo-American aristocratic design.

⑪ The Metropolitan Club, *1916, Bliss & Faville; 1922, expanded*
The Metropolitan Club, a women's club, is one of the finest club buildings in the city. It was designed and expanded by Bliss & Faville in 1916 and 1922. It originally housed the Women's Athletic Club. It is a brick and terra-cotta-clad Renaissance palazzo with a colonnaded loggia. Two large escutcheons bear an intertwined W, A, and C.

The Francisca Club
595 Sutter Street, at Mason

The Metropolitan Club
640 Sutter Street between Mason and Taylor

The Pan Pacific Hotel
500 Post, at Mason;
771-8600

The Olympic Club
524 Post Street, between Mason and Taylor

⑫ The Pan Pacific Hotel, *1987, John C. Portman, Jr. and Associates*
On land owned by the adjoining Olympic Club stands the posh **Pan Pacific Hotel** designed by Atlanta architect-developer John C. Portman, Jr. It opened in 1987 and features luxurious high-tech business conference facilities. Like Portman's own house outside Atlanta, the design motif here is a semi-circular arch with a notch where the keystone would be. The windows have this shape, as do many of the elements inside the building. The hotel is designed around the automobile and features a drive-in area that cuts across the corner site. You must take the elevators to the third floor to see the lobby-atrium. The hotel has 348 rooms arranged around this sixteen-story open space. You may have a drink here or in the lounge on the top floor. The centerpiece sculpture of four dangling bronze figures is by Elbert Weinberg.

⑬ The Olympic Club, *1912, Paff and Baur; 1906 pool pavilion by Henry Schultz*
The light sandstone base of the Olympic Club's Renaissance palazzo catches the eye in this brick-clad district. It also has a notable top story faced in fine, elaborate terra-cotta ornamentation and a sheet metal cornice. One of the best club buildings in the nation, it was designed in 1912 by Paff and Baur, who won a competition staged by the club. Sandwiched between the club and the new Portman Hotel is the low swimming-pool pavilion designed by Henry Schultz right after the earthquake of 1906. The pool inside is surrounded by a two-story colonnade capped by a glass roof, one of the most opulent interiors in the city. For many years this pool had its own pipe all the way out to the ocean to provide it with fresh seawater. The Doric-columned entrance to the clubhouse is designed after that of the Palazzo Massimi in Rome. The marble statues of athletes in the vestibule date from 1912–13 and are by Haig Patigian: to the right is the pugilist Damoxenus, and to the left, Creugas.

The all-male **Olympic Club** has its roots in the German elaboration of gymnastics and the organization of German American *Turnvereine* in the mid-nineteenth century. Twenty-three charter members held their first meeting at the socially elite Lafayette Hook and Ladder Company in 1860.

Across the street is the acclaimed **Postrio** restaurant (see the restaurant listings at the beginning of this chapter.)

The Bohemian Club
625 Taylor Street,
at Post

The Commonwealth Club
of California
Phone 597-6700 for
information about Friday
speeches. These speeches
are also broadcast live
on KQED-FM, 88.5, at
12:30 P.M. Or write to
the club at 595 Market
Street, San Francisco
94105

⓮ The Bohemian Club, *1934, Lewis P. Hobart*

Next to the Olympic Club, the Bohemian Club stands out for its mantle of green ivy over red brick. It is a building built after the fire and completely remodeled in 1934 by Lewis P. Hobart in a discreetly classical Moderne style. The basement of the sloping site contains a large theater. The club dedicatedly maintains the only boxwood hedge downtown. With the vines and the hedges, the clubhouse seems to want to make its own forest on a city corner. On the Taylor Street side is a fine bronze *bas-relief* of Bret Harte characters sculpted by J. J. Mora in 1919. Around the corner on Post Street is the building's bronze cornerstone with the club's emblem—the owl—and motto, "Weaving spiders come not here." It bears the dates 1872, 1909, and 1933. The bronze plaque was designed by Haig Patigian and is one of the finest, if smallest, sculptures in the city, a gift to the observant walker.

The Bohemian Club was organized in 1872 by newspapermen, writers, and artists, hence its name. In a process of social gentrification, it evolved into a businessmen's club with a slant toward the arts. The club stages year-round entertainments in its theater in the base of this building and owns the 2,700-acre Bohemian Grove on the Russian River north of the city, the site of summer encampments and theatricals.

With 2,300 members, all male, the Bohemian Club attracts attention for the great number of business and political movers and shakers who enjoy its hospitality. Perhaps the club's golden age was the early 1900s when it counted among its members Ambrose Bierce, Jack London, Frank Norris, Sinclair Lewis, and photographer Arnold Genthe. In the post-1906 period many of the city's best architects, fine artists, and club members designed and embellished the modern Edwardian city we enjoy today. The Bohemian Club's collection of artwork by members includes the best collection of bronzes, paintings, and fine books created in turn-of-the-century San Francisco.

⓯ The Commonwealth Club of California

Organized in 1903, the Commonwealth Club of California has its roots in the reform movement of early Progressive California. Its Friday lunches with speakers are San Francisco's principal platform for policy statements by major public figures. It is characteristic of how well-organized—and how small—San Francisco is that there should be but one "bully pulpit" in town. The club has 23,500 members and is open to those who subscribe to its purposes: the investigation and discussion of problems affecting the welfare of the Commonwealth of California.

$\mathscr{P}$reliminaries: $\mathscr{T}$our 1b

$\mathscr{P}$arking

Unlike the rest of San Francisco, street parking is often available in the South of Market district. A large city parking garage is at Fifth and Mission Streets. Moscone Center has a garage on Third Street, between Folsom and Howard Streets. Closer to Market Street is the Hearst Garage on Third Street, between Mission and Market Streets.

RESTAURANTS

Max's Diner, catercorner from the back of Moscone Center, recreates the all-American diner with jukebox selectors mounted on the counter and in the booths. Open late; inexpensive. **M and M Tavern & Grill,** a 1939 institution recently modernized. A favorite hangout for newspaper people (the **Chronicle** and **Examiner** are around the corner). Excellent food at a reasonable price; good daily specials; alcohol, of course. **The Acorn Tea & Griddle,** between Eighth and Ninth Streets, a real San Francisco surprise tucked away in a light industrial district (take a taxi). Excellent breads, organic produce, and a modern menu make this a culinary oasis. Informal with a small garden deck in the rear. Serves lunch, tea and dinner, and Saturday and Sunday brunch. Phone about their occasional Tuesday night *prix fixe* dinners where one third of the proceeds are donated to AIDS organizations. Take-out market attached. **Icon Byte Bar & Grill,** a restaurant and bar catering to the online community of South of Market, also known as "Silicon Alley." Internet access, multimedia demonstrations, and great polenta. **Brain Wash Cafe and Laundromat,** on Folsom near Seventh, a concept. (How many cafe-laundromats do *you* know?) An almost painfully hip cafe with an inexpensive, eclectic menu.

Max's Diner, 311 *Third, off Folsom;* 546-6297

M and M Tavern & Grill
198 *Fifth Street at Howard;* 362-6386

The Acorn Tea & Griddle
1256 *Folsom Street;* 863-2469

Icon Byte Bar & Grill
299 *Ninth Street, at Folsom;* 861-2983

Brain Wash Cafe and Laundromat
1126 *Folsom Street, near Seventh Street;* 861-FOOD

Introduction: Tour 1b
The South of Market, from Skid Row to Arts Center

Novelist Jack London, born south of Market Street, described the historic, social, and geographic division of San Francisco: "Old San Francisco was divided by the Slot [the cable car slot that ran down the center of Market Street] ... North of the Slot were the theaters, hotels, and shopping district, the banks and the staid, respectable business houses. South of the Slot were the factories, slums, laundries, machine shops, boiler works, and the abodes of the working class." Many of its nineteenth-century residents were Irish immigrants who crowded into the small frame houses built in the narrow alleys. Slum property was very profitable, and many a wealthy family lived well from its properties in **"Tar Flat."** The city's first concentration of African Americans appeared behind the Palace Hotel, which offered them secure employment. A Japanese immigrant community clustered along narrow Stevenson Street.

The earthquake and fire of 1906 completely leveled the district, but it was rebuilt quickly. By 1907, fifty-eight new transient hotels and eighty lodging houses had sprung up. They were home to merchant seamen, miners, seasonal agricultural workers, and retired men on small pensions. They also housed the drifters, hobos, and alcoholics—life's losers. Around these single-room-occupancy hotels was a network of saloons, inexpensive restaurants, pawnshops, secondhand stores, and employment agencies mainly hiring for temporary out-of-town unskilled jobs. Third Street was called **"Three Street"** and was peppered with bars and bookie joints. Howard Street was branded the "Slave Market" because of its many employment agencies. Leavening this mass were various religious missions and the local headquarters of the Industrial Workers of the World. It was the "other" San Francisco—the wrong side of the tracks. Greek immigrants, who ran numerous small restaurants, and later Filipino immigrants, also lived in the inexpensive district during the early twentieth century.

But the South of Market, the city's backstage, is in immediate proximity to the retail core around Union Square and toward the foot of Market Street to the expanded Financial District. In 1954, hotelier Ben Swig proposed demolishing the heart of the district and building a large convention center, stadium, and huge parking garage. It took a quarter of a century for his dream to become fact. The city proposed to use federal urban renewal funds for the project, but the first property survey did not find a blighted district, just an unfashionable one. So the definition of "blight" was rewritten and the **San Francisco Redevelopment Agency** began demolition in 1966, displacing small businesses and mostly sound buildings. Some of the retired residents, one-time labor activists, organized and began court suits to stop the displacement. They discovered that federal legislation required the city to provide replacement housing, but that this provision had not been enforced since the passage of urban renewal legislation in 1949! The tenants and owners won their case, but the hotel and big business interests still considered a modern convention center vital to the postindustrial city's economy. A deal was struck in 1973, and in exchange for 2,000 replacement units, the Redevelopment Agency condemned a vast swath of land. Eighty-seven acres stretching from **Market to Harrison** Streets, and east of **Third** and west of **Fourth** Streets, were cleared. Then followed the most tangled story of land development in San Francisco's history. The publicly purchased land was sold to private developers for the huge San Francisco Marriott Hotel and office buildings. The proceeds were used to subsidize the construction of a modern convention center and a cultural complex in the center of what was dubbed **Yerba Buena Center**, including a new home for the **San Francisco Museum of Modern Art**, a **Visual Arts Center, Yerba Buena Theater,** and **Yerba Buena Gardens.** The result was the complete transformation of a blue-collar district into a high-class white-collar one. The replacement housing did not begin to make up for the large number of SRO hotels that were lost. The result is that high-art institutions have brand-new homes while the rest of the city is overrun with homeless people. Now we know that San Francisco *needs* cheap hotels, but, of course, can't afford to build them. Yerba Buena Center is a textbook example of the socially unjust transformations taking place in the postindustrial city where public powers are being used to give to the rich and to take from the poor. It was a devil's bargain, and the city has not begun to address the city-wide consequences.

San Francisco Museum of Modern Art
151 Third Street, between Mission and Howard;
357-4000

The Visual Arts Center
Corner of Third and Mission streets;
978-2710

16 **San Francisco Museum of Modern Art**, *1993, Mario Botta, architect;*
Hellmuth, Obata & Kassabaum, architect's of record
Swiss architect Mario Botta's new design for the **San Francisco Museum of Modern Art** is hands down the finest piece of contemporary architecture in San Francisco. Born in Mendrisio, Switzerland, in 1943, he received his professional degree from the University Institute of Architecture in Venice. In this superb $60 million building Botta has achieved the sense of power and clarity of form that are the essence of great architecture. To this strong geometry he has applied textured panels of orange brick that give delicacy to the exterior. The stepped-back, horizontal museum is capped by a black-and-white-striped cylinder cut at an angle. Inside, the great cylinder-atrium rises through the center of the museum and opens to the sky. A grand staircase makes the act of walking through space pleasurable. The five floors of galleries are laid out in a traditional manner that makes walking through them a passage through the evolution of modern art. This fine new building is further commented on in the last entry in Tour 15.

17 **The Visual Arts Center**, *1993, Fumihiko Maki*
Across Third Street, at the southwest corner of Mission Street, is the new Visual Arts Center by avant-garde Japanese architect Fumihiko Maki. This low-slung, gray, almost industrial-looking structure is designed to contain several large and small galleries, a video screening room, and flexible exhibition spaces. It is intended to showcase the works of local artists and groups. This is Maki's first building in the United States.

Yerba Buena Theater
*Corner of Third and
Howard Streets;
978-2787*

Yerba Buena Gardens
*Block bounded by
Mission and Howard,
Third and Fourth streets*

**Moscone
Convention Center**
*747 Howard Street
between Third and
Fourth Streets;
974-4000
Moscone Convention
Center event information,
267-6400*

⑱ Yerba Buena Theater, *1993, James Stewart Polshek*
The black glass and white glazed-brick **Yerba Buena Theater** houses a 750-seat theater for the use of nonprofit companies. New York-based Polshek has designed a determinedly modern, blocklike building that does the best it can with its $10.7 million budget. It is the first freestanding-stage theater to be constructed in San Francisco since the War Memorial Opera House opened in 1932.

⑲ Yerba Buena Gardens, *1993, Omi Lang Associates,
landscape architects; MGA Partners, architects; Maki and
Associates, design consultant*
Between the Visual Arts Center and the Yerba Buena Theater is the entrance to **Yerba Buena Gardens**. This five-acre public space is the centerpiece of Yerba Buena Center and has had the most contentious history of any project ever built in San Francisco. The real purpose of the redevelopment of the huge eleven-acre block was to accommodate an underground extension of the Moscone Convention Center across Howard Street and also the underground ballrooms of the Marriott Hotel across Mission Street. Over these convention facilities are the Visual Arts Center and Yerba Buena Theater, both intended for local nonprofit arts groups. How to design the park in the center and along the west side of the block became the longest-running design game in town. Eventually it was decided to erect a memorial to Dr. Martin Luther King, Jr., as the focal point for the gardens. The result is a huge waterfall fifty feet long and twenty feet high designed by sculptor Houston Conwell. The water pours over dark gray stone-clad walls. Illuminated glass panels are inscribed with quotations of the assassinated civil rights leader. The large central space is called the Esplanade and serves as an entryway for the underground portion of Moscone Convention Center.

⑳ Moscone Convention Center, *1981, 1991 Hellmuth, Obata and Kassabaum;
Third Street addition 1988, Anthony Lumsden of DMJM and Gensler & Associates*
Moscone Convention Center opened in 1981 and was expanded in 1991. Designed by Hellmuth, Obata and Kassabaum, with T. Y. Lin, engineer, the white steel space-frame entrance pavilion facing Howard Street caps enticingly designed escalators and stairs that cascade down to the underground exhibit hall. The hall has three-hundred thousand square feet of space and is the size of six football fields. It was for this building that the city commissioned sculptor Robert Arneson to make a bust of Mayor George Moscone, assassinated in 1978. The piece consists of a large pointillist polychromed ceramic head atop a columnlike base. Everyone liked the smiling bust, but the column was imprinted with a revolver, pierced by bullet holes, and etched with written comments on the killing. It was a superb commemorative work, powerful and true to the violent turning point in the city's history. But Americans like their history sunny and sanitized; the masterpiece was banished. Today it is displayed in the San Francisco Museum of Modern Art.

Between 1988 and 1993, the center's size was doubled, with rooftop meeting space and an underground addition designed by Anthony Lumsden of DMJM and Gensler & Associates. The Third Street side of this expansion is a strikingly clean contemporary design.

San Francisco Marriott Hotel
55 Fourth Street, at Mission;
896-1600

Moscone Center hosts about 10 percent of San Francisco's conventions. The rest meet in the large convention hotels, of which there are many. Conventions began in the 1870s when railroad excursion tickets were sold to fraternal organizations. The first big conventions were the Masons, the Odd Fellows, the Improved Order of Redmen, the Knights of Pythias, and all the panoply of small town and big city fraternal and Civil War veterans' organizations so important in late-nineteenth-century America. Great parades up Market Street were the high points of these gatherings. Showy costumes and brass bands, flags, regalia and horses, carriages and floats passed between temporary plaster classical columns and bunting-draped streets. Some Market Street facades had lightbulbs worked into their ornamentation so that they could be turned on for evening parades.

Today, of course, conventions are usually business, labor, or professional meetings. They are, like the old Improved Order of Redmen conclaves, also intensely political; officers are elected or installed; politicking and palaver and deals flourish. The American genius for voluntary organizations thrives in these associations. They satisfy the political animal in Americans perhaps more than the major political parties themselves.

㉑ San Francisco Marriott Hotel, *1989, Anthony Lumsden of DMJM*
Looming over Yerba Buena Center is this huge, thirty-nine-story, eye-catching, fifteen-hundred-room hotel. Designed by Anthony Lumsden of DMJM, this is the most controversial new building in San Francisco. Some like its jazzy feel, others find it too busy and the silvery glass fan windows that cap it cheap looking. Many think the glitzy design got lost on its way to Las Vegas. It does have one redeeming feature: the View Lounge on the thirty-ninth floor offers spectacular and unusual views of the city. The San Francisco-Oakland Bay Bridge looks beautiful from here at night. And the new San Francisco Museum of Modern Art far below looks like a table top sculpture. The lounge is tall and narrow; its fan-shaped windows reach way up high. Walk around the periphery of the lounge to see all the various views of the city. It is an unusual vantage point and is best experienced at night. Under certain lighting conditions, especially on some late afternoons, the silvery glass reflects the colors in the sky and one can almost forgive the jumbled design for its Oz-like magic.

St. Patrick's Roman Catholic Church
756 Mission Street, between Third and Fourth Streets; Latin high mass offered Sundays at 11 A.M.; 421-0547

Jessie Street Substation
222–26 Jessie Street, visible from Mission Street

Ansel Adams Center: The Museum of Photography
250 Fourth Street, between Howard and Folsom; 495-7000

㉒ St. Patrick's Roman Catholic Church, *1872; rebuilt and remodeled 1909, Shea & Lofquist*

Irish immigrants were the dominant group in the nineteenth-century South of Market; they worked in its factories and warehouses, and lived in its crowded alleys. With their hard-earned money they built this red brick Gothic Revival monument to their faith. The church was battered by the earthquake and gutted by the fire in 1906. When it was rebuilt, steel and poured concrete were used, and beautiful green-veined marble from Ireland was used to line the entrance vestibule. The church has fine stained glass windows. Today a large part of the congregation is Filipino American, the second-largest Asian-Pacific Islander immigrant group in California.

㉓ Jessie Street Substation, *1905, 1907, 1909, Willis Polk*

It was in the South of Market, the backstage for the nineteenth-century downtown, that utilities were located to serve the prestigious uses north of the Market Street divide. An electrical substation was built on this site in 1881. In 1905, famed architect Willis Polk was commissioned by William Bowers Bourn's Pacific Gas & Electric Company to redesign the utilitarian structure. The electrical substation burned in 1906 and was rebuilt in 1907 and enlarged in 1909. It is a steel-frame and reinforced-concrete structure with a red brick veneer. It is trimmed with cream-colored, matte-glazed terra-cotta ornament. A series of great framed windows march toward a tall arched entrance and a smaller heavily decorated doorway. The sculptural group over the smaller entrance is especially fine and shows four cherubs, two of whom are brandishing a torch. Originally the substation was hidden in a narrow alley and surrounded by taller buildings. Demolition for Yerba Buena Center uncovered this architectural jewel. Now a city landmark, it has an undecided future.

㉔ Ansel Adams Center: The Museum of Photography

Located in a converted modernistic concrete building across Fourth Street from the Moscone Convention Center is this gem of a photography museum. Opened in 1989, the museum is operated by the Friends of Photography and named after one of its founders, famed California photographer Ansel Adams. The museum consists of five galleries including one dedicated to Adams' work. The center exhibits nineteenth-century photography, one-artist retrospectives, thematic group shows, and photographic installations utilizing mixed media and video. There is a bookstore here as well specializing in photographic works.

㉕ Crown Point Press

This is where many of the nation's premier artists have their lithographs and prints struck; a wide selection of superb work is offered here along with changing exhibitions.

Crown Point Press
657 Howard Street, between Second and Third; entrance at 20 Hawthorne Street; 974-6273

㉖ Terrain Art Gallery

This intimate gallery, behind the Palace Hotel, shows some of the best of cutting-edge contemporary art.

Terrain Art Gallery
165 Jessie Street, second floor, between New Montgomery and Third; 543-0656

㉗ Old United States Mint, *1869–74, Alfred B. Mullet*

The first U.S. Mint in San Francisco began operations in 1854 and was located on Commercial Street, near Montgomery *(see Tour 2A)*. It proved inadequate to handle the enormous Comstock silver bonanza, and in 1874 this, the second U.S. Mint, opened. Designed by Alfred B. Mullet, the somber Doric-columned structure is built on a foundation of Rocklin, California, granite with walls of British Columbia bluestone. The pyramidal flight of stone steps and the looming Doric portico project an overwhelming image of power. From this busy mint poured a cascade of ringing silver dollars made of Nevada silver and stamped with an "S" for San Francisco. In its vaults (built at street level for ease of handling) was stored a third of the nation's gold reserve until the construction of Fort Knox in the 1930s. The massive building survived the earthquake and fire of 1906 and was saved by mint employees and soldiers who kept the flames away with a fire hose. After the earthquake it was the only financial institution able to open for business, and it served as a temporary bank and administered the relief funds for the ruined city. A new mint was opened in 1937 at 155 Hermann Street, near Market and Duboce, and the "Granite Lady" became federal offices. In 1972, the Treasury Department restored the landmark as a museum. Inside are displays of gold and silver coinage, antique minting equipment, stately reception rooms, and, strangely, Victorian period rooms including a bedroom (in a mint?).

Old United States Mint
88 Fifth Street, at Mission; 744-6830

Burlington Coat Factory Outlet
899 Howard Street, at Fifth; 495-7234

Van Heusen Outlet
601 Mission Street, at Second; 243-0750

Six Sixty Center
660 Third Street, at Brannan;
227-0464

Spaccio
645 Howard Street, between Second and Third, a block from Moscone Convention Center; 777-9797

Esprit Factory Outlet
499 Illinois Street, at Sixteenth; 957-2550
• **Caffè Esprit,** 777-5558

28 *Clothing Factory Outlets*

The vast building at Howard Street at Fifth, **Yerba Buena Square**, houses various small outlet stores on its ground floor and the huge **Burlington Coat Factory Outlet** on its second and third floors. There is much more than coats here, including men's, women's, and children's clothing, underwear, and shoes. There are good buys to be had.

The **Van Heusen Outlet** sells men's and women's shirts. Clustered in the South of Market blocks between Second and Fifth Streets, and Folsom and Townsend Streets, are a number of clothing factory outlets. **Six Sixty Center** is a cluster of some nineteen factory outlets. At 275 Brannan Street, near Second Street, are more factory outlets. **Spaccio** sells Italian men's clothing direct from the manufacturer. Some outlets sell a detailed map of area outlets; a free map is available at the Esprit Outlet (below).

Continuation: Outlets Further South

Located further south of South of Market, in the industrial district off Third Street, is the **Esprit Factory Outlet**. *You can obtain a map to other outlet stores here.* The 22 Fillmore electric trolley and the 15 Third Street bus stop a block from the outlet. This clothing supermarket with its abundance of choice is technoindustrial in image and the-future-now in mood. The Esprit Factory Outlet was designed in 1984 by Esprit's Bruce Slesinger and is one of *the* pieces of contemporary San Francisco environmental design worth examination. The store, the restaurant, and the heavy-duty poured concrete walls around the parking lot invite inspection. Although the handsome parking lot walls are too strong for their purpose, they manipulate the high building technology of today for effect. The heavy disco beat controls the mood inside the store. The clothing racks look like movie studio staging with their heavy aluminum pipes on industrial casters. Special stagelike lights spotlight the clothes. Behind the building **Caffè Esprit** sells salads and pizzas.

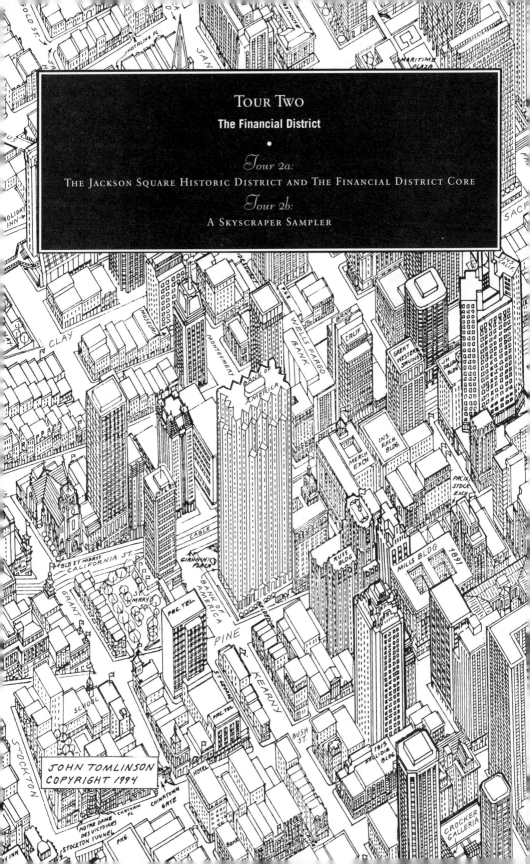

TOUR TWO

The Financial District

•

Tour 2a:
THE JACKSON SQUARE HISTORIC DISTRICT AND THE FINANCIAL DISTRICT CORE

Tour 2b:
A SKYSCRAPER SAMPLER

What These Tours Cover

Preliminaries
Introduction: Dominant Institutions in the Postindustrial City

TOUR 2A:
THE JACKSON SQUARE
HISTORIC DISTRICT AND
THE FINANCIAL
DISTRICT CORE

The Jackson Square Historic District

1. Intersection of Montgomery, Washington, and Columbus
2. 700 Block of Montgomery Street: Gold Rush Survivors
3. 800 Block of Montgomery Street
4. 500 Block of Pacific Avenue: Site of the Infamous Barbary Coast
5. 400 Block of Jackson Street/Balance and Gold Streets/ Hotaling Street: Victorian Commercial Architecture and Antique Row

The Financial District Core

6. The Transamerica Pyramid's Observation Room/Site of the Historic Montgomery Block
7. The Bank of San Francisco
8. The Bank of Canton of California/Pacific Heritage Museum/Grabhorn Park
9. Commercial and Leidesdorff Streets: Post-1906 Cluster
10. Stacking the New Over the Old: 456 Montgomery Street
11. Wells Fargo Bank History Museum/Wells Fargo Bank Headquarters
12. The Bank of California/Museum of the Money of the American West/California Street: The Prestige Address
13. 343 Sansome Street's Roof Garden
14. Union Bank
15. First Interstate Center/The Mandarin Oriental Hotel
16. Merchant's Exchange Building/Grain Exchange Hall/ Coulter Marine Paintings
17. Old Bank of America Headquarters
18. Kohl Building
19. 580 California Street
20. Federal Home Loan Bank
21. Bank of America World Headquarters: Carnelian Room

Continuation
The Embarcadero Center and Nearby

Continuation

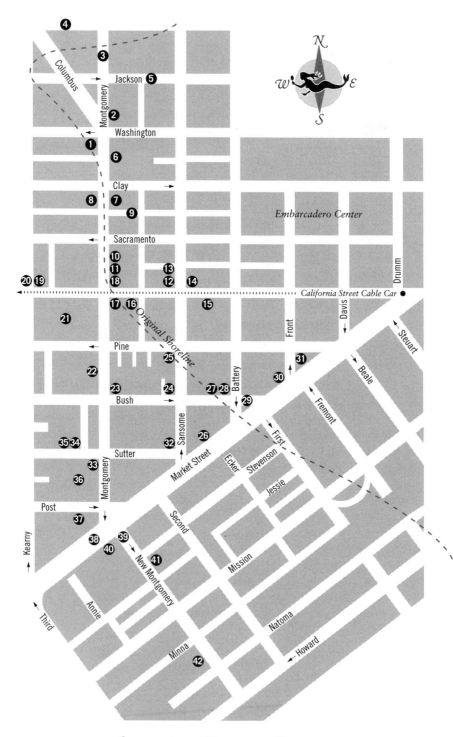

Map of the Financial District

$\mathcal{P}$reliminaries

BEST TIMES TO DO THIS TOUR

Bank hours are Monday to Friday, 10 A.M. to 3 P.M., and that is when you should explore the Financial District. Noontime is people-watching time; Transamerica's **Redwood Park** or the steps around the **BART** subway station near Montgomery and Market are good spots to sit. If you lunch at **Tadich Grill** about 3 P.M., you will not have to wait to be seated (it takes no reservations) and the restaurant will be calm and relaxing. After 3 P.M. the **Carnelian Room** cocktail lounge is open atop the Bank of America. The view from here at sunset and in the afterglow is one of the best in the city. If you visit the downtown at midday, you can take the **California Street cable car** to Drumm Street, cross The Embarcadero to the **Ferry Building,** and take the **Golden Gate Ferry** to **Sausalito** for dinner. This lets you view the city skyline reflected in the water on your return to the city in the evening.

The **Financial District** is, of course, ruthlessly governed by time and corporate etiquette. All this seriousness finds its only tribal release on the last business day of the year, when office workers throw desk calendar pages to the winds and make confetti out of the preceding year. For several days the sidewalks downtown are a mosaic of random, provocative dates, black for business, red for holidays. It seems such a carefree, unbusinesslike thing to do, to throw away one's calendar with its record of the year's work. And so it would be if office workers actually threw *their* calendars out the window. But they don't; when you inspect the pages, all are blank. These are extra calendars stored away for just this ritual of release. So even this "spontaneity" is calculated—cost control managers point to the expense of sweeping up the mess. Humans understand the urge.

Freed Teller & Freed's
In the base of the Embarcadero Center West Tower at Sacramento Street, near Battery; 986-8851

Specialty's Cafe & Bakery
312 Kearny Street, between Bush and Pine; 512-9550

Tadich Grill
240 California Street, between Battery and Front; 391-1849

Jack's Restaurant
615 Sacramento Street, above Montgomery; 986-9854

Parking

The city's **Portsmouth Square Garage** at Kearny and Clay is the least expensive. There is another city garage at **St. Mary's Square**; enter from Kearny north of Pine, across from the Bank of America. Expensive parking is available under the **Bank of America Headquarters**; enter from California Street. On Saturdays parking is free in **The Embarcadero Center** with a validated purchase; on Sundays and holidays parking is free with no purchase necessary.

Transportation

The **California cable line** plunging downhill on California Street from Nob Hill is the most dramatic way to enter the Financial District. The **1 California trolley bus** runs inbound (east) on Clay Street and outbound (west) on Sacramento Street and links the downtown with Nob Hill, Pacific Heights, and the Richmond District. There is also a stark, white-tiled **BART** subway station at Montgomery and Market streets.

RESTAURANTS, CAFÉS, AND BARS

The Financial District has coffee shops, not relaxed cafés. Good take-out coffee is available at **Freed Teller & Freed's,** tucked away in the base of the Embarcadero Center West Tower. A sidewalk window at **Specialty's Cafe & Bakery,** a half-block south of the Bank of America Headquarters, has superb cheese-and-herb breads. A recommended Financial District restaurant is the Buich brothers' **Tadich Grill**. The two-story, green terracotta-clad Tadich Grill was built in 1909 and is attributed to Crim and Scott. Behind a plate-glass window with gold lettering is an agreeably plain interior unchanged since the 1930s. There is a counter as well as tables and booths. It is the oldest restaurant in California and is deservedly popular. It serves charcoal-broiled meats and fresh seafood, including a memorable *cioppino*. It does not take reservations and it closes early. The best time to eat here is about 3 P.M., after lunch and before dinner. **Jack's Restaurant** opened in 1864 and serves French/Continental cuisine in a historic 1907 restaurant building with private rooms upstairs. The main room is trimmed with gilt floral plasterwork. The grilled steaks, chops, and fish are good, as is the wine list. **Sam's Grill** was established in 1867 and has been at its present location since 1946. It is a cozy Financial District institution. **Ernie's**, in the Jackson Square Historic District, serves pricey *nouvelle cuisine* in a plush Victorian environment. **Bix Restaurant and Lounge**, in the Jackson Square Historic District, is a stylish, lively new restaurant in a grandly converted old brick building. Jazz is featured here nightly in this speakeasylike setting. A monumental old wood bar with pillars and arches and cozy booths make the 1912 **House of Shields**, across from the Palace Hotel, a step into the Edwardian past. Their new menu is quite good. A good budget restaurant is **Henry's Hunan**, open Monday to Friday, 9:30 A.M. to 5 P.M. The smoked ham with string beans is excellent.

Downtown's many bars are liveliest weekdays from about 5 to 7 P.M.; they really buzz on Friday after work. A classic Financial District bar is the **Royal Exchange**, across the street from One Embarcadero Center. Here good-looking people in good-looking clothes talk the local *patois*: percentages. **Sutter's Mill** is the Financial District's suit-and-tie gay bar. The most striking new restaurant and bar is the **Cypress Club**, with a wildly postmodern interior and what look like Minoan columns. It's a lively, glossily prosperous scene. The cocktail lounge with the best view is the **Carnelian Room**, atop the Bank of America Headquarters, open to the public after 3 P.M. It is a good place to conclude your exploration with a godlike overview.

SHOPPING

This is not a shopping district, but there are many interesting stores. The **Crocker Galleria** is a three-level upscale arcade of shops and a pleasant place to rest. A few fascinating places pepper the Jackson Square Historic District. **Japonesque Gallery** is outstanding. Here spirit-opening contemporary Japanese sculpture and other artwork is calmly exhibited. Anyone who loves contemporary art should not fail to visit this shrine to the modern aesthetic. **Limn** is an interesting place for contemporary art furniture,

Sam's Grill
374 Bush Street, near Kearny; 421-0594

Ernie's
847 Montgomery, near Pacific; 397-5969

Bix Restaurant and Lounge
56 Gold Street, off Montgomery; 433-6300

House of Shields
39 New Montgomery, between Market and Mission; 392-7732

Henry's Hunan
674 Sacramento Street, near Kearny; 788-2234

Royal Exchange
301 Sacramento Street, at Front; 956-1710

Sutter's Mill
10 Mark Lane, an alley off Bush Street between Kearny and Grant; 788-8377

Cypress Club
500 Jackson Street, at Montgomery; 296-8555

Carnelian Room
Atop the Bank of America Headquarters; 433-7500

Crocker Galleria
50 Post Street, between Kearny and Montgomery; 393-1505

Japonesque Gallery
824 Montgomery Street, between Jackson and Pacific; 391-8860

Limn
457 Pacific Avenue, between Montgomery and Sansome; 397-7474

**William Stout
Architectural Books**
*804 Montgomery Street,
near Jackson; 391-6757*

Antique row
*Along Jackson Street,
between Montgomery
and Sansome*

lamps, and other cutting-edge art goods. **William Stout Architectural Books** is the best architectural and design bookshop in Northern California. This is *the* place to buy books on contemporary California architecture and design. **Antique row,** in the Jackson Square Historic District, is special. Fine English and French antiques are agreeably displayed in Victorian brick buildings along a tree-lined block. (Dress up; otherwise you will be accosted with kindness.) At any one of the shops you can ask for a copy of the Jackson Square Art and Antique Dealers Association brochure/map. This is also a fine block for an evening's stroll. The closed shops leave their lights burning, and the effect is quite domestic.

Introduction: Dominant Institutions in the Postindustrial City

The Financial District fuses money, history, and art, in particular the art of tall buildings. It is the powerful engine that pulls the train of San Francisco. The district specializes in advanced services to capital: banking, legal advice, accounting, insurance, financial analysis, and the smooth, dissimulating art called public relations. It is a synergistic mix of giant corporations and small human-skill businesses. Headquartered here are the city's Big Seven: **Chevron** (oil), **Pacific Gas & Electric**, **Pacific Telesis** (communications), the **Bank of America**, **Transamerica** (insurance), **Bechtel** (engineering and construction), and **Levi Strauss** (clothing). Surprisingly, perhaps three-quarters of the businesses in the imposing downtown highrises employ ten or fewer people. Small business is cumulatively big in San Francisco, but many of these specialized firms directly or indirectly serve the city's giants. Office work employed some 180,000 people in 1992, the largest category of employment in the city. Many here are highly educated and well paid.

San Francisco has been called the "instant city" because of its phenomenal development from a sleepy backwater port of less than a thousand to a booming city of twenty thousand after the Gold Rush of 1849. As the major American seaport on the West Coast (which quickly overtook the older Portland, Oregon), San Francisco attracted Navy and Army headquarters, federal offices, shipping companies, banks, importers, manufacturers, preachers, lawyers, doctors, architects, engineers, photographers, actors, restaurateurs, journalists and writers, prostitutes, and all the other specially skilled people needed to make a city. The Victorian city that developed between the global sea-lanes and the transcontinental railroad became the cultural center of the West. A jerky series of building booms and busts resulted in a chaotic jumble of old and new buildings. Without zoning, the untrammeled controlling force was the price of lots, which was set by a combination of accessibility, notions of prestige, and demand.

The growing city soon abandoned its early center at Portsmouth Square and in what is now the Jackson Square Historic District and migrated onto bay-fill east of Montgomery Street. Banks, then as now, were the institutions that determined the heart of the Financial District. When William Ralston's then-dominant Bank of California built a Renaissance Revival marble palace at California and Sansome in 1866, it determined where prestige would focus. Despite its prominence in the city's layout, Market Street never rivaled California Street as *the* prime address. Luxury retail also moved south from Portsmouth Square to settle along lower Kearny Street in the 1860s and 1870s, in the early 1900s retail shifted westward to Union Square.

The booming Victorian city was an eclectic mixture of architectural styles. The sober Greek Revival of the post–Gold Rush days, still visible in the Jackson Square Historic District, was soon superseded by much fancier stucco-covered brick and timber buildings in the Italianate, Eastlake, Renaissance Revival, Gothic Revival, and mansarded Second Empire styles. From within this brick city a new kind of building erupted in the 1890s: the iron-and steel-frame, brick-clad skyscraper. The first was the **Chronicle Building** at Market and Kearny, built in 1889 for the *San Francisco Chronicle* and designed by the Chicago firm of Burnham and Root. (The building survives under the banal veneer of an unfortunate 1962 modernization.) Today the best remaining example of this first wave of steel-frame construction is the **Mills Building** on Montgomery Street, built in 1891 in the Romanesque Revival style and also designed by Burnham and Root. In 1902 Charles Keeler described these new buildings: "A gratifying feature of the work is the simplicity of design followed in nearly every instance. Costly materials and the most perfect of modern workmanship, combined with good proportions on broad lines, are bound to make the new San Francisco an eminently satisfying city architecturally." What he saw as "simplicity" in 1902 we call "ornamented" today.

The new skyscrapers of the 1890s and turn of the century made possible the vertical expansion of the downtown. They were served by the streetcar system that focused commuter flows in the city and made downtown lots all the more central and valuable. In 1904 the Society for the Improvement and Adornment of San Francisco was formed by the city's business elite under the leadership of banker and former reform mayor James D. Phelan. This private group invited Daniel Burnham and Edward Bennett to come to San Francisco to "blue sky" a modern plan for the city. In 1905 the grandiose Burnham Plan was published, which called for carving a system of Parisian boulevards diagonally across the city's built-up gridiron of streets. The plan also called for a new, monumental civic center, and vast parks in the underdeveloped southwestern section of the city reaching from Twin Peaks to the sea. It was far too drastic a plan ever to be implemented and lacked any suggestion as to just how private-property owners were to be compensated for parting with their land to accommodate the grand boulevards and huge parks.

When the earthquake struck in 1906, the city was in the midst of a great building boom. There were about two dozen steel-frame buildings then in the Financial District and along Market Street. While all were gutted by the fire that broke out after the earthquake, their steel frames survived, and most were reconstructed and stand today. The old brick Victorian buildings, on the other hand, became irreparable shells. Between 1906 and about 1909 San Francisco was an "instant city" for a second time. The Burnham Plan was ignored in the rush to rebuild. Although most of the buildings were destroyed, the patterns of lot ownership and relative prestige were not. A proposal to widen Montgomery Street was thwarted by a single property owner who refused to shave the necessary frontage from his prime lot. By the summer of 1907, six thousand buildings had been completed and three thousand others were under construction. Part of the capital for this boom was money paid out by insurance companies. (This substantial payout depended on a fortunate court decision, which held that it was not the earthquake but the subsequent fire that destroyed the city and that fire insurance policies had to be honored.)

Because the city was rebuilt all at once, the result was an up-to-date Edwardian city of remarkable architectural coherence. The steel-frame skyscrapers of the immediate prefire years set the standards for the rebuilding. Unlike the very earliest tall buildings, which were clad in brick or stone, the postfire steel-frame buildings were clad in lighter terra-cotta tiles, most in a pleasing, softly light-reflecting off-white.

A second and smaller but architecturally creative building boom hit San Francisco in the mid-1920s. This time taller skyscrapers with set-back towers appeared, changing the city's skyline. For the first time, the skyscraper was made to appear to soar upward. **The Shell Building** on Bush Street and the **Pacific Telephone & Telegraph Headquarters** on New Montgomery Street are great examples of this new look. Miller and Pfleuger's celebrated **450 Sutter Street** medical office building of 1929 was the last structure built during this boom, which was ended by the Stock Market Crash of the same year. There was to be little more major building downtown until the 1960s.

In the 1960s investors, city planners, and architects declared war on the traditional city fabric and in a great wave of development—the first of two massive urban renewals—built either isolated towers in "plazas" or put parking garages on the ground level as podiums for large buildings placed atop them. Such city-busting designs gave the choice ground level to automobiles and relegated pedestrians to elevated walkways connecting sterile rooftop plazas. Highrise design hit rock bottom in 1960 with Albert F. Roller and John Carl Warnecke's new **Federal Office Building** in the Civic Center. Here the "tower in a plaza" becomes utterly soul-crushing, an Orwellian, alienating monolith sterilizing an entire windswept block.

Fortunately, in the design of **The Embarcadero Center** with its half-dozen highrises, in the second phase of urban renewal design that began about 1970, ground level was returned to the pedestrian and parking was moved underground, where it belongs in the cosmic scheme. All the city's richest corporations, especially the banks and insurance companies, commissioned grand architectural works, culminating in the dark red granite **Bank of America World Headquarters** of 1969 and the slim, white **Transamerica Pyramid** of 1971. When **Crocker Bank** built its sleek pink granite headquarters in 1982 on the Montgomery, Kearny, Post, Sutter block (today the **Pacific Telesis Tower**), the last of the big hometown corporations built its palatial new tower with a glass-roofed shopping arcade, the **Crocker Galleria**, enlarging and enriching the walker's domain.

Because of the configuration of its recent growth, the "energy" of the office core has "imploded" rather than dissipated as has happened in most American downtowns since the 1950s. The traditional center is still central in San Francisco, and that is the key to the Financial District's attractiveness.

Large new buildings north of Market Street have had to be ingenious to fit into the prime historic blocks. Imaginative construction and preservation projects are making the Financial District ever more complex and layered. When New York's **Citicorp** built its fine new tower at One Sansome, it converted the bank temple on the corner of its plot into the glass-roofed entrance court for the tower. At 345 California Street, where **First Interstate Center** has one of the choicest locations in San Francisco, a brilliant shoehorn job was pulled off by Skidmore, Owings & Merrill in 1987. Here four corner office buildings important to the fabric of the traditional Financial District were preserved and a new tower was built in the center of the block, with elegantly designed sidewalk-level concourses threaded through the block to the tower.

Partial preservation of historic buildings in new projects has a mixed record. The fault has not been in the saving of the old fragments but in the insipidity of many of the new designs. The scale of artifacts saved has jumped from the half-dozen granite walrus heads salvaged from the Alaska-Commercial Building at the **Union Bank** in 1977, to the thirty-five-ton fragment of the richly ornamented cornice of the Holbrook Building, handsomely mounted inside a restaurant in the base of the **Citicorp Center** highrise in 1984. When these bits and pieces of the old city are appropriately handled they add much to the new Financial District, educating people about the value of ornament on buildings and linking the present generation with the city's past.

The city-changing building boom from 1965 to 1985 added 1.4 million square feet of office space a year, increasing the total amount of office space in San Francisco from 26 million to 60 million square feet. The peak of this transforming boom was 1982. While the big hometown banks built the opulent showpieces, most of this growth was financed by insurance companies seeking large, secure investment. Since the mid-1980s, the very finest Financial District architecture has been commissioned by foreign investors willing to spend top dollar to erect premium buildings. By 1986 about 30 percent of San Francisco's Financial District office buildings were foreign-owned. On the crest of this latest wave of investment are **First Interstate Center,** built by Norland Properties, owned by an American insurance company and Middle Eastern investors, and **388 Market Street,** the sleek red granite–clad flatiron building at Market and Pine that was built by Honorway Investments and Hong Kong investors. Both are outstanding works of architectural art.

Such phenomenal growth made continued commercial development *the* hot political issue. The office boom stoked the housing-price boom that quintupled residential real estate values. Tax assessments on a typical home in the city zoomed up 582 percent during the 1970s. Even during the recessionary early 1990s, growth in jobs continued to outpace the production of housing both in the city and in the Bay Area. Widespread choice of independent single living has meant a declining number of people in each unit of housing and therefore a growing need for more units.

It is the *imbalance* between housing and office growth, rather than office growth itself, that is the region's major challenge. San Francisco has led the nation in requiring new office developers to contribute toward the construction of affordable housing, public transit, new open space, and child-care programs to mitigate the impact that office construction has on the rest of the city. Other cities are following San Francisco's lead.

Despite how it looks in the magazine ads, not all San Franciscans are rich. A majority are renters. The rapid escalation in rents precipitated the move to establish rent control in 1979 and to reduce the rate of downtown expansion to 475,000 square feet a year (the equivalent of one thirty-story highrise) in 1986. Some have described this as San Francisco's "surge protector" to moderate the impact of capital investment on the city's office core, and indirectly on its neighborhoods. Building limits protect the value of existing buildings. They have also split the political interests of landlords and developers. The frantic overbuilding of the 1980s, plus an international economic recession, resulted in a cooling of the office real estate market in the 1990s. By 1991, not a single highrise was under construction in the city, something not seen here since 1959. Establishing a quota for new office construction is precedent-setting. Ultimate political-economic questions are at stake here: How can commercial and housing growth achieve balance? Why cannot America produce middle- and lower-income housing? Who is a city for?

The best thing that has happened in downtown San Francisco over the past decade is the now-general recognition of the high architectural quality of almost all of it and the necessity of conserving and adding to it rather than detracting from it. The real works of art, such as the **Pacific Telephone Headquarters**, are today recognized by their owners for what they are. Pacific Telephone's six-year-long restoration of its 1925 terra-cotta-clad Moderne masterpiece is the kind of corporate commitment to the downtown that has created, and that sustains, what is undoubtedly the most pleasant and, though costly, most efficient office core in the United States.

Tour 2a:
The Jackson Square Historic District

*Such was life in the Golden Gate,
Gold dusted all we drank and ate,
And I was one of the children told
We all must eat our peck of gold.*
                Robert Frost, "A Peck of Gold"

The **Jackson Square Historic District** was established in 1971 and consists of approximately four blocks bounded by Washington, Columbus, Pacific, and Sansome streets. It preserves what survives of the post–Gold Rush commercial district and was San Francisco's first historic district.

    Montgomery Street was the original shoreline of the port of Yerba Buena. In the boom that followed the discovery of gold, the young city of San Francisco quickly filled in the cove to make space for piers, warehouses, shops, and offices. Part of this fill consisted of abandoned ships, which still underlie some of the buildings. (**Balance Street**, a short alley between Jackson and Gold streets, is said to be named after a ship buried there when the instant city expanded into the Bay.) Immediately west of the docks, these blocks attracted shops, professional and governmental offices, banks, consulates, assembly halls, and small manufacturing operations. Among the distinguished early San Franciscans who had offices or businesses here were General William Tecumseh Sherman, Colonel Jonathan Stevenson, James King of William, Faxon Dean Atherton, Domingo Ghirardelli, Anson Hotaling, and mayors Charles Brenham and Ephraim Burr.

    As San Francisco grew, its commercial center shifted south. Like a receding tide, prestigious users left the area behind. These quickly old buildings then were rented out to small factories, wholesalers, liquor and tobacco dealers, cigar factories, and later on printing and paper warehouses. When the earthquake and fire struck in 1906, the buildings here were freak survivors. Because the area was no longer prime real estate, owners expediently patched up their buildings but did not significantly alter or modernize them. Pacific Street attracted dance halls, saloons, boarding houses, and prostitutes' "cribs"—earning that part of the district the nickname **Barbary Coast**, after the pirate-infested stretch of the North African coast. The raffish district also saw the opening of The Dash at Pacific and Kearny in 1908 considered the city's first gay bar. (Mona's, the city's first lesbian bar, opened on nearby Broadway in 1936.)

    The Depression of the 1930s weakened the fringe industrial uses that had settled here, and some artists and writers were attracted to the low-rent district. By the 1940s, some buildings on these historic blocks stood vacant. Fortunately, the district was spared wholesale demolition for parking lots, the fate of many Victorian commercial areas near American downtowns. (The historic Montgomery Block, however, was demolished for parking. The Transamerica Pyramid stands on

**William Stout
Architectural Books**
*804 Montgomery;
391-6757*

**Chinatown, North Beach,
Jackson Square Historic
District, Financial District**

**Montgomery
Washington Tower**
655 Montgomery

Tommy Toy's Restaurant
655 Montgomery

Columbus Avenue

Old Transamerica Building
(now Sanwa Bank)

the site today.) In the early 1950s, interior decorators and the wholesale furnishings industry discovered the area and began restoring and improving these intimate blocks with appropriate signage and street trees. After them came architects looking for inexpensive space adjacent to clients downtown. It was the decorator trade that coined the name "Jackson Square," after the concentration of vintage structures along the 400 block of Jackson Street.

Eventually, restaurants, clubs, and advertising and law offices displaced the decorators, who then went on to pioneer the preservation and conversion of the larger red brick warehouses at the base of Telegraph Hill in the 1960s, before skipping south to the former warehouses in the Showplace Square area in the 1970s, where the decorator and furnishings industries today. A few retail shops in Jackson Square, including the outstanding **William Stout Architectural Books** and a cluster of fine art and antique dealers along Jackson Street, retain the district's connection with decoration and design.

❶ *Intersection of Montgomery, Washington, and Columbus*

This intersection is the northern gateway to the Financial District. Four distinct parts of the city touch here: **Chinatown** to the west, **North Beach** to the north, the **Jackson Square Historic District** to the east, and the **Financial District** to the south. In the late nineteenth and early twentieth centuries this was the heart of San Francisco's bohemia. A display case in the lobby of the **Montgomery Washington Tower** tells something of the story of this district when it was a low-rent artists' colony. Enter the door to the left near **Tommy Toy's Restaurant** and turn to the right-hand wall. Here are photos and memorabilia of this lost bohemia. The building is a mixed-use commercial, office, and residential tower and was designed in 1984 by Kaplan McLaughlin Diaz. **Columbus Avenue**, originally Montgomery Avenue, was cut across the city's grid in 1873. Property had to be condemned and many buildings moved to make way for it. This important intersection, the "hinge" between the Financial District and North Beach, attracted several fine Italian American–owned banks during the post-1906 reconstruction. Three of them survive. The centerpiece is the white terra-cotta-clad **Old Transamerica Building**, now Sanwa Bank, built in 1909 for the Banca Populare Operaia Italiana Fugazi, which was organized right after the earthquake and fire by John F. Fugazi, members of the Italian American community, and William H. Crocker, president of Crocker National Bank. The flatiron (so called for its triangular shape) was originally designed by Field and Kohlberg as a two-story building. In 1916, a third story with a now-lost cupola was added by architect Italo Zanolini. The circular porticoed entrance at the corner is the focal point of the design. In 1929, the Fugazi Bank was merged into A. P. Giannini's Bank of Italy (which later became the Bank of America), and this building continued as a branch bank until 1931. In 1938, the building became the headquarters of Giannini's bank holding company, the

Transamerica Corporation, which had been organized in 1928. The landmark remained Transamerica's headquarters until the completion of the Pyramid across the intersection.

Columbus Savings Bank
700 Montgomery
(now K-101 Radio)

On the northeast corner of Washington and Montgomery is the gray-green Colusa sandstone old **Columbus Savings Bank** (now K-101 Radio), designed by Meyer and O'Brien in 1905 and built after the earthquake and fire of 1906. It is an elegant Beaux Arts design with a slightly rounded corner and engaged Ionic columns. The Columbus Savings Bank was also organized by John F. Fugazi, who had started a travel agency in 1859 and then branched out into banking while sending home the remittances of Italian immigrants. Isaias W. Hellmen, the president of the Nevada Bank, had an interest in this institution. Columbus Savings was also eventually absorbed into Giannini's Bank of Italy.

1 Columbus/
622 Washington
Northwest corner of
Washington and
Columbus

Canessa Building
708-10 Montgomery
Street

722 Montgomery Street

Unnoticed, and threatened with demolition, is **1 Columbus/622 Washington**, a suave, two-story, classically colonnaded flatiron building on the northwest corner of Washington and Columbus. It, too, is a post-earthquake Beaux Arts design, and it completes this important three-building cluster. Rather than being demolished, it should be preserved and incorporated into any new structure built on the cleared land behind it.

❷ *700 Block of Montgomery Street: Gold Rush Survivors*

The oldest row of post–Gold Rush survivors is along the east side of the 700 block of Montgomery, between Washington and Jackson streets. At 708-10 Montgomery Street is the **Canessa Building**, built right after the 1906 fire. It has a white glazed-brick facade and four round windows along its top. It was originally built for the Canessa Printing Company. Number 710 was once the home of the Black Cat Bar, one of San Francisco's most famous bohemian rendezvous. Owner Sol Stoumen described his patrons as "merely members of the bohemian intelligentsia who gather at the Black Cat to discuss art and semantics, in the best San Francisco tradition." The Black Cat was famous for its out-of-the-closet Halloween costume parties and for attracting police harassment. In 1951 the California Supreme Court ruling in the Black Cat case allowed homosexuals to congregate in bars. The festive bar closed forever on Halloween in 1963.

The building at **722 Montgomery Street** was built in 1851 by Henry W. Halleck, an engineer who devised a novel foundation for brick buildings built on landfill, consisting of a redwood "raft" eight feet thick. The building's first recorded tenant was Langerman's tobacco warehouse. It was later converted into the Melodeon Theater and presented, among others, singer Lotta Crabtree. Later tenants included commission merchants, an auctioneer, a Turkish bath, and in the 1880s a medical establishment specializing in hydrotherapy. In 1958 lawyer Melvin Belli bought the old building and gussied it up New Orleans style. The original stucco was stripped to reveal the brickwork and an antique French postbox was attached to the facade.

728 Montgomery Street

Golden Era Building
730-732 Montgomery Street

744 Montgomery

Bank of Lucas, Turner and Co.
802 Montgomery Street

Number **728 Montgomery Street**, originally the Genella Building, is a three-story, Italianate brick and timber structure erected in 1853–54 on the foundation of an 1849 building. This site is the birthplace of Freemasonry in California; Lodge No. 1 met here on October 17, 1849, right after the Gold Rush. Later its upstairs hall was used by the Odd Fellows. From the 1880s to the 1930s, artists' studios occupied the upper stories. Artist Jules Tavernier entertained Oscar Wilde here during his visit to San Francisco in 1882. Arthur Matthews, Emil Carlson, Maynard Dixon, and perhaps Dorothea Lange are some of the important California artists who had studios here in later years. A plaque affixed to the old Transamerica flatiron across the street records that on that site the first Jewish religious service in San Francisco was held on Yom Kippur, September 26, 1849.

Number 730-732 Montgomery Street is the **Golden Era Building**, built about 1852 on the foundations of an 1849 structure destroyed in the fire of 1851. The cast-iron pilasters on its facade are dated 1892 and are a later addition; the pilasters on the rear of the building facing Hotaling Place are dated 1857. *The Golden Era*, an early literary weekly that published work by Mark Twain and Bret Harte, was edited here.

On the corner stands **744 Montgomery**, a larger building built in 1965 with blank red brick panels in a modern style that once housed the Playboy Club. Its facades were redesigned in 1982 by J/W Associates to blend better with the historic district. This was the site of the banking firm of Pioche et Bayerque, who financed the Market Street Railroad, the San Francisco and San Jose Railroad, the Sacramento Valley Railroad, the San Francisco Gas Works, and the Spring Valley Water Company, all important San Francisco enterprises. Today the ground floor houses an antique shop.

❸ 800 Block Of Montgomery Street

• Bank of Lucas, Turner and Co., *1853–54, Reuben Clark*

On the northeast corner of Montgomery and Jackson streets, is the two-story base of the originally three-story **Bank of Lucas, Turner and Co.**, built in 1853–54 and designed by architect Reuben Clark. The building cost the princely sum of $82,000. This St. Louis–based bank was briefly headed by William Tecumseh Sherman, who resigned his army commission in 1853 to come to California. The building's first-floor facade is covered in rusticated granite; its brick walls originally were stuccoed, scored, and painted to imitate stone. Soon after the construction of this severe Italianate design, the financial district of the city shifted to Battery Street (and later to California Street). The building was home to the Sacramento Rail Road, the West's first railroad. After the earthquake and fire of 1906, its top floor was removed. In the 1970s the building housed the West Coast office of the National Trust for Historic Preservation and also the first office of the Foundation for San Francisco's Architectural Heritage. Today William Stout's Architectural Books, Northern California's best architectural and design bookstore, is on the ground floor.

• **801 Montgomery Street/Cypress Club**, *1985, Robinson, Mills and* | **801 Montgomery Street**
Williams

Across Montgomery Street, at the northwest corner of Jackson, is a **Cypress Club**
new five-story brick-veneer building with clocks at the corner. It was *500 Jackson Street, at*
designed by Robinson, Mills and Williams in 1985 to blend in with *Montgomery; 296-8555*
its historic context. The narrow Montgomery Street end has bay | **555 Pacific Avenue**
windows, something new to this area but associated with the city at
large. The Jackson Street facade has heavily enframed paired windows somewhat
reminiscent of lower Manhattan's cast–iron architecture. Behind the mosaic panels
on the ground floor is the trendy **Cypress Club** whose voluptuous interior was
designed by Jordan Mozer and Assocates in 1988–90. The most striking features are
the Minoanlike columns and the wraparound mural; even the dishes are custom
designed here. Mozer himself has described it as "an overstuffed mohair sofa meets
a 1948 Hudson." It is a consummate expression of the fun some designers are
having in the ruleless 1990s, and the restaurant attracts a stylish crowd.

The rest of this block is lined with more historic red brick structures. At 824 Montgomery is **Japonesque Gallery**, a treasury of advanced Japanese
sculpture and art. It is a quiet Zen-soaked oasis of the best of the modern Japanese
aesthetic. **Ernie's Restaurant**, an elegant San Francisco institution, is across the street,
near Pacific Avenue.

❹ 500 Block of Pacific Avenue: Site of the Infamous Barbary Coast

Those interested in San Francisco's bawdy past may want to make a slight detour to
visit the now-quiet site of what was once the rip-roaring Barbary Coast, a name that
still lives in countless sham-sinful bars. When this was a left-behind district in the late
nineteenth and early twentieth centuries, it attracted a strip of saloons, dance halls,
target-shooting galleries, and brothels. A guide to the city published in 1878 located
each dive and then protested: "We give the precise location so our readers may keep
away." San Francisco police took a realistic view of the needs of the thriving seaport
and actually issued the prostitutes who worked here identification cards and had the
police surgeon examine the women for diseases. The wide-open district achieved
great notoriety, or infamy, and a visit to "Terrific Pacific" drew men from all over
the West. The district got the nickname "Barbary Coast" after a dangerous, pirate-
infested shore off North Africa. Two dozen saloons were packed into this one block.
As part of the Progressive movement in San Francisco, a red-light abatement act was
passed in 1914 and the police were forced by reformers to rescind their permissive (if
sensible) policy. Dancing permits were revoked where liquor was sold, and the brothels were shut down. Prostitution did not disappear, of course; it dispersed, mostly to
the Tenderloin north of Market Street and west of Union Square. Only one interesting architectural relic remains of the infamous Barbary Coast. At **555 Pacific Avenue**
is the recessed entrance vestibule of the old Hippodrome bar and dance hall, a Barbary
Coast survivor with plaster bas-reliefs of dancing girls.

Solari Building West
472 Jackson Street

**Solari Building East
(Larco's Building)**
468–70 Jackson Street

440–44 Jackson Street

Yeon Building
*432–34–36 Jackson
Street*

Balance Street

In the 1930s, Pierino Gavello, a restaurant owner, began buying up most of the faded block. He proclaimed it the International Settlement and announced that he would turn it into a restaurant row with food from around the world. But just before World War II honky-tonks and B-girls reappeared. When the war came, the M.P.s made the block off-limits to soldiers and sailors. Gavello later rented much of his property to interior decorators who were willing to improve their spaces on their own (Gavello did not believe in making renovations). Thus began the district's contemporary rebirth as a tasteful locale for designers, and later lawyers, advertising agencies, and now fashionable restaurants and bars. Return to the intersection of Montgomery and Jackson streets.

❺ *400 Block of Jackson Street/Balance and Gold Streets/ Hotaling Street: Victorian Commercial Architecture and Antique Row*

The block of Jackson Street between Montgomery and Sansome streets, the heart of the Jackson Square Historic District, is interesting because it shows the shift from the plainer commercial architecture of the 1850s to the fancier styles of the 1860s. The north side of the block is dominated by sober 1850s buildings, the south side by more elaborate Italianate buildings of a decade later. Today this block harbors a collection of the finest antique shops in the city.

At 472 Jackson Street is the old two-story French consulate known as the **Solari Building West**. It was constructed in 1850–52 and is, architecturally, perhaps the most important Gold Rush–era building in the district. Its severe brick and timber architecture and its original second-floor cast-iron shutters make it much like the Wells Fargo Express offices built in the Gold Country. The building backs up on Gold Street, where its brick construction and granite still can be inspected. While other buildings in the district are more eye-catching, this one in its purity of design better displays the typical commercial designs built by Yankee merchants.

Next door is 468–70 Jackson Street, the **Solari Building East**, or **Larco's Building**, built in 1852 by Nicholas Larco, a prominent Italian American businessman. At different times it housed the French, Spanish, and Chilean consulates, along with the offices of the Italian Benevolent Society and *La Parola,* an Italian language newspaper. Number **440–44 Jackson Street** was built in 1891 as a stable for the horses that drew the cars along part of the Presidio and Ferries Railroad. Its second floor was removed in 1907 and the façade remodeled in 1955. The **Yeon Building** at the corner of Balance Street is one of the handsomest on the block. It was built after the 1906 earthquake and fire on the foundations of the Tremont Hotel of 1855. It is distinguished by an arcade of five arches along its first floor.

The narrow alley here is named **Balance Street**, supposedly after the ship *Balance* that is said to be buried here. As the Gold Rush city expanded into the Bay, old ships were used as fill. **Gold Street**, at the opposite end of Balance, is a narrow alley that was once lined with warehouses. Most are now offices. At 56 Gold Street, behind an unprepossessing front decorated with a big blue neon martini glass, is **Bix**, a stylish restaurant and lounge with a massive wooden bar. There is jazz here nightly and the wonderful feeling that comes from being hidden away in a speakeasylike supper club. Return to Jackson Street.

To the left (east), beyond the four-story building at 414 Jackson, is a two-story in-fill building at **408 Jackson Street** that was built in 1953 as the district was reviving. It demonstrates how modern designs, when sensitively handled, can add to historic districts without being mock antique. It also shows how modern designers introduce plants and vines into once all-brick environments. The last building in the row, on the corner of Jackson and Sansome, is the **Grogan-Lent-Atherton Building**. It was built in 1859 and rebuilt after being damaged in 1906. In its early days it was home to numerous real estate, mining, and stock broker movers and shakers including Faxon Dean Atherton (after whom the elite suburb of Atherton is named) and William M. Lent, who helped open up the Comstock silver lode.

Cross the street to see the south side of Jackson Street, lined with ornate Italianate commercial buildings from the 1860s. They are the rare surviving companions to the city's many rows of Italianate houses. Next to the parking lot at Sansome and Jackson is number **407 Jackson Street**, a three-story building constructed in 1860 and used by the Ghirardelli Company as an annex for the manufacture of chocolate. Number **415–31 Jackson Street** was built in 1853 and later became the first Ghirardelli chocolate manufactory. Architect William Mooser altered the building in 1887 and 1896, perhaps adding the cast-iron storefront. (In 1894 the Ghirardelli operation moved to the Old Pioneer Woolen Mill at what is now Ghirardelli Square; *see Tour 5*.) Number 435–41, the **Medico-Dental Building**, was built in 1861 over the hulls of two ships abandoned during the Gold Rush. Its cast-iron pilasters are ornamented with *caducei*, the staff with entwined serpents that is appropriately both the emblem of Mercury, the god of commerce, and the medical profession.

The next three buildings flanking Hotaling Street, numbers **443–45, 451–55, and 463–73 Jackson Street**, were all at one time part of Anson Parsons Hotaling's liquor, trading, and real estate business. These substantial masonry buildings replaced simpler frame buildings. Hittell's guidebook of 1888 noted that "year by year the wooden buildings that form the landmarks of the early days are being crowded out by substantial brick and iron edifices.... The leading business blocks are built up of brick, with the front on the ground floor of iron, which allows nearly all the width to be occupied for windows and doors. The architecture is elegant and varied. The ceilings are high; the glass is large plate."

Gold Street

408 Jackson Street

Grogan-Lent-Atherton
Building
*400 Jackson Street,
at Sansome*

407 Jackson Street

415–31 Jackson Street

Medico-Dental Building
435–41 Jackson Street

443–45, 451–55, and
463–73 Jackson Street

Villa Taverna
27 Hotaling

Two-story **445 Jackson** was built about 1860 and was originally the Tremont Stables. It has its original iron shutters on the ground floor and elaborate frames around its second-floor windows. The most elaborate building in the row is **451–55 Jackson**, erected in 1866 in the Italianate style. It is built of brick covered in scored stucco painted to look like stone, with exaggerated quoins at its corners to give the illusion of masonry construction. Its ground floor has cast-iron pilasters and iron shutters; its upper floors have windows with alternating arches and triangular pediments over the windows, hallmarks of the Italianate style, the first of the fancy Victorian styles popular in San Francisco. Here Hotaling housed his collection of books and paintings. The building escaped the fire of 1906, leading one wit to pen the jingle, "If as they say God spanked the town for being over frisky, why did he burn the churches down and spare Hotaling's whiskey?"

Across the alley is **463–74**, the **Hotaling Annex**, built about 1860 and also decorated in the Italianate style. In the 1930s this building was the headquarters of the Federal Artists and Writers projects and later housed artists' studios when this was part of San Francisco's bohemia. The row ends with 744 Montgomery, a much larger building from 1965, originally in a starkly modern style, which was "historicized" in 1982 to better fit with its context.

Contrasting the Hotaling buildings with number **472 Jackson Street**, the plain, two-story red brick building across the street, neatly sums up the evolution from the simple brick structures of the Gold Rush days to the ornate buildings characteristic of the Victorian era. Commercial buildings became ever more decorated and drenched with ornament. Montgomery and Market streets were lined with them by the late 1880s, but all were lost in 1906, leaving a gap in the architectural history of the city between these survivors of the mid-1860s and the reconstructed office blocks of the 1890s. (To see High Victorian commercial architecture in the Bay Area you must go to the 400 block of downtown Oakland's Ninth Street, between Broadway and Washington. There one block survives as a monument to High Victorian commercial architecture in the Bay Area.)

Walk down Hotaling Street toward the looming Transamerica Pyramid. This one-time service alley is now lined with antique shops. At 27 Hotaling is the gray granite paving-block facade of the **Villa Taverna**. A marble lintel over the door depicts a woman holding wheat and poppies. This is one of the city's private dining sanctums. Cross Washington Street at the crosswalk to go to the Pyramid.

The Financial District Core

6 The Transamerica Pyramid's Observation Room/
Site of the Historic Montgomery Block

Transamerica Pyramid
*600 Montgomery Street
at Washington;
Observation Room on
27th floor, call ahead;
983-4000*

- **Transamerica Pyramid**, 1972, *William Pereira and Associates*

The slim, white, 853-foot–tall **Transamerica Pyramid** is the tallest office building (Sutro Television Tower is the tallest structure) in San Francisco and is the signature building on San Francisco's contemporary skyline. In the evening, with all her lights turned on, she is as glamorous as a movie star. Designed by Los Angeles architect William Pereira and Associates, the building was begun in 1969 and completed in 1972. The forty-eight–story structure is capped by a hollow, 212-foot spire lighted from within, probably the largest architectural ornament of our time. Its prominent site cost $8 million, and the building itself $36 million. Changing art exhibits are presented in the lobby. An express elevator catapults you to an observatory on the twenty-seventh floor that is open free during business hours. (Don't be disappointed—the observatory only consists of four windows looking north. But the view is exceptional; the Jackson Square Historic District that you have just walked looks like a toy. You can also see from here how Telegraph Hill has been cut and graded for bayfill.) Immediately east of the Pyramid is **Redwood Park**, a gated oasis designed by Tom Galli and landscaped with eighty redwoods from the Santa Cruz Mountains, making the corporate headquarters a human-made mountain with its own transplanted forest at its foot.

The Pyramid was initially designed to be fifty-five stories and one thousand feet tall but was downsized after vigorous protests. It was the brainchild of then-chairman John R. Beckett, who wished to give the hard-to-visualize conglomerate a memorable corporate image. In this he succeeded.

The Pyramid pops into view in the most unexpected places throughout the city. It is especially dramatic when lighted on winter nights, serving as the city's giant Christmas tree. From across the Bay, its graceful form counterbalances the flat-topped mass of the city's new highrises and makes the San Francisco skyline memorable. The Pyramid stands on the northern edge of the highrise district on the city's original shoreline and will never be obscured by other highrises to the north.

The Pyramid has a slope angle of five degrees. Its curtain wall consists of three-thousand quartz-aggregate concrete panels weighing three-and-a-half tons each. Its windows are on pivots so that they can be washed from inside the building. The largest floor, the fifth, is 145 feet on each side with 21,025 square feet; the smallest floor, the forty-eighth, is only 45 feet square. The "wings" on the two sides of the building house eighteen elevators on the east side, and emergency stairs and a smoke tower on the west side. The building has an advanced life-safety and fire protection system linked to an underground command post. Its foundation is a concrete-and-steel block, nine feet thick, weighing more than 30,000 tons, at the bottom of a 52-foot-deep excavation. Some fifty firms, mostly law and banking, along with Transamerica's own headquarters, occupy the building. More than fifteen hundred people work here.

The Bank of San Francisco
550 Montgomery Street,
at Clay

Transamerica was founded by A. P. Giannini in 1928 as a bank holding company. In the 1950s it divested itself of its bank stock, and in the 1960s it evolved into the archetypical corporate conglomerate. At one time it and its subsidiaries sold insurance, made loans, developed snapshots, moved furniture, flew airplanes, rented cars, manufactured turbines, leased containers, and distributed movies. Insurance, however, was long its major business, and the corporation has restructured itself as a financial services and insurance company. In 1992 it had assets of $32.3 billion and 10,700 employees.

The Pyramid stands on the site of the historic Montgomery Block, San Francisco's first prestige office building. Designed by engineer Henry W. Halleck in 1853, the four-story brick office sat on a twenty-two-foot-thick "raft" of redwood logs sunk in the mud. The ambitious building cost $3 million and became the best address in the West. It housed the law firm of Halleck, Peachy, and Billings(!), mining companies, stock brokers, and realtors. It also housed the U.S. Army Corps of Engineers, the city's first law library, the Adams Express Company's bullion vaults, the offices of the Pacific and Atlantic Railroad, and two early newspapers, the *Alta California* and the *Daily Herald,* among other tenants. In 1856 it housed the Second Committee of Vigilance. Adolph Sutro housed his collection of 250,000 books there. In the second-floor office of attorney Oliver Perry Stidler, Dr. Sun Yat-Sen drafted the proclamation of the Republic of China. Its elegant Bank Exchange Saloon was a celebrated meeting place and dispensed its famous Pisco punch to Robert Louis Stevenson, Bret Hart, and Ulysses S. Grant. Mark Twain is said to have met the fireman Tom Sawyer in the basement steam baths.

When the business district shifted south, the Montgomery Block lost its cachet and the faded "Ark of Empire" became the favorite location for low-rent artists' studios. Nicknamed the "Monkey Block," it was frequented by Ambrose Bierce, Frank Norris, Joaquin Miller, Gelett Burgess, George Sterling, and Jack London. Eventually the Block housed some seventy-five painters, sculptors, writers, photographers, and musicians. The rugged building with its rich historic and artistic associations survived the earthquake and fire of 1906 only to be demolished for an ignominious parking lot in 1959. In 1969 the Transamerica Pyramid was built on the history-soaked site.

❼ The Bank of San Francisco, *1908, Shea and Lofquist*

Facing the Pyramid on the southeast corner of Clay Street is the nine-story **Bank of San Francisco** with its opulent banking hall. The building was built in 1908 to designs by Shea and Lofquist as the headquarters of A. P. Giannini's Bank of Italy. It is a prime example of Beaux Arts architecture and a great favorite with architecture buffs. It has a rusticated granite base and terra-cotta cladding on its upper stories. The rich marble and decorative plaster banking hall has fine bronze fittings, including elaborate old tellers' cages from the days when bank security consisted of bars, not cameras.

Catercorner to the Bank of San Francisco, at 601 Montgomery Street, inconspicuously placed along the dark Clay Street wall, are five bronze plaques commemorating the Overland Mail Company, better known as the Pony Express. It linked San Francisco with St. Joseph, Missouri, from April 3, 1860 until October 26, 1861. While sailing 'round the Horn took ninety days, and Atlantic and Pacific steamers via the Panama land link took thirty days, this express service with its 190 stations and 120 riders covered 1,966 miles in relays that took only ten to thirteen days. The fastest time was seven days and seventeen hours when President Lincoln's first inaugural address was conveyed to an anxious California.

The Bank of Canton of California
555 Montgomery Street

Pacific Heritage Museum
608 Commercial Street;
399-1124

8 **The Bank of Canton of California,** *1984, Skidmore, Owings & Merrill*
Across Montgomery Street is the dusty Texas-pink, granite-clad headquarters of **The Bank of Canton of California** completed in 1984 and designed by Skidmore, Owings & Merrill. This seventeen-story bank headquarters is a strong, smooth, rectangular block capped by a three-step pyramidal mechanical penthouse ornamented with small gold-leafed plaques. The large, clear glass windows have narrow, muted-red frames. Inside is a large contemporary banking hall behind geometric metal grilles recalling the historic banking temples of the Financial District. The subtly gold-accented hall has a coffered ceiling and a large, four-paneled geometric mural in tan, beige, and rust. The elevator lobby is a high white octagonal drum with a shallow dome that produces an echo when a person speaks from the bull's-eye marked out in the colored granite paving. The building is a contemporary interpretation of traditional San Francisco bank buildings. The Bank of Canton of California has been located on this block since the 1930s. Its Chinatown branch is in the historic Chinese Telephone Exchange pagoda of 1909 (*see Tour 3*).

• **Pacific Heritage Museum/Grabhorn Park,** *1875, William Appleton Potter; 1984, Page, Anderson and Turnbull, restoration*
Around the corner at 608 Commercial Street is the entrance to the Bank of Canton's superb **Pacific Heritage Museum** in the restored U.S. Subtreasury building of 1875. Originally designed as a four-story brick building by Treasury architect William Appleton Potter, the building was gutted in 1906 and reconstructed as a one-story structure. It stands on the site of the first U.S. Branch Mint, which was established in 1854 in the wake of the Gold Rush. When the new Bank of Canton was built, the landmark Subtreasury was elegantly restored and converted into the Pacific Heritage Museum by Page, Anderson and Turnbull.

This gem of a museum houses changing exhibits on the artistic, cultural, and economic links across the Pacific. Pale, calm colors and plush, light carpeting make this museum a downtown oasis. In addition to its fascinating exhibits, the museum has a permanent display on the history of the Subtreasury with a cutaway section through the old structure, architectural plans, and historic photographs. In the basement is the brick vault and the guard's walk, a narrow corridor around the bullion

Grabhorn Park
608 Commercial Street

Chinese Historical Society Museum
650 Commercial Street;
391-1188

Union Ferry Depot

The Embarcadero Center

565 Commercial Street
(old Pacific Gas &
Electric Station J)

566 Commercial Street

556 Commercial Street

555 Commercial/
215 Leidesdorff/
560 Sacramento

vault. A few steps west up Commercial Street is the new **Grabhorn Park**, a pocket park with a curious modern sculpture by Pepo Pichler. This park was built by the developers of 505 Montgomery Street across Commercial Street. The park was once the site of Edwin and Robert Grabhorn's celebrated small press. Further up is the **Chinese Historical Society Museum** (see Tour 3).

9 *Commercial and Leidesdorff Streets:*
Post-1906 Cluster

Some may wish to make a half-block detour east, back across Montgomery Street to the intersection of Commercial and Leidesdorff streets, to see a post-1906 cluster. Narrow Commercial Street was not part of the original plan of the city and was cut through in July 1850, from the Central Wharf to Grant (then Dupont) Avenue. It was lined with substantial New York–like brick buildings and quickly became an important business and banking center. Look west, uphill, to see Chinatown and one of the city's last brick-paved streets. Visible just above the landscaped archway, to the east is the tower of A. Page Brown's **Union Ferry Depot**, built in 1895–1903. The light-colored highrises that bracket the now toylike tower are part of **The Embarcadero Center**, a complex of highrises and a hotel designed in 1970 by Atlanta architect John C. Portman, Jr. and Associates. Pedestrian concourses between the towers continue the line of Commercial Street to the Sausalito Ferry across The Embarcadero.

Visible one building east of Montgomery, at **565 Commercial Street**, is the monumental facade of the old **Pacific Gas & Electric Station J**, built in 1914 to the designs of Frederick H. Meyer, with a large cartouche over its great wood and glass doors. The substation was converted first into a nightclub and more recently into offices and a copy shop. Across the narrow street, at **566 Commercial**, is a narrow, three-story brick building with white stone trim around a large Gothic window in its top two stories. Designed by Wright, Rushforth and Cahill and built in 1907, it was once the location of Andrew Hoyem's Arion Press. The pleasing brick building at **556 Commercial**, with its checkerboard of alternating orange– and buff–colored bricks, was designed by Charles Rousseau and also built about 1907. This area was once the center of San Francisco's important printing industry. The **555 Commercial/215 Leidesdorff/560 Sacramento** building was designed by Albert Pissis and was the printing plant of Britton and Rey, famous San Francisco printers and lithographers.

10 *Stacking the New Over the Old*

456 Montgomery
Montgomery and
Sacramento Streets

• **456 Montgomery Street,** *1983, Roger Owen Boyer and Associates; 1908, Howard and Galloway; 1908, Albert Pissis*
On the southeast corner of Montgomery and Sacramento streets is **456 Montgomery**, a twenty-four–story highrise perched atop two small historic bank temples. This highrise was designed by Roger Owen Boyer and Associates in 1983 and is one of several examples of partial, or facade, preservation in the new Financial District. The small granite building at the corner with Tuscan columns (now Coast Federal Bank) was built for the Italian-American Bank in 1908 to designs by Howard and Galloway, (John Galen Howard was the architect of the fine Beaux Arts buildings at the University of California, Berkeley, including the monumental campanile.) The old bank is a steel-frame and concrete building with monolithic granite columns. The other small bank (today Imperial Bank) under the 456 Montgomery tower was originally the Anton Borel Bank and was designed in 1908 by Albert Pissis, one of the most important San Francisco architects at the turn of the century. It, too, has monolithic granite columns, these in the Corinthian order.

Wells Fargo Bank History Museum
420 Montgomery Street, between California and Sacramento; 396-2619

The modern highrise is notable for its column-free interiors: the walls of the new structure are load-bearing. While the preservation of the old banks was a good idea, and the modern silver tower is competent, the entrance between the historic banks is unsatisfactory despite its soothing waterfall and sunken patio café.

11 *Wells Fargo Bank History Museum*

Not more than ten feet from its original location is the glass-walled entrance to the **Wells Fargo Bank History Museum,** an adjunct to the bank headquarters around the corner on California Street. A plaque set in the sidewalk in front of the glass wall shows the first Wells Fargo & Company bank in 1852. This fascinating museum recounts the history of the California Gold Rush which made San Francisco a great city. The centerpiece of the History Room is a fine red-and-yellow stagecoach made in Concord, New Hampshire. Exhibits and maps explain the discovery of gold and Wells Fargo's role as an express company that carried treasure from the Sierra foothills to the instant metropolis on the Bay, and from there back East. Gold nuggets, gold dust, strongboxes, and other mementos fill the showcases here. It is worth lingering here and seeing everything. Upstairs, in the museum's mezzanine, is a reproduction of a stagecoach that you may sit in while listening to a tape of a nineteenth-century English traveler's description of just how uncomfortable stagecoach travel was. Also here in a display case built into the wall is a small photograph of Black Bart the versifying "PO8" who held up twenty-seven stagecoaches between 1875 and 1883. A handkerchief he dropped at one holdup led bank detectives to Charles E. Boles in San Francisco. A sample of his verse is displayed. In the wall here are sliding panels containing the Wiltsee collection of early-California covers, folded letters with stamps or franks from Gold Rush towns.

**Wells Fargo Bank
Headquarters**
464 California Street

464 California Street

The Bank of California
*400 California Street,
at Sansome*

• **Wells Fargo Bank Headquarters,** *1959, Ashley, Keyser, and Runge*
You can walk through the museum, through a corridor, and into the headquarters of the bank, which faces California Street. A second stagecoach stands in the modern bank lobby. Wells Fargo is the oldest bank in California. On March 18, 1852, upstate New Yorkers Henry Wells and William George Fargo and their associates met in New York City to form a joint stock association "for the purpose of carrying on [an] Express and Exchange business [between] the City of New York and San Francisco [and] other Cities and Towns in California." Wells, Fargo & Company began its banking and express business on July 13, 1852, on Montgomery Street, a few feet from the museum. By 1855 Wells Fargo had fifty-five offices and was the major express company in California; by 1890 it had 2,600 agencies nationwide.

In 1905 the express business in New York was severed from the banking business in San Francisco. In that same year, Bavarian-born Isaias W. Hellman merged Wells Fargo Bank with his Nevada National Bank. Hellman had come to America at sixteen to work as a clerk in his cousin's dry-goods business in the small village of Los Angeles. In the 1860s he posted a sign in a corner of the store that read, "I. W. Hellman, Banker." In 1870 he made a fortunate marriage to Esther Neugass, the daughter of a New York and London banking family related to the Lehmans. He moved to San Francisco and bought silver baron James G. Fair's Nevada Bank. He merged Wells Fargo with his Union Trust Company in 1923. Hellman held interests in some fifteen California banks, Los Angeles and San Francisco street railways, and Southern California real estate. In 1901, during the heyday of the trusts, he obtained control of the California wine industry. When the earthquake devastated the city in 1906, Hellman checked his deposits in eastern banks and announced to the press, "It will only take one-third of the Hellman resources to pay off the depositors of the Wells Fargo Nevada Bank and the Union Trust Company. The Hellman surplus will be $30 million. Every dolar of this will be used for the rebuilding of San Francisco." I. W. Hellman died in harness at seventy-seven. One of his favorite mottos was, "Work is a very necessary and good habit."

In 1960 Wells Fargo Bank took over the American Trust Company and moved its headquarters to bland, gray-granite **464 California Street,** built in 1959 by Ashley, Keyser, and Runge for American Trust. In 1986 Wells Fargo Bank nearly doubled in size when it bought the Crocker Bank from the British Midland Bank, making Wells Fargo the number three bank in California and the tenth largest bank in the nation.

⑫ The Bank of California/Museum of the Money of the American West, *1907, Bliss & Faville; 1967, Anshen and Allen, highrise*
Walk through the Wells Fargo headquarters lobby to emerge on the 400 block of California, the historic epicenter of California banking. The curious black iron object on the sidewalk in front of the automatic tellers is a Victorian hitching post. Across the narrow Leidesdorff Street is the glass base of the modern highrise adjoining the classical banking temple of **The Bank of California**. Founded in 1864, The Bank of California

very early had branches in Oregon and Washington, making it the first West Coast bank. When the then-dominant bank built at the corner of California and Sansome in 1866, it determined the heart of the banking district. Previously, this corner had been the site of the Tehama House, a hotel popular with Army officers including Ulysses S. Grant, Joseph Folsom, and William Tecumseh Sherman.

Museum of the Money of the American West *in the basement of The Bank of California*

The Bank of California was D. O. Mill's and William Ralston's bank. Ralston was the financier behind many of California's earliest industrial enterprises, including San Francisco's first woolen mill, first iron mill, first dry dock, the enormous Palace Hotel, the San Francisco Sugar Refinery, the New Montgomery Street extension, the Sherman Island reclamation in the Delta, and the vast California Theater. He was California's first great empire builder. His more cautious partner, William Sharon, wrote "In building the Palace Hotel he wanted to get some oak planks for it and he bought a ranch for a very large sum of money and never used a plank for it.... I said to him, 'If you are going to buy a factory for a nail, a ranch for a plank, and a manufactory to build furniture, where is this going to end?' "

Alas, it ended one day when the bank was examined and found seriously overextended. That afternoon Ralston went for his customary swim off Aquatic Park and drowned. His funeral was the biggest social event in the city.

The bank survived Ralston's swim. In 1907 it commissioned Bliss & Faville to design a grand Corinthian temple built of steel and granite. It is the grandest banking temple in a city noted for its banking temples and was modeled on McKim, Mead, and White's long-lost Knickerbocker Trust Building in New York City. It is surrounded on three sides by great windows and Corinthian columns. Inside is a great banking hall with sixty-foot-high ceilings. Tennessee marble lines an interior capped by a magnificent coffered ceiling. The three walls of windows admit a filtered, muted light. Famous California sculptor Arthur Putnam carved the mountain lions that guard the vault.

In the basement, near the imposing circular vault door, is a jewel of a collection known as the **Museum of the Money of the American West**. Displayed here among other precious items are examples of "necessity coinage," privately struck gold coins that circulated before the establishment of a United States Mint in San Francisco. The historic $50 octagonal gold slug of 1851 and smaller octagonal gold coins are on display, as well as the extraordinarily beautiful Saint-Gaudens double eagle $20 gold coin, and also special coins minted for the Panama-Pacific International Exposition of 1915 with the Bohemian Club's owl on the reverse. One section of the museum is devoted to Nevada's Comstock silver lode of the 1860s, which the Bank of California helped finance; another tells the story of Adolph Sutro's famous tunnel which drained the silver mines and made his fortune.

In 1967, Anshen and Allen designed the compatible highrise that adjoins the temple and that houses the bank's offices. The tower's concrete panels echo the fluting of the granite columns. The roof of the bank became an outdoor garden entered from the highrise (see illustration, next page). It is one of the best marriages of new and old architecture in San Francisco. Today the historic Bank of California, after long being controlled by the French Rothschilds, is owned by Tokyo's Mitsubishi Bank.

The Bank of California, **at the center of the banking district, fuses
Bliss & Faville's 1907 Corinthian temple with Anshen and Allen's 1967 fluted highrise.**

- *California Street: The Prestige Address*

California Street was laid out wider than the other downtown streets north of Market and cuts back from the foot of Market Street near the Ferry Building, through the Financial District, and straight up Nob Hill out west to Pacific Heights. Historically, it was always a prestigious address, both at its downtown and at its western, residential end. The California cable car line had the largest, most luxurious cars, and all along this well-run line elaborate houses were constructed. West of Nob Hill, in Pacific Heights, California Street still separates the poshest residential neighborhoods to its north from the rest of the city. West of Franklin Street, California Street still has many large often-overlooked Victorian houses.

343 Sansome Street's Roof Garden
Accessible from fifteenth floor

Union Bank
370 California Street, northeast corner of Sansome

⓭ 343 Sansome Street's Roof Garden, *1929, Hyman & Appleton; 1990, Johnson/Burgee, remodel and addition*
Up Sansome Street, behind the Bank of California's temple, is this new highrise blending an Art Deco building constructed for Crown Zellerbach paper company in 1929 with a new building commissioned by the Gerald D. Hines Interests from John Burgee with Philip Johnson. The beige-colored Art Deco structure is itself a building with a complex history. It was built as an eight-story structure in 1908 and had five stories added onto it in 1929, along with its interesting ornament. That building was gutted and wedded to a taller building in 1990. The Johnson/Burgee design is a pleasing, if retardaire, postmodern Chicago School design with simplified Louis H. Sullivan–like details. The lobby of **343 Sansome** contains a curious gallery off to its right-hand side that was the elevator lobby of the 1929 remodel. Here are displayed artifacts uncovered when the new building was built. The relics probably date from the great fire of 1851 that leveled the Gold Rush city. A **roof garden** open to the public was built atop the Art Deco tower and is accessible from the fifteenth floor of the new building. There are interesting views of the Financial District core from here, including slices of the Bay, a piece of the streamlined San Francisco–Oakland Bay Bridge, the penthouse of the neighboring Wells Fargo Bank headquarters, the Transamerica Pyramid, and the twin booms of the Mandarin Hotel at 345 California Street. The pleasant terrace gives you an office worker's view of the Financial District. Return to California Street.

⓮ Union Bank, *1977, Skidmore, Owings & Merrill*
Across Sansome from The Bank of California is the headquarters of the **Union Bank,** designed by Skidmore, Owings & Merrill in 1977. The large glassed openings and columnlike elements of the design seek to relate the modern building to the Corinthian temple it faces. At the side entrance between the tower and its California Street neighbor is a row of granite walrus heads saved from the historic Alaska Commercial Building, which once graced this corner. A plaque here, in a finely carved white marble frame also salvaged from that old landmark, tells something of the Alaska Commercial Building's history.

First Interstate Center/
The Mandarin
Oriental Hotel
345 California Street

Merchant's Exchange
Building/Grain Exchange
Hall/Coulter Marine
Paintings
465 California Street,
corner of Leidesdorff

The Union Bank has its roots in the agency of the Yokohama Specie Bank opened in San Francisco in 1886. By 1988 Union Bank was the sixth largest bank in California. It is owned by the Bank of Tokyo, Ltd. Japanese banks have recently supplanted British banks as the major foreign owners of California banks. By that year five of the eleven largest banks in the state were Japanese owned. (By 1986, eight of the world's ten largest banks were Japanese.) San Francisco, in the nineteenth century a gateway for British capital seeking investment in the resource-rich American West, has become ever more closely linked with Japan in this century.

⑮ First Interstate Center/The Mandarin Oriental Hotel, *1987, Skidmore, Owings & Merrill*

Cross California Street to the mid-block entrance of the **First Interstate Center**, designed by Skidmore, Owings & Merrill and completed in 1987. Flanking the deep slot entrance to the new tower are, to the right, the J. Harold Dollar Building of 1920 designed by George Kelham (now the Pacific Bank) and, to the left, the Robert Dollar Building of 1919 by Charles McCall. First Interstate Center's flag-capped, diamond-shaped towers rise forty-seven stories from the middle of this prime block. At 724 feet this is the third-tallest office building in San Francisco. It cost $225 million to build. The building preserves vintage office buildings at the corners of the block. A T-shaped pedestrian concourse with retail shops threads through the building, which has thirty-one floors of office space and an eleven-story luxury hotel in twin towers. Twin booms fly large flags.

This complex project is worth looking at from several angles. Its lobby is simple but elegant and paneled in African mahogany. The pedestrian concourse is lavishly clad in gray granites from Sweden and Sardinia, deep-red Swedish granite, polished black African granite, and gray and pink mottled granite from India. It is lighted by some of the finest new light fixtures in the city. The tower itself is clad in both dark and light gray granite, which mask the building's bulk. The building uses dark colors at its base and lighter colors at its top to relate to its two very different contexts, the streetscape and the skyline. The modernistic booms surmounting the towers are illuminated at night. The building adds a new accent to the city's skyline without mimicking forms from the past. **The Mandarin Oriental Hotel** occupies the top eleven floors with the glass "skybridges" between the two towers.

⑯ Merchant's Exchange Building/Grain Exchange Hall/Coulter Marine Paintings, *1903, Willis Polk*

The **Merchant's Exchange Building** is one of the most important prototypical office buildings in San Francisco. It was designed by Willis Polk, the local architect of the Chicago firm of D. H. Burnham and Co., in 1903 and reconstructed after the earthquake and fire of 1906. It contains some of the finest public art in San Francisco. (While Julia Morgan had her offices in the building, there is no evidence that she did the post-fire rebuilding.) Today, among other tenants, the Merchant's Exchange Building houses the San Francisco Chamber of Commerce, the Merchant's Exchange Club in the basement, and the Commercial Club on the top floors.

Pass through the twin-columned entrance into the marble lobby with its elaborate elevator doors and fine ship models. A skylight here reveals a large light court. At the end of the lobby is the entrance to the great **Grain Exchange Hall**, today the Financial District branch of First Interstate Bank. This room was originally the center of commercial life on the West Coast. News of ship arrivals was transmitted from the belvedere on the roof to the merchants in the exchange hall. Here complete information was kept on every Pacific Coast ship from start to finish of every voyage. Shippers, ship owners, ship chandlers, warehousers, exporters, and importers gathered here to do business. This great space was considered the "Forum of San Francisco." On April 29, 1910, $4 million was raised in two hours in a mass meeting held here to launch the great Panama-Pacific International Exposition of 1915. In plan, the Grain Exchange Hall is like the porch of a temple. Looking through the entrance there are four giant columns, and beyond them, a series of large **oil paintings** by marine painter **William A. Coulter** and one by **Nils Hagerup.** The paintings are full of color and emotion. Coulter was born in Ireland in 1849 to a seafaring family. He went to sea as a cabin boy and then as an able-bodied seaman. He later studied art in Europe and was an illustrator for the *San Francisco Call*. He devoted much of his art to the history of maritime shipping in Northern California, and the post-1909 group of paintings here, which tells the history of this historic seaport, is his masterpiece.

• *Port Costa,* by Coulter. A view through the Silver Gate, where the American and Sacramento rivers enter San Francisco Bay. Sailing vessels ride at anchor while a hay scow and two barges towed by a stern-wheeler head for San Francisco. The agricultural riches of California's great Central Valley flowed down these river routes to the entrepôt of San Francisco on their way to world markets.

• *Honolulu Harbor,* by Coulter. The steppingstone between San Francisco and Asia and a major focus of San Francisco investment was preboom Honolulu, shown here, a small seaport at the base of towering green volcanoes. Pristine Waikiki Beach and Diamond Head are seen to the right. A Matson steamship loaded with island sugar steams toward the viewer and San Francisco. An outrigger canoe returns, from fishing, to Oahu.

• *Arrived, All Well,* by Coulter. Shows the sailing ship *W. F. Babcock* of the Dollar Line (note the flag with its dollar sign) being towed into the harbor as the sun pierces the late-afternoon fog. Small ships dot the harbor. On the horizon, red brick Fort Point guards the entrance to the Bay; Telegraph Hill with its Gothic castle appears to the far left.

• *Full and By,* by Coulter. The wonderfully named ship *Dashing Wave* cuts through a blue sea with rain squalls to the right and dappled clouds above. She is passing the Tatash Light carrying a cargo of redwood lumber destined for San Francisco. North Coast redwood and Oregon pine and fir were used to build San Francisco's elaborate Victorian houses.

Old Bank of America
Headquarters
1185 California/300
Montgomery Street

Kohl Building
400 Montgomery Street

580 California Street

• *War Time*, by Coulter. Shows the launching of the freighter *Cotati* at the Hunters Point shipyards in the southeast corner of San Francisco. The other vessels riding at anchor sport geometrical World War I camouflage patterns, while an early airplane flies overhead.

• *Northwest Passage, 1903–06*, by Nils Hagerup. Depicts the tiny one-masted schooner-rigged sloop *Gjoa* commanded by Danish captain Roald Amundsen, the first vessel to make the long-sought-after Northwest Passage from the Atlantic to the Pacific. The fearless ship with its seven sailors plunges through Arctic swells off a bleak coast. Amundsen discovered the passage and determined the location of the magnetic North Pole on his three-year expedition. Today the historic ship is at Norway's National Maritime Museum, after sitting for many years beached near the ocean end of Golden Gate Park.

17 **Old Bank of America Headquarters,** *1922, George Kelham; 1941,*
L. J. Hendy, addition
Next door to the Merchant's Exchange, at the southeast corner of California and Montgomery streets, is **485 California/300 Montgomery**. Its grand banking hall, now subdivided into offices, was modeled on a Roman basilica, originally not a church type but a large meeting hall used for law and public administration. Plaster bulls and bears decorate the hall's frieze. The columns here have been given a *scagliola* finish in imitation of veined marble. This hall and the original building were designed by George Kelham in 1922 for the American National Bank. In 1941 this became the **headquarters of the Bank of America,** the building's exterior was remodeled in a sober classicism, and an addition was added on the Pine Street end designed by L. J. Hendy. The fine Moderne lobby at 300 Montgomery dates from this reworking and expansion. The remodeled building presents giant Ionic colonnades on three sides.

18 **Kohl Building,** *1901, Percy and Polk; 1907, Willis Polk, reconstruction*
Across California Street, on the northeast corner of Montgomery Street, is the gray **Kohl Building,** originally the Alvinza Hayward Building. It was designed by Percy and Polk in 1901 in an H shape. While its base has been remodeled several times, the upper stories and elaborate cornice survive from the original design. It was an early "fireproof" steel-frame structure and survived the earthquake and fire of 1906 with no fire damage above the fourth floor, making it a unique survivor. It was reconstructed by Willis Polk in 1907. Its brick curtain walls are clad in gray Colusa sandstone. The rich cornice and giant order at the upper stories are fine examples of Edwardian design.

19 **580 California Street,** *1983, Johnson/Burgee*
The much ballyhooed postmodernist Philip Johnson has not been a good thing for San Francisco. His harlequin-pattern Neiman-Marcus store, the cutesy gazebo in front of cylindrical 101 California Street, and the faceless statues here that look like the Grim Reaper are all pure kitsch. Office towers should be serious works of up-to-date archi-

tecture, not frivolous pastry decoration such as this. The hideous statues by Muriel Castanis that crown this twenty-three-story office building were not an auspicious return of ornament to downtown buildings. This postmodern French Chateau skyscraper confection has an acceptable and practical arcaded entrance most appropriate on this windy corner; it is detailed like a 1920s design. The wall treatment, with its very slightly bowed out windows and light-colored granite facing, is acceptable, even if it misunderstands the architectural patterns of San Francisco's Financial District. But the pseudo-mansard glass roof with its ridiculous cresting and ominous statuary is just rampant bad taste.

Federal Home Loan Bank
600 California Street, northwest corner of Kearny

Bank of America World Headquarters
555 California Street, between Montgomery and Kearny

20 **Federal Home Loan Bank,** *1990, Kohn Pederson Fox Associates*
This postmodern essay clad in light gray Sardinian granite is acceptable enough but is not great architecture. The building's best features are the decorations it recycles from the past. Mount the steps to the corner entrance. In the vestibule are some fine 1930 reliefs by Lee O. Lowrie including a surveyor embracing an Art Deco skyscraper. In the lofty lobby are two oil paintings by Peter Ilyin done in 1938 for the San Francisco Building at Treasure Island's Golden Gate International Exposition. The painting on the left depicts San Francisco's downtown from the Bay; that on the right shows Fisherman's Wharf and Russian Hill from a fishing boat. They are light and airy and project a modernist vision of the city as an almost geological formation. A handsome postmodern case designed by Po Shun Leong and crafted of many exotic woods holds interesting Chinese ceramics dug up on the site in 1988 when the foundations were dug for the new tower. They probably come from a Chinese store destroyed in the great fire of 1851. Chinatown *(see Tour 3)* is immediately across Sacramento Street from the back of this modern tower.

21 **Bank of America World Headquarters: Carnelian Room,** *1968,*
Wurster, Bernardi & Emmons; Skidmore, Owings & Merrill; Pietro Belluschi, consulting architect
The dominant building on the city's skyline and still the dominant financial institution in California, the **Bank of America World Headquarters** occupies the full block between California and Pine, Montgomery and Kearny streets. Rising up fifty-two stories (779 feet) and containing 1.8 million square feet of prime office space, the dark red granite-clad tower was designed in 1968 by Wurster, Bernardi & Emmons, and Skidmore, Owings & Merrill, with Pietro Belluschi as design consultant. It was completed in 1970–71. In 1985 the landmark highrise was bought by San Francisco real estate magnate Walter H. Shorenstein for $660 million, the highest price ever paid for one building in this country. By 1987 Shorenstein was reported to own twelve million square feet of office space in San Francisco, Houston, Kansas City, Los Angeles, and other American cities, and to manage roughly 30 percent of the commercial real estate in San Francisco's Financial District.

A.P. Giannini Plaza
553 California Street

Carnelian Room
Top of the Bank
of America,
555 California Street,
between Montgomery
and Kearny;
433-7500

The Bank of America World Headquarters—despite its disruptive dark color so at odds with the rest of this light-reflecting city—is one of the most magnificent tall buildings of our time. Along with the Transamerica Pyramid (also erected by a Giannini-founded corporation) and St. Mary's Roman Catholic Cathedral, it is one of the great architectural monuments of the boom that transformed San Francisco in the go-go 1970s. Rising abruptly from its granite-paved plaza, the huge building has zigzag facades of two-sided bay windows, which do not look particularly large from outside but which are very large from within. This sawtooth facade is curiously reminiscent of the 1937 Art Deco concrete abutments that anchor the suspension cables of the Golden Gate Bridge. While regular along the tower's base and midsection, these bays are irregular at its top, giving the building a subtly animated profile within its simple box shape. The tower is most dramatic from the narrow passage on Montgomery Street between the lowrise, freestanding banking hall and the preserved California Commercial Union Building of 1921 at the corner of Montgomery and Pine. From this compressed space the tower seems to soar in splendid isolation like a superb sculpture, which it is. The building is sheathed in 3.5-inch-thick slabs of mirror-polished carnelian granite from South Dakota. Late in the day, under certain light foggy atmospheres, when the sun's rays strike the prismlike facades at low angles, the red polished granite and glass reflect the light in beams that seem to emanate from within the building. The dark structure is then transformed into a gleaming crystal in a moving, diaphanous atmosphere. Occasionally, at sunset, it becomes a glittering shaft of gold rising out of the white cubist cityscape. This is powerful architecture for a powerful institution.

On the California Street side of the tower is the **A. P. Giannini Plaza**, with a plush auditorium underneath it. Standing in the plaza is the sleek, black Swedish- granite sculpture executed by Masayuki Nagare entitled *Transcendence*. (Irreverent San Franciscans, however, have dubbed it "the banker's heart.") Over time, greenery and benches have been introduced here, softening the pharaonic monumentality of this cold, granite-paved space.

A. P. Giannini was born in 1870, the son of a Genoa-born San Jose hotel owner who died when the boy was very young. His mother then married Lorenzo Scatena, a produce wholesaler who moved the family to San Francisco. Here A.P. went into his stepfather's business and became a partner at nineteen. He proved to be a whiz with numbers and with people. In 1892, at twenty-two, he married Clorinda Cuneo. In 1904, with Antonio Chichizola and others, he founded his own bank, serving, at first, Italian Americans. Soon it began to court other immigrant groups, such as the Portuguese and Chinese, that established WASP banks disdained. In serving the "little fellow," a great bank was built. By 1921 it was the largest bank in the West, and in 1930 it shed its immigrant beginnings and proudly rechristened itself the Bank of America (adopting the name of a New York City bank established in 1812 that Giannini had acquired in 1928). The new Bank of America became a key instrument in financing the municipalities, ranches, and industries of California, including Hollywood movies.

After this walk exploring the heart of the banking district, from the Gold Rush survivors of the Jackson Square Historic District to the opulent steel-frame towers of the present, it is appropriate to end with an elevator ride to the top of Bank of America's tower. After 3 P.M., the Bankers Club atop the commanding Bank of America is open to the public as the **Carnelian Room**, a cocktail lounge and restaurant. It has one of the finest views in the city, especially memorable at sunset.

Continuation:
The Embarcadero Center and Nearby

- **The Embarcadero Center**, *1967–81, John C. Portman, Jr. and Associates*

You can continue Tour 2A by walking down California Street to Battery for an exploration of **The Embarcadero Center** complex, which includes an array of shops, boutiques, restaurants, and cafés. However, those with an interest in skyscraper design would do better to skip ahead to *Tour 2B, A Skyscraper Sampler*, which continues from the Bank of America World Headquarters through the Financial District and across Market Street to the new San Francisco Museum of Modern Art in Yerba Buena Center.

The Embarcadero Center is approximately five blocks from Sansome Street, between Sacramento and Clay, with an L-shaped extension to California and Market streets. The four office towers, were designed in 1967-81 by John C. Portman, Jr. and Associates.

- **One Embarcadero Center**, 45 stories

- **Two Embarcadero Center/Site of the Vigilantes' Fort Gunnybags,** 35 stories

Facing Two Embarcadero Center, across Sacramento Street, is a low wall with a handsome bronze plaque mounted on it. The tablet is capped by an all-seeing eye with wings, the emblem of the **Committee of Vigilance**, and was designed by Newton J. Tharp in 1903. It marks the spot where Fort Gunnybags stood, the fortified warehouse that became the headquarters of the Second Committee of Vigilance in 1856. Sometimes called "the businessman's revolution," the Vigilante movement erupted three times in San Francisco—in 1851, 1856, and 1877—and it presented itself as a response to out-of-control crime. In all three instances it was led by merchant William T. Coleman. This extra-legal movement actually pitted the city's elite merchants against its working–class immigrants, in particular the Irish Democratic political machine that had taken over city government. In 1851 the Vigilantes lynched four men, whipped one, and deported twenty-eight. The 1856 episode took place at the same time that nativist "Know Nothing" movements were sweeping other cities in the nation. In San Francisco it styled itself the Peoples Party, a probusiness political organization that took over the city government a year later and held power until 1867.

The Embarcadero Center

One Embarcadero Center
Battery and Sacramento streets

Two Embarcadero Center/ Site of the Vigilantes' Fort Gunnybags, *Front and Sacramento streets*

Three Embarcadero Center
Davis and Sacramento streets

Four Embarcadero Center
Drumm Street at the foot of Sacramento

Alcoa Building

Golden Gateway

- **Three Embarcadero Center,** 35 stories

- **Four Embarcadero Center,** 45 stories

The Embarcadero Center, recently expanded west of Battery Street, today consists of six office towers, two major hotels, and some 175 retail shops, boutiques, restaurants, cafés, and galleries. It is virtually a satellite city, perhaps the best of its kind. San Francisco was fortunate that when urban renewal moved downtown it had the large, obsolete, architecturally undistinguished, low-rise produce and wharfside warehouse district to condemn and expand into.

Two very different phases of urban renewal design are displayed here and across Clay Street. The first, cruder phase north of Clay Street, designed between 1959 and 1964, produced the dark, X-braced **Alcoa Building** and the banal concrete highrise boxes of **Golden Gateway**, both set atop massive, unrelieved parking podiums. Skidmore, Owings & Merrill's Alcoa Building was deliberately set to block the view corridors of Front and Merchant streets. There is a very fine Henry Moore sculpture, *Knife Edge Figure*, in the unpeopled sculpture garden on the west side of the Alcoa Building.

The second wave of urban renewal learned from the city-busting mistakes of the first. In John C. Portman, Jr. and Associates' Embarcadero Center, parking was put underground where it belongs and the sidewalk level of the complex's podiums designed to draw in pedestrians. The old line of Commercial Street was carried through the four-block megaparcel of assembled blocks as an internal walkway. Three levels of restaurants, shops, and terraces linked by pedestrian bridges over intervening streets and garnished with a collection of modern sculpture serve as the base for four thin, slablike towers. Louise Nevelson's thirty-four-ton CorTen steel *Sky Tree* at Three Embarcadero Center, facing Sacramento Street between Davis and Drumm, is probably the best sculpture here.

The site plan set the office towers along the north edge of the parcel, putting the three-level podiums with their terraces atop them on the sunny side of the site. In section the towers look like slightly splayed playing cards. This gives each floor from ten to fourteen corner offices rather than the usual four. The general styling of The Embarcadero Center's towers with their accentuated thinness and vertical striped effect is reminiscent of Rockefeller Center in New York, still the finest of modern in-city megadevelopments. One Embarcadero Center, the westernmost tower of Embarcadero Center, between Battery and Front streets, is set slightly off the axial arrangement of the three other towers, a bit like the former RCA Building in New York. All four towers line up with their skinny side to the city, thereby disturbing the fewest views from residential Nob Hill to the west. In every way these big buildings did everything they could, including adopting a light color, to fit into the city while introducing the radically larger scale of contemporary redevelopment.

• **Hyatt Regency Hotel and Five Embarcadero Center,** *1973*
The splashiest space in The Embarcadero Center is the **Hyatt Regency Hotel's** seventeen-story **atrium**. This modern space is quite active with cafés, bars, and people. The great globelike sculpture is *Eclipse*, by Charles O. Perry. (The Embarcadero BART and Muni Metro stations are right outside the hotel on the Market Street side, as is the terminus of the California Street cable line.)

• **The Royal Exchange,** *1911, Righetti & Headman; 1972, Ron Kaufman, restoration*
The Royal Exchange, across the street from One Embarcadero Center, is a large, stylish, welcoming, Financial District watering hole. The bar fills the ground floor of a 1911 Edwardian commercial building designed as a warehouse by Righetti & Headman. In 1972 developer Ron Kaufman reinforced the building with exposed interior steel bracing (painted yellow and visible through the upstairs windows) and converted the building to offices with the new-old Royal Exchange perfectly fitted into the handsome original cast-iron and plate-glass Edwardian storefront.

• **Old Federal Reserve Bank**, *1924, George Kelham; 1991, Studios Architecture/ Kaplan McLaughlin Diaz, restoration/adaptation*

• **Embarcadero Center West**, *1988, John C. Portman, Jr. and Associates*

• **Park Hyatt Hotel,** *1988, John C. Portman, Jr. and Associates*
The Embarcadero Center has been a success and has expanded to the west, where it has bought, restored, and redesigned the starchy **Old Federal Reserve Bank** designed by George Kelham in 1924. Two new buildings, **Embarcadero Center West**, a thirty-three-story tower with a whittled top, and the twenty-four-story **Park Hyatt Hotel**, were built to either side of the neoclassical Old Fed in 1988. The new buildings are also by John C. Portman, Jr. and Associates, with Studios Architecture and Kaplan McLaughlin Diaz as associate architects for the restoration work on the Old Fed. These new elements of Embarcadero Center remain three separate blocks within the old city grid, not assembled, multiblock megaparcels. Thus the latest wave of city building (under the strong hand of the Department of City Planning) has come back to appreciate the basic city pattern it once did everything to erase.

It is a fine piece of city-mending, which is the hallmark of the best present-day projects, that the Old Federal Reserve Bank has been "turned around." Once the sharp edge of the Financial District, with its giant portico facing Sansome Street to the west and its utilitarian armored-car entrance facing Battery Street and the Produce District to the east, it has been transformed into a link between The Embarcadero Center and the banking core through the addition of a second giant Ionic portico at the eastern, Battery Street, side of the building. The Sansome Street lobby has colorful murals by Jules Guerin. An interesting sliced-up bronze statue stands on the Sansome Street steps.

Hyatt Regency Hotel and Five Embarcadero Center
Foot of California Street, at Drumm

The Royal Exchange
301 Sacramento Street, at Front

Embarcadero Center West
255 Battery Street, at Sacramento

Old Federal Reserve Bank of San Francisco
400 Sansome Street

Park Hyatt Hotel
333 Battery Street, at Clay

Russ Building
235 Montgomery Street,
between Pine and Bush

Mills Building and Tower
220 Montgomery,
at Bush

Tour 2B: A Skyscraper Sampler

San Francisco's compact downtown is a choice sampler of sky-scraper architecture, one of America's most distinctive inventions. Historically, after New York and the "Windy City," it had the third largest concentration of tall buildings in the country. This second tour highlights some of the most interesting of these steel-frame structures, from the Bank of America World Headquarters through the Financial District and across Market Street to the Palace Hotel, the Moderne Pacific Telephone and Telegraph skyscraper at 140 New Montgomery Street, and the new San Francisco Museum of Modern Art. It highlights all the important architectural styles from the 1890s to the 1990s.

22 Russ Building, *1927, George Kelham*
Long the tallest skyscraper in the West, the thirty-one story Gothic Revival **Russ Building** has lost none of its beauty. The building's tower is a grace note on the horizon, and the east, or back, side of the building facing Nob Hill is nicely detailed. It was designed with an E-shape to provide natural light and ventilation. A bronze oval set into the floor of the entrance vestibule depicts an archer. The bronze elevator indicator with its moving lights is informative and artistic, one of the downtown's best kinetic sculptures.

23 Mills Building and Tower *1891, Burnham and Root, Chicago School office block; 1908, Burnham & Company/Willis Polk, reconstruction; 1914 and 1918, Willis Polk, Bush Street additions; 1931, Lewis P. Hobart, tower addition*
A massive round Romanesque arch at 220 Montgomery Street marks the emphatic entrance to this historic and handsome office block. Built around a light-filled central court, this is the first entirely steel-frame building erected in San Francisco. Its lobby has been handsomely restored, and contemporary art works are displayed in its ground-floor corridor. On its Bush Street side is a compatible series of additions culminating in the first tower addition to a San Francisco landmark, Lewis P. Hobart's fine twenty-two-story **Mills Tower**. The building is worth careful scrutiny for its superior exterior finish. Above its two-story white Inyo marble base, large, plain, yellowish-buff Roman brick areas set off intricate terra-cotta decoration.

This powerful monument was built by Darius Ogden Mills, founder of the first bank in the West and later of the Bank of California. It is a fine example of what is known as the Chicago School of commercial architecture. It long housed the downtown municipal law library and was the center of legal activity in the city. (Today it houses the **Mills Law Library**, a service of the building's landlord.) Later, insurance companies were prominent tenants. The Sierra Club was incorporated in an office here in 1892 when this was a brand-new building. In 1898 Paul Elder's bookshop and publishing house was located here during the artistic high point of book publishing in the West. The massive block survived the earthquake of 1906 with little damage but was gutted by the fire that broke out afterward. Turn left at Bush Street.

㉔ Chevron/Former Standard Oil of California Headquarters, *1922, George Kelham; 1948, Harry Thomsen, addition*

There was a fascination with Italian Renaissance design in the United States in the 1920s. The gardens of the elite, public libraries, campuses, and some office buildings dressed themselves in suave Italian style. This very fine, reticent but luxurious design is probably modeled after York and Sawyer's winning competition design for the Federal Reserve Bank of New York. In 1948, as Aramco was developing Saudi Arabia, Harry Thomsen designed an identical wing that made the L-shaped building a U-shape. The top of the building, with its corbeled cornice, attic, and red tile roof recalls Renaissance Florentine city palaces. In 1964 and 1975 the energy giant built two newer towers on Market Street, moving the chairman's office there. **Chevron**, as it is known today, is the richest corporation headquartered in San Francisco.

Former Standard Oil of California Headquarters
225 Bush Street, southwest corner of Sansome

200 Bush Street
northwest corner of Sansome

Pacific Coast Stock Exchange/ Stackpole Statues
301 Pine Street, southwest corner of Sansome; Stock Exchange not open to the public.

• **200 Bush Street,** *1912, 1916, Benjamin G. McDougall*

225 Bush Street was the second Standard Oil Company building in San Francisco. The first is across the street at **200 Bush Street**, on the northwest corner of Sansome. This Beaux Arts office building was built in 1912 and had two top floors added in 1916. Designed by Benjamin G. McDougall, it was one of the most sumptuous office buildings of its day. In 1916 *Architect and Engineer* gushed "It expresses to a nicety the princely character of one of the world's wealthiest corporations and it impresses the visitor most profoundly with the importance, the perfection, and the power of this most efficient and most successful of all America's business organizations." Walk north up Sansome Street to Pine. On the southwest corner is the templelike Pacific Coast Stock Exchange with its two monumental statues.

㉕ Pacific Coast Stock Exchange, *1915, J. Milton Dyer*
   Stackpole Statues, *1933, Ralph Stackpole*

This temple to money and art has a complex history. The sober gray granite temple trading hall with the Doric colonnade facing Pine Street was designed by J. Milton Dyer of Cleveland and built in 1915 to house the United States Subtreasury. When the government vacated the temple after the Stock Market Crash of 1929, the **San Francisco Stock Exchange** moved in and commissioned Miller and Pfleuger to update the building. They added Moderne touches to the design, including the octagonal bas-reliefs along the attic story of the temple, and engaged **Ralph Stackpole** to create two colossal sculptural groups, which were unveiled on New Year's Eve in 1933. The one on the right is entitled *Man and His Inventions*, the one to the left is *Mother Earth*. They are fine examples of 1930s figurative public art.

• **The City Club/155 Sansome Street**, *1930, Miller and Pfleuger; 1931, mural by Diego Rivera*
Miller and Pfleuger also designed a twelve-story, granite-clad office tower behind the trading hall with facilities for the Stock Exchange Club atop it. Its entrance is at 155 Sansome Street. Over the door, carved in high relief, is **Ralph Stackpole's** muscular figure representing *The Progress of Man*. The opulent lobby is faced with black marble and has a gold leaf ceiling with a geometric star pattern. Upstairs (not open to the public) is the luxuriously appointed Moderne Stock Exchange Club, today **The City Club**. A large mural by **Diego Rivera** in the two-story stairwell of the club depicts an *Allegory of California* as a great mother figure. Occasionally the Mexican Museum, arranges tours to see this important mural. Return to Bush Street and turn left (east).

㉖ 1 Bush Street/Hambrecht & Quist Building *1959, Hertzka and Knowles; Skidmore, Owings & Merrill; plaza by Lawrence Halprin & Associates; fountain by David Tolerton*
A very fine work of architecture but a disastrous piece of urban design, the high-quality **Hambrecht & Quist Building** (originally built for the Crown-Zellerbach paper company) first introduced the deadly "tower in a plaza" idea to the new San Francisco that emerged about 1960. The building boasts a handsome glass skin and a mosaic-clad elevator and stair tower, facing Market Street and placed outside the office tower. Admired by many and put in a class with Lever House in New York City by some, this rectangular tower on a full triangular block brought Le Corbusier's *Ville Contemporain* of 1922 and *Ville Radieuse* of 1935 from fantasy illustration to urban actuality. The idea was to completely break away from the city as it had evolved over eons and to have buildings stand apart in a new form consisting of towers rising out of large open spaces with lower buildings and complex traffic routes between. What was actually banished in this Puritan vision was the continuous ribbon of commerce and sidewalk-life-producing activities that had always crowded their way down busy downtown streets. When built in groups—or more typically, when randomly scattered about American downtowns with a vast backwash of parking lots all around—this idea has made contemporary American downtowns repellent to pedestrian life.

Number **1 Bush Street** is arranged like two contrasting pieces of sculpture in a shallow granite bowl; the green glass rectangular tower "converses" with the low, round building set like a flat, folded steel chrysanthemum in the southwest corner. The pavilion building was originally a bank branch; today it houses The Sharper Image. The artfully paved sunken plaza with its fine stainless-steel wall fountain by David Tolerton has no benches. Blocks of a city developed as freestanding islands sterilize the urban environment. What is remarkable about this development is its low density considering the size of the site. Spread out over the entire triangular plot, this would be a six-story building. This "underutilization" of the site threatened the building with demolition when Crown-Zellerbach was swallowed by a corporate raider. To preserve this modern monument, the city made the building a landmark.

㉗ 130 Bush Street, *1910, MacDonald and Applegarth*
This twenty-foot wide, eleven-story, bay-windowed Gothic Revival skyscraper clad in intricate, cream-glazed terra-cotta is one of San Francisco's three narrowest skyscrapers and looks like an ornate hinge between its two large neighbors. Bay windows are exceedingly rare in the post-1906 Financial District but they work well here.

㉘ Shell Building, *1929, George Kelham*
The **Shell Building** both knits with the surrounding buildings of the city and soars in a graceful, artistic tower from its corner site. Clad in sepia-glazed terra-cotta with blue-green cast-concrete spandrels, the building is designed to emphasize its verticality. Moderne dishlike ornaments flood-lit at night cap the tower. Abstracted shell designs are worked into the ornament inside and out in reference to the client. The small lobby is quite handsome and was recently restored. The office floors upstairs were built with movable partitions. This urbane tower follows the model of Eliel Saarinen's Chicago Tribune Tower Competition entry, which won second place and was never built but which influenced many forward-looking designers.

㉙ Mechanic's Monument, *1895, Douglas Tilden, sculptor; Willis Polk, architect*
This heroic group shows five well-muscled men punching a hole in a metal plate with a large press. It was the gift of James Mervyn Donahue in memory of his father, Peter Donahue, who established the state's first iron works in 1850. The sculptor was Douglas Tilden, a gifted deaf mute. Architect Willis Polk designed the fine granite pedestal. It is one of the finest pieces of public statuary in the city and is unusual in honoring workingmen. Bronze plaques set in the sidewalk here mark the original shoreline of Yerba Buena Cove, the original anchorage that was quickly obliterated as the city expanded eastward onto bayfill.

• **Market Street: Main Stem and Great Divide**
1847, Jasper O'Farrell, extension of city plan; 1971–78, Market Street Beautification Project by Mario Ciampi, Lawrence Halprin & Associates, John Carl Warnecke and Associates
Market Street was laid out by Irish-born civil engineer Jasper O'Farrell in 1847 and aligned not to the existing city grid to its north, which it cuts across at a 36-degree angle, but to Twin Peaks, its visual terminus. Why O'Farrell did this he never explained; its effect has been to make traffic connections across Market Street difficult and to divide the city into the prestigious middle and upper class north of Market and the industrial and working class south of Market.

The Central Pacific Railroad's "Big Four" organized the **Market Street Cable Railway**, which opened in 1883. It eventually ran lines up Market and out Valencia and Castro streets south of Market, and also up Market and out west on McAllister, Hayes, and Haight streets, through the Western Addition to Golden Gate Park. The narrow cable conduit slot down Market Street became, figuratively,

130 Bush Street

Shell Building
*100 Bush Street
at Battery*

Mechanic's Monument
Bush Street at Market

Market Street

Shaklee Terraces
444 Market Street,
between Bush and Front

388 Market Street Flatiron
on Market Street between
Front and Pine

the social dividing line in San Francisco society, as "South of the Slot" increasingly became a working-class "other city."

Later the municipality itself built a competing transit line down Market Street, and for many years four sets of tracks busy with streetcars made crossing Market Street and boarding streetcars risky business. Department stores came to mid–Market Street in the 1890s and some bank headquarters moved here between 1900 and 1920. After the fire of 1906 and into the 1920s, Market Street between Golden Gate and Van Ness avenues became the street for movie palaces. The 120-foot-wide street was described in the WPA guide of 1940 as a "streamlined array of neon signs, movie-theater marquees, neat awnings, and gleaming window glass." Below Montgomery Street, Market Street was a much quieter zone of railroad and steamship companies, nautical supplies, and transient hotels.

When the Muni Metro/BART subway was built under Market Street in the early 1970s, the sidewalks and pocket parks along Market were redesigned by Mario Ciampi, Lawrence Halprin & Associates and John Carl Warnecke and Associates with a $24.5 million bond issue approved in 1968. Unfortunately, it is a graceless design, even though granite was lavishly used. The only positive note was the replication of the 1917 "Path of Gold" streetlights with their three elegant lamps designed by Willis Polk, Arthur Putnam, and Leo Lentelli, the handsomest street furniture San Francisco has ever seen. The bas-relief panels at their base are entitled The Winning of the West and are Putnam's work.

30 **Shaklee Terraces**, *1982, Skidmore, Owings & Merrill*

The undulating, silvery, aluminum-clad **Shaklee Terraces** relates creatively to Market Street's diagonal, though not successfully to its 1908 neighbor. The top of the tower is a series of set-back, glassed-in terraces with trees, looking out over San Francisco Bay. It is one of the few contemporary towers to use its top in this way; mechanical equipment monopolizes the top of most highrises. Cross Front Street.

31 **388 Market Street Flatiron**, *1986, Skidmore, Owings & Merrill*

This red-granite-clad flatiron building is the jewel of late 1980s highrise construction in San Francisco and the magnificent flagship of the flotilla of flatiron buildings on the north side of Market Street. The sophisticated, luxuriously understated design fuses a wedge and a cylinder in a teardrop-shaped building, rounded at both ends. The subtly faceted, cylindrical Front Street end echoes the shape of Philip Johnson and John Burgee's colossal, cylindrical 101 California Street tower across Pine Street. Number **388 Market** is clad in polished deep-red granite mounted on precast concrete panels. Its flat and curved clear-glass windows are set in narrow aquamarine metal frames. The building is a layer cake of uses: underground parking for 120 cars, a two-story retail base with a pass-through from Pine to Market Street, sixteen floors of offices, mechanical equipment floors, and six floors containing one- and two-bedroom condominiums on top. Number 388 Market was granted permission for additional floors by the city because of its incorporation of housing. A shallow dome on the roof masks cooling equipment; this is a building designed to be attractive when looked down upon from its taller neighbors. It was built by Honorway Investment Corporation of Hong Kong. Cases in the lobby display fine Chinese ceramics. Retrace your steps two blocks up Market Street to the west to Market, Sansome, and Sutter streets.

Citicorp Center
1 Sansome Street, at Sutter and Market

Hunter-Dulin Building
111 Sutter Street, at Montgomery

㉜ Citicorp Center, *1910, Albert Pissis, London Paris Bank; 1921, George Kelham, bank temple expansion; 1984, William Pereira and Associates, highrise and bank temple adaptation; 1915, A. Stirling Calder statue*
Enter the cold but impressive white marble–faced forecourt to the fine 1984 tower built within the granite shell of the Beaux Arts London Paris Bank of 1910. Tables and chairs set out here are a good place to rest. The statue presiding over the space is one with much meaning for San Francisco. It is A. Stirling Calder's *Star Figure* sculpted for the great Panama-Pacific International Exposition of 1915. A woman in clinging drapery stands lightly on a globe with her hands held over her head in a diamond pattern framing a rayed, starry headdress.

The tower designed by William Pereira and Associates is sleek and clean. Its light, rounded corners and the windowlike openings at its top create a design that is both assertive and contextual. The wraparound corner windows exploit the best view edges of tall buildings. Despite its large horizontal windows, the building wall seems predominantly a light-reflecting white. This is a "smart building," that is, it incorporates into itself an "electronic nervous system" of communication and computer services for its tenants.

The construction of the new tower involved the retention of the fine exterior of the 1910–21 bank temple and the saving of a thirty-five-ton section of the richly decorated cornice of MacDonald and Applegarth's fine 1912 Holbrook Building which occupied the tower's site. That impressive architectural fragment makes a dramatic sculpture/memento mounted on the back wall of the restaurant tucked into the base of the tower. A panel on the lobby wall nearby tells the stories of the Anglo and London and Paris National Bank. An Aubusson tapestry of 1971 by Alexander Calder entitled *Le Lezard et le Tetard* brightens the lobby.

Citicorp is the largest bank in the United States and is headquartered in New York City in a distinctive 1977 slant-topped tower. **Citicorp Center** in San Francisco is owned by Citicorp and Dai-ichi Mutual Life Insurance Company, Japan's second-largest insurance company. Walk up Sutter Street and cross Montgomery.

㉝ Hunter-Dulin Building *1926, Schultze and Weaver*
The **Hunter-Dulin Building** is a stately, beige terra-cotta-clad castle in the air whose copper-trimmed top is now enjoyed mostly from the plain tall buildings that surround it. Sam Spade had his fictional detective offices in this Romanesque/châteauesque skyscraper.

Former French
Bank Building
110 Sutter Street,
at Trinity

Hallidie Building/
American Institute of
Architects Gallery
130 Sutter Street;
AIA Gallery on 6th
floor; Monday to
Friday, 9 A.M. to 5 P.M.;
to inquire about
changing exhibits,
phone 362-7397

Crocker Galleria/
Pacific Telesis Tower
1 Montgomery Street;
50 Post Street

㉞ Former French Bank Building, *1902, Hemenway & Miller;*
1907, 1913, E. A. Bozio, complete remodel and addition
This gray-green Colusa-sandstone-clad Beaux Arts skyscraper is
opulent, assured, and very beautiful. The green copper spandrels
and cornice are quite elaborate. Built in 1902, the building was
extended down Trinity Alley and elaborately reworked in 1907
when the French Bank moved in. It is part of an especially fine row
of buildings along this block of Sutter Street. The ground floor
columns are ornamented with a shield and a caduceus, the emblem
of Mercury, the Roman god of commerce.

㉟ Hallidie Building/American Institute of Architects Gallery, *1917,*
Willis Polk; 1979, Kaplan McLaughlin Diaz, restoration and
compatible ground floor
The **Hallidie Building** is the centerpiece of this beautiful block and
is considered to be the world's first **glass curtain wall facade**. It
was built as an investment property by the Regents of the University
of California and named after a fellow Regent, the developer of the
cable car, Andrew Hallidie.

From an architectural-historical point of view, this is the single
most important building in San Francisco. Its metal and glass curtain wall is hung a
foot beyond the reinforced concrete structure. (The term "curtain wall" refers to the
fact that the facade does not help support the building but rather is hung in front of
the building like a protective curtain.) Here Willis Polk used metal and glass in a way
that reveals the protective nature of the modern wall. Framing this bold "frontless"
building are graceful Regency-inspired fire escapes and a heavy-looking (but actually
light) sheet metal Venetian Gothic cornice capped by a white flagpole.

In 1979 Kaplan McLaughlin Diaz designed the restrained, close-to-
original Post Office and bank shopfronts that make an appropriate metal and plate-
glass base for the building. Glass is what this building is about; it is in its way San
Francisco's most important "window." The top floor is now the office of the San
Francisco chapter of the **American Institute of Architects**, and its **gallery** hosts interesting changing exhibitions of cutting-edge contemporary design. Cross Sutter Street to
the entrance of the Crocker Galleria.

㊱ Crocker Galleria/Pacific Telesis Tower, *1908, Willis Polk, bank at 1 Montgomery;*
1982, Skidmore, Owings & Merrill, tower, galleria, and rooftop park
Facing the Hallidie Building is the entrance to the barrel-vaulted **Crocker Galleria,**
designed by Skidmore, Owings & Merrill in 1982. Enter the glass-roofed galleria. You
can rest here; there are also public restrooms on the third level. When Crocker Bank
redeveloped the block, it preserved the sumptuous banking hall at 1 Montgomery,
designed by Willis Polk in 1908, and demolished the ten-story office tower above it.
Over the bank it built a rooftop park accessible from the third level of the galleria (the
entrance is near the central escalators). Utilitarian Lick Place, a narrow service alley
that once ran through the block, became the site for this complex of shops. At the

corner of Post and Kearny, a pink granite–clad, thirty-eight-story tower was built that has since been renamed **Telesis Tower**. This classic, chamfered highrise's granite sheathing is both polished and rough-finished, creating a subtle checkerboard pattern. The tower reflects the lights and atmosphere of the city in ever-changing ways. **Circolo Restaurant and Champagneria**, on the third level of the galleria, serves moderately expensive Italian cuisine. The murals in its bar came from the Old Poodle Dog, a famous San Francisco restaurant. Some window tables offer a view of the Hallidie Building across Sutter Street. Walk through the galleria and out to Post Street.

Circolo Restaurant and Champagneria
Crocker Galleria;
362-0404

Mechanics' Institute Library
57 Post Street;
421-1768

View of the Humboldt Bank Tower
783–85 Market Street, near Fourth Street

㊲ Mechanics' Institute Library, *1909, Albert Pissis; painting by Arthur F. Mathews in lobby*
Across from the Crocker Galleria is the fine gray-stone-clad Beaux Arts building that houses the **Mechanics' Institute Library,** a subscription library formed by the merger in 1906 of the Mechanics' Institute Library founded in 1854 and the Mercantile Library Association founded in 1852. Both collections, alas, were destroyed in the great fire. The second and third floors house the library assembled since then. In the lobby is a fine 1909 painting by Arthur F. Mathews entitled *The Arts* that depicts the Muses inspiring workers who erect a grand dome much like those of the later Panama-Pacific International Exposition of 1915. At the back of the lobby, behind a metal grille door, is one of the finest staircases in San Francisco, a corkscrew spiral of iron and marble. The Mechanics' Institute Library welcomes new members and is an oasis of civility in San Francisco. A slot to the left of the building, between the library and the brooding McKesson Tower at 1 Post Street, leads out to Market Street.

㊳ View of the Humboldt Bank Tower, *1907, Meyer and O'Brien*
Visible to the west up Market Street is the ornate top of the eighteen-story Beaux Arts **Humboldt Bank Building**. It was under construction when the earthquake hit and was redesigned with stronger latticed steel girders. This was the first building contract let after the catastrophe. Capped by a fanciful dome, the building is faced in sandstone and terra-cotta. It is in actuality a long narrow slab, but its Market Street frontage is treated like a freestanding tower. It is today a rare survivor and lends a note of Edwardian fantasy to the city's skyline.

Sheraton-Palace Hotel
2 *New Montgomery Street, at Market Street*

Kyo-ya Restaurant
Closed Saturday and Sunday; 392-8600

39 *New Montgomery Street*

New Montgomery Street was the first attempt to pull San Francisco's downtown across Market Street. It was a privately cut-through street on land owned by Asbury Harpending and William Ralston, using $2 million of the Bank of California's money. Ralston built the great **Palace Hotel** in 1875 on the southwest corner of Market and New Montgomery, putting the hotel's entrance on his own New Montgomery Street. (The new Palace Hotel built in 1909 preserved that orientation.) "New" Montgomery Street was intended to extend prestigious Montgomery Street, the city's principal business street, to the south, across Market, but only recently has the prime office district expanded there. Cross Market Street to the entrance of the Palace Hotel.

40 Sheraton-Palace Hotel, *1909, Trowbridge and Livingston; 1915–25, additions, George Kelham; 1991, restoration and addition, Skidmore, Owings & Merrill and Page & Turnbull*

The elegant Grand Edwardian **Palace Hotel** and the fine ten-story Monadnock Building to its right, designed by Meyer and O'Brien, both conform to the height limits on Market Street set by the city between the summer of 1906 and April 1907. That Paris-inspired law briefly limited building heights to one-and-one-half times the width of the streets they faced, an almost always agreeable building height. In the pressure to rebuild after the fire, this regulation was rescinded.

Constructed on the site of the historic Palace Hotel, which opened in 1875 and burned in 1906, the new Palace Hotel of 1909's most famous amenity is the splendid art-glass-roofed **Garden Court**, one of the finest Beaux Arts spaces in the nation. This grand room is especially attractive at night with its elegant chandeliers lit and its fancy plasterwork subtly illuminated. Also worth seeing is **Maxfield's**, a plush, mahogany-paneled bar with a glowing, enamellike Maxfield Parrish mural of the Pied Piper and his hapless followers. Brass and glass vitrines along the carpeted main corridor display memorabilia from the grand hotel's palmy past. *This* is a grand hotel! It was the social epicenter of the West and is still the favored location for the introduction of young women to San Francisco society. President Warren G. Harding died of apoplexy here on August 2, 1923 (was it the bill?). Walk down the main corridor and exit to the left, through the New Montgomery Street entrance. **Kyo-ya Restaurant** and sushi bar is at the rear corner of the hotel: elegant and expensive.

㊶ Sharon Building/House of Shields, *1912, George Kelham*

Across New Montgomery Street from the Palace Hotel is the nine-story Beaux Arts **Sharon Building** designed by George Kelham in 1912. In its ground floor is the **House of Shields**, an unchanged Edwardian bar and restaurant redolent of the turn-of-the-century city's strictly masculine downtown. A high ceiling, imposing fine wood bar, booths and upstairs tables, and decorative light fixtures of draped women holding stalks of lightbulbs make this a fly-in-amber Edwardian interior, the real thing. A modern Californian menu has matched the fine decor with good food (lunch only, and perfect at 1:30 P.M. after the rush; no dinner). This is a great place to relax after your exploration of San Francisco. While modern design is alive and well in the city, it is the rare Edwardian spaces such as this one that best capture the flavor of sophisticated San Francisco.

Sharon Building/ House of Shields
39 New Montgomery Street; 392-7732

Pacific Telephone and Telegraph Company Headquarters/ Telecommunication Museum
140 New Montgomery Street; Open Monday to Friday, 9 A.M. to 3 P.M.; free.

㊷ Pacific Telephone and Telegraph Company Headquarters/ Telecommunication Museum, *1925, Miller and Pfleuger, A. A. Cantin*

Built as the **headquarters of PT&T,** this F-shaped office tower was once the largest corporate office building on the West Coast and long stood in splendid isolation south of Market Street. Clad in light gray terra-cotta, the soaring design culminates in flowerlike ornaments, stern eagles, and an exclamatory flagpole. (Originally it was capped by a light whose color forecast the weather.) A painstaking six-year restoration brought this masterpiece back to perfect condition. The lobby, with its bronze doorway, black marble, and intricate plaster ceiling with pheasants and Chinese cloud patterns, is a knockout.

    A small **Telecommunication Museum** has recently been opened off the lobby. The Telephone Pioneers of America, a service group of Pacific Bell employees, runs the museum.

**San Francisco Museum of
Modern Art**
151 Third Street

Continuation:

San Francisco Museum of Modern Art

The Pacific Telephone and Telegraph Company Headquarters is one block from the new **San Francisco Museum of Modern Art**. Walk through Minna Street, the alley to the right of the phone company, to get to Third Street and the new museum (*See Tours 1 and 15*).

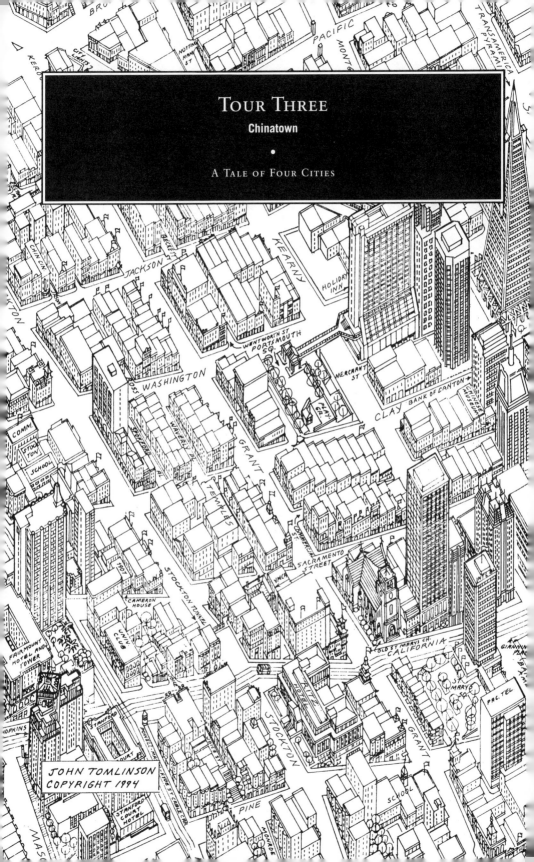

TOUR THREE
Chinatown

•

A TALE OF FOUR CITIES

JOHN TOMLINSON
COPYRIGHT 1994

What this Tour Covers
Preliminaries
Introduction: A Tale of Four Cities

Tour 3:
Chinatown

1. Chinatown Gate/Grant Avenue
2. Sing Chong and Sing Fat Buildings
3. Old St. Mary's Roman Catholic Church and Rectory
4. St. Mary's Square/Statue of Sun Yat-Sen
5. 700 and 800 Blocks of Sacramento Street
6. Commercial Street/Chinese Historical Society of America Museum/ Pacific Heritage Museum
7. Portsmouth Square: Yerba Buena's Plaza/ The Birthplace of San Francisco
8. Holiday Inn Financial District/ Chinese Culture Foundation Gallery
9. 700 Block of Washington Street/Buddha's Universal Church
10. Wentworth Street: Victorian Vice
11. Old Chinese Telephone Exchange/Bank of Canton
12. *Detour:* Grant Avenue between Washington and Clay/ Site of William Richardson's Trading Post of 1835
13. Grant Avenue from Washington to Jackson Street
14. 700 Block of Jackson Street/Jewelry District
15. Ross Alley
16. *Detour:* Spofford Street
17. Waverly Place Associations and Temples Cluster
18. Stockton Street from Sacramento to Clay: The Real Chinatown
19. St. Mary's Chinese Catholic Center / First Presbyterian Church
20. Chinese United Methodist Church/ Chinese American Citizens Alliance
21. Stockton Street Tunnel

Continuation
Four Directions in the City, or the Last Rural Chinatown

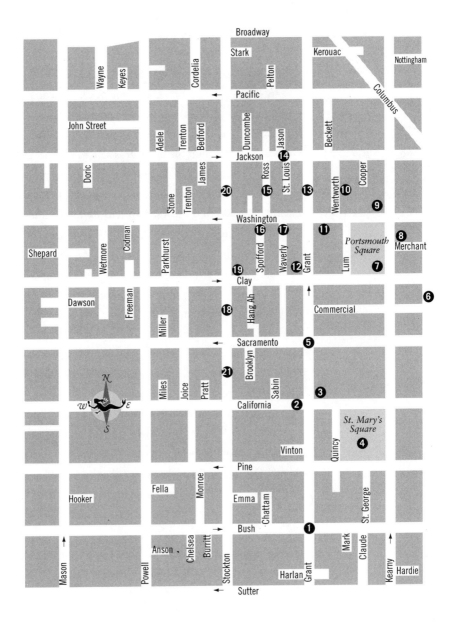

Chinatown

Portsmouth Square garage

City garage
*Sutter and Stockton
between Union Square
and Chinatown*

City garage,
*in North Beach over
the Police Station at
766 Vallejo, between
Stockton and Powell*

Preliminaries

**BEST TIMES TO
DO THIS TOUR**

Chinatown's peak time is Saturday, from 10 A.M. to 3 P.M. Everything in Chinatown is going full blast then, especially food shopping. Chinatown is one of the parts of San Francisco open latest into the night. It is safe to use the alleyways in Chinatown, and it is a necessity to use them to see behind Chinatown's façade. The hours that the **Chinese Historical Society of America Museum** and the **Tin How** and **Norras** temples are open (Tuesday to Saturday, 12 to 4 P.M.) are the best time for the explorer. To the knowledgeable San Franciscan there is no bad or boring time in Chinatown, for new discoveries pop up on every single exploration.

The noisy, festive, debt-settling Chinese (Lunar) New Year usually occurs in February, just when the quince in California's great Central Valley is budding. The most beautiful morning of the year in Chinatown is when the first quince arrives and you see elderly men bearing the leafless branches with the pearly pink buds to their rooms. For information on the Chinese New Year Parade write to the **Chinese Chamber of Commerce**.

For Chinatown's district and family associations and tongs, lucky-numbered "Double Ten," the tenth day of the tenth month, October tenth, is when every important building breaks out its flags and turns on the electric lights that outline it.

Walks

The **Chinese Culture Foundation** in the Holiday Inn Financial District offers several walks. The Chinese Heritage Walk is on Saturday at 2 P.M.; the Chinese Culinary Walk and Luncheon is weekdays at 11 A.M.

Parking

It is not easy to find street parking in Chinatown. Avoid unnecessary frustration by garaging your car. If the **Portsmouth Square garage** is full, try the strategically placed **city garages**. On bustling Saturdays there is free parking in **The Embarcadero Center** garages with a mini-mum validated purchase in the center; on Sundays and holidays parking is free in The Embarcadero Center. From there it is an easy three-block walk up narrow Commercial Street to Portsmouth Square and the heart of Chinatown.

Transportation

For the bus traveler, the key transit line is the **30 Stockton electric trolley bus,** which links Chinatown with Union Square to the south and with Aquatic Park and Fisherman's Wharf to the north. The **California Street cable car** line bisects Chinatown. It is one of San Francisco's special moments when the twin Chinese roof pagodas pop up at California and Grant on the east slope of Nob Hill. The place to ride is an outside bench facing north when the car stops athwart Grant Avenue. The vista opens before you like a door. Grant Avenue, San Francisco's first street, is a minicanyon stage set alive with Chinese signs and festive architectural trumpery mostly built between 1909 and 1929.

RESTAURANTS

The hole-in-the-wall **House of Nanking** serves excellent, inexpensive Chinese food. Go at an off hour to avoid waiting, though you will probably find the line entertaining, if lines can entertain you. Recommended. The large **New Asia Restaurant** is popular for its great variety of *dim sum* (especially the steamed dumplings), served from 8:30 A.M. to 3 P.M. daily. **The J&J Restaurant** serves good Cantonese dishes. **New Sun Hong Kong Restaurant** is popular with Chinese Americans and has good window tables for people-watching. For its historic 1920 decor (check out the chandeliers!), not for its bland, humdrum cooking, the **Far East Cafe** is worth seeing.

Beyond Chinatown

The newer, more elegant restaurants are outside touristic Chinatown. **Tommy Toy's Chinoise Cuisine** is an opulent Chinese restaurant with an excellent kitchen; expensive. **Harbor Village Restaurant** is an upscale Cantonese/Mandarin restaurant. **Yank Sing** is an upscale restaurant with excellent *dim sum*. **The Mandarin** is an elegant setting and the

House of Nanking
919 Kearny, near Jackson; 421-1429

New Asia Restaurant
772 Pacific Avenue, east of Stockton; 391-6666

The J&J Restaurant
615 Jackson Street, between Grant and Kearny; 981-7308

New Sun Hong Kong Restaurant
606 Broadway, at the corner of Grant and Columbus; 956-3338

Far East Cafe
631 Grant, near California; 982-3245

Tommy Toy's Chinoise Cuisine, *655 Montgomery Street, at Washington; 397-4888*

Harbor Village Restaurant
Four Embarcadero Center, Sacramento and Drumm; 781-8833

Yank Sing
427 Battery Street, between Clay and Washington; 781-1111

The Mandarin
900 North Point Street, in the Old Woolen Mill at Ghirardelli Square; 673-8812

Hunan Restaurant
*674 Sacramento Street,
between Kearny and
Montgomery; 788-2234*

Tai Chi Restaurant
*2031 Polk Street, near
Pacific Avenue; 441-6758*

Yet Wah Mandarin Cuisine
*2140 Clement Street at
Twenty-third Avenue;
387-8040*

Gump's, *240 Post Street,
near Union Square*

Kee Fung Ng Gallery
*757 Grant Avenue,
between Sacramento and
Clay; 434-1844*

The Wok Shop
718 Grant Avenue

The Ying Company
*1120 Stockton Street,
between Sacramento and
Jackson; 989-3797*

Ellision Enterprises
*1758 Stockton Street
below Sacramento;
982-3881*

Clarion Music Center
*816 Sacramento Street
near Waverly Place and
Pacific; 391-1317.*

Eastwind Books & Arts
*1435A Stockton Street,
near Columbus, in the
basement level of the
EurekaBank Building;
772-5877*

Eastwind Books & Arts
*633 Vallejo between
Columbus and Stockton
in North Beach;
772-5899*

pioneer gourmet Chinese restaurant in San Francisco. Ask for a table with a view of the Bay. **Hunan Restaurant,** on the edge of the Financial District near Chinatown, is a modest place with excellent spicy Hunan dishes, and inexpensive; closes early. **Tai Chi Restaurant** offers Hunan and Mandarin dishes until 10 P.M. Reasonable and tasty. **Yet Wah Mandarin Cuisine,** in the Richmond District, serves *dim sum* on Sundays. Popular with Chinese American families at midday on Sundays, it is excellent and reasonable.

SHOPPING

Gump's is the oldest Asian art dealer in the city. See the Union Square Tour *(Tour 1)* for other Asian antique shops. **Kee Fung Ng Gallery** can custom-make a personalized chop, a soapstone seal in a brocade case. They make unusual souvenirs or gifts. **The Wok Shop** sells Chinese cooking equipment and cookbooks. They will ship your purchases home. **The Ying Company** sells woks, cooking equipment, china, tea, and like goods. Not fancy, just real. **Ellision Enterprises,** near the Stockton Street Tunnel, sells herbs at fair prices. Rich *silk brocade* is the thing to look for in Chinatown, as is yellow-gold jewelry and spinach-green jade. There are many shops to choose from; comparison shop. The better goods and prices tend to be off Grant Avenue on side streets. **Clarion Music Center** carries gongs, cymbals, drums, and traditional Chinese stringed instruments. Posters here announce Chinese musical recitals and programs by the Chinese Orchestra of San Francisco. **Eastwind Books & Arts** has the best and widest selection of books in Asian languages. It also sells calligraphic brushes and inkstones. The latest English-language books on Asian American themes are at the other Eastwind store in North Beach. Cookbooks, art books, serious Asian American histories, literature, travel guides; it's all here.

Introduction: A Tale of Four Cities

The *Ying On Labor and Merchant Benevolent Association* at 745 Grant Avenue, near Clay, was built right after the earthquake and fire in 1906 for A. B. Ware and remodeled with an elaborate chinoiserie facade in 1920.

Chinatown is old and Chinatown is new. It is not a jumble or a chaos; it is a pattern of changing patterns. If one listens with the ears of a historian over a century and a quarter, the happiest sounds today are the squeals of Chinatown's many children in the lively school playgrounds. Chinatown has never had so many children with such bright prospects. The glory of Chinatown is the dedication and seriousness of so many of its students. The culture of the Chinese and Chinese Americans respects learning, and the results are to be seen in the substantial Asian American population of California's universities.

Today Chinatown is best understood as the complex overlay of four "cities": (1) the old Chinese ghetto-become-neighborhood with its 20,000 residents, half of them elderly, who live on San Francisco's oldest blocks almost in the shadow of the Financial District's highrises; (2) the cultural "capital city" for the Bay Area's affluent, assimilated Chinese Americans who descend on it on Saturdays; (3) a special shopping district for non-Chinese San Franciscans; and (4) a visitor-pleasing tourist attraction. Today Chinatown is one of the densest neighborhoods in the nation with some 160 people per acre: second only to New York City's Chinatown. Seventy-five percent of its residents are foreign-born; the comparable citywide proportion is 28 percent. The median household income here is about ten thousand dollars, one-third the median income of the city as a whole.

The population history of Chinatown has been a dramatic J-shaped curve. From the Gold Rush through the 1870s a large migration of mostly single male laborers came to San Francisco and the American West, as well as to Canada and Peru. With the Chinese Exclusion Act of 1882, the nation's first racially restrictive immigration measure, the Chinese American population aged without replacing itself and San Francisco's Chinese population fell from 26,000 in 1881 to 11,000 at its nadir in 1920. There were vacant storefronts on Chinatown's side streets in the 1920s, hard as that is to imagine today. In 1943, during World War II when the United States allied with China against Japan, the Chinese Exclusion Act was repealed by Congress, though war in the Pacific and a very small quota of 105 Chinese a year kept migration minimal.

The first migration streams from China to San Francisco were from four regional dialect groupings within Guangtung Province in southern China. A series of disastrous floods in the Pearl River Delta downriver from Canton propelled a virtual diaspora of Cantonese-dialect-speaking people all around the Pacific Basin. These are the *huagiao,* the Overseas Chinese. Historians estimate that some 2.5 million people emigrated from China between 1840 and 1900. Between 1852 and 1882, many mostly male Chinese laborers and a few merchants and labor brokers came to San Francisco.

"Mayflower" migrants from the three districts of Nomhai, Punji, and Shunteh, wealthy commercial and agricultural districts near Canton, dominated. In 1851 they organized as the Canton Company, also known as the Sam Yup Association, or the "Three Districts." The organizers were well-wired merchants who dominated the economic life of the expatriate community. Peasant migrants also came from less advanced areas further from Canton, speaking a different dialect. They felt oppressed by the Sam Yup and organized as the Sze Yup or "Four Districts" in the same polarizing year. In 1852 migrants from Heunghan, Tsengshing, and Tungken organized as the Young Yo Company. Hakka speakers from Xin'an withdrew from the Young Yo Company to form the Sun On Company, later the Yan Wo Company.

Just as within the larger American society where different immigrant groups carved out different economic niches—Italian Americans in truck gardening, or Greek Americans in coffee shops, for example—so, too, the tongs and associations within Chinatown established (and fought over) different economic turfs. In 1984, historian John Kuo Wei Tchen sketched the general pattern:

A hierarchy of businesses developed along economic and district-of-origin lines. Wealthier Sanyi tended to control the larger, commercially successful companies, such as export-import firms. Nanhai District people monopolized the men's clothing and tailoring trade, in addition to butcher shops. Neighboring Shunde District folk controlled the overalls and workers' clothing factories. Chinese hailing from the Zhongshan District, the second largest population of Chinese in California, controlled the fish businesses and fruit-orchard work, and predominated in the women's garment, shirt, and underwear sewing factories. The Siyi, or Four District people, by far the largest and poorest group of Chinese, controlled the low end of the business pecking order in occupations such as laundries, small retail shops, and restaurants. Up until World War II, class affiliations within Tangrenbu [Chinatown] were largely predetermined by district of origin.

Most important associations were controlled by Chinatown's tiny merchant elite. These merchants profited as the intermediaries between labor-starved large American corporations of the nineteenth-century West (railroads, land reclamation companies, commercial farms, mines, and early factories) and the limitless reliable labor pool of China. Most Chinese immigrants were poor but healthy and motivated young men who came to America for a brief time to better their chances back home. They came across the Pacific on the "credit-ticket" system. Under it Cantonese and Hong Kong merchants lent peasant sojourners their passage of forty to fifty dollars. On this side of the ocean, San Francisco merchants oversaw the payment of the principal and the interest on the loans and also contracted out the laborer in gangs to American employers. When they contracted the labor, San Francisco's Chinese merchants also made exclusive arrangements to sell supplies to the small armies of Chinese workers working all over the arid, frontier West. To oversimplify a very complicated reality, the Sam Yup grew rich brokering the labor of the Sze Yup.

All the various Chinatown associations were small empires worth fighting over. They levied dues and exercised other social controls over individual immigrants. Most eventually owned real estate, if only their headquarters in Chinatown, and it was no small thing to have the choice ground-floor store. Much more important, some of these associations had the power to grant or deny the exit permits issued by the steamship companies. The fee for these permits varied from a couple of dollars to ten or twenty dollars in the mid-1880s. Because the early migration to California was of sojourners, men who planned to go back home and marry and have a family, this was an important "tax power." (This exit permit system continued until 1949 when passage to by-then Communist China ceased.)

Cutting across the so-called "nonvoluntary associations" based on family or birthplace were often equally nonvoluntary "voluntary associations" called tongs, which were workers' and merchants' guilds with labyrinthine and competing interests. There were legitimate tongs and also criminal tongs, which ran Chinatown's protection rackets, gambling, loan-sharking, and prostitution.

During the height of anti-Chinese hysteria in California in the early 1880s, Chinatown's mutually suspicious key associations formed an umbrella association. "Uniting" the most important of the district associations in what became known as the Chinese Six Companies—officially the Consolidated Chinese Benevolent Association—in 1882 (incorporated in the State of California in 1901) made that organization the cockpit for personal and group political, economic, and social contention.

Romantic old Chinatown, then, was a tense place. When tensions ran high violence erupted within California's Chinatowns. This violence came from within, between rival Chinese groups inside the ghettos. The domination of the Sam Yup grew more resented overtime, as Chinese immigrants became more Americanized. The dean of contemporary historians of Chinatown, engineer and writer Him Mark Lai, wrote in 1987 that:

> During the nineteenth century and early twentieth century, when tong wars erupted frequently and Chinatown was a jungle where the strong preyed on the weak and unprotected, many larger clan associations organized into two branches. One, administered by the elders, had jurisdiction over affairs affecting the entire clan, while the other acted as the clan association's defense unit against outside threats to members' interests. In many respects this latter was akin to a secret society in behavior.

Inside the Chinese Six Companies (which actually numbered seven, and briefly eight), there was intense conflict. Once again, the smaller associations like the Sam Yup, Young Wo, and Kong Chow, which had a greater proportion of wealthy merchants, dominated. The system was an oligarchy run by intermarried merchant families. This rankled the members of the populous Ning Yung Association, the one with the largest membership and whose exit permits accounted for about half the Six Companies' income. In 1928 the Ning Yung Association temporarily withdrew from the Six Companies and withheld its contributions. In 1930 the Six Companies rewrote its bylaws to apportion the fifty-five seats on its board according to the number of registered members in 1926. This gave the Ning Yung one less member than half the board and reduced the Sam Yup, Young Wo, and Kong Chow to a total of thirteen board seats among them. The new arrangement also set the president's term at two months, to be rotated every other term between Ning Yung and all the others. The American notion of representation based on population, not status or wealth, became the method for apportioning power inside the Six Companies.

As Chinese immigration dwindled, and as individual assimilation took place—and it does in America—parochial clan and regional attachments weakened. With the republican revolution in China in 1911, San Francisco's Chinese men cut off their queues, ancient symbols of Manchu domination. In the 1920s traditional Chinese dress disappeared in favor of Western, if uniformly dark and somber, garb. Dating and personal choice in marriage partners gradually replaced family-arranged unions. After 1933 tong warfare faded away. While the Chinese were, practically speaking, segregated within Chinatown until the late 1940s, some assimilation nonetheless took place. The post–World War II era saw the economic and social advance of Chinese Americans. The nullification of California's antimiscegenation law in 1948 and the striking down of racially restrictive covenants in the sale of California real estate in the same year emancipated Chinese Americans and other Asian Americans. In 1949, when the Nationalist government retreated to Taiwan, an influx of Mandarin-speaking professionals and wealthy merchants fled Red China to San Francisco. Chinese Americans made impressive gains in income and status and surpassed the median national income level by 1960.

In 1965 the Civil Rights Act was passed and the United States began to break through the psychological and legal barriers of its historic racial antipathies and to put a positive spin on the reality of its multiracial society. In the same year, immigration quotas were reconfigured to reflect a multiracial reality and to permit more Asian immigration. From 105 a year, quotas for Chinese grew to 20,000 per year by 1970. By that time, 56 percent of Chinese Americans were in white-collar occupations.

Since the late 1970s, more and more Chinese from Vietnam, along with other Southeast Asian peoples, have arrived in San Francisco. Many have sidestepped Chinatown. This latest wave has found rents cheaper in the Tenderloin than in high-priced old Chinatown and has formed a new, loosely sprinkled Vietnamese Chinatown southwest of Union Square. By 1970, 52 percent of all San Franciscans of Chinese ancestry were foreign-born. The new immigration laws favor migrants with skills and/or capital, and the recent migration includes many highly skilled people with education. This wave is Americanizing and suburbanizing faster than all its predecessors.

Chinatown's uniquely dense associational history is spelled out across the façades of its principal buildings. Originally a makeshift adaptation and overcrowding of the ramshackle "discarded" buildings of Mexican Yerba Buena and early American San Francisco of 1840–60, the quarter was owned by white landlords. Of 153 pieces of property in Chinatown in 1873, only ten were Chinese owned. All the rest were leased from Anglo Americans, Franco Americans, Italian Americans, and German Americans. In 1904, of 316 parcels, only twenty-five were owned by Chinese-Americans.

Early Chinatown saw little "Chinese architecture" but did see a distinctly Chinese way of decorating and treating buildings. Big red paper lanterns were hung from balconies and cornices, signboards were affixed, posters appeared plastered to walls, and a Chinese "look" was given to the old Italianate buildings.

Ramshackle old Chinatown was completely wiped away by the fire of 1906. When the district was rebuilt by non-Chinese absentee landowners, between 1906 and about 1929, a newer, cleaner—if still extraordinarily dense—early-twentieth-century city of remarkable consistency emerged. These new buildings conformed to better municipal building laws that required brick or concrete construction in the "congested district." The resulting Edwardian buildings are the stuff of today's Chinatown.

Over time two things happened. Chinese Americans, particularly associations, bought their lots and buildings, and plain brick buildings of the 1906–15 period were enriched to varying degrees with chinoiserie, especially the upper floors where associational meeting halls and a few temples were located. Periods of building or remodeling are recorded in the dates on their parapets.

While European architecture indulged in chinoiserie in the late-eighteenth century and sporadically in the late-nineteenth century, the post-earthquake and fire chinoiserie in San Francisco was something essentially local and new. There were no Chinese American architects during this period, and San Francisco's established "Anglo" architects turned their hands to stage-set Chinese remodels and encrustations of varying degrees of elaborateness.

The twin-gateway pagoda-capped buildings at California and Grant, and the old Pacific Telephone Exchange, all of 1909, set the architectural standards for others to follow all the way (almost) to the present. In the 1909–29 era, building outlines and features such as balconies and pagoda cornices were studded with lightbulbs that could be turned on for festive occasions. San Francisco's Beaux Arts–trained or–influenced architects were adaptable designers, and they collectively left a remarkable legacy of "San Francisco Chinese" architecture. The thing to look for in Chinatown is the Edwardian city under the layers of chinoiserie. Those who look above the shopfronts will see tight rows of expressive façades set like masks on a high shelf. Connoisseurs will observe changes in the chinoiserie itself, particularly the introduction of zappy neon trimming in the late 1940s.

In the early 1970s new Chinese-style designs were built by Chinese American architects, including Clayton Lee's **Bush Street Gate**, Ed Sue's **Citicorp Savings** at 845 Grant, and the new **Post Office** and **Kong Chow Temple** at Stockton and Clay streets.

In the late 1980s some Chinatown buildings, both new and remodeled, introduced supermodern stainless steel facades, which, alas, in this climate are not stainless. Relentlessly blatant shopfronts are also spreading in Chinatown, with completely open fronts, harshly overlighted exposed interiors, and industrial roll-down steel doors. Vintage 1906–29 shopfronts disappear every month before this apparently unstoppable trend. These open-front shops with their paranoid roll-down steel doors increasingly deaden the streets at night. (Such solid steel roll-down doors should only be permitted in industrial districts, not on shopping streets, which should remain welcoming at night.) Remodelings in Chinatown are so drastic that the observer must constantly be checking old favorites and intensely enjoying them. For they only *seem* lost in time. Chinatown ought to be a landmark San Francisco Historic District, but it is not one. All the research has been done for landmarking, and there is no doubt in anyone's mind that Chinatown qualifies as a local, state, and even national landmark. But many building owners here have a "new is always better" attitude and prefer radical modernization to conservation or restoration. Too many shop owners want their vintage shopfronts to look like the open ones they see in suburban malls. They do not see that what they have is unique and irreplaceable. The proposed Chinatown landmark district has been stalled since 1985. Meanwhile the district's architectural character erodes month by month, shopfront by shopfront. Only in the United States would a city permit a world-recognized visitor attraction to be chewed up piece by piece through ignorance. On the issue of landmarking, Chinatown is where the whole country was in the 1950s when so much was lost. Already much of the block of Grant Avenue across from Old St. Mary's Church looks like the worst parts of Times Square.

Chinatown's **Portsmouth Square** is the forgotten seed of this great city. Few realize when they park in its banal 1960 underground garage that this was San Francisco's birthplace, its Mexican-era plaza. Here Mexican governor José Figueroa of Alta California authorized *alcalde* Francisco de Haro to engage Swiss ship captain and engineer Jean Jacques Vioget to plot out a town in 1839. This was done to regularize and shape the spontaneous settlement sprouting around sandy-bottomed Yerba Buena Cove, where William A. Richardson, an English trader married into a Mexican landowning family, had built a trading post in 1835.

Jean Jacques Vioget laid out a checkerboard settlement with a central plaza facing the public beach where goods were landed. His layout accommodated the two already-existing groups of buildings: a string of half-a-dozen one-story adobes along what is now Grant Avenue, and a cluster of Yankee frame buildings on the shoreline at what is now Clay Street between Montgomery and Kearny. Grant Avenue's original name was *la Calle de la fundacion*. The area Vioget laid out is today bounded by Pacific Avenue to the north, Sacramento Street to the south, Grant Avenue to the west, and Montgomery Street to the east. The small block sizes, narrow street widths, and small lot sizes are preserved in today's Chinatown.

Inexplicably, Vioget did not make right-angled blocks, but rather blocks 2.5 degrees off square, forming trapezoids. (This peculiarity was later corrected.) Each of Vioget's blocks was divided into six lots. The central plaza—now Portsmouth Square—was never a full block. Vioget built himself a house across from the southeast corner of the plaza, on the corner of Kearny and Clay streets. The town's only official map, inscribed with lot holders, was hung behind the bar of a plaza saloon.

When war broke out between the United States and Mexico in 1846 over the annexation of Texas, the U.S. Navy swiftly occupied Alta California. On July 9, 1846, Navy Captain John B. Montgomery of the war sloop U.S.S. *Portsmouth* raised the Stars and Stripes in the plaza of Yerba Buena and took possession of the port. He appointed one of his officers, Washington A. Bartlett, as the first United States *alcalde*.

The peace treaty with Mexico that ceded the vast Southwest to the United States was signed on February 2, 1848. Days before, on January 4, gold had been discovered by John Marshall at Coloma in the foothills of the Sierra. It was in Portsmouth Square on May 12, 1849, that Samuel Brannan, editor of the *California Star*, announced the discovery of gold. When President Polk formally announced the discovery to Congress in Washington, the famous California Gold Rush began. With the Gold Rush stampede, the fly-speck port exploded. Landfill quickly spread out into the shallow cove and on it the new American city developed. *(See Tours 2A and 2B.)*

❶ Chinatown Gate, *1970, Clayton Lee*

At Grant and Bush stands the **Chinatown Gate** designed by Clayton Lee in 1970. The green-tiled-capped gate with its triple portals makes a monumental announcement of Chinatown's elaborate Grant Avenue to the north. The building on the northeast corner of Grant and Bush at **400 Grant** was built as the Friedman Hotel and Mandarin Cafe in 1913 in a French Baroque style. In 1924 Ashley & Evers added its Chinese-style top with a small pagoda tower.

Beyond the Chinatown gate you will begin to notice the elaborate **Dragon Lights**, the fine streetlights that line Grant Avenue. They were designed by W. D'Arcy Ryan and installed in 1925 as Chinatown became a noted tourist attraction. Golden dragons whose tails wrap around the poles grasp the bases of lamps with their jaws. At **445 Grant Avenue**, midblock on the left, is the KHC Plaza, though fortunately there is no "plaza" here. It is the ill-conceived fusion of the facade of the old Shanghai Low Nightclub of 1922, designed by the O'Brien Brothers, with a brutally ugly 1985 six-story addition behind. There is no excuse for the blocklike balconies and the general bleakness of this intrusive building.

Across the street, on the southeast corner of Grant and Pine and with a fine corner pagoda tower, is **450–64 Grant Avenue**, now China Station but originally the old Peking Bazaar. This building was designed by Sidney B. and Noble Newsom, successors to an important Victorian architectural firm in California. Built in 1921, its upper floors retain their fine design, while the ground floor was indifferently remodeled recently and the original shop interior, alas, was lost.

The view east down Pine Street, at Grant, is terminated by the handsome pair of the old Matson Building and the Pacific Gas & Electric headquarters. The Matson Building on the left, capped by an open tower, was designed by Bliss & Faville in 1921. It was the former headquarters of the Matson Shipping Lines and once housed the mainland offices of Hawaii's Big Five corporations. The old Pacific Gas & Electric headquarters on the right was designed by Bakewell and Brown in 1925. It is distinguished by a giant order of columns capped with urns on its upper floors. (PG&E built a modern tower behind it on Mission Street in 1971.) Both buildings are clad in terracotta and are handsome examples of dignified 1920s corporate architecture.

The block of Grant between Pine and California is lined on both sides with fine Edwardian buildings that have surprisingly little chinoiserie. On the northeast corner of Grant and Pine, at **500 Grant**, is one of the few bay-windowed buildings in Chinatown. It was built in 1910. Adjoining it is **506–10 Grant**, the Tai Chong Company Building, designed by Righetti and Kuhl in 1907. This narrow building has fine brickwork on its upper stories and an old shopfront and intact shop interior on the ground floor. While slightly altered, the shopfront retains the handsome design of postfire Chinatown tourist shops.

2 **Sing Fat Building, Sing Chong Building ("Trade Mark"),**
1907–08, T. Patterson Ross and A.W. Burgren
California and Grant, where the cable car bisects Chinatown on its
way from the Financial District to Nob Hill, is one of the spots every
visitor will remember and every San Franciscan treasures. Here hills,
cable cars, and architecture seem to say "San Francisco" to everyone.
East meets West in the architectural counterpoint between the red
brick Gothic Revival tower of Old St. Mary's Roman Catholic
Church and the twin Chinese pagoda-capped buildings on Grant.

Sing Fat Building
*555–97 Grant Avenue,
southwest corner of
California*

**Sing Chong Building
("Trade Mark")**
*601–25 Grant Avenue,
northwest corner of
California*

In 1905 John Partridge organized the U.S.
Improvement and Investment Company, whose stated purpose was to buy up Chinatown
and relocate its residents to distant Hunter's Point. He claimed that by widening Grant
Avenue and expelling the Chinese, the value of the real estate here could be increased
from $6 million to $25 to $30 million. Nothing came of this early private "urban
renewal" scheme. Instead, when Chinatown burned in 1906, the ideas of Chinese
American merchant Look Tin Eli prevailed. It was his dream to rebuild Chinatown as
an "Oriental City" with Chinese-style architecture. The San Francisco Real Estate Board
endorsed the notion and recommended that the overwhelmingly white property owners
of Chinatown "have their buildings rebuilt with fronts of Oriental and artistic appearance." The splashy twin buildings at the highly visible intersection of California and
Grant were among the first to display the new style. The Journal *Architect and Engineer*
wrote in 1908 that

> To [architect T. Patterson] Ross and [engineer A.W.] Burgren more than any
> other architectural firm in San Francisco must be credited the responsibility for
> the radical changes that have been followed in the style and construction of
> buildings in the Oriental district. Where previously the rigid lines of cheap occi-
> dental building construction had provided perpendicular walls, now the fan-
> tasy of the Far East has been borrowed and in the Chinatown of today the
> pagoda style quite generally predominates.

Old St. Mary's Roman
Catholic Church and
Rectory
600 California Street,
at Grant

St. Mary's Square/
Statue of Sun Yat-Sen
California at Grant

③ Old St. Mary's Roman Catholic Church and Rectory

1854, Craine and England; 1907–09, reconstruction; 1969, Welsh & Carey; 1964, Skidmore, Owings & Merrill, rectory

St. Mary's epitomizes part of San Francisco's unique history, for its brick is said to have "come around the Horn" and its granite base is said to be from China. Old St. Mary's was the first Roman Catholic cathedral on the Pacific Coast and had been dedicated by 1854, by Archbishop Joseph Sadoc Alemany. It was built on land donated by pioneer banker John Sullivan, whose wife lies buried in its crypt. The Irish-dominated Catholic church, unlike the Protestant churches, did little missionary work among the Chinese in Chinatown. This did not change until 1903. In 1894 a new St. Mary's was built on fashionable Van Ness Avenue, and the old one became a Paulist Fathers' church. Old St. Mary's was gutted in the 1906 fire and rebuilt, expanded in 1929, burned again in 1969, and rebuilt a second time. (Its interior is not noteworthy.) Under its clock is the stern inscription "Son Observe the Time and Fly from Evil." This message was placed here to face the brothels that once stood across the street in what is today St. Mary's Square. The church's most American touch is something no one "sees": the black steel tower atop the brick tower with its large gold cross outlined with light bulbs. The handsome rectory on the downhill California Street side with its courtyard was designed by Skidmore, Owings & Merrill in 1964.

④ St. Mary's Square/Statue of Sun Yat-Sen, *1955, John Jay Gould; 1960, landscape by Eckbo, Royston and Williams; Statue of Sun Yat-Sen, 1938, Beniamino Bufano.* Across California Street from Old St. Mary's is this tucked-away city park with its fine statue of Sun Yat-Sen. Today the park is the landscaped roof of a city parking garage designed by John Jay Gould and built in 1955. Its landscaping was designed by Eckbo, Royston and Williams in 1960 and is a good example of landscape design from that period. There is a fine view of the Bank of America tower from here. Standing in the square is a statue of **Sun Yat-Sen** (1866–1925) by Beniamino Bufano, commissioned by the New Deal's Work Projects Administration and placed here in 1938. The stream-lined statue is made of stainless steel and pink granite and is a fine example of the public art of the period. Facing it across the square is a Chinese-style open-work bronze screen commemorating Americans of Chinese ancestry who gave their lives for America in World War I and II.

Agitation for a park to replace the brothels clustered here was begun by Father M. Otis in 1895; the park was purchased by the city in 1906 after the earthquake. Unfortunately, the construction of a dark gray slab of a building by the Pacific Telephone Company in 1967 south of the park robs it of sunlight. The wall-like building is a monument to the insensitive city planning of the 1960s. Such a light-blocking structure would not gain city approval today. Return up to Grant Avenue.

At 631 Grant Avenue is the **Far East Cafe**, which was established in 1920 and is the Chinatown restaurant with the most evocative "old Chinatown" interior, if an unfortunately bland tourist cuisine. The exterior gives no hint of the high-ceilinged interior with its dark wood wainscotting and curtained private booths in the back. Most remarkable are the old electric chandeliers of phantasmagoric ornateness. The murals on the walls are banal except for the one that depicts the Chinese Pavilion at the Panama-Pacific International Exposition of 1915. This was one of the earliest "Chinese" buildings in San Francisco.

5 *700 and 800 Blocks of Sacramento Street*

One of the most interesting buildings here is not Chinese. On the southeast corner of Grant and Sacramento, at **654–70 Grant Avenue,** is the three-story Edwardian hotel with interesting window surrounds designed by Stone and Smith in 1907 for A.P. Giannini and S. Scatena. Giannini was the founder of the Bank of Italy, later the Bank of America. Catercorner to it is the **Lowry Estate Building** of 1906, with a Bank of America branch in its modernized ground floor. On its second floor, entered from Sacramento Street, is the **Gold Mountain Sagely Monastery** recently established by the Dharma Realm Buddhist Association. While the building is not historic or especially attractive, the monastery conducts Buddhist ceremonies.

The downhill 700 block of Sacramento, between Grant and Kearny, was the first block where Chinese immigrants were able to rent rooms and establish a toe-hold in San Francisco. In the nineteenth century it was known as "Tong Yen Gai," or Street of the Chinese. Today it still boasts both the Chinese Chamber of Commerce and the Nam Kue Chinese School. First Sacramento, then Dupont (now Grant), then Jackson between Kearny and Stockton became Chinese. Unlike all of San Francisco's other ethnic enclaves, Chinatown has never moved, only grown.

Downhill, at 728–30 Sacramento Street, is the **Chinese Chamber of Commerce,** designed in 1912 by R. J. Patcha and elaborated in 1925 by J. E. Freeman. Though not particularly impressive, it does have a loggia and pagoda cornice, and it is of historic significance, since the formation of this organization in 1908 signified the bridging of the deep rifts inside Chinatown between the Sam Yup and the Sze Yup. Across the street, at 755-65 Sacramento, is the **Nam Kue School** with its front courtyard, an extravagant gesture in dense Chinatown. This after-hours Chinese language school was founded by merchants from the Fook Yum Tong, some of Chinatown's wealthiest men. The building was designed by Charles E. J. Rogers in 1925 and opened with a staff of four teachers from Pekin University. It is a unique design in Chinatown. Return to Grant Avenue.

Far East Cafe
631 Grant Avenue

654–70 Grant Avenue

Lowry Estate Building
Grant at Sacramento

Gold Mountain Sagely Monastery
800 Sacramento Street; 421-6117; Buddhist ceremonies Monday to Friday at 6:30 P.M. and Saturday and Sunday at 12:30 P.M.

Chinese Chamber of Commerce
728–30 Sacramento Street

Nam Kue School
755-65 Sacramento

746–48 Commercial Street

681–83 Commercial Street

**Chinese Historical Society
of America Museum**
*650 Commercial, in the
basement; 391-1188*

Pacific Heritage Museum
*608 Commercial Street;
362-4100*

**⑥ *Commercial Street/Chinese Historical Society
of America Museum/Pacific Heritage Museum***

Half a block up Grant is the right-hand turn down into Commercial Street. Commercial Street and nearby Merchant Street, as their names if not their buildings record, were among Gold Rush San Francisco's prestige business addresses. The block of Commercial below Grant is still paved in red brick, one of the last such streets in the city. The distant flat part of Commercial to the east was originally Long Wharf, a two-thousand-foot-long wharf built out into Yerba Buena Cove. Commercial and Merchant streets were cut through existing blocks and privately developed. They were originally lined with costly brick commercial buildings. By the 1870s many of the old-fashioned buildings were occupied by Chinese shoe, slipper, and cigar factories and laundries. It became Chinatown's own "industrial district." Until 1908 the Chinese Six Companies was on this street.

After 1906 the street was rebuilt and partially occupied by brothels. The two-story French Baroque Dubois Building at **746–48 Commercial Street**, with the heavy iron gate, was designed by Righetti & Kuhl and may have been built as a "fancy house." Number **681–83 Commercial Street**, the Anna Giselman Building, designed by William Curlett and Son in 1908, is intact and shows just how handsome San Francisco's ordinary post-fire buildings were. At 650 Commercial, in the basement, is the **Chinese Historical Society of America Museum**. This small and agreeable museum displays mementos, work tools, artifacts, and photographs of the Chinese pioneers in California. A fine series of photo panels explains the migration of the Chinese and the evolution of Chinese American culture in the United States. An old lacquered wood Taoist altar from Napa carved in 1889 is decorated with crimson bunting and orange gold-flecked paper banners. A shrimp-cleaning machine and a wheelbarrow made of wood and wire display the ingenuity of Chinese craftsmen. Some fine old green, gold, and black carved wood signs are hung here and there. Linger here and you get a feeling for the work and endurance of the early Chinese migrants, and a better appreciation of the history of this part of San Francisco. The Chinese Historical Society of America presents lectures and publishes a journal for sale here on Chinese American history.

At 608 Commercial Street is the **Pacific Heritage Museum** on the site of the West's first mint. This museum mounts changing exhibitions on the broad theme of the history of the economic, cultural, and artistic interchanges across the Pacific. Inside you can see the old vaults and a display on the history of the building as well as first-rate changing exhibits often featuring fine Asian art and fascinating historic artifacts. This is one of the finest specialized museums in California. (For more information, see the entry for the Bank of Canton of California and Pacific Heritage Museum in *Tour 2A*.) Return up Commercial Street, turn right on Kearny Street, and walk half a block to Portsmouth Square.

❼ Portsmouth Square: Yerba Buena's Plaza/The Birthplace of San Francisco, *1960, Royston, Hanamoto and Mayes; 1993, park redesign*

Half a block downhill from Grant Avenue is **Portsmouth Square.** This popular park, now known to most as the roof of a city parking garage, was the birthplace of the City of San Francisco. Laid out by the Swiss-born surveyor Jean Jacques Vioget in 1839, the small grid of the port centered on this open space, the town's plaza. This was the center of the Mexican-era port known as Yerba Buena, named after a wild mint that grew in the sand dunes here. The Mexican Custom House once stood here. It was in this plaza that Captain John B. Montgomery raised the American flag when the United States took the settlement from Mexico on July 9, 1848. It was named Portsmouth Square after Captain Montgomery's ship, the sloop *Portsmouth*. It was here that the discovery of gold was announced by Samuel Brannan on May 12, 1849, triggering the famous Gold Rush. In this square the Vigilantes hanged their victims in 1851. The first American public school was erected here. The saloons of the Gold Rush city once ringed the square. In the early days of the city, the City Hall stood across the narrow street on the west side of the square.

In the historic park is the **Robert Louis Stevenson Monument** designed by Bruce Porter and sculptor George Piper and dedicated in 1897. This handsome monument consists of a fine granite base capped by Piper's bronze model of the galleon Hispaniola from Stevenson's *Treasure Island*. The shaft is inscribed with excerpts from his "Christmas Sermon." Its lengthy inscription is worth reading.

Beginning in 1942, San Francisco excavated its few downtown parks to build underground parking garages. Portsmouth Square was hit in 1960 and the unfortunate decision is now irreversible. (North Beach's Washington Square was to be next but escaped when San Franciscans protested turning over their precious parks to the voracious automobile.) The park was refurbished in 1993 and more structures were placed in it. Perhaps some day it will be all buildings. Retired Chinese American men in particular enjoy the park and gather there to chat and play cards and Chinese chess.

In 1994 sculptor Thomas Marsh's bronze version of the *Goddess of Democracy*, the statue that stood in Tianamen Square in Beijing in the Spring of 1989, was erected in Portsmouth Square.

❽ Holiday Inn Financial District/Chinese Culture Foundation Gallery, *1971, Clement Chin, John Carl Warnecke and Associates*

The downtown side of Portsmouth Square faces Kearny Street, one of the first streets to be widened in San Francisco in a process that continues very slowly but steadily. The Holiday Inn was an urban renewal project exempt from the City Planning Commission's design review procedure. It was built on former public land, the site of the old police headquarters and courts building. The hotel's pedestrian bridge unnecessarily intrudes into the park. In the 1960s public space was up for grabs in San Francisco. On the third floor of the Holiday Inn is the Chinese Culture Foundation

Buddha's Universal Church
720 Washington Street
Tours of the temple are
given Sundays between
1 and 3 P.M.

733 Washington

737-39 Washington

Gallery, which hosts changing exhibitions of Chinese American and Chinese art. The foundation also conducts tours of Chinatown. Except for the Holiday Inn and the intrusive Empress of China Restaurant, built in 1966 on the west side of the square, the buildings embracing Portsmouth Square preserve the scale of the nineteenth-century city. Almost all date from the period of rebuilding in 1906–09, after the earthquake and fire.

⑨ 700 Block of Washington Street/ Buddha's Universal Church, *1952, Campbell & Wong*

This modern white temple was designed by Campbell & Wong in 1952. While an International Style building, it has a recessed penthouse with a meeting room just like traditional Chinatown association buildings. The teak-trimmed entrance is simple and pleasing. The foyer has a brass wall screen of Buddha seated under the *bodhi* tree.

At **733 Washington**, just up from the park, is Jackson Produce, an original shopfront dating from 1912 and designed by William H. Crim, Jr. Here, seemingly lost in time, is a bit of old Chinatown unchanged, an Edwardian shopfront with Chinese lettering. Such antique shopfronts are an endangered species in Chinatown. In fact, perhaps by the time you read this guide, this historic business will be gone.

At **737-39 Washington** the old Arata Hotel, now the Silver Restaurant, is a 1906 building radically remodeled and given a stainless steel cladding that is quickly discoloring. Chinatown is about a generation behind the rest of San Francisco in understanding the value of its vintage architecture. What happens here to commercial buildings today used to happen to Victorian houses all over the city.

⑩ *Wentworth Street: Victorian Vice*

While most tourists simply pour down Grant Avenue in a straight line from Bush to Broadway, the diligent explorer threads through Chinatown's many side streets and narrow alleyways to get behind the tourist façade and experience the residents' district. The alleys in Chinatown are safe by day or night. Even in 1888, Hittell's guidebook noted that "Ladies unaccompanied by gentlemen can venture into Chinatown in the daytime with entire safety, and in the evenings are in as little danger as in some streets of the city occupied exclusively by white inhabitants." Because they attract fewer tourists, alleyways tend to be much plainer than Grant Avenue and preserve more of the feel of Chinese Chinatown. They are part of the first of Chinatown's four "cities," that of the twenty thousand residents and workers of the district. Wentworth Street, the alley between Washington and Jackson east of Grant, is a typical example.

In nineteenth-century American cities, alleyways inside blocks were often lined with working-class housing while middle-class houses were built facing the wider main streets. Chinatown, North Beach, and the South of Market districts preserve this old pattern. Ghettos then, as now, often also harbored the city's vice, especially gambling and prostitution, and in Chinatown, the infamous opium dens.

Despite the popular images of Victorian society as straight-laced, San Francisco and most other American cities had well-known red light districts. In San Francisco in the late 1880s, the alleys inside the blocks near Pacific and Grant harbored many of San Francisco's brothels. Most catered to white prostitution, but some served Chinatown's overwhelmingly male population. In 1909 the Police Commission decided on a policy of strict segregation and contained most prostitution in a zone from Sacramento to Broadway and from Kearny to Stockton. This created a joint-tenancy between Chinatown and the brothels. The city Board of Health conducted periodic medical examinations and even issued the "working girls" identification cards. Eventually pressure from some church groups led the city to abandon this system of regulated toleration. It was not until the purification campaigns of the Progressive era and America's entry into World War I in 1917 that prostitution was driven underground. Of course prostitution did not evaporate, it simply dispersed to other areas, in particular to what today is called the Tenderloin, west of Union Square. It is in Chinatown's byways that some of its oldest businesses survive. The old façade of **Quong Sang Chong & Company** is such a spot. Here the window displays exotic imports such as sharks' fins.

Quong Sang Chong & Company
24 Wentworth Street

Old Chinese Telephone Exchange/Bank of Canton
743 Washington Street

⓫ Old Chinese Telephone Exchange/Bank of Canton, *1909, C. W. Burckett, engineer*
Pressed between two neighbors is one of Chinatown's most delightful concoctions, the old Pacific Telephone and Telegraph Company's Chinatown Exchange, built in 1909. It is one of the most "Chinese" of Chinatown's buildings and epitomizes the efforts to make rebuilt Chinatown an "oriental city." This was probably the only telephone exchange in the United States operated in a foreign language. Its originally male operators were required to be proficient in English and five Chinese dialects: the Som Yup, Say Yup, Geung Son, Gow Gong, and Aw Duck dialects. Since there is no Chinese alphabet, the Chinese telephone directory was arranged by streets. The street with the most subscribers came first and that with the least last. The earliest male operators lived in quarters on the building's second floor; later operators were female and lived in their own homes. The Bank of Canton has carefully preserved this very important building, and its interior has been converted for the bank.

⓬ Detour: *Grant Avenue Between Washington and Clay/ Site of William Richardson's Trading Post of 1835*

The middle section of Grant Avenue is the heart of tourist Chinatown, an industry that employs neighborhood residents in its kitchens and stockrooms and Chinese American small businessmen from other parts of the city as owners and managers. Its restaurants are not noteworthy and its shops run to trinkets and souvenirs made in Taiwan. This part of Grant is lively until late at night.

Citicorp Savings
845 Grant Avenue

823 Grant Avenue

William A. Richardson's
adobe trading post

At 845 Grant Avenue is Chinese American architect Ed Sue's **Citicorp Savings** of 1970. In that decade several important Chinese-style buildings were built in Chinatown as the district enjoyed a burst of business prosperity. This bank with its well-proportioned gatelike façade is perhaps the best of its period. The gold-glazed roof tiles and guardian lions came from Hong Kong and Taiwan. If you backtrack about a half-block further south down Grant Avenue you can pass the architecturally unremarkable Dick-Young Apartments at **823 Grant Avenue**, which were built for the Adams Investment Company in 1907 and designed by W. D. Woodruff. This building is ordinary by Chinatown standards; however, its site is considered the approximate location of William A. Richardson's adobe trading post erected in 1835, the first building on Yerba Buena Cove and considered the birthplace of the settlement that became the City of San Francisco. A rarely spotted plaque here records this important fact. Return to Grant.

⓭ *Grant Avenue from Washington to Jackson Street*

The northern end of Grant Avenue from Washington to Broadway has several poultry and fish vendors who cater to the Chinatown market. These blocks are alive with shoppers early in the morning; later in the day tourists fill the sidewalks. Grant Avenue was called Dupont Street in the early days but had its name changed to honor the general and president, during the first decade of this century when merchants and reformers sought to "clean up" the image of this part of the city. Some elderly Chinese Americans still refer to the street as "Dupong Gai."

In the pre-1948 days of racially restrictive convenants in the sale of real estate, Chinatown was tightly circumscribed. Major streets like Kearny and Broadway were "white," while Chinatown began several lots inside those lines. As happened in New York City, Little Italy and Chinatown both located in the oldest parts of the city right next to each other. In San Francisco, wide Broadway was the dividing line between the two. Teenage toughs enforced these sharp social divisions and beat up those who strayed from their turf. But Italian Americans assimilated faster than Chinese immigrants, and second- and third-generation San Franciscans of Italian ancestry moved into the Marina in the 1920s and out to the truck gardens in the southern districts of the city, slowly draining North Beach of its Italian flavor. Chinatown, in contrast, was reinvigorated after 1965 by a new wave of immigration, and Chinese Americans began buying property in North Beach and along Broadway. Today both sides of Broadway are Chinese-American in character.

⓮ *700 Block of Jackson Street/Jewelry District*

At Grant and Jackson walk uphill half a block, turning left into Ross Alley (the second alley you pass). In this vicinity was Li Po-Tai's alley, named after Chinatown's most successful nineteenth-century herbalist who amassed considerable real estate inside Chinatown. Li Po-Tai and his assistants were said to see from 150 to 300 patients a day; in his clientele were such notables as Leland Stanford and Mark Hopkins. Rumor put his income at $75,000 a year.

When Chinese did buy real estate, they had to   **Ross Alley**
pay a premium for it. In 1873 the Real Estate Circular reported that
a lot on Jackson Street had been sold to Chung Hoon Hoy et al. for   **14 Ross Alley**
$9,000, which worked out to nearly $500 per front foot. As the edi-   **36 Spofford Street**
tor noted, "When Chinamen either lease or purchase property here
they are always made to pay a very high price." The Circular also
noted that Chung had borrowed $5,000 from the Odd Fellows' Bank to build on the
lot and that this was "the first instance, in our recollection, of a Chinaman borrowing
from a savings bank." Today nearly all of Chinatown is owned by Chinese Americans,
but this is a relatively recent development.

At either end of Ross Alley are clusters of small jewelry stores catering to Chinese Americans and the influx of traditionalistic new Chinese immigrants to
San Francisco. There are more than fifty jewelry stores in Chinatown alone. Comparison shoppers can find here some of the best souvenirs of their visit to San Francisco,
though prices are not low. The Chinese market prefers a yellower gold than the
American market; jade, of course, has always been coveted here. Fine spinach-green and
pale lavender jade pendants entice the window-shopper. The elaborate gold objects in
red cases and frames are meant not for wearing but for display and are presented at
anniversaries and other family occasions.

15 *Ross Alley*

Long neglected by the city, Chinatown's alleys have been repaved and improved since
1980. The formation of the Ross Alley Improvement Association (a most San
Franciscan tradition, these neighborhood improvement associations) has brought
municipal investment even here. At **Ross Alley**, between Numbers 22 1/2 and 32, is the
Golden Gate Fortune Cookie Company. A few storefront garment factories also operate here. At **14 Ross Alley** is the Sam Bo Trading Company with a modern yellow-and-
red plastic sign and an old Edwardian door with an oval glass insert. Inside is a universe
of Chinese religious goods: statues, banners, lanterns, hangings, plaques, scrolls, small
shrines, and Buddhas. This is where Chinese American shopkeepers themselves shop
for the small shrines with the red electric vigil lights often seen in Chinese shops. At
the Washington Street end of the alley is another cluster of jewelry shops. Cross
Washington and enter Spofford Street, another narrow alley.

16 Detour: *Spofford Street*

Spofford is an alleyway of perhaps not scenic importance but of real historic interest.
The clacking of *mah jong* tiles is sometimes heard here. Halfway up the alley at **36
Spofford Street** is a small red door with old gold lettering on its glass pane reading
"Chinese Free Mason" with a compass and square insignia and "CTK" in place of
the usual Masonic "G." It is the headquarters of the Chee Kung Tong, housed in a 1907
building designed by Charles M. Rousseau. This secret society was organized about
1853 and incorporated in 1879. In 1904 Dr. Sun Yat-Sen stayed here and utilized the
society's newspaper, *The Chinese Free Press,* as his political platform for some six

33 Spofford Street

**Hip Sen Tong/
Universal Cafe**
*824–26 Washington
Street*

years. From here Chinese American support was generated for the overthrow of the Manchus in China. When the revolution erupted in China on October 10, 1911 this building became the American outpost from which government notes were sold. On November 5, 1911 nearly all the associations in Chinatown hauled down the triangular yellow standard of the Manchu dynasty with its dragon and hoisted the modern red, white, and blue flag of the new Republic of China. This remains the flag of Nationalist China (Taiwan) and is the flag that still flies from Chinatown's many flagpoles on festive occasions.

At **33 Spofford Street,** attached to a 1907 building designed by the O'Brien Brothers, is the signboard of the Chinese Laundry Association. Laundry work was one of the economic niches that Chinese immigrants carved out for themselves in the hostile climate of nineteenth-century San Francisco. In 1888 some three thousand Chinese laundrymen were at work in the city. The laundrymen's tong sought to protect the Chinese from discriminatory municipal taxation and to regularize competition. The tong set rules specifying the minimum number of shopfronts between laundries and also arbitrated disputes within the industry.

Spofford was the scene of several violent confrontations between warring criminal tongs in the 1900s. The formation of the General Peace Association in 1913, and the dwindling of the population of Chinatown in the 1920s, led to a diminution in tong warfare. The last outburst was in 1933 during the depths of the Great Depression.

At the end of Spofford, on the west-side St. Mary's Playground wall, are four fine *murals* painted by Aratani in 1986 depicting Chinatown residents. If you have taken this detour, return along Spofford Street and, at Washington, turn right and walk half a block downhill to the beginning of Waverly Place.

⑰ *Waverly Place Associations and Temples Cluster*

Two-block-long Waverly Place is perhaps Chinatown's most intriguing pocket and is worth careful examination. It houses two of Chinatown's most interesting temples. Before this area became part of Chinatown it was called Pike Street, named by Dr. Augustus J. Bowie in honor of his wife's Maryland family. In the late nineteenth century it was lined with brothels, but these were replaced by a string of Chinese association buildings after the catastrophe of 1906. To see the buildings here to their best advantage, walk down the east (downtown) side of Waverly Place and look across the street at the elaborate row on the west side of the narrow street. This exploration begins with the buildings on the north side of Washington Street that look down Waverly Place, continues down two-block Waverly Place, and includes the Chinatown YMCA on Sacramento Street.

- **Hip Sen Tong/Universal Cafe,** *1910, O'Brien Brothers; 1960, Stephen Lee*
A 1910 Edwardian building, remodeled in 1960 by Stephen Lee, with a pagoda cornice.

- **Chan, Woo, Yeun Family Association**, *1909, Walter K. Yurston; 1920, A. A. Cantin*

This elaborate façade looks down Waverly and defines one end of the street. It was built in 1909 for Goong Quon Cheong, described as a "Chinese capitalist." In 1920 the building passed to the Oak Tin Benevolent Association, which raised the ceiling on the top floor and commissioned A. A. Cantin to design an exuberant metal canopy, balconies, penthouse, and cornice with the date "1920" inscribed on it. The facade uses tile, marble, and glazed brick and is an outstanding example of San Francisco chinoiserie.

- **Golden Dragon Restaurant**, *1906, architect unknown*

On the corner is a plain post-fire brick building that has had its cornice removed and its ground floor covered in green ceramic tile. To complete its "improvement," gold-colored anodized aluminum windows have been inserted.

- **Commercial/Residential Building**, *1906, architect unknown*

This building was also built immediately after the earthquake and shows how plain Edwardian Chinatown was. Its brick facade has been stuccoed, scored, and painted to look like stone. The ground floor has two shopfronts, one still original and one modernized.

- **Wong Gow Building**, *1906, Emil Guenther*

Above its modern backlit plastic sign is a handsome pale yellow brick Edwardian façade with a fine dark green fire escape and dark green window sash. The gold leaf characters on the second-story windows are striking. The pale yellow, dark green, and gold color scheme present classic old Chinatown at its best.

- **Yick Keung Benevolent Association/Hop Sing Tong**, *1909, W. J. Cuthbertson*

Above the modern black granite facing of the ground floor with its bronze lettering and sun design is a brick façade painted a bright shade of sherbet green. The railings of the three balcony–fire escapes have a vaguely Chinese design. The octagonal mirrors affixed to the railings are intended to confuse any evil spirits that want to invade the premises. The building is capped with a pagoda cornice and a flagpole. Under the cornice is a green marble tablet with gold Chinese characters. Among the building's occupants is the Sinocast radio and television studio.

- **Yee Fung Toy Family Association**, *1908, Hamilton Murdock*

This four-story association building was built with cast-iron columns and girders and sports a light yellow brick façade. Its original windows are effectively painted with dark green frames and red sashes and doors. The top-story meeting room has an open loggia with a pagoda cornice and flagpole. Its interior was described in the April 1908 *Architect and Engineer:*

Chan, Woo, Yeun Family Association
834–40 Washington Street

Golden Dragon Restaurant
823–33 Washington Street, corner of Waverly

Commercial/Residential Building
151–55 Waverly Place

Wong Gow Building
143–47 Waverly Place

Yick Keung Benevolent Association/Hop Sing Tong
137–41 Waverly Place

Yee Fung Toy Family Association
131 Waverly Place

Tin How Temple/Sue Hing
Benevolent Association
Temple hours 10 A.M. to
5 P.M. and 7 to 9 P.M.
daily; donation requested;
123–29 Waverly Place;
391-4841

Solid walnut doors, with iron thresholds, lead into the large assembly room [on the top story], which has an oak floor, decorative skylight screen, and is resplendent with imported carvings, screens, hangings, draperies, altar stand, furniture, vases, etc. Off this room is a committee room of equal splendor.

Ching Chong Dong Building
117–19 Waverly Place

Sometime in the 1940s, probably, the entrance was decorated with fine green and maroon ceramic tile and a pagoda hood.

- **Tin How Temple/Sue Hing Benevolent Association**, *1911, O'Brien Brothers*

The top floor of this building contains what is probably Chinatown's most evocative room: The Tin How Temple.

The building is a classic example of the multiuse "layer cake" of Chinatown: There is a shop on the ground floor, association offices on the second and third floors, and the temple on the top floor. The building was designed by the prolific O'Brien Brothers in 1911, though its ground floor has been remodeled with unattractive 1960s dark tiles imprisoning two old Corinthian pilaster capitals. The light-yellow brick façade has two open loggias, one on the third and the other on the top floor. Sandwiched between these is the plain second floor. The loggias have composite columns and marble door surrounds with black characters emblazoned on them. The loggias and balconies are painted a brilliant yellow with red trim. Attached to the balconies are modern plastic signs reading "Tin How Temple." The top two floors are also outlined with lightbulbs. Everything that could happen to a Chinatown building happened to this one.

Visitors may climb the narrow stairs to see the **Tin How Temple**, founded in 1852 and dedicated to Tien Hon, the Goddess of Heaven. Sailors, travelers, fishermen, wandering minstrels, actors, and prostitutes look to her for protection. She is the protectress of the sojourner and has long been an appropriate presence in this immigrants' colony. The temple houses antique fragments from other Chinese temples destroyed when the Chinese were driven out of remote towns in Northern California in the 1880s. Pious families donate the tins of vegetable oil used to keep the temple lights burning. Oranges are a favored offering because they are a pun on the Chinese word for "wealth"; similarly, the word for tangerines sounds like "luck" in Chinese. Nineteenth-century San Franciscans called these temples "joss houses" after the pidgin English term for God derived from the Portuguese, Dios.

- **Ching Chong Dong Building**, *1907, J. E. Freeman*

The euphonious Ching Chong Dong Building is a handsome Edwardian red-brick structure with yellow-brick bands across its façade and over its windows. The cheap plastic lettering clashes with the historic façade; gilded wooden letters would be appropriate. For many years the Chinese Times was housed here and posted the day's paper in the ground floor windows for all to read.

• **Norras Temple/Lee Family Association**, *1907, J. E. Freeman*
Above the altered ground floor is a very fine façade of yellow brick
with white terra-cotta trim enframing the windows and running in
bands across the width of the building. (The third-floor Norras
Temple has inexplicably painted its terra-cotta seafoam green.) The
building boasts its original windows, and also fine metal brackets
and railings on its balconies. It has a coffered cornice with a
Baroque parapet and a white flagpole. On the third floor is the
Norras Buddhist temple; its altar with gold-colored Buddhas is surrounded by incense, flowers, and offerings. Trance-inducing tapes
of gongs, bells, and drums are played here.

Norras Temple/Lee Family Association
109–11 Waverly Place Temple hours 9 A.M. to 4 P.M. daily; donation requested.

Gee Family Association
101–05 Waverly Place

Eng Family Benevolent Association
53–65 Waverly Place, corner of Clay

Ning Yung Benevolent Association
41–45 Waverly Place

Wong Family Benevolent Association
37–39 Waverly Place

• **Gee Family Association**, *1907, Jules Lambla; 1948, Uguste Ortion*
On the corner of Waverly and Clay is this three-story stuccoed
building painted a light lime green. It is most notable for its neon-
trimmed entrance canopy and pagoda cornice.

• **Eng Family Benevolent Association**, *1907, architects unknown; 1948, remodeling*
On the southwest corner of Waverly and Clay is the bay-windowed
Eng Family Benevolent Association, a 1907 building remodeled in 1948. It is hand-
somely painted in pink, ivory, green, red, and yellow (which looks better than it reads).
There are very few bay-windowed buildings in Chinatown; this one has corner bays
with neon-trimmed pagoda tops, an architectural amalgam uniquely San Franciscan.
The loggia, pagoda cornice, and Mission parapet were decorated in 1948 and faced
in pink and maroon tile. If that is not festive enough, everything is trimmed in neon.
This is the best late 1940s chinoiserie in San Francisco.

• **Ning Yung Benevolent Association**, *1907, T. H. Skinner*
This building originally housed the Chinese Merchants' Association. It has a red brick
façade trimmed with white brick and cast-iron ground-floor pilasters. It is most
notable for its fine sheet-metal balustrade-parapet with a large cartouche bearing the
legend "07." The ground floor and second floor aluminum sash windows are weak
and disrupt the original design.

• **Wong Family Benevolent Association**, *1911, F. H. Howard, builder*
Above the remodeled ground floor with its odd juxtaposition of carnelian granite and
pale aqua-green tile is a fine façade of white glazed brick with three balconies and an
emphatic parapet. The parapet boasts three large white stars and a flagpole. Again,
the modern dark aluminum windows detract from the design.

**Bing Kong Tong/
Chinese Masonic Temple**
29–35 Waverly Place

**First Chinese Baptist
Church**
*1–15 Waverly Place, at
Sacramento*

Chinatown YMCA
855 Sacramento Street

• **Bing Kong Tong/Chinese Masonic Temple**, *1911, O'Brien Brothers*
Here, too, the new ground floor of cheap stucco and weak aluminum windows clashes with the fine original architecture above. This is the Chinese Masonic Temple, as is evident by the neon compass insignia suspended in the loggia. The facade's yellow brickwork is set in raised bands. The lunettes on the third floor are inset with streaked art glass. The top-floor loggia has what might be called Chinese-Doric columns and a fine pagoda cornice in green, yellow, and red. But oh, the shopfront!

• **First Chinese Baptist Church**, *1908, G. H. Moore; 1931, George E. Burlingame*
This emphatic red clinker brick church, with offices above, served a Baptist congregation organized in 1880 in rented rooms on Portsmouth Square. The church moved to this site in 1888, and the American Baptist Home Mission Society of New York built this building two years after the earthquake. In 1931 a compatible third floor was added, and in 1980 the chapel was remodeled and a contemporary stained-glass window facing Sacramento Street was commissioned.

After examining each of Waverly Place's buildings individually, look back to see this landmark row as a whole. The east side is lined with plain post-earthquake buildings, only one of which has any chinoiserie. Some of these buildings still have their old wood and glass shopfronts painted the traditional green.

• **Chinatown YMCA**, *1925, Meyer & Johnson*
The Waverly Place landmark row is concluded by the gate of the Chinatown YMCA of 1925 designed by Meyer & Johnson. This concrete building has been described as Chinese Classical in style and has fine ornamental touches, including Chinese-style terra-cotta decorations around its entrance. The walls of the playground have been covered with murals by Victor Q. Fan depicting Chinese pioneers, Pacific Island peoples, and Asian Americans as scientists and professionals shown against the San Francisco skyline.

⓲ *Stockton Street from Sacramento Street to Clay: The Real Chinatown*

Wide Stockton Street is not as scenic as narrow Grant Avenue, but it has an important past and a lively present. Today Stockton is the location of several of the most important cultural and political institutions serving the Bay Area's large Chinese American population. This is the "capital city," the second of Chinatown's four "cities." Stockton is also the premier shopping street for Chinese culinary needs. Fish, meat, and vegetable shops abound here. Street vendors sell tangerines and old Chinese American women sell homemade Chinese tamales. It is a lively scene.

Few know that Stockton Street was San Francisco's first fashionable address. As the haughty, blue-and-gold-bound *Social Manual of San Francisco* explained in 1884

In spite of the prevailing lack of repose [San Francisco high] society began to show signs of combined effort in 1852. Its first attempt of importance was on Stockton Street north of Washington where some dwellings and a few scattering churches going to ruin still show traces of ancient grandeur.

But *le Boulevard Stockton* very quickly lost its cachet; the city grew explosively and fashion jumped to Rincon Hill, South of Market.

Chinese Central High School
827–29 Stockton Street

The Chinese Six Companies
843 Stockton Street
Main Hall open 2 to 5 P.M. on weekdays.

- **Chinese Central High School**, *1914; 1970, Stephen Lee, entrance pavilion and roof*
A few doors up Stockton is **Victory Hall**, the home of the **Chinese Central High School**. The two-story school was built as the Chinese Christian Institute in 1914. In 1970, a one-story entrance pavilion with a green-tile pagoda roof designed by Stephen Lee was added. The ancestor of this school was the Ta Ching Shu Yuan organized in 1884; its trustees were the Chinese Six Companies. Chinese American parents interested in preserving Chinese language and culture have long supported after-hours schools for their children.

- **The Chinese Six Companies**, *1908–09, Cuthbertson and Mahoney*
Up Stockton toward the tunnel is this exuberant building housing the most famous association in Chinatown, the association of district associations formally known as the **Chinese Consolidated Benevolent Association** but popularly known as the **Chinese Six Companies**. This elaborate building was constructed in part with forty thousand taels of silver (twenty thousand dollars) in relief funds sent to Chinatown by the imperial court after the earthquake of 1906. The money was not used for that purpose but rather for the construction of this Chinese school building with its ground-floor meeting hall. The building is alive with color: yellow, bright green, Chinese red, and sky blue. Two pairs of stone guardian lions flank the entrance with its freestanding, green tile-roofed gateway ornamented with dragons, birds, and fish. The main doors are painted Chinese red, the luckiest color. Climb the stairs and enter the raised porch. The building's façade is an interesting juxtaposition of straightforward, utilitarian elements, such as pillars and fire escapes, overlaid with bright colors and rich ornament. The sky-blue glazed tile is especially attractive.

The building's main hall is laid out like a courtroom with a rail and swinging gate separating the public vestibule from the room itself. A stained-glass and gilded wood screen with a central niche covers the back wall. The old tile floor has a ruglike design. Three long central tables are set in the middle of the room and fine rosewood Chinese armchairs are ranged around its four sides. Art Deco lamps are suspended from the unfortunately modernized ceiling. Small American and Nationalist Chinese flags on streamers crisscross the room. It is a space with a severely formal presence and is worth a peek. In its early years the Six Companies wielded much power both within Chinatown and among the Chinese Americans across the United States. Disputes between associations were arbitrated here. The association also served to witness contracts and property sales. In the late nineteenth century, the Chinese elite managed to establish a kind of cultural extraterritoriality by winning unofficial recognition from the white civic elite.

United States Post Office and Kong Chow Temple
Stockton and Clay streets
Temple open 9 A.M. to 4 P.M. daily.

Kuo Ming Tang Headquarters
830–48 Stockton Street

St. Mary's Chinese Catholic Center/ Holy Family Roman Catholic Church
902 Stockton Street, at Sacramento; Sunday Masses in English at 9:30 A.M.; Cantonese at 11 A.M.

First Presbyterian Church
925 Stockton Street; Sunday morning services in Mandarin at 9 A.M., English at 10:45 A.M., and Cantonese at noon

• **United States Post Office and Kong Chow Temple**, *1977, Ed Sue*

On the southwest corner of Stockton and Clay is the tan-colored **Kong Chow temple** designed by Ed Sue. An elevator in the building lobby takes you to the temple on the top floor. Note the huge antique bronze urn with the dragon handles. Chinese pioneers from the Kong Chow district, one of the Chinese Six Companies, established their first San Francisco temple in 1857. The patron deity here is Kuan Ti, who presides over the seventeen gods and goddesses of the temple. Many of the furnishings are antique and worthy of examination. By shaking the canisters with their divination sticks until one falls out, devotees determine the most auspicious days for business dealings and travels. In a small room behind the altar ancestor tablets are arranged in racks in memory of the dead. From the temple's balcony there is a good view down Stockton to the Bay. Visible to the north up Stockton are the masts of the Balclutha of 1886 and the C. A. Thayer, built in 1895, and wooded Angel Island. The post office on the ground floor houses some fine old gilded Chinese signs from the old Post Office that faced Portsmouth Square.

• **Kuo Ming Tang Headquarters**, *1915, D. J. Patterson; 1932, remodel; 1993, façade redesign*

Facing the elaborate Six Companies across Stockton is the **Kuo Ming Tang Headquarters,** a three-story building built in 1915 and remodeled in 1932 and 1993. This political party has its roots in Dr. Sun Yat-Sen's republican movement of the early twentieth century, which triumphed in 1911. Later it became the party of Generalissimo Chiang Kai Shek, whose Nationalist regime retreated to Taiwan in 1949. The KMT publishes the Young China Daily from 49–51 Hang Ah Alley behind this building.

⓳ St. Mary's Chinese Catholic Center/Holy Family Roman Catholic Church, *1920,*

At the northeast corner of Stockton and Sacramento streets is the four-story **St. Mary's Chinese Catholic Center** and Schools, which serves the Chinatown neighborhood. Tucked on the Sacramento Street side is the little-noticed **Holy Family Roman Catholic Church,** a small neighborhood chapel.

• **First Presbyterian Church**, *1907, H. Starbuck*

Protestant churches conducted several missions in Chinatown to Christianize and Americanize its inhabitants. The Presbyterian Board of Foreign Missions founded a church in San Francisco in 1853 and built a church on this site in 1857. This Classical Revival church with Ionic pilasters, portico, and pediment was designed by H. Starbuck and erected the year after the earthquake. It is a rare design in Chinatown today and of great importance to the history of the post-fire quarter.

㉒ Chinese United Methodist Church *1910, Henry H. Meyers*
On the northwest corner of Stockton and Washington streets is the
pagoda-and-cross capped Chinese Methodist Episcopal Church
designed by Henry H. Meyers in 1910. This congregation was organized in 1868 by Reverend Otis Gibson following his return from
ten years of missionary work in China. Gibson was a vigorous
defender of the Chinese Americans in their darkest days of perse-
cution. This post-earthquake building originally housed a chapel,
a school, and an orphanage for young Chinese girls rescued from
prostitution.

Chinese United Methodist Church
1001-11 Stockton Street

Chinese American Citizens Alliance
1044 Stockton Street

Stockton Street Tunnel

• **Chinese American Citizens Alliance**, *1920, Charles E. J. Rodgers*
On the opposite side of Stockton, midblock, is the four-story **Chinese American Citizens
Alliance** building built in 1920 and designed by Charles E. J. Rodgers. It is a thoroughly
American design typical of the rebuilt city. This building houses the first civil rights
organization founded by Chinese Americans, organized as the Native Sons of the
Golden State in 1895. It assumed its present name in 1915. The organization battled
successfully in the courts to protect the rights of native-born Americans of Chinese
ancestry. In 1898, in the landmark case United States v. Wong, the Supreme Court
affirmed citizenship by right of birth in the United States regardless of race. The organization of the CACA marked the emergence of Chinese Americans into the larger society outside the Chinatown ghetto. Inside this building is a framed copy of the 1946 law
that repealed the Chinese Exclusion Act of 1882, and the pen used to sign it. The CACA
was active in the effort to secure Chinatown's first playground in 1925.

㉑ Stockton Street Tunnel, *1914, Michael M. O'Shaughnessy*
Visible south up Stockton is the "triumphal arch" entrance to the Stockton Street
Tunnel designed by City Engineer Michael M. O'Shaughnessy in 1914. It was one of
the urban improvements spurred by the Panama-Pacific International Exposition of
1915. It shows how handsome the City Beautiful municipal improvements were, under
longtime mayor James Rolph, Jr.

*Continuation: Four Directions in the City, or
the Last Rural Chinatown*

Here you have the choice of taking the 30 Stockton trolley bus either south through
the tunnel to Bush Street (see below), Union Square, Market Street, and south across
Market Street to Moscone Convention Center (Tour 1), or alternatively north to
Columbus Avenue, North Beach (Tour 4), and further on to Fisherman's Wharf,
Aquatic Park, and Fort Mason and the GGNRA (Tour 5), before continuing west
through the Marina District's civilized Chestnut Street. The line ends at Broderick and
North Point streets, one block from the 1962 concrete replica of Bernard Maybeck's
romantic "temporary" Palace of Fine Arts of 1915. Or, you may walk up the flight of

French Consulate
540 Bush

Goethe Institute
530 Bush

Notre Dame des Victoires
Roman Catholic Church
566 Bush Street;
French Mass on Sundays
at 10:30 A.M.

stairs at the tunnel's entrance to emerge a short block from the California Street cable car line leading west up Nob Hill (Tour 7), or east, downhill, to the heart of the Financial District (Tour 2). At the foot of California Street are Market Street, the Ferry Building, and the Golden Gate Ferry to Sausalito.

500 Block of Bush Street: Memories of the French Pioneers

Also accessible by the flight of stairs at the entrance to the Stockton Street Tunnel, and walking two blocks south, is Bush Street, which in the 1850s was favored by French immigrants and was nicknamed Frenchmen's Hill. Today the Chancery of the **French Consulate** is at 540 Bush in a modern solar-conscious building designed by Storek & Storek in 1979. Next door is the **Goethe Institute** at 530 Bush, with its German library and English- and German-language cultural programs in part of a fine 1916 utility substation, which was built by W. Garden Mitchell in 1916 and converted in 1982 by Storek & Storek.

The only souvenir of the early French settlement is the twin-towered church of **Notre Dame des Victoires Roman Catholic Church**, built in 1913 and designed by Louis Brochoud after a church in Lyon. It was San Francisco's French national Roman Catholic church and was established in 1856. It has a fine 1915 organ and conducts sung masses in French on Sundays at 10:30 A.M. The treasure in the church is a sixteenth-century Flemish tapestry of Christ at the Mount of Olives.

Further Afield: Locke, California, The Last Rural Chinatown

If you are interested in the history of the Chinese soujourners outside of San Francisco's Chinatown, consider visiting Locke, California, a small Delta town on the Sacramento River northeast of San Francisco. Locke was built about 1915 for the Chinese laborers who raised the levees, built the railroads, and planted crops in the early Delta. It consists of a narrow main street lined with plain, two-story balconied buildings like an old Western town. It is of historical and architectural interest as the last rural Chinatown in California and is listed in the National Register of Historic Places. Take scenic Highway 160 along the Sacramento River to Walnut Grove, and cross the bridge to Highway E 13 north.

Jasper Place **looking south from Filbert Street with typical post 1906 alley flats and apartments. Fire codes prohibited bay windows on narrow streets.**

What This Tour Covers

Preliminaries

Introduction: The Essential San Francisco

North Beach

**TOUR 4:
NORTH BEACH
AND
TELEGRAPH HILL**

1. Columbus Avenue from the Transamerica Pyramid to Broadway
2. Columbus Tower/Sentinel Building
3. City Lights Bookstore
4. Vesuvio Café
5. Mural of San Francisco Scenes
6. The Broadway Entertainment Strip
7. St. Francis of Assisi Roman Catholic Church
8. The Bank of America/North Beach Museum/ EurekaBank
9. Fugazi Hall/Casa Coloniale Italiana
10. Washington Square: The Ideal Park
11. Sts. Peter and Paul Roman Catholic Church

Telegraph Hill

12. Old Telegraph Hill Dwellers Association Clinic
13. Jasper Alley
14. Upper Grant Avenue Shops and Café Strip
15. To Coit Tower/Coit Tower/Panorama and WPA Murals/ Other Important San Francisco Murals
16. Greenwich Steps/Julius Castle Restaurant
17. Malloch Apartment Building
18. Filbert Steps and Darrell Place/Napier Lane
19. Levi's Plaza: Levi Strauss & Company Headquarters

Continuation

Fisherman's Wharf, or Skyscrapers and the Downtown

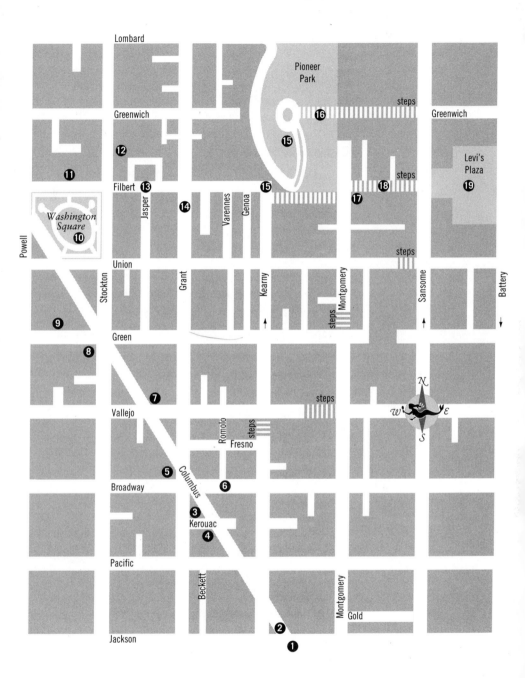

North Beach to Telegraph Hill

City Parking Garage
*Over the Police Station,
on Powell at Vallejo*

Preliminaries

BEST TIMES TO DO THIS TOUR

The best times are when the North Beach Museum is open (see below). It is like the neighborhood's attic and is full of informative memorabilia. If you come on a Friday or Saturday night, have dinner reservations ahead of time. On Columbus Day there is a grand parade down Columbus Avenue. This being San Francisco, the highlight is usually the Chinese American St. Mary's School Drum and Bugle corps.

Parking

In North Beach there is a **city parking garage** tucked away over the Police Station on Powell at Vallejo. Paid off-street parking is also at **699 and 721 Filbert** Street, just west of Washington Square. Telegraph Hill has very little parking. There is a small lot at the top of the hill at Coit Tower; good at night but there's usually a long line to enter it during the summer. These are two neighborhoods where it is best to walk and then take a taxi or the 42 Downtown Loop bus at the end of the tour.

Transportation

The **30 Stockton electric trolley bus** crosses Columbus Avenue and stops at Washington Square before continuing down Columbus to Fisherman's Wharf. The **Powell-Mason cable car** line links Union Square with Mason and Union streets a block west of Washington Square. The **39 Coit bus** links Washington Square in North Beach with Coit Tower atop Telegraph Hill and then returns downhill and continues to the Wharf. At the end of this walk the **42 Downtown Loop bus** runs north, on Sansome Street to the Wharf, and south, on Battery Street to the Financial District and Market Street.

RESTAURANTS, CAFÉS, AND BARS

San Francisco and Berkeley have more good cafés than any other American settlements. North Beach's *caffès*—Italian, not French—are frequented by natives, newcomers, and visitors. Each has its own particular personality and clientele. You are sure to find one just right for you. Every San Francisco neighborhood now has its own café(s), but North Beach's were first and are still probably the most fun. People read, page through the want ads, write, and chat. At the Caffè Trieste and others, tables are shared when the place fills up. It's a natural way to meet the locals.

Caffè Roma, in the 1920s this was an Italian bakery. The then owner had J. G. Giribone paint scenes of *putti* engaged in confectionery-making on the walls and ceiling. Mercury with his bag of gold shares the ceiling with a blond goddess and *putti* scattering sweets from the painted skies. When Sergio Azzollini opened the Caffè Roma, he restored the delightful artwork. Window seats here are great people-watching spots. The caffè serves breakfast and pizza, pasta, and salads and is perhaps the best for visitors who want to taste North Beach today; an airy, welcoming place. Opened in 1956, **Caffè Trieste** is a San Francisco institution. Every Saturday from noon to 2 P.M. there is Italian singing and spontaneous entertainment. The jukebox features operatic favorites. Next door, the Trieste roasts and sells its own coffees. **The North End Caffe**, features live jazz several nights a week. Open daily, **The Savoy-Tivoli**, an open-fronted café, has a restaurant inside; good cappuccino; lively and noisy on weekends. **Mario's Bohemian Cigar Store Café** has excellent cappuccino and a nonyuppie ambiance. Inexpensive meatball sandwiches and *frittatas*, a local crowd. Good view of the church across the park. Ed and Mary Etta Moose's new restaurant, **Moose's Restaurant,** is hands down the best new place in North Beach. Behind San Francisco artist Ward Schumaker's zappy blue neon sign of a moose head is a beautiful, airy, modern interior designed by Eden & Eden. Chef Lance Velasquez has created a superb menu of contemporary California dishes with an Italian theme. Sophisticated

Caffè Roma
414 Columbus Avenue, near Vallejo; 391-8584

Caffè Trieste
601 Vallejo Street, at Grant; 392-6739

The North End Caffe
1402 Grant Avenue, between Green and Union; 956-3350

The Savoy-Tivoli
1434 Grant Avenue, between Green and Union; 362-7023

Mario's Bohemian Cigar Store Café
566 Columbus Avenue at Union, facing Washington Square; 362-0536

Moose's Restaurant
1652 Stockton Street, between Union and Filbert, facing Washington Square; 989-7800

Fior d'Italia Restaurant
601 Union Street, corner of Stockton across from Washington Square;
986-1886

Firenze by Night Ristorante
1429 Stockton Street, near Columbus;
392-8585

Grazie
515 Columbus Avenue, near Union; 982-7400

Entree des Artistes
1630 Powell Street, near Green; 397-4339

Molinari's Delicatessen
373 Columbus Avenue, at Vallejo; 421-2337

Victoria Pastry Company
1362 Stockton Street, corner of Vallejo Street;
781-2015

Panelli Bros. Delicatessen
1419 Stockton Street, near Vallejo; 421-2541

Panama Canal Ravioli Factory
1358 Grant Avenue, near Green; 421-1952

R. Iacopi & Company Meat Market and Deli
1462 Grant Avenue, at Union; 421-0757

Italian French Baking Company of San Francisco
1501 Grant Avenue, at Union; 421-3796

Biordi Art Imports
412 Columbus Avenue, near Vallejo; 392-8096

Columbus Cutlery
358 Columbus Avenue, near Vallejo; 362-1342

yet fun; advance reservations recommended. Founded in 1881, **Fior d'Italia Restaurant** is San Francisco's oldest Italian restaurant and is a favorite of the Italian American Establishment; *Il Cenacolo* meets here. **Firenze by Night Ristorante** serves good Northern Italian dishes. **Grazie**, good salads and pastas. **Entree des Artistes**, an attractively decorated traditional San Francisco space serving chef Jacky Robert's excellent dishes. Budget diners should check out **Mario's Bohemian Cigar Store Café**.

Delicatessens, Etc.

Molinari's Delicatessen. The real thing, with a transporting, caloric aroma, Molinari's manufactures its own ravioli and tagliarini, and makes it own fine salami. San Francisco's uniquely mild climate is ideal for the curing of Italian dry salami; traditional makers cure their pungent pork and bulk meat sausages for forty-five days. Excellent made-to-order sandwiches for take-out. Established in 1914, **Victoria Pastry Company** is San Francisco's best Italian bakery and specializes in *gâteau St. Honoré* and in *zuccotto,* a Tuscan sponge cake filled with surprises; also rum cakes, *cannoli,* and *panettone.* **Panelli Bros. Delicatessen** has excellent made-to-order sandwiches; good for picnic fixings for travelers on a budget. **Panama Canal Ravioli Factory** was established in 1915; makes excellent ravioli, noodles, and sauce. **R. Iacopi & Company Meat Market and Deli**, established in 1910, makes Sicilian, Calabrese, and Tuscan-style sausages; also superb ricotta cheese *tortas* of many different kinds. **Italian French Baking Company of San Francisco** makes excellent breads and *panettone.*

SOME SHOPS

Biordi Art Imports. Carries hand-painted Italian dinnerware and ceramics and gourmet cookware. Gianfranco Savio's shop is the best in its line; and they will ship. This is probably the best shop in North Beach. **Columbus Cutlery**, owned by Pietro and Otillia Malattia. Their tiny shop sells, sharpens, and repairs all kinds of scissors, shears, razors, clippers, and knives. If they don't have it, it isn't made. **Postermat**. Sells the now-expensive perception-altering posters by such artists as Rick

Grifflin, Wes Wilson, Stanley Mouse, Alton Kelly, and Victor Moscoso. They were created to promote mid-1960s rock shows at the Fillmore Auditorium, Avalon Ballroom, and The Family Dog. **Settemezzo**, painfully hip leather jackets, militant modern shoes, and sexy jeans. **Eastwind Books**, a vast selection of all the best books on Asian history, literature, and arts. This is the company's English-language branch; Asian-language books are at the shop at 1435A Stockton, below Columbus, in the basement of the Eureka Federal Bank/North Beach Museum building. **Figoni Hardware**, an old-fashioned hardware store. Inside are wooden floors and shelves stacked with small boxes. Good for Italian kitchen implements.

Postermat
401 Columbus Avenue, at the corner of Vallejo; 421-5536

Settemezzo
419 Columbus Avenue, between Vallejo and Green; 398-4664

Figoni Hardware
1351 Grant Avenue; 392-4765

Introduction: The Essential San Francisco

Tucked in the sunny, wind-sheltered valley between Telegraph and Russian hills, North Beach is one of San Francisco's oldest neighborhoods and has seen many changes. Originally and briefly a fashionable part of town, it lost its appeal for the middle class as newer districts were made accessible by the cable cars. Shortly after fashion abandoned the area, it became the city's Latin Quarter with a mixed population of working-class Irish, Chilean, Peruvian, French, Spanish, Mexican, Basque, and Portuguese immigrants. Jammed between the docks and the downtown, the area became increasingly industrial when bayfill expanded the district north of Bay Street, obliterating sandy North Beach. (Today North Beach has no beach.) Railyards and factories including the Del Monte cannery and the Ghirardelli chocolate factory located here and employed many Italian American immigrants.

       The first Italian colony settled in the poor, congested blocks south of Broadway along Pacific, Jackson, Washington, and Clay streets, in what is today's Jackson Square Historic District. The cutting through of Columbus Avenue in 1872 displaced part of this population and propelled it north of Broadway to Upper Grant Avenue and the western slope of Telegraph Hill. The Yankees, Germans, and Irish who had previously occupied these blocks drifted away, and the Italian presence grew stronger, turning the Latin Quarter into Little Italy. By 1889, the *San Francisco Real Estate Circular* reported that "the stores remind one of a street in Naples." Italian, French, Swiss, and German immigrants "of the poorer class" predominated. They bid up the value of the real estate in this faded slum. **St. Francis of Assisi Roman Catholic Church** became the religious center of this colony. While there were but five thousand Italian Americans in San Francisco in 1890, by 1939 some sixty thousand were packed into North Beach. In 1931 there were five Italian-language newspapers in North Beach. Unlike the East Coast's Italian migration, San Francisco's Italian immigrants were predominantly northerners from Liguria, Lombardy, and the Piedmont, especially Genoa, Turin, and Milan.

California was promoted as the "American Italy" and many city residents began to move out of the congested city to farm the land. Italian Americans established truck gardens, vineyards, and orchards all over California. Santa Rosa in Sonoma County, for example, and the nearby Napa Valley became noticeably Italian American. Italian American truck gardens were familiar sights in the outlying undeveloped parts of San Francisco itself in what is now the Civic Center, Mission, Ingleside, and Bayview districts. Italian Americans captured the fishing industry, driving out the Chinese, who were relegated to marginal shrimping operations. Others founded export-import companies, opened restaurants, or began food-processing businesses. Scavenging (garbage collection) also became a money-making Italian American enterprise in San Francisco, organized as a collective.

Italian Americans did not stay trapped in the ghetto. During the prosperity of the 1920s many moved up and out, in particular to the nearby Marina District developed on the site of the 1915 Panama-Pacific International Exposition. After World War II mobility accelerated. It was partly because the neighborhood was "decongesting" that the beats found low rents here in the 1950s. Proximity to downtown also drew young office workers to North Beach's convenient apartments and flats. Today the Italian heritage is evident in a few venerable institutions, restaurants, old businesses, and social groups such as *Il Cenacolo,* but it no longer dominates the neighborhood. Instead, booming Chinatown has spilled across Broadway and moved up Stockton into North Beach. By 1990, North Beach was 47 percent white and 46 percent Asian American. (Latinos comprise 4 percent, and African Americans 3 percent, of the total neighborhood population.)

Bohemian San Francisco

The unbohemian *Oxford English Dictionary* defines the bohemian

> as the gipsy of society; one who either cuts himself off, or is by his habits cut off, from society for which he is otherwise fitted; especially an artist, literary man, or actor, who leads a free, vagabond, or irregular life, not being particular as to the society he frequents, and despising conventionalities generally. (Used with considerable latitude with or without reference to morals.)

Bohemians first appeared in Paris in the mid-1840s. Since the gypsies in France were traditionally from Bohemia, the Parisian press dubbed them "bohemians." Novelist Henry Murger defined Bohemia as an imaginary region "bordered in the North by hope, work and gaiety, on the South by necessity and courage, [and] on the West and East by slander and the hospital."

San Francisco had a milquetoast bohemia of literary dabblers and light-weight poets in the 1890s. This bohemia lived on then-inexpensive Russian Hill and slummed in cafés and bars near Pacific Street and the waterfront. The architect Willis Polk was a member of *les jeunes* ("the young"), as this coterie styled itself. Frank Norris, the well-born, Harvard-educated naturalistic novelist, was the only important writer to emerge from this genteel bohemia.

Another bohemia took root on Telegraph Hill in the 1920s in a cluster of shacks on the east side of the hill. In the depressed 1930s, left-wing radicals found North Beach one of their low-rent havens. Protest songs flowered; some painters took the social crisis of the time as their theme. The painters who worked with Ralph Stackpole on the 1934 **murals in Coit Tower** created a major monument of the period. Although no important literature came out of this era of political and class struggle, the visual arts flowered vividly.

The San Francisco bohemia that was most significant, however, was that of the beats of the mid-1950s. These gypsies from bourgeois postatomic America introduced sexual and racial variety in their free-floating subculture, and drugs too. Cool jazz was its music, black was its basic color, red wine and caffeine were its drugs of choice. San Francisco's North Beach emerged as one of three poles around which this movement drifted. New York's Greenwich Village and Los Angeles' Venice Beach, all faded areas with low rents that sprouted jazz clubs, were the other two beat magnets. Besides breaking America's race lines—a contribution of immense future importance—this movement's prophetic monument is Allen Ginsberg's poem, *Howl*, an apocalyptic vision of the madness of atomic warfare. A famous municipal obscenity trial of 1957 cleared the book—and gave it great publicity. The trial provoked the classic newspaper headline "THE COPS DON'T ALLOW NO RENAISSANCE HERE."

Amazingly, poet Lawrence Ferlinghetti's **City Lights Books**, and the funky **Vesuvio Café**, survive from the beat days. The beatnik bohemia of the mid-1950s existed in the corners and cracks of the ethnically mixed lower-middle-class North Beach apartment district. Beatniks evolved a distinctive "look": goatees and berets for the men, and black toreador pants and tops for "chicks." They created an argot—hip talk—which owed much to black jazz musicians. It was a night-creature culture based on staying up late. This bohemia had its painters, but it's the poets who have lasted. It was never a mob scene like the later hippie wave in the Haight-Ashbury. There were always only a few beats, and they were generally despised, much like the punks of today.

Today, San Francisco's bohemia is scattered, linked together by clunker automobiles, beat-up motorcycles, and redundant delivery trucks. The North Mission area, a gray zone between the South of Market and the Inner Mission, is its "center." Rock music is its chief art, though there is some painting, sculpture, and performance art as well. Videos, alas, seem to have erased the written word. The contemporary bohemia's events are announced by severely black-and-white photocopied posters taped to utility poles in the North Mission, near the South of Market rock clubs on Eleventh Street, and along lower and upper Haight Street.

There also is a vaguer, looser (more sane and healthy) "bohemia," a bohemia of the heart we might call it, and it is an important part of the character of this city. San Franciscans revel in human variety and are a bit more open to people of different persuasions. The working definition of a well-adjusted San Franciscan is that he or she is a bohemian at heart (but has a steady day job).

Tower Records
At Columbus and Bay streets; 885-0500

Montgomery-Washington Tower
655 Montgomery Street

Thomas Bros. Maps
550 Jackson Street, at Columbus; 981-7520

Purple Onion
*140 Columbus
(no telephone)*

❶ *Columbus Avenue from the Transamerica Pyramid to Broadway*

Originally named Montgomery Avenue, and cut across the existing grid of streets and houses retroactively in 1872-73, Columbus Avenue is one of the very few concessions San Francisco's street plan has made to the city's undulating topography in its old core. Renamed Columbus Avenue in recognition of the large Italian American colony in North Beach and along the industrial northern waterfront, the wide street is visually anchored by the **Transamerica Pyramid** at its southeast end and by **Mt. Tamalpais** in Marin County, across the Bay, to the northwest. The walk up the gentle rise of Columbus to Broadway passes between the Jackson Square Historic District to the east and Chinatown immediately west.

This entire quadrant of the city burned to the ground in 1906. It had been the Victorian city's slum district. As North Beach quickly rebuilt between 1906 and about 1915, it built with new, more stringent building codes. The even scale and coherent pattern of North Beach is due to these then-advanced codes. Mostly three to four stories high, the flats, apartments, hotels, and shops that were built then almost all survive. Columbus Avenue is San Francisco's greatest Edwardian boulevard, though few see it as such. The most interesting post-1906 buildings were built on the many triangular lots along prominent Columbus Avenue. Each one of these buildings is unique. Many have small entrance vestibules with mosaic floors paved with fragments of the destroyed Victorian city. This is a rewarding street to walk along, all the way to The Cannery near Fisherman's Wharf. Hip new shops have begun to pop up here and there along the boulevard. There is always something new and undiscovered here. **Tower Records** way down near Fisherman's Wharf, but a natural progression from North Beach, has a large selection of many kinds of music, including opera and classical music, and is open late.

At the corner of Washington and Columbus, is the **Montgomery-Washington Tower** designed by Kaplan McLaughlin Diaz in 1984. It is a mixed-use building with shops and offices and with condominiums on top. Under its arcade, through the gold revolving doors to the left inside the lobby and on the right-hand wall, is a display case entitled "Local Color." Here old photos and memorabilia memorialize the time when this was San Francisco's bohemia. Walk up the right-hand (east) side of gently sloping Columbus Avenue. (*See Tour 2A* for the history of these buildings.) East of Columbus, on Jackson Street, is **Thomas Bros. Maps**, a good place for maps and reproductions of old views of San Francisco. At 140 Columbus, between Jackson and Pacific on the east side of the street and down a steep flight of stairs, is the famous **Purple Onion** nightclub, now a venue for cutting-edge rock music on Friday and Saturday nights. With its mirrored walls, red booths, and parquet dance floor, this is a real part of San Francisco's entertainment history. Lenny Bruce and Woody Allen got their start here. Now it features local bands like the Ovarian Trolley and the Phantom Surfers.

② Columbus Tower/Sentinel Building, *1905–07, Salfield and Kohlberg*

North on Kearny, at the diagonal of Columbus Avenue, rises the cupola of the flatiron Columbus Tower designed by Salfield and Kohlberg before the earthquake and finished after it. It is a landmark building clad in gleaming white tile and sporting fine green, copper-clad bay windows. It has long been a favorite building in San Francisco. Its top floor housed turn-of-the-century political boss Abe Ruef's thriving real estate brokerage business after his release from San Quentin prison. Movie producer Francis Ford Coppola bought and restored the building in the 1970s. A new six-story building designed by William D. Podesto and Associates was built behind Columbus Tower in 1988. Modern corner bay windows fill out the profile of this triangular plot. Across Pacific Avenue, still on the right-hand side of Columbus, is the dead-end stub of old Adler Alley, recently renamed Saroyan Place. At number 12 is **Specs Museum Cafe**, Richard "Specs" Simmons' "first class toilet" crammed with memorabilia, smoke, and local characters.

Columbus Tower/ Sentinel Building
906 Kearny Street at Columbus

Specs Museum Cafe
12 Saroyan Place, at Columbus; 421-4112

City Lights Bookstore
261 Columbus Avenue below Broadway; 362-8193.

Vesuvio Café
255 Columbus Avenue, across the alley from City Lights Books; 362-3370

③ City Lights Bookstore

Poet Lawrence Ferlinghetti opened City Lights in 1953, one of the earliest paperback bookstores anywhere. As he recently reminisced, "We opened up the pocketbook shop to pay rent on this literary magazine we were doing. The magazine folded but the bookstore kept going. We stayed open to midnight. Just couldn't get the door closed." The shop was named after Charlie Chaplin's film and its image of the "little man against the cold cruel world." This landmark bookstore occupies the ground floor and basement, where there are chairs for browsers. It has books, avant-garde magazines, and a definitive selection of little magazines. City Lights is also a publishing house with a distinguished series of pocket poetry books, including *Howl*, among many other titles. Poets Lawrence Ferlinghetti, Gary Snyder, Allen Ginsberg, and Gregory Corso were among the original beats. The store and publishing house thrives.

④ Vesuvio Café *1913, Italo Zanolini*

Across narrow Kerouac Alley is the only other surviving beat haunt in the city. It is located in the ground floor and mezzanine of the old Cavalli Italian-language bookstore, an erudite pressed-tin landmark of the post-fire rebuilding designed by Italo Zanolini and built in 1913. This is San Francisco's most elaborate sheet-metal façade. Inside, the bar has a magpie decor. The front tables are a good place for people-watching.

Mural of San Francisco Scenes, *606 Grant Avenue, at Broadway and Columbus*

New Sun Hong Kong Restaurant

Finocchio Club
506 Broadway, near Kearny; 982-9388

St. Francis of Assisi Roman Catholic Church
610 Vallejo Street, off Columbus

❺ Mural of San Francisco Scenes

On the northwest corner of Broadway and Columbus is a four-story Edwardian building at 606 Grant Avenue with large murals showing San Francisco scenes and jazz musicians, painted by Bill Weber and Tony Klass in 1988. On the ground floor is the **New Sun Hong Kong Restaurant,** a restaurant popular with Chinese Americans.

❻  *The Broadway Entertainment Strip*

Broadway, wider than most San Francisco streets, was the principal route to the passenger docks in San Francisco's earliest years. Like long-distance bus terminals now, such areas attracted transients, low-life bars, and cheap hotels. A block south of Broadway, "Terrific" Pacific Street thrived with dives and whorehouses, later to be romanticized as the "old Barbary Coast." This red-light district was "abated" in 1914 and completely shut down in February, 1917 when the United States entered World War I. The construction of the Broadway Tunnel under Russian Hill in 1952 and of the Embarcadero Freeway in 1962 (since removed), which dumped all its traffic onto Broadway, made Broadway accessible from all over the Bay Area and sparked a boom in nightclubs and restaurants along this strip. In a city under continual gentrification, Broadway seems to be perversely sliding backward. The topless club craze that took off in 1964 and that lasted until the early 1970s is long over. Video porn seems to have found a niche in the blocks downhill from Broadway, appropriately enough backing up on Pacific and the one-time Barbary Coast. Broadway is in one of its eternal transitions. Theater districts are like that, going dark between acts.

The **Finocchio Club** offers male actresses in a polished and fun revue. Established in 1936, this had been a speakeasy during Prohibition. Joseph Finocchio, who died in 1986, once commented that "all my fellas conduct themselves in a ladylike manner."

Broadway west of Columbus is now fully absorbed into Chinatown, but a cluster of old Italian American shops and one key venerable landmark, **Fugazi Hall**, survive in the blocks near Vallejo and Stockton.

❼ St. Francis of Assisi Roman Catholic Church, *1860; rebuilt after 1906*

This historic Franciscan church was founded on June 12, 1849 and was the first Roman Catholic parish established in California after the Spanish missions. Bishop Joseph Sadoc Alemany, the Bishop of Monterey, resided here from 1850 to 1854, before Old St. Mary's Cathedral was completed on California Street, at Grant Avenue. The present light-painted Gothic Revival church was built in 1860. It was gutted by the 1906 fire and was rebuilt shortly thereafter within the original brick walls. It was one of the important early focal points of the Italian colony. Today this landmark church is considered redundant by the Roman Catholic archdiocese, and it has been closed. Its fate is undecided. The steps here are a good spot to rest and people-watch. Walk one block up Columbus, turn left (west), and walk one block up Green Street almost to the corner.

8 The Bank of America, *1927, H. A. Minton*
This one-story Art Deco corner bank shows how artistically the architects of the 1920s manipulated reinforced concrete. The upper part of the building has faces worked into its decoration. It is a fine period piece and was designed by H. A. Minton in 1927. The architect's rendering of the building is hung on the wall to the left as you enter. The locally founded bank was especially proud of the branches it built in North Beach. Another elegant branch, now a Carl's Jr. fast-food place, stands on the triangular lot at Broadway and Columbus.

• North Beach Museum/EurekaBank
The Art Deco Cavalli Building was unattractively altered for the bank and the insertion of basement-level shops, including the excellent Eastwind Books and Arts. This is their Asian-language store; English-language books are at 633 Vallejo, just west of Columbus. Inside the bank on the mezzanine upstairs is a gem of a small museum devoted to the history of North Beach. In changing exhibits it recounts the story of the Italian-American community and of Chinese American North Beach as well. This intimate museum is filled with heirlooms and old photographs that evoke old Little Italy and the many other cultural currents that have swirled through these historic blocks. This is one of the city's hidden treasures and is the best window into historic North Beach. An informative panorama of San Francisco in 1862 hangs on the landing.

9 Fugazi Hall/Casa Coloniale Italiana, *1913, Italo Zanolini*
Since 1975, theatrical producer Steve Silver's zany **Beach Blanket Babylon** has been staged in the intimate theater on the ground floor.

Most of the important ethnic groups in San Francisco in the nineteenth and early twentieth centuries built at least one community meeting hall. By 1910, people of Italian descent probably accounted for about eight percent of the city's population. Novelist Virgilio Luciani noted in that year that "Nothing was missing from the city's Little Italy—two daily newspapers, monthly magazines, weeklies, the church, the Dante Alighieri Society with an Italian school, mutual aid societies, athletic and drama clubs, travel agencies, banks, restaurants and large stores, and there were even large book and stationery stores." This thriving community began to produce men of wealth by the early twentieth century. John F. Fugazi, born in Milan of Genoese parents in 1838, came to America and became rich as the promoter of a popular hair lotion. He then organized a travel agency and moved over into banking. To counteract the parochial regional divisions—*campanillismo*—within the Italian American community, he gave it this splendid building in 1912. It was designed by Como-born Italo Zanolini and has a rich buff brick façade decorated with elaborate terra-cotta ornament, crowned by a central niche with a bust of the lushly bearded donor. The façade looks like the frontispiece of an old volume and is very Old World in flavor. It seems to burst with pride in high Italian culture. The theater inside is now

The Bank of America
1455 Stockton Street, at Columbus

North Beach Museum/ EurekaBank
1435 Stockton Street, near Columbus, upstairs

Fugazi Hall/Casa Coloniale Italiana
678 Green Street, between Columbus and Powell

Beach Blanket Babylon
Phone 421-4222 for
ticket information

Museo Italoamericano
Building C, Fort Mason,
Laguna Street at Marina
Boulevard; 673-2200

Washington Square

host to the long-running musical show **Beach Blanket Babylon**. Fugazi Hall has a *trompe l'oeil*-decorated basement banquet hall and offices upstairs for several Italian American philanthropic and cultural organizations, including the Italian Welfare Agency, organized in 1916. Today this agency serves the needs of the neighborhood elderly. The hall is the major secular landmark of San Francisco's important Italian American community, a community now integrated into every aspect of city life. Upstairs, on the third floor, is a photographic exhibit in the Italian Heritage Room (open during regular business hours).

There is a **Museo Italoamericano** in Building C, Fort Mason, Laguna Street at Marina Boulevard.

⑩ *Washington Square: The Ideal Park*
1847; 1955, Lawrence Halprin & Associates

Placid, green **Washington Square** surrounded by its pale, light-reflecting buildings, with the twin spires of Sts. Peter and Paul floating over it, is one of the finest parks in the United States. Washington Square's current landscape design dates from 1955 and is both simple and agreeable. A light screen of varied trees surrounds the square while a large sunny lawn spreads out at its center. The square is the lowest depression between Telegraph and Russian hills. It was reserved as a park by Jasper O'Farrell in 1847 and never saw serious attempts at private encroachment, something highly unusual for a nineteenth-century San Francisco park. Pressure to convert the park into playing fields was relieved by the creation of the North Beach Playground one block north in 1910. (The movement to put parking garages under downtown parks came as far as Washington Square, but was fortunately stopped.)

On the Columbus Avenue side of Washington Square is the bronze statue by Haig Patigian in honor of the city's volunteer firemen, erected in 1933 with part of Lillie Hitchcock Coit's bequest. The statue of Benjamin Franklin in the center of the park was the gift of H. D. Cogswell in 1879. Cogswell was a prosperous dentist and active prohibitionist. The long-dry taps at the base of the monument are inscribed "Cal Seltzer," "Vichy," and "Congress," though they provided only ordinary tap water.

Stockton Street, bordering the park, was an early fashionable residential address, the "Pacific Heights" of a much smaller city. Washington Square was then only an open lot with a low board fence around it and a flagpole dead center. When Columbus Avenue was cut through in 1872, clipping off the southwestern corner of the block, the park was landscaped with irrigated lawns and sheltering rows of densely planted conifers like Christmas trees. A new flagpole and fence were erected and a small keeper's kiosk built at Columbus and Union, near today's bus stop. In the 1860s, Washington Square was the only island of green that city dwellers could walk to.

What is best about Washington Square today is the generally peaceful mood of all the very different kinds of people who use it almost around the clock. It is what a park is supposed to be, a piece of sky and grass and momentary release from the urban world. The plan of the park is fine in its unpretentiousness and in its openness to sunlight. Retired men sit on the benches facing Union Street; Chinese American families take their tots to the sandbox play area in the northwest corner of the park; and passersby sit on the benches facing the lawn on the path parallel to Stockton Street. Young people like spots on the central lawn. Washington Square is filled with human life of all ages and conditions.

Sts. Peter and Paul Roman Catholic Church
666 Filbert Street

Old Telegraph Hill Dwellers Association Clinic
1736 Stockton Street, near Filbert

⓫ Sts. Peter and Paul Roman Catholic Church, *1922, Charles Fantoni*
The twin spires of Sts. Peter and Paul Roman Catholic Church, illuminated at night, float over the north side of the square. It was designed in 1922 by Charles Fantoni in the Romanesque style and was two decades in construction. Sts. Peter and Paul was San Francisco's Italian-language parish and is served by the Salesians of St. John Bosco, whose special mission is the instruction of boys from the poor and laboring classes. At its dedication in 1924 this church was hailed as "a monument which glorifies God, and reflects honor upon our City, our colony and our far away Italy." The stately church is also a manifestation of the prosperity San Francisco's Italian American colony achieved, principally through cornering wholesale fish and produce markets. Originally St. Peter's church, it was known as "the Church of the Fishermen" and has inside it a painting of *La madre del Lume*, Our Lady of Light, the patroness of Porticello. The naive painting shows the Madonna and Child; the Madonna is lifting a sinner by the arm from out of the pit of the inferno. Processions depart from here for Fisherman's Wharf and the annual blessing of the fishing fleet early each October. In 1881, the parish added St. Paul to its name. It did this because the Italian Masonic Lodge was making inroads among anticlerical Italian immigrants and the church wished to enlist the aid of the fiercely argumentative Paul.

This steel-frame and concrete building is actually two buildings in one: a large church with a grammar school wrapped around its nave. The inscription that runs across the façade is from the opening line of Dante's *Paradise*, "The glory of Him who moves everything penetrates and glows throughout the universe." The original plan was to cover the façade with mosaicwork showing Columbus discovering America and Dante writing *Paradise*. The interior is quintessentially Italian in its people-crowded feeling. Even when empty, the church seems full of people because of all the statues and images; it is as gregarious as Italian American culture itself. The altar is an impressive extravaganza, a heavenly city of sumptuous marble spires and life-size angels.

⓬ Old Telegraph Hill Dwellers Association Clinic, *1907, Bernard Maybeck; many later alterations*
This is an important building in the history of San Francisco, for it represents the beginning of the movement to create voluntary grassroots neighborhood associations, today a fundamental way in which politically active San Franciscans are orga-

Jasper Alley
Off the 500 block of
Gilbert Street, between
Stockton and Grant

nized. Architecturally, the building is interesting for its distinguished early pedigree as a 1907 design by Bernard Maybeck, much expanded and altered by perhaps a dozen architects since then. In imagery rustic or Swiss, its small courtyard with its one tree achieves a sense of separation from the city streets. Today converted to architects' offices, it is a good reminder of the great flexibility and adaptability of frame buildings.

The building opened as a settlement house clinic founded by two upper-class San Francisco women, Alice Griffith and Elizabeth Ashe. The center fought overcrowding in the slums, vaccinated children, ran baby clinics, and cared for the sick during three major flu epidemics. It called for better sanitation and health conditions in the crowded tenements of the immigrant newcomers, for conditions were bad in the tenements of the poor. Little Italy disappeared when life got better and its people moved up and out.

⓭ *Jasper Alley*

Off the 500 block of Filbert Street, between Stockton and Grant, is **Jasper Alley**, a typical neighborhood side street. The flats and apartments in North Beach's narrow alleys were forbidden to have bay windows by the city's fire code. Today many of these buildings house working-class Chinese American families. In the rebuilding after the fire in 1906, the very old city pattern of building working-class housing along alleys inside blocks and middle-class housing on the wider streets at the periphery of blocks was preserved. Multiclass blocks are something later real estate trends almost obliterated. Until quite recently, it was always thought an advance to segregate classes in order to create homogeneous tracts. Survivals such as this of an older, multiclass city form are instructive of how to create lively cities that serve many different kinds of people.

⓮ *Upper Grant Avenue Shops and Café Strip*

Grant Avenue from Broadway to Greenwich is perhaps the most interesting inexpensive shopping/browsing street in San Francisco both for visitors and residents. In form, it is the classic Edwardian city of three-story, bay-windowed frame buildings with shops along the ground floor and apartments and hotels above. The uniform architecture creates a narrow street with sides "corrugated" by bay windows. A strong and even cornice line holds the sky and defines the visual edge of the mini-canyon. The sidewalks are narrow and the shops all of the same general small size creating an environment that is intimate, like a village. Some vintage shopfronts survive here with their tile work, long an Italian American specialty in the building trades.

Faded here and there, not swank, Upper Grant Avenue's shops are great hunting grounds for unusual items. The relatively low-rent storefronts strung out continuously along both sides of the narrow street are a changing mix of old-time Italian American businesses (just a few are left), antique stores, interesting offbeat shops, new Chinese American stores, storefront offices and garment factories, and services such as dry cleaners and small grocery stores catering to Telegraph Hill and North Beach residents. A light sprinkling of contemporary clothes shops and art galleries enlivens this potpourri.

Travelers who need postcards should check out **Quantity Postcards** with its twenty thousand old and new postcards. **Grant Antiques** also has good hunting. **The Saloon** at Grant and Fresno Alley, right above the diagonal of Columbus, looks and smells just like its name and presents good rock, blues and jazz. Up Grant is the **Lost & Found Saloon,** a bit of a dive but also a place where the music cooks; they serve up live blues and rock with no cover charge. This was once the famous Coffee Gallery, a beat hangout.

Quantity Postcards
1441 Grant; 986-8866

Grant Antiques
1415 Grant; 864-2611

The Saloon
1232 Grant, at Fresno Alley; 989-7666

Lost & Found Saloon
1353 Grant; 397-3751

Coit Tower

275 Telegraph Hill Boulevard

⓫ *To Coit Tower*

The stairs at the head of Filbert Street are the most direct path up steep Telegraph Hill. Walk along the shoulder of Telegraph Hill Boulevard to **Coit Tower**. The alternative is the convenient and scenic 39 Coit bus, which runs every twenty minutes and stops at Union Street near Columbus, on the south edge of Washington Square, or along Stockton between Filbert and Lombard. Sit on the driver's side for the best view as the bus climbs Lombard and swings onto curvy Telegraph Hill Boulevard. The pale stucco apartments, flats, and houses of Telegraph Hill are neat and tidy light-reflecting facets of this cubist cityscape. The sudden view of the blue Bay and its distant shores makes this short ride memorable. Now a posh enclave, Telegraph Hill was once solidly working class with Irish American dock-workers on its east face and Italian American fishermen on its north face, all living in modest cottages. If you take the bus, where Telegraph Hill Boulevard swings in a loop at the head of Lombard, you pass a granite monument with a bronze plaque dedicated to Guglielmo Marconi, the inventor of wireless telegraphy. The memorial was placed here by public subscription in 1938 shortly after the inventor's death. Immediately behind it, at **275 Telegraph Hill Boulevard**, is architect Gardner A. Dailey's own house designed in 1942. This elegant modern stucco design blends in so well with its neighbors that few notice it. Dailey was one of the Bay Area's greatest designers, and in this subtle building he masterfully utilized the views from the site and incorporated roof terraces into the original design. Striving to be rigorously pure and modern, he eschewed adding bay windows. His widow, however, ended up adding one to the back of the house.

Coit Tower/Panorama/
WPA Murals
Summit of Telegraph
Hill; Tower and murals
open 10 A.M. to 5 P.M.
daily; fee

• **Coit Tower/Panorama/WPA Murals,** *1933, Arthur Brown, Jr.;*
1934, WPA murals, various artists

Coit Tower stands atop Telegraph Hill, Robert Louis Stevenson's "peak in the wind." Pioneer Park on the hill's summit is one of the oldest parks in the city. Originally a barren hilltop, this 295-foot hill got its name from a semaphore built here in 1850 to advise merchants in the port of the approach of ships. It functioned for only three-and-a-half years before an electric telegraph station was built on Point Lobos, at the entrance to the Golden Gate, making the primitive semaphore obsolete. During Gold Rush days, the residents of this then-remote port thronged the summit of the hill every two weeks to watch the arrival of the Pacific Mail steamer with its letters and newspapers from home. In 1876 a group of civic-minded businessmen, wanting to celebrate in some tangible way the nation's centennial, purchased four lots at the top of the hill for twelve thousand dollars and donated them to the city to create Pioneer Park. Later purchases by the city considerably expanded the park and in 1901 Park Superintendent John McLaren began planting trees here.

Lillie Hitchcock Coit, a pioneer San Franciscan, was brought to San Francisco as a child in 1851. She developed a life-long fascination with fires and firemen. As a young girl, she was made a honorary member of the Knickerbocker No. 5 Fire Company. A southern sympathizer during the Civil War, Coit spent the war years first in the South and then in Paris. Eventually she returned to San Francisco, and when she died in 1929 she left a hundred thousand dollars to the City of San Francisco "to be expended in an appropriate manner for the purpose of adding to the beauty of the city which I have always loved."

The Coit Advisory Committee used the funds to erect the statue to volunteer firemen that stands in Washington Square and to construct an observation tower atop Telegraph Hill. Arthur Brown, Jr., the architect of City Hall, was commissioned to design the 210-foot-tall reinforced concrete tower, which was completed in 1933. In form, the tower is a giant fluted column with an arcaded observatory at its top. So that it would appear vertical to the human eye, the tower is slightly tapered and is eighteen inches smaller in diameter at its top than its base. In style, Coit Tower might be called "stripped classical." (Despite what some will tell you, the tower is not modeled on a firehose nozzle.) Over the entrance to the tower is a high-relief plaque by sculptor Robert Howard showing the phoenix rising from its ashes. San Francisco adopted this emblem after the devastating fires of the 1850s that repeatedly destroyed the Gold Rush city. Each time the city rebuilt with better buildings.

An elevator carries the visitor to a landing from which thirty-seven steps lead to the open loggia, at the top of the tower, with its splendid view. The panorama here embraces the entire north Bay from the Golden Gate in the west to the Contra Costa hills in the east. The construction of a tall apartment building on the north side of the hilltop led to the first height limits in San Francisco in 1931 "so that skyscrapers would not interfere with the view from or detract from the beauty of the Coit Memorial." (In 1963, a forty-foot, or four-story, height limit was imposed on all the northern waterfront to prevent a Miami Beach-like wall of Bay-front highrises from destroying the views from the rest of the city.)

• **Panorama/View of The San Francisco-Oakland Bay Bridge**, *1933–36*
Begun during the depth of the Depression, the great bridge was built by the State of California and financed by the New Deal Reconstruction Finance Corporation. Its gifted designers were Charles H. Purcell, chief engineer; Charles E. Andrew, bridge engineer; and Glenn B. Woodruff, design engineer, with Timothy Pfleuger, consulting architect. It was completed in November 1936 for $70 million. The two elegant suspension bridges, each a 2,310-foot span, are joined in the middle of the channel by a man-made concrete pier "island" that extends 220 feet below the Bay. The four great steel piers of the suspension bridges have great X-braces that create an overlapping diamond pattern as you pass under them.

While the Art Deco Golden Gate Bridge is the great crowd pleaser in the Bay Area and is virtually the symbol of San Francisco, the streamlined San Francisco-Oakland Bay Bridge's twin silver suspension spans are the connoisseur's bridge. Steel bridges, especially the great works of the 1930s, are the great artistic monuments of our mobile people. There is something at once stripped down and basic and yet graceful, thoughtful, and pure about the design of the four piers of the San Francisco–Oakland Bay Bridge. They are among architect Timothy Pfleuger's finest works. It persuades us that it is steel in as strong, economical, and elegant a disposition as possible. Every rivet counts. The Bay Bridge has the always persuasive beauty of simplicity.

The Murals of Coit Tower

It was originally intended that a restaurant or an exhibit hall would occupy the ground floor of Coit Tower, but neither came to pass. Instead, in 1934 San Francisco artist Bernard Zakheim contacted Dr. Walter Heil, a San Franciscan then serving in President Roosevelt's New Deal, urging that the interior of the tower be embellished as a relief project for local artists. Heil, head of the Public Works of Art Project (PWAP), liked this idea and the result was the first relief work project for artists sponsored by the federal government. Twenty-five master artists and nineteen assistants were commissioned to cover the interior with frescoes depicting the working life of California. All received the monthly salary of ninety-four dollars. The work was accomplished in eight-and-a-half months and produced one of the most important pieces of public art in California. Though the Coit Tower frescoes are unified in narrative conception, each section was done by different hands and a few vary markedly in style. Some panels are straightforwardly documentary, while others are militantly political. The frescoes are well worth careful examination.

• *American Eagle*, artist unknown. Enter the tower and look over the inner archway leading to the elevators. A pair of penetrating eyes surrounded by clouds, lightning, rain, the sun, and the moon stare at the viewer like the eyes of God the Creator in a Byzantine apse. An American eagle adorns the arch itself. Step to the left and follow the frescoes in a clockwise direction.

• *Animal Force and Machine Force*, Ray Boynton. This panel flanks the doorway on both sides of the inner north wall. On the left is the ancient source of power, human and animal muscle. The fishermen pulling their heavy nets from the sea repeat an ancient fresco theme. In a small niche a young boy reads the dedication book for Coit Tower. To the right of the doorway a modern hydroelectric dam harnesses elemental forces for the modern world's work.

• *California Industry: Timber and Dairying,* Gordon Langdon. On the outer wall, in the northeast corner, is Langdon's depiction of a sawmill processing redwood trees into milled lumber. Look carefully in the mill to find the primitive worker's graffito on a pillar, a wry reference to the roots of art.

• *Farmer and Cowboy,* Clifford Wright. Flanking the east window are Wright's figures holding implements of their trade. The two figures represent the classic struggle in the West between the rancher's desire for open ranges and the farmer's need for fenced-in fields.

• *California,* Maxine Albro. Across the inner east wall is Maxine Albro's synthesis of California agricultural scenes. From left to right are wheat farming (California's first important crop and the basis of much of the wealth of Victorian San Francisco), flower-raising, and viticulture and winemaking.

• *Department Store,* Frede Vidar. On the outer wall, in the left southeast corner, is Vidar's panel showing a soda fountain, a wine shop, and a department store with clerks and customers. Fear and foreboding of the coming war permeate the soda fountain. One woman hides behind another as if afraid of a photographer. In the background a woman reads a newspaper with headlines of Hitler and of the destruction of Diego Rivera's controversial murals in New York City's Rockefeller Center.

• *Banking,* George Harris. On the outer wall, in the right southeast corner, is Harris' fresco showing lawyers reading in a law library, armed guards protecting a bank vault, and the interior of the Grain Exchange Board. The downward sloping line on the graph in the Grain Exchange tells the story of the Great Depression.

• *Stockbroker and Scientist,* Mallette Dean. Flanking the south window are two figures with symbolic tools of their professions. The man who creates intellectual capital—the scientist or inventor—and the man who makes ideas economic realities—the investor or entrepreneur—frame the window looking down on the skyscrapers of the Financial District. A light switch on the wall is incorporated into the scientist's observatory.

• *City Life,* Victor Arnatoff. On the inner south wall is Arnatoff's great synthesis of San Francisco in the 1930s. This complex scene is the apex of the cycle and shows various parts of the city as they looked in the 1930s. A newsstand occupies the center of the composition. The man with the hat at the right staring at the viewer is Ralph Stackpole, the artist in charge of the overall conception of the fresco cycle. A car crash has taken place in front of the Stock Exchange. A holdup is in progress as the indifferent city crowd hurries by. The city's varied people is the theme: silk-hatted capitalists, sailors, laborers, policemen, and thieves all animate the city streets. Hovering over all this activity is a stock exchange ticker with market quotations. Note the three newspapers that surround the prosperous-looking businessman in the brown homburg. He is reading the New York stock tables while a women's legs peek out from under the paper clutched under his arm. He stands on a cheap tabloid depicting a gangster slaying. They symbolize money, sex, and death.

- *Library*, Bernard B. Zakheim. On the outer wall, in the left southwest corner, is Bernard B. Zakheim's controversial depiction of workers reading in the library's periodical room. Most of the newspapers are Communist or socialist periodicals whose headlines record the political and social crises of the day. The most prominent figure is reaching for Marx's *Capital*. A happy hedonist among these politically passionate readers relishes a girlie paper.
- *News Gathering*, Suzanne Scheuer. On the outer wall, in the right southwest corner, is Suzanne Scheuer's fresco showing the editorial office, linotyping, composing, printing, and selling of the *San Francisco Chronicle*. A reporter with his back to the viewer hands his story in to his editor. The frame around the small window shows the printing of the separate colors for the Sunday comics. A newsboy stands to the left with the finished product. On the windowsill is a copy of the *San Francisco Chronicle* with the headline ARTISTS FINISH COIT TOWER MURALS.
- *Surveyor and Steelworker*, Clifford Wright. On the outer wall flanking the west window are Clifford Wright's two figures representing mental and physical labor.
- *Industries of California*, Ralph Stackpole. On the inner west wall is Stackpole's large fresco depicting in realistic detail California industries from canning to steel to chemicals. Diego Rivera's influence on the artists is strongest here. The NRA blue eagles on the sacks refer to the New Deal's attempts to organize the devastated American economy.
- *Railroad and Shipping*, William Hesthal. On the outer wall in the northwest corner is William Hesthal's pairing of land and sea transport.
- *California Industrial Scenes*, John Langley Howard. On the outer north wall is John Langley Howard's fresco showing construction, oil drilling, mining, and panning for gold. Striking black and white miners mass menacingly before the viewer. A poor migrant family with its battered car is camped out in the open, panning for gold in California's worked-over streambeds. They are the object of the curiosity of the idle rich who have come slumming in their yellow limousine. The hungry mongrel and the pampered poodle eye each other, summing up the class conflict. Looming over the squalid migrants' camp is a modern hydroelectric dam and a sleek streamlined train representing the theme of technological advance and social collapse.
- *Social Revolution*, John Langley Howard. Over the inner lintel of the door leading outside is the little-noticed conclusion to the cycle. In the cramped space over the door, a vast wheatfield moves under a stormy, lightning-streaked sky. The wheatfield below is ablaze; out of the flames rises the clenched fist of social revolution.

To the left of the front door is a scrap of paper with a quip from President Franklin Roosevelt on his return from a fishing expedition, "I'm a tough guy. I learned a lot from the barracudas and the sharks."

The Coit Tower murals were completed just as San Francisco entered one of its most acute crises. A longshoremen's strike that July turned into a four-day general strike after police shot down two union members. Politics and paint became an explosive combination when rumors began circulating about the "subversive" frescoes. The city's Art Commission ordered a hammer and sickle removed from one fresco and then decided to close the tower until tempers in the city cooled. The Artists' Union

Beach Chalet
far western end of Golden Gate Park, facing the Ocean Beach

Rincon Center
101 Spear Street, at Mission Street

City College
50 Phelan Avenue

The City Club
155 Sansome Street

The San Francisco Art Institute
800 Chestnut Street, on Russian Hill

Greenwich Steps

picketed the locked monument. Finally, in October, the frescoes were opened to the public. Rarely has public art so touched the nerves of San Francisco the way these murals did during the polarized year of 1934.

Other Important San Francisco Murals

San Francisco's second important WPA fresco cycle was painted in 1936–37 by Lucian Labaudt and is located in the **Beach Chalet** at the far western end of Golden Gate Park, facing the Ocean Beach (*see Tour 13*). Those murals depict play and recreation, complementing these on work and industry. **Rincon Center**'s former Rincon Annex Post Office, built in 1940 and designed by Gilbert Stanley Underwood in the Moderne style near the foot of Mission Street, has an important and in its day controversial mural cycle painted in 1941–48 by Anton Refregier. They tell the history of San Francisco in an unflinching way. A large mural by Diego Rivera on the theme of *Pan American Unity*, painted in 1939 for the Pan Pacific Exposition held on Treasure Island, is now located at the new library at **City College** in the Ingleside District west of Twin Peaks. **The City Club** has a Rivera mural as well (*see Tour 2B*). **The San Francisco Art Institute** on Russian Hill has yet another Rivera mural (*see Tour 6*).

16 Greenwich Steps

Leave Coit Tower, turn right, and cross the road to the light pole; here you will find the head of **Greenwich Steps**, a street right-of-way too steep to pave. The hidden stairs are embowered in greenery and give access to secluded houses and apartments. In the nineteenth and early-twentieth centuries, the east face of the hill was inhabited by Irish American dockworkers who labored on the bustling piers below. In 1888 one woman described how hard it was to locate a particular shanty in this jumble:

> It requires some physical exertion to mount a Telegraph Hill stairway, but that is nothing in comparison with the mental effort necessary in finding one's way after reaching the top. We jump a ditch that serves as an open channel for sewage, make a detour around a pile of tomato cans, bring up a blind alley that purports to be a street leading directly to the house we seek, try a path that ends abruptly on the edge of the cliff, and narrowly escape a landslide that goes careening down the bluff, and which has lost its precarious hold just a moment too soon to give us a free toboggan ride....

Small local grocery stores catered to the isolated hillside residents. Goat trails webbed the steep slopes. There were many empty lots on the hill then, and the cheap real estate within hiking distance of the cafés and bars along Pacific and

Broadway drew a small band of artists to the hill. Where Greenwich meets Montgomery, Harry Lafler, an artist and newspaperman who also sold real estate, built a fenced cluster of five cottages known as The Compound. It became a gathering place for writers such as local poet George Sterling. Later the isolation, splendid views, and good weather began to attract others to the hill.

Julius Castle Restaurant
1541 Montgomery Street;
362-3042

Malloch Apartment Building
1360 Montgomery Street

In 1931 Montgomery Street was graded, split into two levels, and paved. The construction of Coit Tower gave the hill a new image and new houses and apartments began to pop up here and there. Better garbage service and landscaping also spruced up the hill. By 1939 some quite artistic buildings were constructed and the hill tipped toward those with "the longing for bohemia…whose income permits them to be comfortably daring." The same observer noted then that the once-working-class hill "is well on the way to becoming smart." Telegraph Hill was one of the first areas in San Francisco to undergo what today is called gentrification. While only a few shingled shacks remain today, the explorer can find here and there relics of the hill's early days. In 1986 the **Telegraph Hill Historic District** was established to preserve the surviving small-scale hill cottages.

• **Julius Castle Restaurant**, *1921, Louis Mastropasqua*
At the head of Montgomery is crenellated **Julius Castle**, a restaurant with a splendid view, built in 1921 and designed by Louis Mastropasqua, a gifted Italian American architect and cartoonist for *La Vita Italiana*. In the 1920s a turntable in front of the restaurant was the only practical way to turn autos around on the narrow street. (Today the restaurant has valet parking.) Walk up the lower side of Montgomery. The retaining wall here has been heavily planted and gives the illusion of a park.

🔢 **Malloch Apartment Building**, *1936; 1939, Irving W. Goldstine*
On the corner of Montgomery and Filbert streets is one of San Francisco's Art Deco treasures, a four-story apartment house built in 1936 and remodeled in 1939 by Irving W. Goldstine. Lauren Bacall sheltered Humphrey Bogart in *Dark Passage* (1947) here. Large *sgraffito* panels decorate the building. Facing Montgomery is a stevedore holding a globe with the Bay Bridge and Coit Tower visible at his feet. Above him are three Manila Clippers, the earliest air link across the Pacific, inaugurated in 1936. At the other end of the façade is a Spanish conquistador. On the Filbert Street side is a panel with a female figure representing California with a rainbow and a map of the state. A sun sets in a zigzag landscape. The entrance is decorated with an etched glass window with the obligatory leaping gazelle. Streamlined corners, glass blocks, and a railing along the top of the building make this a quintessential piece of Moderne design.

34–36 Darrell Place

228 Filbert Street

224 Filbert

222 Filbert

10 Napier Lane

22 Napier Lane

(18) *Filbert Steps and Darrell Place*

Filbert Steps and Darrell Place, along with Napier Lane, lined with simple Victorian cottages and embowered in gardens, is one of San Francisco's most-loved enclaves. Another street right-of-way too steep to pave, Filbert is made accessible by wooden stairs. The perpendicular gardens here, filled with flowers and carpeted with baby tears, are a labor of love for the **Filbert Steps** residents who continue the efforts begun by Grace Marchant many years ago. The modest cottages, lush plantings, and sweeping views of the Bay, all so close to the downtown's skyscrapers, sum up the best of San Francisco.

At **34–36 Darrell Place**, the narrow passage to the left near the head of the stairs, is David Weingarten/ACE Architects' condominium building built in 1986. Set in a row of ordinary, flat-front apartment buildings, this hard-to-see postmodern essay has a giant half-arch into which are spliced the entrances to the two units. The upper stories have a canted façade with bay windows. A fragment of a heavy cornice is set over the archway's giant "keystone." It is an exciting, inventive design.

At **228 Filbert Street** is a Gothic Revival cottage built in 1873 by an Englishman from Jersey in the stevedore business. It replaces an earlier shanty. Further down the steps, at **224 Filbert** at the corner of Napier Lane, is an 1863 cottage thoroughly restored and improved in 1978. This simple vernacular cottage is one of the oldest on the hill and gives a taste of the first wave of building here. Before its restoration by architect-owner Robert J. Fogel it was in a decrepit state; today it charms all who see it. On the opposite corner of Filbert Steps and Napier Lane is **222 Filbert**, a simple frame building that once housed Michael Thornton's grocery store and "blind pig," an unlicensed saloon. Legend has it that some of the cottages here were used to "shanghai" sailors. "To shanghai" was a verb coined in early San Francisco.

• *Napier Lane*

Napier Lane, originally Napier Alley, is a short boardwalk, one of the last in the city, lined with cottages and modest apartment buildings. Pots of flowers bloom here all year long, and sleek cats patrol their intricate territories. Number **10 Napier Lane** is a one-story, Italianate house built in 1885 and is typical of the working-class housing that once predominated on the hill. Its precipitous exterior staircase creates interesting patterns. The gaps between the Napier Lane cottages permit glimpses of gardens, porches, and roof decks that spill down the eastern face of the hill. The cottage at **22 Napier Lane** was built about 1875 and restored in 1994.

At the bottom of Filbert is a cliff-clinging concrete staircase built in 1972 to replace the rickety wooden staircase that once gave access to Sansome Street and the piers down below. The stairs traverse a former quarry. Rock excavated from Telegraph Hill was used to fill behind the city's seawall to make space for warehouses that backed up the once-busy piers. In 1878 a heavy rainstorm uncovered traces of gold near the Filbert Steps and a brief flurry of gold fever struck the hill. While the "gold rush" turned out to be brief, the quarry of rock was long profitable and was not stopped until several houses at the edge of the excavation slid down into the pit. Today aromatic wild fennel, red valerian, and yellow and orange nasturtium cling to the rocks. Visible from here is the roof of the four-story **H. G. Walters Warehouse** with a Moderne house, garden, and guest house perched on its roof.

 The red brick former warehouse district at the foot of Telegraph Hill, between Sansome and The Embarcadero, is one of the oldest sections of San Francisco. Three blocks from here, on Front Street flanking Vallejo, are the twin **Gibb Warehouses** built in the 1850s, among the oldest buildings in the city. The district has seen dramatic change since the 1960s. When shipping moved across the Bay to the Port of Oakland's modern container cargo facilities, the solidly built warehouses here were converted first into furniture showrooms and architects' and designers' offices and then, as real estate values continued to escalate, into offices. All the former warehouses and factories that line the waterfront in an arc from Broadway to Ghirardelli Square have been converted to new uses in the postindustrial city.

H. G. Walters Warehouse

Gibb Warehouses,
101 Vallejo Street and
915 Front Street

Levi's Plaza: Levi Strauss & Company Headquarters
1155 Battery Street

Stern Building, Italian Swiss Colony wine warehouse

Il Fornaio Restaurant
1265 Battery Street;
986-1505

⑲ Levi's Plaza: Levi Strauss & Company Headquarters, *1982*
Hellmuth, Obata & Kassabaum with Howard Friedman and Gensler &
Associates; 1982, Lawrence Halprin and Omi Lang, landscape architects
Cross Sansome and enter landscape architect Lawrence Halprin's handsome park at the heart of **Levi's Plaza**, the corporate headquarters of **Levi Strauss & Company**. An attractive fountain here hewn out of a rough chunk of granite is a good place to rest. Buried under this bayfill are Gold Rush ships abandoned when their crews took off for the mines. The brig *Palmyra* lies buried underground near the Levi's Plaza fountain. The lowrise, five-building complex was designed by Hellmuth, Obata & Kassabaum with Howard Friedman and Gensler & Associates in 1982. It is designed to blend with both the old warehouse district of which it is a part and the cubist jumble of Telegraph Hill's houses behind it. Levi's Plaza also incorporates the fine old **Italian Swiss Colony wine warehouse** at the corner of Battery and Greenwich designed by Hemenway & Miller in 1903. Today it houses the fine **Il Fornaio Restaurant**.

 Levi Strauss & Company is one of San Francisco's best-known firms. Its products have carried San Francisco's initials on their copper rivets around the world. The company has its roots in a clothing import business begun in 1850 by David Stern. Stern invited his brother-in-law, Bavarian-born Levi Strauss, to join him in 1853 and Levi Strauss & Company was born. In 1871 Jacob W. Davis, a Reno, Nevada saddlebag maker who purchased duck twill from Levi Strauss, secured the seams of heavy work pants with copper saddlebag rivets. The next year Davis and Levi Strauss applied for a patent for an "improvement in fastening pocket openings,"

Levi Strauss Factory and Design Center,

*In the Mission District
250 Valencia, between
Duboce and Fourteenth;
Phone 565-9159 for
tour information and
reservations; tours on
Wednesdays at
10:30 A.M. and 1 P.M.*

Fog City Diner

*1300 Battery Street;
982-2000*

which was granted the following year. The company began the manufacture of denim overalls that were sold throughout the West. Today Levi Strauss is one of the world's largest apparel manufacturers, with about a fifth of the denim jeans market.

Levi Strauss also offers tours, by appointment, of its factory and design center at **250 Valencia**; reservations must be made in advance. The one-and-a-half hour tour includes a BBC documentary on the company, a museum of memorabilia on the famous jeans, and a look at the design department.

The **Fog City Diner** is located across the street from the plaza in a chrome and neon evocation of a traditional diner, designed by Pat Kuleto in 1985.

Continuation: Fisherman's Wharf, or Skycrapers and the Downtown

The 42 Downtown Red Arrow Loop bus runs north up Sansome Street and The Embarcadero to Columbus and North Point, one block from The Cannery and Fisherman's Wharf *(Tour 5)*. On Battery Street the 42 Downtown Gold Arrow Loop runs south to Battery and California in the Financial District *(Tour 2)* and the California Street cable car line, and then to Market Street.

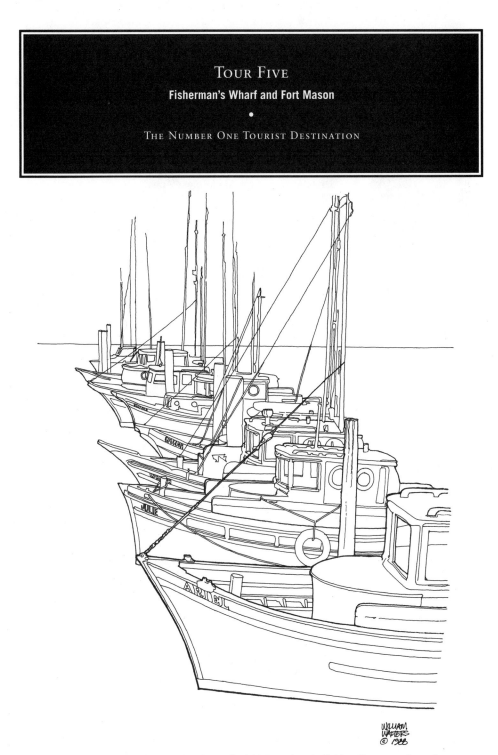

The oldest, most graceful, wooden boats in San Francisco's fishing fleet are given the most visible berths, those facing the 200 block of Jefferson Street, between Taylor and Jones.

What This Tour Covers
Preliminaries
Introduction: The Number One Tourist Destination

TOUR 5:
FISHERMAN'S WHARF
AND
FORT MASON

❶ Taylor Street Wharf, Crab Pots, and Restaurant Row
  A U.S.S. *Pampanito*/U.S. Navy Vessels/Pier 45
  B Ferry Slips/Alcatraz Island
  C Jefferson Street Amusement Zone
  D Pier 39

❷ The Historic Fishing Fleet

❸ Fish Alley

❹ The Cannery/Haslett Warehouse

❺ Hyde Street Pier/Historic Ships

❻ Victorian Park/Hyde Street Cable Car Turntable

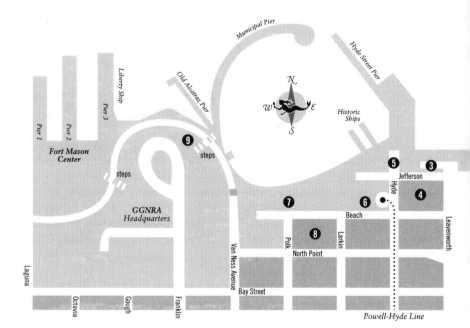

7 National Maritime Museum/Aquatic Park Casino/
Municipal Pier/Aquatic Park

8 Ghirardelli Square

9 Fort Mason Center ("Fort Culture")/
Golden Gate National Recreation Area Headquarters/
Liberty Ship S.S. *Jeremiah O'Brien*

Continuation

Golden Gate Promenade to Fort Point and the Presidio

Preliminaries

Pier 39 Garage
On Beach, between Powell and Stockton

Anchorage Garage
At Jones, between Jefferson and Beach

Scoma's Fisherman's Wharf
Pier 47; 771-4383

Castagnola's Restaurant
286 Jefferson Street; 776-5015

Alioto's Restaurant
286 Jefferson Street; 673-0183

A. Sabella's Restaurant
2766 Taylor Street, at Jefferson; 771-6775

Fishermen's Grotto
9 Fisherman's Wharf; 673-7025

Tarantino's Restaurant
206 Jefferson Street; 775-5600

Franciscan Restaurant
Pier 43 1/2; 362-7733

Sabella & La Torre
2809 Taylor Street; 673-2824

Pompei's Grotto
340 Jefferson Street; 776-9265

Tokyo Sukiyaki
225 Jefferson Street; 775-9030

BEST TIMES TO
DO THIS TOUR

Very early in the morning, from 4 A.M. to 8 A.M. the Wharf is a fish distribution center with fish arriving by boat and truck to be sold and shipped throughout the region. Almost no one comes to watch the action at Pier 45 and almost hidden **Fish Alley** (across Jefferson Street from The Cannery, between Leavenworth and Hyde streets). By 11 A.M. the tourist shops are open. Restaurants at the Wharf tend to stay open later than those in the rest of the city. Summer, of course, is the most crowded time here. Winter is probably the best season at the Wharf. Every October, at the time of the celebration of the **Madonna del Lume** and the blessing of the fishing fleet, the Wharf holds a weekend **Festa Italiana** with food, music, entertainment and fireworks. Phone 673-3782 for dates and information.

Parking

Not surprisingly, parking can be frustrating in the Fisherman's Wharf area. It's best to come by public transit or taxi. At peak times, the most likely available unmetered parking is at the foot of Van Ness Avenue at the far west edge of the Wharf, a block west of Ghirardelli Square. Other unmetered zones with no time restrictions are on the blocks east of Powell and north of Bay streets (though the city may change this). There are paid parking lots on Jefferson, between Taylor and Powell. The **Pier 39 Garage** has the highest rates and the highest occupancy because signs point cars that way. The **Anchorage Garage**, at Jones and Beach, has seven hundred spaces. There are three hundred spaces under **Ghirardelli Square**; enter from Beach or Larkin streets.

Transportation

Many visitors take the **cable cars** from down-town to the Wharf. The **Powell-Hyde line** is much more scenic than the **Powell-Mason**. Scrutinize the cars' signs, for otherwise they are identical. The alternative transit route from downtown is the **30 Stockton trolley bus** from Sutter and Stockton streets, a block north of Union Square. The **39 Coit bus** links Washington Square in North Beach with Coit Tower atop Telegraph Hill and the Wharf going as far as North Point and Taylor streets. The **42 Downtown Loop bus'** Red Arrow Loop links Sansome Street near Levi's Plaza at the base of Telegraph Hill with the Wharf via The Embarca-dero and Bay Street. *Within* the Wharf the **19 Polk bus** runs west along Jefferson Street to Ghirardelli Square, and east on Beach Street. There is "owl service" on the **15 Third bus** on North Point Street, between Taylor and Mason, to Market Street downtown.

SOME FISHERMAN'S WHARF RESTAURANTS **Scoma's Fisherman's Wharf**, at the foot of Jones on Jefferson. **Castagnola's Restaurant, Alioto's Restaurant**, on Taylor, established in 1925. **A. Sabella's Restaurant. Fisherman's Grotto**, Fisherman's Wharf(on Taylor). **Tarantino's Restaurant. Franciscan Restaurant**, on The Embarca-dero. **Sabella & La Torre**, on Taylor Street near Jefferson. **Pompei's Grotto**, on Jefferson Street. **Tokyo Sukiyaki**, Jefferson Street at Taylor serves sashimi, sushi, and seafood. **McCormick & Kuleto's Seafood Restaurant**, Beach Street side of Ghirardelli Square, a superb new restaurant with sweeping views of the Bay; ask for a Bay-view table.

Some of San Francisco's best seafood restaurants are not located at the Wharf. **Scott's Seafood Grill & Bar**, one of the best in San Francisco, is located at 2400 Lombard Street on the corner of Scott. The **Hayes Street Grill**, on Hayes Street, known for its impeccably fresh fish, is located near the Civic Center. **Elka**, located in Japantown, is outstanding and serves "definitive seafood" (*see Tour 9*).

A fun place for music is **Lou's Pier 47**, near the foot of Jones and a block from the entrance to Fish Alley. It boasts "cool music and hot food."

McCormick & Kuleto's Seafood Restaurant
At Ghiradelli Square;
929-1730

Scott's Seafood Grill & Bar
2400 Lombard Street,
on the corner of Scott;
563-8988

Hayes Street Grill
324 Hayes Street;
863-5545

Elka
1625 Post Street;
922-7788

Lou's Pier 47
300 Jefferson Street,
near the foot of Jones;
771-0377

Introduction:
The Number One Tourist Destination

San Francisco's northern waterfront, from **Fisherman's Wharf** to **Fort Mason**, is one of the glories of this city, for it offers something for everyone, from the bustling carnival of the Wharf to quiet pierheads and windy bluffs with some of the most beautiful views of San Francisco Bay's ever-shifting colors and moods.

Fisherman's Wharf is San Francisco's single most popular visitor destination and attracts some eleven to twelve million people a year. Though it began to draw a few visitors in the late nineteenth century who came to watch the Italian American fishermen repairing their nets and working on their boats in this then-industrial district, today's booming tourist district is actually little more than thirty years old and is more contemporary than historic. Fisherman's Wharf is much more complex than most people think, though everyone notices the difference between the happy honky-tonk at one end and the spacious green parks at the other.

In 1853 Harry Meiggs built a long wharf near the foot of present-day Powell Street. Shipbuilders were active here in the 1860s along the sandy **North Beach** (now approximately Bay Street). With the construction of the Great Seawall, North Point Cove was quickly filled in. All the flat blocks from Bay Street north are landfill that soon obliterated the North Beach. With the filling of the cove, businesses moved here: lumber yards, warehouses, a woolen mill, chemical works, a gas lighting plant, and the Selby Lead and Smelting works. Later the California Fruit Canners Association and the **Ghirardelli Chocolate Company** built large factories on the northern waterfront. Piers and railyards served this important industrial zone.

In 1900 the fishing fleet was moved from the foot of Union Street, near present-day Levi's Plaza, to the foot of Taylor Street where a remnant survives today. **Fish Alley**, across Jefferson Street from The Cannery, between Leavenworth and Hyde streets, survives today like a fossil embedded in the bustling restaurant, retail, and hotel district. In the nineteenth century Italian Americans achieved a virtual monopoly in San Francisco's seafood industry. The hard and unpredictable work of fishing first drew Northern Italians from Genoa, who at one point comprised eighty percent of the fishermen. The Genoese captured the trade from the pioneer Chinese and developed the fleet and the operational structures of markets and fish wholesaling. By the early 1900s, however, the northerners were superseded by Neapolitans, Calabrians, and most important, Sicilians, whose descendants continue as the most important group of fishermen, dealers, and now restaurateurs. The Italian American fishermen developed a spirit of cooperation and camaraderie—*campagnismo*—that brought together fishermen from the same province against both the unpredictable elements and the unpredictable competition. Specializations evolved, with the Genoese engaged in deep-sea tuna-fishing for the statewide California market while the Sicilians caught most of the freshwater and inshore fish for the San Francisco market. Since the 1970s, some Vietnamese Americans have joined the ranks of San Francisco commercial fishermen.

Over time the progressive fishing-out of the Bay, nearby rivers, and the immediate coast has sent the fishermen farther and farther north. Today San Francisco's fishing fleet is only a pale, antiquated shadow of what it once was. Today the harbor at Eureka, California, far to the north near the Oregon border, has a substantial fishing fleet crowded around a genuine, working fisherman's wharf. San Francisco's fleet has become an atmospheric adornment to the booming tourist district that has been developed here since the 1960s. Long gone are the days when colorful *feluccas* with their three-cornered sails dotted the Bay. No longer does the fleet return at sundown "like a flock of sea birds scudding on the wind to their roost."

In 1958 the **International Longshoremen and Warehousemen's Union** built a handsome modern headquarters at 400 North Point Street, at the corner of Mason, designed by architect Henry Hill and engineer I. Thompsen. This stolid blue-collar bastion inadvertantly became famous when, in January of 1966, Ken Kesey and his Merry Pranksters hosted a Trips Festival here. Thousands of the new bohemians showed up, dropped then-legal acid, and spaced out on rock music and colored lights. The word *hippie* was born. San Francisco was in for big changes. Over the next decade San Francisco changed from a mixed blue-and-white collar town to one increasingly white collar. Blue-collar jobs in places like Fisherman's Wharf were replaced with low-paid retail jobs catering to tourists along the northern waterfront, or high-paying white-collar jobs in the new highrise Financial District. The transformation was dramatic here along the once-industrial Bay front, where a cluster of popular hotels replaced old railyards in what seemed a twinkling of the eye. The modernistic **I.L.W.U. hall** remains, but not many of the jobs it was built to serve. The big change in the district began in the 1960s and 1970s as tourism boomed while industrial maritime activities shifted to the expanding Port of Oakland across the Bay. The opening of **Cost Plus Imports** in 1958, the adaptation of the old **Ghirardelli Chocolate factory** to a major shopping complex in 1968, the rebuilding in 1968 of the 1907 California Fruit Canners Association's red brick cannery as The Cannery, a restaurant and shopping complex, and in 1978, the development of Pier 39 completely transformed the Wharf and made it *the* major tourist destination in San Francisco, an almost-instant attraction more attractive than the historic city itself. Today the San Francisco Port Commission derives more than half of its revenues from the leases to the parking lots, shops, and restaurants of Fisherman's Wharf. Securing these long-term leases is one of the great political plums in postindustrial San Francisco.

This is perhaps a good place to tell the story of San Francisco's famous foghorns, one the city's distinctive musics. After 1857, cannons boomed from the shore every half hour to guide ships during the frequent fogs that blanket the coast here. Later a giant bell was installed. In 1903, the Coast Guard began placing some fifty diaphragm foghorns around the Bay. In the 1930s single-tone diaphragm foghorns were installed. Each had its own tone and the melancholy music they created, coming from all directions in the all-obscuring fog, was wonderful to hear. Their basso profundo *beeee-ohhh* reverberated around the Bay until 1992. In that year the Coast Guard decided to replace the foghorns with modern high-pitched electronic beepers having all the melodiousness of car alarms. San Franciscans were

Note: *This chapter is divided into two parts, both of which begin at the Taylor Street Wharf:*

A **The lettered attractions** *trace a path to the east and cater to mass tourism. They end at popular Pier 39.*

2 **The numbered entries** *beginning with 2 trace a path west toward Ghirardelli Square and Fort Mason's Golden Gate National Recreation Area; these sites are more historic and environmental in character.*

It is possible to walk along the Bay front all the way from the Hyde Street Pier's historic ships to Fort Point in the Presidio. This is a bracing and highly scenic 3.5-mile hike much favored by nature lovers.

stunned. It was as if our favorite opera singer had lost his voice. What would happen next? Replace the cable cars with diesel buses? Vote Republican? San Franciscans suffered a collective identity crisis. After protests, the Coast Guard's solution was to allow the nonprofit U.S. Lighthouse Society to reactivate the Alcatraz foghorn. (The Golden Gate Bridge and San Francisco–Oakland Bay Bridge operate their own foghorns, which we can be sure will never be "improved" away.) So San Francisco got her foghorns back. The stately, measured music of the foghorns continues to waft over the fog-shrouded Bay like the profound laments of very old souls.

1 **Taylor Street Wharf, Crab Pots, and Restaurant Row**

The oldest center of attraction at Fisherman's Wharf is the row of fish stalls, outdoor crab pots, and waterfront restaurants at Taylor and Jefferson streets. Many of these restaurants look down on the fishing fleet and across the wide Bay. Walkaway crab cocktails seem to have been first promoted by Tomaso Castagnola in 1916. He got the idea from the stand-up chowder stands that once served the fishermen and market workers who had to eat on the run as they sold their perishable catch in the early morning. An arcade of crab pots lines a block of Taylor and part of Jefferson Street. The special treat here is sweet Dungeness crab trapped in pots along the Northern California coast. The traditional way for a San Franciscan to greet New Year's Day is with cracked crab and California white wine. Other seafood specialties served in the restaurants here are king and silver salmon; sea bass; ling, rock, and black cod; sand dabs; rex, and petrale sole; mackerel; ocean perch; halibut; abalone; and squid. Tiny flavorful shrimp and Olympia oysters from Washington State are also prized. A much favored local dish is cioppino, a shellfish and seafood stew flavored with tomatoes and white wine.

Many of the restaurants along this strip bear the names of locally prominent Italian American families who have moved over the generations from fishing to restaurants. Many of these restaurants are open until midnight and offer validated parking. Most post their menus at their entrance. Ask for a window table. There are more than a hundred eating places here. A partial list appears in the restaurant section at the beginning of this tour.

A **U.S.S.** *Pampanito* **/U.S. Navy Vessels/Pier 45**

Massive Pier 45, at the foot of Taylor on The Embarcadero, is one of the last vestiges of the working wharf and still serves the fishermen and fish brokers who crowd it before daybreak. Four large sheds and public parking occupy the big pier behind its Gothic Revival bulkhead building. You should walk to its end for an expansive view of the Bay. On the pier's east side the *U.S.S. Pampanito* is moored, a *Balao*-class submarine built in 1943 at Portsmouth Naval Shipyard, New Hampshire. She operated at a depth of six hundred feet, made six patrols, and sank five Japanese ships. Operated by the National Maritime Museum Association and opened to the public in 1982, she has exhibits onboard and a self-guided audio tour.

Pier 45 is also a favored berth for **U.S. Navy vessels** when they visit San Francisco (open to the public between 1 and 4 P.M. on Saturday and Sunday; free).

U.S.S. *Pampanito*/
U.S. Navy Vessels/Pier 45
Open daily, 9 A.M. to
9 P.M.; $3 for adults,
$2 for children
929-0202.

Jefferson Street

Pier 39

B **Ferry Slips/Alcatraz Island**
See Tour 16 for Alcatraz Island and the Preliminaries at the front of this guide for ferry routes.

C *Jefferson Street Amusement Zone*

Jefferson Street is Fisherman's Wharf's amusement strip lined with high-volume T-shirt and souvenir shops and wax museums. The two blocks from Taylor to Powell are the epicenter of all this activity. Jefferson has a populist mix of attractions, especially for young people, that makes it a magnet for vacationing families. During peak summer periods an estimated three thousand people per hour stroll by here, making Jefferson one of the most heavily traveled pedestrian corridors in the city. Street performers are drawn by the milling crowds. Entrepreneurial young boys stand on milk crates holding poses that they change intermittently with mechanical precision.

D **Pier 39**, *1978, Walker and Moody*
At the east end of the Jefferson Street strip is **Pier 39**, a shop and restaurant complex designed in 1978 by Walker and Moody surrounded by a large marina of white sailboats with blue canvas covers. Modern Pier 39 is built over a 1905 pier on Port Commission property under a controversial sixty-year lease. Its design features an enticing central walkway designed to draw the stroller down its length and past shops built out of recycled lumber from the old pier shed. The pavilion to the right of the entrance of the pier is a lively, noisy place of bumper cars and video games. At the far end of the pier is a delightful, gaily colored, two-level Venetian carousel that plays grand old-time oom-pah-pah music. Pier 39's best feature is its sweeping views of the Bay and Telegraph Hill with the downtown highrises popping up over it. The little-used perimeter walkway has wonderful views and is usually quite quiet. The loud barking you are likely to hear is from the herd of California sea lions that has taken a fancy to the marina just west of Pier 39. The randy and vocal sea lions call back and forth and have become an accidental visitor attraction.

② *The Historic Fishing Fleet*

San Francisco's historic fishing fleet ties up at the piers between Taylor and Hyde, north of Jefferson Street. The area is most active very early in the morning. By about 8 A.M. the catch has been sold and the fishermen and brokers are on their way home. Of the approximately 140 vessels berthed here, only 80 are licensed fishing boats and only about half of those are active year-round; twenty-five years ago, the Wharf had some 300 fishing boats. While the Wharf still lands about twenty million pounds of fish, possibly five to ten times that amount comes in by truck to supply the Bay Area's restaurants and fish markets.

Helen Throop Purdy described old Fisherman's Wharf in 1912:

If the fleet is out, you will find some of the fishermen left behind to mend their nets, festooning them along the wharf to dry, or busy about their boats—always picturesque—their love of color displayed in bright shirts, in red and blue Tams, or in their gay little boats, painted rainbow colors, bright blue, yellow, green or striped. And if you happen upon just the right time to see the fleet, the sight is unforgettable—dozens of these bright boats with their tawny, three-cornered sails like a flock of great, yellow butterflies as they glide over the water.

The Italian fishermen recreated in America their traditional vessel, the *felucca*, a narrow, fast, lateen-rigged ship with an ancient Mediterranean lineage. Over time, a new kind of fishing boat evolved in Northern California known as the "Monterey clipper" with a graceful, curved bow. Look carefully at the row of small fishing boats given "front row" berths facing Jefferson, between Taylor and Jones. They are the fragile descendants of the old fleet, industrial antiques well worth conserving.

While very few visitors perambulate it, the Port Commission has made every effort to open the water edge of the Wharf to pedestrians. You may walk all along the edge of the water up and down the wooden wharfs. Sleek seals (who eat only seafood and disdain bread) glide in and out among the boats. Seagulls and black cormorants fish here too. The small wood fisherman's chapel at the end of Pier 49 has one stained-glass window, over the door so that it is seen on exiting. It depicts a ship's steering wheel.

③ *Fish Alley*

A block up Jefferson Street, across from the foot of Jones, is **Fish Alley**, one of the last fragments of the working Fisherman's Wharf. Its proper name is **Tonquin Street** and it is built over a small sand and mud shoal named after the ship *Tonquin*, which was wrecked here in 1849. If you poke down half a block here you will be rewarded with a "backstage" view of the real Wharf with fishing boats tied up for the day and perhaps a seal quietly gliding through the still water. You will note that few tourists go even half a block off the beaten track to see the Real Thing.

④ The Cannery/Haslett Warehouse, *1907-09,*
Philip L. Bush; 1968, Joseph Esherick and Associates

Illusion is one of architecture's most effective methods. In the rebuilt Cannery the illusion is that this is an old industrial structure adapted in an *ad hoc* way for shops and restaurants. Its visitor-pleasing courtyards and internal mazes give the sense of unplanned reworkings over time. In reality, however, The Cannery, the brain-child of San Franciscan Leonard V. Martin, is an entirely new rein-forced concrete building constructed in 1968 and designed by Joseph Esherick and Associates. It is neatly inserted within the four brick walls of engineer Philip L. Bush's California Fruit Canners Association cannery built in 1907–09. Escalators take the browser up the levels of an open-air maze of shops; there are good views of the Bay from the top of the added third floor. The **Cannery Wine Cellars** has a good selection of California wines and will ship your purchases. On the third floor of the Cannery is the **Museum of the City of San Francisco**, which opened in 1991. It has earthquake memorabilia and some interesting artifacts but is not the caliber of museum the city deserves.

The courtyard on the west side of The Cannery was originally the railroad spur that served the peach cannery and its warehouse. The **Haslett Warehouse** was also designed by Philip L. Bush, between 1907 and 1909. Its monumental western brick wall faces Victorian Park across Hyde Street. The Haslett Warehouse has been publicly owned since 1963, when it was pur-chased by the Maritime Museum. Today it is a part of the Golden Gate National Recreation Area. It would be the perfect location for a combination National Maritime Museum on the ground floor, facing the Hyde Street Pier, and a serious museum of San Francisco facing the cable car turntable at Hyde and Beach streets. Today it sits in limbo awaiting flusher National Park Service budgets.

⑤ *Hyde Street Pier/Historic Ships*

The **Hyde Street Pier** at the foot of Hyde, near the cable car turntable, is one of San Francisco's most historically evocative places. The **Maritime Store** at the entrance to the pier has an outstanding selection of books and posters associated with ships and the sea, ship models, and the best regional guides. You may also obtain the National Park Service's excellent free map of the Golden Gate National Recreation Area here, which is useful if you wish to hike along the Golden Gate Promenade, explore the Presidio, or visit the redwoods in Muir Woods National Monument in Marin County across the Golden Gate.

The Hyde Street Pier was built to serve the Sausalito and Berkeley ferries, which mostly ceased operating after the Bay and Golden Gate bridges were built. (Today the Sausalito ferry departs from the Ferry Building at the foot of Market Street.) Eventually the pier became the mooring for a fleet of five historic ships, three

**The Cannery/
Haslett Warehouse**
*2801 Leavenworth Street
between Beach and
Jefferson Streets*

Cannery Wine Cellars
The Cannery; 673-0400

Museum of the City of San Francisco
*The Cannery, third floor;
Open Wednesday to
Sunday, 10 A.M. to
4 P.M.; free*

Haslett Warehouse

Hyde Street Pier

Maritime Store
*Open from 9:30 A.M.
to 6 P.M. daily;* 775-2665

Victorian Park/Hyde Street Cable Car Turntable
Hyde Street at Beach

Buena Vista Café
2965 Beach at Hyde;
474-5044

of which visitors may board. These historic ships recall the days when San Francisco Bay was an animated scene of sail and steam, and ships both great and small crowded the West Coast's most important harbor. Scattered along the pier are other exhibits including an ark (a flat-bottomed barge with a cottage built atop it used as a floating summer house), and the Victorian office of Tubbs Cordage furnished as it was a hundred years ago.

Tied up here is the sidewheel ferry *Eureka*, built in 1890 and once the world's largest passenger ferry. The white-painted *Eureka* was powered by a four-story steam engine and today carries a fleet of historic automobiles and trucks. Nearby is the *C. A. Thayer*, a wood-hull, three-masted schooner built in 1895 to carry lumber from the Pacific Northwest to booming San Francisco. Also tied up here is the hay-scow *Alma*, launched in 1891, a flat-bottomed, shallow-draft workhorse used to carry hay and lumber around the Bay. The ocean-going steam tug *Hercules*, appropriately named, towed sailing ships out to sea. The *Wapama* is a 1915 steam schooner that carried both cargo and passengers.

The steel-hulled, three-masted, square-rigged sailing ship *Balclutha*, launched in Glasgow, Scotland in 1886, was named for the ancient Gaelic name for the site of Dumbarton, Scotland, the home of Robert McMillan, her original owner. She made her maiden voyage around Cape Horn to San Francisco and served in the deep-water trade carrying wine and spirits from London, hardware from Antwerp, and coal from Wales. Returning to Europe she carried California wheat. She is a typical British merchant ship of the late Victorian era. After 1899 she flew the Hawaiian flag and transported lumber from Puget Sound to Australia, returning with coal for the locomotives of the Southern Pacific Railroad. From 1902 until 1930 she engaged in the Alaska salmon trade, carrying cannery supplies and up to three hundred men north for the fishing season. In 1906 she was renamed *The Star of Alaska;* she made her final voyage for the Alaska Packers Association in 1930, the last square-rigger in the salmon trade. From 1933 to 1952, she was gaudily painted and used as a showboat; eventually she was laid up on the Sausalito mud flats. In 1954, before she could be sold for scrap, she was purchased by the San Francisco Maritime Museum, which restored her original name and undertook a complete rehabilitation of the historic ship. The local shipping industry and eighteen labor unions participated in the year-long project. She opened as a part of the museum in 1955 painted her original colors.

6   **Victorian Park/Hyde Street Cable Car Turntable**, *1960, Thomas D. Church*
The Hyde Street cable car line is the most scenic of the three surviving lines and ends at the turntable in Victorian Park. The park was designed by Thomas D. Church in 1960 with a formal arrangement of a double row of benches facing each other and a central flower bed. The landscaping of the 5.6-acre park is kept low so as not to block the sweeping view of the Bay. The **Buena Vista Café** on Beach at Hyde, facing the park, is a fine bay-windowed Edwardian commercial-residential building of 1911 designed by August Nordin. This is a characteristic San Francisco Edwardian building. The café, opened in 1941, is reputed to be the place where Irish coffee was first served in the United States, in 1952. (Caffeine, alcohol, and butterfat; is there anything more?) This is a fine place for an early morning breakfast.

❼ National Maritime Museum/Aquatic Park Casino, *1939,*
William M. Mooser III
At the west end of Victorian Park is the white, streamlined **Aquatic Park Casino** built in 1939 by the WPA and designed by William M. Mooser III. Since 1951 it has been the home of the **Maritime Museum,** now part of the GGNRA. The Casino, one of the great Streamline Moderne buildings in the West, was designed in imitation of a luxury liner. (It was never intended for gambling and was always meant to be a park building.) The rectangular, three-level reinforced concrete structure has semicircular ends. Each level is stepped back, giving the appearance of a ship's decks. Porthole windows, steel railings, and cowl ventilators complete the nautical theme.

National Maritime Museum/Aquatic Park Casino, *Beach Street at the foot of Polk; Open daily 10 A.M. to 5 P.M. except Monday;* 556-8177.

Municipal Pier in Aquatic Park

Ghirardelli Square
900 North Point Street; 775-5500

The building is flanked by bleachers, two streamlined towers intended for public address systems, and two restrooms set quite far apart. The entire site was landscaped to match the building, and a man-made beach was created facing Aquatic Park where there was once a railroad trestle and a polluted bayshore. The complex was intended to accommodate five thousand bathers daily, but the water is too cold and few came. (You will, however, spot some hardy, cold-blooded swimmers here from the nearby swimming and rowing clubs.) The building is enlivened with WPA art works. Sargent Johnson carved the greenish slate decorations around the entrance, and Hilaire Hiler painted the vivid murals depicting undersea life in the lobby.

The Casino was closed for many years until the Maritime Museum was established by Karl Kortum in 1951. The nautical building is filled with ship models, artifacts, and old paintings and photographs that make San Francisco's history as a seaport come alive.

• Municipal Pier/Aquatic Park
The construction of the curved, 1,850-foot-long **Municipal Pier in Aquatic Park,** between 1929 and 1934, and the addition of the Casino together make this one of the finest waterfront parks in any American city. The Muni Pier is a quiet spot. Asian American fishermen favor it, as do San Franciscans seeking peace and quiet and a spacious view of the Bay. The view from here is stunning on a clear night.

❽ Ghirardelli Square *, 1866, William M. Mooser; 1900–22,*
William M. Mooser II; 1962–68, Wurster, Bernardi & Emmons; John Matthias;
Lawrence Halprin & Associates, landscape architects; Ruth Asawa, fountain
Ghirardelli Square is a San Francisco landmark in several senses. Its handsome old red brick factory buildings are architectural landmarks; its fine old electric sign is a visual landmark; and its conversion into shops and restaurants was an economic landmark in the evolution of the postindustrial city. Visitors are sure to enjoy strolling here, shopping in its sixty quality shops and dining in one of its dozen restaurants serving an international array of cuisines.

Domingo Ghirardelli, born in Rapallo, Italy, came to Gold Rush San Francisco in 1850 via Peru and began the manufacture of chocolate in a shop now in the Jackson Square Historic District. His sons expanded the business and in 1893 pur-

Clock Tower building
*on the corner of North
Point Street and Larkin*

Mandarin Restaurant
673-8812

chased this then-remote block with the 1866 Pioneer Woolen Mill designed by William M. Mooser, one of the oldest factories in the West. Around that old building (placed at an eccentric angle because it was oriented to the original shoreline, not the city's street grid) Domingo's sons began the construction of a model factory. Architect William Mooser II, son of the designer of the Woolen Mill and father of the designer of the Aquatic Park Casino, designed the crenellated complex in stages between 1900 and 1922. The buildings were constructed of brick and timber with cast stone trim. Eventually the buildings ringed the block, leaving a central lawn where workers ate lunch when the weather permitted. The last building in the complex was the **Clock Tower building**, whose ornament was modeled on that of the château at Blois. Its vestibule has a mosaic of an eagle, the Ghirardelli trademark, and antique millstones from the old chocolate works downtown. The great electric sign reading "Ghirardelli" capped the factory in 1923 and was visible to passenger ships entering the Bay.

Advances in technology made the old plant obsolete and a modern chocolate plant was built across the Bay in San Leandro. For a while it seemed that the historic factory would be replaced by highrise apartments. William M. Roth, a civic-minded San Franciscan and heir to the Matson shipping fortune, bought the block to prevent its demolition and then cast about for a new use for it. He decided to create a shop and restaurant complex. He added an underground garage, completed the ring of red brick buildings with new ones designed by Wurster, Bernardi & Emmons, and created a series of landscaped terraces designed by Lawrence Halprin & Associates. John Matthias designed the small red-brick pavilion buildings with the fanciful roofs in the center of the complex. Thus Ghirardelli Square is a fusion of new *and* old buildings, not simply the adaptation of existing structures. The use of two contemporary designers, not just one, avoided the monotony so prevalent in today's large new developments—an innovation only a few later developers have followed.

To create a focal point for the Square, sculptor Ruth Asawa was commissioned to design *Andrea* in 1968, the refreshing fountain of nursing mermaids surrounded by water, lily pads, tortoises, and dancing frogs. Bill Roth wanted to preserve even the aroma of the old chocolate works, and while that wasn't possible, some of the old German machinery was saved and installed in the ground floor of the Clock Tower building behind the Ghirardelli Ice Cream Parlor. Built into the wall are three cacao-bean roasters, belt-driven chocolate mills, giant mixers, and conching machines.

The most interesting interior in Ghirardelli Square is that of the superb **Mandarin Restaurant** located on the top floor of the old Woolen Mill. The old brick-and-timber interior was retained, enhanced with tile floors, and filled with fine Chinese art. For a sweeping overview of the Square and all of Fisherman's Wharf, take the elevator or climb to the top of the glass-enclosed stairs of the Chocolate Building in the far southwest corner of the Square, near the Gaylord India Restaurant.

Art lovers may wish to make a detour to see **872–80 North Point Street**, a half-block east of Ghirardelli Square. Behind the Dutch door is a narrow passageway leading to a surprising hidden garden surrounded by art and rug galleries and designers' studios. This lush courtyard is a prime example of Northern California's infatuation with plants. Vine-draped decks, porches, and staircases surround what was originally just another back yard, but which here has been transformed into a jungle of greenery with a soothing, trickling fountain. Tucked away here is **North Point Gallery**, a virtual museum of nineteenth-century California landscape painting with examples of grand mountain scenery and views of California a century ago. The art shown in this intimate gallery is one of the best windows into the history of the West.

9 **Fort Mason Center ("Fort Culture")/**
Golden Gate National Recreation Area (GGNRA) Headquarters/
Liberty Ship S.S. *Jeremiah O'Brien*

At the foot of Van Ness Avenue, near the entrance to the Municipal Pier, is a narrow pathway. Just past the curving that climbs the bluff of **Fort Mason**, today the headquarters of the **Golden Gate National Recreation Area**, established in 1972. (There are automobile entrances to Fort Mason at Bay and Franklin streets and at Laguna and Beach streets that lead to a large free parking lot.) On this bluff, with its spectacular views of the Bay, Spanish soldiers from the Presidio built a small battery in 1779 that they christened Batería San José. In 1850, Black Point, as the Yankees called it, perhaps because of the dark laurel that grew here, was one of the three important U.S. Army reservations created within San Francisco by President Millard Fillmore. The Army did not immediately occupy the point, so squatters built houses here. In 1863 the squatters were removed and the commanding site was terraced for batteries as part of the system of harbor defenses. Recent archaeological excavations have uncovered part of these Civil War–era batteries. Eventually, a Rodman cannon from the Smithsonian Institution will be mounted here. Fort Mason became the headquarters of the commanding general of the U.S. Army in the West during the Indian wars in the interior.

The three large Victorian houses on the wooded bluff, built between 1855 and 1863, are still officers' housing. A cluster of seven Victorian enlisted men's houses built between 1864 and 1891 survives on the west, or inland, side of Franklin Street. Nearby McDowell Hall, built in 1877 as the commandant's residence, is today an Officers Club. The name "Fort Mason" was adopted in 1882 in honor of Colonel Mason, the military governor of California from 1847 to 1849.

The in-harbor fortifications were soon obsolete, though Fort Mason remained an administrative and logistical center as the Quartermaster's Depot. Three substantial piers were constructed in 1912, and large warehouses behind them three years later. All were connected with the port's Belt Line Railroad by a tunnel under the bluff. The post saw its peak activity during World War II as a point of embarkation for 1.6 million soldiers who passed through here on their way to the Pacific Theater. Today, at Pier 3 East, the Liberty Ship **S.S.** *Jeremiah O'Brien* is moored, the last unaltered Liberty Ship of the 2,751 launched between 1941 and 1945. She serves as a memorial to the men of the U.S. Merchant Marine.

872–80 North Point Street

North Point Gallery
885-0657

Fort Mason Center ("Fort Culture")/ Golden Gate National Recreation Area (GGNRA) Headquarters/ Liberty Ship S.S. *Jeremiah O'Brien, Phone 979-3010 for information.*
S.S. *Jeremiah O'Brien Open daily from 9 A.M. to 3 P.M.; $2 adults, $3 children, $5 family. 441-3101*

Golden Gate National Park Association, *Fort Mason, Building 201, San Francisco 94123-1308; 776-0693*

The Magic Theater
441-8822

Greens Restaurant
Fort Mason Building A.
Open for lunch daily;
dinner Tuesday to
Sunday; reservations
advised; 771-6222

The military was the only institution with the foresight and the power to make public reservations in the Bay Area in 1850. Vast stretches of shoreline including the scenic Marin Headlands and islands such as Alcatraz were reserved for harbor fortification and slowly developed and landscaped over a century of occupation. But changes in technology and high costs made these in-city installations redundant.

Proposals were floated by developers to build on these waterfront sites, but local environmental groups saw the magnificent properties as part of the national heritage and as potential parks for the Bay Area's five million residents and millions of visitors. The late San Francisco Congressman Philip Burton, one of the most powerful, abrasive, and principled members of Congress and a staunch environmentalist, enthusiastically supported that concept and made this park his local monument. Over the objections of the traditionalists in the National Park Service who did not want national parks inside cities, Congressman Burton forced the creation of the GGNRA in 1972. It was assembled from a core of historic lands and buildings no longer needed by the military. Burton did not stop there. His Omnibus Parks Bill of 1980 put more land into parks than anyone in the history of the nation. Today, the GGNRA is one of the nation's most popular national parks. The 1902 hospital in the center of the post is today GGNRA Headquarters; the information center here stocks maps and brochures; call 556-0560 for information. A bronze statue of Congressman Burton has been erected at Fort Mason facing the Golden Gate.

To insulate the new urban national park from politics, the independent, nonprofit Fort Mason Foundation was formed to manage the facilities. The Fort Mason Center opened in 1977 and sponsors fairs, festivals, and exhibits. The piers and warehouses at Fort Mason became home to more than fifty nonprofit visual and performing arts, cultural, and environmental organizations. This book can only lead you to this Ali Baba's cave of culture. **The Magic Theater** is just one of the many treats here. Write or phone the **Golden Gate National Park Association** for information on the many wonderful happenings here all year long.

One of Fort Mason's most popular features is the San Francisco Zen Center's **Greens Restaurant**, a gourmet vegetarian restaurant with a splendid view of the Golden Gate.

Continuation: Golden Gate Promenade to Fort Point and the Presidio

From the Hyde Street Pier to Fort Point near the Golden Gate Bridge is the 3.5-mile footpath of the Golden Gate Promenade along the scenic, breezy northern shore of San Francisco. The path is especially popular with joggers. It passes through Aquatic Park, Fort Mason, the marina in Gashouse Cove, flat Marina Green, Crissy Field, the old Coast Guard station in the Presidio, and then along the granite seawall to historic Fort Point, begun in 1853 and completed in 1861. Looming above the fort is the monumental south tower of the magnificent Golden Gate Bridge (*see Tour 14*).

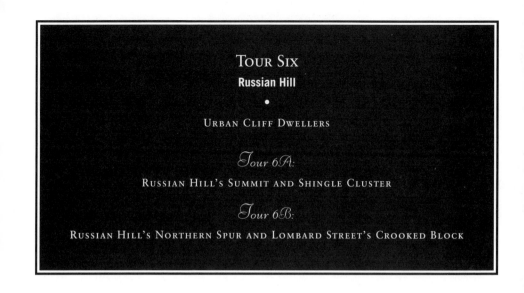

TOUR SIX
Russian Hill

•

URBAN CLIFF DWELLERS

Tour 6A:
RUSSIAN HILL'S SUMMIT AND SHINGLE CLUSTER

Tour 6B:
RUSSIAN HILL'S NORTHERN SPUR AND LOMBARD STREET'S CROOKED BLOCK

Russian Hill viewed from Sacramento and Mason streets
near the Fairmont Hotel atop Nob Hill.
The brick building in the valley with the arched windows is the
Cable Car Powerhouse and Museum at Washington and Mason streets,
built in 1887 and rebuilt in 1907.

What These Tours Cover
Preliminaries
Introduction: Urban Cliff Dwellers

**TOUR 6A:
RUSSIAN HILL'S
SUMMIT AND SHINGLE
CLUSTER**

1 Hyde and Union: Edwardian Commercial Crossroad
2 Union and Leavenworth: Post-Fire Apartments
3 1101 Green Street
4 1000 Block of Green Street
5 The Summit Apartments
6 945 Green Street
7 Macondray Lane
8 1821 Jones Street
9 Vallejo Street Improvements
10 Russian Hill Place
11 The Marshall Houses
12 The Hermitage
13 Williams-Polk House
14 Florence Street Pueblo Revival Group and the
     Livermore House
15 1000 Block of Broadway

Continuation
Chinatown and North Beach, or Nob Hill

**TOUR 6B:
RUSSIAN HILL'S
NORTHERN SPUR AND
LOMBARD STREET'S
CROOKED BLOCK**

16 1100 Block of Filbert/Steepest Paved Street
17 2115-29 Hyde Street
18 Greenwich Street Stub/Alice Marble Tennis Courts
19 Fannie Osbourne Stevenson House
20 The Crooked Block/1000 Block of Lombard Street
21 The San Francisco Art Institute

Continuation
Fisherman's Wharf, North Beach, Chinatown, or Union Square

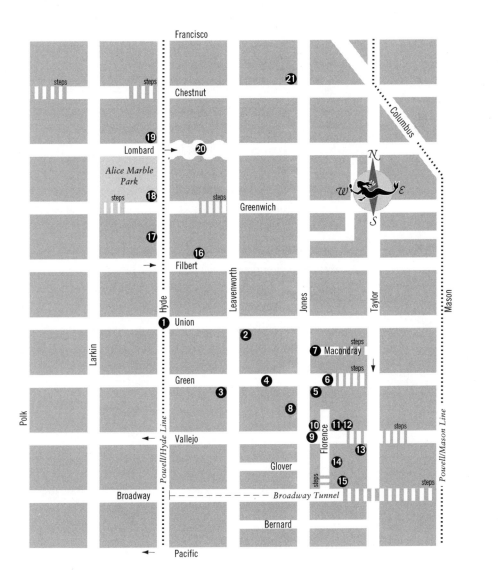

Russian Hill

San Francisco Art Institute
800 Chestnut, at Jones

Tower Records
Columbus and Bay

Preliminaries

THE BEST WAY
TO SEE
RUSSIAN HILL

Russian Hill is a quiet residential island in the sky overlooking the historic core of San Francisco. The best way to see it is slowly, on foot, step by step. Large tour buses are barred from the hill's steep streets and it is unlikely that drivers will enjoy negotiating the hill's extremely sharp grades and surprise dead ends. With more cable car trackage than in any other part of San Francisco, you can combine cable car rides and walks.

Pick almost any route zigzagging across the hill's two summits, looking back frequently as you walk for retrospective views. Climb the landscaped staircases where street grades become too steep for anything but stairs. Pay attention to the abstract patterns created by wooden stairs and glassed-in sunporches on the backs of so many buildings. Note the penthouses added here and there to exploit the panoramic views and how rooms and bay windows "lean" toward distant vistas. Peek over, but do not open, garden gates for glimpses down the unexpected front gardens that survive here and there on the hill. Take the time to let the sweeping views from the steep intersections seep in. Above all, do not rush. The hill will open itself only if given time.

Russian Hill is worth a second, evening, stroll once you've become familiar with it in daylight. The views of the downtown's lit-up glass highrises—with the slim Transamerica Pyramid standing away from the mass and the inky blue-black Bay with its necklace of twinkling orange lights and great illuminated suspension bridges—seem all the more brilliant from the dark, abrupt streets of Russian Hill. The hill is safe to walk about on at night, though the sidewalks will seem deserted. The view from the roof deck of the modern addition to the **San Francisco Art Institute** is splendid. Two blocks downhill, at Columbus and Bay, at the edge of the Fisherman's Wharf district, is **Tower Records**, open until midnight seven days a week and stocked with the city's largest selection of recordings.

Parking

Russian Hill is best approached by cable car or taxi to its summit. Do not expect to find a parking space here because there aren't any; parking is limited to two hours between 8 A.M. and 9 P.M. for those without neighborhood residential parking stickers.

Transportation

The **41 Union electric trolley bus** links Russian Hill with North Beach, Chinatown, and then the Financial District and Embarcadero Center. Going west, the 41 Union line passes between the north slope of posh Pacific Heights and the well-to-do Marina District and serves the lively restaurant and shopping district along **Union Street**. Both the **Powell-Mason and the Powell-Hyde cable car lines** serve Russian Hill. The Powell-Hyde line is the most scenic and traverses the steepest hills. *(See the entry on cable cars in the Preliminaries chapter at the front of this guide.)*

RESTAURANTS, CAFÉS, AND BARS

There are a few restaurants sprinkled on Russian Hill, particularly down Hyde from Union Street. They generally serve a neighborhood clientele. **Le Petit Café** is a neighborhood oasis. A very fine Italian restaurant at the summit of the hill in a quiet setting, **Allegro** has dinner seven days, and prepares box lunches; excellent. The **San Francisco Art Institute Café** has a splendid view of the Bay and is, of course, frequented by art students. **Swensen's Ice Cream** has the best ice cream on Russian Hill; a favorite with the hill dwellers. The nationwide chain began here in 1948.

Le Petit Café
2164 Larkin, at Green;
776-5356

Allegro
1701 Jones Street, at
Broadway; 928-4002

San Francisco Art Institute Café
800 Chestnut; 749-4567

Swensen's Ice Cream
southwest corner of Union and Hyde streets;
775-6818

Introduction: Urban Cliff Dwellers

Russian Hill rises from the center of the old city and enjoys views of almost everything that is quintessentially San Franciscan: the serene Bay, the great bridges, Alcatraz, Angel Island, the Financial District towers, Coit Tower atop Telegraph Hill, and the green Presidio. It is the part of San Francisco best served by the historic cable cars. The famous hill is diverse, beautiful, tranquil, and very classy. It's the kind of neighborhood where you might overhear someone practicing the cello on a quiet morning.

Russian Hill appears as a name on U.S. Coast Survey maps as early as 1859. The Russian Hill Neighbors Association defines the neighborhood as the thirty-four blocks bounded by **Taylor, Pacific, Polk,** and **Francisco** streets. The hill merges with Nob Hill to the south at Pacific Avenue. Its summit is at Vallejo Street between Taylor and Jones, with an elevation of 294 feet. To the northwest, at Hyde and Lombard, is the hill's northwest spur with dramatic views of the north Bay and the Golden Gate.

In 1850 minister Bayard Taylor described a San Francisco winter seen from underdeveloped Russian Hill: "When the floating gauze of mist had cleared off the water, the sky was without a cloud for the remainder of the day, and of a fresh, tender blue, which was exquisite relief to the pale green of the hills." Taylor took to climbing the hill "just in the rear of the town" from where the harbor, the strait into San Pablo Bay, the Golden Gate, and the horizon of the Pacific could be seen. He wrote that "[O]n the top of the Hill are the graves of several Russians, who came out in the service of the Russian [fur trapping] company, each surmounted with a black cross, bearing an inscription in their language. All this ground, however, has been surveyed, staked into lots, and sold, and at the same rate of growth the city will not be long in climbing the hill and disturbing the rest of the Muscovites."

Years ago, excavations for retaining walls near Jones and Vallejo uncovered some unidentified graves that might have been those of the pioneer "Muscovites."

Jasper O'Farrell's rigid gridiron of blocks was projected over the abrupt hill creating some streets too steep to pave, which end in stairways. (The steepest paved street in San Francisco is on the downtown side of Russian Hill, the 1100 block of Filbert between Leavenworth and Hyde streets.) Old photographs show sturdy, well-maintained fences guarding Russian Hill's unbuilt lots from the encroachment of squatters. No public reservations for open land or parks were provided for in the original city survey of Russian Hill; the city has had to buy sites over time for public needs. Ina Coolbrith Park was bought by the city in 1858 for a school site and a schoolhouse stood there from 1864 to 1877. The green summit block bounded by Hyde, Larkin, Greenwich, and Lombard, today the **Alice Marble Tennis Courts**, was a reservoir property of the private Spring Valley Water Company acquired by the municipality in 1930 when it bought the water company.

In 1861, Captain David Jobson erected a forty-foot wooden observation tower on the hill's summit. The ex-mariner become real estate dealer charged two bits to climb up his tower though there was little to be seen from its top that couldn't be enjoyed from the ground. It seems that San Franciscans could not really enjoy a view that cost nothing. Large blocks of land on the hill were owned by Nicholas Luning, an old-time banker who boasted that he never improved a foot of his property; land speculation was his specialty.

Houses were built all around the hill before development crept up its steep slopes. Not until the Presidio & Ferries Railroad's cable line on Union Street came to the top of the hill in 1880 did the summit become popular as a place to live. The cable line on Mason Street was not built by the Ferries & Cliff House Railway until 1888. The dramatic north-south Hyde Street cable line that descends to Victorian Park opened as an extension of the California Street Cable Railroad as late as 1891.

Russian Hill's initial population was not wealthy like that on Nob Hill's redeveloped summit; houses much like those built anywhere else in the Victorian city popped up on its slopes. A few houses had large gardens and fine views of the growing city and the crowded harbor below. The low land costs here permitted a unique cluster of artistic buildings and gardens to appear on the summit block bounded by Taylor, Broadway, Jones, and Vallejo streets. At the head of the street, where a handsome concrete balustrade and cliff-edge park are today, the Reverend Joseph Worcester built an inexpensive, one-story redwood and shingle cottage in 1890 that looked down on the city. Worcester was a Swedenborgian minister from Massachusetts with a mystic love of nature. His deliberately simple cottage with its exposed wood introduced a new aesthetic and philosophy to overdecorated Victorian San Francisco. Influenced by the Arts and Crafts Movement, some houses and interiors such as Worcester's strove to look "natural." (His influential cottage was demolished for a highrise that was never built. The fine **Church of the New Jerusalem** that he commissioned from A. Page Brown in 1895 is perfectly preserved in Pacific Heights. It is included in Tour 15 among the city's great interiors.) Those with small budgets but advanced tastes were attracted to the summit of the hill. The Worcester cottage and the nearby "Marshall houses" built by one of his parishioners were joined by other brown-shingled houses and flats that were built over the years by Horatio P. Livermore, who owned much of the block at the Vallejo summit. Livermore and other Russian Hill dwellers commissioned some of San Francisco's best architects to design artistic houses here, many set behind gardens and under what grew to become tall trees. Working-class housing appeared along the eastern slope facing North Beach. By the time the earthquake and fire came in 1906, Russian Hill had attracted her share of artists. During the conflagration of 1906, writer James Hopper passed over Russian Hill: "Upon the top of the Jones Street hill, in the middle of the street, the only thing standing in that direction for miles was a piano. A man was playing upon it. I could see his hands rising and falling, his body swaying. In the wind his long black hair and loosened tie streamed. The wind bore the sounds away from me, but in a lull, I finally heard the music. It was Saint-Saëns's *Danse Macabre.*" By 1919, Edward A. Morphy noted that the top of Russian Hill "harbors that perhaps not wholly unconscious pride of superiority to its environment which is the privilege of every place that becomes the abode of the intellectuals."

But the block or two of Russian Hill featured here and in architectural histories (and only partially visible from the sidewalk) are not really the most important phase of Russian Hill's development. That came after the earthquake and fire of 1906 cleared away almost all of the hill's buildings. It is the post-1906 rebuilding that is the stuff of contemporary Russian Hill. And it is too easily overlooked, for extraordinary buildings do not make a city; the texture of its "ordinary" ones, the buildings most people live in and use, count most. In place of the small cottages and large single-family houses that had covered most of the prefire slopes of Nob and Russian hills, apartment houses were built between 1906 and the 1920s. Most of these frame buildings were two to four stories high. There was a small eruption of isolated 1920s "Spanish" and later 1930s Art Deco concrete highrise apartment buildings as well. In 1939, Charles Caldwell Dobie complained that Russian Hill was attracting "ten-story apartment buildings which house millionaires, writers of best sellers, and opulent bootleggers."

Pre-1974 city planning permitted tall buildings on the tops of hills to help "define" them, and to preserve views from the slopes. Along Green Street on the summit of Russian Hill a spine of very large highrises was built to take advantage of the commanding views. They are the last of their kind to be built, for masses of such buildings (and their occupants' automobiles) threatened to overwhelm the neighborhood. Russian Hill residents and property owners, better educated than most and familiar with the power of city zoning, pressed the city to impose a reasonable height limit that would allow for multiunit develop without turning the hill's streets into canyons of skyscrapers. After much agitation, a forty-foot height limit was imposed on the hill in 1974. Over time this four-story limit was extended to virtually all of San Francisco's residential neighborhoods. Thus Russian Hill's active citizens spearheaded the conservation of San Francisco's neighborhoods and traditional housing stock through modern height limits.

Tour 6A:
Russian Hill's Summit and Shingle Cluster

❶ *Hyde and Union: Edwardian Commercial Crossroad*

Hyde Street cable line

29 Russell Place

The **Hyde Street cable line** was built in 1891 as an extension of the California Street Cable Railroad. It was built to link Russian Hill residents with the Union Square retail district, not to serve Fisherman's Wharf and Aquatic Park, its current pole of attraction. Because this cable line was built so late and cut a north-south crosstown path over the older east-west cable lines, the Hyde Street grip, the man who operates the lever that holds or releases the moving cable, has to drop his cable more than any other gripman. Where transit lines crossed, as at Hyde and Union, corner buildings (allowed to cover 100 percent of their lots—inside lots had to leave back yards) were built with commercial uses on their ground floors and affordable apartments on their second, third, or fourth floors. At Hyde and Union, where **Swensen's Ice Cream** store takes one corner, this pattern survives.

The commercial establishments clustered here, food markets, laundries, the ice cream place, cafés, restaurants, and shops, serve a local clientele. Today the Union and Hyde intersection is insulated by congestion. San Franciscans do not drive here because there is no place to park; tourists pass through it on the packed cable cars without daring to get off. Thus the residents have this intersection to themselves, more or less.

To literary historian Don Herron, **29 Russell Place**, the simple, gabled, brown-shingled cottage on a nearby side street off Hyde Street, between Union and Green, is "one of the most important literary sites in post–World War II America." It was here, in 1952, in Neal and Carolyn Cassady's attic study, that Jack Kerouac drafted three of his major works, *On The Road*, *Visions of Cody*, and *Doctor Sax*. (Carolyn Cassady described this *ménage à trois* in her 1976 memoir *Heart Beat*.)

❷ *Union and Leavenworth: Post-Fire Apartments*

The intersection of Union and Leavenworth should be carefully "danced." Look down all the corners of the intersection from the sidewalk. (Pedestrians have the right of way at these crosswalks, but some drivers do not know this, or do not obey it. Be careful.) The views here are exceptional and give you a taste of why apartments on Russian Hill are so sought after. To the north down Leavenworth is Alcatraz and wooded Angel Island State Park behind it. To the east is the summit of Telegraph Hill with Coit Tower, one pier of the silver Bay Bridge to the right, the Contra Costa hills, and on a clear day, pyramidal Mt. Diablo on the far horizon. San Francisco has historically placed parks on hilltops, and schools near parks, if possible. Here the classic pattern of San Francisco's white and green building and park development is displayed dramatically. Most of the distant peaks and ridges are parks as well, giving the dense, white-cube city a permanent frame of green.

1101 Green Street

1111–33 Green

1088 Green Street

Feusier Octagon House
1067 Green

The reconstruction-era buildings of two to four stories on the southwest corner of Union and Leavenworth epitomize the basic fabric of post-1906 Russian Hill. The even rhythm of their bays pulls all the buildings together. This row of three-story, bay-windowed flats is a classic example of how fine postfire reconstruction was. These are outstanding blocks of great regional architecture. Rising from the summit a block away is a tall, bleak concrete highrise from the boom of the 1960s.

3 1101 Green Street, *1930, H. C. Baumann*

At the southwest corner of Leavenworth and Green rises the white, Art Deco shaft of 1101 Green, a twenty-story reinforced concrete apartment building designed by the prolific H. C. Baumann and completed in 1930. The elegant tower has a heavily ornamented neo-Churrigueresque entrance and lobby on the high corner. Shallow bay windows project from the skyscraper. Its rooftop utility penthouse is styled to complete the building's profile. Generous wall space, painted a light-reflecting white, makes even such a huge building blend with the city like one crystal longer than the others in a cluster. The garage entrance is minimalized in the design, tucked downhill and covered with an opaque (not a see-through) door. In every way this building is superior in design to the residential highrises that came after it in the 1960s and 1970s.

Next door, at **1111–33 Green**, a complex of Tudor-gabled, bay-windowed apartments are built atop a high retaining wall. The walls here show how drastically the hill was graded.

4 *1000 Block of Green Street*

The 1000 block of Green Street, to the left between Leavenworth and Jones, has at its heart a cluster of eleven setback houses, flats, and apartments with fenced front gardens. Each building is in a different architectural style. Street trees further the garden enclave feeling. The structures are set like small volumes between the great bookends of the flanking concrete highrises. The sudden contrast in the scale of buildings here makes this a very American space; a place developed by individuals each with varied, clashing imaginations.

Standing to the left of its concrete highrise neighbor, the Tudor Revival former Engine House No. 31 at **1088 Green Street** was built in 1908 and designed by City Architect Newton J. Tharp. It was deactivated in 1952 and bought by philanthropist Louise S. Davies in 1958. She restored it and permits the Russian Hill Neighbors and the Scottish-American St. Andrews Society to use it for meetings. In 1978 she donated it to the National Trust for Historic Preservation.

The most curious building on the block is the **Feusier Octagon House** across the street, built in 1859 and given an added story and a mansard roof with an octagonal cupola in the 1870s or early 1880s by produce merchant Louis Feusier. It has a high basement and is built out of an early concretelike material. Its form follows that suggested by phrenologist Orson S. Fowler in his *A Home for All*, a book touting octagonal houses as healthier to live in. (A frame octagonal house near Union Street's shops has been preserved by the Colonial Dames of America; that **Octagon House** is open to the public.)

Next door, **1055 Green Street** was built about 1866 and then completely reworked by Julia Morgan in 1915 for importer and merchant David Atkins. Morgan transformed a simple Italianate house into a stucco Beaux Arts villa with an entrance recessed under the *piano nobile* with its arcade of windows. The house sits in a garden.

The O'Brien House at **1045 Green Street** next door was built about 1867 in the Italianate style and remodeled with brown shingles and a cupola in the Craftsman style. It looks like it was originally a firehouse, but it was always a dwelling. The house was bought by John O'Brien, an employment and real estate agent, in 1875. His son, Charles W. O'Brien, a postman, added the shingles and the turret between 1910 and 1916. A side bay window was added later.

At **1039–43 Green Street**, behind a vintage iron fence, is a three-story, three-flat Italianate building with an unusual exterior staircase. It was built in 1885 and designed by the often showier Newsom Brothers, Samuel and Joseph Cather. Four buildings down the block and hidden behind and above its ivy-covered garage is **1011 Green Street**, best seen from across the street. This interesting house was designed by Roland I. Stringham in 1925. It creates privacy for itself with its garage and marked setback. Its brown shingles are elegantly complemented with black-painted trim. An iron bracket braces its brick chimney.

At **1020 Green Street**, across the street, there is a fine contemporary stucco house and three-car garage with Tuscan pillars and a slate roof. Visible over the low wall here is the elegant house itself with a copper-domed entrance, a slate roof, and simple modern windows. A flagstone-surrounded pool glints in the front yard.

At **1030 Green Street**, behind a brick wall and a green hedge, is a fine Pueblo Revival house designed in 1913 by Oscar Haupt. This two-story stucco residence has a square turret and a recessed side entrance with a Tuscan arcade. **1040 Green Street** was built in 1912 to designs by Llewellyn B. Dutton. It combines Colonial Revival features with a stucco exterior. The detached garage was added in 1953.

The jewel of the block is **1050 Green Street**, the George A. Bos Apartments, designed by Lewis P. Hobart in 1913. This five-story, Classical Revival stuccoed apartment building is one of the most elegant small buildings in San Francisco. Hobart studied at the École des Beaux Arts in Paris between 1901 and 1903. Here he brought a Parisian feel to a San Francisco apartment house. Its black wrought-iron front door is beautiful at night when lighted from behind. The simple garden is startlingly effective in creating an aristocratic air. The building backs up on Macondray Lane at the summit's edge and enjoys fine views to the north. Walk east on Green Street toward the modern base of The Summit Apartments.

Octagon House
2645 Gough
Open to the public on the second Sunday and the second and fourth Thursday of each month, from noon to 4 P.M.; free; 441-7512

1055 Green Street

1045 Green Street

1039–43 Green Street

1011 Green Street

1020 Green Street

1030 Green Street

1040 Green Street

1050 Green Street

The Summit Apartments
999 Green Street

945 Green Street

947 Green Street

1950 Jones Street

15–17 Macondray Lane

❺ The Summit Apartments, *1965, Claude Oakland & Associates*
Looming up at the southeast corner of Jones Street is this thirty-one story 1965 residential highrise designed by Claude Oakland & Associates and built for Joseph Eichler, the developer of much of the middle-class stucco housing in the Sunset District in the 1940s and 1950s. Eichler reserved a two-story penthouse atop the spectacularly placed tower for himself. In the 1960s, high-art buildings strove, and succeeded, in setting themselves apart from their urban context. The Summit Apartments is a sculpted piece of futuristic design, quite successful if contemplated in the abstract. It stands on its corner and presents a vast, blank, multistoried parking structure to the neighborhood.

The highrise's design was so ambitious that it created a space with a fine view but no use. Atop the garage is a dead "park space" underneath the tower visible from the stairs at the end of Russian Hill Place. The design of the glass tower—if glass residential towers are appropriate in San Francisco, an arguable proposition—is very well done. The tower has the air of a movement perhaps best called "Brasilia Modern."

❻ 945 Green Street, *1927-28, Bos and Quandt*
Just east of The Summit Apartments is a rocky outcropping that pinches Green Street. In the *cul-de-sac* at the end of this block of Green there are box-seat views of Telegraph Hill and the Bay. The tall apartment building at **947 Green Street** was built in the late 1920s. It cut off the view of 1000 Vallejo on the next block. To spite the view-blocking tower, the owner of 1000 Vallejo built **945 Green Street**. It was designed right before the Crash in 1927–28 by Bos and Quandt. Number 945 Green is higher than its neighbor and built in an L-shape to further obstruct the intruder's views. In those days there were no height limits in San Francisco. Retrace your steps back out Green Street to Jones Street and walk right, downhill, to the entrance of Macondray Lane.

❼ *Macondray Lane*

Between Jones and Taylor streets, below Green Street, is Macondray Lane, a landscaped pedestrian oasis that ends in steep wooden stairs lined with pleasing houses, flats, and apartments. At the corner of Macondray Lane is **1950 Jones Street**, an apartment building built in 1907–08 by contractor Otto A. Craemer. The typical Edwardian shape is clothed in painted shingles, making a deliberately Russian Hill building. The building has polygonal bay windows at its corners and bay windows along its two sides. It steps down the Jones Street slope and has a recessed entry capped by a broken pediment.

Only one of the lane's buildings, **15–17 Macondray Lane**, painter Giuseppe Cadenasso's house, survived the 1906 fire. Many of the existing buildings were built over the next three years during the reconstruction boom.

At **68 Macondray Lane** is Charles Bovone's brown-shingle house, built in 1908 and designed by Louis Mastropasqua. Bovone came from Italy in 1884 and became a maker of cut glass and curved glass for curved bay windows such as the one protruding from the second floor of his own house. The house has been converted into several apartments.

The Taylor Street end of Macondray was the furthest westward extent of Italian American North Beach about the turn of the century. Many who lived here were natives of Genoa. Local painter Giuseppe Cadenasso, Genoa-born, who rose from a waiter to head of the Mills College art department, was the artistic luminary among early residents. Today Macondray Lane has a varied white-collar population. The lane's geography, if not its population, has been memorialized in Armistead Maupin's 1978 slice-of-gay-life *Tales of the City* as "Barbary Lane."

At **36 Macondray Lane** is a good contemporary clapboard house. The wooden stairs at the east end of Macondray Lane offer a sweeping view of the Bay with the typical flat, gravel-covered roofs of San Francisco apartments, their galvanized metal chimneys in the foreground. This is the real San Francisco. Retrace your steps back through the embowered lane to Jones Street and walk one-and-a-half blocks uphill to Jones and Vallejo.

8 1821 Jones Street, *1916, Fabre and Hildebrand*
Just before the ramp to the left that rises to the 1000 block of Vallejo Street is 1821 Jones Street, a fine three-story house with two archways on its ground floor. One shelters the front door, the other the garage. An elegant *piano nobile* with a balcony and neoclassical detailing marks the third floor along with, most unusually, a bay window and a similarly shaped open balcony. This is a unique and sophisticated design for a San Francisco townhouse, an ideal design for a city building. It was designed by Fabre and Hildebrand and built in 1916.

9 Vallejo Street Improvements, *1915, Willis Polk & Company*
At Jones and Vallejo streets are the elegant concrete retaining wall, automobile ramps, and sidewalks of the Vallejo Street improvements designed by Willis Polk & Company in 1915. These high-style improvements were paid for not by the city but by the adjoining property owners, organized by Horatio P. Livermore, who owned several lots here and who built the buildings flanking the ramps. Livermore was an engineer-entrepreneur who built irrigation systems in the San Joaquin Valley and the hydroeletric system that powered Sacramento's streetcars. One of the companies he founded became part of the giant Pacific Gas & Electric Company. To the east are the backs of four townhouses on Russian Hill Place designed by Willis Polk. To the south are 1805 Vallejo Street and **1740** and **1742 Jones Street**, three stucco houses designed by Charles W. McCall in 1915. This block of Vallejo is narrow and passes between high embankments leading to a balustraded turnaround. Steps embowered in greenery zigzag down the eastern escarpment of the hill to Taylor Street.

Russian Hill Place

The Marshall Houses
1036 and 1034
Vallejo Street

⑩ *Russian Hill Place*

Off this summit block of Vallejo are privately built Russian Hill Place and Florence Street, two quiet *cul-de-sacs* sheltering sophisticated architecture. Norman Livermore engaged Willis Polk to design the row of four Mediterranean villas along **Russian Hill Place** backing up on Jones Street in 1915. In 1926 the Livermores deeded brick-paved Russian Hill Place to the city as a public right of way. Russian Hill Place ends in a short staircase with a view through the bottom of The Summit Apartments.

⑪ The Marshall Houses, *circa 1884*
Numbers **1036 and 1034 Vallejo** are known as the Marshall houses and were built in 1889 for a parishoner of Joseph Worcester's. The two gable-roofed, brown-shingled houses peek from behind their protective walls. They were among the earliest shingled houses on Russian Hill and seem to hark back to New England.

JOHN TOMLINSON COPYRIGHT 1994

⑫ The Hermitage, *1982, Esherick, Homsey, Dodge & Davis*
Although the Livermore family began to sell its properties on
Russian Hill in the 1950s, subsequent owners have been careful to
preserve the buildings and gardens here and to change them only
minimally. The last Livermore family development was Putnam Livermore's construction of the contexturalist, brown-shingled **Hermitage**, designed by Esherick, Homsey,
Dodge & Davis and built in 1980–82. This four-story, seven-unit condominium building adopts as its ornament the square-section urns of Willis Polk's 1915 balustrade. It
sits on the edge of the cliff and looks down on the city. This was the site of Joseph
Worcester's shingled cottage with its simple redwood interiors that introduced the
Craftsman aesthetic to Russian Hill and San Francisco. The view from the balustraded
turnaround here is splendid.

The Hermitage
1020 Vallejo Street

Bird's-eye view of the summit of Russian Hill

Williams-Polk House
1013–19 Vallejo Street

Florence Street

1071 Vallejo Street

35, 37 and 39 Florence Street

40 Florence Street

⓭ Williams-Polk House, *1892, Polk & Polk*
Near the head of the Vallejo Street staircase, behind a fence and embowered in trees, is the brown-shingled medieval jumble of the **Williams-Polk House** looking like an old country house, not a city dwelling. It is one of Russian Hill's most distinctive cliff dwellings. This duplex was built in 1892 for Mrs. Virgil Williams and designed by Polk & Polk. Dora Norton Williams was the widow of painter and teacher Virgil Williams, one of the founders of the School of Design, now the San Francisco Art Institute. Mrs. Williams lived in the western half of the house, Willis Polk in the eastern half. This twin-gabled house was Polk's first "rustic" design. Bands of simple, white-painted casement windows stretch across the two stories of the building at a uniform height concealing a three-foot difference in the floor levels in the two separate units. From the Vallejo stairs, two stories and an attic with a windowed gable are visible; the back of the building, which faces a panoramic view of the downtown, has six stories and is a loose piling of rooms with balconies and terraces looking like a random accumulation of hillside shacks. (A good distant view of this brown-shingle jumble can be had from the northeast corner of Taylor and Jackson streets.) Its interior used natural unvarnished redwood and is cabinlike and homey. California architectural historians revere this building, though to the layman it may not look all that special.

⓮ *Florence Street Pueblo Revival Group and The Livermore House*

Starting in 1913, Horatio P. Livermore began the construction of a row of stucco Pueblo Revival–style houses along one-block-long **Florence Street**, between Vallejo and Broadway. They form a remarkable stucco cluster, a quiet *cul-de-sac* garnished with meticulous landscaping.

The interesting cubic Pueblo Revival design at **1071 Vallejo Street,** southwest corner of Florence, was designed in 1912 by Charles F. Whittlesey for Norman Livermore. It is a U-shaped, two-flat building with an entrance court facing Florence Street. The building has a bold, manipulated design. In 1947 it lost its rough pebble-dash stucco to a smoother finish. In the 1910–20 period Whittlesey designed **35, 37 and 39 Florence Street** for the same client. These stucco designs have fine doors and entry windows. The carefully trained landscaping in front of these houses is meticulously kept.

Across the street and behind a low wall is **40 Florence Street,** the brown-shingled Livermore house begun in 1865 and much enlarged and enhanced over time. It was expanded and remodeled by Willis Polk in 1891. In 1990 Robert A. M. Stern again expanded and remodeled the house, giving it its present appearance. Shaded by a Monterey cypress and lushly landscaped, the brown-shingled house with its forest green trim is the epitome of Russian Hill's continuous and now high-style architectural identity. The low brick wall capped by its see-through dark green fence with roses and vines is a model for security and privacy yet generosity to the passer-by.

15 *1000 Block of Broadway*

Florence Street ends in a steep staircase leading down to Broadway; the view of the downtown's highrises is fine from here. Most of Broadway's traffic passes under the hill in a tunnel built in 1952; up here, it is a dead-end street. Cross Broadway at the retaining wall to the opposite side of the street to look back north. The sidewalk here is so steep it is partly stepped. The high concrete retaining wall built in the early 1890s when Broadway was graded served as a buffer for the summit block when the fire swept the city in 1906.

1032 Broadway

1020 Broadway

1629 Taylor

Nuestra Senora de Guadalupe

Grace Episcopal Cathedral

Behind the noble old tree to the left is **1032 Broadway**, the Atkinson House; built in 1853, it was added to about 1860 and remodeled about 1893 by Willis Polk. It is an E-shaped Italianate house with long, narrow windows and bracketed gables built around the tree and set in a fine garden. The Atkinson House is the oldest and most intact house on the Vallejo Street summit. At some point it was stuccoed without losing its ornamentation. Catherine Atkinson, the original owner's daughter, conducted a salon here in the 1890s. Here Gelett Burgess and the rest of *Les Jeunes* discussed art and gossiped. The roomy old house was later converted into a private school but is today again a private dwelling. (Please respect the privacy of the residents.)

Downhill, surrounded by trees and greenery are the three metal chimneys of **1020 Broadway**, a superb brown-shingled Craftsman house designed by Albert Farr in 1909 for Ethel Parker Roeder. It was built with another house, **1629 Taylor**, around the corner, for a brother and sister who had grown up in their grandparents' house on the corner lot. That house was demolished for a large garden when the Farr houses were finished. It is very modern, a real break from Victorian design.

Continuation: Chinatown and North Beach or Nob Hill

From here you have two choices: You may walk downhill on Broadway, past the twin towers of the now-closed **Nuestra Senora de Guadalupe** Roman Catholic Church (designed in 1906 and 1912 by Shea & Lofquist) and across the tracks of the cable car on Mason Street to Chinatown *(Tour 3)* or to North Beach's café and restaurants *(Tour 4)*; or you can walk the six relatively flat blocks of Taylor Street south to **Grace Episcopal Cathedral** and the summit of **Nob Hill** *(Tour 7)*. If you choose this second option, be sure to look back toward Russian Hill from the corner of Taylor and Jackson streets. This corner offers a good view of the back of the Williams-Polk house and its cascade of rooms spilling down the steep slope.

Tour 6b:
Russian Hill's Northern Spur and
Lombard Street's Crooked Block

2115–29 Hyde Street

**View Tower at
2238 Hyde Street**

The Powell-Hyde cable car can take you to the intersection of Hyde and Filbert streets where this walk begins. Or you can take the 45 Union-Stockton trolley bus, which will drop you off at Union and Hyde one steep block south of Hyde and Filbert.

16 *1100 Block of Filbert Street/Steepest Paved Street*

This precipitous block of Filbert Street has a grade of 31.5 percent and is the steepest paved street in San Francisco. Its sidewalks became shallow steps. Directly east is Telegraph Hill capped by Coit Tower. The flat island to its left is man-made Treasure Island built for the Golden Gate International Exposition of 1939 and now a U.S. Navy base.

17 **2115–29 Hyde Street**, *1910, Stone and Smith*

Midblock between tall apartment buildings is the Tudor-Craftsman complex built in a U-shape with a cascading brick staircase. Built in 1910 to designs by Stone and Smith, its clinker-brick base, projecting upper floors, and protruding beam ends make a strong impression. Russian Hill was developed with quite a few courtyard apartment buildings between about 1910 and 1940, the same years when bungalow courts were popular in Los Angeles.

18 *Greenwich Street Stub/Alice Marble Tennis Courts*

The block of Green bounded by Hyde, Larkin, Lombard, and Greenwich streets was the site of a Spring Valley Water Company reservoir and became municipal property when the city bought the water company in 1930. It has been planted with pines and other wind-resistant trees and provides the summit of the hill with its largest park. For the walker, the special experience here is walking into the brick-paved stub end of Greenwich Street, at Hyde, along the south edge of the park, turning around, and walking back to Hyde. As you return east, up the slight hump in the road, Coit Tower atop Telegraph Hill seems to grow up out of the ground. The hilltop-to-hilltop view is remarkable. If you walk along the path at the west edge of the park heading north there are fine views of the forested Presidio to the west, the Bay and the Golden Gate Bridge, and serene Mt. Tamalpais.

The summit blocks of Hyde are lined with large apartments buildings built before the imposition of height limits. The slim **View Tower at 2238 Hyde Street**, between Greenwich and Lombard streets, is a sixteen-story, bay-windowed steel-frame sliver built in 1927 on a standard house lot. It rises out of the middle of its block like a mathematical model of maximum floor-area ratio. Such a building could not be built today.

⓳ Fannie Osbourne Stevenson House, *1900, Willis Polk; later additions*
Rarely noticed across the street from the head of the crooked block is the palatial bulk of **1100 Lombard Street**, at the northwest corner of Hyde, Willis Polk's Fannie Osborne Stevenson house of 1900. Much added onto and adapted over time, this rambling house was built for Robert Louis Stevenson's widow. Remembering Italy, California architects looked to the Mediterranean in their stucco buildings at the turn of the century.

⓴ The Crooked Block/1000 Block of Lombard Street
The 1000 block of Lombard Street, between Hyde and Leavenworth, is nicknamed "the crookedest street in the world." It has eight switchbacks in its one-block descent. It was a little-used cobbled street with a 27 percent grade until 1922, when the corkscrew design was installed by the city as a way of making the street accessible to automobiles. Carl Henry, the founder of the Owl Drug Company, who owned lots on the block, was the first to propose the design. City engineer Clyde Healy designed the road with a 16 percent grade. The municipality paid for the grading and the paving and the lot owners facing the block paid for the fancier-than-usual brick steps and plantings and agreed to pay for the garden maintenance. The street achieved its purpose of making the lots accessible, thus increasing their value.

The crookedest street suffers from overpopularity. Because it *is,* as an advertisement could for once say honestly, "a unique driving experience," it attracts far too much traffic. It has turned out to be a mistake to promote a major tourist attraction in the middle of a residential area. And in this case the impact is on the *opposite* slope of the hill; summer traffic backs up on Lombard, where cars over heat and sometimes catch fire. Because the street is a public way maintained by public funds, there is principled objection to closing it or restricting its use. Scenic it is, sensible it is not.

When looking at the street, be sure to look at the buildings that define it as well. Most are stucco flats and apartments with clean, modern lines built since the 1940s. While none is outstanding individually, as a group they make a distinctive block that can only be San Franciscan.

Off this tourist-happy crooked block is **65 Montclair Terrace**, an elegant International Style house designed by Gardner A. Dailey in 1938. Now draped by a bougainvilea vine, its clean lines, various view-catching terraces and top-floor loggia represent a high point in environmentally-sited Bay Area architecture. A short staircase at the end of Montclair Terrace leads to Chestnut Street.

Fannie Osbourne Stevenson House
1100 Lombard Street, northwest corner of Hyde

The Crooked Block
1000 Block of Lombard

65 Montclair Terrace

The San Francisco
Art Institute
*800 Chestnut Street at
Jones; Information,
749-4564; events
information, 749-4588*

Rivera Gallery

Walter McBean Gallery

㉑   The San Francisco Art Institute, *1926, Bakewell & Brown;
1969, Paffard Keatinge Clay, addition*

This institution, clinging to the side of the hill at Chestnut and Jones, continues to draw artists and art students to Russian Hill. The San Francisco Art Institute is well worth seeing and makes a perfect conclusion to an exploration of the hill. The school's concrete "monastery" with a tower was built in 1926 by Bakewell and Brown. A high wall sets off the school from the street. Inside, around an intimate courtyard, hangs student work, often cutting-edge things of real interest. A modern concrete addition in 1969 by Paffard Keatinge Clay has a rooftop deck with a superb view.

The San Francisco Art Institute was established in 1871. In 1893 Edward F. Searles gave it the gingerbread-castle Mark Hopkins House atop Nob Hill, where the Mark Hopkins Hotel stands today. (This was the first time a great San Francisco house was donated for a philanthropic purpose.) In the 1906 fire, that house was destroyed and the school built a temporary frame building on the site. It then sold the corner to the builder of the Mark Hopkins Hotel, taking the money to buy a lot and erect the new school on Russian Hill. Here master San Francisco architects Bakewell & Brown designed the working art school of studio spaces, a library, offices, and galleries around a courtyard and a tower. The result is one of the finest Spanish Colonial Revival–style buildings in San Francisco. There is a 1931 Diego Rivera mural in the **Rivera Gallery** showing the artist (with his ample backside to the viewer) painting a mural in honor of the American workman. The mural's donor, William Lewis Gerstle, is the man in the black homberg hat flanked by the architects holding their plans. Student work is displayed in the gallery, which is open Tuesday through Saturday.

The Art Institute presents art exhibits in its two galleries. The principal gallery is the **Walter McBean Gallery** off the rooftop courtyard. Lectures and films are presented in the auditorium. The utility pole in front of the entrance to the Art Institute on Chestnut Street is a good place to check for flyers announcing the events that can't afford to advertise. The roof deck of the 1969 addition is the perfect place to rest and look out over the city and the Bay. There is a café here that is open to the public. The students often look like works of neoprimitive art themselves.

Continuation: Fisherman's Wharf, North Beach, Chinatown, or Union Square

Fisherman's Wharf *(Tour 5)* is just down the Jones Street hill. Columbus Avenue and North Beach *(Tour 4)* are to the east down Chestnut. The 30 Stockton trolley bus runs on Columbus and can take you north, through the Wharf, to Chestnut Street neighborhood shopping strip and eventually the Palace of Fine Arts, or south, to Chinatown *(Tour 3)* and through the Stockton Tunnel to Union Square *(Tour 1)* downtown and further south to Yerba Buena Center and the Moscone Convention Center.

View of Huntington Park, **donated in 1915
and previously the site of the Colton, later Huntington, Mansion, which burned in 1906.
To the north is the 1100 block of Sacramento Street, with residential highrises and a two-story
Edwardian building remodeled in 1968 by Ted Moulton as a French-style townhouse.**

What This Tour Covers
Preliminaries
Introduction: The Enduring Imprint of the Railroad and Silver Barons

Continuation
Eastern Pacifc Heights, Chinatown, Russian Hill,
Fisherman's Wharf, or the Financial District

TOUR 7:
NOB HILL
SUMMIT

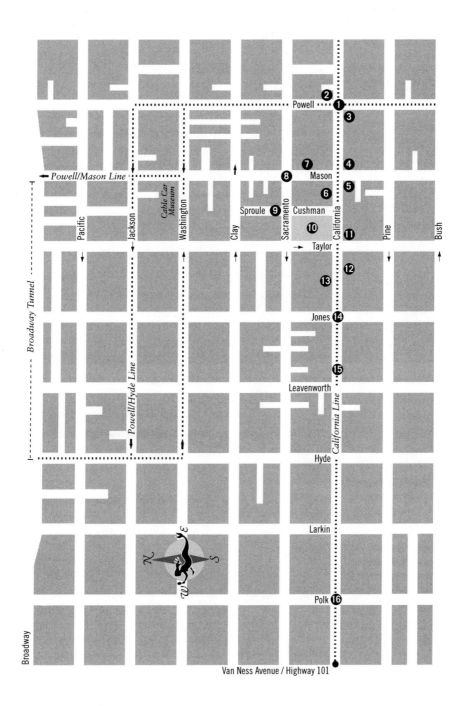

Nob Hill

Preliminaries

St. Mary's Square Garage
*On Kearny between Pine
and California*

The Fairmont Garage
At Powell near California

The Crocker Garage
*On California between
Mason and Taylor*

**BEST TIMES TO
DO THIS TOUR**

Grace Cathedral has a magnificent Holy Eucharist and choral service is celebrated on Sundays, with a coffee hour afterward that invites you to mingle with San Franciscans. Evening prayer is offered daily in the Chapel of Grace, with a choral service, Evensong, on Thursdays. Carillon recitals are on Sundays and Wednesdays and Friday; fine concerts are held frequently.

Walking the outside sidewalks of the summit block bounded by California, Mason, Sacramento, and Taylor streets makes a fine, level evening constitutional and lets you look out over the twinkling lights of the city and the ink-blue Bay. At Christmastime festive lights decorate the hotels and Huntington Park.

Parking

City-owned **St. Mary's Square Garage** is the least expensive; hop the **California cable car** for the three steep blocks uphill to Powell. The **Fairmont Garage** is near where this tour begins. The **Crocker Garage** is on California, between Mason and Taylor at the crest of the hill; there is also a garage under the **Masonic Auditorium** at California and Taylor across the street from Grace Cathedral.

Transportation

All cable lines cross at Powell and California. The **California Street cable car line** serves Nob Hill. The **1 California electric trolley bus** goes outbound up Sacramento Street from the Financial District through Chinatown, up to the crest of Nob Hill, and down to Polk Street; the line continues into Pacific Heights, the Richmond District, and almost to the Palace of the Legion of Honor overlooking the Golden Gate. Inbound the 1 California travels on Clay Street, and terminates at Drumm Street and the Embarcadero Center.

RESTAURANTS, CAFÉS, AND BARS

The ideal way to begin this walk is with breakfast or lunch at the **Big Four Restaurant and Bar** in the Huntington Hotel weekdays or on weekends. The Big Four is also a virtual museum of railroad and silver baron memorabilia and captures the spirit of the historic hill. **Vanessi's** Italian restaurant, off the courtyard at California and Jones, is a great place to eat lunch or dinner; the lively counter has a view of the cooking. **Le Club**, in the Clay-Jones Tower at Clay and Jones streets, serves fine French cuisine; expensive. The **New Orleans Room** at the Fairmont Hotel showcases great jazz artists; the **Cirque Bar**, also in the Fairmont, has Art Deco circus murals from 1934 and has recently been restored. Cocktails at the **Top of the Mark** is a local tradition.

Polk Street, at the western foot of the hill, has many moderately priced restaurants and one lunch-time jewel, **Swan Oyster Depot**, serving the best cold seafood and hot clam chowder in San Francisco at its old marble counter; a San Francisco tradition since 1912.

Big Four Restaurant and Bar
in the Huntington Hotel at California at Taylor;
771-1140

Vanessi's
1177 California Street; off the courtyard at Jones;
771-2422

Le Club
1250 Jones, in the Clay-Jones Tower at Clay; 771-5400

New Orleans Room
At the Fairmont Hotel;
772-5259

Cirque Bar
At the Fairmont Hotel;
772-5101

Top of the Mark
Entrance on California Street, below Mason;
392–3434

Swan Oyster Depot
1517 Polk Street, near California; 673-1101

Introduction: The Enduring Imprint of the Railroad and Silver Barons

Wealth, power, beauty, spirituality, and exclusivity characterize the summit of **Nob Hill.** In a city of hills, this is the most famous one. Like the center of a carousel, Nob Hill seems to stand still in a more elegant time while all around it the city changes. There is a European, and faintly French, flavor to the hill. Nob Hill rises 339 feet above sea level and its grand buildings loom over the Financial District the way a baron's castle looks down on a village. It is one of the places in San Francisco that is a part of every American's mental geography.

Three waves of development have swept over this steep hill. The first saw the construction of ordinary frame houses on the sandy, hard-to-climb hill. (Before the cable car, the rich preferred level streets.) Nob Hill, then known as the California Street hill, was sprinkled with modest houses on small lots, one of which was to attain a curious fame. There were also some early fancy houses on the hill: in the late 1850s, William Walton, a wealthy merchant, built a big house at Taylor and Washington streets, William T. Coleman of Vigilante fame built what contemporaries described as a Roman villa in a walled garden, and Senator George Hearst, father of the mining and publishing magnate, built a "Spanish" palace of white stucco.

The invention of the cable car in 1871—and the simultaneous emergence of great railroad and silver mining fortunes—led to a second wave of building on the hill. Andrew Hallidie's invention conquered the steep hills and made their summits choice real estate rather than hard-of-access backwaters. In 1876 the city granted a franchise to the **California Street Cable Railroad,** and service began in 1878. Among the early investors in the line was Leland Stanford of the Central (later Southern) Pacific Railroad. The *San Francisco Real Estate Circular* predicted in 1876 that "The wire-cable mode of propelling street cars being susceptible of use on the very steepest of hills, where horses could not possibly be used, will prove ultimately to be one of the most valuable aids to increase of San Francisco's real estate values ever devised. Much of the most beautiful real estate in this county is situated on the highest hills. ... It will ... in future, be possible to have a residence on the steepest side-hills, commanding panoramic views, and still be in a place that will be quickly, easily, and cheaply accessible."

The transcontinental railroad's **Big Four** were all from Sacramento: **Leland Stanford,** a wholesale grocer, **Charles Crocker,** owner of a dry goods store, **Collis Huntington,** who began as a peddler at the age of fourteen, and **Mark Hopkins,** owner of a hardware store. In 1861 these merchants incorporated the Central Pacific Railroad and successfully lobbied for generous subsidies in Washington. The railroad was pushed as a war measure during the Civil War, and both cash and a baronial endowment of Western lands were obtained by the corporation. Construction began in 1863 and the last spike was driven at Promontory, Utah on May 10, 1869. A sign displayed in San Francisco boasted: CALIFORNIA ANNEXES THE UNITED STATES. Historian Hubert Howe Bancroft wrote that "from the middle 1870s to 1910 the major share of the profit of virtually every business and industry on the Coast was diverted from its normal channel into the hands of the railroad and its controlling group."

Leland Stanford bought up all the parcels on the block bounded by California, Powell, Pine, and Mason streets, kept the downtown-facing half of the block for himself, and sold the uphill half to his partner Mark Hopkins. Together they built the formidable granite retaining wall on the Powell, Pine, and Mason streets sides of the block with Sierra granite from the railroad's quarry at Rocklin. This impressive granite retaining wall, along with the reconstructed Flood Mansion, are what principally remains of the grand Nob Hill mansions. The third member of the railroad's Big Four, Charles Crocker, bought up all but one elusive lot on the block bounded by California, Taylor, Sacramento, and Jones streets. The existing buildings were demolished and in their place rose some of the grandest showplace houses in the West.

Robert Louis Stevenson described the summit of Nob Hill in 1882:

> The great net of straight thoroughfares lying at right angles, east and west and north and south, over the shoulders of Nob Hill, the Hill of palaces, must certainly be counted the best part of San Francisco. It is there that the millionaires are gathered together vying with each other in display. From thence, looking down over the business wards of the city, we can descry a building with a little belfry, and that is the Stock Exchange, the heart of San Francisco: a great pump we might call it, continually pumping up the savings of the lower quarters to the pockets of the millionaires on the Hill.

It was sometime in the 1870s that the hill got its famous name. "Nob" is a variation on the plain English word *knob* meaning an isolated rounded hill or mountain. It is one of those simple, matter-of-fact, almost brutal mining-era names that dot the West. The sandy hill became the epicenter of wealth in nineteenth-century California. The railroad and silver barons stamped the hill with the indelible cachet that has survived earthquake, fire, shifting real estate patterns, and even the income tax.

Nob Hill's mansions were not destined to be occupied for long, nor did they prove to be very happy homes. Mark Hopkins died in his railroad car in Arizona before occupying the fantasy his wife had hallucinated. "Bonanza Jim" Fair's marriage shattered before he got to build his house on his prime block. Charles Crocker's domain was spoiled by one man who would not sell him his lot with its modest house. (Crocker proceeded to build a thirty-foot-high spite fence around three sides of hold-out Nicholas Yung's house.) Senator Stanford lost his only son. A bitter lawsuit brought by Mrs. Colton, who lived where Huntington Park is today, exposed the systematic political corruption on which the railroad millions were based.

Nor did contemporary San Franciscans react with awe to the architectural excesses that crowned the hill and lorded over the city. The *Real Estate Circular* branded them "all gingerbread, ignorance, and bad taste" and protested that all such structures did was "bury capital." Crueler still were the comments of Alfred Cohen, who when accused of misappropriating railroad money used the courtroom to recite an imaginary soliloquy by one of the magnates: "I will build myself a mansion, which I will set upon a hill. I will upholster and furnish it so that visitors shall be filled with doubt whether it is designed for a haberdasher's shop or a stage scene for a modern furniture drama.... I will buy pictures from the galleris of the Medicis and employ Mr.

Medici himself to make the selections. I will show the world how an intelligent patron of the arts and literature can be manufactured by the process of wealth out of a peddler of needles and pins ... I shall strut along the corridors of the Palace Hotel a living, breathing, waddling monument of the triumph of vulgarity, viciousness and dishonesty."

What the moralists decried the earthquake and fire of 1906 wiped away. The best place to experience what the hill looked like in its heyday is the diorama of the Nob Hill summit in 1906 that is at the **Presidio Army Museum**. The best interior in the state recalling the showy piles is the superbly restored Italianate-style **Crocker Art Gallery**, designed by Seth Babson in 1873 for Charles Crocker's brother, Edwin Bryant Crocker, in Sacramento.

In the third wave of building on the hill the lost Victorian houses on the slopes of the hill were quickly replaced by income-producing apartment houses built on the 25-foot-by-100-foot single-family house lots. They are nearly all frame and incorporate bay windows that project out over the sidewalks, making the apartments seem larger from within and giving the hilly blockfronts a corrugated profile. They blanket the slopes of the hill and, along with contiguous Russian Hill and North Beach, create one of the most coherent Edwardian districts in the nation. These buildings have always housed moderate-income people, singles and couples mostly, many of whom work downtown.

The big parcels on the summit, sites of the lost mirages, were slower to be rebuilt. The Fairmont Hotel opened a year to the day after the catastrophe, and the brownstone Flood mansion was soon remodeled for the Pacific-Union Club. The Crocker family donated its block to the Episcopal church. But it was not until the mid–1920s that large hotels, many originally residential hotels, were erected on the commanding hill. The Episcopal cathedral was begun in the 1920s, but not completed until the 1960s.

A burst of highrise construction in the 1960s saw tall buildings sprout along the Jones Street spine. The image of the hill began to shine brightly again. There were no height limits on the hill before 1968, and after that date the height limits were extremely generous. The threat that highrises would blanket the slopes of the hill as well as the summit led the neighborhood to organize to push for the reduction of height limits in two steps, in 1979 and 1986. A new six-story height limit now preserves the even-scale, moderate-income slopes and will prevent overcongestion of the summit.

Nob Hill's highrises today house the well-to-do and luxury hotels, while the apartment buildings on the slopes house people of modest income. Today, about half the population of the hill as a whole is Chinese American, and Chinese Americans own perhaps 80 percent of the apartment buildings on the north and west slopes of the hill. The famous hill is today a lively, varied, and very San Franciscan neighborhood accommodating many races, classes, and cultures.

*California and Powell Cable Car Transfer Point/
View of San Francisco-Oakland Bay Bridge*

**California and Powell
Cable Car Transfer Point**

University Club
*800 Powell Street, at
California*

**The Stouffer Stanford Court
Hotel/Site of the
Stanford Mansion**
905 California Street

The intersection of **California and Powell** streets is one of the natural gathering spots for visitors to San Francisco. It is here that the three surviving cable car lines intersect and transfers can be made. It is worth carefully crossing this lofty intersection and looking down from each corner. Visible at the foot of California Street is the red brick bulk of the 1916 former Southern Pacific railroad headquarters designed by Bliss & Faville. The Southern Pacific railroad's predecessor was the western section of the first transcontinental railroad, the utility that made the United States a continental market. It was the dominant corporation in nineteenth-century California and much of the arid West. This was the railroad, steamship, and real estate company controlled by the Big Four.

Beyond the old SP building rises one of the piers of the streamlined Bay Bridge, which was carefully placed to terminate the vista down the California Street hill. (*See Tour 4, entry 12, for the sleek bridge.*) This is one of San Francisco's too-few protected view corridors.

2 University Club, *1912, Bliss & Faville*
On the northeast corner of California and Powell stood Leland Stanford's opulent stables. In 1912 Bliss and Faville designed the red brick University Club, a men's club designed in the style of a Florentine Renaissance city palace. It is a dignified, reticent design, typical of the image favored by many of the men's clubs built in San Francisco between 1906 and the 1920s.

Visible at the foot of Powell, across the now-quiet Bay, is wooded Angel Island State Park (*see Tour 16*). Far in the distance is the silver, utilitarian Richmond–San Rafael Bridge.

3 The Stouffer Stanford Court Hotel/Site of the Stanford Mansion, *1911, Creighton Withers; 1972, Curtis and Davis*
At the southwest corner of California and Powell, with glass-enclosed conservatories added, is the solid-looking Stanford Court Hotel. Built in 1911 to designs by Creighton Withers, it was completely reconstructed inside in 1972 by Curtis and Davis when the former apartment house was converted into one of the city's finest hotels. The great dark granite wall along Powell Street is all that remains of the Stanford mansion that once rose here. Sepia **murals** in the lobby beyond the entrance court painted by Mark Evans and Charley Brown in 1992 depict various San Francisco scenes, including the summit of the hill in the late nineteenth century with the Stanford mansion to the left and the Hopkins extravaganza to the right.

Leland Stanford was born in Watervliet, New York, in 1824 and practiced law in Wisconsin before moving to California in 1852 to join his five brothers in a retail grocery store. He moved to Sacramento, the state capital, and helped organize the Republican party there. He was elected governor in 1862 and supported the Union cause and railroad interests.

**The Mark Hopkins Hotel/
Site of the Hopkins
Mansion**
*999 California Street,
at Mason*

With four other Sacramento merchants Stanford launched the Central Pacific Railroad, for which he became the public spokesman. In Washington, the transcontinental railroad was pushed as a war measure with a generous congressional subsidy of ten square miles of federal land for every mile of track laid. In 1864 the railroad's promoters had a bill passed that defined mountains by soil composition, not elevation, because subsidies were higher for rail-laying over mountains. As Oscar Lewis wrote in *The Big Four*, "Any group who could move the base of the Sierra Nevadas twenty-five miles westward into the center of the [Central] valley and could net a half-million dollars by the exploit would bear watching."

Stanford took to his millions with enthusiasm. His horse-breeding ranch and country house, now the campus of Stanford University, consisted of 7,200 acres of the finest land in California. His vineyard in Tehama County embraced 55,000 acres on the Sacramento River; his Gridley Ranch spread over 21,000 acres in Butte County. He lived the sobriquet "railroad baron" to the hilt. In 1876, with his redoubtable wife Jane, he commissioned S. C. Bugbee to design his Nob Hill mansion, a brown-painted Italianate pile that he had Eadweard Muybridge photograph inside and out. It *was* a "modern furniture drama."

The Stanfords doted on their only child, Leland Stanford, Jr. He was privately tutored and traveled extensively. He began a boy's hoard of rare and wondrous things: interesting stones, miniature steam engines, crystals, an inquisitive boy's magpie collection of wonderful curiosities. It became a small private museum. Then, at fifteen, young Leland died in Florence while on a European tour with his parents. The Stanfords decided to endow a university in the boy's memory. Today, in a remarkable room at the University Museum at Stanford University in Palo Alto, south of San Francisco, you can see some of the things that the young boy collected in his parents' Nob Hill mansion and that his compulsive mother saved (*see Tour 16*). That his childlike curiosity, the most marvelous of capacities, should be the genesis of a now world-renowned seat of learning is happy indeed.

4   The Mark Hopkins Hotel/Site of the Hopkins Mansion, *1925, Weeks & Day*
Up the hill from the Stanford Court Hotel, at the southeast corner of California and Mason, is the famous Mark Hopkins Hotel designed by Weeks & Day. This commanding location was the site of the ornate Mark Hopkins mansion. All that remains of it are the granite retaining walls, including a stone turret with an iron finial on the Pine Street side that capped the stable. The redwood Stick-style Hopkins Mansion was the most ostentatious of all the Victorian houses built in California—no small claim. It was a monument not to the plain-living, vegetarian Mark Hopkins, who liked to cultivate his own garden, but to his splashy wife, Mary.

Mark Hopkins was another upstate New Yorker who came west with the Gold Rush. With Collis P. Huntington, he ran a hardware business in Sacramento serving the miners in the hills. He was one of the early investors in the Central Pacific Railroad and served as its treasurer. He moved to San Francisco, where he was content to live in a relatively simple frame house. But his cousin-wife Mary had grander ideas. She had a passion for possessions and eventually accumulated great houses in New York City, Massachusetts, and Block Island, along with the architectural mirage on Nob Hill. The California Street castle was a phantasmagoria of turrets, gables, pinnacles, and chimneys with a great Gothic-style glass conservatory on its Mason Street side. One wit claimed that if all the gingerbread was chopped off there would be no house left. When Mark Hopkins died, in 1878, his widow married Edward T. Searles, a young interior decorator she met when building her Great Barrington chateau. After his wife's death, Searles donated the house to the University of California for use by the San Francisco Art Institute. It made a splendid bonfire in 1906. Afterwards the Art Institute built a temporary school here before selling the property and moving to Russian Hill (*see Tour 6.*).

Top of the Mark

Morsehead Apartments
1001 California Street

Mason Street Townhouse Row
831–49 Mason Street

900–08 Pine

Weeks & Day designed the lofty Mark Hopkins Hotel for Comstock mining engineer George D. Smith in 1925. It is a twenty-story, steel-frame, buff brick and terra-cotta-clad building notable for the urbane way that it defines the southeast corner of the summit of the hill. Its brick-paved plaza and ornamental terra-cotta entrance pillars with their great lamps make a welcoming gesture to arriving guests. The tall central tower and its two wings are accented with Gothic Revival ornament, an appropriate if unconscious recall of the lost Hopkins extravaganza. It was built as a residential hotel but has since become one for travelers. In 1939 Timothy Pfleuger designed the hotel's rooftop cocktail lounge, the famous **Top of the Mark** (since remodeled inside and out with an intrusive, if understandable, band of windows).

⑤ Morsehead Apartments, *1914, Houghton Sawyer*
On the southwest corner of California and Mason stands the elegant Morsehead Apartments designed by Houghton Sawyer in 1914. This French-style, six-story building is one of the handsomest in San Francisco. It originally had only five apartments with the Morseheads occupying the top two floors. The shallow bays at its corners echo the oval rooms within. Its lobby is ornamented with statuary and mosaic work.

• Mason Street Townhouse Row, *1917, Willis Polk*
Down the Mason Street hill from the Morsehead Apartments are 831, 837, 843, and 849 Mason Street, an urbane row of townhouses designed by the ubiquitous Willis Polk in 1917. The elegant detailing of these four identical row houses is typical of the period before the World War I.

Visible across Pine Street, on the southwest corner of Mason, is **900–08 Pine**, a characteristic four-story, bay-windowed apartment building designed in 1915 by the prolific firm of Rousseau and Rousseau, designers of many of the city's postfire apartment buildings. The vista down Mason, cutting through the raffish Tenderloin at the bottom of the hill, is terminated by the diagonal of Market Street. Beyond is Potrero Hill. All the layers of American society exist along Mason Street, from the uppercrust atop the hill to the underclass at Market Street with the middle classes in the blocks between.

1021 California Street

Pacific-Union Club/
Flood Mansion
*1000 California Street,
at Mason*

• **1021 California Street**, *1911, George Schasty*

Up California Street from the Morsehead Apartments is a discreet three-story townhouse that steps down the hill to a five-story rear. It was designed in 1911 by New Yorker George Schasty for Herbert Law, the patent-medicine millionaire who eventually owned the Fairmont Hotel across the street. The diminutive building was once described as standing "like a quiet, well-dressed child among grownups." It was highly unusual in the rebuilding after 1906 for single-family dwellings to be built on Nob Hill. The fire and earthquake propelled wealthy San Franciscans westward away from the core and out to new townhouses in Pacific and Presidio heights, or south down the San Mateo Peninsula to gated estates.

6 **Pacific-Union Club/Flood Mansion**, *1886, Augustus Laver; 1909–11, Willis Polk; 1934, George Kelham*

The dark Connecticut brownstone **Pacific-Union Club** at the northwest corner of California and Mason streets is social San Francisco's ultimate bastion. This gentleman's club occupies the reconstructed **Flood Mansion** originally built in 1886 and designed by Augustus Laver for James Clair Flood. Flood was born in 1826 of Irish immigrant parents in New York and came to California in 1849. With his partner William S. O'Brien he opened the Auction Lunch, a saloon on Commercial Street near the Financial District. There the two men rubbed shoulders with mining stock speculators they soon outmanipulated in the frantic stock market. They ended controlling mines in Nevada's Comstock silver lode and formed the famous Consolidated Virginia Mine. Soon after they quit bartending, they had an income of a half-million dollars a month. With his wealth, Flood built this impressive stone mansion atop Nob Hill and a great estate in Menlo Park, on the San Mateo Peninsula.

Perhaps because of the rage for brownstone in his native New York City, Flood commissioned Augustus Laver to build his mansion of that material. Laver, an Englishman trained in London, migrated to Canada and with two partners won the competition for the new Parliament Building in Ottawa. He also designed the Roman Catholic Cathedral in Montreal. In the mid-1860s he moved to New York City, where with another partner he won the competition for the new capitol at Albany. In 1870 he moved once again, this time to San Francisco. Here he won the competition for the grand new City Hall begun in 1878 and lost in the 1906 cataclysm. He also secured the commission for both Flood's country and city houses.

The Flood Mansion is one of the great landmarks of San Francisco. It was the only Nob Hill palace built of stone, not wood, and its gutted shell survived once the flames of 1906 had passed over the hill. The building is in the Italianate style, a style introduced by London's Pall Mall men's clubs. The Flood Mansion is important because it monumentalizes the style adapted for the Victorian city's ubiquitous redwood-built middle-class row houses. You will see the same window design in inexpensive redwood in the surviving Victorian districts in the city. The now-green bronze fence and the side gates off the main stairs show Laver's more fanciful side. This is the finest Victorian metalwork in San Francisco (matched only by the later Beaux Arts metal work inside the 1915 City Hall). The fence's design has a rocking flow and seems to move as you walk beside it. It was said that Flood employed one man full-time just to polish his $30,000 fence.

When the fire swept the hill, the Floods departed for Pacific Heights (*see Tour 8*), where two more Flood Mansions were subsequently built, both in light colors. The half-block site with the gutted ruins was purchased by the Pacific-Union Club; a $900,000 bond issue floated among the 450 members of the club financed the acquisition. Substantial remodeling was undertaken by architect Willis Polk, a club member. The first thought was to pull down the walls, but Polk preferred to preserve them and to modify the structure. The tower was lowered and two spreading wings added to the building, giving it more restful proportions. Windows inserted at the third story show where an additional story was inserted into the originally two-story building. Inside, Polk designed club rooms as opulent as any back East. In the basement, on the Mason side, he inserted a Minoan-columned plunge with an electrically illuminated stained-glass ceiling that ranks among the most astounding private rooms in San Francisco.

The Pacific-Union Club was incorporated in 1881 as a consolidation of the Pacific Club, founded in 1852, and the Union Club, founded in 1854, and is considered one of the most exclusive men's clubs in the West. When members die, its powder blue flag with the club monogram is flown half-staff from the flagpole that caps the tower.

The Fairmont Hotel and Tower
950 Mason Street, between California and Sacramento

❼ The Fairmont Hotel and Tower *1902–06, Reid Brothers; 1907, Julia Morgan, restoration; 1962, Mario Gaidano, tower addition*
The grand Fairmont Hotel and Tower occupies the block assembled by another Nevada silver baron, James Graham Fair. Born in County Tyrone, Ireland, in 1831, Fair migrated to Illinois before joining the Gold Rush in 1849. From a successful quartz mining operation Fair moved to Nevada silver, where in association with Flood and partners Mackay and O'Brien he helped develop the Comstock lode with its fifty-foot vein of silver, thus earning the nickname "Bonanza Jim." Like many other mining magnates, Fair invested heavily in San Francisco real estate and reputedly owned sixty acres of downtown and South of Market property that he barely maintained. Fair had himself elected senator by the Nevada legislature and held the seat from 1881 to 1887. His marriage shattered in 1883 before he got to build his city mansion.

Fair's daughter, Theresa Alice (Tessie), decided to build a grand hotel on the Nob Hill block, the first hotel on the hill. She commissioned James and Merritt Reid to design a steel-frame, terra-cotta-clad Beaux Arts monument. Construction began in 1902, but building proceeded slowly on the 600-room hotel and it consumed more money than Tessie anticipated. In 1906 Herbert and Hartland Law, patent-medicine millionaires, bought the unfinished building in exchange for the Rialto and Crossley buildings on New Montgomery Street.

Before the hotel opened, while crates of furniture sat inside it, the earthquake struck on April 18, 1906. When the subsequent fire claimed the City Hall, the mayor and the emergency Committee of Fifty repaired to the unfinished hotel. In its ballroom Brigadier General Frederick Funston, commandant at the Presidio, announced his plans to dynamite firebreaks across the city to stop the fire from consuming the western districts. At dawn on April 19 the fire advanced up the hill, destroy-ing all the great mansions and gutting the unfinished hotel. Gertrude Atherton described the scene: "I forgot the doomed city as I gazed at the Fairmont, a tremendous volume of white smoke pouring from where the roof had been, every window a shimmering sheet of gold; not a flame, not a spark shot forth. The Fairmont will never be as demonic in its beauty again."

The Laws engaged Julia Morgan to restore the ruined hotel. A garden terrace was built on the Powell Street side of the hotel with a view of the rebuild-ing city below. With feverish work, the great hostelry was completed and opened one year to the day after the earthquake, on April 18, 1907. The elite Merchants' Association held a grand dinner in the ornate dining room that consumed six hundred pounds of turtle, thirteen thousand oysters, and five thousand dollars worth of wine and champagne.

In 1927 financier John S. Drumm of the American Trust Company built an opulent three-bedroom penthouse designed by Arthur Upham Pope atop the hotel. Its circular library had a ceiling painted with the constellations of the night sky; its game room was tiled like a Persian pleasure dome. When Prohibition ended, the Fairmont engaged Timothy Pfleuger to design an Art Deco cocktail lounge off the lobby. **The Cirque Bar** is decorated with murals on the theme of the circus painted by Esther, Margaret, and Helen Bruton against a gold-leaf background.

During World War II, the Fairmont and the other great hotels in the city were taken over by the military and their staffs unionized. The hotel's greatest hour came after the war when San Francisco's War Memorial Opera House was chosen as the place where the United Nations charter was signed. Secretary of State Stettinius headed the U.S. delegation and occupied the Fairmont's penthouse. Stettinius, the U.S.S.R.'s Molotov, the United Kingdom's Eden, and China's Soong, representatives of another Big Four, conferred at the Fairmont.

In 1945 Benjamin H. Swig and a partner bought a controlling inter-est in the grand hotel and began renovating it. Dorothy Draper was commissioned to redecorate the lobby in 1947, a design that is still intact and is now a period piece of late-1940s *luxe*. In 1962 an indifferent modern twenty-two story tower with 252 rooms was added to the hotel.

To tour the hotel, enter by the main entrance. The grand lobby's pat-terned carpet with swirling leaves makes one a bit giddy. The columns here are covered in golden marble. Follow the corridor to the immediate left, then turn right at the sign to the tower elevators. (Off this corridor is the usually locked Main Ballroom, origi-nally the Main Dining Room, with its wedding-cake plasterwork. It is a great *belle époque* interior.) On the corridor walls is an extensive, if depressing, collection of pho-tographs of Nob Hill after the fire. Farther down, the corridor jogs to the left; in the corner is a splendid watercolor rendering of the Reid Brothers' original design for the Powell Street façade, a fine work of art itself. At the end of the corridor are plain gold-colored elevator doors leading to the Crown Room atop the Tower. Take this agreeably slow glass-walled elevator up and then back down. San Francisco's Financial District highrises seem to grow up out of the ground as you ascend. The panorama of the city, the Bay, and its ring of coastal hills is breathtaking.

Come back out through the lobby to Mason Street and turn to the right, to the intersection of Mason and steep Sacramento Street.

 View From Sacramento and Mason Streets

The intersection of Mason and Sacramento streets offers dramatic views. Down the slope of Mason to the north is the red brick **Cable Car Powerhouse** with its bottle-shaped chimney. In the distance is Russian Hill with its dark shingled houses. The white church with the twin towers is **Nuestra Señora de Guadalupe**, built in 1906–12, the first reinforced concrete church in the city. It marks the spot of the Gold Rush-era Latin Quarter where many Chileans and Peruvians lived.

The corner building at 1000 Mason Street with the brick-paved court and the curiously small windows is the **Brocklebank Apartments**, designed by Weeks & Day and completed in 1926. Like the Mark Hopkins Hotel by the same architects, it graciously defines one corner of the hill's summit. It was the pride and joy of Mrs. M. V. B. MacAdam, who set out to build an apartment house "which would be a credit to San Francisco and myself." She oversaw every step of its design and erection; the architects must have had great patience. During the boom of the 1920s she sank her entire fortune into this project. To furnish its 277 rooms, she sold off an apartment house on Sutter Street and forty-six "sand-lots" out on the beach. Most unhappily, her one million dollar loan was foreclosed during the dark days of the Great Depression. Even the furnishings in her own apartment were threatened. As she wrote years later in her sad memoir, "Added tears are futile: so, with outward calm I passed through the door which closed upon my little world wherein I had lived in supposed security." The Brocklebank's entrance pillars and lamps are especially handsome.

9 *1100 Block of Sacramento Street*
- **Park Lane Apartments**, *1924 Edward E. Young*
- **1150 Sacramento Street**, *1987, Rony Rolnizky*

Walk west up Sacramento Street, passing the **Park Lane Apartments** on the corner designed in the Moderne style by Edward E. Young in 1924, to **1150 Sacramento**. This was the first building on the summit of the hill under the new sixty-five foot height limit. Designed by Rony Rolnizky and completed in 1989, it contains forty-five condominiums and has a fanciful parapet echoing the general shape of the nearby Park Lane Apartments. Contextural design is the current trend in San Francisco.

Nuestra Señora de Guadalupe

Brocklebank Apartments
1000 Mason Street

Park Lane Apartments
1100 Sacramento, corner of Mason

1150 Sacramento Street

The Nob Hill Community
Apartments
1170 Sacramento Street

1182 Sacramento Street

1190 Sacramento Street

Huntington Park/Site of
the Colton Mansion
*California Street at
Taylor*

• **The Nob Hill Community Apartments,** *1958*

Across Sproul Lane rises this eighteen-story condominium tower built before height limits were imposed on the hill. A driveway circles through the ground-floor level of the tower. Along its west side is a sliver of a garden.

• **1182 Sacramento Street,** *1908; 1968, Ted Moulton*

This bijou townhouse is one of the most-noted confections on Nob Hill. It is best appreciated from Huntington Park across the street. Its façade is ornamented with mahogany pillars and fancy cast-iron grilles over plate-glass French windows. From across the street the illusionist effect of the converging lines on its mansard roof is quite effective. Like the lost Nob Hill Victorian palaces, its roof is trimmed with cast-iron cresting. It is actually an extensively reworked postfire, two-flat building constructed about 1908. In 1968 it was remodeled by Ted Moulton for Edward T. Haas. Not the sort of building architects admire, it is more a stage set than architecture. It can best be described as a High Decorator 1960s version of an eighteenth-century French *hôtel particulier.*

• **1190 Sacramento Street,** *1954, Angus McSweeney*

Next door, on the northeast corner of Sacramento and Taylor, is an International Style, twelve-story highrise designed with a slight flavor of Miami Beach by Angus McSweeney in 1954. It is a fine example of a not-much-appreciated period of building in San Francisco. (It manifested the courage of its design convictions when it was painted pink.)

⑩ Huntington Park/Site of the Colton Mansion, *1915*

Huntington Park is one of San Francisco's landscape jewels and is an agreeable island of peace and sunlight that serves as the public center to this private hill. It was the site of the David Colton mansion built in 1872. The white-painted, Renaissance-style mansion was unique among the millionaires' palaces in that it was the only one that showed any architectural restraint. Its low granite retaining walls survive to define the park.

David Colton was born in Maine and came to California in 1850. He made his first fortune from the Amador gold mine and became a leader in California Democratic politics. He was a vice president of the Southern Pacific Railroad and was derisively branded by the newspapers the one-half of the "Big Four and a Half." When he died in 1878, his widow became embroiled in nineteenth-century California's most notorious lawsuit when the surviving Big Four contested the estate. At the sensational trial, Mrs. Colton entered into evidence a series of six hundred letters from Colton to Collis P. Huntington detailing how the railroad had bought elections, bribed congressmen, and ruled the political destiny of the Golden State. The trial revealed the corruption on which the Nob Hill palaces were built. A bitter but victorious Mrs. Colton left San Francisco in the 1880s.

Strangely enough, Collis P. Huntington bought the Colton mansion in 1892. It stood until 1906. After the fire, the lot stood empty until 1915 when Huntington's widow donated the half-block parcel for a city park stipulating that it be named in honor of her first husband. The park was most likely designed by John McLaren. Its simple design is curiously like that of a great house. Axial paths divide the park into four quadrants. At the center is a copy of Taddeo di Leonardo Landini's **Tortoise Fountain** of 1581 erected by Pope Alexander VII in Rome's Piazza Mattei. The front quadrants of the park, where parlors would be located in a great house, are occupied by formal lawns, one with a small bronze sculpture of children entitled *Dancing Sprites.* The rear quadrants of the park are occupied by the children's playground just the way children's rooms were placed in the back of Victorian houses. It is a most agreeable design for a park and was retained when a public-private partnership restored the park under the leadership of the Nob Hill Association in 1984. One very Nob Hill touch is the pillared and red-tile-roofed toolshed, which looks like a small temple.

The Huntington Hotel
1075 California, at Taylor

Big Four Bar and Restaurant, *at the corner of Taylor Street*

California Masonic Memorial Temple/ Masonic Museum
1111 California Street Masonic Museum open daily 10 A.M. to 3 P.M.

11 **The Huntington Hotel**, *1924, Weeks & Day*
Across California Street facing the park is the unostentatious Huntington Hotel, one of the very finest in San Francisco. Built in 1924 and designed by Weeks & Day as a residential hotel, the Huntington stands on the site of Mrs. Tobin's pre–1906 residence. The clublike **Big Four Bar and Restaurant** at the corner of Taylor Street is a virtual museum of nineteenth-century Nob Hill and well worth dressing up to savor. This atmospheric interior was designed by Sid Del Leach in 1976. The Huntington's doorman's shrill, hollow whistle calling for taxis is a familiar sound on the hill.

12 **California Masonic Memorial Temple/Masonic Museum**, *1958, Albert F. Roller*
The slick, white Vermont marble-clad California Masonic Memorial Temple and Auditorium stands on the southwest corner of California and Taylor streets. It was designed by Albert F. Roller and was dedicated in 1958. On its façade is a bas-relief depicting four figures representing the four branches of the armed services. Adjoining them is a frieze of fourteen figures engaged in a tug-of-war between the forces of good and evil.

A terrace at the Taylor Street side of the Temple gives a view of the city below. Sheltered by the entrance portico are two twenty-three-foot high marble pillars, one supporting a globe and the other the heavens. They are supposed to represent the twin pillars of the porch of the Temple of Solomon. Inside the lobby is a huge historical window executed by Emile Norman and Brooks Clement in 1957. The central figure represents a Mason with his ceremonial apron. Above him is the Masonic All-Seeing Eye. A brochure available in the lobby explains some of the window's symbolism. The window consists of a sandwich of Plexiglass holding thousands of bits of stained glass, metal, parchment, felt, linen, silk, foliage, agates, shells, and, along the bottom of the design, gravel and soil from California's fifty-eight counties and the islands of Hawaii.

Grace Episcopal Cathedral and Close/Site of the Crocker Mansions

The second floor of the Temple houses the Masonic Museum. A terrace here lets you look down on the postfire apartment houses that line Pine Street below. The top floor of the Temple houses the offices of the Grand Lodge and the Grand Master. The heart of the building is a 3,165-seat auditorium and concert hall used for musical programs and Masonic ceremonies. Architecturally, this is a good example of stripped classical 1950s design, perhaps the dullest period for formal (as opposed to zappy commercial) design in California's architectural development.

This corner was the site of the A. N. Towne Residence, a Colonial Revival house built in 1891. Its marble portal survived the catastrophe of 1906 and was the subject of a famous photograph framing the city's ruins entitled *The Portals of the Past*. The portal was saved and moved to Golden Gate Park's Lloyd Lake (*see Tour 13*). There it serves as one of only two memorials to the great earthquake and fire. The other memorial is the depressing late–WPA 1941–48 mural by Anton Refregier in the former Rincon Annex Post Office at 99 Mission Street, one block from the foot of Market Street, now part of Rincon Center.

⓭ Grace Episcopal Cathedral and Close/Site of the Crocker Mansions
- **Cathedral**, *1928–33, 1936–41, Lewis P. Hobart with Ralph Adams Cram; 1961–64, Weihe, Frick & Krause with W. Fox*
- **Crocker Courtyard and Chapter House**, *1994, William Turnbull Associates*
- **Diocesan House**, *1935, Lewis P. Hobart*
- **Cathedral School for Boys**, *1966, Rockrise and Watson*

Grace Cathedral is the seat of the Episcopal bishop of California, whose diocese originally embraced the entire state but which today consists of the San Francisco Bay Area. The cathedral and its grounds occupy the block assembled by another of the Big Four, Charles Crocker. Crocker was yet another upstate New Yorker who came to California, this time by way of Indiana, seeking gold in 1850. He opened a store in Sacramento, joined three other local merchants, and supervised the construction of the Central Pacific Railroad. He commissioned Arthur Brown to design a great Second Empire–style house here in 1877 where the nave of the cathedral stands today. He gave the uphill half of the block to his banker son William H. Crocker, who built a Queen Anne–style mansion in 1888. When the Crocker houses were lost in the 1906 fire, the family donated the block to the Episcopal church.

Grace Cathedral was essentially built in three stages to designs by Ecole des Beaux Arts–trained Lewis P. Hobart. The building was finally completed and consecrated in 1964. Hobart modeled his church on thirteenth-century French Gothic designs, chiefly Notre Dame in Paris. The cathedral is 329 feet long and 162 feet wide at the transepts; its two towers rise 174 feet. The gilded cross atop the spire is 247 feet above street level. The cathedral faces Huntington Park and downtown. While antique in image, it is modern in construction; the danger of earthquakes led to the use of concrete and steel rather than stone.

Outside the cathedral, in the central east portal, hang copies of Lorenzo Ghiberti's bronze doors to the Baptistry in Florence, known as the *Doors of Paradise*. Enter the cathedral through the door under the Children's Tower to the left. The modern baptismal font was designed by Hans and Norman Grag in 1964. Walk down the center aisle; the altar, also designed in 1964, is made of blocks of California granite with a California redwood tabletop. Richly embroidered frontals often drape the altar. The flanking candlesticks of bronze, steel, and gold are symbolic of San Francisco's motto: "Gold in peace, steel in war." Particularly beautiful are the needlepoint kneelers designed by Mona Spoor and made by the women of the diocese. They show California wild flowers and the coats of arms of California's Episcopal dioceses. Beyond the sanctuary and its high altar is the choir with its Gothic-style stalls. The Grace Cathedral Choir of men and boys was founded in 1913 and sings every Sunday and Thursday. The eagle-topped oak choir lectern was carved by Gutzon Borglum in 1908.

The beautiful predominantly blue central windows in the apse were designed by Charles Jay Connick in 1931 and show Christ the Light of the World (left) and Christ the Good Shepherd with a lamb (right). The sixty-seven stained-glass windows in the cathedral are mostly from two periods. The traditional leaded windows are mostly the work of Connick and were executed in the 1930s; the modern 1960s windows are made of faceted, or chipped, glass set in concrete. Turning away from the altar and looking back toward the entrance the cathedral's most splendid window can be seen: the twenty-five-foot wide rose window made at the Gabriel Loire studios near Chartres, France. Designed in 1964, it makes vivid St. Francis of Assisi's mystical thirteenth-century *Canticle of the Sun*. At the center of this wheel of light is Brother Sun. Circling the sun clockwise are the Chi Rho, the first two letters of the Greek title *Christ*, then come air, stars, and Sister Moon (top), the fruits and flowers of Sister Earth (right), Sister Death (right center), Sister Water (bottom), Brother Fire (lower left), and Brother Wind with two birds (upper left). This canticle is Francis' great vision of the harmonies in Nature:

The Canticle of the Sun
Most loving and almighty Lord,
Yours is the power and blessing forever.
To You be honor in each of your creatures,
But first of all in radiant brother Sun.
How quietly he tumbles shadows into dawn,
and warmth into our blood.
Be praised, my Lord, in faithful sister moon.
By her the tides and seasons run,
with her the stars spill across your skies.
Be praised my Lord, in the bellows of the winds.
In their channels scarlet leaves and windmills twirl and dance.
And be praised my Lord, by lowly sister water,
pure wine of your creation.

She babbles and banters in golden streams,
making us young again in baptism and in rain.
Be honored, my Lord, by stately brother fire.
He it is who purifies our souls,
and brings us homeward in the dark.
In his friendship men recline to crackling warmth and mellow wine.
Be praised, my Lord, in spinning earth, in worms and churning surf.
Exalt, my Lord, in green and red, in dark and evening's end.
Tumble down, my Lord, in colored glass, in grass and chimes and horns.
Be praised my Lord, in sunly voices, scents and sounding songs.
And, yes, my Lord, be praised in chaff, in aching lives, on bloody trees.
For it is You who make coins thick, and cast hope on unknown seas.
O praised and blessed be You, my Lord.
Let us give You thanks and awake with the dead.

Francis of Assisi (1182–1226)

Ranged along the blind arcade of the south aisle wall (California Street side) are a series of wax tempera and gold-leaf murals by John H. DeRosen executed in 1950, including one showing St. Francis receiving St. Clare on a mystical, starry night. The later murals closer to the entrance are by Antonio Sotomayor and were completed in 1983 in acrylic on canvas. On a wall opposite the California Street entrance and up a few steps is a rare late-Romanesque Catalan crucifix carved about 1260.

Nearby is the Chapel of Grace, a gift of the Crocker family and the first part of the cathedral to be completed. The chapel is closed except for services and is protected by a fine wrought-iron grille made by one of America's greatest metal craftsmen, Samuel Yellin, in 1931. The chapel altar is French and dates from circa 1430. Above it hangs a three-paneled, Flemish oak reredos made for Hambye Abbey in Flanders in 1490.

The stained-glass windows of Grace Cathedral depict moderns as well as ancient saints. The "Human Endeavor" series of faceted Loire windows incorporates in its designs Albert Einstein (with his famous formula $E = mc^2$), astronaut John Glenn, Supreme Court Justice Thurgood Marshall, medical reformer William H. Welch, social worker Jane Addams, poet Robert Frost (born in San Francisco in 1874), plantman Luther Burbank, President Franklin Delano Roosevelt, architect Frank Lloyd Wright, labor leader John L. Lewis, industrialist Henry Ford, and philosopher and educator John Dewey. These windows are located in the clerestory (upper) section of the nave toward the front towers.

Exit from the door under the Singing Tower, so called because it houses a carillon of forty-four bronze bells cast in Croydon, England in 1938. The largest bell weighs six tons and rings the hour. There is a columbarium housing the ashes of the dead in this tower. To the left is the new Helen Russell **Crocker Courtyard and Chapter House** designed by William Turnbull Associates and completed in 1995. Facing Taylor Street is the **Diocesan House**, designed by Lewis P. Hobart, and built in 1935. At the northwest, uphill, corner of Sacramento and Jones is the **Cathedral School for Boys** designed by Rockrise and Watson in 1966. It is a congenial modern work with a small entrance court and utilizes its roof for a playground.

Cathedral Apartments
1201 California Street

On a less Christian note, between the Diocesan House and the new Chapter House is the approximate site of the cottage that Nicholas Yung refused to sell to Charles Crocker. Furious, Crocker built an infamous thirty-foot-high spite fence around three sides of Yung's property depriving him of sunlight. In 1877, Denis Kearney, the fiery leader of the Workingmen's party, led a mass protest against Crocker's fence. Vigilantes chased and clubbed the protesters back down the hill to the South of Market flats. Not until 1904, after Yung's death, were Crocker's heirs able to buy the lot and assimilate the holdout parcel.

Chambord Apartments
*1298 Sacramento Street,
at Taylor*

Clay-Jones Apartments
1250 Jones Street

Le Club
*1250 Jones Street, at
Clay; 771-5400*

You can walk back through the cathedral and exit by the door to California Street near the Chapel of Grace. At the corner of California and Jones, cross California Street to the southwest corner.

⑭ *Views From California and Jones Streets*

On the southwest corner of California stands the **Cathedral Apartments** built in 1930 and designed by Weeks & Day in the "Hollywood Spanish" style. The tan concrete tower is enlivened by an ornate Churrigueresque Revival terra-cotta entrance pavilion on California Street.

From this corner, look south down Jones Street for a view of the Tenderloin's apartment buildings, the South of Market district in the valley, and Potrero Hill beyond. This is historically the working-class side of the city.

Look north up Jones Street for a view of the billowing bay windows of the **Chambord Apartments**, built in 1921 and designed by James F. Dunn. Like the Morsehead Apartments across from the Mark Hopkins Hotel, this elegant building features oval living rooms stacked at the corners. Their shape is expressed in the billowing corner bays. As originally designed, each floor had two units, each unit consisting of the oval living room, a bedroom with a bay window, a dining room, a kitchen, and a bath. All the rooms branched off an elevator foyer. Though small, the apartments were designed for formal entertaining and provided an opulent standard for single living. The top floor was originally a single C-shaped unit arranged around an open court. In 1926, when Herbert E. Law bought the building, this floor was altered and an undistinguished sixth-floor penthouse was added.

Beyond the Chambord Apartments can be seen the radio tower atop the Clay-Jones Apartments. The intersection of Clay and Jones streets is the highest point on Nob Hill and is 338 feet above sea level. The **Clay-Jones Apartments** is one of the earliest residential highrises in San Francisco and still one of the best designed. It is a slender, Art Deco shaft designed by Albert H. Larsen in 1929. Its radio tower serves taxi companies. It was converted into condominiums in 1973. Inside its ground floor is **Le Club**, a swank French restaurant with mildly Art Deco decor.

Polk Street

California Hall

California Culinary Academy
Call 771-3500 for lunch or dinner reservations.

From here you can catch the California Street cable car either east, to the Financial District, or west, to funky Polk Street with its shops, inexpensive restaurants, and raffish street scene.

⑮ *California Street and the Cable Car: The Western Slope of Nob Hill*

The bay-windowed, post–1906 apartments that march down the slopes of Nob Hill are among San Francisco's most important and least appreciated buildings. They are, as a matter of fact, almost invisible to San Franciscans, being so coherent as a group that most only notice the exceptions. Constructed between 1906 and about 1917, these Edwardian buildings are not quite old enough to be considered antique and so are merely old. As with Victorian houses in the 1950s, many owners "renovate" and "improve" them rather than restore them. Sadly, their sometimes elaborate wood-sash windows are being replaced with unsightly metal ones. Since 1979, rent control has dampened speculation in these buildings. Limited street parking and a general lack of garages (these close-to-downtown areas were built during the heyday of public transit and before middle-class city dwellers owned automobiles) has discouraged more affluent renters from favoring this area. These "disadvantages" work to keep the apartments relatively affordable.

The buildings owe their configuration—the rhythm of their bay windows and back yards that create open spaces for light and air—to "tenement laws" agitated for by public health advocates. The coherence of this district is also a result of the fraternity of architects in Edwardian San Francisco, who largely agreed on how to build within the city-mandated building envelope. The aim of these designers was to create individual designs within a formula and to work out plans that were efficient but had style.

⑯ *Polk Street*

At the base of Nob Hill and parallel to once-aristocratic Van Ness Avenue is **Polk Street**, one of San Francisco's many lively commercial strips that developed along old streetcar lines. The California Street cable line intersects the 19 Polk bus, which runs south on Polk Street to City Hall and the Civic Center and north to Ghirardelli Square, Fort Mason, and Fisherman's Wharf. In the Victorian era, Polk Street catered to the carriage trade atop Nob Hill and along Van Ness. South of California Street, Polk attracted many German Americans who called the artery "Polk-strasse." Today the only sign of that era in the street's history is the monumental **California Hall**, originally the German National Community Hall, designed by Frederick H. Meyer and built in 1912. This splendid German Renaissance Revival building at Polk and Turk with its elaborate terra-cotta façade was the finest ethnic hall in San Francisco, befitting the progressive, successful, rapidly assimilated German American community. Today it houses the **California Culinary Academy**.

Frank Norris's naturalistic novel *McTeague: A Story of San Francisco,* published in 1899, was set on Polk Street. McTeague hung his giant gold tooth from his second-floor dental parlor at Polk and California and watched the crowds below:

> Evening began: and one by one a multitude of lights, from the demoniac glare of the druggists' windows to the dazzling blue-whiteness of the electric globes, grew thick from street corner to street corner…. Now there was no thought but for amusement. The cable cars were loaded with theatergoers—men in high hats and young girls in furred opera cloaks. On the sidewalks were groups and couples—the plumbers' apprentices, the girls of the ribbon counters, the little families that lived on the second stories over their shops, the dressmakers, the small doctors, the harness makers—all the various inhabitants of the street were abroad, strolling idly from shop window to shop window, taking the air after the day's work.

Hotel Wently
1214 Polk Street, at the corner of Sutter

Royal Theater

Swan Oyster Depot
1517 Polk, just north of California

Field's Book Store
1419 Polk Street, between California and Pine

Freed, Teller, and Freed's
1326 Polk Street, between Pine and Bush.

Polk Street is still animated, though after the fire of 1906 and the loss of the great mansions, the carriage trade drifted to other streets. The nondescript former **Hotel Wently** was a nest of beats in the late 1950s. Today Polk Street is characterized by inexpensive restaurants, ultratrendy clothing shops, and a sprinkling of gay bars. Its south end abuts the Tenderloin and attracts hustlers, especially at night.

The street architectural "sleeper" is the façade of Miller and Pfleuger's **Royal Theater**, an Art Deco sheet metal delight designed in 1925 but inexplicably neglected. It undoubtedly once had built-in lighting. Almost next door is **Swan Oyster Depot**, the perfect spot for a bowl of superb clam chowder (lunch only). **Field's Book Store** is an island of calm and specializes in metaphysical books. At 1326 Polk Street, between Pine and Bush, is the street's treasure, a landmark-quality, one-story circa 1910 commercial building housing **Freed, Teller, and Freed's** coffee, tea, and delicacies emporium. Its interior is a delight, a virtual museum and a rare commercial survivor from the Edwardian era.

Continuation: Eastern Pacific Heights, Chinatown, Russian Hill, Fisherman's Wharf, or the Financial District

From either California and Polk at the bottom of the hill, or California and Jones at the summit, you can walk one block north to Sacramento Street to catch the 1 California trolley bus west to Sacramento and Octavia streets, the entrance to Lafayette Park and the beginning of the Eastern Pacific Heights walk *(Tour 8)*. Going east, the 1 California trolley bus takes you to Chinatown *(Tour 3)* and Embarcadero Center. From California and Taylor, where Grace Cathedral stands, you can walk north up Taylor Street to Russian Hill *(Tour 6)*. On Polk Street, the 19 Polk bus goes north to Ghirardelli Square and on to Fisherman's Wharf. The California Street cable car can take you east to the Financial District and the Ferry Building *(Tour 2)*.

The high Victorian and Edwardian mansion group
of the northwest corner of California and Franklin streets. Left to right:
1834 California (1876 and 1895), 1818 California (1876),
1701 Franklin (1895), and 1735 Franklin (1904)

What This Tour Covers
Preliminaries
Introduction: Victorian and Edwardian Landmarks

TOUR 8:
EASTERN
PACIFIC HEIGHTS

1 Lafayette Park/Panoramas
2 Washington Street Houses/Phelan Mansion/
    Washington Tower
3 Spreckels Mansion
4 2006 and 2000 Washington Street Community Apartments
5 Gough Street Townhouses and Victorians
6 St. Regis Apartments
7 Clay Street Moderne Flats/1950 Clay Street
8 Golden Gate Spiritualist Church
9 California and Franklin Victorian and Edwardian Mansion
    Group: Edward Coleman House, Lilienthal-Pratt
    House, Wormser-Coleman House, Bransten House
10 First Church of Christ, Scientist/
    Franklin Street Apartment Buildings
11 Haas-Lilienthal House Museum/The Foundation for
    San Francisco's Architectural Heritage
12 Greenlee Terrace Apartments
13 Matson-Roth Houses/German Consulate
14 2000 Block of Jackson Street
15 Whittier Mansion
16 2000 Block of Pacific Avenue: Victorian Cluster
17 2400 Block of Octavia Street Victorians
18 1940 and 1960 Broadway: Luxury Apartment Towers
19 2000 Broadway/2040 Broadway
20 The Hamlin School/James Leary Flood Mansion
21 Bourn Mansion
22 Joseph Donohoe Grant Mansion: School of the Sacred
    Heart/James Leary Flood Mansion: Convent of the Sacred
    Heart High School/Andrew Hammond Mansion:
    Stuart Hall School for Boys
23 View of the Palace of Fine Arts and the Golden Gate
24 Vedanta Society Temple

Continuation   Bus Connections, the Bay, and Upscale Shopping

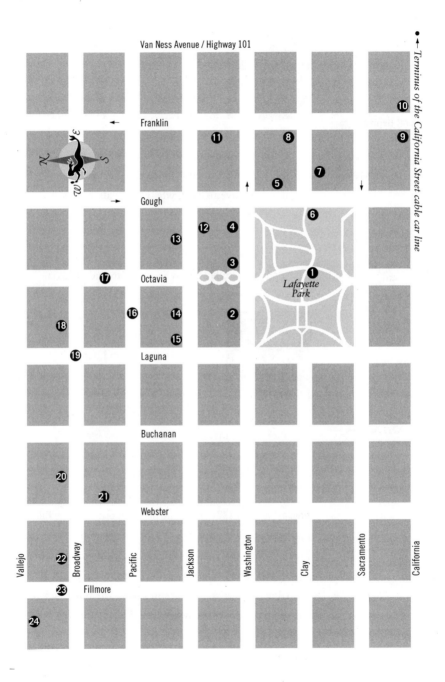

Eastern Pacific Heights

Preliminaries

Haas-Lilienthal House
2007 Franklin Street
441-3004; Open
Wednesday from 12:30
P.M., Sunday from
11 A.M. to 5 p.m.

The Foundation for
San Francisco's
Architectural Heritage
441-3004

T. Z. Shiota
3131 Fillmore; 929-7979

Perry's
1944 Union; 922-9022

La Mediterranée
2210 Fillmore, near
Sacramento; 921-2956

Sherman House
2160 Green Street,
between Webster and
Fillmore; 563-3600

Harris' Steak House
2100 Van Ness Avenue,
at Pacific; 673–1888

Hard Rock Café
1699 Van Ness Avenue,
at Sacramento; 885-1699

> **BEST TIMES TO DO THIS TOUR**

The **Haas-Lilienthal House** is open on Wednesday and Sunday. **The Foundation for San Francisco's Architectural Heritage** also conducts walking tours of Pacific Heights and other neighborhoods.

Parking

Parking is usually available along Sacramento Street on the southern edge of Lafayette Park, where this walk begins.

Transportation

For public transit to the tour starting point from downtown take the **1 California trolley bus** to Sacramento and Octavia.

> **RESTAURANTS, CAFÉS, AND BARS**

At the end of this tour, an easy walk downhill takes you to Union Street with its many fine shops, restaurants, and bars. Next door is **T. Z. Shiota**, a treasury of Asian art. A popular spot is **Perry's** with good hamburgers and salads and a lively bar. The other option at the end of this walk is to walk south on Fillmore (or catch the **22 Fillmore** trolley bus) to Upper Fillmore's shops and restaurants. An excellent choice here is **La Mediterranée**, serving Armenian and Mediterranian salads and specialties; inexpensive. An elegant place to dine in Pacific Heights is the **Sherman House**. Set in an 1876 Italianate mansion decorated by Billy Gaylord, this fine French restaurant is the perfect place for dinner or Sunday brunch, with views and a Tommy Church–designed garden; expensive. **Harris' Steak House** is a fine skylighted Edwardian space and probably the best steak place in town. The **Hard Rock Cafe** draws tourists to this immensely popular (if standardized) rock-and-roll-themed hamburger palace.

Introduction
Victorian and Edwardian Landmarks

Pacific Heights is San Francisco's elite residential section. It is cool, quiet, clean, and aloof. Like all enclaves of the very wealthy, you rarely see pedestrians here, just the occasional dog walker, repairmen, and delivery people. Fine imported automobiles glide down its lightly traveled streets between manicured trees. The district is sharply defined and embraces the blocks in the Western Addition bounded by California Street to the south, Van Ness Avenue to the east, Green Street to the north, and Presidio Avenue to the west. It divides into two parts at Fillmore Street, where the 22 Fillmore trolley bus runs. Eastern Pacific Heights, closest to the downtown and the oldest half, saw most of its Victorian mansions replaced with swank apartment houses after about 1910. Western Pacific Heights, on the other hand, remains mostly single-family dwellings, though many large buildings now have more than one unit. In eastern Pacific Heights one great Victorian house now open to the public, the **Haas-Lilienthal House**, lets the explorer glimpse a preserved interior from the late nineteenth century. Two other adapted great houses, the **Convent of the Sacred Heart High School** and the **Hamlin School**, are occasionally accessible to the public for special events. There are also a few bed and breakfasts in the neighborhood; see the preliminaries in the front of this guide in addition to the beginning of this chapter for listings.

Even when these were only barren hills in the late 1860s, it was clear that Fashion would come to rest here once transit linked it with the downtown. In the first subdivision of these blocks, the lots in Pacific Heights were deliberately larger than in the other city neighborhoods so that they could accommodate much bigger houses. While other neighborhoods have seen ups and downs in lots and real estate, Pacific Heights lots, in particular, have always held their value.

Hill-conquering cable cars turned the Victorian city inside out. In the beginning of settlement, the very best streets were the most level ones. Horsecars and ferries began to change that pattern, drawing the wealthy away from the increasingly congested and polluted center. The cable cars completed the revolution by drawing people to the edge of the city, fringes previously sprinkled with the shanties and shacks of the poor. Bankers, shippers, wholesalers, and lawyers once clustered along Stockton Street or South of Market on Rincon Hill moved out to the edge of the city. The elite Protestant churches and the Roman Catholic cathedral followed their powerhouse congregations west.

By the early 1880s, the blocks near **Lafayette Park** and **Alta Plaza** were the most prestigious streets to live on and luxurious houses clustered on "the heights." The *Real Estate Circular* reported in 1882 that "Nine-tenths of the demand for property for fine residences or cheaper homesteads during the past year has been in the Western Addition. That portion of it between Van Ness, Pierce, California and Pacific streets has been by far the most favored section, for large residence sites on the one hand and for the best medium class homesteads on the other."

The Social Manual of San Francisco described the social ordering of San Francisco's neighborhoods in 1884: "... a greater uniformity in reception days prevails from year to year. The rule is as follows: Mondays, the hotels, Tuesday, Nob Hill and Taylor Street to the north, Wednesday, Rincon Hill, South Park and the streets near the Mission, Thursday most of Pine, Bush, Sutter, and parallel streets, and the greater part of Van Ness Avenue, Fridays, Pacific Avenue and adjacent streets as far as the Presidio."

San Francisco had been a relatively open economy and society after the Gold Rush 1850s. But the depressed 1870s saw social mobility in San Francisco slow (though it never stopped) and social distinctions harden. It was from the visiting lists of the residents of the grand houses of the Victorian city that the *Social Register* was later compiled. San Francisco's first society list was published in 1880 and was in two parts: Christians, then "Hebrews." According to it, Jews accounted for 20 percent of San Francisco society. (The Christian list, interestingly, included two Jews.) Very soon, San Francisco's *Social Register* ran but one religiously integrated alphabetical list. German Jewish merchants, in particular, after flirting with the streets near the Panhandle in the Haight-Ashbury the early 1880s, bought, if they could, in Pacific Heights. Some wealthy Roman Catholic Irish and others built large showy houses with gardens in the sunny Mission District in the 1870s. But by the next decade, with Nob Hill's summit too small to contain all the mansions of the wealthy, the focus of the most stylish overflow was Pacific Heights.

Because all of the Victorian houses, and some of the later houses, employed servants, more races and classes mingled, or were "layered," in Pacific Heights than elsewhere in the city. In the late Victorian era, Irish American girls were often the parlor maids and occasionally cooks. German women were most often cooks, and as such, the rulers of the servant roost with the best room in the attic. Chinese men were widely employed as laundrymen and had separate basement rooms. In the first decade of this century, some house servants were young Japanese American men. Only a few truly grand houses had European butlers and chauffeurs.

Some of the palatial mansions in Pacific Heights ended up being mainly *for* the servants. The baronial turn-of-the-century rich preferred to live on their fog-free country estates on the San Mateo Peninsula rather than in their city houses. In the 1890s the *Real Estate Circular* decried the closed-up mansions on California Street as "palaces of ease" for their servants.

Harriet Lane Levy, in her classic memoir, *920 O'Farrell Street,* listed the many nations and races that served an upper-middle-class household in San Francisco. The baker was German; the fish man, Italian; the grocer, a Jew; the butcher, Irish; the steam laundryman, a New Englander. The vegetable vendor and the regular laundryman who came to the house were Chinese. Levy left one sharp snapshot of Maggie, the lively Irish American cook in a Polish Jewish household as remembered by a perceptive little girl:

> The kitchen offered the social potentialities of a ballroom, and Maggie missed none of them. Twice a day the tradesmen or his emissary knocked at the kitchen door. In the morning he took the order, in the afternoon he delivered

it. The grocer, the baker, the steam laundryman, the fish man, the chicken man, the butcher boy, came twice a day proffering a salty bit of conversation or a flashing glance of fire. Bent over the sink, Maggie Doyle aimed a shaft of repartee over her left shoulder in invitation, or she buried her scorn in a bowl of dough, or she leaned lightly against the jamb of the door in coquettish intimacy with the man who pleased her.

The scarcity of household servants after World War I, and more important, the much simpler tastes among new generations of the already-established rich, led to a quick evaporation of the more cumbersome of society's rituals, especially the "at homes" and their attendant calls. In the 1920s the rich emancipated themselves from the time-consuming socializing of their parents and grandparents and took up tennis, swimming, and golf instead. At the same time, the gargantuan endless-course feasts of the Victorians were supplanted by less elaborate dinners. The very rich stopped building freestanding palaces in the city and erected more "modest" residences or took floors or large apartments in anonymous swank community apartment buildings with more security and privacy.

Eastern Pacific Heights' great Victorian piles were one by one torn down for apartments as the modern rich inherited too-large and, to them, gloomy old houses they had no wish to live in. The good views, good transit links with the Financial District, and good name of the district led to the replacement of many obsolete Victorian mansions with apartment buildings starting perhaps about 1910 and cresting in the 1920s. A few fine Art Deco apartment buildings went up here even during the depressed 1930s. More apartments were built after the revival of building in the 1950s, with very bulky, often less attractive highrise buildings in the 1960s and 1970s. Since the 1980s, condominium building in Pacific Heights has been "contextural" and more conscious of the character of the neighborhood.

While the architecture in Pacific Heights is described in guides because it is visible from the street, the finest aspect of Pacific Heights is the special gardening tradition that flourishes here, marked by plants in containers, ivy trained against trellises, and mostly always green, easily maintained plantings. The invisible back gardens and landscaped decks are the jewels of Pacific Heights. Ruby-throated hummingbirds dart among their flowers, a few of which are in bloom nearly every month of the year. Frederick Law Olmsted's sharp eye for landscape noted this San Franciscan tradition as early as 1866:

> Strangers, on their arrival in San Francisco, are usually much attracted by the beauty of certain small gardens, house courts, and porches, and, if they have any knowledge of horticulture, they perceive that this beauty is of a novel character. It is dependent on elements which require to be seen somewhat closely.... It is found in the highest degree in some of the smallest gardens in the more closely built and densely populated parts of the town, in situations where park trees would dwindle for want of light and air.

There is a lot of privacy in Pacific Heights, as in most elite neighborhoods, even though its population density is quite substantial and its buildings cheek-by-jowl. There is only one day of the year when Pacific Heights is "open," Halloween after dinner to about 8 P.M. Then pumpkins glow in the windows (or, more tastefully, are heaped uncut with corn stalks near the front door) and parents take their small children trick-or-treating door to door. Lighted doorways to lighted parlors open and close, candies are handed to children, and pleasantries are exchanged with neighbors rarely seen. Otherwise, Pacific Heights' inhabited mansions are best seen in the evening when one blind is cocked and you can catch a glimpse of slivers of rooms richly paneled in warm woods and decorated with antique statues and pots of orchids.

Van Ness Avenue, the eastern edge of Pacific Heights, was laid out as part of the Western Addition in 1854 not as a highway but as a spacious, quiet boulevard for mansions. (At 125 feet, it is the widest street in the city.) The lots along it were large, the corner ones especially so. Prestigious Protestant congregations and the Roman Catholic cathedral built along Van Ness Avenue, following their elite congregations west. By 1892 Van Ness was described as "our one show street, purely a residence section." Van Ness Avenue was well served by east-west cable lines, but no noisy transit line disturbed the elegant street itself with its impressive blocks of gingerbread mansions. A proposal by a syndicate to construct a trolley line down Van Ness in 1892 by "men rich enough to be honest," as the press put it, united the property owners here in opposition to the transit invasion. But Van Ness Avenue was slowly infiltrated by commerce in the 1890s with some hotel-boardinghouses, society doctors, and fashionable dressmakers and hairdressers operating on the street.

When the 1906 earthquake struck and the downtown caught fire, city and Army engineers decided to use Van Ness Avenue as a firebreak. They dynamited all the grand houses on the east side of the street. Though the fire did jump over the break to Franklin Street along some blocks, the line was generally held here. Had this not been done, the entire city could have been consumed. Immediately after the fire, Van Ness Avenue shifted to commerce. At the edge of the surviving residential districts, large and small retailers leased the lots and the few surviving big houses on the west side of the avenue and built temporary stores, which during the rebuilding did a great deal of business.

When the department stores and rest of the retail district around Union Square was ready for occupation about 1909–10, retail skipped back downtown. Van Ness Avenue's large corner lots became ideal sites for luxury automobile showrooms with repair shops attached. During the 1920s, when automobiles were still luxuries, a stately row of elaborate landmark-quality auto showrooms was built along Van Ness. The beige, multistory, cubelike, former Don Lee Cadillac building at **1000 Van Ness** at O'Farrell, built in 1921 and designed by Weeks & Day, is the most interesting. More popular is the former Earl C. Anthony Packard temple at **901 Van Ness** at Ellis, designed by Bernard Maybeck in 1928. While car servicing and repair continues in smaller garages on the side streets between Van Ness and Polk (some of these are the sites of old livery stables), most car buying has moved off the boulevard. Van Ness Avenue has been designated by the city as a site for multistory housing and several large projects have been built. It is a good location for large apartment and condominium buildings, and the reintroduction of residential uses on the street is making Van Ness ever more attractive to pedestrians. With the pedestrians come movie theaters, electronics and furniture stores, and restaurants and cafés.

    The hidden jewel of the avenue is the interior of **St. Luke's Episcopal Church**. Designed by Benjamin G. McDougall and completed in 1910, this white Gothic Revival church has an intimate interior surrounded on four sides by large, glowing stained-glass windows of angels.

❶ Lafayette Park/Panoramas, *1855, John T. Hoff, city surveyor; circa 1910, paths and retaining walls*

Twin palms announce the entrance to Lafayette Park at the crest of Octavia and Sacramento streets. Four-block square Lafayette Park crowns the highest point in Pacific Heights; its crest is 378 feet above sea level. It enjoys fine views, both of Twin Peaks to the southwest and of the Bay to the north. This 12.7-acre hilltop park was one of a series of large parks reserved in the Western Addition when the city expanded west in 1855. The pattern of large, mostly four-block parks between Larkin and Divisadero streets north of Market was probably the best balance of buildings to park space San Francisco has seen in her history. The hilltop parks—Lafayette Park, Alamo Square, and Alta Plaza—occupy commanding sites with sweeping panoramas of the Bay or the city. They are also related to one another visually: you can stand in one and look out to the green of the others. The squares placed in the valleys have had a more complex history than the hilltop parks. Eventually east-west streets were run through them and houses, schools, and recreational facilities were built over parts of some of them. But they, too, have become part of a larger design attracting sports facilities and active recreation, while the hilltop parks have evolved into places of quiet contemplation. Lafayette Park is most active about 5:30 P.M. when office workers return home and take their dogs out for a walk. City dwellers socialize while their dogs run around. This park is also a favorite with sunbathers.

    The Western Addition Survey Commission of 1855 exceeded its mandate, resulting in decades of litigation, by ignoring the ordinance that expressly limited parks to one block "corresponding in size to the adjoining block." In December 1864 Samuel W. Holladay, a former City Attorney, began legal action against the city when he claimed the summit of Lafayette Park, the highest, choicest spot in the entire Western Addition. In December of 1867, the court found in Holladay's favor and he began construction of a large white house, Holladay's Heights, which became a mecca for local and literary society. In what was to be a crucial error the city failed to appeal this decision to a higher court.

    The anomaly of a private mansion in the center of a public park attracted notice. In the 1870s an action of ejectment was brought by the city against Holladay. By this time, he had built his house, planted gardens, and constructed fences on the summit. When the issue went all the way to the Supreme Court in Washington, it found in favor of Holladay and barred the city from further litigation. A compro-

2100 Washington Street

2108 Washington Street

2120 Washington Street

The Mary Phelan Mansion
2150 Washington Street

mise with later claimants to property within the park resulted in the construction of the Beaux Arts apartment building on the east side of the park facing Gough Street. Holladay's intrusive house was not torn down until 1936.

Though the city litigated over the park, it did not do much to improve it in the Victorian period. In 1890 Lafayette Park was described as "mostly an unimproved sand hill." About 1910 the city began to grade and plant the park. It was landscaped in the English style with large lawns falling away from a wooded peak. The lawn surrounded by trees at the summit was the site of Holladay's mansion.

2 *Washington Street Houses/ Phelan Mansion/ Washington Tower*

This block on the view ridge across from Lafayette Park, served by the Washington-Jackson cable line until 1956, was one of the finest addresses in Pacific Heights as Fashion marched westward. At the corner of Washington and Octavia streets is **2100 Washington Street**, a fine white, French-style city mansion. Its Octavia Street side is especially impressive and makes a fine pair with the French-influenced Spreckels Mansion. Its front yard has been walled in and an attractive pergola introduced at its entrance.

Next door to the west is red brick **2108 Washington Street**, a house with a complex history. It seems to have been built between 1875 and 1885 for Frank Griffen and stood near the Spreckels wall. In 1921 it was moved to this site and in 1925 was completely remodeled by architect Lewis P. Hobart and faced in red brick. Today it is a Georgian Revival building. The fine first-floor bow "window" solarium that stretches across the front was added in 1988. This house has walled in its front yard for privacy.

White **2120 Washington Street** is a Classical Revival box built in 1908 for the president of a lumber company. It banished bay windows from its facade, though one appears on the west side of the house facing the Phelan Mansion.

- **The Mary Phelan Mansion,** *1915, Charles Peter Weeks*

James Duvall Phelan, scion of a wealthy Irish Catholic banking family, built this palazzo for his sister Mary after the fire of 1906 destroyed the family home at Seventeenth and Valencia streets. It was designed by Charles Peter Weeks and completed in 1915 in time for the great Exposition. The buff brick Renaissance Revival mansion was the scene of elaborate receptions. The glassed-in loggia was a later improvement. Neither Senator Phelan nor his sister ever married; James had his own suite in the house.

James Duvall Phelan served as a Democratic reform mayor of San Francisco from 1894 to 1902, and as U.S. senator from California from 1915 to 1921. As mayor he was the first to use substantial bond issues to improve the city and was the first to begin landscaping the city's neglected neighborhood parks. He was active in the City Beautiful movement and led the Association for the Improvement and Adornment of San Francisco that funded the unexecuted Burnham Plan of 1905. He was chiefly responsible for the imposing Merchant's Exchange Building on California Street (*see Tour 2A*), and also built the handsome Phelan Building at Market, O'Farrell, and Grant streets. In the aftermath of the earthquake and fire of 1906 he helped run the Relief Committee. He was the principal benefactor in the construction of imposing St. Ignatius Church adjoining the campus of the Jesuit University of San Francisco, his *alma mater*. Today the Mary Phelan Mansion is a Buddhist monastery.

Villa Montalvo
P.O. Box 158, Saratoga 95071; (408) 741-3421

Washington Tower
2190 Washington Street

Spreckels Mansion
2080 Washington Street, at Octavia

James D. Phelan also built an elaborate estate south of San Francisco in Saratoga, nestled aganist the Santa Cruz Mountains. **Villa Montalvo**, a Mediterranean villa constructed in 1912, sits in 175 acres of grounds landscaped by John McLaren of Golden Gate Park fame. Bachelor Senator Phelan made his country place a center of social, political, and artistic life in California. He was a great patron of the arts, and when he died he left Villa Montalvo as a retreat for artists and as a house museum. Concerts, art exhibitions, theater, and poetry are also presented there.

• **Washington Tower**, *1960, Heiada & Muir*
On the corner of Washington and Laguna, behind a glitzy sidewalk, is highrise Washington Tower, a Miami-modern import of 1960 on the site of the lost Irwin mansion. It makes no effort to relate to its surroundings.

❸ Spreckels Mansion, *1913, MacDonald and Applegarth*
The palatial reinforced-concrete, white Utah limestone–faced mansion at Washington and Octavia streets was built in 1912 for Adolph and Alma de Bretteville Spreckels. It occupies almost half a block and is distinguished by paired columns, French windows, and balconies with richly scrolled metal balustrades. *Putti* uphold escutcheons over the windows and under the balconies.

Adolph Spreckels was one of the many sons of German-born sugar magnate Claus Spreckels, who came to control all the sugar refineries in San Francisco. Claus developed a vast sugarbeet operation in the Salinas Valley and moved on to finance a Hawaiian sugar kingdom and to control much of its cane production and shipping. His son Adolph followed him into the sugar business.

In 1908, at age fifty, Adolph married twenty-four-year-old San Francisco–born Alma de Bretteville. (Young Alma had studied nights at the old Mark Hopkins Institute of Art, and one of her instructors, Robert Aitken, selected her as the model for the figure of Victory that tops the **Dewey Monument** in Union Square.) Together Alma and Adolph had this grand house built before the opening of the 1915 Panama–Pacific International Exposition. The great fair could be seen on the Bay front below from the mansion's north windows. When the lots were accumulated for the grand house, Mrs. Spreckels insisted on saving and moving from them six Victorian houses that sat on Jackson, and two facing Washington Street. In 1924 the Spreckels gave the **California Palace of the Legion of Honor** in Lincoln Park, also designed by *Ecole des Beaux Arts*–trained George A. Applegarth, to San Francisco; Mrs. Spreckels

2006 Washington Street

2000 Washington Street

2040 Gough Street

2030 Gough Street

2004-10 Gough Street

additionally gave the museum its fine collection of Rodin sculptures. (*See Tour 14.*) Today the grand pile is the home of novelist Danielle Steel and her large family.

4 **2006 and 2000 Washington Street Community Apartments**

Immediately east of the Spreckels Mansion is the elegant, ten-story, salmon-colored apartment building at **2006 Washington Street.** Designed by C. A. Meussdorffer in 1925, this concrete building is one of the finest "community apartment" houses, if not *the* finest, ever constructed in San Francisco. (Community apartments are in cooperative apartment buildings where tenants are shareholders in the corporation that owns and maintains the building.) Each floor is a separate unit as large as a sizable house. The original residents included oil man Roscoe Oakes and his wife Margaret (who donated choice paintings by Rembrandt to the de Young Museum), Dean Witter, founder of the stock brokerage firm, and several members of the Schilling family, of Schilling spices.

The building is designed to face not the streets but the low-rise Spreckels Mansion and the Golden Gate to the west. Between it and the Spreckels Mansion there is a large garden with a curving, brick-paved ramp leading to an underground garage. A figure of Pan playing his pipes decorates the garage approach. As with many of San Francisco's most sophisticated traditional buildings, it is painted all one color, with no emphasis given to its decorative elements. The building's salmon color has a warm glow at sunset. Green trees peek out from a roof garden.

Next door is **2000 Washington**, on the corner of Gough, built in 1922 and also designed by C. A. Meussdorffer. While less showy, this fine seven-story, seven-unit, Beaux Arts apartment building is another luxurious building with fine views to the north out over the Bay. It, too, is painted in one color, a soft gray; only its metalwork is painted a contrasting black.

5 **Gough Street Townhouses and Victorians**

Of the 1960s apartment buildings on the southeast corner of Gough and Washington, the less said the better. Such bleak designs will probably experience facelifts in the future since their location is so superior to their architecture. Past them is a pair of fine townhouses, **2040 Gough Street**, a red brick Georgian Revival house, and **2030 Gough Street**, a Tudor Revival stucco design. These early-twentieth-century houses fill out more of their lot than Victorians did and were built with ample garages underneath them. The two dissimilarly styled houses share a similar form and join to create a U-shaped garden space.

The Belden-Buck House at **2004–10 Gough Street** is a large Queen Anne built in 1889 and designed by T. C. Matthew and Son. This very fine frame house is a great example of a late Victorian San Francisco upper-class residence. The design features a central chimney that rises through the center of the façade and a set of cylindrical bays, two stories high on the right and one story on the left. The whole design is an essay in asymmetrical disposition of building elements. Between the first and second floor is a large carved masklike face set in carved foliage. A large stained-glass window depicting the Bay is set in the west side of the house next to the present parking area. Art-glass windows were used on the sides of houses to let in light but to obscure the view of neighboring side walls. At **2000 Gough Street**, on the northeast corner of Clay, stands a fine Eastlake–Queen Anne house built in 1886. The old house has been much expanded to the rear with decks and added rooms that you can see from Clay Street.

6 St. Regis Apartments

Built into the edge of Lafayette Park is 1925 Gough Street, the **St. Regis Apartments**, a midrise Beaux Arts luxury apartment house built in 1907 and designed by C. A. Meussdorffer. It is surrounded on three sides by parkland and enjoys a unique location. It is the heir to the many claims made to a string of lots within the park. The city, in a compromise, permitted the construction of this building in order to secure the rest of the properties for incorporation into the park.

7 Clay Street Moderne Flats/1950 Clay Street

The steep block of Clay between Gough and Franklin streets enjoys fine views of Nob Hill's highrises and the tops of the Financial District's highrises on the other side of the hill. On the south side of Clay is a group of three three-flat apartment houses built about 1938: numbers **1977–79–81, 1969–71–73, and 1963–65–67 Clay Street**, designed by Martin Rist. These fine stucco flats are set back from the sidewalk in a staggered pattern with attractively landscaped planter-gardens set in front of them. They do not have bay windows; instead they sport wrap-around corner windows, with shallow, false balconies set beneath them. At their garage bases, the buildings have steel columns and curved walls with glass blocks. Portholes decorate the setback garage doors.

Across Clay is the black canvas canopy of **1950 Clay Street**, a beige and tan highrise concrete apartment building in the Art Deco style, designed by Baumann & Jose and built in 1930. This swank design features a splashy Art Deco lobby with a metal grille and plate glass door, bay windows, and an Art Deco roofline with jazzy ornament. Even during the depressed 1930s some construction continued in Pacific Heights and on Russian Hill, oftentimes the best residential highrise construction the city was ever to see.

8 Golden Gate Spiritualist Church, *circa 1900*

On the corner of Franklin and Clay streets, with its entrance on prestigious Franklin Street, is the restrained, white Classical Revival house built at the turn of the century for a member of the Crocker family. Edwardian reticence and the reaction against the late Queen Annes resulted in restrained designs such as this archetypical example.

2000 Gough Street

St. Regis Apartments
1925 Gough Street

**1977–79–81,
1969–71–73, and
1963–65–67 Clay Street**

1950 Clay Street

Golden Gate Spiritualist Church
1901 Franklin Street at Clay; 885-9976

Edward Coleman House
1701 Franklin Street,
corner of California

The gumdrop shrubbery around the building and the unadorned lawns on the graded embankments are traditional. The wood house is intended to look like stone, as is the cement-stuccoed brick retaining wall around the high lot. A few minimal alterations were made when the house was converted into a church. Note the way this lowrise mansion sets off the Art Deco wall of highrise 1950 Clay to its west.

The founder of this Spiritualist church was the Reverend Florence S. Becker, a medium who organized a congregation in 1924. Spiritualists affirm that "communication with the so-called dead is a fact, scientifically proven by the phenomena of Spiritualism."

9 *California and Franklin Victorian and Edwardian Mansion Group*

This group of great houses and rare gardens is best studied first from across the busy intersection. (Be careful here; Franklin is a one-way speedway north to the Golden Gate Bridge.)

- **Edward Coleman House**, *1895, W. H. Lillie*

This 1895 house is a high point in San Francisco architecture and building. Designed by W. H. Lillie in what is now called the Queen Anne style, it is late Victorian domestic perfection and one of the most beautiful old buildings in San Francisco. Its great round corner tower with curved glass windows accommodates very large bays attached to the principal rooms. In its massing and the arrangement of its component parts, the house shows how Victorian architects turned the corner of an important block, giving the intersection of two important streets a sense of definition and the inhabitants splendid views of their surroundings.

The fine, expansive corner mansion was finished inside with choice woods. **Edward Coleman**, who built this house, owned the Idaho Gold Mine in Grass Valley, California, and made another fortune in timber. The adjacent lot on Franklin Street was bought for a garden. The house survived the years of active hatred of "Victorian monstrosities" because it was bought by the Bransten family, the owners of 1735 Franklin, the red brick townhouse immediately to its north, in order to preserve that house's sunlight and view.

Over the years, 1701 Franklin became a pleasant boardinghouse and later a card club. In 1975 it was restored and converted into law offices. At that time the original gray color of the house was changed to contemporary colors that accentuate the wreath and garland plaster scratchwork bands decorating the house. The conical roof of the round corner tower is capped by an elaborate finial so that the outline of the building comes to a fine flourish on the skyline. The high front porch facing Franklin is light and elegant and incorporates subtle curves. A peek through the window of its elegant front door (this is now an office, not a private home) reveals the house's central hall. The outer vestibule is paneled in golden oak and has a fine frieze of garlands, wreaths, and torches.

• **Lilienthal-Pratt House**, *1876, architect unknown*
1818 California Street Bed and Breakfast
The **Lilienthal-Pratt House** sits atop a graded lot with a high retaining wall capped by a black iron fence; garages were inserted in 1988. The front stairs march straight up to the front door. A sunny, flower-filled garden flourishes along the east side of the house. The building has a flat roof with a very impressive cornice along its top. (Flat roofs evolved in San Francisco because the climate is so mild here with no snow and only occasional heavy rains.)

Lilienthal-Pratt House
1818 California Street Bed and Breakfast
1818 California Street
Phone 885-1818 for information and reservations.

Wormser-Coleman House
1834 California Street

The richly ornamented façade is enlivened with redwood ornament. The general aim was to imitate stone buildings, thus the quoins along the corners. The building is not a simple rectangle in its floor plan; there is a slightly projecting set-back "wing" along the right-hand side of the house. In completed rows of such houses, this "slot" allowed ventilation of the rooms in the middle of the house and also permitted reflected sunlight to filter into the house's dark midsection. This 1876 Italianate Victorian house is worth close attention because it is the "ideal type" of the San Francisco Victorian row house, slightly blown up in size.

This style of house is called Italianate in San Francisco because of the Renaissance Revival details adopted from the Pall Mall London men's clubs of the 1840s. The Italianate style was sometimes referred to as "London Roman" in nineteenth-century San Francisco. Slant-sided windows were in vogue during the Italianate era. (In the Eastlake and Stick styles that followed the Italianate style in the 1880s, the bay window was pushed out into a rectangle to capture more space. In the Queen Anne style of the 1890s, bay windows reached their most elaborated form and became smooth semicircles or three-quarter circles at corners with curved panes of glass.)

The Lilienthal-Pratt House was a wedding gift from Louis Sloss to his daughter Hanna and her husband, Ernest Lilienthal. Sloss formed the Alaska Commercial Company and secured the concession to harvest seal skins off the Aleutian Islands. This became the foundation of a great fortune. The house was later broken up into apartments. Today the elegant Italianate has been restored and redecorated as the **1818 California Bed and Breakfast Inn.** Walk up the California Street hill to the neighboring mansion.

• **Wormser-Coleman House**, *1876, architect unknown; 1895, additions and remodeling by Percy & Hamilton*
Standing in unusual isolation on its double lot, this great house with its imposing granite and marble stairs is an amalgam of an 1876 Italianate style house (the right-hand side) greatly expanded and partly remodeled in 1895 with a Queen Anne round corner tower by Percy & Hamilton. The 1876 house was built by **Isaac Wormser**, a pioneer merchant and the "W" in S&W Fine Foods. In 1895 the house was bought by **John C. Coleman**, a gold miner and utilities investor and the brother of the man who built the corner Queen Anne. Active in telephone, gas, and railroad companies, Coleman was also a director of the California Street Cable Railroad that served his mansion. In the wake of the 1906 earthquake and fire, this house served as the temporary headquarters of the cable line.

Bransten House
1735 Franklin Street

First Church of Christ, Scientist
1700 Franklin Street, at California

For many years the quiet house was preserved by Miss Persis Coleman in its original light gray color scheme, with black window sash and green shades. New owners have freshened up the stately house with agreeable, light colors and enhanced the garden with many young trees. The great symmetrical tree is a mature Norfolk pine, one of the many exotic plants imported by the Victorians to enliven their treeless city. Return to the corner of California and Franklin and turn right up Franklin Street. As you repass the corner Coleman House you will note the beautiful lavender stained-glass window on the north side facing the garden.

* **Bransten House**, *1904, Herman Barth*

The red brick Georgian Revival **Bransten House**, built in 1904, presents a severe and plain façade to Franklin Street. A modern house, it is quite different from the Victorians all around it. It is much simpler looking, calmer, even introspective. This long, narrow house was designed to face the south side of its lot and the garden of the neighboring Coleman House. Many turn-of-the-century San Francisco houses pushed the front door back to the middle of the house, creating more space for a grand parlor facing the street. Centered in the façade is a framed window with Ionic columns and a segmented arch pediment.

Having designed their house to take advantage of the garden next door, the Branstens eventually bought the neighboring mansions at 1701 Franklin and 1818 California to prevent their demolition for apartment buildings, thus protecting their own sunlight and garden view.

The Bransten House was a wedding gift from the William Haases of 2007 Franklin Street when their daughter Florine married Edward Bransten in 1904. Edward Bransten's company was MJB Coffee. Florine continued to live here as a widow from 1948 to 1973, three blocks away from her sister, Alice Haas Lilienthal.

⑩ First Church of Christ, Scientist, *1911, Edgar A. Matthews*

On this prominent corner at the edge of the burned district, the Christian Scientists built this fine church, notable for its subtle and sophisticated use of color. The exterior of the sober Tuscan Revival church with its corner tower is clad in tapestry brick of a generally light yellowish color. Set into the brickwork is fine polychrome terra-cotta. The roof is clad in green glazed tiles. Green copper eaves and soffits circle the church. Over the front doors are inset windows of streaked art glass rich with color. Inscriptions over the doors read: "God is Spirit," "God is Life," "God is Truth," 'God is Love."

The fine square tower of the First Church of Christ, Scientist converses with the round tower of the Coleman House across the street, making a gateway to Pacific Heights for the stream of traffic pouring up one-way Franklin.

• **Franklin Street Apartment Buildings**, *1912, architect unknown*
Between 1906 and 1930, upscale apartment buildings replaced most of the Victorian houses of eastern Pacific Heights. This five-story, bay-windowed apartment building has a slightly French feeling to it. The floor plans of such units are almost always intelligently laid out. Commodious rooms and "ancillary" amenities such as foyers, glass interior doors, walk-in storage closets, and built-in storage furniture in kitchens and baths produced a compact, civilized standard of urban accommodation, particularly for singles and couples. These buildings are the real stuff of eastern Pacific Heights. Viewed from across the Bay or from the Sausalito ferry, they are the countless facets of white, cubist San Francisco.

Franklin Street Apartment Buildings
1740 Franklin Street

Haas-Lilienthal House Museum/The Foundation for San Francisco's Architectural Heritage
2007 Franklin Street
Heritage also conducts walks in the city, an annual open house tour, and other educational programs; 441-3004

⓫ **Haas-Lilienthal House Museum/The Foundation for San Francisco's Architectural Heritage**, *1886, Peter R. Schmidt; 1928, Gardner A. Dailey, wing and garage*
Tours of the interior of the turreted Haas-Lilienthal House afford a glimpse of a Pacific Heights Victorian as it was lived in by one San Francisco family from 1886 to 1972. **Alice Haas Lilienthal**, born a year before her parents built this house, lived here until her death in 1972. She preserved her family house on the once-fashionable street as all the buildings around were demolished for apartment buildings.

Architect Peter R. Schmidt's 1886 design takes the standardized floor plan of the typical San Francisco row house and increases it in all dimensions to fit this larger, upper-middle-class lot. The house has evolved over time. The front parlor was remodeled in the 1890s with a warm, yellow Sienna marble fireplace. The middle parlor is paneled in wide boards of fine redwood and has a red Numidian marble-faced hearth. The dining room is late 1880s in feel, with golden oak wainscotting and embossed wallpaper walls. The kitchen has an old sinkboard, servants' call box, and original simple plaster walls and wood cabinets and wainscotting. The stove dates from the 1920s, when many appliances were modernized and an elevator was installed. A compatible wing with a garage downstairs was added in 1928 and designed by Gardner A. Dailey.

In 1974, Alice Haas Lilienthal's heirs donated the old house to **The Foundation for San Francisco's Architectural Heritage**, founded in 1971 and a member-supported, nonprofit organization dedicated to the preservation of buildings and places important to San Francisco's architectural and historic character. Heritage operates the Haas-Lilienthal house as its headquarters and opens the principal rooms of the landmark to the public for guided tours.

The best view of the Haas-Lilienthal House is from across Franklin Street, at the northeast corner of Clay, looking northwest. From there the long south wall can be seen, along with the building's four gables. The manipulated gables make it appear that the building has a pitched roof; it actually has a flat roof. The corner turret with its framed windows is strictly decorative; its windows are some ten feet off the unfinished tower floor. If you walk north up Franklin to look at the facade frontally, a curious thing happens: The house seems to fold up into a tense, compressed design. Viewed from this angle, the facade becomes an ascending series of three triangles; the porch gable, the false central gable, and the conical roof of the turret with its triangular-pedimented window. The houses of this period—1886 to 1889—were the most wildly imagined residential designs California ever saw. They used all the basic geometric forms: rectangles, cylinders, and triangles combined in boldly interpenetrating combinations.

Haas-Lilienthal House

⓬ Greenlee Terrace Apartments, *1913, Arthur J. Laib*

Greenlee Terrace
Apartments
1925–55 Jackson Street

From about 1900 through the 1920s, courtyard complexes were built in San Francisco and Los Angeles in prestigious neighborhoods. Almost pueblolike, these flats step up the hill. Stucco and theater produce a most agreeable regional architectural "set" combining Mission Revival and Craftsman imagery. Designed as cells within the city, the building creates a strong sense of place and apartness. The palm-landscaped stairs are private and not part of the public sidewalk. The design can be amply enjoyed visually from across the street without entering it. The landscaping here adds much to the islandlike feeling of this complex.

Matson-Roth Houses/
German Consulate
*1950 and 1960
Jackson Street*

2010 Jackson Street

2020 Jackson Street

⓭ Matson-Roth Houses/German Consulate, *1918, circa 1924, Walter Bliss*

This sophisticated pair of orange brick Georgian Revival townhouses forms a U that shelters an elegant garden. The two were built by the widow of Swedish-born shipping magnate William Matson. Matson forged a great shipping company, Matson Navigation, and also developed California oil fields and had extensive investments in Hawaii. After his death in 1917, Mrs. Matson built 1960 Jackson Street, the larger house to the left of the court, for herself. About 1924, she built 1950 Jackson Street for her daughter and son-in-law, Mr. and Mrs. William P. Roth. After Mrs. Matson's death and the Roths' purchase of Filoli, the William Bourn estate on the San Mateo Peninsula (*see Tour 16*), the twin houses were sold. For some time they were most appropriately the Swedish consulate. In 1987 they were bought, restored, and adapted for the German consulate. The houses enjoy fine views of the entrance to the harbor. William M. Roth, the builder's grandson, developed Ghirardelli Square in the 1960s.

⓮ *2000 Block of Jackson Street*

The 2000 block of Jackson Street, between Octavia and Laguna, has an eclectic array of houses, apartments, and condominiums from the Victorian to the modern period. The second house in, **2010 Jackson Street**, is a two-story neoclassical contemporary house with two statues and a pergola on its second story. It was built by socialite billboard heir George Kleiser, Jr. It features a private central court and was designed by Ted Moulton in 1960; the upper floor was added in 1988 and designed by George Livermore. In front of the reticent house is a very fine white granite and black iron low front fence preserved from the Victorian house that once stood here.

The Classical Revival yellow brick mansion at **2020 Jackson Street** was built for I. W. Hellman, the founder of the Union Trust Company and principal stockholder in Wells Fargo Bank. It dates from about 1902 and was designed by Reid Brothers. Here again Edwardian self-control dominates. A formal Ionic colonnade lines the side entranceway. The front door has a fine iron grille. Immediately after the earthquake and fire in 1906, this house became the temporary headquarters of Wells Fargo Bank.

2030 and 2040 Jackson Street

2045 Jackson Street

Whittier Mansion
2090 Jackson Street, at Laguna

2030 and 2040 Jackson Street, a pair of Mediterranean-style houses, form another U-shape. Decorated bays, grillework balconies, and emphatically molded ornament create idealized architectural images of California as reinvented in the early twentieth century.

Across the street, behind the classical balustrade of the back of the 1915 Phelan Mansion, is a new house at **2045 Jackson Street** completed in 1988 to designs by Hornberger, Worstell & Associates. This commodius residence with lofty ceilings presents an air of classical formality. Though it looks like stone or concrete, it is conventional frame and stucco. Copper-crowned chimneys and two oval windows make a picturesque, postmodern skyline. This is a sophisticated design that does not attract too much attention to itself. Glimpsed between the pair is the back of the buff brick Phelan Mansion with its loggia and horizontal picture window looking out over the Bay.

⓯ Whittier Mansion, *1896, Edward R. Swain*
The red Arizona sandstone-clad **Whittier Mansion** was designed by Edward R. Swain in 1896 for William Frank Whittier, partner in a large paint and glass company. Whittier was a Maine man who came to San Francisco in 1854 at twenty-two. He became a director of what is today Pacific Gas & Electric Company. Whittier's house is unusual in San Francisco for its steel-reinforced brick walls and red stone facing. Swain designed a house that incorporated all the latest mechanical equipment. There was an electric converter to change city streetcar power to house current, an Otis hydraulic elevator, combination gas and electric lighting fixtures, a central heating system, and a large attic water-storage tank. The house rode out the 1906 earthquake, suffering only toppled chimneys. For many years this was the home of the California Historical Society, which has since moved to the Yerba Buena Center area (*see Tour 1*). Walk down steep Laguna Street and turn right (east) onto the 2000 block of Pacific Avenue with its Victorian cluster.

⓰ *2000 Block of Pacific Avenue: Victorian Cluster*

Pacific Heights has always had some construction, even during hard times. Thus this neighborhood has more different architectural styles than any other in San Francisco. The 2000 block of Pacific Avenue is something of an architectural zoo. Two large Hollywood Spanish apartment blocks stand on the northwest corner of Pacific and Laguna on the view side of the block. Victorian houses on view corners were more likely to be replaced with apartment buildings than were houses on the nonview side of the street, a pattern that is evident on this prime block.

A cluster of turreted Victorian houses from the 1890s survives along the south side of the block with an interesting medieval Tudor stucco house in their midst. At **2027 Pacific Avenue** is an Eastlake-style house designed by W. H. Wickersham in 1890. The three Queen Anne houses at **2019, 2021, and 2023 Pacific Avenue** were also built in 1890. Here and there on the eclectic block are drab 1960s motellike apartments built during the decade when San Francisco temporarily lost her architectural uniqueness to bland, cheap designs.

At the corner of Pacific and Octavia, at **2000 Pacific Avenue**, is a real treasure, a fine Queen Anne–Colonial Revival house of 1894 with a round corner bay, designed by Henry Burns. The house has fine art glass in its vestibule and in its first-floor enframed window. The Octavia Street side of the house has a spectacular stained-glass window inset with "jewels."

2027 Pacific Avenue

2019, 2021, and 2023 Pacific Avenue

2000 Pacific Avenue

2405 to 2415 Octavia Street

1940 and 1960 Broadway

2000 Broadway

 2400 Block of Octavia Street Victorians

Here Octavia Street plunges downhill. If you look back uphill you can see the landscaped islands in the brick-paved block of Octavia flanking the Spreckels Mansion. The west side of the 2400 block of Octavia Street harbors a fine row of 1890s Queen Anne Victorians. The five similar-looking houses at **2405 to 2415 Octavia Street** were designed by William Hinkel in 1892. At Broadway turn left (west).

18 1940 and 1960 Broadway: Luxury Apartment Towers, *1925, 1923, Bos & Quant*

On the view side of the 1900 block of prestigious Broadway stand 1940 and 1960 Broadway, two elegant and unusual ten-story apartment towers both designed by Bos & Quant. Number **1940 Broadway** dates from 1925 and **1960 Broadway** from 1923. Both are built of steel and concrete and embellished with 1920s decoration. They positively exude Old Money. There is an interesting view between the two towers from across Broadway with partial views of two fancifully detailed apartment buildings on Vallejo Street downhill. Here is a grouping of the best 1920s apartment buildings.

19 2000 Broadway, *1973, Backen, Arrigoni & Ross*

The twelve-story unpainted concrete highrise at 2000 Broadway, at the northwest corner of Laguna, introduced a new style to Pacific Heights: 1970s Concrete Brutalism. The base of its Laguna Street side and its Broadway-facing bays display a remarkable gracelessness. The rectangular projecting bays along elegant Broadway have stingy little slit windows and present mostly concrete to the street. If the façade almost looks like the back of an industrial building, that is because the west side of the tower, facing the Golden Gate, is the "front" of the complex with metal-sash floor-to-ceiling windows looking to the view. The central court that cuts through the dense stack of units is more like a light well than a courtyard. The freestanding concrete entrance canopy with the proud address "2000 Broadway" has all the subtlety of a child's block set. Unpainted gray concrete is a particularly offensive material in San Francisco. It ages unattractively and is dull and depressing in fog or rain. This is the kind of design that gave modern architecture a bad name and that led to architectural preservation in the 1970s and the postmodern reaction of the 1980s.

2040 Broadway

The Hamlin School/James Leary Flood Mansion
2120 Broadway

2129 Vallejo Street

• **2040 Broadway**, *1987, Frizell Hill Moorehouse*
The blockbuster towers of the 1960s and 1970s have been out-lawed by recent zoning. Today, a kind of "contexturalist" zoning requires recent buildings to fit into their environment, so that build-ings in Pacific Heights tend, for example, to be the average height of their neighbors; if the neighbors are set back from the street, so will the new building be. Four-story 2040 Broadway was built in 1987 to designs by Frizell Hill Moorehouse and has twelve units. It might be described as being in the postmodern French mansard style. A gas lamp burns over the entrance and the cornice is garnished with heroic-sized grape clusters.

㉑ The Hamlin School/James Leary Flood Mansion, *1901, Julius Krafft*
The gray **James Leary Flood Mansion** is one of San Francisco's great Edwardian man-sions. Its lines are quiet, expansive, dignified. Built of wood, it is designed to look like a stone palazzo. It sits behind extraordinarily fine monolithic white granite entrance pillars and a now-green bronze fence. The front stairs and landings are made from sin-gle large pieces of the finest Raymond, California granite. Seen from the foot of the steps, the facade of the classically detailed house creates a stacked-up pyramid of forms: the porch, loggia, and horizontal third-floor window pile one atop the other. The twin gray marble lions guarding the steps are nicknamed **Leo** and **Leona**. A peek through the elaborate grille over the front door reveals the golden-oak and red-brocade–paneled central hall.

The most remarkable interior is the red lacquer–paneled, bamboo-ceilinged Chinese Room with green silk-lined walls. An elaborate Chinese-style man-telpiece here has sea-green marble. There were once many of these Chinese-style rooms in San Francisco's mansions; this is one of the last original interiors of its kind to sur-vive. A porte cochère stands at the west end of the house, and a driveway leads behind the mansion. From there the mosaic-tiled solarium, which projects from the back of the house, can be seen. The view of the Bay from here is splendid.

Today the building, now called Stanwood Hall, houses offices and classrooms of the **Hamlin School**. Directly below are the rooftop playgrounds of the new Hamlin school building, McKinney Hall, at **2129 Vallejo Street**, designed by Wurster, Bernardi and Emmons in 1967 in a simple, pure Bay Region version of the International Style. In 1970 Walker and Moody designed a science building, Jennie Mae Hooker Laboratory, which is tucked behind the Vallejo Street building.

Mr. and Mrs. James Flood and his sister Cora Jane—"Miss Jennie"—moved into the house in 1906 after the earthquake and fire gutted the brown-stone Flood mansion atop Nob Hill (today the Pacific–Union Club). Eleven years later, James Leary Flood built another mansion a block west at 2222 Broadway. He and his wife moved there in 1913 and gave this house to Miss Jennie. She retired to the Fairmont Hotel in 1924, and in 1928 Mrs. Edward B. Stanwood, head of the Sarah Dix Hamlin School, bought the mansion from the Regents of the University of California, converting its principal rooms into classrooms and the third-floor servants'

quarters into rooms for boarders. Founded in 1863 as the Van Ness
Seminary, the school is the oldest nonsectarian independent school
for girls west of the Mississippi. It became a nonprofit educational
institution in 1955 and is today an independent day school for some
three hundred girls. Walk to Webster Street, turn left, and approach
the dark red brick Bourn Mansion.

21 Bourn Mansion, *1896, Willis Polk*

The imposing, dark clinker brick townhouse built for William Bowers Bourn in 1896
is one of the most forceful house designs in San Francisco. The façade has at its center one large, ornately framed window with a shallow stone balcony. The entrance is
a "tunnel" set under this overpowering focal point. While conventionally described as
"Georgian Revival," it is perhaps better called Manipulated Georgian. From
Broadway, the baronial house presents double gables and a formidable array of towering chimneys. Inside the rusticated ground floor were two waiting rooms, one light
and airy and French for ladies, another dark and masculine in the Craftsman style for
gentlemen. Beyond the central hall an imposing staircase rises to the second floor, the
piano nobile. Beyond a reception area embellished with Bruce Porter peacock murals
was Bourn's stately parlor, with a monumental marble mantelpiece and at the north
end a great bay window with a view of the Golden Gate.

Willis Polk designed several monumental buildings for Bourn: this
house, the Empire Cottage at the Empire Gold Mine in Grass Valley in 1897–98, the
Jessie Street Substation for PG&E, off Mission Street near Yerba Buena Gardens, in
1905–09, and the great Georgian Revival estate of Filoli in the San Mateo watershed
lands in 1916. (*See Tour 16.*)

Bourn inherited a Gold Rush mining fortune and eventually controlled the Spring Valley Water Company (which provided San Francisco with all its
water, at a high price) and became president of the San Francisco Gas Company. In
1888 he built the largest stone winery in Napa Valley, today the Christian Brothers
Greystone Cellars, in St. Helena. Bourn's princely taste also resulted in PG&E's elegant substations, tucked away in alleys throughout the city. (See *Tour 16.*)

㉒ **Joseph Donohoe Grant Mansion: School of the Sacred Heart**, *1910, Hiss and Weekes; 1948, conversion into girls' elementary school*

• **James Leary Flood Mansion: Convent of the Sacred Heart High School**, *1912, Bliss and Faville; 1940, Timothy Pfleuger, conversion into convent and girls' high school*

• **Andrew Hammond Mansion: Stuart Hall School for Boys**, *1905, architect unknown; 1956, conversion into boys' elementary school*

The greatest single private conserver of great San Francisco architecture is the **Convent** and **Schools of the Sacred Heart**. The three great mansions at Broadway and Webster Street are an outstanding architectural grouping: two large red-brick mansions frame the set-back pink Tennessee marble Italian Renaissance palazzo built by James Leary Flood in 1913, the stateliest house ever erected in San Francisco.

To the right of the Flood Mansion, at the northeast corner of Webster, is the red brick and limestone **Joseph Donohoe Grant Mansion** designed in 1910 by Hiss and Weekes for the heir to a dry goods fortune. Two giant urns flank its semi-circular entry. In 1920 Grant helped found the Save-the-Redwoods League; there is a J. D. Grant Redwood Grove in Del Norte State Park named in his honor. In 1948 the mansion was added to the **School of the Sacred Heart**. It serves today as a girl's elementary school.

Designed by Bliss and Faville and built with a budget that knew no bounds, the **Flood Mansion** (now the Convent of the Sacred Heart High School) is the equivalent of a great hotel in its equipment and scale. The façade of the steel-frame building is clad in the finest stonework in San Francisco. The carefully matched blocks of Tennessee marble form a smooth background for the delicate carving that surrounds the entrance and the great windows. Two spiraled Corinthian columns frame the metal and plate-glass front door. A peek through the superb wrought-iron grille allows a view down the immense, 140-foot-long entrance hall paved with Rosato Vicenza marble, ending in a bay window overlooking the Golden Gate. A side gate near the children's playground to the right is usually open, and you may turn the corner and view the great *cortile*. This magnificent space originally had a large reflecting pool and a fountain. The tree ferns here came from the Australian pavilion at the 1915 Exposition. When the house was unobtrusively converted into a school by master architect Timothy Pfleuger in 1940, the elaborate arcaded bay of the drawing room was filled in with stained-glass windows for the school chapel.

To the left of the earlier, white Flood Mansion, at 2222 Broadway, is the **Andrew Hammond Mansion**, an Edwardian red brick townhouse built about 1905 for a lumber and railroad magnate. In 1956 it was converted into Stuart Hall School for Boys. Walk to the corner of Broadway and Fillmore.

㉓ *View of the Palace of Fine Arts and the Golden Gate*

From the corner of Broadway and Fillmore, looking west, there is a view down into a small valley filled with opulent houses with mature back gardens. This is one of the choicest residential pockets in San Francisco. About halfway down the steep block of Fillmore between Broadway and Vallejo, with its stepped sidewalk, a sweeping panorama of the north Bay and the Golden Gate opens before you. This area was known as Harbor View in the nineteenth century. Today's white, lowrise Marina District at the base of the hill was a tidal marsh filled in for the Panama–Pacific International Exposition of 1915. The great ocher dome of Maybeck's **Palace of Fine Arts** floats over the west end of the Marina (*see Tour 14*). Green forests blanket the Army Presidio. There is a good profile view of the Art Deco Golden Gate Bridge from here.

Vedanta Society Temple
*2323 Vallejo Street;
Open daily for
meditation, 8 A.M.
to 7:30 P.M.; ring the
bell for access;* 922-2323

2963 Webster Street

㉔ **Vedanta Society Temple**, *1955, Henry Gutterson*
The pitched slate roof on the southwest corner of Vallejo and Fillmore is the New Temple of the Vedanta Society of Northern California. This austere late Art Deco concrete temple was designed in 1955, perhaps by Henry Gutterson. A flower-filled garden on the steep slope behind the temple is visible from the lobby stairs as you ascend to the temple itself. Inside the truss-roofed temple all is still. Diffused light filters through the frosted glass windows and illuminates the carved altar with its five figures. The symbol in the circle is "Om." Comfortable chairs with bent plywood frames fill the room. This is an ideal place to meditate.

Vedanta is a religion based on the philosophical texts known as the *Upanishads*. A booklet available here explains the teachings of Vedanta, which sees religion not as a matter of doctrine or belief but as realization of God-consciousness. Swami Vivekananda, a disciple of Sri Ramakrishna, brought Vedanta from India to the West in the 1890s.

The Old Temple is at **2963 Webster Street**, at the corner of Filbert, in the Marina district. Designed in 1905 by Joseph A. Leonard, it is an extraordinary bay-windowed Edwardian building with an upper story crowned with extravagant domes. There is no other exterior like it. Today it serves as the Society's monastery.

Continuation: Bus Connections, the Bay, and Upscale Shopping

To return to the Lafayette Park starting point from the end of this walk at Fillmore and Broadway, take the **22 Fillmore** trolley bus south to Fillmore and Sacramento, then transfer to the 1 California trolley bus heading east (downtown) on Sacramento back to Lafayette Park.

The 22 Fillmore trolley bus, which runs north and south through Eastern Pacific Heights, connects several points near the end of this tour. Heading north the 22 crosses Union Street, with its restaurants and shops, and ends across the street from the Bay, along the continuation of *Tour 5* that connects Fisherman's Wharf and Fort Mason with the Presidio. Headed south on Fillmore the 22 passes Upper Fillmore's restaurants and shops and the edge of Japantown *(Tour 9)*. At Fillmore and Sacramento you can catch the 1 California trolley bus headed west and get off at Laurel Street. On Laurel walk one block north to the elegant antique shops, galleries, and restaurants of outer Sacramento Street. Here you can experience San Francisco taste at its most sophisticated.

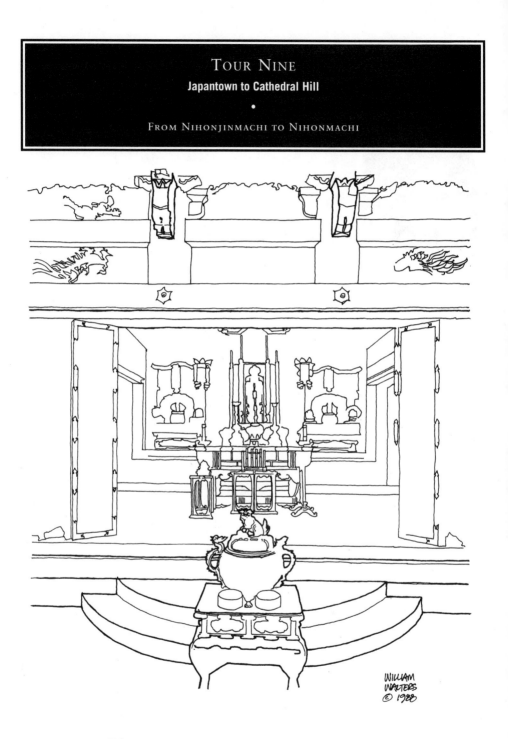

The altar of the Buddhist Church of America
on the second floor at 1881 Pine Street, at Octavia, dedicated in 1938 and designed
by Gentoko Shimamato, is perhaps the most beautiful room in Japantown.

What This Tour Covers
Preliminaries
Introduction: From Nihonjinmachi to Nihonmachi

Continuation
Bus Connections to Downtown, or out to the Cliff House

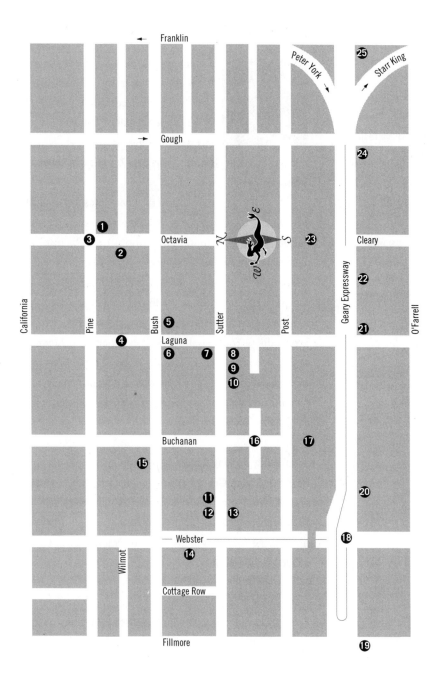

Japantown to Cathedral Hill

Preliminaries

Buddhist Church
1881 Pine Street, at
Octavia; 776-3158

The Soto Zen
Mission Sokoji
1691 Laguna Street

Cherry Blossom Festival
Japan Center, 1520
Webster Street; phone
922-6776 for information

City Parking Garage
under Japan Center

St. Mary's Cathedral
Gough Street, at Geary

BEST TIMES
TO DO
THIS TOUR

Sunday at 10 A.M. is the most convenient time to see the fine interiors of Japantown's temples. Start with the second-floor sanctuary of the stupa-capped **Buddhist Church**. The traditional recessed altar here is modeled on one in Kyoto and is remarkably beautiful. **The Soto Zen Mission Sokoji** on Laguna opens at 1 P.M.

Every April the **Cherry Blossom Festival** presents two weekends of festivities including a parade of costumed performers; write for more information. Each August, a weekend **Nihonmachi Street Fair** is held in the Japan Center and the **Buchanan Street Mall**. First held in 1973, the fair gathers a large multiracial but predominantly young Asian American audience to listen to a diverse program performed by Asian, black, brown, and white artists doing rock, soul, salsa, Polynesian, and Japanese music. Over forty nonprofit community organizations participate, many from the Western Addition as well as Japantown, and many performing arts groups, singers, musicians, and dancers perform.

Parking

A large **City Parking Garage** is located under Japan Center and can be entered from Geary Expressway headed west, between Laguna and Webster, and from Fillmore Street between Geary and Post. Parking here puts you at the end of the tour. **St. Mary's Cathedral** has a large free sunken parking lot entered from Gough Street headed south, at Geary.

Transportation

From Union Square, take the **3 Jackson trolley bus** west on Sutter Street and alight at Sutter and Octavia, in front of the Queen Anne Hotel; walk two easy uphill blocks north to Octavia and Pine and the Buddhist Church entrance around the corner on Pine.

RESTAURANTS

Elka, adjacent to the Miyako Hotel, boasts "definitive seafood." It may be the finest new restaurant in restaurant-rich San Francisco, and it certainly is,the best restaurant in Japantown. Artistic contem-porary interior. Make reservations well ahead of time; expensive but superb. **Isobune** in Japantown. Lunch and dinner daily; moderate. Sushi and other Japanese dishes. **Yoshida-Ya**. Dinner daily; moderate. A traditional menu including sushi, tempura, teriyaki, sashimi, and yakitori. **Yamato** near Grant Avenue and Chinatown. Lunch Tuesday to Saturday, dinner Tuesday to Sunday. Traditional menu and a sushi bar; bamboo-mat floor or table seating. **Kabuto Sushi** on Geary Boulevard, near Fifteenth Avenue in the Richmond District. Dinner Wednesday to Saturday to 2 A.M., Sunday to 11 P.M.; not only open late but active then. **Kyo-Ya Restaurant**, elegant and expensive.

SHOPPING

A few Japantown shops are mentioned in the tour, in the Nihonmachi Mall and Japan Center entries. **Soko Hardware Company** and the **Kinokuniya Bookstore** are especially noteworthy. Some shops outside Japantown are **Jeanne's Bonsai**, on Lake Street in the Richmond District. Open since 1972; has a large selection of tree varieties; will ship. **Kozo Paper**, on Castro Street, near Eighteenth Street in the Castro District, carries unbelievably beautiful handmade and printed Japanese papers; also notebooks, small boxes, and art objects covered in artistic Japanese paper.

Elka
1611 Post Street, near Laguna; 922-7788

Isobune
1737 Post Street, between Buchanan and Webster; 563-1030

Yoshida-Ya
2909 Webster Street, off Union Street; 346-3431

Yamato
717 California Street; 397-3456

Kabuto Sushi
5116 Geary Boulevard; 752-5652

Kyo-Ya Restaurant
at New Montgomery and Jessie streets, in the back corner of the Palace Hotel; 392-8600

Soko Hardware Company
1698 Post Street, at Buchanan; 931-5510

Kinokuniya Bookstore
In the West Building of the Japan Center; 567-7625

Jeanne's Bonsai
43 Lake Street, between Second Avenue and Arguello; 387-9492

Kozo Paper
531 Castro Street, near Eighteenth Street in the Castro District; 621-0869

Theatre of Yugen
2840 Mariposa Street,
near Alabama; 621-7978

Asian American Theater Company, *405 Arguello at Clement; 751-2600*

Asian American Dance Performances
2403 Sixteenth Street; 552-8980

AMC Kabuki 8 Theaters
located at Post and Fillmore in the western end of the Japan Center; 931-9800

ENTERTAINMENT

Theatre of Yugen was founded in 1978 by Yuriko Doi; specializes in Noh and Kyogen Japanese the ater but performs contemporary non-Japanese theater as well. Founded in 1973, the **Asian American Theater Company** company presents contemporary plays, often about the multiracial and generational experience of young Asian Americans. The **Asian American Dance Performances** was organized in 1974 and both performs and teaches dance. **AMC Kabuki 8 Theaters**, in the western end of the Japan Center. The small theater here is like a screening room and presents unusual films. Occasionally the San Francisco Film Society has screenings here, as do community arts groups. Inexpensive validated parking on weekdays after 5 P.M. and on weekends.

Introduction:
From Nihonjinmachi to Nihonmachi

Japantown is a small slice of the 1850s Western Addition, a sandy valley developed between the 1870s and the 1890s as the city's population grew by more than a hundred thousand. It was the first major middle-class expansion beyond the congested, accidentally built up, mostly jerry-built downtown. Developers built one to six row houses in groups along street car routes according to standard plans. Both native-born Americans and newly successful immigrants bought houses here. There was a notable infusion of Germans, Christian and Jewish, and of Irish Catholics. After the disruptions of the earthquake, about 1909, a zone along Post and Sutter streets from Franklin to Fillmore streets became the center of San Francisco's Japantown.

Like a historical yin and yang, the evolution of San Francisco's Chinatown and Japantown seem an almost too neat set of opposites. Chinatown is old, rooted, expansive, ad hoc, busy, and "exotic"; Japantown is new, diffused, smaller than it once was, planned, quiet, and actually quite American. Although both Chinese and Japanese immigrants suffered discrimination in the past and are successful today, their histories as communities in San Francisco have been remarkably divergent.

Some of these differences are rooted in the histories of China and Japan themselves. While China was a disintegrating empire in the nineteenth century, Japan was a strong and rising power. The weak and disorganized Chinese imperial government exercised little real control over emigration while the Japanese state was highly organized and, until the Meiji revolution in 1868, forbade its citizens to leave the country. Once Chinese went overseas, they were more or less on their own; Japanese emigrants, on the other hand, were long the object of concern of the mother country. Then too, Chinese emigration was quite large, continuing from the 1850s until exclusion in the 1880s; the Japanese migration was smaller and briefer in its first phase.

A striking feature of the Japanese migration is the careful distinctions made within Japanese American society among the different generations. Every immigrant group to America, of course, knows the tensions inherent in the second, American-born generation that looks back to its "old country" parents and outward to the larger society. Among the Japanese Americans these distinctions were refined: the *issei* were the first generation immigrants; the *nisei*, the second generation; the *sansei*, the third generation; the *yonsei*, the fourth generation; and today, the *shin issei*, the post-1965 migration.

When Japan dropped her policy of isolation in 1868, a small migration to the United States began that included some political exiles and students seeking modern skills and educations. American cotton and rice were traded for Japanese skills. In 1870 the Japanese government established a consulate in San Francisco, America's chief port on the Pacific. Seven years later the *Fukuin-Kai*, the Japanese Gospel Society, was established in Chinatown by the Chinese Methodist Mission. Many of the earliest Westernizing Japanese students embraced Christianity as part of their individual modernization. But this migration, though important, was only a trickle.

The first substantial Japanese migrations were to Hawaii, where the newly developed, American-owned sugar plantations were starved for labor. Most immigrants were young male agricultural workers under contract who intended to return to Japan after accumulating some savings. Some stayed on the islands, eventually becoming the single largest ethnic group there. Their descendants account for a bit less than a third of modern Hawaii's population.

From Hawaii some Japanese moved on to California to work in the fields. The impetus for a substantial migration to California came only after the Chinese Exclusion Act took effect in 1884; by 1890 two thousand Japanese had migrated to the United States. Most worked in agriculture and horticulture, where they achieved reputations as skillful workers. A few bought or leased land and became growers themselves, employing their fellow countrymen; others organized wholesale and retail produce outlets. As the Chinese communities in California shrank, between 1900 and 1930 the Japanese migration grew fivefold. The peak of migration occurred between 1901 and 1908, yet even at the time of their highest incidence in the population, Japanese immigrants and native-born composed only 2.1 percent of the population of California. In San Francisco in 1910 there were but 4,518 Japanese, less than 2 percent of the city's population.

Before the earthquake of 1906, two clusters of Japanese settlement existed in San Francisco. The one most noticed by outsiders was adjacent to and mixed in with Chinatown along Grant Avenue from Sutter to Sacramento streets. This settlement was characterized by small art goods shops and restaurants, with the proprietor's family often living over the store. The market in San Francisco for silks and Asian art gave this colony its financial base. A second and larger Japanese cluster was located in the working-class South of Market area along narrow Stevenson and Jessie streets, from Fourth to Seventh streets, and on Sixth Street from Stevenson to Bryant. Here were workers' hotels, restaurants, shops, Japanese baths, missions, and all the usual services found in immigrant ghettos. Boardinghouse owners there often doubled as small-scale agricultural labor contractors. The third and nonresidential focus of the Japanese community was in the Financial District, east of Sansome Street, where Japanese banks, shipping companies, and the larger import-export firms located to facilitate trans-Pacific trade. A leader in this sector was the Yokohama Specie Bank, which opened an agency in San Francisco in 1886 (the parent of today's Union Bank; *see Tour 2A*).

The great earthquake and fire completely destroyed both the Chinatown and South of Market Japanese American districts. The Chinatown cluster, because of the unchanged focus of the tourist trade and art goods business there, reestablished itself in its former location, and by 1941 there were some forty Japanese American-owned shops in the southern end of Chinatown. The South of Market neighborhood did not come back; that district became increasingly devoted to warehouses and light industrial uses. A small cluster of Japanese hotels, boardinghouses, and service businesses located around South Park, in the South of Market block between Second, Third, Bryant, and Brannan streets. This pocket flourished between 1907 and 1930 because of its proximity to the piers, where immigrants debarked.

The largest Japanese American concentration, however, settled in the old Victorian Western Addition between Van Ness Avenue and Fillmore Street, today's Japantown. It was here that the *Nihonjinmachi,* "Japanese people's town," took root and flowered, covering thirty blocks by 1940. The Victorian Western Addition had escaped the great fire and enjoyed a great boom from 1906 to about 1909, becoming one of the busiest shopping zones in the city as San Franciscans restocked their wardrobes and new homes. Rents soared in the temporarily overcrowded neighborhood. But as the city quickly rebuilt east of Van Ness Avenue—and as middle-class districts expanded in the Outer Mission and elite housing was built in Presidio Heights—the Western Addition decongested and the real estate market there dropped. As the Japanese-language newspaper *Shin-Sekai* (*The New World*) editorialized in May 1906, only a month after the fire:

> The Japanese here in San Francisco are not financially able to lease new structures which will be built on the fire-wracked sites. They will therefore have little choice but to seek rentals such as those in the Fillmore District that survived the earthquake and fire. Rents, however, in the Fillmore District are still extremely high as they are on [Upper] Market Street. But as new buildings are completed and become available in the city, rents in the Fillmore District will be forced down, and the Japanese will gradually occupy the buildings in that area.

This prediction proved accurate. Old houses were adapted with shops and restaurants inserted at the ground floor and apartments above. Italianate Victorian houses sprouted Japanese shop signs in Roman lettering. Residences (some with rear gardens), boardinghouses, churches, temples, schools, clubs, businesses, restaurants, newspapers, and all the other support services of an almost complete community filled the fancy old Victorians. By 1910 the Western Addition was the center of Japanese American social life, and in 1922 a Nihonjinmachi Improvement Association was organized by the area's businessmen.

Even though the citizens and government of Japan had been the largest foreign contributors to earthquake relief in San Francisco in 1906—more than all other nations combined—an irrational wave of virulent racism swept over San Francisco as Japanese Americans inherited the brunt of anti-Chinese agitation. This was the period of strong anti-Asian sentiment among Progressive politicians in California and in 1905 the Asiatic Exclusion League was formed to lead this movement.

Japanese immigrants believed in education and even older boys enrolled in the city's public schools to learn English. Japanese American parents refused to enroll their children in the segregated Chinese public school. A furor over Japanese American boys sharing classrooms with young white girls erupted. Though there were only ninety-three Japanese students in the public schools, a wave of anti-Japanese hysteria was whipped up by politicians and the press. Hooligans began stoning Japanese American San Franciscans. In October of 1906 the San Francisco School Board ordered all Japanese, Korean, and Chinese students to attend the segregated Oriental School in Chinatown. The Japanese government protested and an international incident erupted. President Theodore Roosevelt intervened in the local San Francisco situation. In a compromise, the Japanese government struck its famous "Gentlemen's Agreement." Under this originally secret agreement, the Japanese government shut off the immigration of laborers; in return, young Japanese American children were allowed to attend the "white" public schools. The results were dramatic. In 1907, 30,200 Japanese came to the United States, in 1908, 5,000, and by 1910 only 2,000 migrated to the United States.

California continued to press Washington for further measures against the Japanese. In 1913 the Alien Land Law was passed in California, depriving Japanese Americans of the right to buy farmland. This was done despite, or perhaps because of, their great reputation as agriculturists. As the *San Francisco Chronicle* noted in 1918, "The Japanese farmer in California has always been a great developer and improver." *Issei* farmers, barred from naturalization, circumvented the iniquitous law by vesting title to their land in their *nisei,* American-citizen children. From 1924 to 1952 Japanese immigration was banned by the United States.

As time went on the *nisei* were caught in a double bind. Urged by their education-revering parents to excel in their studies and to attend college, they found when they graduated that no matter how skilled they were, racist barriers kept them from the jobs they were trained for. Many were forced back to work in family-owned shops and small businesses.

With the Japanese attack on Pearl Harbor in 1941, anti-Japanese hysteria overwhelmed California. On Monday, December 8, every *issei* bank account in America was frozen. Overnight, 1,500 *issei,* the leaders of their communities, were interned by the F.B.I. Under pressure from the U.S. Army commanding general in California and with the urging of Governor Earl Warren, President Franklin Roosevelt signed Executive Order 9066, which forcibly uprooted 112,000 Japanese Americans, *aliens and citizens alike,* from the West Coast's cities and shipped them to hastily built detention camps deep in the Western deserts of California, Utah, and Idaho. (Many San Franciscans were sent to Topaz Relocation Center in Utah.) Two thirds of those interned were American citizens. They had committed no crime nor engaged in treasonable activities or espionage.

San Francisco's Japantown was completely emptied in the spring of 1942. Businesses and homes were sold in haste at bargain prices. The neighborhood did not stay empty long; war workers flooded the city in 1942 looking for housing. For the first time, a significant number of these migrants to San Francisco were black. Henry Kaiser's shipyards brought one to three trainloads of new workers to the Bay Area every day for six months. Black workers were recruited in Texas, Louisiana, Arkansas, and the Western South. In 1940 there were but 4,846 black San Franciscans, a bare .8 percent of the population; by 1950 there were 43,460, making up 5.6 percent of the city's inhabitants. Fillmore Street became the commercial and cultural spine of San Francisco's first sizable black neighborhood. While that era's jazz clubs are long gone, some of the black Protestant churches organized then (and earlier) continue today.

Upon their release in 1945, Japanese Americans found their former neighborhood already occupied. Some picked up the threads of their interrupted lives and reopened Japanese restaurants and shops in old Japantown. But most scattered and moved into the Richmond District (now the San Francisco district with the most Americans of Japanese descent), the Sunset, and the suburbs of the East Bay and Peninsula. Japantown's forty blocks shrank to a half dozen. California's panicky forced exile of Japanese Americans ironically served to accelerate their integration into American society by dispersing the ghetto. Today Japantown has many businesses, churches, clubs, and housing complexes for the elderly, but it is not the population center of the post-war Japanese Americans; diffuse suburbia is.

The United States–Japan peace treaty signed on September 8, 1951 in San Francisco's Opera House officially ended the "Great Pacific War." A new, non-racist Immigration and Naturalization Act was passed the following year. By the early 1970s, Asians constituted nearly one fifth of all immigrants to the United States. In 1987 there were some 12,000 San Franciscans of Japanese ancestry.

"Blighted" Victorian Japantown felt the brunt of a massive urban renewal program in the 1950s and 1960s. A master plan by Vernon DeMars called for the bulldozing of the Geary Street Expressway from Franklin to Fillmore and the wiping away of twenty-two blocks of "substandard" Victorian buildings. The drastic A-1 Urban Renewal Project sliced through the black slum and isolated Japantown north of Geary Boulevard.

The A-1 project displaced 4,000 households and carved a mid-twentieth-century automotive city through the "obsolete platting" of the Victorian city grid. North-south Western Addition streets were in many places closed for parks or were assembled into superparcels for gargantuan new development.

Where once there were blocks lined with bay-windowed Victorian houses and shops, St. Mary's Cathedral, Japan Center, and the Geary Expressway together act as a great concrete wall that runs down the center of the old multiracial Western Addition. The Redevelopment Agency's projects replaced low-income communities of blacks, Japanese Americans, and Filipino Americans with racially integrated but middle-class renters, shifting the black poor from the central Western Addition to new developments at Hunters Point, the city's most remote corner.

Though it is rarely noticed, urban renewal worked to the great benefit of San Francisco's churches. The state used its power of eminent domain to forcibly buy up private properties, demolish buildings, consolidate small lots into large parcels, and then sell the properties at low cost to private developers and community organizations, including many local churches.

Buddhist Church of San Francisco
1881 Pine Street at Octavia; English service Sundays at 9:30 A.M., Japanese service at 1:30 P.M.; 776-3158

A second wave of urban renewal in Japantown fifteen years later destroyed most of the remaining Victorian buildings north of Post Street facing the Japan Center. When they were demolished, and their small businesses and affordable housing displaced, modern Japanese-style buildings were erected. Continuing urban renewal's war on the "outmoded" nineteenth-century street grid and its sidewalks, a pedestrian **Nihonmachi Mall** was built on the block of Buchanan between Post and Sutter. This was filled with unmaintained planters and unwalkable cobbles, some fine Ruth Asawa benches, and now-dry CorTen steel fountains. Thus redeveloped Japantown has a "center" with a "plaza" and a "mall," all on vacated public streets, the three worst things that can happen to San Francisco's historic and working urban fabric.

Many of the new buildings in Japantown are of cheap stucco trimmed with "Japanesque" wood trim and are aging all too rapidly. There are, alas, precious few gardens to distract from the uninspired architecture.

Concurrent with all this upheaval, dislocation, and massive public and private reinvestment in the heart of the old Western Addition, the surviving Victorians all along its edge skyrocketed in value. Working couples, straight and gay, bought the abused asbestos-shingle-covered Victorians along Japantown's north fringes and restored them. The blocks climbing up toward California Street and Pacific Heights became completely gentrified as fine old redwood houses were restored and meticulously landscaped.

1 **Buddhist Church of San Francisco**, *1938, Gentoko Shimamato*

This plain, Roman Baroque, light-colored corner building designed by *nisei* architect Gentoko Shimamato has stage-set broken pediments applied to its façade and gives little hint of the rich temple within. This is despite the small *stupa* (dome and finial) that caps the blocklike multiuse building. Little noticed by the stream of auto traffic that pours west out Pine Street, the *stupa* contains what are said to be relics of the Buddha given to the Buddhist Church in America in 1935 by the King of Siam.

Up a broad staircase is the second-floor *hondo,* or worship hall. This superb room with its recessed gilded altar flanked by painted screens of peacocks is modeled on that of the mother church in Kyoto. The plain, unornamented timbers are inset with intricate gilded ornamented panels carved in Kyoto. It is a sumptuous yet calm room, one of the most beautiful in San Francisco.

**Buddhist Churches
of America**
1710 Octavia Street
Buddhist Bookstore
*Open Monday to
Saturday, 9 A.M. to
5 P.M.; 776-7877*

**Binet-Montessori School/
Former Morning Star
School**
1715 Octavia Street

**St. Francis Xavier Roman
Catholic Mission for the
Japanese**
*1801 Octavia Street,
at Pine; English mass
Sundays at 10 A.M.;
Japanese mass the third
Sunday of each month
at 11 A.M.; 346-7309*

This church's congregation became multiracial as other San Franciscans were attracted to Buddhism. When the Japanese and Japanese American congregation members were banished to Topaz Relocation Center in Utah's harsh desert, white members continued the corporate life of the congregation and maintained the building, inside of which Japanese American members deposited important possessions. Upon their release, the building served as a hostel for returning Japanese and Japanese Americans.

• **Buddhist Churches of America**, *1971, Miles Suda*
This blank stucco building has mounted on its façade a copper wheel of life with eight spokes. The **Buddhist Bookstore** on the second floor is open Monday to Saturday.

2 **Binet-Montessori School/Former Morning Star School** *1929,
Henry A. Minton*
This handsome school building designed in 1929 by Henry A. Minton is from the golden years of school construction in California. It should be looked at from across Octavia Street for its unique façade to be fully appreciated. This light beige three-story building with brown window frames is styled in Japanese dress. Green tile roofs have upturned eaves, an arched entrance is treated like a grate, and at the very top is a colossal green copper "cloud" finial. A green copper madonna and child with Japanese features stands in an ornate white niche in the center of the façade, making the entire building a pagoda/shrine. Inside is a large ground-floor gymnasium with two floors of classrooms above, in an ideal size for a school. The school's playground is at the southwest corner of Pine and Octavia.

3 **St. Francis Xavier Roman Catholic Mission for the Japanese**, *1932–39,
Henry A. Minton*
This modest California Mission-style stucco church with understated Japanese elements serves Japanese American Roman Catholics from all over the Bay Area. The white stucco frame building has a green tile roof with turned up eaves and a richly decorated dark green Japanese-style gatelike entrance porch. Its square tower with restrained pagoda roof capped by a wrought-iron cross converses with the *stupa* across the intersection. This 1930s church preserved and reuses, from the Victorian house that once stood here, the granite front steps and the retaining wall, with its black iron fence.

The building is a combination church and rectory built over a ground-floor social hall and offices. Its small sanctuary is simple and calm. Richly colored stained-glass clerestory windows depict St. Francis Xavier and other Roman Catholic missionaries to Asia. The 1930s liturgical furnishings are spare and handsome. Despite its Jesuit saint name, the church was built by the Order of the Divine

Word, a German missionary society. In keeping with the name of **1801–63 Laguna Street**
the order, the shell-like painted wooden *baldacchino* over the sim-
ple freestanding altar acts as a sounding board and reflects the   **1800–32 Laguna Street**
priest's words out into the intimate chapel. The church's most inter-
esting feature is the garden that surrounds it on three sides. This is one of the best
California gardens in Japantown. It is very much a low-maintenance garden, but with
its artistically trimmed shrubbery and one pine tree it recalls the way that Japanese
migrants to California took to its botanic possibilities as gifted gardeners and
successful growers.

4 *1800 Block of Laguna Street Victorian Group*

The 1800 block of Laguna slopes gently downward and, beyond the modern buildings at Pine and Laguna's southeast corner, is lined on both sides by restored bay-windowed Victorian houses. This is a unique cluster even in the Victoriana-rich Western
Addition. On the west side of the street at numbers **1801–63 Laguna Street** are eleven
Eastlake or Stick-style houses built in 1889 by William Hinkel. Gables and turrets
pierce the western skyline. Most have been restored after a long decline; a couple still
have the asbestos shingle "improvements" of the 1930s and 1940s. Note the different
ways the first-floor bay window was designed with various mullion patterns and edg-
ings of colored "flash glass." Shingles enrich the upper stories of some houses. The corner house at the southern end of the complete row has an elaborate two-story bay
window capped by a fancy gable projecting over the Bush Street sidewalk.

Facing them, on the east side of the block at numbers **1800–32
Laguna Street**, are six Italianate row houses with slant-sided bay windows built in
1877 by The Real Estate Associates. In an earlier, more chaste style, the Italianates here
face the more decorated later Eastlake or Stick-style row. Most of these houses have
had garages tucked beneath them. The trimmed street trees blend with the many small
front gardens and potted plants. This street landscaping is a relatively recent achievement concurrent with the gentrification of this block starting in the 1960s—the
Victorian city had a stark appearance and very few street trees.

The Real Estate Associates first sold unimproved lots in the 1860s
and then began building row houses in the 1870s. Eventually they built about one
thousand houses, mostly in the Western Addition and the Mission. Down payments
on these houses ranged from 25 to 50 percent of the average $7,000 cost, with the rest
paid in one to twelve years in monthly installments. Architectural historian Anne
Bloomfield calculated that the cost of the building broke down roughly at about one-
third for wages, one-third for lumber (fir, pine, and redwood), one-eighth for millwork
(windows, doors, stairs, and ornament), and one-fifth for plumbing, paint, glass, brick,
tile, marble, and hardware. Only especially elaborate Victorian houses were individually architect-designed.

Old Bush Street Synagogue
1881 Bush Street,
near Laguna

Konko Kyo Church of
San Francisco
1909 Bush Street, at
Laguna. Services in
English and Japanese
Monday to Saturday,
7:15 A.M., 10:30 A.M.;
service in English Sunday
at 10:00 A.M. On the
third Sunday of May the
grand ceremony for the
Principal Parent of
the Universe is held;
on the third Sunday
of November is the
ceremony honoring
founder Konko-Daijin;
931-0453

❺ Old Bush Street Synagogue, *1895, Moses J. Lyon*

The Venetian-Moorish redwood gingerbread façade of the former conservative synagogue of congregation **Ohabai Shalome** (Lovers of Peace) is well worth seeking out. Designed by Moses J. Lyon in 1895, this is a unique survivor in post-1906 San Francisco. Behind the lacy façade with its Romanesque portal, tracery of Venetian columns, and two square Moorish towers is a vaguely Romanesque sanctuary with a U-shaped gallery. The carved and gilded wood setting for the ark survives; in the apse over the ark is a choir loft. The sanctuary has an especially lofty ornamented plaster ceiling curved to enhance the hall's acoustics. Originally, the men sat in the pews on the main floor facing the ark and women sat in the U-shaped gallery, facing one another.

The old synagogue has had a varied, quintessentially San Franciscan history and is something of a "Rosetta stone" of San Francisco's distinctive east-west multiracial and multicultural religious history. The little wood building with delusions of Venetian stone grandeur was built by fifty European conservative Jews who seceded from congregation Emanu-El in 1863. After meeting in a synagogue on Mason Street a block west of Union Square, the congregation built this new synagogue in 1895. Following its congregation west, in 1934 the synagogue moved a third time to the Richmond District. The old synagogue was sold to a Japanese Buddhist sect known as Soto Shu, followers of the Zen priest Teraro Kasuga. In the 1940s it briefly served a Christian congregation.

After the return of some Japanese Americans to the neighborhood in 1944, the **Sokoji Zen Temple** was established here. (It moved to a new temple in 1984; *see entry for Soto Zen Mission Sokoji later in this tour.*) Buddhist priests sat facing each other on the raised stage leading sonorous, trance-inducing chants punctuated by occasional gongs. **The San Francisco Zen Center** evolved from a group of young white residents of the Western Addition who met here to study *zazen* meditation under Shunryu Suzuki. In 1973 the San Francisco Redevelopment Agency bought the run-down building and leased part of it to the Go Club. This architectural rarity deserves sensitive restoration and a compatible new use.

❻ Konko Kyo Church of San Francisco, *1973, Van Bourg, Nakamura, Katsura and Karney*

This modern Japanese-style temple is a two-story steel-frame, wood and stucco building, designed in 1973 by Van Bourg, Nakamura, Katsura and Karney. It uses the post-and-lintel form of traditional Shinto architecture; a dramatic Japanese roof with projecting timbers is modeled on the Grand Shrine at Ise, Japan. Social rooms, a kitchen, and a tea ceremony room occupy the ground floor under the sanctuary. The temple itself is an austere room with a beautiful pale wood altar on which offerings of food, flowers, sprigs of greenery, and bottles of rice wine are symmetrically placed. There is a separate ash vault. The light-colored polished wood altar is perhaps the best piece of new design in Japantown and is sparsely decorated with fine bamboo curtains with great silk tassels. Over the altar alcove is a golden disk, the *yatsu-nami,* the Konko symbol of divine light. Tucked over the front entrance is a balcony room used for martial arts.

The Konko religion was founded in 1859 by Ikigami Konko-Daijin, a forty-two-year-old farmer who recovered from a serious illness. (Konko translates as "the teaching of the golden light.") It uses the prayers, rituals, and robes of Shintoism.

After the bland stucco boxes inflicted on the city from the 1950s to the 1970s, architects have returned to the design of Edwardian flats building, modified this time around by ground-floor garages. The traditionally bay-windowed and ornamented building at **1740 Laguna Street** is brand new but would be taken by most to be a turn-of-the-century building. Next door is a structure built seventy years earlier when the optimal three-story, bay-windowed San Francisco building was first perfected.

1740 Laguna Street

Christ United Presbyterian Church
1700 Sutter Street, at Laguna; Sunday services in English at 10 A.M. and Japanese at 11:15 A.M.; 567-3988

Soto Zen Mission Sokoji
1691 Laguna Street, at Sutter; Zazen meditation Wednesday 6:30 to 7:30 P.M.; closed August; Phone 346-7540 for Sunday schedules

Nichi Bei Kai Cultural Center
1759 Sutter Street

7 Christ United Presbyterian Church, *1972, Wayne Osaki*
The American Presbyterian Church was among the most active in missionary work in Japan, Korea, and China in the late-nineteenth and early-twentieth centuries. Many of the ambitious young Japanese men who migrated to California in the early-twentieth century, especially those who came as students at the great California universities, were Japanese Christians—Presbyterians at that. Though the church's interior is pleasing and refined, its exterior is reticent to the point of dullness. The brown wood trim, thin square tower, and large diagonal skylight hardly counter the blandness of the white stucco building.

8 Soto Zen Mission Sokoji, *1984, VBN Corporation*
This modern Japanese-style Buddhist temple with projecting roof timbers forming an X was designed by the VBN Corporation and completed in 1984. It is built of cinnamon-stained wood and light yellow stucco. Under the exposed wood eaves over the entrance is a thin wood tablet with fine calligraphy in white and light seafoam green, perhaps the most artistic sign in Japantown. The spare interior was designed for *zazen* meditation and is furnished with black and white cushions.

9 Nichi Bei Kai Cultural Center, *1972, Mitsuru Tada & Associates*
One of the most Japanese of the urban renewal Japantown designs is this set-back, three-story, stucco and wood "traditional" frame building with shingle trim tucked into a Victorian block. Designed by Mitsuru Tada & Associates, it features a small Japanese garden with a stone lantern behind a rustic fence. It is disappointing in the new and "better" urban renewed Japantown to find so very few gardens, and even fewer constantly manicured and maintained ones. Very much like the rest of San Francisco, the strategy in Japantown is plant it and forget it; thrive or die. There is a tea room on the third floor open to the public.

Japanese American
Citizens League
1765 Sutter Street;
921-5225

Western Addition YWCA
1830 Sutter Street

⑩ Japanese American Citizens League, *1973, Van Bourg, Nakamura, Katsura and Karney*
This new building fuses traditional San Francisco frame architecture with contemporary Japanese elements such as the circular second-floor window. While less literally "Japanese" than most of the post-urban-renewal Japantown designs, it is one of the more successful. It was designed by Van Bourg, Nakamura, Katsura and Karney in 1973.

The Japanese American Citizens League (JACL) emerged as a civil rights organization in 1930 from local and regional organizations of *nisei*. It worked for rapid Americanization and assimilation into mainstream American society. Its creed is "better Americans in a greater America." The top leadership of the JACL removed to Salt Lake City before the government instituted the travel freeze that preceded relocation to camps in the interior. The JACL urged Secretary of War Henry Stinson to form the volunteer Japanese American combat units that subsequently distinguished themselves in World War II. During the immediate postwar years, the JACL emerged as the most important Japanese American civil rights organization.

⑪ Western Addition YWCA, *1912, Julia Morgan*
Sutter Street was Japantown's important institutional street during the period between the earthquake and World War II, analogous to Chinatown's Stockton Street. Architect Julia Morgan's 1912 Japanese Branch YWCA at 1830 Sutter Street is actually an eclectic frame and stucco building somewhat Craftsman, or perhaps Tudor, in flavor. The interestingly walled-in structure has a high tile-capped wall and tile roof with upturned eaves. It is one of the earliest examples of "Japanese style" design. The light-greenish-color mottled roof is quite fine. The walled forecourt shelters a typical San Francisco side entrance and front stairs.

The original interior is substantially intact. In the 1930s this was known as the Japanese branch of the YWCA and along with all the usual activities of a Y taught traditional Japanese dance and ceremonies, martial arts, and flower arranging. During the war, the building served war workers who flooded San Francisco's crowded Western Addition. With the release of the Japanese Americans from detention, the Y and the neighborhood's churches and temples served as hostels and relocation facilities.

⑫ Japanese Cultural and Community Center of Northern California/ CFB–Japanese American History Room, *1987, Wayne Osaki*
Next door to the YWCA is one of the best and latest Japantown designs, Wayne Osaki's Japanese Cultural and Community Center of Northern California, built on a Redevelopment Agency–cleared site. Owned and operated by a consortium of community groups, its purpose is "to preserve and transmit to future generations the Nikkei community's unique history and heritage." The center is constructed of brown timbers with white stucco panels over a cracked-pattern granite base. A fine modern three-part Japanese roof clad in flat brown tiles with a copper ridgepole caps the build-

ing. Various community service organizations and activities are housed here and serve neighborhood residents and Japanese Americans from all over the Bay Area. The ground floor, with the easiest access, is reserved for the senior center; upstairs are offices and a large meeting room where space is rented to various cultural, artistic, educational, recreational, physical fitness, and social service organizations. The center plans to expand to the rear with a community hall/gymnasium with bleachers. The donor wall in the lobby is distinctive.

Japanese Cultural and Community Center of Northern California/ CFB–Japanese American History Room
1840 Sutter Street; CFB–Japanese American History Room, a fine historical archive, is open by appointment, 921-1485; For center programs, phone 567-5505

⓭ 1825 Sutter Street *1878, Italianate row house*
At 1825 Sutter Street is a characteristic two-story, bay-windowed San Francisco Italianate row house built in 1878. Captain and Mrs. John Cavalry were its first owners. The house was first restored in the 1960s and then was restored again with invisible additions to the rear. It was imaginatively landscaped in 1983. The oak white (slightly eggshell) monochromatic color scheme elegantly displays the house's restrained redwood ornament. The green boxwood grid of a front garden sets off a black steel abstract sculpture entitled *Streetlight*, by James Nestor, again a rare gesture to the city. There are several fine surviving 1870s Victorian row houses and sets of flats on this side of Sutter Street, all carefully restored since the late 1960s.

1825 Sutter Street

Vollmer House
1735–37 Webster Street

⓮ Vollmer House: Victorian High Point, *1885, Samuel and Joseph Cather Newsom*
The ornate, steeple-capped Eastlake row house at 1735–37 Webster Street is one of the most elaborate surviving Victorian architectural works in San Francisco. Architects Samuel and Joseph Cather Newsom here took the basic San Francisco row house box with its standard interior and applied to it one of the richest redwood gingerbread façades ever confected in San Francisco. Like their Carson Mansion of 1884–85 in Eureka, California, the architectural ornament here projects far from the wall plane of the building, giving it a pronounced three-dimensional effect. The right-angled bay window and all the other windows are framed by pipestem colonnettes. The entrance porch is capped by elaborate spindlework and a carved basket of flowers. The projecting ornamental gable with its sunburst ornament sports an inventive pyramidal steeple with a round ball finial.

In the mid–1970s, the Redevelopment Agency shifted gears and turned to restoring rather than demolishing the Victorians left along the fringes of its vast swath of cleared Western Addition blocks. The newly founded Foundation for San Francisco's Architectural Heritage worked to find buyers to restore the houses, and the Redevelopment Agency moved them.

This landmark building has had a peripatetic history. It was built as a single-family dwelling in 1885 at 773 Turk Street, near Franklin, and was once block from the edge of the 1906 fire. Over the years it was converted into a rooming-house with about two dozen inexpensive units and a manager's office/flat inserted

2101–21½ Bush Street

Stanyan House
2006 Bush Street

2000–12 Bush Street

where the basement flat is today. When its "blighted" block was condemned in 1975 by the Redevelopment Agency in order to build Opera Plaza on Van Ness Avenue, this old house and eleven others were jacked up, put on wheels, and towed by night twelve blocks west to the other side of the A-2 Western Addition redevelopment area.

It was a tight fit squeezing this house between its neighbors—part of the left bay had to be shaved off. Despite its extraordinary façade, the house as originally built was plain inside with only a fancy spindlework archway in the main hall. (This is a private residence and should be left undisturbed.)

The corner building at Webster and Bush streets, **2101–21½ Bush Street**, is a two-story Italianate clapboard building with a corner shop and a five-sided corner bay window that projects out over the public sidewalk at the second floor. Visible in side view is the extension to the building. The steplike profile of these three Victorians is typical of the way the Victorian city's individually–built frame buildings fit together to form whole blocks. Corner lots were usually larger and more expensive and saw the construction of either grander, more expensive houses (many of which have since been torn down) or a combination of shops and residences, many of which survive. This shopfront was handsomely faced in maroon and black tiles with a thin yellow band, probably in the 1940s.

⑮ Stanyan House, *circa 1852*
One of the oldest houses in San Francisco, this house dates from the immediate post-Gold Rush city and shows how simple the first wave of Victorian house building was. It makes a dramatic contrast with the Newsom brothers' Vollmer House of 1885. It was owned by the family of San Francisco supervisor **Charles Stanyan**, who had a hand in the creation of Golden Gate Park and the Haight-Ashbury, where a street was named for him. This house originally sat in a large corner garden. It is typical of the gable-roofed, open-porch, clapboard houses, many built with imported lumber, that New Englanders and other Easterners built in sandy San Francisco in the early 1850s. The steep pitch of its roof proved to be unnecessary in a climate where it rarely rains and never snows.

Flanking the Stanyan House at **2000–12 Bush Street**, near Buchanan, are two two-story, bay-windowed Eastlake or Stick-style flats buildings built by the Stanyans about 1885 as income property. They exhibit the classic San Francisco row house form: flat rooflines, bay windows rather than open porches, and machine-carved ornamental redwood trim.

16 **Nihonmachi Mall**, *1971–80, Okamoto-Liskamm with Van Bourg/Nakamura & Associates, Japantown master plan; 1976, Okamoto & Murata/Van Bourg Nakamura, mall design; Ruth Asawa, fountains*

Nihonmachi Mall
1700 Block of Buchanan Street, between Sutter and Post

Post Street is the dividing line between the A-1 Western Addition redevelopment area to the south and the A-2 Western Addition redevelopment area, of which the **Nihonmachi Mall** is a part, to the north. In the first wave of urban renewal, total demolition consolidated blocks into huge parcels on which monumental concrete buildings could be built. Reaction against this drastic approach resulted in a second wave of downscaled projects.

Genji Kimonos and Antiques, *22 Peace Plaza, corner of Buchanan behind Union Bank; 931-1616*

Japan Center
Three blocks bounded by Post, Geary, Laguna, and Fillmore streets; 922-6776

The Nihonmachi, or Buchanan Street, Mall wiped away many vintage Victorians that had been adapted over time to Japanese shops and restaurants. These small businesses were displaced by demolition and then the construction of this modern "Japanese village" arrangement with a central paved mall. A stark modern concrete-and-timber Japanese gate faces Sutter Street at the north end of the mall and a tall square tower faces Post Street at the south end of the vacated block. Rough granite paving blocks are laid to create a "river" where the street once was. Ruth Asawa's two fine CorTen steel fountains, which look like folded steel flowers, are usually dry, but are among the best new public art in the city. (She and schoolchildren also made the lively ornamented sidepanels of the benches here by casting dough figures in concrete.) As malls go, this one probably has potential, though real streets and sidewalks are always superior for San Francisco shopping districts. The modern wood-and-stucco Japanese-style buildings grouped here have a human scale and agreeable intricacy but do not seem to be aging well. The center of the mall seems unfinished: "arms" where Hemlock Alley should continue resolve instead into clusters of unsightly dumpsters.

The modern square tower building is the former Kokusai Theater (since converted to a fast food outlet) designed by Rai Okamoto & Associates in 1971. Facing it at 1698 Post Street at Buchanan is the well-stocked **Soko Hardware Company** designed by Van Bourg/Nakamura in 1980. (*Soko* is the Japanese word for *San Francisco*.) The finest shop in the mall is treasure-filled **Genji Kimonos and Antiques**.

17 **Japan Center**, *1968, Minoru Yamasaki and Van Bourg/Nakamura & Associates; Yoshiro Taniguchi with T. Y. Lin, Kulka, Yang & Associates, engineers, Peace Pagoda*
This five-acre complex houses a large parking garage, a sixteen-story hotel, and lowrise shops, restaurants, art galleries, a major bookstore, professional offices, travel agencies, a Japanese bath, a cineplex, and originally the Japanese Consulate. It is a period piece of sterile 1960s mall design, a monument to the bad city planning and worse architecture of 1960s urban renewal. Eminent domain was used to clear the three blocks; revenue bonds financed an eight-hundred-car city-operated parking garage on the ground level. The air rights over the garage were sold to Honolulu insurance magnate Masayuki Tokioka, who formed a joint venture with Nippon Railway Company and a theater company.

Ginza Discount Imports
In the East Building
992-2475

Ikenobo Ikebana Society
In the Kintetsu Building;
Open Tuesday through
Saturday, call for hours;
567-1011

The International Art
Guild Society
On the right-hand side of
the Webster Street bridge;
567-4390

Townhouse Living
1825 Post Street, in the
Kinokuniya Building;
563-1417

Asakichi Japanese
Antiques and Art
On the first floor of the
West Building; Open
Monday; 921-2147

Kabuki Hot Springs
1750 Geary Boulevard,
in the West Building;
Open Monday to Friday,
10 A.M. to 10 P.M., and
Saturday and Sunday,
9 A.M. to 10 P.M.; Shiatsu
massage weekdays after
2 P.M. and after 10 A.M.
on weekends; 922-6000

Japan Center's one accent is the Peace Pagoda, a gift from the people of Japan. Its twelve rectangular pillars support five copper-clad roofs. Above the topmost roof is a *karin,* a nine-ringed spire, supporting a *hoshu,* flaming golden ball. The pagoda's design is adapted from that of the twelve-hundred-year-old Pagoda of Eternal Peace in Nara, Japan. The former reflecting pool has been planted as a garden (fountains on roofs *always* leak).

Some of the best shops in the Japan Center include **Ginza Discount Imports** in the East Building, which is trinket city. In the Kintetsu Building, the **Ikenobo Ikebana Society**, immediately to the left before the floor rises for the Webster Street bridge, carries books on flower arranging, implements, and containers. It also displays fine flower arrangements in its show windows. **The International Art Guild Society**, a hole-in-the-wall art gallery on the right-hand side of the Webster Street bridge, has nineteenth-century and contemporary Japanese prints, some quite fine. **Kinokuniya Bookstore**, in the West Building, second floor, has a large stock of Japanese and English language books, excellent art books, and guides to Japan, as well as some inks, brushes, and paper. **Townhouse Living**, in the Kinokuniya Building, carries a good selection of Noguchi paper lamps. On the first floor of the West Building, in front of the castle model, is **Asakichi Japanese Antiques and Art.**. The **Kabuki Hot Springs**, located in the West Building, is a Japanese-style bathhouse with private and communal baths. Costs are from ten dollars for the communal bath and sauna to sixty–five dollars for a private room and a one-hour massage. The entrance to the hot springs is located on Geary Boulevard, outside the Japan Center. Some Korean American businesses have leased shopfronts along the Geary Boulevard side of the Japan Center.

18 *The African American*
   Western Addition's Divisadero Street

While urban renewal fundamentally changed the Western Addition there are still reminders of the African American population that clustered here starting in the 1940s. Across from the old Fillmore Auditorium is **Jack's**, a neighborhood blues bar. If you wish to see something of African American San Francisco today, take the 38 Geary bus west to Divisadero Street and then transfer to the 24 Divisadero bus headed south. (If you stay on the 24 Divisadero bus you can get to the heart of the Castro district and Tour 11.) The commercial strip along Divisadero, from about Ellis to Oak streets, is the most African American shopping strip in San Francisco. Here are shops and restaurants catering to the Western Addition's African Americans as well as others. **Brother-in-Law's Bar-b-que** is tasty. (Further afield, in the South of Market district, is **Big Nate's Bar-be-que**; take-out and delivery.) The San Francisco **African American Historical and Cultural Society** is at Fort Mason.

The Western Addition became an African American neighborhood during the 1940s as war industries drew rural Southerners to the West Coast's booming factories. The detention of the Japanese Americans emptied part of this old Victorian district and the newcomers moved in. Massive urban renewal projects in the 1960s demolished much of the run-down, low-rent, nineteenth-century district, and the new racially integrated housing that was built was more expensive than the housing it replaced. Rising rents have squeezed out many working class people, especially African Americans. Prosperous middle-class African Americans continue to move to the suburbs along with so many others. The result has been a steep decline in the city's African American population, from 96,098 in 1970 to 79,039 by 1990. There is a widening income gap between whites and the blacks who remain in the city. In 1970, African American salaries averaged 60 percent of what whites made; by 1993, it had dropped to 45 percent of white incomes. San Francisco is not immune from the alarming trends in American society generally. African Americans have made great strides in San Francisco since the 1960s in terms of breaking barriers in employment and politics. Today many African Americans add their artistic talents to this multicultural city.

Jack's
1601 Fillmore Street;
675-3227

Brother-in-Law's Bar-b-que
705 Divisadero, near
Grove; 931-7427

Big Nate's Bar-be-que
1665 Folsom Street,
between Twelfth and
Thirteenth streets;
861-4242

African American Historical and Cultural Society
In Building C at Fort
Mason; 441-0640

Geary Expressway
Geary Boulevard from
Franklin to Broderick
streets

Fillmore Auditorium
1807 Geary Boulevard,
at Fillmore

• **Geary Expressway**, *1950s, San Francisco Redevelopment Agency; by Vernon DeMars, master plan*
The Japan Center turns its back to the **Geary Expressway**, which cleared a wide swath from east to west, linking the downtown with the middle-class Richmond District to the west. The expressway project, built to Vernon DeMars' master plan, included the demolition and redevelopment of all the flanking blocks of Geary from Franklin to Broderick streets. A narrow pedestrian bridge was flung across the busy expressway at Geary and Webster streets and a two-block underpass for automobiles constructed at Geary and Fillmore streets. On the underpass walls are four brightly colored metal graphics installed in 1986. The two designs on the south wall, a West African cow and a Ghanan *gye nyame*, or spirit symbol, face two Japanese *mon*, or family crests, one with a yin-yang design and the other a crab.

⑲ Fillmore Auditorium, *1912, Reid Brothers*
Fillmore and Geary was once a very lively crossroads. On the southwest corner stands a blocklike, three-story, yellow brick building with all its original upper-floor windows intact. There are shops on the building's ground floor; the **Fillmore Auditorium** is upstairs. Over the years, the Fillmore Auditorium has been the venue for a great many events. Promoter Bill Graham leased the hall in 1967 and staged the first of his six-days-a-week "Summer of Love" rock concerts. On June 20, 1967 Graham debuted with the Jefferson Airplane, Gabor Szabo, and Jimi Hendrix here. This first rush of the psychedelic San Francisco sound was accompanied by novel light shows projected on the walls. This building deserves to be a city landmark, for it has had a critical role in modern San Francisco's cultural identity.

Fillmore Center
*Three blocks bounded
by Fillmore, Steiner,
O'Farrell, and Turk
streets*

**Consulate General of the
People's Republic of China**
*1450 Laguna Street,
at Geary Boulevard*

St. Francis Square
*Geary Boulevard from
Webster to Laguna streets*

Transit Hop

At this point it is best to catch the **38 Geary bus** at the southeast corner of Geary and Fillmore. Head uphill five blocks east and alight at the top of the crest, at Geary and Gough, in front of modernistic St. Mary's Cathedral. The sites listed below are all on the 38's route and can be seen adaquately from the bus.

㉟ Fillmore Center, *1988–89, Daniel, Mann, Johnson & Mendenhall; Lifescapes, Inc., landscape architect*
The peak-roofed towers visible south of Geary Expressway, east of Fillmore Street, are part of **Fillmore Center**, a nine-acre residential and commercial complex consisting of 1,113 rental units in five-story apartment buildings and four sixteen-story towers; there are also 1,260 covered parking spaces. These sandy blocks composed one of the city's principal black neighborhoods until the forces of eminent domain and the Redevelopment Agency combined and razed them in the 1960s. The new highrises try to relate to the city's patterns in their bay windows but are too large to fit in with the valley's lowrise profile.

㉑ Consulate General of the People's Republic of China
The anonymous white stucco complex at the southeast corner of Geary and Laguna was built for the Salvation Army but has since been bought by the People's Republic of China for its consulate general. The red flag with yellow stars flies here in neutral nondescript territory, far from Chinatown with its predominantly Nationalist sympathies.

㉒ St. Francis Square, *1962, Marquis & Stoller; Lawrence Halprin & Associates, landscape architect*
From the 38 Geary bus, on the right, or south side of Geary Boulevard, are the cypress trees bordering the parking lots of **St. Francis Square**, a co-operative housing project developed by the Pacific Maritime Association and the International Longshoremen's and Warehousemen's Union. St. Francis Square's brave-new-world design took San Francisco's evolved residential pattern and turned it inside out. Parking lots create a no-man's-land on the Geary Boulevard perimeter, while freestanding rows of housing designed by Marquis & Stoller face away from the public street and sidewalk and into the landscaped interior of the block. It is not a city-wise design.

㉓ The Sequoias, *1969, Stone, Marraccini & Patterson*
Across Geary Boulevard is **The Sequoias**, an elegantly designed white concrete tower standing on a horizontal base. It is a large retirement and hospital facility built by Northern California Presbyterian Homes. Designed in 1969 by Stone, Marraccini & Patterson, it must have made a beautiful architectural model. The residential tower with views and the "floating" hospital base are artistically fused. The design is a modern sculpture blown up to gargantuan size, a classic architectural design of its day. Standing alone on a mountain slope it would be splendid, but built as a two-block concrete wall, artistic as it is, it sterilizes its adjoining blocks. The Sequoias is best appreciated from a

helicopter, or driving east on Geary Boulevard, not by a mere pedestrian living in the neighborhood.

24 **St. Mary's Roman Catholic Cathedral of the Assumption**, *1971, Pietro Belluschi, Pier Luigi Nervi, and McSweeney, Ryan & Lee; John Staley, landscape architect; Gyorgy Kepes, stained glass; Richard Lippold,* baldacchino
San Francisco has had three Roman Catholic cathedrals: Old St. Mary's at California and Grant between the Financial District and Chinatown, which still stands; a great red brick "plant" of impressive proportions built on Van Ness Avenue between 1887 and 1891, which burned in 1962; and today's novel monument at Geary and Gough, completed in 1971 atop Cathedral Hill.

St. Mary's Roman Catholic Cathedral's travertine-clad form rises from a square base to become an equal-armed Greek cross surmounted by a thin silver cross. The four "seams" in the reinforced concrete cupola are filled with abstract stained-glass windows representing fire to the west, sky to the north, water to the east, and earth to the south. Because the cathedral was placed on a vacated block of O'Farrell Street when the Redevelopment Agency assembled this two-block superblock, the gleaming white cathedral is visible from the very heart of downtown.

The splendor of the building and its importance for our time lie in its interior. The great cupola imagined by Pietro Belluschi and engineered by master Italian engineer Pier Luigi Nervi joins four hyperbolic paraboloids in a triangular coffered dome that soars upward 190 feet. The entire structure rests on four gracefully formed freestanding piers. The vast cupola has all the eloquence and elegance of a sublime mathematical discourse. Bands of clear glass around the perimeter of the square plan "open up" the church and bring views of the city to the congregation. You should perambulate the vast space examining it slowly from various angles. If there are no services, walk directly under the cupola and look up and all around. The concrete pedestal for the organ is poured concrete become art. Walk the perimeter of the cathedral with its view of the finely detailed great green copper dome of Bakewell & Brown's opulent City Hall to the southeast.

This was the first Roman Catholic cathedral built after the liturgical reforms of the Second Vatican Council in 1962. The priest celebrating the mass faces the congregation across a simplified but luxurious stone altar. The austere altar has a raised stone platform devoid of ornament backed by a fine dark wood screen that makes the robed celebrants stand out. A gold cross hangs above the altar. Over that the cathedral's glory, Richard Lippold's *baldacchino,* a silver rain of thin glinting rods, falls like a shower of light on the altar.

The St. Mary's complex includes more than its 2,500-seat sanctuary. Directly under the cathedral is a 1,200-seat auditorium and a ring of meeting rooms and offices. Built into the sloping two-block site on the downhill side facing Ellis Street is Cathedral High School, a rectory, and a convent.

The Sequoias
1400 Geary Boulevard, between Gough and Laguna

St. Mary's Roman Catholic Cathedral of the Assumption
1111 Gough Street at Geary Boulevard; Open 6:45 A.M. to 5 P.M. Sunday masses at 7:30, 9, and 10:30 A.M. and 5 P.M., the 11 A.M. mass is sung, and the 1 P.M. mass is in Spanish; 567-2020

First Unitarian Church
1187 Franklin Street,
at Starr King Way;
Services Sunday at
11 A.M.; for other
programs, phone
776-4580.

㉕ First Unitarian Church , *1887–89, George W. Percy; 1967–68, Callister, Payne & Rosse; landscape architect, John Carmak*

This old stone Romanesque church is tucked artfully into what is essentially a large triangular traffic island. A brilliant addition was designed by Callister, Payne & Rosse and built between 1967 and 1968. While the old church at the corner of Franklin and Geary is routine, if venerable, the modern addition is both inventive and deliberately regional. The contemporary concrete-with-redwood-trim complex has two human-scaled courtyards, one courtyard is surrounded by a new chapel, parish offices, comfortable meeting rooms, an auditorium, and a kitchen; the second is the focal point of a two-story elementary school. One of the best contemporary designs in San Francisco, this building represents the humane, nature-oriented qualities of the best Bay Area design. The Callister, Payne & Rosse design is important for visitors who wish to see distinctively Bay Area modern architecture.

The First Unitarian Church in San Francisco has been at the forefront of religious, cultural, political, economic, and social reform since its organization in the wake of the Gold Rush. The first Unitarian service was conducted in San Francisco on October 20, 1850, and the Unitarian society was organized in 1852. In the 1860s, under its famous minister Thomas Starr King, the First Unitarian Church was the first to open its pulpit to all faiths. King is buried under the white marble tomb facing Franklin Street, under the corner palm. Over the years First Unitarian's pulpit has been distinguished by Ralph Waldo Emerson, Julia Ward Howe, Edward Everett Hale, Charles Eliot, David Starr Jordan, and many others. Ecumenical efforts in San Francisco have always been strongly supported here, and this congregation and reform Temple Emanu-El hold a joint Thanksgiving Day service.

Continuation:
Bus Connections to Downtown, or out to the Cliff House

The **38 Geary** bus stops at the corner of Geary and Gough in front of St. Mary's Cathedral. This line can take you east to Union Square downtown *(Tour 1)* and further on to Market Street and the Transbay Terminal. Across Geary Boulevard, the 38 Geary bus going west can take you through the Richmond District to Sutro Heights Park and near the Cliff House and Land's End *(Tour 13)*.

TOUR TEN
Mission Dolores and the Mission District

•

THE REVOLVING DOOR INTO AMERICAN SOCIETY

Mission Dolores,
built of adobe to the designs of Father Francisco Palou and completed in 1795,
has withstood two great earthquakes. In the earthen plaza in front of this church the
Native American peoples once performed their dances.

What This Tour Covers
Preliminaries
Introduction: The Revolving Door into American Society

TOUR 10:
MISSION DOLORES
AND THE
MISSION DISTRICT

① Sixteenth Street: The Mission's Oldest Street/ Basilica of San Francisco

② Mission Dolores Chapel, Museum, and Old Cemetery

③ Old Notre Dame School/Site of Costanoan Rancheria

④ Chula Lane and Abbey Street Victorian Cottages

⑤ 3639–41 Seventeenth Street

⑥ Dolores Street Palms and Landscaping

⑦ Mission High School

⑧ Mission Dolores Park/Downtown Panorama

⑨ Dolores Street from Cumberland to Liberty

⑩ 100 Block of Liberty Street

⑪ 827 Guerrero Street

⑫ Liberty Street between Guerrero and Valencia/ Valencia Street: Feminist Epicenter

⑬ Lexington Street Victorian Enclave

⑭ La Casa de la Raza/Parking Garage

⑮ 3243–45 Twenty-First Street

⑯ Twenty-Second Street/Mission Street Warehouses

⑰ Old St. John's Lutheran Church Victorian Group/ Iglesia de Santa Maria y Santa Marta

⑱ Mission District Mural

⑲ Capp Street Victorian Row

⑳ La Iglesia Presbiteriana de la Mision/Mission United Church

㉑ Twenty-Fourth Street Latino Shopping Strip

㉒ Balmy Street Murals

㉓ BART Station and Mural

㉔ Mission Cultural Center/Teatro Mision

㉕ *Homage to Siqueiros* Mural

Continuation
Downtown, or Noe Valley and the Castro District

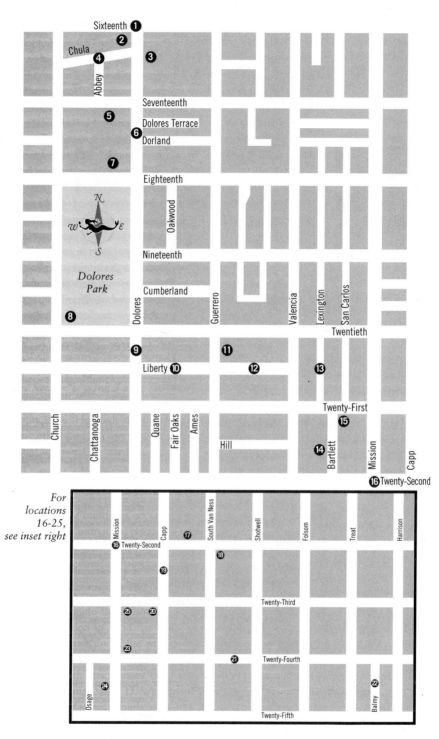

Mission District

$\mathscr{P}$reliminaries

Mission Dolores
3321 Sixteenth Street,
at Dolores; Open daily
9 A.M. to 4 P.M.;
621-8203

Mission Economic
Cultural Association,
2601 Mission Street,
ninth floor,
San Francisco 94110;
phone 826-1401.

Open Studio/SF,
1800 Market Street,
suite 252,
San Francisco, CA 94102

BEST TIMES
TO DO THIS TOUR

Weekdays at 7:30 A.M. mass is said in the historic old mission; the Saturday 5 P.M. mass is also celebrated there. Sunday services are in the less- interesting adjoining basilica; the noon mass there is sung in Spanish. The old mission is generally open daily; see listing below for seasonal variations in hours; donation requested. Sunday mornings are good times to explore the neighborhood; churches are open, families are on their way to worship, the neighborhood is relaxed and happy, and no trucks rumble through the streets.

Since 1966, on the first weekend of May there is a *Cinco de Mayo* parade in the Mission. On Memorial Day weekend there is a festive *Carnaval* parade and salsa ball. On the second Sunday of September Twenty-fourth Street hosts the *Festival de las Americas* Latin American Independence celebration. November 1st is the *Dia de los Muertos* procession. For information on these events contact the **Mission Economic Cultural Association.**

On one October weekend each year some of the painters, photographers, sculptors, weavers, and other artists with studios all across the city host **Open Studio/SF** and present their art. This is a rare opportunity to see not only a great variety of arts and crafts but the sometimes more interesting environments that artists live in. For dates, cost, and a map, write for more information.

$\mathscr{P}$arking

Street parking is available on Sixteenth Street, between Valencia and Guerrero; take BART back to your car at the end of the walk. There is a parking lot on Twenty-fourth Street at the corner of Capp and a large garage on Bartlett Street between Twenty-first and Twenty-second streets, under the Casa de la Raza.

Transportation

The Muni Metro **J Church** streetcar runs under Market Street and then emerges above ground to intersect Church and Sixteenth streets; from there walk one block east on Sixteenth to Mission Dolores. Or take **BART** to the Sixteenth Street station and walk three blocks west to the mission, passing what may be the heart of contemporary bohemia near the Roxie Cinema at Sixteenth and Valencia.

RESTAURANTS AND CAFÉS

Café La Boheme has the spirit of the North Beach cafés of the 1950s. Local artists' works hang on the walls. **Café Babar** is open from 5 P.M. to 2 A.M. (proper bohemian hours), and serves beer, wine, and espresso; jazz every Wednesday night; open-mike poetry every Thursday.

Interesting restaurants continue to pop up along low-rent Guerrero and Valencia streets, as well as Mission Street. These are not high-class restaurants: their plastic-tablecloth decor is both "south of the border" in feeling and thoroughly working class in reality. The best taco, burrito, and Mexican beer place is **La Taqueria** across the street from the Mission Cultural Center. Many worlds overlap here: *cholos* and cops, tourists and hip-hoppers, bohos and blue collars. An excellent place for crepes is **Ti-Couz**. A San Francisco tradition is the Christakes family's **St. Francis Fountain**. Opened in 1918, the St. Francis makes its own ice cream (twenty flavors), toppings, and hand-dipped chocolate candies. Taped to the cash register is a small sign that warns: "Life is uncertain, eat dessert first." In the North Mission is the **Rite Spot Café**, a hang-out for local artists.

SHOPPING

Used, left-wing, feminist and lesbian, children's, Latin-American, and labor-oriented books and newspapers are what the low-rent Mission offers uniquely, in a cluster near Sixteenth and Valencia streets and here and there throughout

Café La Boheme
3318 Twenty-fourth, near Mission; 285-4122

Café Babar
994 Guerrero, near Twenty-second; 282-6789

La Taqueria
2889 Mission Street, between Twenty-fourth and Twenty-fifth; 285-7117

Ti-Couz Creperie
3108 Sixteenth Street, between Guerro and Valencia; 25-CREPE

St. Francis Fountain
2801 Twenty-fourth Street, corner of York; 826-4200

Rite Spot Café
2099 Folsom, near Seventeenth; 552-6066

Modern Times Bookstore
888 Valencia Street, between Nineteenth and Twentieth; 282-9246

Discoteca Havana
*3000 Twenty-fourth, at
Harrison; 826-9214*

Discolandia
*2964 Twenty-fourth, near
Alabama; 826-9446*

La Palma Mexicatessen
*2884 Twenty-fourth, at
Florida; 647-1500*

Casa Lucas Market
*2934 Twenty-fourth, near
Alabama; 826-4334*

Lucca Ravioli
*1100 Valencia, at
Twenty-second; 647-5581*

Rainbow Grocery
*1899 Mission, at
Fifteenth; 863-0620*

Groger's Western Wear
*1445 Valencia, at
Twenty-fifth; 647-0700*

Mission Cultural Center
*2868 Mission, near
Twenty-fifth; Phone
821-1155 for programs*

La Peña Cultural Center
*3105 Shattuck Avenue
in Berkeley;
(510) 849-2568*

Roxie Cinema
*3117 Sixteenth, near
Valencia; 863-1087*

**The Marsh—A Breeding
Ground for New
Performance** *1062
Valencia Street, near
Twenty-second;
641-0235*

Artists' Television Access
*992 Valencia Street,
near Twenty-first;
824-3890*

the neighborhood. At any local bookstore secure a copy of *A Book Lover's Guide to the Mission,* which lists and maps the many unusual bookstores, cafés, and art galleries that cluster here. **Modern Times Bookstore** has books in English and Spanish and specializes in contemporary Latin American literature and left-wing books and newspapers; a good place to taste the radical tradition of the Mission.

Discoteca Havana has Caribbean and samba records. **Discolandia** is good for salsa and Central American rhythms.

Shops along Twenty-fourth street offer the best regional selection of Central American tropical produce, spices, and condiments. **La Palma Mexicatessen** has handmade tortillas and a fine assortment of dried chiles. The open-fronted **Casa Lucas Market** imports a dozen different kinds of bananas. Alas, the Mexican bakeries along Twenty-fourth are ordinary. **Lucca Ravioli** has its own pasta manufactory visible through a sidewalk window. **Rainbow Grocery** is an ultimate synthesis of progressive politics, expanded consciousness, and organic food.

Mission Street lost most of its big furniture stores to the freeways; along Valencia, Guerrero, and Mission there are some secondhand stores. **Groger's Western Wear** carries pointy-toed cowboy boots, Stetson hats, bolo ties, a fine array of fancy gold and silver belt buckles, boot tips, and traditional, brand-name Western wear; it's worth going out of the way for if you seek authentic Western duds.

ENTERTAINMENT

Founded in 1977, the active **Mission Cultural Center** neighborhood institution has classes, galleries, art and dance studios, and a theater. It presents Latino art exhibits and houses the 150-seat **Teatro Mision. La Peña Cultural Center,** across the Bay in Berkeley, hosts a wide variety of artistic, musical, and theatrical events. The **Roxie Cinema** is the epicenter of the Mission's contemporary bohemia; unusual films. Several cafés and restaurants cluster here; nearby is a concentration of used book shops. **The Marsh—A Breeding Ground for New Performance** presents new performance art and comedy. Attended parking is nearby on Twenty-first and Bartlett, near Valencia. **Artists' Television Access** is a multimedia gallery that also presents weekly screenings of cutting-edge films and videos. Not like the major networks. **Women's Building/Edificio de Mujeres** presents a wide variety of women's, progressive, and peace programs in funky Dovre Hall, home to many women's organizations. **Theater Artaud** New theater, dance, and music in a converted industrial building. **Theater Rhinoceros** Cutting-edge gay theater in the basement of the San Francisco Labor Temple. **New Performance Gallery** Modern dance and theater. **Intersection for The Arts** Avant-garde theater, performance art, and readings. **Esta Noche** is a gay bar popular with Latino transvestites.

Galleria de la Raza/Studio 24 A showcase for contemporary Chicano and Latino artists; the adjoining gift shop has Mexican folk art and cards. **Tzin Tzun Tzan** has the largest selection of Mexican folk art in the Bay Area, including large ceramics and furniture.

Precita Eyes Mural Arts Center offers a slide show and walking tour of the Mission's murals. The **Mexican Museum** is at Fort Mason. A part of the outstanding Nelson Rockefeller Mexican folk art collection is housed here; changing exhibits.

Levi Strauss & Company, on Valencia Street between Thirteenth and Fourteenth, offers a forty-five-minute tour with a film on the history of Levi jeans on Wednesdays; reservations are best made a week ahead. This garment factory was built in 1906 and made Western-looking in 1970 by Howard Friedman. Philanthropist Rosalie Stern leased to the city the land in front of the building, now Levi Strauss Playground, for $1 a year, to improve conditions in the congested neighborhood.

Women's Building/Edificio de Mujeres
3543 Eighteenth Street, near Valencia; 431-1180

Theater Artaud
450 Florida Street, at Seventeenth; 621-7797

Theater Rhinoceros
2926 Sixteenth Street, near South Van Ness; 861-5079

New Performance Gallery
3153 Seventeenth Street, at Shotwell; 863-9834

Intersection for The Arts
466 Valencia Street; 626-2787

Esta Noche
3079 Sixteenth Street, between Mission and Valencia; 861-5757

Galleria de la Raza/Studio 24
2857 Twenty-fourth Street, near Bryant; 826-8009

Tzin Tzun Tzan
1020 Murray Street, Berkeley; (510) 644-1088

Precita Eyes Mural Arts Center
348 Precita Avenue; Phone 285-2287 for reservations

Mexican Museum
Fort Mason, Building D; 441-0404

Levi Strauss & Company
250 Valencia Street, between Thirteenth and Fourteenth; 565-9153

Introduction: The Revolving Door into American Society

The **Mission** and the **Presidio** are the two oldest Spanish foundations in what became the city of San Francisco. If you look at a map of the Mission, you will notice that **San Jose Avenue** angles idiosyncratically through the regular grid of streets south of Twenty-second Street. Once part of the San Jose Road, **El Camino Real** was established by the Spanish military along animal and Native American trails to the south. Near where this trail crossed Mission Creek (which gave access to Mission Bay and then San Francisco Bay), at today's Camp and Albion streets, the original mission site was selected by Lieutenant José Joaquin Moraga on June 28, 1776. The first mission church was a simple brush shelter. It was the sixth of the twenty-one missions established in Spanish Alta California. Father Font's diary records that

> Passing through wooded hills and flats with good lands, in which we encountered two lagoons and some springs of good water, with plentiful grass, fennel, and other useful herbs, we arrived at a beautiful arroyo which, because it was Friday of Sorrows [the Friday before Palm Sunday], we called the Arroyo de los Dolores. On its banks we found much and very fragrant manzanita and other plants, and many wild violets. Near it the lieutenant planted a little maize and chickpeas to test the soil, which to us appeared very good ...

Because the ground at the original location was too soft to support a heavy adobe church building, the mission was relocated about a block and a half to the west to the present site on Dolores near Sixteenth Street.

The Mission period of California history, from the 1770s to the mid–1830s, is very difficult to uncover, buried as it is under a distorting, pious romanticism that began in the 1880s. The coming of the gray-clothed Franciscan friars from the convent of San Fernando in Mexico City was not the salvation but rather the utter obliteration of the native peoples. Absolute cultural contempt was accompanied by smallpox and other "new" diseases that wiped away virtually the entire race of native peoples in a couple of generations. For them, the Christians' God of Love was accompanied by extinction.

The tribe that the Spanish cavalry and Franciscan friars gathered at **Mission Dolores** was known as the **Ramaytush**, one of the peoples whom the Spanish called the **Costanoan**, or coast people. The Costanoans embraced eight languages and ranged over the San Francisco peninsula, the East Bay, and as far south as the Salinas Valley and Big Sur. Before the arrival of the Spanish, Ramaytush was spoken by about 1,400 people in what is now San Francisco and San Mateo counties. Most early explorers were struck by the great variation of tribes in the Bay Area, which was an intricate patchwork of different language groups. The San Francisco mission embraced eighteen recognized tribes by 1816. They seem to have migrated to this region about A.D. 500, probably from the San Joaquin–Sacramento delta. Before the coming of the

Europeans, these peoples had a relatively simple material culture. Their houses and rafts were made of tule rushes, and their diet was based on acorns, salmon, and shellfish. They conducted controlled burnings each fall to promote seed-bearing annuals and to increase the grazing for deer and antelope. Tribelet chiefs might be either men or women, though the office was usually inherited patrilineally. Warfare was conducted against neighboring tribes with bows and arrows.

The Spanish soldiers forced the tribes to abandon their favorite sunny places around the Bay and to cluster in rancherías, European-dominated villages near the mission churches. Here they saddened, sickened, and died. The aboriginal existence of the last triblets disappeared for the most part by about 1810. Louis Choris observed in 1816 that "After several months spent in the mission, they usually grow fretful and thin, and they constantly gaze with sadness at the mountains which they can see in the distance." By 1850 a United States Indian Agent found but one survivor, Pedro Alcantara, who lamented, "I am all that is left of my people—I am alone."

The Mission District became a revolving door into American society. The history of the succession of its peoples is in microcosm the history of the city, and to a degree, that of the state of California. Native American tribes, Spanish explorers and colonists, Mexican settlers, and Yankee squatters have all lived here. Following the Yankees in the 1860s came a substantial wave of German and Scandinavian immigrants. In the 1870s, some streets in the Mission, such as **Howard** (now South Van Ness Avenue) and **Guerrero**, began to attract grand houses, mansions even. But this was short-lived as Pacific Heights solidified its position as the elite district. By 1898 *The Real Estate Circular* noted "how obediently fashion's behests are obeyed" as the foggier northwestern heights triumphed over the sunnier Mission valley. Middle-class and working-class houses filled up most of the Mission. When the large Potrero industrial district immediately to the west began expanding in the 1900s, the neighborhood became more and more blue collar and less and less middle class. When Italian American North Beach and the Irish American South of Market were destroyed by the earthquake and fire of 1906, many Irish and Italian workers moved into the neighborhood. "The Mish" became bigger and more insular and even developed its own accent, said to be something like that of Brooklyn. The Mission became something of a "city within the city"; with the stores, services, and theaters along Mission Street, locals had little reason to go downtown to Market Street.

Because San Francisco has had longstanding trade links with Pacific Coast Central American coffee-exporting ports, there was, even in the mid-nineteenth century, a trickle of Latin immigration to the city. Elite Latin American families came to vacation in the Victorian city. Latin American workers began to settle in the South of Market district close to the United Fruit Company docks and the big coffee roasters. While Mexican immigrants tended to work in the agricultural interior of California, Central Americans gravitated to this port city. Immigration from El Salvador, Nicaragua, and the Panama Canal Zone began in the early twentieth century. It declined during the depressed 1930s but began again with World War II and post-war prosperity. **Sixteenth Street** in the north Mission emerged as the first distinctively Latino shopping strip, with restaurants and bakeries. As migration increased the Spanish-speaking population moved deeper into the Inner Mission. While it is not a rigid pattern, Mexican immigrants tend to dominate in the poorer core of the Mission east of **Mission Street,** between Seventeenth and Twenty-fourth streets. Central Americans are more in evidence west of Mission Street and in the more middle class Outer Mission south of Army Street. The **Excelsior** and **Crocker-Amazon** neighborhoods near the southern city limits have a noticeable concentration of Salvadoran, Nicaraguan, and other Central American small proprietors. By 1950, Central Americans outnumbered Mexican-born San Franciscans. The civil wars in El Salvador and Nicaragua and the brutal repression in Guatemala propelled many more Spanish-speaking migrants north in the 1980s.

Between 1950 and 1970, the Latino population in the low-rent Mission doubled every ten years, going from 11 percent in 1950 to 45 percent by 1970. (These were also the decades when the children of the older immigrant groups became throughly assimilated and suburbanized.) In 1990, the Latino population grew to 52 percent, an increase of 23 percent since 1980. Today the "non–Hispanic"white population accounts for 29 percent, Asians and Pacific Islanders 13 percent, and African Americans 4 percent of Mission residents. There are at least eighteen distinct groups of Latinos in the Mission today. The fancy license-plate frames sold in Mission Street shops proudly proclaim "Soy de Peru, Nicaragua, Guatemala, El Salvador, Honduras, Colombia, Costa Rica, Panama" and then get more specific for Mexico: "Soy de Guadalajara, Jalisco, Durango, Nayarit, Sinaloa, Michoacan, Guerrero, or Distrito Federal." This very varied migration has made political mobilization difficult in the Mission. Though Latinos make up about 15 percent of the city's population, they are only 6 percent of the voters. The new Mission, unlike the Irish American Mission of the turn of the century, has relatively little political clout and Latinos have had very limited success in electing city Supervisors (aldermen).

The adult Latino population of the Mission is remarkably hard working. Many work as janitors, roofers, day laborers, or in the city's many hotels and restaurants. (Latino cooks prepare much of the Italian and other cuisines in San Francisco.) These low-paid workers in this high-cost city face a difficult situation. In many couples both parents work long hours, which means that many youths here grow up unsupervised and on the streets. The Mission is seeing an increase in youth gangs, often based on nationality. The plague of grafitti here is due in part to these gangs marking "their" territory. The Roman numerals you see represent the Mission's numbered streets where various cliques hang out. The city needs more creative recreation and cultural programs and much more support for public schools in the Mission.

Pockets of the Mission are experiencing gentrification, especially on quieter side streets along its edges. Some lesbian couples favor the narrow sidestreets east of Valencia Street. However, heavy traffic on the principal streets, and the contemporary overcrowding of the neighborhood, limit its appeal to professionals and this keeps the area working-class. The latest change in the ever-changing Mission is the increase in the number of Chinese American landlords and merchants in the neighborhood. Many have opened inexpensive shops along the northern end of Mission Street and some have begun buying apartment houses as investments. The Mission has never stood still; the revolving door keeps revolving.

① *Sixteenth Street: The Mission's Oldest Street*

Basilica of San Francisco
Sixteenth Street and Dolores; Sunday masses held at 8, 10, and 12 A.M. (in Spanish); 621-8203

An ornate Churrigueresque Revival basilica rises on the southwest corner of Sixteenth Street and Dolores. This was the site of the old adobe mission quadrangle begun in 1782. Old surveys show that the complex extended out into what is now Sixteenth Street. The *convento*, or priests' quarters, adjoined the mission chapel and connected with a storehouse. Behind the quadrangle were gardens, orchards, and a vineyard. During the mission era, a string of adobe houses sprang up along what is now Sixteenth Street from Dolores to Guerrero, on the trail to the port at Yerba Buena (today's downtown). After the priests abandoned the mission in the 1830s, this small Mexican settlement continued to grow slowly. Records indicate that as late as 1844 some Native Americans continued to live in a community, with a *mayordomo*, or administrator, at the former mission. In that year the Mexican inhabitants here unsuccessfully petitioned the governor at Monterey to declare the settlement a pueblo and to grant house lots. Among the petitioners were **Francisco de Haro, Francisco Sanchez, Francisco Guerrero, Jesús Noe, Cand'llo Valencia,** and **José Bernal,** all of whom eventually had their names given to Mission streets. The governor refused; instead, over time, the former mission lands were granted as ranchos, many to former soldiers.

In the late 1840s, Yankee squatters turned the mission complex into a hotel, gambling den, and small brewery. Far from the settlement at Yerba Buena, the "over the line" Mission attracted duels, bear baiting, bull fights, and horse racing. The Catholic Church did not regain the old mission and two plots containing the former mission gardens and orchards until 1857. In 1861, after the mission had been returned to the church, the *convento* had a second story added and became a seminary. In 1876 the *convento* was demolished for the opening of Sixteenth Street and the erection of a now-lost red brick Gothic church that was dedicated on the mission's centennial.

- **Basilica of San Francisco,** *1913; 1926*

The basilica was begun in 1913 and remodeled with fanciful towers in 1926 for the sesquicentennial of the founding of the mission. (The title "basilica" is an honor conferred by the pope. Pius XII conferred this dignity in 1952, and a pontifical red and gold umbrella and papal coat of arms flank the altar.) The basilica is worth looking at from the outside and comparing with its venerable neighbor, Mission Dolores. As a whole, with its strong diagonal from the top of the tallest basilica tower to the small wall shrine to the Virgin in front of the old cemetery, this is one of the most beautiful blockfronts in San Francisco.

Mission Dolores Chapel, Museum, and Old Cemetery
*320 Dolores Street;
Open May to October 31,
9 A.M. to 4:00 P.M.;
November to April 30,
10 A.M. to 4 P.M.;
New Years' and Easter,
10 A.M. to 1 P.M.
Masses held in the old
mission weekdays at
7:30 A.M. and Saturday
at 5 P.M.; 621-8203*

② Mission Dolores Chapel, Museum, and Old Cemetery, *1783–95; Francisco Palou; 1918, restoration by Willis Polk*

The old mission, officially the **Mission San Francisco de Asis,** is one of the great historical and architectural treasures in San Francisco and has been recently restored. It was begun in 1783 and completed in 1795 and survived both abandonment in the 1840s and 1850s and the great earthquakes of 1868 and 1906. It has seen sensitive preservation, including a thorough restoration by Willis Polk in 1918. In 1992, the mission began a fund-raising campaign to conserve this important monument. Historically Irish and Italian, today half of San Francisco's population of 165,000 church-going Roman Catholics are Spanish-speaking. It is also interesting to note that many of the parishioners of Mission Dolores in the 1990s are openly gay or lesbian.

The mission was designed by Father Francisco Palou, who is buried near its south wall in the adjoining cemetery. It was the sixth in the chain of twenty-one Franciscan missions that extended from San Diego to San Francisco Solano (Sonoma). The chapel is built of adobe, a building technique introduced to California by the Spanish. The soft contours and powdery surface of the adobe have been covered with a hard cement stucco coating to preserve the building from rain. Paired, engaged columns decorate the facade, making this a Baroque design. The three original bronze bells carried overland from Mexico in the 1820s still hang in their niches. A narrow wooden balcony runs across the front of the church and a deep overhang shelters the church facade. In front of the chapel, where Dolores Street runs today, was an earthen plaza with a large cross.

Enter the old mission by a door to the left. Inside, the cool mission, 22 feet wide and 114 feet long, with walls 4 feet thick, feels as ancient as it is. When the eye travels down to the end of the dim church, it is dazzled by the painted and gilded altar and its *reredos* (background), a piece of Baroque Spanish art strained through distant Mexico. Old statues and paintings fill the room; an old Mexican statue of Saint Francis occupies a prominent place to the left. The church is now only infrequently used for mass, but it still serves as the baptistery for the parish, and there is a fine Victorian marble font to the side. The hand-wrought altar rail and the ironwork around the font are probably from the mission workshops. The door of the tabernacle with its picture of Christ came from Spanish workshops in Manila, another part of the vast Spanish empire linked to Acapulco, Mexico, by the famous Manila galleons. Lieutenant José Moraga, the leader of the June 1776 colonizing expedition, is buried within the church.

The most interesting artistic feature of the mission is the ceiling. It is patterned after Costanoan basket designs and is the most interesting ceiling in the city. It employs earth tones in a chevronlike design painted over the beams and the flat ceiling. The design appears differently when seen straight up than when looked at in perspective. It is the only memento of the lost arts of the extinct Costanoan peoples.

Leave the chapel through the door to the right of the altar. Outside is a modern Mission-style veranda with an interesting series of pictures of what the mission looked like at various stages in its history. In the small museum tucked behind the chapel is a glass window in the left-hand wall that allows a glimpse of the adobe construction underneath the modern white stucco. Mounted high on the wall is a model of how the struts and the ridge-joints of the rafters were originally bound with rawhide thongs. (In the restoration of 1918, they were augmented with steel supports.) Mementos of the old mission are housed here. Alas, thieves stole the original silver chalices and monstrance of the Franciscan missionaries. Behind the museum is a well-designed courtyard with a fountain and restrooms installed in 1978.

Old Notre Dame School/ Site of Costanoan Rancheria
347 Dolores Street

The old cemetery adjoins the mission to the south; originally it covered a larger area. Here are buried some 5,500 Costanoans and many pioneers: Spanish, Mexican, and Yankee. After 1857 the parish was a heavily Irish American one, and many of the tombstones here record that migration. The highrise marble obelisks of the rich face Dolores Street, while humbler tombs, most unmarked, are in the back of the plot. Burial next to the wall of the church was reserved for priests and governors; Captain Luis Antonio Arguello, the first Mexican governor of Alta California, and Francisco de Haro, the first *alcalde* (mayor) of San Francisco, are buried here, as well as Father Palou.

At some time in the present century a grid of concrete paths was laid out over the cemetery. Recent "improvement" of the plantings has been naïve, though the fragrant roses are welcome. The most interesting monument in the cemetery is in the far corner toward the front: a large brown sandstone Victorian extravaganza decorated with firemen's helmets and upside-down torches. Here lies James "Yankee" Sullivan, an Irishman, who, it was said, hanged himself while awaiting trial by the Vigilance Committee of 1856. James P. Casey and Charles Cora, two other victims of the vigilantes, are also buried here. The dazzling white wall of the mission is often the foil to the clinging bougainvillea, which bursts in magenta sprays.

❸ Old Notre Dame School/Site of Costanoan Rancheria, *1907, Theodore W. Lenzen*
At 347 Dolores Street, across from the mission, is the former **Notre Dame High School** and Convent of the Sisters of Notre Dame de Namur, which closed in 1981. Founded in 1868, it was the first girls' school in San Francisco. That building was dynamited in 1906 to save the old mission across the street from the fire. In 1907 the present mansard-roofed building was designed by Theodore W. Lenzen and constructed on the old foundations.

The block on which this old school stands was one of the two parcels flanking Dolores Street granted by the United States government to the Catholic Church and Bishop Alemany in 1857. Between here and Valencia Street was the *rancheria* established by the Spanish authorities to "civilize" the wandering Native American tribes, members of the Penutian language family who originally ranged over the San Francisco peninsula, the East Bay, and as far south as Big Sur and Soledad. Their prehistoric population has been estimated at seven thousand; by 1910 they were extinct. No signs, of course, remain from their primitive settlement, but this is a potentially important archaeological zone in San Francisco and merits identification and protection.

445 Church Street

4 *Chula Lane and Abbey Street Victorian Cottages*

37 Abbey Street

34–40 Abbey Street

Past the shrine to the Virgin Mary in the cemetery wall and to the right is **Chula Lane**. Walk up Chula Lane to **Abbey Street**, a quiet *cul-de-sac* of modest Victorian houses. Cars slow to a crawl here and children play in the streets. To its residents the Mission is a honeycomb of out-of-the-way back streets such as these. Up Chula Lane the houses are set at a sawtooth angle to the sidewalk. The lots and house placement reflect the *ad hoc* subdivisions that survive here and there within the regular, square-block grid extended into the Mission Addition in the early 1850s.

3639–41 Seventeenth Street

Dolores Street palms

Beyond the nearby parking lot at **445 Church Street** is the back of the modest white stucco and green panel headquarters of the Roman Catholic archdiocese of San Francisco, built in 1955. This is the general location of the Native American burial ground.

From Abbey Street the tile-clad dome of the tower of Mission High School can be seen in the distance. Number **37 Abbey Street** is a simple, one-story, flat-front Italianate. Facing it, at Numbers **34–40 Abbey Street**, is a plain three-story frame building with four units of a type known locally as Romeo flats because of the open stairway's balcony at the second floor.

5 **3639–41 Seventeenth Street**, *1874, Italianate House*

Number **3639–41 Seventeenth Street** is a classic two-story, bay-windowed Italianate house built in 1874, now the Dolores Park Inn Bed and Breakfast. It has a small front garden softened with ferns, fuchsia, and jade plants. Its side wall is visible from the sidewalk. This is the house type that has, in the last twenty years, again become the architectural trademark of San Francisco.

6 *Dolores Street Palms and Landscaping*

In 1904 the Outdoor Art League, a pioneer city beautification group and part of the reformist, Progressive wave that swept San Francisco during the first decade of this century, urged the "improvement and adornment" of barren Dolores Street. The stately date palms were planted by Golden Gate Park's John McLaren about 1910. The **Dolores Street palms** make elegant a street solidly lined with houses, flats, and apartment houses and sprinkled with churches. In the landscaped median is a cast-iron replica of a mission bell on a pole that looks like a shepherd's crook. In the earliest days of leisurely motor touring, the California Women's Club marked El Camino Real with these emblems. Each marker originally had a sign posting the number of miles to the next mission.

The bay-windowed, three-story frame flats and apartments that line this part of Dolores Street were mostly built between 1907 and 1929 in the area burned in 1906. It is a most agreeable street to walk or drive along. The buildings preserve the old Victorian house lot sizes, which give the blocks a human scale of twenty-five-foot building fronts. Wide Dolores Street was where the great fire was stopped in 1906. Thus the buildings to the west of the street are predominantly Victorian and those to the east Edwardian, mostly apartments and flats. On the northeast corner of Dolores and Seventeenth streets, at **395–97–99 Dolores Street**, is a typical post-1906, three-flat building with round corner bay windows. Facing it across Seventeenth Street, at **400 Dolores Street**, are two new three-flat buildings completed in 1993. Designed by John Bauman, their general form and detailing echoes the traditional Edwardian buildings of the neighborhood. Their slant-sided bays and double-hung sash windows relate perfectly to old San Francisco. Only their column-framed garage doors tell they are contemporary. This is a good example of the care with which many contemporary developers approach building in historic San Francisco neighborhoods.

395–97–99 Dolores Street

400 Dolores Street

Mission High School
3750 Eighteenth Street

**Mission Dolores Park/
Downtown Panorama**
*Between Dolores and
Church, Eighteenth and
Twentieth streets*

7 Mission High School, *1926, John Reid, Jr.; 1972–76, J. Martin Rosse*
On Eighteenth Street facing Mission Dolores Park is this large, red tile-roofed high school with a lofty and richly ornamented tower. It was designed by John Reid, Jr., the architect responsible for many of San Francisco's finest school designs. (That he was Mayor James Rolph's brother-in-law does not seem to have hurt his career.) Plain walls and rich ornament concentrated at the entrance and tower make a stark, effective contrast. Here the simple white-walled, arcaded, red-tile-roofed imagery of the early California missions was adapted for a modern structure—the imagery of adobe in modern reinforced concrete and factory-cast terra-cotta ornament. The school was completely reconstructed and its ornament more securely fastened in the 1970s as part of the seismic upgrading of all the public schools in California.

In the prosperous 1920s, Mission-style architecture became immensely popular in California. The early colonial days provided a unifying architectural image of white stucco walls and red tile roofs. Many then-unfashionable Victorian houses had their gingerbread stripped away and were coated in stucco. With red tile fringes attached to their cornices, they became weirdly vertical "adobe" buildings. The Mission style has been the region's favorite style, judging simply by the number of attempts at it. Fortunately, mediocre Mission is always better than mediocre anything else. And, embowered in semitropical vegetation, the total effect is almost always pleasing.

8 Mission Dolores Park/Downtown Panorama, *1861, Jewish cemeteries; 1905, city park*
These two blocks were originally purchased in 1861 for the cemeteries of the Emanu-El and Sherith Israel congregations. Cemeteries occupied much of the high ground west of Divisadero in the nineteenth-century city and formed a barrier to the city's expansion by the turn of the century. They and some fenced-in amusement grounds and beer gardens were the best landscaped parts of the sandy Victorian city before Golden Gate Park was developed in the 1870s. The Jewish cemeteries here in the Mission District were bought by the city in 1905 to provide a park in the congested Mission. Later,

Second Church of Christ, Scientist
655 Dolores Street

Golden Gate Lutheran and Samoan Church
601 Dolores Street

751–53 Dolores

United States Mint

after a long political struggle, the city refused to permit new burials within its limits, forcing the cemeteries west of Divisadero to relocate to a valley in Colma, south of the city line. The remains in Dolores Park were transferred to the new burial grounds.

In 1905 a park was laid out here to serve the populous Mission District. Today, **Mission Dolores Park** is the largest park in the Mission. The landscape plan is agreeable and open with groups of palms in the corners and an axial path along the line of Nineteenth Street. An unfortunate little park building mars the very center of the park. Also more a blight than an ornament is the massive concrete monument with a replica of Mexico's "liberty bell" installed at Dolores and Nineteenth streets in 1962. The bell itself might have been attractive in the park, but the useless concrete "plaza" is unnecessary and provides concrete where there should be grass.

Up the slope, on the west side of the park, is an indifferent bronze statue of Miguel Hidalgo y Castilla, the priest who is considered the George Washington of Mexico. A streetcar line was hidden in a depression along the western edge of the park in 1915. From the elevated corner at Twentieth and Church streets there is an impressive panorama over the downtown to the northeast and the Bay beyond. On Church Street, just south of Twentieth, is a gold-painted fire hydrant, one of the few that provided water during the earthquake and fire of 1906. Every April 18, on the anniversary of the catastrophe, the hydrant gets a new coat of gold paint. Dolores Heights, with its agreeable mixture of small houses and rich vegetation, rises to the southwest.

⑨ *Dolores Street from Cumberland to Liberty*

Walk up Dolores Street to Cumberland Street opposite the south side of the park. On the corner is the cream-colored, slate-domed, Beaux Arts **Second Church of Christ, Scientist,** competently designed by William H. Crim, Jr., in 1915. It makes a nice contrast with its red-brick Gothic Revival neighbor, **Golden Gate Lutheran and Samoan Church**. The two churches show the change from Victorian to Beaux Arts taste: from medieval to classical models and from red brick to white stone or stucco.

On the southeast corner of Dolores and Liberty streets, at **751–53 Dolores,** is an exuberant Edwardian two-flat building with round corner bay windows capped by a shallow dome with a ball on top. It is nicely trimmed with the standard decorative touches of the 1900s, including a cornice with garlands and swags.

From Dolores and Liberty there is a sweeping view north down palm-lined Dolores Street. The fortresslike, streamlined Moderne **United States Mint** visible in the distance was designed by Los Angeles architect Gilbert Stanley Underwood and built atop Blue Mountain in 1937. American and Filipino coins were struck here; today this mint produces only proof sets for collectors and is not open to the public. *(See the Old Mint at Fifth and Mission, Tour 1.)*

⑩ *100 Block of Liberty Street*

The eighteen blocks between the lines formed by Dolores to Mission and Twentieth to Twenty-third streets comprise the **Liberty Hill Historic District**, established by the city in 1987. Owners of buildings must secure Certificates of Appropriateness to alter exteriors visible from the public streets. The houses on Liberty Street are worth looking at. This is one of the Mission's architecturally richest streets; the gardens add a lot to the block. Number **159 Liberty Street**, a large Italianate house atop a high retaining wall, was built by Judge Daniel Murphy in 1878 during the brief period when some thought the Mission's "warm belt" might develop into a suburban luxury district. But the conquest of the steeper hills by the cable car in the 1870s turned the tide of fashion north, and Pacific Heights with its marine views became the poshest residential district. The Murphy house is one of the largest houses in the Mission and is noted for the visit to it made in 1896 by Susan B. Anthony, an early leader of the woman-suffrage movement. It has since been subdivided into many units.

The row of houses downhill from number 159 displays several of the styles once popular in San Francisco. **Number 151–53**, the house immediately to the east, was probably built around 1917 on what had been the side yard of number 159. Built in an aggressive Craftsman style, it is typical of the housing built after World War I in the East Bay and in the western districts of the city, especially the Inner Richmond.

Next down the hill, **123 Liberty Street** is a good example of the Queen Anne style of the 1890s, with scratchwork plaster ornament and a round corner tower. Numbers **121–21A, 117–19, and 111–15 Liberty Street** are three Stick-style houses of the 1880s. Last in the row, **109 Liberty Street**, is a flat-fronted Italianate built in 1869 with elegant window moldings and a side garden.

The south side of the block, with its view of the city, attracted the fancier houses, while more modest houses were built on the north side. Number **110 Liberty Street** is a late Queen Anne–Tudoresque house from the 1890s with a gable roof. At the turn of the century, flats and apartment houses were built on the corners of the main streets in the Mission such as the one at **850–52 Guerrero Street**. They define the side streets by enclosing them, creating a roomlike effect within each side street.

Liberty Hill Historic District
*Dolores to Mission
and Twentieth to
Twenty-third*

159 Liberty Street

151–53 Liberty Street

123 Liberty Street

**121–21A, 117–19, and
111–15 Liberty Street**

109 Liberty Street

110 Liberty Street

850–52 Guerrero Street

827 Guerrero Street

⑪ **827 Guerrero Street**, *1881, architect unknown; 1890, remodeled as a Moorish Queen Anne by Samuel Newsom*

The dramatic house at 827 Guerrero Street with the Moorish or Moon Gate entrance with new wrought-iron roof cresting was built in 1881 and then much expanded and remodeled in 1890 by Samuel Newsom. It has a round bay, stage-set balconies, fine art-glass windows, a jerkinhead variation on the gable to the left, and a vaguely *Arabian Nights* air. Note the rich texture of the walls; virtually every surface, and originally the roof as well, was treated as an opportunity for pattern and ornament. The entrance arch is much like the main hall arches in Samuel and Joseph Cather Newsom's

70 Liberty Street

58 Liberty Street

Old Wives Tales
*1009 Valencia Street,
near Twenty-first;
821-4675*

900 block of Valencia

great Carson Mansion of 1884–85 in Eureka, California, the greatest surviving Victorian mansion in the state. There is a fine garden here with many topiary trees. Today this is Agape House, a residence for the mentally ill and AIDS dementia patients.

12 *Liberty Street Between Guerrero and Valencia*

The next block down Liberty Street is dense with Victorian treasures. The trees at midblock create a sudden oasis of green. At **70 Liberty Street**, a three-story, bay-windowed Italianate with bay windows on both sides of a central entrance was built in 1872 for the owner of a woodworking mill and box factory. (The 1920s Gothic-style lamps are a later garnish.) Next door is equally impressive **58 Liberty Street**, another bay-windowed Italianate with a center hall. It was designed by S. C. Bugbee and Son in 1876 for a commission merchant. This house has an unusual "jog" in its fac nade; the left-hand side juts out further than the center and right-hand side. The Bugbees designed some of the largest of the now-lost Nob Hill mansions in the 1870s. Both these houses sit on double-width lots more usual in Pacific Heights than the Mission. These grand houses were among the first to be restored in the Mission in the 1970s. Both are now subdivided into apartments. Walk to the end of the block and Valencia Street.

• *Valencia Street: Feminist Epicenter*

Heavy through-traffic along Valencia and Guerrero streets has created relatively unattractive and therefore low-rent commercial strips, and this has attracted chronically low-profit progressive bookstores, peace groups, left-wing political organizations, and evangelical churches. In the 1930s, the Communist Party had its offices on Valencia and sponsored rallies in Garfield Square.

Valencia Street, sandwiched between the gay male Castro and the low-rent Mission, has emerged as the epicenter of the women's movement. **Old Wives Tales** opened in 1977 and is a nerve center for "womens visions and books" and for children's books. Guides and information can be secured here on Valencia's feminist and lesbian businesses, activities, and restaurants.

Not on this walk, but one-half block off Valencia, at 3543 Eighteenth Street, is the **Women's Building/Edificio de Mujeres**, in Dovre Hall, originally built as a Norwegian American meeting hall. The building houses many women's, gay and lesbian, peace, and progressive groups and is the setting for meetings, lectures, films, and other programs. A mural painted across the entire building by Juana Alicia and a host of other women artists in 1995 is one of the best new art works in the city. From the beats of the 1950s to the cultural, sexual, and health care politics of the 1990s, San Francisco has harbored within herself the active yeast of contemporary progressive culture.

The east side of the **900 block of Valencia**, between Twentieth and Twenty-first streets, harbors a string of six two-story, bay-windowed Italianate houses all built between 1875 and 1877 by the Real Estate Associates, mid-nineteenth-century

San Francisco's largest developer and house builder. They are surviving elements from the largest pieces of town planning and building the Real Estate Associates achieved. In 1875 the associates,
essentially William Hollis and partners, bought the block bounded
by Mission, Valencia, Twentieth, and Twenty-first streets and cut
two narrow streets, today Stevenson and San Carlos streets, through it. They subdivided the parcel into 120 house lots. On Mission and Valencia streets, the Real Estate
Associates surveyed large lots and built Italianate villas that sold for about $7,400. All
have been demolished. On Valencia Street standard middle-class two-story, bay-windowed Italianate row houses were built that sold for about $5,800. This row survives.
Lots and houses on Twentieth and Twenty-first streets were slightly smaller and
cheaper; those on the narrow interior streets were smaller still. These houses sold typically to craftsmen, small proprietors, and teachers for about $3,700 on San Carlos
Street (closer to Mission) and $3,350 on Lexington Street. Corner lots, the largest and
most expensive of all, were developed with mixed commercial-residential buildings for
grocers who lived over their shops. They averaged a high $9,990.

Missionaries of Charity Queen of Peace Convent
974 Valencia

Lexington Street

Modern Times Bookstore carries new international—especially Latin
American—literature and progressive books. It is an island of calm with comfortable
chairs and a mother lode of free newspapers and flyers reflecting what's happening in
radical circles in the Mission. A sort of Christian Science Reading Room for the left,
Modern Times sponsors lectures and readings.

At 974 Valencia, over the entrance to a bay-windowed Edwardian
apartment building, is the small white and blue sign of Mother Teresa's **Missionaries
of Charity Queen of Peace Convent** quietly established here in 1985. These Roman
Catholic nuns are dedicated to serving the poorest of the poor and dying. At 992
Valencia is **Artists' Television Access**.

⓭ *Lexington Street Victorian Enclave*

The contrast between palm- and residence-lined Dolores Street and stark Valencia with
its auto shops is dramatic. East of Valencia, heading downhill, the character of the streets
changes from what was originally professional and middle-class housing on the high
ground to lower-middle-class and working-class housing on the flat land.

Lexington Street can be seen as California's first tract housing. The
small-scale, speculator-subdivided side streets in the Mission, blessedly free of through
traffic, harbor architecturally coherent and socially diverse residential enclaves. Side
streets like Lexington, which is only three-and-a-half blocks long, have a strong sense of
visual definition and an intimate sense of place. The closed-in vistas of the narrow streets
define a cell within the larger neighborhood. Most of the two-story, flat-front Italianate
houses here were built between 1876 and 1877. There are some bay-windowed houses
as well. Though built as single-family houses, they were easily and neatly subdivided into
upstairs and downstairs flats when buildings became absentee-owned investment properties. Among the first owners here were a bookkeeper, a master mariner, a theatrical
and musical manager, a waiter, and a plasterer. When Victorians were out of favor from
the 1920s to 1960s some of these houses were drastically modernized. Today, of course,
the trend is toward facade restoration and interior modernization.

La Casa de la Raza/
Parking Garage
50 Bartlett Street

3243–45 Twenty-first
Street

Bay View Federal Bank
2601 Mission Street

⑭ La Casa de la Raza/Parking Garage, *1987, Conrad & Associates*
On Twenty-first Street, at the head of Lexington Street, are fifty-one units of state-financed, low-income housing built over a three-level, two-hundred-stall city parking garage. Public housing *has* evolved—even though construction of it has dwindled to almost nothing. At least the central "open space" of this compound is gated. (It is debatable, however, whether housing should be built over concentrated auto exhaust.) The building's chief urban design fault is not its featureless windows, or the cheap appliquéed mock Victorian sunrise designs in the gables, or even the brutality of the block-long Bartlett Street side of the garage; it is the unforgivable interruption of the continuous shopping strip along Twenty-second Street on the other side of the block.

⑮ 3243–45 Twenty-first Street
On the corner of Twenty-first and Bartlett is a remarkable two-family Eastlake house at **3243–45 Twenty-first Street**, which has settled unevenly into the soft ground. It was built in 1883 for $4,000 for George Pattison. The lathe-turned redwood ornament on this house is emphatic and strong. Robust designs and durable materials—redwood rather than cheaper cast plaster and sheet metal—marked the best buildings of the booming 1880s. This house represents the high-water mark of Victorian house design in San Francisco. The porch is especially robust.

⑯ *Twenty-Second Street / Mission Street Warehouses*

Looking north up Mission Street from Twenty-second you'll see San Francisco's best surviving cluster of old neon and electric signs, attached to a string of movie theaters and furniture stores. They create steeplelike vertical accents down the long commercial strip. The Moderne "New Mission" of 1916 has a later tall, streamlined sign; the "Cine Latino" of 1923 has a sign in the shape of a knight's helmet. Both, unfortunately, are dark. The "El Capitan" of 1928 survives as a facade, but its auditorium was demolished for a parking lot in the 1960s. "Starlight Furniture" boasts a rare old illuminated sign. Looking to the south, down Mission, you can see the streamline Moderne "Grand Theater" of 1940. Great neon signs were beacons of attraction on 1920s-to-1950s main streets. Mission Street's great theaters deserve to be revived.

Mission Street from Twentieth Street south to the San Mateo County line is one of San Francisco's "sleepers." Because Mission Street did not burn in 1906, layers of San Francisco history can be seen along this old land route into the city.

On the southeast corner of Mission and Twenty-second streets is the **Bay View Federal Bank** tower erected in 1963. This nine- story glass and quartz aggregate clad slab is quite out of place in the lowrise district. Its lower section is shielded by a riot-proof metal grill behind which there is a dark, dreary minigarden. A large parking lot for the tower eats into the neighborhood on the Capp Street side.

⑰ Old St. John's Lutheran Church Victorian Group/Iglesia de Santa Maria y Santa Marta

Down Twenty-second are the lacy Gothic spires of St. John's Lutheran Church, the centerpiece of a remarkable Victorian cluster. The cornerstone of the church is engraved "1900: Ev. Luth. St. Johannes Kirche," though in style the conservative church belongs to the nineteenth century. It is a pleasing piece of nineteenth-century carpentry with convincing ornament: a stone cathedral translated into redwood for a German-speaking congregation. Alas, its rose window has been lost, but that can be reversed someday. Today it houses the Iglesia de Santa Maria y Santa Marta, a Latino Protestant congregation.

On the corner to the left of the church is **3144–46 Twenty-second Street**, an L-shaped, three-story, Eastlake-style building. The typical corner storefront has 1930s tile splash panels. To the right of the church is **3126 Twenty-second Street**, the parsonage, a fine two-story, bay-windowed Italianate house with a parish office built over its front lawn that brings the building out to the sidewalk. Behind a lattice fence next door is **3118–22 Twenty-second Street**, a charming one-story, flat-front Italianate cottage with a uniquely ornamented parapet. It is perched atop a garage inserted in the 1920s. The old cottage has been beautifully restored and adapted into two units. The simple pergola "carport" alongside leads to an iron gate through which can be glimpsed a delightful oasis of a garden with a carriage-house cottage at its back.

Old St. John's Lutheran Church Victorian Group/ Iglesia de Santa Maria y Santa Marta

3144–46 Twenty-second Street

3126 Twenty-second Street

3118–22 Twenty-second Street

Mission District Mural
southeast corner of Twenty-second Street and South Van Ness Avenue

⑱ Mission District Mural, *"Inspire to Aspire: Tribute to Carlos Santana," 1987, Michael Ríos, Carlos Gonzalez, Johnny Mayorga*

Exploding in vivid colors on the southeast corner of Twenty-second Street and South Van Ness Avenue facing a corner parking lot is a vibrant "neo-Aztec" mural entitled *Inspire to Aspire: Tribute to Carlos Santana*, painted by Michael Rios, Carlos Gonzalez, and Johnny Mayorga in 1987. It depicts Latino musicians, Mexican *mariachis,* plumed serpents, a mandala, and an Aztec pyramid set before the San Francisco skyline with the Transamerica Pyramid. Chicano murals first emerged in the *barrios* of East Los Angeles in the late 1960s. From there the idea spread to the East Bay, where militantly political and revolutionary themes dominated. In San Francisco, which has seen murals come and go in black, hippie, Latino, Chinese, and Filipino neighborhoods, the murals have had sunnier themes, in particular music and dancing. This is one of the best of what is by its nature an ephemeral art. It was funded by the city. Return to Capp Street and turn left.

⑲ *Capp Street Victorian Row*

The most extensive row of identical Stick-Eastlake houses is on the east side of Capp between Twenty-second and Twenty-third streets. All were built between 1889 and 1894 by Australian-born architect T. J. Welch for developer Mary E. von Schroeder. Of the fifteen houses, ten are substantially intact. The row is very beautiful, its mass-produced woodwork lacy and fanciful. The "flash glass"—small colored squares sur-

767–69–71 Capp

La Iglesia Presbiteriana de la Mision/Mission United Church
Twenty-third and Capp streets

rounding the main window pane—survives on many of them. One house has been shingled, three "improved" with asbestos shingles, and one stuccoed and fringed with red tiles, probably in the 1920s. On the corner of Twenty-third Street, at number **767–69–71 Capp**, is a three-story, Eastlake-style commercial and flats building with fine corner bay windows. Capp Street is fortunate to retain its handsome 1920s streetlights.

20 La Iglesia Presbiteriana de la Mision/ Mission United Church, *1891, Percy & Hamilton*

At Twenty-third and Capp is the Mission United Presbyterian Church designed by Percy & Hamilton in 1891. It is an excellent example of the Romanesque shingle style and boasts a fine tower, recently restored. Organized in 1868, this was the first "suburban" Presbyterian congregation in San Francisco. The church flourished during the second half of the nineteenth century, attracting many well-to-do members. After 1900, factories and warehouses expanded into the area and middle-class families began to drift toward the suburbs down the peninsula or across the Bay to Oakland. The fire of 1906, which destroyed adjoining parts of the Mission and all of the heavily working-class South of Market, accelerated the change. Surviving houses were profitably subdivided and the old mixture of middle class and working class in the district tipped toward being solidly working class. The recent restoration of Mission United Church is a heroic achievement and marks a turning point for the Mission District. One man, Winchell T. Hayward, made all the difference in this restoration miracle.

To the east of Capp Street on filled-in Mission Bay was San Francisco's—and the West Coast's—first large industrial zone. Iron works, breweries, sugar refineries, lumber mills, and factories of all kinds grew along the Bay shore and the railroad tracks. Many of the Mission's immigrant residents walked to jobs in those factories.

21 Twenty-Fourth Street Latino Shopping Strip

The commercial strip of Twenty-fourth Street from Mission east to about Bryant Street is the axis of Latino shopping and restaurants in San Francisco. Twenty-fourth Street's Nicaraguan, Salvadoran, Costa Rican, and other Latin-American restaurants and shops reflect one of the West's most complex Latino community. War and disruption in Central America have steadily fed migration to the Bay Area. Many exiles have opened small businesses and employ fellow Latinos. Here are old ladies with the immemorial faces of peasant Central America, an abundance of exotic tropical fruits and vegetables, and a full spectrum of Spanish-speaking businesses and services. It's a street where the restaurants have plastic tablecloths, artificial flowers, and mementos of home.

At the southeast corner of Twenty-fourth and South Van Ness is a fine mural entitled *Golden Dream of the New World,* showing Latin dancers with a background of cleverly painted Victorian houses. It was executed by Daniel Galvez in 1984.

㉒ *Balmy Street Murals*

Balmy Street, a service alley on the south side of Twenty-fourth, between Treat and Harrison, is lined with board fences, garage doors, and a few small tenements. Be cautious exploring this unfrequented alley. Hidden here is a series of murals begun in 1973 on the political agony of contemporary Central America. They are the work of *Placa*, Chicano slang for "graffiti," a group of some forty artists and community workers. The murals are quite varied and repay individual examination; some, unfortunately, have attracted spray-can graffiti, the Mission's 1990s environmental blight.

BART Station and Mural
Mission Street at Twenty-fourth Street

Galeria Museo
open Tuesday to Sunday, 10 A.M. to 5 P.M.

After seeing the murals return to Twenty-fourth Street. Three and a half blocks further east is the **Galería de la Raza**, a showcase for contemporary Latino artists. It can provide you with a pamphlet listing the Mission's many fine murals. Next door is **Studio 24** with Mexican and Central American folk art and Latin American literature, the best place for souvenirs of your day in the Mission.

㉓ **BART Station and Mural**, *1973, Hertz and Knowles. Mural: 1975, Michael Ríos, Tony Machado, and Ricardo Montez*

Both the Sixteenth and Twenty-fourth Street BART stations were designed by Hertzka and Knowles in 1973. Above ground they are equally unattractive: brick-paved holes in the ground. The aboveground mural at the Twenty-fourth Street station, now increasingly masked by trees, was painted in 1975 by Michael Ríos, Tony Machado, and Ricardo Montez. In a biting allusion to the .5 percent sales tax used to finance BART, a sleek silver BART train is shown resting on the backs of the people. BART, originally intended to "improve" the Mission by introducing the construction of highrises, instead galvanized the Mission to thwart the demolition and displacement of urban renewal. In 1968 the Mission Coalition Organization brought together some two hundred neighborhood groups and local interests to press for city policies that would preserve the small businesses and affordable housing characteristic of the district. With conservationist city building controls, BART now serves the Mission rather than the Mission serving BART. But the Mission needs more investment in its existing public facilities and private buildings in the 1990s. The overcrowding of the neighborhood is obvious in the poor condition of too many buildings.

㉔ **Mission Cultural Center/Teatro Mision**

Housed in a four-story converted furniture store is this vital community arts organization founded in 1977. The vibrant mural on the facade is by Carlos Loarca, Manuel Villamor, and Betsie Miller-Kusz and was painted in 1982. There is an art gallery here, the **Galeria Museo**, on the second floor with changing exhibits. The *Teatro Mision* performs here, as do many touring Latin American musical and dance groups. The center also hosts literary programs in both Spanish and English and provides a platform for both local and Latin American writers. The center is funded by government, corporations, foundations, and the income from classes and performances. It has an active arts program and a productive silk-screening studio. Here you can experience the multicultural ferment of the Mission today.

La Taqueria
2889 Mission Street;
open daily, 11 A.M. to
9 P.M., to 8 P.M. on
Sunday

2844 Mission Street

Homage to Siqueiros Mural
2701 Mission Street

La Taqueria is across the street. It is the best taco and burrito restaurant in the city (and has take-out).

(On the west side of Mission Street is an architectural curiosity, an old pioneer, two-story, gable-roofed house jacked up over a later shopfront at **2844 Mission Street**. It may date from the 1860s and the early Anglo settlement of Mission valley. It's an anomaly worth preserving. Mission Street is full of surprises for those who look carefully.)

㉕ Homage to Siqueiros Mural, *1974, Chuy Campesino, Luis Cortázar, Michael Ríos, and David Alfaro*
Inside a branch of the Bank of America at Mission and Twenty-third streets is a fine 1974 mural by Chuy Campesino, Luis Cortázar, Michael Ríos, and David Alfaro entitled **Homage to Siqueiros,** depicts the present-day Latino population of the Mission. In the tradition of Mexican muralists, it is a people-crowded didactic work: a swirling exhortation to work, struggle, and study.

Continuation: Downtown, or
Noe Valley and the Castro District

From the Bank of America either turn back to the Twenty-fourth Street BART station to get back downtown *(Tour 1)* quickly or take the 14 Mission trolley bus on Mission Street headed north. The 14 Mission is a study in the ethnic and social variety of working-class San Francisco. The 48 Quintara bus on the north side of Twenty-fourth Street heads west on Twenty-fourth to Noe Valley *(Tour 11)*. At Twenty-fourth and Castro, you can transfer to the 24 Divisadero bus to get to Castro and Market streets and Muni Metro.

TOUR ELEVEN
The Castro and Noe Valley

•

OLD BOTTLES, NEW WINES

A row of Queen Anne—style cottages,
designed by John Anderson and built in 1897 on the south side of
the 500 block of Liberty Street, between Castro and Noe streets.

What This Tour Covers
Preliminaries
Introduction: Old Bottles, New Wines

Continuation
Pacific Heights, or the Mission District

TOUR 11:
THE CASTRO
AND
NOE VALLEY

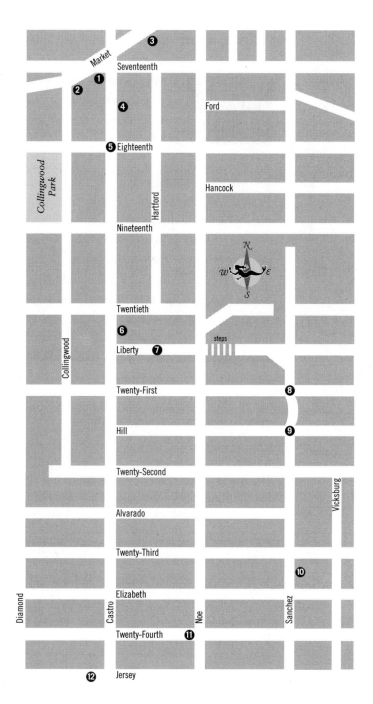

The Castro and Noe Valley

Preliminaries

**The Metropolitan
Community Church**
*150 Eureka Street, near
Nineteenth; Protestant
services Sunday at 9 A.M.
(High Church), 11 A.M.,
and 7 P.M. (Baptist-
Pentecostal); 863-4434*

**Most Holy Redeemer
Roman Catholic Church**
*100 Diamond, near
Eighteenth; Mass
Saturday at 5 P.M.,
Sunday at 7:30 A.M. and
10 A.M.; 863-6259*

Dignity, *Celebrates mass
at Seventh Avenue
Presbyterian Church,
1329 Seventh Avenue
(between Irving and
Judah), Sunday
at 5:30 P.M.; 681-2491*

Sha'ar Zahav,
*220 Danvers Street,
near Nineteenth Street;
Friday Shabbat services
at 8:15 P.M. the second
Saturday of each month
at 10:30 A.M.; 861-6932*

Castro Street Fair
*Phone for information
467-3354*

**BEST TIMES
TO DO THIS TOUR**

Daytime Saturdays and Sundays from about 11 A.M. to 3 P.M. are when people are out—and this should be a tour of people as much as buildings.

Churches and Synagogues

To see the serious—and joyous—side of gay San Francisco, attend one of the several active gay congregations' services here, especially if you are nongay or nonreligious. This is where the spirit listeth now. **The Metropolitan Community Church** conducts Protestant services on Eureka Street, near Nineteenth. **Most Holy Redeemer** Roman Catholic Church on Diamond, near Eighteenth, has many gay parishioners who seem to be infusing Roman Catholicism with love. **Dignity**, a gay Catholic organization, celebrates mass at Seventh Avenue Presbyterian Church, on Seventh Avenue between Irving and Judah. **Sha'ar Zahav**, which means "Golden Gate," has its Reform synagogue on Danvers Street, near Nineteenth Street. All these congregations welcome visitors.

Special Events

The **Gay and Lesbian Freedom Day parade** takes place on the last Sunday in June. It has become the biggest event in San Francisco's annual calendar of celebrations. (But then every day is gay and lesbian freedom day in San Francisco.) **The Folsom Street Fair**, South of Market, is on the last Sunday in September. It has become ever more popular in the last few years. The **Castro Street Fair** is on the first Sunday in October. Every November 27 there is a candlelight march from the Castro down Market Street to City Hall to honor the memory of assassinated Mayor George Moscone and Supervisor Harvey Milk.

Parking

There are city-owned, metered, mini parking lots near the Castro Theater on Castro between Seventeenth and Eighteenth and, around the corner, on Eighteenth between Castro and Collingwood. Parking is tight here; it's best to take the Muni or a taxi.

Transportation

During the summer season and into the fall, **historic trolleys** run up Market Street terminating at Castro and Market (*see Tour 1*). At other times take the **Muni Metro L, M, or K** subway under Market Street to Castro Station; this is how the locals get to work downtown. The more scenic aboveground **8 Market trolley bus** also runs Market to Castro Street. In 1995, the new **F streetcar** line opened linking the Transbay Terminal with Market and Castro. Eventually that line will be extended to the Ferry Building, and then Fisherman's Wharf. Taxis are often available at Castro Street just below Market, near the Castro Theater.

Village Deli Cafe
495 Castro, near Eighteenth Street;
626-2027

Thailand Restaurant
438 A Castro Street, upstairs, between Market and Eighteenth;
863-6868

Pasqua Coffee Bar
4094 Eighteenth Street, just off Castro; 626-6263

Elephant Walk
500 Castro, at Eighteenth

Harvest Ranch Market
2285 Market Street, at Noe; 626-0805

Cafe Flore
2298 Market Street, at Noe; 621-8579

Detour
2348 Market, east of Castro; 861-6053

RESTAURANTS, CAFÉS, AND BARS

The Castro has many inexpensive cafés and restaurants, several with window tables so you can watch the passing scene. The **Village Deli Cafe** has simple food and good window seats. **Thailand Restaurant** has tasty Thai cuisine, including a fine salmon dish; a few tables look out over the active block below. A new and pleasant spot is the **Pasqua Coffee Bar**; it has an outside bench facing the sidewalk. **Elephant Walk** is an attractive, airy cocktail lounge that serves lunch and brunch; it has a piano player, a relaxed, mixed clientele, and window seats. A great salad bar popular with buffed locals, superb breads, and gourmet foods are available at **Harvest Ranch Market**. **Cafe Flore** has been described as "a glass terrarium of Queers with attitude." The coffee and pastries are only average, but not the pierced patrons; serves brunch. The gay bar of the moment is **Detour**; painted black, smoky, bisected by a chain link fence, and with *very loud* cutting-edge rock, techno, and hip-hop music. The *Severe Queer Review* described it as looking like a high school set for *West Side Story*. But high school wasn't at all like this.

Barney's Gourmet Hamburgers, *4138 Twenty-fourth Street, between Castro and Diamond;* 282-7770

Panos', *4000 Twenty-fourth Street at Noe;* 824-8000

Meat Market Coffeehouse *4123 Twenty-fourth Street;* 285-5598

Rat and Raven Bar *Twenty-fourth Street*

Ixia Flowers, *2331 Market, at Noe;* 431-3134

Worn Out West, *582 Castro;* 431-6020

Soho Gallery *548 Castro;* 252-0294

Kozo Paper, *531 Castro, near Eighteenth;* 621-0869

A Different Light Bookstore *489 Castro Street;* 431-0891

Out of Hand, *1303 Castro near, Twenty-fourth;* 826-3885

Star Magic, *4026A Twenty-fourth Street;* 641-8626

Xela, *3925 Twenty-fourth Street;* 695-1323

Streetlight Records *3979 Twenty-fourth Street;* 282-3550

Little Bean Sprouts *3961A Twenty-fourth Street;* 550-1668

Small Frys *4066 Twenty-fourth Street;* 648-3954

In Noe Valley try **Barney's Gourmet Hamburgers.** It serves more than hamburgers and has a pleasant outdoor patio. A bit fancier is **Panos',** serving lunch, brunch, and dinner. The **Meat Market Coffeehouse** is a favorite hangout for newspaper-reading Noe Valley locals. The **Rat and Raven Bar** attracts a college crowd.

SHOPPING

Both the Castro and Noe Valley have interesting shops. Some of the best shops are on the **2300 block of Market,** south side, between Sixteenth and Seventeenth streets. The very latest in clothing, accessories, furniture, and flowers cluster here. **Ixia Flowers** is probably the most creative flower shop in the city; amazing window displays. Castro and Eighteenth streets have a half-dozen modern men's clothing shops with clunky black shoes (*so* correct), radical hip-hop fashion, and outspoken T-shirts. (For example, muscle shirts with small printing over the left nipple that reads: "It's MISTER Faggot to you.") **Worn Out West** has new and used masculine clothing; leather upstairs; a butch museum. **Soho Gallery** has a good selection of cards. **Kozo** has beautiful handmade Japanese papers and also boxes, notebooks, and other items wrapped with them. Gay and lesbian visitors especially should not fail to browse in **A Different Light Bookstore,** one of the very best specialized bookstores in this literate city. The local free gay newspapers, many fliers and handbills, and posters here are the best window into what's happening *now*.

Twenty-fourth Street in Noe Valley also has good browsing. The shops are inclined toward environmental and third-world consciousness. **Out of Hand** is probably the best shop for contemporary crafts in the city. **Star Magic** sells astral accouterments and "celestial music." **Xela** ("Shayla") has beads and many different earrings. **Streetlight Records** has new and used recorded music and specializes in out-of-print records. **Little Bean Sprouts** and **Small Frys** have artfully designed children's clothes.

ARTS AND ENTERTAINMENT

The sidewalk scene is the best entertainment here no matter what your gender preference. As the French say: "The crowd on the boulevard never grows old." The new Queer movement and the increased presence of lesbians have added new spice to the gay Castro. By far the most popular entertainments here are the imaginative screenings at the **Castro Theater**. If audience participation bothers you, the Castro's not for you. The best club is **Josie's Cabaret and Juice Joint**. Josie's is a vegetarian restaurant/juice bar cabaret that presents theater and music Tuesday to Friday, and queer comedy Saturday and Monday nights. Acts like the Pomo Afro Homos appear here. The **Cafe du Nord** is located in the basement of the Swedish Society Hall built in 1907. Jazz, salsa, mambo, and many other musics cook here; dinner, entertainment, and dancing. Gay and lesbian art is varied and vibrant in San Francisco. **Theater Rhinoceros**, in the Mission District, is one important venue. Look in the free newspapers available at **A Different Light Bookstore** for new theater, dance, music, and performance art.

The catastrophe of AIDS has spurred much new art and expression (and a vast array of social services) in San Francisco. The Names Project's AIDS **Memorial Quilt** has its Visitor's Center and Panel Workshop on Market Street, not far from Castro. Here new panels are created and old ones conserved. Visits and donations are welcome. It has become the Castro's, and the nation's, most moving communal art work.

The **Harvey Milk–Eureka Valley branch of the San Francisco Public Library** has an extensive gay and lesbian section including complete runs of the local gay newspapers. The new Main Library in the Civic Center is the home of an important **Gay and Lesbian Center**. San Franciscan Jim Hormel's generosity has kicked off the $1.6 million fund-raising campaign, and Barbara Grier and Donna McBride have donated their extensive collection of gay and lesbian literature.

Castro Theater
429 Castro, between Market and Eighteenth Streets; 621-6120

Josie's Cabaret and Juice Joint
3583 Sixteenth Street, at Market; 861-7933

Cafe du Nord
2170 Market Street, at Sanchez; 861-5016

Theater Rhinoceros
2926 Sixteenth Street, near South Van Ness Avenue in the Mission District; 861-5079

A Different Light Bookstore
489 Castro Street; 431-0891

Memorial Quilt Visitor's Center and Panel Workshop
2362 Market Street, not far from Castro 863-1966

Harvey Milk–Eureka Valley branch of the San Francisco Public Library
3555 Sixteenth Street, near Noe and Market; 554-9445

Gay and Lesbian Center
Opening in Spring 1996 Main Library in the Civic Center; 557-4566

Introduction: Old Bottles, New Wines

Find out who you are, and then become it.

Quentin Crisp

Change is the only constant in life and few parts of San Francisco have seen as great a change as Eureka and Noe valleys. Here fine old buildings have been lovingly restored and given new life. Along with Twin Peaks, these valleys were originally part of the four-thousand acre Rancho San Miguel granted to Mexican San Francisco's last *alcalde*, or mayor, **José de Jesús Noe**, in 1845. With the arrival of the Yankees came a wave of land speculation. In 1854 John M. Horner bought most of the virtually undeveloped ranch for ninety thousand dollars and platted out Horner's Addition, a grid of blocks from Castro to Valencia and from about Eighteenth to Thirteenth streets. The rest of the San Miguel Ranch became the property of two French speculators, Pioche and Bazerque, and their American partner, Parsons. Twin Peaks was absorbed into the vast real estate empire of Adolph Sutro by 1880.

The main north-south streets in Horner's Addition were named after early Mexican ranchers: **Castro, Noe, Sanchez, Guerrero**, and **Valencia**. This subdivision was slow to develop since it was far from the downtown and hard of access, while there were still many empty lots much closer to downtown. Small dairy ranches, truck gardens, and a few brickyards and sanitariums were built here. In 1864 the Eureka Homestead Association incorporated. These cooperative associations bought blocks of property, which they then subdivided into house lots and sold to members or to contractor-builders who erected wooden Victorian houses. Comfortable Victorian houses began to appear, first in the valleys, then on the slopes. In 1868 the *Real Estate Circular* reported

> An active demand has been noticeable for lots lying within the bounds of Eighteenth, Twenty-Sixth, Valencia and Castro streets. This locality is occupied with rolling hills and tableland, and heretofore has not been in favor with purchasers .... But the perfect nature of its title, the fine view which is obtained from most of the land, and the good drainage which it will have, have lately operated favorably in elevating its prices.

The real boom in house building followed the opening of the Castro Street segment of the Market Street Cable Railway in 1887. This line linked the Ferry Building at the foot of Market with Twenty-sixth Street in Noe Valley. The Castro Street line had some of the steepest grades of any cable line with an 18.4 percent grade between Twenty-second and Twenty-third streets.

With a transit system in place, lower-middle-class families flocked to these sunny valleys. The relatively high rates of San Francisco workers' pay were reflected in these comfortable dwellings. German, Scandinavian, and later more and more Irish American families clustered here. Many were Roman Catholic and the local churches became important neighborhood institutions, as were the many corner groceries and saloons.

The area has never suffered real neglect, and with every year the gardens behind the houses and the pruned trees along the sidewalks soften more of these precipitous streets. Because San Francisco's marine views are justifiably famous, the "inland" cityscapes are frequently overlooked. In these valleys, where Victorian houses lie draped over the furrowed slopes of Twin Peaks, remarkable views of nothing but nineteenth-century houses with twentieth-century gardens are memorable to all who look for them.

After the boom of the 1920s, during which new banks and a fancy movie theater were built on Castro Street, the neighborhood saw little improvement. Like all American inner-city neighborhoods, Eureka and Noe valleys went into a relative decline after World War II. FHA-backed mortgages and the spread of the automobile drew many of the children raised in cities to the expanding suburbs. Irish Americans continued their historic southwestward drift across the city and out to Daly City and Pacifica. Eureka and Noe valleys began to fade.

All this changed in the early 1970s as downtown San Francisco's highrise boom took off. From a commercial and industrial city with many ethnic blue-collar workers, San Francisco began a rapid transformation into a postindustrial city marked by a shift from manufacturing and an explosion in white-collar office work and service industries. The factories left for technological and cost reasons: new one-story plants were practical to build only on cheap land beyond the suburbs. But as industry and jobs left, skyscrapers and office work increased.

These economic and employment shifts were accompanied by dramatic social and cultural changes. The spread of college education, in particular, uprooted young people from their birthplaces and took them to schools often quite far from home. Upon graduation few returned home; most looked for skilled jobs in the cities. The migration of suburban-bred singles back into the heart of the old, culturally attractive cities accelerated. Because of its small size, this migration has been most noticeable in San Francisco. As the total population of the city drifted downward by 5 percent between 1970 and 1980, the number of people between twenty-five and thirty-four exploded by more than 25 percent. Many were highly educated, energetic, and ambitious, and they revitalized San Francisco with the most important of all forms of capital: human capital.

This new migration had a curious quality; while relentlessly modern, it had a real appreciation of old architecture, especially Victorian houses. In fact, the new migrants loved these buildings more than many natives, who saw them as obsolete. In the 1950s and 1960s an almost invisible movement of middle-class gay men began buying faded Victorians in Pacific Heights. Then "Lower Pacific Heights" (the blocks south of California Street) drew buyers, then Dolores Heights, then Noe Valley, then the Castro. In the 1970s a sudden wave of restoration swept San Francisco. New migrants refurbished old houses and made them resplendent. Many young gay men and gay couples made their living by buying, restoring, and then selling Victorian houses, only to buy more faded real estate to propel the process further. Between 1973 and 1976, vintage houses in San Francisco quintupled in value.

There was more to it than real estate, important as that religion remains. Gays in particular, feeling the social liberation of the 1970s—in 1973, the American Psychiatric Association dropped homosexuality from its lists of mental disorders, and in 1975 California decriminalized adult consensual sexual relations—registered to vote and formed active political clubs. This changed the face of politics in what had been an old-fashioned, ethnic-based political system. In 1972 San Francisco was the first American city to pass an ordinance forbidding discrimination in employment and housing on the basis of sexual orientation. **Harvey Milk**, a New York–born camera-store owner from the Castro, became the first openly gay man elected to public office in 1977. The soundest estimate of the gay and lesbian population today is that it comprises 17 percent of the total population, or between 110,000 and 120,000 persons. Two-thirds are gay men and one-third lesbians. Educated and committed, gays and lesbians are thought to make up from 20 to 25 percent of the city's voters.

History, however, is the unexpected, quite often the brutally unexpected. With the eruption of acquired-immune-deficiency syndrome (AIDS) in 1981, a deep sea change began in the Castro and in San Francisco generally. The party-hardy seventies were succeeded by the sober eighties and now the coping-with-it nineties. Gay culture has evolved. A remarkable proliferation of social service agencies has emerged, many in the Castro, but in other parts of San Francisco as well. Hospices for the dying, home care for the ill, public education on hygiene for the living, and counseling for the anxious have sprung up to face the crisis. In the Names Project memorial quilt, where survivors create individual panels to celebrate those they have loved, a unique kind of communal art has been created. While one must always mistrust tricks with language—without clear language, there can be no clear thinking—the Castro can be said not to be dying from AIDS, but living compassionately with it. In the face of unspeakable loss a remarkable compassion has emerged.

Best of all, in the 1990s a new generation has migrated to San Francisco and it is changing the faces on the streets and the art that is being created here. Aggressively calling themselves "Queers," this feisty generation's members have been shaped by AIDS ACT-UP activism, postmodern culture generally, and the harder economic times of the present. (Virtually no young person can afford to buy a run-down Victorian house today.) Lesbians have also become much more visible and effective in contemporary San Francisco. The 1990s are a new world and San Francisco continues to be the epicenter of social change. The most radical change of all might be the casual integration of Queer culture with postpunk straight youth. The hottest dance clubs today are much less gender-segregated than they were in the 1970s. Boys and boys, girls and girls—even, are we ready?—boys and girls dance together in today's underground clubs. The races are less segregated in these venues as well. There is an emerging gay Asian American presence making itself felt, especially in the art world. San Francisco continues to be ahead of the curve culturally.

The social changes in Noe Valley, over the Castro Street hill, have been less attention-getting but just as profound as those in the Castro. New vigor has come to this old part of town. Babies are back in vogue, and many professional families with young children live here. This is a discernibly committed-to-the-city population, including many artists and writers. They contribute to one of the most agreeable neighborhoods in San Francisco. By 1987 writers Cyra McFadden, Warren Hinckle, and Armistead Maupin had settled in Noe Valley. As McFadden notes, "Busy little fingers are typing all over the place." Fortunately the noise is not too loud and the side streets on the southern slope of the hill remain quiet, serene, and well worth random exploration.

Ferry Building

Sutro Television Tower

Muni Metro Station
Castro and Upper Market Streets

 1 *Market and Castro Streets*

Castro Common Condominiums
2425 Market Street

At Castro Street, Market Street is deflected from its course by the base of the Twin Peaks hills that rise at the center of the San Francisco peninsula. The Castro Street cable car turntable once stood near here. Beautiful Canary Island palm trees have recently appeared full grown here at the head of Market Street as part of the construction of the F streetcar line. The foot of Market, at the eastern end, is marked by the tower of the 1896 **Ferry Building**. At the western end is the **Sutro Television Tower** built in 1973, a handsome (if controversial) piece of utilitarian design.

• **Muni Metro Station**, *1974, Reid and Tarics*
Under this busy intersection is the **MUNI Metro station** designed by Reid and Tarics in 1974, the cheeriest underground transit station in San Francisco, far lighter in feeling than the ponderous BART stations built about the same time. It is, however, as devoid of life as any American transit station. The orange brick and inventive graphics look better than they sound. The landscaped stairway-entrance to the station is known as **Harvey Milk Plaza** and is marked by an unattractive bronze plaque in honor of the assassinated city supervisor. Stairs lead to the busy intersection of Market and Castro. When the Castro community is angry, or joyous, it has become traditional to spontaneously block traffic at this major intersection. San Francisco drivers have learned that it is not the end of the world; out-of-town motorists can't get over it.

2 **Castro Common Condominiums**, *1982, Daniel Solomon and Associates*
Immediately west of the Metro entrance, down a brick-paved pedestrian bridge, is the transparent white and gray grid fence of **Castro Common**, condominiums designed by Daniel Solomon and Associates in 1982. Solomon, a professor of architecture at the University of California at Berkeley, is one of the best of the new designers active today. When this roughly T-shaped parcel was developed, the mature symmetrical Norfolk pine was preserved, adding much to the appeal of the project. The grid fence continues the street wall and makes a counterpoint to the square grids employed in the building itself. The building is broken up into three separate sections linked by a courtyard and set over a parking garage.

Castro Common is the best architectural play on the curious fascination with square grids that overtook graphic design in the early 1980s. Built of common materials, this building is a model of how architecture can be wholly new yet mesh smoothly with San Francisco's established character. It is instructive to compare this piece of high art with the vernacular building backs and sides visible next door.

400 Castro Street

Twin Peaks Bar

California Federal Bank
444 Castro Street

The Castro Theater
429 Castro Street;
621-6120

❸ 2300 Block of Market Street Shops

The south side of Market Street, between Sixteenth and Seventeenth, houses the most interesting of the Castro shops. Costly and ferociously up-to-the-nanosecond, they display both men's and women's clothing, furnishings, electronic goods, and flowers-become-art. Here the latest trends are showcased in old shopfronts (a few with "design statement" interiors), making this one of the most interesting window shopping strips in Northern California. (The north side of Market is much less interesting.)

❹ 400 Block of Castro Street

At the southwest corner of Castro and Market streets, at **400 Castro Street**, is a rounded corner building designed by Edward T. Foulkes in 1921 and long occupied by the Bank of America. Originally this was a more ornate building with elaborate terra-cotta ornament. It was stripped at some point to make the building look more modern. Today it houses a take-out food place and has meeting spaces for gay organizations.

On the opposite, southeast, corner stands the **Twin Peaks Bar** with its projecting sheet-metal sign showing the profile of the hills. While not an architectural monument, it is a sociological one. It was the first openly gay bar with floor-to-ceiling plate glass windows looking out on the world.

Halfway down the block is the **California Federal Bank** designed in 1985 by Neeley Lofrano. This was built for Atlas Savings, the first, and short-lived, gay-founded bank. The building is a parody of a typical bay-windowed Edwardian and has a white-painted steel open-work front standing before a glass and mirror façade. It has two second-story "bay windows" and an open-work pedimented gable with a mirrored gable behind. Trick façades with mirrors seem particularly inappropriate for financial institutions, though in this case it turned out to be ominously prescient.

Next door to the transparent bank is a standard bay-windowed Edwardian that was stripped of this classicizing ornament and covered with stucco in a Moderne mode. It is a not unpleasing face-lift. You will probably see many rainbow flags here and elsewhere in the Castro. Designed in San Francisco by Gilbert Baker in 1978, the colorfully affirmative rainbow flag has become a territorial marker in gay neighborhoods across the country and around the world.

• **The Castro Theater**, *1922, Timothy Pfleuger; 1937, marquee modernized and vertical neon sign added*
Fantasy *is* appropriate for movie palaces, and Timothy Pfleuger's Castro Theater is one of the best such efforts in the Bay Area. Built as a flagship theater of the pioneer movie-exhibitor Nasser family, this Spanish Renaissance extravaganza is marked by a giant blind window flanked by elaborate ornament and surmounted by an empty niche. Its splendid neon-trimmed marquee and giant vertical sign added in 1937 have become an icon for the reborn neighborhood. One newcomer to the neighborhood described

seeing the sign like being an immigrant seeing the Statue of Liberty for the first time. The Castro has an elaborate, intact interior; the plaster ceiling has been made to look like the inside of a tent with swags, ropes, and tassels. The theater hosts imaginative screenings and is one of the venues of the San Francisco Film Festival.

Bank of America
501 Castro Street

527–33 Castro Street

Architecture, however, is not likely to be what attracts most of the attention here. It's the street life that makes the Castro special, a lively street scene of mostly gay young men shopping, doing errands, chatting, bar-hopping, milling about. There is a palpable energy to the street that everyone notices. More gay women are visible on Castro Street in the 1990s, though the population here is still mostly male and mostly young. Styles are often radical. The Queer look has displaced the now-historic clone style.

❺ *Castro and Eighteenth Streets: Castro Village*

The Castro is sometimes referred to as Castro Village, no doubt after Greenwich Village in New York City. The intersection of Castro and Eighteenth is its heart. In its urban form, if not in population, Eureka Valley is a microcosm of the typical nineteenth-century California town, consisting of a grid of residential streets, with one, Castro Street, as a transit and commercial strip. One block behind this commercial strip is the local church and grammar school with its park and ballfield. All else is housing. The Castro hill is crowned with charming peak-roofed cottages built in rows in the 1890s. The hill's silhouette looks as if it was cut with pinking shears. Now painted a variety of colors, this is one of the most distinctive views in San Francisco.

On the southeast corner of Castro and Eighteenth streets (with the **Elephant Walk** bar in the corner space) is a commercial-residential building designed by John Davis Hatch in 1912. It is mildly Secessionist in its upstairs architectural treatment. Facing it across the street is a **Bank of America** branch that was formerly a Hibernia Bank branch, a reminder of the originally dominant population in the neighborhood. It has a neoclassical corner building built in 1929 and a modern glass addition designed in 1979 by Robert Sarnoff. The new wing is cut back at a forty-five degree angle, the design signature of the late 1970s. In this space the Castro erects its neighborhood Christmas tree—the Christmas lights along Castro Street are some of the best in the city. This corner is often the site of ironing-board-equipped petitioners circulating the latest political broadsides in this politically energized neighborhood. The bench at the bus shelter here is a convenient place to sit and watch the passing parade.

The flanking blocks of Eighteenth Street have many small shops and inexpensive eating places. In 1993, the Castro had thirteen bars within a short walk of this intersection.

At **527–33 Castro Street**, beyond the bank, are the semicircular bay windows of the three-story Komsthoeft Building built early in this century. It was originally a bakery and the old brick ovens remain in the back; since then the ground floor has been converted into a minimall of boutiques, and a restaurant has been inserted at the rear. **Kozo Paper** here carries fine handmade Japanese papers.

580–84 Castro

Isak Lindenauer Antiques
4143 Nineteenth Street,
near Collingwood;
552-6436

701 Castro Street

711–33 Castro Street

563–79 Liberty Street

571–73 Liberty Street

533–59 Liberty Street

513–29 Liberty

At **580–84 Castro**, on the northwest corner of Nineteenth Street, is a Stick-style commercial and residential building designed by the prolific Fernando Nelson in 1887. More of his houses are up the hill. Up the block to the west, tucked in an old storefront is **Isak Lindenauer Antiques**, a veritable museum of pricy Craftsman and Arts and Crafts oak furniture (known in California as Mission style), art pottery, and hammered-copper artifacts.

 **6** *700 Block of Castro Street Victorians*

If you don't wish to climb steep hills, catch the 24 Divisadero bus going uphill and alight at Twentieth Street. Between Twentieth and Liberty, on the east side of Castro, is a group of Victorian houses designed by Fernando Nelson. Born in New York in 1860, Nelson built some four thousand Victorian houses in the city. He reduced house-building to a formula, going so far as to call his two house types "A" and "B." On the southeast corner of Castro and Twentieth is **701 Castro Street**, a whimsical one-story Queen Anne cottage with a round corner tower built by Nelson for himself in 1897. It was originally in the back of the lot and had a stable underneath it for Nelson's work horse. A later owner moved the house to the corner and built brick garages underneath.

Immediately up the hill at **711–33 Castro Street** is an outstanding row of five flats and houses, one a Queen Anne and the others Stick style, all built by Nelson in 1897. Some boast Nelson's "deluxe $5 front door." The curiously shaped donut capitals of the porch columns were Nelson's signature. These houses all sport modern color schemes that pick out their gingerbread. Their dramatic false gables with sunburst ornaments emphasize verticality and create an animated profile. There is a great view here, and more gardens as you climb the hill.

 7 *500 Block of Liberty Street/Liberty Street Steps*

Unlike the twentieth century, when quiet side streets are preferred to busy through streets for houses, in the Victorian era cable-car-served streets were preferred to lateral pedestrian streets. Liberty Street harbors the peak-roofed cottages seen from Castro and Eighteenth streets. A decade after the main streets were built up with multistory houses, less costly one-story cottages filled the side streets. These cottages were built by developers for speculative sale to prosperous "mechanics." John Anderson built the peak-roofed Queen Anne cottages at **563–79 Liberty Street** in 1897. Number **571–73** was later made a two-flat building with the addition of a second story. Another row of eight cottages at **533–59 Liberty Street** was built by Carlson and Anderson in the same year. The five larger cottages uphill with the gingerbread drips and donut capitals at **513–29 Liberty** were built by the prolific Fernando Nelson in 1897.

At Liberty and Noe streets is a good view of a white Moderne flats complex at **741–51 Noe/482–95 Liberty Street**, built about 1940. The simple white stucco boxes step up the hillside quite agreeably. It is one of the most ambitious Moderne developments in any San Francisco neighborhood. Climb the landscaped steps and look back. Spread out before you is a panorama few spectators get to appreciate: San Francisco's overlooked "inland" cityscape. Pale houses and dark green trees cover the steep amphitheater of hills. The grassy slopes of Twin Peaks are due west. Sutro television tower rises in the distance. The afternoon fog often stops at Twin Peaks, leaving this slope in the sunshine. Houses of every period, style, color, and shape merge; at night the lights in the houses make these hills look like heaps of diamonds. From the top of the Liberty steps, Potrero Hill, San Francisco Bay, and the Contra Costa hills appear to the east.

**741–51 Noe/
482–95 Liberty Street**

Casa Ciele
3690 Twenty-first Street

Also at the top of the steps is **Rayburn Street**, lined with garages and very simple houses. Follow it to Twenty-first Street and walk up the slight incline to Sanchez Street. Simple houses with elaborate gardens line the block.

⑧ *Downtown Panorama*

At the northwest corner of Twenty-first and Sanchez there is a startling view of the new downtown highrises. The dark Bank of America and the white Transamerica Pyramid make a perfect contrasting pair from this high vantage point. The white peaked-hat structure is St. Mary's Cathedral. A red- tile-roofed church with a dome and twin towers of different heights rises in the valley below next to a long, low, rectangular structure with a tile roof; this is Mission Dolores (*see Tour 10*). The great green dome in the middle distance caps Bakewell & Brown's City Hall of 1915 in the Beaux Arts Civic Center. To the far left are the residential highrises of Pacific Heights with always-changing San Francisco Bay beyond.

On the northeast corner of Sanchez and Twenty-first is the **Casa Ciele**, a Tudor cottage nestled under old pine trees. It was built in 1929 by Mayor "Sunny Jim" Rolph, who served as mayor from 1911 to 1930, and then as Republican governor of California until his death in 1934. The "cottage" is said to have been Rolph's love nest in which he ensconced his mistress. Rolph built the splendid City Hall below and many of San Francisco's finest public buildings and schools during his long reign. Rolph sold the house in 1932 for about $38,000. In 1994 the asking price for the property was an astronomical $1.75 million. The fountain of Leda and the Swan was installed by a later owner.

From the red fire-alarm box on the southeast corner of the intersection is a fine view of historic Mission Valley below, Potrero Hill with its peak-roofed cottages, the calm Bay, Oakland, the Contra Costa ridge, and Mt. Diablo, the highest peak in the region.

849 Sanchez Street

Noe Valley Ministry
1021 Sanchez Street,
between Elizabeth and
Twenty-third streets;
Sunday worship at
10 A.M.; 282-2317

⑨ *Panorama of Victorian Neighborhoods*

A century ago this rocky hill was used for grazing sheep and goats. It has had more than its share of names: Dolores Heights, Sanchez Street Hill, Noe Hill, Liberty Hill, Mineral Springs Hill, and Nanny Goat Hill. At **849 Sanchez Street**, on the northeast corner of appropriately named Hill Street, is a simple, two-story streamlined Moderne stucco house with porthole windows built in 1938. It has been enlivened with modern abstract stained-glass windows.

Catercorner from this house is a fine panorama to the south of densely built Noe Valley. The tall needlelike steeples rise from St. Paul's Roman Catholic Church at Twenty-ninth and Church streets, built in 1890. Its bells can be heard pealing out over the quiet valley. The wind, and an occasional distant truck or bus shifting gears, are the only other sounds heard atop this "peak in the wind" set in the center of the busy city. Hilltop parks, some forested, some on open hills, frame the horizon. This is what is so beautiful about San Francisco.

⑩ Noe Valley Ministry, *1888, Charles Geddes*
Three blocks down the hill is the steeple of the **Noe Valley Ministry**, a Stick style church with a Gothic-style porch designed by Charles Geddes and dedicated in 1889. It cost $3,880 to build. The congregation was first known as the Noe Valley Presbyterian Church but changed its name to the Lebanon Presbyterian Church shortly thereafter. Geddes was born in Halifax, Nova Scotia and came to California in the 1850s. He evolved from a carpenter to a builder to an architect. Though its woodwork may seem rich to us, this is a plain building for its period. The church's gable has three different shingle patterns. After 1906 the church was jacked up, enlarged, and a ground floor with meeting rooms added. The church was restored in the late 1970s and painted a pleasing pearl gray and white. Today the revitalized church serves as Noe Valley's informal community center and is used for worship, concerts, lectures, a co-op nursery school, senior programs, dance and exercise classes, and local merchants' meetings, and it is the home of the neighborhood newspaper, *The Noe Valley Voice*.

The wide, quiet streets and sidewalks lined with small, light-colored houses have a pleasing serenity that is the quintessential "feel" of so many of San Francisco's clean, tucked-away neighborhoods. Behind these vintage houses are carefully tended gardens even more peaceful and remote. Hummingbirds and typewriters are the loudest sounds.

⑪ *Twenty-Fourth Street Commercial Strip and "The Emerald Enclave"*

José de Jesús Noe built his adobe ranchhouse in the mid-1840s near the intersection of Twenty-fourth and Noe streets. With the coming of the Castro Street cable car in 1887, Twenty-fourth Street became the shopping strip for the valley. Today Noe Valley is a post-hippie, post-Vietnam, post-sexual-revolution, post-mellow zone with organic food, spiritual books, charts of the heavens, and imported gourmet foods. Young families and strollers enliven the street. The shopping strip includes a small supermarket, shops, local services, bookstores, restaurants, and cafés. See the beginning of the tour for some suggestions. **Out of Hand** contemporary crafts is special.

Dubliner
3838 Twenty-fourth Street

Noe Valley Branch Public Library
451 Jersey Street; 695-5095

The pressures on a street like Twenty-fourth are more intense than casual visitors imagine. A great concern in San Francisco is the preservation of moderate-rent housing such as the apartments on the upper floors of mixed commercial-residential buildings. The City Planning Commission does not permit the conversion of upstairs residential units to higher-income retail or office use. There are also limits on new bars and restaurants lest those more profitable uses drive out all the other community-serving businesses. Both the local merchants and the surrounding residents have active organizations that zealously monitor changes on the fragile street. What looks so "natural" to the visitor is not that way at all; "success" can spoil a street as fast as poverty. San Francisco's neighborhood commercial strips are a continual balancing act between change and continuity.

The blocks from **Twenty-first** to **Twenty-fourth**, and from **Castro** west to **Grandview**, are San Francisco's "emerald enclave." Nearly one in four of the residents of the eastern slope of the hill claims an Irish heritage on at least one side of the family. (City-wide, about 10 percent of San Franciscans were of Irish lineage in 1990; in the 1880s, fully one-third of the city was Irish American.) **St. Philip's Roman Catholic Church** on Diamond Street is the spiritual center of this world. Several Irish American bars along Twenty-fourth Street, including the **Dubliner**, make convivial gathering places for the locals. While young urban professionals seem to dominate the newer shops and restaurants, the local bars retain a working-class feel. Less visible are the many lesbian couples who also favor Noe Valley.

12 Noe Valley Branch Public Library, *1916, John Reid, Jr.*
One block south of Twenty-fourth and Castro is the **Noe Valley Branch Library**, dedicated in 1916. It is a little gem, a model of the appropriate scale for neighborhood facilities. The building is the result of steel magnate **Andrew Carnegie**'s farseeing philanthropy. Carnegie was the one robber baron who was a secularist at heart; rather than endow churches, he decided to elevate the intellectual level of his adopted country. He launched a program that spread free public libraries, both great and small, across the United States and in his native Scotland as well. He paid for elegant buildings if communities would agree to fill them with books and keep them open. In this way he enticed local involvement and created what is very often still the finest architectural work in many small American towns.

The Noe Valley Branch Library is slightly set back from this quiet street with small trees in front of it. It is faced in light yellow brick and is handsomely ornamented terra-cotta. It has four engaged columns across its facade framing large windows. Swags and garlands with open books between them enrich the façade. It is an intimate temple to knowledge and an ideal neighborhood oasis of culture. Inside, along with the usual departments, is a special women's collection, imprints from

Bay Area small presses, and the Noe Valley Community Archives. The work of some of Noe Valley's many artists is sometimes displayed here. Evening lectures make it "the people's university." Over the entrance to the library is an open book and the San Francisco Public Library's motto: "Life without literature is death."

Continuation: Pacific Heights, or the Mission District

From Twenty-fourth Street you can return via the 24 Divisadero bus to Market and Castro and continue to Pacific Heights (*Tour 8*). Or you can board the 48 Quintara bus heading east on Twenty-fourth Street to the Twenty-fourth Street BART station and the Mission District (*Tour 10*).

TOUR TWELVE
The Haight-Ashbury
•
ANTHROPOLOGICAL WILDLIFE REFUGE

Mixed shops, hotels, and apartments
were built along the streetcar lines in the nineteenth century;
at the southeast corner of Haight and Masonic stands 1200 Masonic Avenue,
designed in 1896 by W. H. Lillie. In 1895–96, Cranston and Keenan designed
the row of Queen Anne houses that marches south up Masonic Avenue.

What This Tour Covers
Preliminaries
Introduction: Anthropological Wildlife Refuge

TOUR 12:
THE
HAIGHT-ASHBURY

1. Spencer House Bed and Breakfast Inn
2. 1100 Block of Haight Street
3. Buena Vista Park
4. Buena Vista Avenue West
5. Java Street, Masonic Avenue, and Waller Street/ Victorian Rows
6. Haight Street Commercial Strip
7. Haight and Ashbury Streets
8. Golden Gate Park Panhandle
9. 1700 Block of Oak/400 Block of Clayton
10. 500 Block of Cole Street
11. Park Branch Public Library and Mural
12. Page and Shrader Streets

Continuation

Some Haight Street Landmarks, or Golden Gate Park

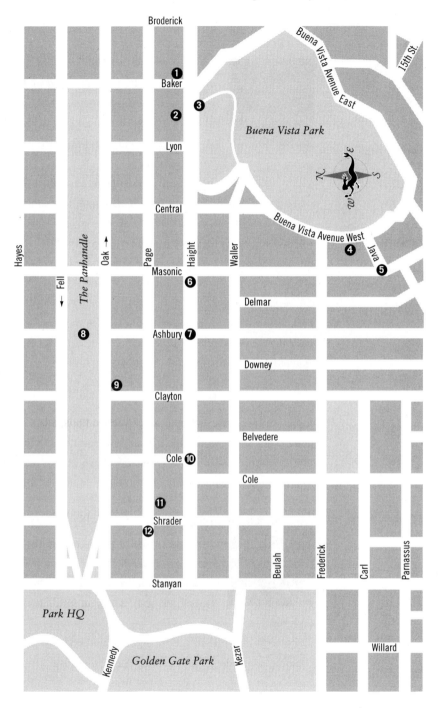

The Haight-Ashbury

Haight-Asbury Street Fair
661-8025

Dish
1398 Haight, at Masonic;
431-3534

Zare
1640 Haight Street;
861-8868

Cha Cha Cha
1801 Haight Street;
386-5758

Tassajara-Just Desserts
1000 Cole, corner of
Parnassus; 664-8947

Preliminaries

BEST TIMES
TO DO
THIS TOUR

The fog over the Haight burns off late and comes back early; midday between 11 A.M. and 3 P.M. is the sunniest time here. Saturday about 1 P.M. is when the teen-age shoppers are loose, and cafés and stores then are a *tableau vivant* of postpunk urban culture.

The Haight is most alive during the summer when many Americans and foreigners come here looking for hippies. The **Haight-Ashbury Street Fair** every summer is always worth checking out for new forms of urban life as well as old standbys like Deadheads and bikers; phone for information.

Parking

Parking is easiest on weekdays. You will see some law breakers park their cars across the pedestrian crosswalks; please do not emulate them.

Transportation

Muni's **6 Parnassus, 7 Haight, and 71 Haight-Noriega bus lines** all link Haight Street with Market Street downtown. The **N Judah bus** (not streetcar) runs every thirty minutes down Haight to Market Street from midnight to 6 A.M.

RESTAURANTS,
CAFÉS, AND BARS

Dish is popular for Sunday brunch. **Zare** serves California cuisine with a Mediterranean influence and is probably the best restaurant here; pleasant interior and back patio. **Cha Cha Cha** serves Caribbean/ Mexican food and is lively and popular.

There are many coffee places and ice cream and cookie vendors along Haight Street. A neighborhood retreat away from hectic Haight is **Tassajara-Just Desserts**. The N Judah Muni Metro streetcar links this hidden, agreeable valley with Market Street and the downtown.

CLUBS AND MOVIES

A postpunk art set gathers at **The Thirsty Swede** with live bands on week-ends; contemporary underground rock. All have loud sound systems and draw young, black-clad crowds mostly in their twenties. The **Achilles Heel**, a pleasant "Victorian" pub, has comfortable seats and tables with views of the street scene. The **Red Vic Movie House** is run as a collective and screens films you won't see at a multiplex; comfortable sofa seating; café next door; mellow local crowd.

SHOPPING

Haight Street, with some 180 small, individual shops and only a few chain store outlets, preserves the Edwardian pattern of long, narrow, ground-floor shops with plate-glass windows that face the sidewalk. This is the ideal retail space both for individual shops and as a sequence of varied, changing businesses that pulls the walker down the sidewalk like frames in a movie.

The "head shops" on Haight today are fakes conjured up to cater to the tourist demand for things hippie. Two shops for tarot cards, crystals, oils, and related ritualistic paraphernalia are **Touch Stone** and **Uma's Occult Shop**; both are on the walk between Haight and the Panhandle.

Haight Street is a museum of American fashion and has many clothing shops, with both new and vintage garments. Lately it's been shoes, shoes, shoes; always black and clunky and sometimes almost orthopedic. **Ambiance** has romantic dresses, blouses, and skirts for women along with tighter numbers. **Solo Fashion** emphasizes Bay Area and Los Angeles dress designers including some one-of-a-kind designs. **Daljeet's** carries fetish boots, bondage gear, and radical fashion. The oversized, baggy styles popular with skatepunx can also be found on the street. If you have a teenager on your gift list, you could do worse than to get him or her something "rad." **The Taming of the Shoe** carries shoes your mother will not approve of. If all this hard-core postpunk fetish fashion makes you yearn for the softer Sixties, try **Dharma**, with throwback

The Thirsty Swede
1821 Haight Street;
221-9008

Achilles Heel
1601 Haight Street,
at Clayton; 626-1800

Red Vic Movie House
1727 Haight Street;
668-3994

Touch Stone
1601A Page Street,
southwest corner of
Ashbury; 621-2782

Uma's Occult Shop
1915 Page Street, near
Shrader; 668-3132

Ambiance
1458 Haight Street;
552-5095

Solo Fashion
1599 Haight Street;
621-0342

Daljeet's
1744 Haight Street;
752-5610

The Taming of the Shoe
1736 Haight Street;
221-4453

Dharma
1600 Haight Street;
621-5597

Buffalo Exchange
1555 Haight Street;
431-7733

Wasteland
1660 Haight Street;
863-3150

Reckless Records
1401 Haight Street,
at Masonic; 431-3434

Recycled Records
1377 Haight Street;
626-4075

Rough Trade
1529 Haight Street;
621-4395

Comic Relief
1597 Haight Street;
552-9010

Naked Eye
533 Haight, between
Fillmore and Steiner;
864-2985

Bound Together Anarchist
Collective Bookstore
1369 Haight Street;
421-8355

Austen Books
1687 Haight Street;
552-4122

The Booksmith
1644 Haight Street;
863-8688

Great Expectations
Bookstore
1512 Haight Street;
863-5515

Indian print cottons, Deadhead tie-dyed tops, beads, and water pipes. The **Buffalo Exchange** is probably the best of the many thrift shops. **Wasteland**, in the old Superba Theater of 1911, is another American *shmatta* museum.

The small record shops on and off Haight, such as **Reckless Records**, cater to the Bay Area teen and college market and sell music that is loud, hard, fast, and short. Other shops are **Recycled Records**, which has soul and jazz in addition to rock, and **Rough Trade**. Most of the labels sold here will never cross over into the mainstream. What the Haight is listening to is aired over **KUSF radio**, 90.3 FM, college radio broadcasting from the nearby Jesuit University of San Francisco.

Comix rule on Haight, OK? Perhaps we can look at them as art. **Comic Relief** has gory comix you won't believe along with "graphic novels" and self-published local pulp. Further away on truly bohemian **Lower Haight** is **Naked Eye**, with underground comix, homo 'zines, biker and tattoo mags, out-of-print flics, and trash videos. The oxymoronic **Bound Together Anarchist Collective Bookstore** was organized in 1976; check here for events flyers and free newspapers. For literate San Franciscans, the happiest trend on Haight is the proliferation of book shops, both new and used. Catering to the neighborhood's many readers and resident writers are, for example, **Austen Books**, **The Booksmith**, and **Great Expectations Bookstore**.

Introduction:
Anthropological Wildlife Refuge

"Nebraska Needs You More."

Sign in the window of the
Psychedelic Shop, October 1967

The Haight gave its name to an epoch. The 1960s lastingly altered the social composition and political consciousness of this Victorian district. The Haight today is the most left-wing of San Francisco's neighborhoods, just as the west-of-Twin-Peaks districts are its most conservative. Nothing in its nineteenth-century history pointed in this direction. A provocative description of the **Haight-Ashbury**—or at least of the youthful street scene along Haight Street—is that of community organizer Calvin Welch, who has described his neighborhood as "an urban lifestyle and archaeological dig in which you can find all the urban social movements of the last forty years .... There are punks, hippies, remnants of the beats, antiwar health faddists, prowar joggers, skinhead skateboarders .... name it." The Haight also has gays, anarchists, real estate agents, blacks, teenagers, French tourists, bikers, English expatriates, hobos, and yuppies. Here and there, wandering the cold streets like survivors from a lost tribe, are gray-haired hippie survivors and young, wannabe, tie-die-garbed neohippies. The Haight is San Francisco's most culturally diverse neighborhood, more a living anthropological wildlife refuge than a dead "dig."

The Haight-Ashbury, as its hyphenated name implies, consists of two distinct areas: the Haight itself, located along the commercial strip of **Haight Street** and the flats along the **Golden Gate Park Panhandle**; and **Ashbury Heights**, a fancier district south of Haight Street that climbs the slopes of Buena Vista Heights. All of this land was originally part of the municipally owned Outside Lands west of Divisadero Street, but was claimed by squatters. In 1865 the Supreme Court ruled that the City of San Francisco was the legal successor to the Mexican pueblo of Yerba Buena and that as such it was the rightful heir to the 17,000 acres of the pueblo's Outside Lands. In 1866 Congress affirmed municipal title to the sand dunes north of today's Wawona Street from Divisadero to the Pacific Ocean.

But court rulings and congressional confirmation only put the vexed question of the ownership of the land west of the built-up city in the hands of the city's politicians. All the Outside Lands were claimed by somebody—in many cases several somebodies, since all could see that the city would have to expand westward and that great profits would be made when sand dunes became city lots. The squatters who claimed this land were not a ragtag bunch of small holders; many were substantial citizens active in state and municipal politics who hired men to build shacks and fences in order to claim ownership. The state legislature had to approve any disposition that the city made of these lands, and the big land speculators had a firm grip on the state legislature in Sacramento.

Frank McCoppin was the supervisor who represented the eleventh ward, which included the Outside Lands, from 1859 to 1866. He was one of the earliest advocates of the creation of a major "pleasure ground" in the park-starved city. In 1866 he was elected mayor and decided to secure a park through the settlement of the Outside Lands question. He brought the principal land claimants together in a secret meeting to hammer out a deal, asking the "squatters" how much land they would give up to the city in return for clear title to the rest of the tract. The smallest amount they were willing to surrender was 10 percent; John B. Felton was willing to give up 25 percent. In the final deal 10.75 percent of the Outside Lands was reserved to the city, chiefly for the creation of Golden Gate Park, Buena Vista Park, a handful of other parks, and school and firehouse lots. Ninety percent was turned over to the squatters. Some ended up with parcels of twenty, fifty, or as many as one hundred blocks. The city had to go even further to get the consent of the politically well-wired speculators; it had to agree to compensate those who claimed what became the public reservations. To do this a one-time assessment of 10.75 percent of the appraised value of the land was made on the 80.25 percent to pay off the "dispossessed" 10.75 percent. This left the municipality with no profit, only the costly obligation to develop its sandy one tenth into a grand park. Clearing title touched off wild speculation in Outside Lands lots that raged for about eighteen months before collapsing in 1869.

A dispute arose over the shape of the 10 percent reserved by the city for Golden Gate Park. Supervisors Monroe Ashbury and Charles Clayton wanted the great city park to begin at Divisadero and to cut straight west to the Ocean Beach. But the valley between Divisadero and what became Stanyan Street was closest to the city and had the best soil. Supervisors **Charles H. Stanyan, A. J. Shrader**, and **R. Beverly Cole** managed to whittle down the eastern end of the park into a one-block-wide **Panhandle** and to push the eastern edge of the main park ten blocks west to Stanyan Street. This benefited politically well-connected land speculators. Governor **Henry Huntly Haight** signed the necessary state legislation confirming the oddly shaped park. Both the heroes and villains in the piece had streets named after themselves in what became the Haight-Ashbury. Haight Street was named for Yale-educated lawyer Governor Haight.

In 1870 work began on landscaping the Panhandle and the eastern end of Golden Gate Park. In 1883 the Haight Street cable car line built by Southern Pacific Railroad opened. It terminated at Haight and Stanyan; nearby was the depot of the Park and Ocean Railroad that went out along the southern edge of the park to Ocean Beach. A private baseball field was laid out at Stanyan and Waller in 1887, and an amusement park called The Chutes was built on Haight between Clayton and Cole in the 1890s. All these attractions brought people out to the western edge of town and led to the construction of a cluster of hotels, restaurants, and bars at this transfer point. (**The Stanyan Park Hotel**, built in 1904 and handsomely restored in 1983, dates from this era.) Thus, the park end of the Haight evolved as an amusement park.

In the 1880s, houses began to be built along the Panhandle, Victorian high society's favorite carriage drive, and on Ashbury Heights. The late 1880s and early 1890s were the heyday of the Queen Anne style and roughly three-quarters of the 1,160 Victorian houses in the neighborhood are Queen Annes. They are characterized by gable roofs, round towers and turrets, and elaborate redwood gingerbread and plaster ornament.

The earliest residents of the Haight-Ashbury were a cosmopolitan mix of Americans and successful immigrants. There was a noticeably Jewish flavor to the Panhandle area in the 1880s, when that was a new neighborhood. The census of 1900 recorded American-born and German, Irish, Swedish, Scottish, Swiss, Australian, and French homeowners with some black, Japanese, and Chinese live-in domestics in the largest houses. The devastation of the downtown districts in 1906 touched off a building boom in the undamaged Haight. The neighborhood was filled with the sounds of the sawing of wood and the pounding of nails. More flats, hotels and small apartments appeared along Haight Street itself between 1906 and 1915 over ground-floor shops. Haight Street finally filled in with more than a hundred businesses. Anita Day Hubbard wrote in 1924 that "there is a comfortable maturity about the compact little city that San Francisco knows as Haight-Ashbury ... [A] nice upholstered, fuchsia garden sort of grown-up-ness, just weathered enough to be nice, and new enough to be looking ahead to the future instead of sighing futilely over the past."

Then during the Depression of the 1930s the neighborhood began to decline as maintenance was deferred and buildings faded. From an upper-middle-class suburban fringe, in the 1880s, the area changed into a working-class inner-city district by the 1930s. By 1939 only 10 percent of the Haight's houses were still single-family dwellings; most properties were owned by absentee landlords. During the World War II boom, when the city's factories were working at capacity but housing stopped being built, many of the Haight's roomy old Victorians were subdivided.

When the city Redevelopment Authority began wholesale demolition of the Victorian Western Addition slums, poor black families began to move into the Panhandle area, the next neighborhood over. In 1950 the black population between Oak and Waller and Stanyan and Baker was 3 percent; in 1960, 17 percent; and in 1970, 50 percent. Rents in the Haight stagnated and it became a relatively cheap place to live. Meanwhile, on the other side of the city, in North Beach, the tourist boom began to drive up commercial rents and to displace the beatniks. Some drifted to the Panhandle area. A small "postbeat" subculture emerged in the flats and slowly spread up the slopes toward Ashbury Heights. By 1962 a significant but unpublicized bohemian subculture was suffused through the Haight, though, of course, it was never in the majority. The first hip business was the **Blue Unicorn Café** at 1927 Hayes, north of the Panhandle, which opened in 1963.

Things came to a head in January 1966 when Ken Kesey hosted a Trips Festival at Longshoreman's Hall near Fisherman's Wharf (of all places). Thousands showed up, dropped acid, and spaced-out on rock music and light shows. The word *hippie* was born. Through a new kind of music, psychedelic rock, the pacific hippie message spread around the country and the world. The "San Francisco Sound" emerged and people wore flowers in their hair and passed them out to San Franciscans on their way to work downtown. On January 14, 1967 the Human Be-In/Gathering of the Tribes was celebrated at Golden Gate Park's old Polo Field and the new bohemia got its first media attention.

In the Haight, Victoriana came back in decor and dress. Lithographs of Hindu icons, dancing elephants with many heads, served as signs of some half-perceived cultural confusion. Rock posters took turn-of-the-century Viennese lettering and clashing color combinations to make vibrant posters for bands with names like The Charlatans, The Chocolate Watch Band, Quicksilver Messenger Service, the Electric Flag, Big Brother and the Holding Company, Blue Cheer, Jefferson Airplane, and the enduring Grateful Dead. Drugs, music, polymorphous sex, vivid art, and visionary poetry swirled in a multisensory mix.

Some of the Haight's Victorians were painted in strong colors: red, yellow, green, brown, black, purple, violet, and dark blue, with every different architectural feature painted to stand out. Façades and interiors were painted with the strong coloring of masks. It was the first time the colors of San Francisco's old houses had been changed from their traditional light-reflecting pale colors.

In 1967 *Time* magazine announced that the Haight was the "vibrant epicenter of America's hippie movement" and publicity turned the attention of America's footloose youth to this beautiful Victorian neighborhood with its mature parks and foggy summer weather. An avalanche of young people—the police claimed 75,000—descended on the fragile scene. During the spring of 1967, the Gray Line began taking tourists in sealed buses on the "Hippie Hop: the only foreign tour within the continental limits of the United States." Hippies trotted alongside the buses, which were crawling their way through the traffic jam of gawkers, holding mirrors up to the bus windows.

As Charles Perry, the best historian of the "Summer of Love," wrote in *Rolling Stone*

> The actual composition of the Haight was diverse. Among the things that brought people were traditional bohemian impulses of artistic self-assertion and the romantic search for mystery and authentic experience; the search for non-violent social forms; curiosity about the meaning of psychedelics; the lure of the drug marketplace, for both customer and dealer; rejection of a comfortable social upbringing; loneliness and rejection in other communities; uncertainty about goals; desire to evangelize, organize or bust the people already in the Haight; and the sheer momentum of the phenomenon.

Along with the day-trippers and "plastic hippies" came violent individuals, drug dealers, and the mentally deranged. The hippie pastoral dream became a nightmare. On October 6, 1966, the State of California had made LSD illegal and hippies became outlaws. A quick downward spiral of drug abuse devastated the hippie subculture as drug users became drug addicts. Many OD'd. On October 6, 1967, the Diggers staged a "Death of Hippie" march. What was left of the countercultural Haight was wiped out by a suspicious flood of cheap heroin in 1970–71.

By the early 1970s Haight Street looked like skid row. All the beauty was gone; only the bumbling burnouts remained. About a third of the shopfronts were empty. City health inspectors began closing down the unsanitary communes. Police busted the dealers. The city instituted a Rehabilitation Assistance Program in 1973 whereby city inspectors examined buildings in the Ashbury Heights area, tallied up deficiencies, and then offered property owners subsidized loans to bring their buildings up to code. The city also rezoned large parts of the neighborhood to reduce the number of units permitted in new construction. This made restoration of vintage buildings economically attractive. Along Haight Street the unnatural commercial depression induced speculators to pick up buildings and to "flip" them. The wild house inflation of the mid–1970s that raged citywide rescued the Haight from decay. Between 1973 and 1978 real estate prices increased from 100 to 500 percent.

Two streams of new residents revitalized the Haight, young urban professionals and gays. Grocery stores and taverns are the surest barometers of a neighborhood; by 1979 gay bars outnumbered straight ones five to three along Haight Street. Owner-occupancy increased from 14 percent to 54 percent between 1970 and 1977. Neighborhood organizations were revitalized by these new homeowners. The spiraling rents also made the Haight a center of agitation for citywide rent control, which was adopted in 1979. Today the Haight is the most left-wing of the city's neighborhoods. A particular sore point with radical residents is the threat of chain stores on funky Haight Street. The construction of a chain drug store on the strip was frustrated when the building that was to house it was fire-bombed while it was under construction. The insanity of setting fires in an all-frame Victorian district was roundly condemned by more level-headed residents.

House colors all over the Haight have become more sophisticated as real estate values have escalated. Pleasing combinations of pale colors—with a lot of white used for windows and trim—reflect warm-colored light onto the streets and into the apartments. The near-universality of using white for windows and trim produces a Wedgwoodlike effect of white raised ornament over varying light background colors.

In the early 1980s the Haight saw a brief moment when some thought that the street would shift to luxury boutiques and tony restaurants and become another Union Street. But the more ambitious restaurants failed to draw a city-wide clientele and the neighborhood would not support pricey *nouvelle cuisine*. By the late-1980s the Haight street commercial strip settled down to a lively, viable mixture of radical (or nostalgic) clothing stores, inexpensive restaurants, and many new and used bookstores and record shops.

The 1990s have seen further change. While the fine Victorian houses on the side streets command astronomical prices and are ever more cared for and improved, the Haight Street shopping strip can be a depressing sight late at night. Teen-age runaways, throw-away children, and aggressive, unattractive punk youth from all over the Bay Area find Haight Street one of the few places in the now-gentrified city where they can "hang." But it is not a romantic sight to those who remember the optimistic hippie flowering to see shivering youngsters sleeping in doorways next to discarded hypodermic needles. The east end of Golden Gate Park has become a problem zone attracting derelicts and drug abusers. The want-to-be-tolerant residents of the Haight have organized to discourage drug dealers from taking over their neighborhood. High rents on Upper Haight have propelled the new bohemians of the 1990s to colonize the Lower Haight, the blocks from Fillmore to Divisadero quite far from the old Haight-Ashbury. Some of the hippest cafés and alternative shops now cluster there. No, the 1990s are not at all like the 1960s.

Spencer House Bed and Breakfast Inn
1080 Haight Street;
626-9205

1801 Haight/
1–3 Buena Vista East

One Baker Street

15, 17, 19, and 21 Baker Street

1128 Haight Street

1132–34–36 Haight Street

1144–46 Haight Street

❶ Spencer House Bed and Breakfast Inn, *1895, Frederick P. Rabin*
On the northeast corner of Haight Street at Baker is the three-story corner turret of the elegant **Spencer House** built in 1895. This imposing Queen Anne–style house was designed by German-born Frederick P. Rabin for John Spencer. It is one of the most opulent houses built in this part of the city. It is unusual for its triple-sized corner lot and for being freestanding and ornamented on all four sides. Its corner tower is squared at its base, octagonal at the second and third floors, and capped by a faceted, conical roof. The stained glass transoms in the first-floor Palladian windows with their soft canary-yellow glass and transparent faceted "jewels" glitter invitingly at night. The front porch is sheltered by triple Richardsonian-Romanesque arches. A white marble stoop leads to a mosaic entryway and wood-grained front doors.

The house is now a bed-and-breakfast inn, and passersby can sometimes peek into the golden-oak paneled vestibule with its crazy-pattern parquet floors. The interior of the mansion has been perfectly restored and furnished with antiques. Luxuriant palms flourish in the narrow side garden to the east. It is worth walking half a block down Baker and looking back at the Spencer House to admire the manipulation of its roof forms and its very fine side bay.

Across Haight, on the triangular lot formed by Buena Vista East, is **1801 Haight/1–3 Buena Vista East**, a flatiron with a corner turret built in 1894 and designed by John J. Clark. The black iron fence here is a rare original survivor. This intersection, with its four turrets, serves as a dramatic gateway to the Haight-Ashbury.

Across Baker at **One Baker Street** on the northwest corner of Haight is a modern twenty-two unit building built around a courtyard. It is in a mock Victorian style with a weak roofline and a silly "cap" over its corner bay. Down Baker on this side is a row of Eastlake style houses. Numbers **15, 17, 19, and 21 Baker Street** were designed by Hugh Keenan and built in 1890. This fine row has curious porch columns with silhouette flower patterns. Number 21 was restored in 1994; number 19 awaits the eventual restoration that rising real estate values will no doubt someday induce.

❷  *The 1100 Block of Haight Street*

The flat block of Haight between Baker and Lyon streets facing Buena Vista Park was prime real estate in the Victorian era and attracted fine architecture. At **1128 Haight Street** is a Queen Anne house built in 1891. Now apartments, it has a fine, decorated cylindrical corner tower. Number **1132–34–36 Haight Street** is a three-flat Edwardian built about 1910 with semicircular bay windows. At **1144–46 Haight Street** is a pair of Queen Anne flats with another corner tower. A complex grid pattern is worked out through the porch hood, front doors, transoms, porch paneling, and in the design of the top lights of its double-hung windows. This is an outstanding example of how important window design was to Victorian architects.

Return to Haight and Baker and the corner stair-   **Buena Vista Park**
case entrance to Buena Vista Park. Looking east there is a view over
the city to the Bay, Oakland, and the Contra Costa hills.

❸ *Buena Vista Park*

Enter **Buena Vista Park** from the stairs at Haight and Baker and take the path to the
right. As you climb, there is a sudden, superb view: the white Transamerica Pyramid,
Lafayette Park's treetops, the dark, slate-covered dome of Temple Sherith Israel of 1905,
the green terraces of Alta Plaza with forested Angel Island behind it, the twin piers of
the Golden Gate Bridge against the high hills of Marin County, and the trees and H. A.
Minton's 1932 Gothic Revival tower of Lone Mountain College (now part of the University of San Francisco). Keep walking uphill and to the right to the small children's
play area built in 1975. The grand twin-towered church in the distance with the dome
and square campanile is Jesuit St. Ignatius on the campus of the University of San
Francisco, designed by Charles J. I. Devlin and built in 1914. On the far horizon rises
Mt. Tamalpais in Marin County. Immediately below the park, on Haight Street, is the
warm yellow brick and red-tile roofed Tuscan Revival façade of the Third Church of
Christ, Scientist designed by Edgar A. Matthews in 1918. The church is enriched with
terra-cotta ornament. The band of trees between the two churches is Golden Gate
Park's Panhandle.

Buena Vista Park was originally known as Hill Park and was
reserved by the city in 1867 as a part of the Outside Lands. Its summit is 569 feet above
sea level and the park covers 36.5 acres. The city paid $88,250 to squatters with claims
to the hilltop in the state legislation that established Golden Gate Park. Originally
almost treeless, the summit of the park was one of the chief visitors' overlooks of the
nineteenth-century city. Forestation, including the preservation of a grove of native
oaks, began about 1880. The name Buena Vista Park was adopted in 1894. About 1910,
park neighbors organized an improvement club to press the city for improvements of
the park and the road around it, and in 1913 the handsome new staircases, paths, and
tennis courts were dedicated.

Though it looks wild, Buena Vista is essentially man-made. John
McLaren oversaw the park's forestation. Some of the trees were planted by school children on Arbor Day with seedlings provided by Adolph Sutro. Monterey cypress, Monterey pines, several kinds of eucalyptus, redwoods, acacia, and Australian tea trees
flourish here. There are also some madrone, toyon, deodar cedars, Torrey pines, Italian
stone pines, and Japanese black pines.

From the play area with its sweeping view, walk down the path out
of the park to its perimeter sidewalk. You pass a grove of native California oaks to the
left and an eclectic array of houses and apartments across Buena Vista Avenue West.
Walk uphill on Buena Vista Avenue West.

Richard Spreckels Mansion
737 Buena Vista Avenue West

731 Buena Vista West

639 Buena Vista West

635 Buena Vista West

615 Buena Vista West

601 Buena Vista West

595–97 Buena Vista Avenue West

1482 Masonic Avenue

1450 Masonic Avenue

❹ *Buena Vista Avenue West*

Richard Spreckels Mansion, *1897, Edward J. Vogel*
Another of the grand houses built facing the park is the Richard Spreckels house of 1897, designed by Edward J. Vogel in the neo-Georgian/Colonial Revival style for Richard Spreckels, the nephew of sugar magnate Claus Spreckels. The house has a columned semicircular porch, white marble steps, a tall iron gate to its right, and dramatic, flaring sheet-metal chimneys. Paired oak doors are set back in the entrance vestibule. Immediately next door is **731 Buena Vista West,** a Queen Anne–style house. It is notable for its wild front porch protective iron grille, executed by E. A. Chase in 1979.

Buena Vista Avenue West, developed a decade later than the blocks down the hill, is notable for the great variety of its architecture. At **639 Buena Vista West** at Frederick Street is a classic stucco box with an elegant entrance built in 1913 by owner-builder Eugene N. Fritz. At **635 Buena Vista West** is another stucco house, with elegant French windows and a fine cornice, also built by Eugene N. Fritz in 1913. Number **615 Buena Vista West** is a shingled Tudor house with an elaborate central bay. This house is now several units. Between it and its neighbor is a curious view of the seemingly free-floating shingled onion dome and odd copper chimneys added to the top of 1450 Masonic Avenue, a block away.

At **601 Buena Vista West** is a Queen Anne house with a tower built in 1895 by William H. Armitage. Note the smooth curve where the tower meets the front wall. At **595–97 Buena Vista Avenue West**, on the southeast corner of Java, is a modern, horizontal, two-flat building designed about 1950 by Henry Hill, one of the Bay Area's modernist designers. Originally of all unpainted wood, its "natural" finish did not weather well, and its window frames have been painted. At narrow Java Street, turn right to busy Masonic Avenue.

❺ *Java Street, Masonic Avenue, and Waller Street/Victorian Rows*

Java Street is a short one-block connector to **Masonic Avenue**. It has a good view of the planted eucalyptus forests of Mt. Sutro, once part of Adolph Sutro's vast real estate holdings. **Masonic Avenue** is a busy street lined with fine houses, with lush greenery and many flowering plants in pots and in the small plots in front of the houses. At **1482 Masonic Avenue** at the corner of Java is a large shingled house with black trim, a strange column to the left, and a projecting third floor. The house incorporates hints of the Mission Revival in its welcoming porch. (Postmodernists have nothing on this design!) Down the hill on the same side of the street is **1450 Masonic Avenue**, a Queen Anne house with a tower designed in 1891 by A. J. Barnett. Modern copperwork panels have replaced the plaster scratchwork at the cornice and first floor and contemporary stained-glass windows have been added to the tower at the second floor. A contemporary sculpture/house number stands in the yard. This is the house whose onion dome

and copper chimneys were visible from Buena Vista West. The building is an amalgam of Victoriana and vaguely hippie artwork.
Number **1430 Masonic Avenue**, next door almost hidden under its
trees, is a fine turn-of-the-century house with a clinker brick base
and classical detailing.

  About two-thirds down the block on the right-
hand side is a row of six Eastlake row houses at **1322–42 Masonic
Avenue**, built in 1891 and identical in form, though they are now
painted in a variety of color schemes. They were designed by Robert
Dickie Cranston for developer J. A. Whelan in a somewhat *retardaire* style. The houses are set on high bases that emphasize their verticality. They originally had false gables and cast-iron cresting on
their roofs. Note the applied ornamental "sticks" that seem to rise
from the base straight to the cornice. In the 1920s, when the Haight-
Ashbury was comfortable but a bit faded, such houses were described as sitting "with
their poker faces like close-mouthed Yankees refusing to divulge any secrets."

  At Waller and Masonic are several choice rows. The house on the
southwest corner, at **1301–03 Waller Street**, sits on a dramatic base and has curved glass.
It and its neighbor, **1307–09 Waller Street**, were built in 1901. A row of houses—**1315,
1321–23, 1327–29,** and **1333–35 Waller Street**—were all constructed in 1896, again for
developer J. A. Whelan. All the houses here, varying from single-family residences to
flats, are set on high bases and have gable roofs and a lush embroidery ornament. Note
the central medallion at the second floor of 1315 Waller. These houses represent the
highwater mark of ornament in San Francisco architecture. Number 1321–23 was
"improved" with stucco when Victoriana was unfashionable but has since had an
emphatic, neo-Victorian façade applied, with a giant urn of flowers in the middle of the
second story. This decoration has the courage of its convictions and looks quite good;
most people will never suspect that it is not original. Number 1333–35, the last in the
row, was more conventionally restored in 1988. When the misimprovements of the
façade were removed, the "ghosts" of the original ornament were revealed and new
ornament was custom-made.

  Across from the Waller Street row, on the northwest corner of
Masonic and Waller where Masonic Avenue widens, stands **1265–67 Masonic Avenue**,
a suave corner house on a yellow brick base with a three-quarter round bay window
at the corner. The bay has curved glass, a design motif picked up in the semicircular
porch opening. A very fine small stained-glass window with a semicircular hood is
placed on the smooth first-floor façade facing Masonic. The double-hung windows here
are more horizontal than vertical and make the house more restful than its exaggerat-
edly vertical neighbors. Along its Waller Street side march four semicircular bays in an
even rhythm. The house dates from the late 1890s when San Francisco architects were
striving to design houses with more elegant, restrained ornament.

  Across Masonic Avenue, on the east side of the block, is one of the
most spectacular rows of Queen Anne houses, the **1200 block of Masonic Avenue** from
Waller to Haight. There, prime lots on the sunny side of prestigious Masonic Avenue

1430 Masonic Avenue

1322–42 Masonic Avenue

1301–03 Waller Street

1307–09 Waller Street

1315, 1321–23, 1327–29,
and 1333–35 Waller
Street

1265–67 Masonic Avenue

1200 block of Masonic
Avenue

1244–46 Masonic Avenue

1200 Masonic Avenue

1398 Haight Street

were developed by Robert Dickie Cranston and his partner Hugh Keenan in 1895–96; number **1244–46 Masonic Avenue** was designed in the same year by Martens and Coffey. The row is distinguished by "witch's cap" turrets, some round, some faceted. Softer colors have succeeded the somewhat garish paint schemes of the hippie period.

 6 *Haight Street Commercial Strip*

On the southeast corner of Masonic and Haight stands turreted **1200 Masonic Avenue** (see illustration at begining of this tour), a mixed commercial and residential building erected for a Mrs. Bogart, a cashier at the *San Francisco Examiner*. A dentist's parlors occupied the second-story corner bay. This Queen Anne was designed by W. H. Lillie in 1896. Facing it across Masonic are much plainer brick commercial buildings on the southwest and northwest corners of Haight and Masonic, designed by Meyers and Ward for the Goldberg Bowen Company in 1904–05. The corner building houses the painfully hip Reckless Records; check here for events flyers. (Suddenly: Modern Youth!)

A peculiarity in the development of the Haight was that the John H. Baird Estate owned a blocks-long swath along both sides of Haight Street that it did not sell to developers until the early 1900s. The result is that today's neighborhood is a sandwich consisting of plainer Edwardian commercial-residential buildings, built between 1900 and 1915 along Haight Street, which are flanked by fancier 1880s–90s Victorian housing along the streets to either side.

On the fourth, northeast corner of Haight and Masonic stands a mixed commercial residential building at **1398 Haight Street**. For many years it was a corner drugstore, and many of the original fittings survive in the restaurant. In 1967 this became the site of the Drogstore café, a celebrated hippie hang-out. It's said that the café wanted to keep the name "Drugstore" along with its apothecary-jar decor, but that the police insisted on an alteration in the name, hence "Drogstore." Today **Dish** is one of the better eating places in the Haight, and a popular place for brunch. It has preserved the original turn-of-the-century interior, decorating it with different dishes, thus the name of the restaurant. Also near Haight and Masonic, at 1371 Haight Street, upstairs, were the offices of *The San Francisco Oracle*, the mystical, quietist underground newspaper that was the voice of the hippie Haight. Its multicolor inks and psychedelic art work invented the graphic look of much subsequent 1960s art.

Haight and Ashbury Streets

Ben & Jerry's Ice Cream
249-4685

A block west down Haight Street is the famous intersection of **Haight** and **Ashbury**, the coordinates that gave this neighborhood its name and which were adopted to refer to the hippie bohemia that blossomed here a generation ago. A recent and fitting addition to the neighborhood here is **Ben and Jerry's** ice cream shop. (Those with a particular interest in the shrines of the hippie era will want to make a detour one block uphill on Ashbury Street, past Waller, to **710 Ashbury Street**, the former Grateful Dead house. The Dead were busted here on October 2, 1967 as attitudes toward the hippies began to change. This is a private residence; please do not disturb the residents. Conveniently enough, the Haight-Ashbury Legal Clinic was across the street at 715 Ashbury.) The very fine Queen Anne row from **704 to 714 Ashbury Street** was built about 1890 and designed by the active Robert Dickie Cranston. While similar in design, each façade has its particular variations. Both sides of this block are lined with three-flat buildings marked by bay windows held up by decorative brackets.

710 Ashbury Street

704 to 714 Ashbury Street

1550–42 Page Street

461 Ashbury Street

459 Ashbury Street

431 Ashbury Street

429 Ashbury Street

    Touch Stone, an "occult" shop on the southwest corner of Ashbury and Page, is one of the few shops that continue the hippie sensibility. At the northwest corner of Ashbury and Page is a row of five houses, **1550–42 Page Street**. These Queen Annes were designed in 1891 by the ubiquitous Cranston and Keenan. The corner house is particularly fine, with a wood-grained entry that has squat Romanesque columns, elegant hardware, and a shallow, bow-shaped second-floor porch. The side wall facing Ashbury has a decorated chimney, decorative panels, and projecting bays with textured plasterwork on their undersides. Three of the houses have been badly altered. You can still see their second-floor arched porches.

    Number **461 Ashbury Street** at the northwest corner of Page is distinguished by a lovely oval corner bay window with curved glass. Three houses down is **459 Ashbury Street**, with two overly ornamented "Victorian" garages. Above them rises a splendid Queen Anne building of 1893 by Cranston and Keenan with a bulging second-floor porch featuring a semicircular arch. The whale weathervane is an inauthentic modern addition. Such houses often had wood or iron finials, but not weathervanes. Past the apartment building is **431 Ashbury Street**, a cottage on a raised basement with a square bay and interesting "outrigger" porch brackets. One-story houses are unusual in the Haight; the land was too expensive for that kind of house. Next to it is **429 Ashbury Street**, a three-story, gable-roofed Eastlake house designed in 1891 by the Shipman Brothers. The original owner was a deputy superintendent of streets for the city. This lacy façade has a beautiful porch hood and eye-catching spindlework and columns at its second floor corner.

Golden Gate Park Panhandle

1705 Oak Street

1711 Oak Street

1759 and 1763 Oak Street

❽ *Golden Gate Park Panhandle*

At the foot of Ashbury is the **Golden Gate Park Panhandle**, lined with mature eucalyptus trees. The Panhandle was one of the first parts of the park to be landscaped, in 1870, and was originally enclosed by a fence that was locked at 9 P.M. The Panhandle was laid out with a now-lost carriage drive, The Avenue, that had three small "islands" of plantings. Here San Francisco's High Society went for afternoon carriage drives to see and to be seen. San Francisco's swells thronged the Panhandle to see the ladies and show off their mounts. One gossipy description of the scene from the 1882 *San Francisco News Letter* ran

> A closed carriage [passed], carrying Mrs. C. and Miss C.C., of Sutter street, both robed in exquisite costumes fresh from New York. M., the lawyer, he of the flowing locks, was their attendant cavalier. S.W.'s family in an open carriage, driven by his son R., Mrs. R. expanding more and more daily, in comfort and happiness. R.L. on horseback, Judge H. and family in a carryall. Gov. S[tanford]'s beautiful turn-out—gold-mounted harness and perfectly appointed servants making it a feature of the crowd; Mrs. S., dressed in mourning, was accompanied by Miss G., of Sacramento.

In 1906, immediately after the earthquake and fire, the Panhandle and park became a refuge for fleeing families. Eleven babies were born here the first night. Tents and later wood cottages eventually housed thirty thousand refugees. During the hippie period, the Panhandle was the scene of outdoor rock concerts that caused heavy wear-and-tear on the fragile landscape. Today the Panhandle is somewhat seedy. Wanderers in buses and beat-up cars are drawn here as one of the last refuges of 1960s-style seekers. The painted vehicles are sometimes quite wonderful. An inscription spotted here recently read: "Spirit is the Journey, Body is the Bus." The derelict and homeless are also drawn to the Panhandle. From the very rich to the very poor, the Panhandle has experienced a complete revolution of Fortune's wheel.

❾ *1700 Block of Oak/400 Block of Clayton*

The block of Oak Street facing the Panhandle between Ashbury and Clayton streets harbors a cluster of fine Victorians. Number **1705 Oak Street** was designed by Maxwell G. Bugbee in 1893 and has stucco and horizontal windows. Number 1709 Oak Street is a superb shingled house with a streamlined first floor and a brick arched entrance; the two-story upper section juts out with a second-story bay window and a third-story, look-out-style gable window. It was designed by the zappy Joseph Cather Newsom in 1890; note the fancy shinglework. Number **1711 Oak Street**, much simpler, is a delightful one-story Queen Anne cottage on a raised basement built by Adolph Lutgens in 1896, a late date for such a small building on a prime street. Numbers **1759 and 1763 Oak Street** are looming, three-story buildings with swallow's nest stuccowork in their gables; they were designed by architect W. H. Lillie in 1891.

On the southeast corner of Oak and Clayton is **400 Clayton Street**, the McFarlane House, designed by Coxhead and Coxhead in 1895 and built for $7,261. Engaged Corinthian columns and an off-center entrance create a formal yet quirky Mannerist façade on Clayton. Over the small front door is a broken pediment with an oval window and a rich garland ornament. The double-hung windows in the "wings" of the façade are stretched out to create a horizontal effect.

400 Clayton Street

401–07 Clayton Street

409 and 411 Clayton Street

1700 Page Street

1727 and 1726 Page Street

1762 Page Street

1767 Page Street

1768 Page Street

1777 Page Street

Up the 400 block of Clayton are more architectural treasures. On the southwest corner stands **401–07 Clayton Street**, a group of four Eastlake designs by J. B. Hall built in 1894–95. Note their pronounced gables. These four houses cost a total of $4,900. Numbers **409 and 411 Clayton Street** are by Soule and Hoadley and date from 1893. Number **409 Clayton** is a wild Queen Anne with balconies; it was once called 409 House, with reading and meditation rooms on the first floor, psychiatric counseling on the second floor, and the offices of *The Journal of Psychedelic Drugs* in the attic. Today it houses various community organizations including the San Francisco Information Clearing House and a neighborhood newspaper (back copies usually available). Number **411 Clayton** has an oval spindlework screen and a basket of carved flowers and exuberant foliage in its gable. This row of fine vintage houses is terminated by **1700 Page Street** on the northwest corner of Clayton and Page, an egregious thirteen-unit apartment building with ground-floor parking. Peek through its entrance grate for what can only be called barracks architecture. Such "higher and better" uses threatened much of the Haight in the 1960s, until zoning rules were rewritten in the 1970s, to prevent such disruptive redevelopment.

Another instructive contrast is offered by **1727 and 1726 Page Street**, on opposite sides of the street. Number 1727 is a robustly ornamented Eastlake cottage on a raised basement built for M. Wiegman in 1889. It has a beautiful front door with incised wood panels and colored flash glass, also with incised ornament. The overly enthusiastic paint scheme is modern. Facing it is 1726 Page with a yellow brick veneer, sandpaper stucco panels, ugly yellow glass windows, and a heavy metal fire escape characteristic of the early 1960s.

Number **1762 Page Street** was designed by Edward R. Swain in 1895. Here fake "colonial style" mullions have been added to the double-hung windows in a most inappropriate "East Coast antique" manner. Number **1767 Page Street**, set between larger flats buildings and with a tall redwood tree in its small front yard, is a fine Edwardian house with a round corner tower and a smooth curve where the tower meets the flat façade. Its narrow clapboard is set flush.

Also in this block of vintage buildings is **1768 Page Street**, a modern building with two-story, generously proportioned bay windows but too much bleak cement at the ground level and too large a garage door. Designing in-fill buildings in Victorian districts is difficult. While it is desirable to accommodate parking on the ground floor, such overlarge garage doors are disruptive. A generous porch and suave detailing complete the design. Fanciful **1777 Page Street** was built in 1894 by the pro-

500–06 Cole Street

508, 510, 512, and 516 Cole Street

1677–79–81 Haight

Park Branch Public Library and Mural
1833 Page Street
There is a public
restroom here;
666-7155

lific Cranston and Keenan as Robert Dickie Cranston's own home. It is distinguished by decorative plasterwork and owls' heads. Poor 1794 Page Street, on the northeast corner of Cole, is a corner Victorian with its corner bays brutally stripped and stuccoed. The house has been gated and a garage artlessly inserted.

⑩ *500 Block of Cole Street*

On the southeast corner of Page and Cole streets stands **500–06 Cole Street**, designed by Cranston and Keenan in 1899. This almost wildly expressive Queen Anne does a clever job of tucking four upper flats and two ground-floor flats onto a corner lot, making the result look like a single mansion. The U-shaped front stairs lead to the porch with its Richardsonian columns and redwood ornament. The third floor is marked by an unusual turret set between two gables. Delicate ribbons and garlands decorate the tower.

Up the block toward Haight Street is yet another Cranston and Keenan row, **508, 510, 512,** and **516 Cole Street**, built in 1899. The last house in the cluster, 516, boasts a particularly lacy façade with fine bay windows. Elaborate mullions decorate the upper windows, while the lower pane is plain for unobstructed views of the street. Notice what a large proportion of the façade is devoted to windows.

Visible at the head of Cole Street, across Haight at **1677–79–81 Haight**, is a Parisian style shop-and-flats building with a flower shop on its ground floor designed by South-of-Market-born architect James F. Dunn in 1904. It is a rare building type in the city some promoters called the "Paris of America" in the early 1900s. (That was a political code word for open vice, it seems.)

⑪ Park Branch Public Library and Mural, *1909, McDougall Brothers*
Return to Page Street and walk west toward Golden Gate Park. At 1833 Page Street, tucked away inconspicuously, is **Public Library Branch No. 5**, the Park Branch, an elegantly proportioned, light yellow brick library with a terra-cotta–framed entrance and oak and glass doors designed by the McDougall Brothers in 1909. Inside is a large reading room with windows on all four sides. These plain windows are handsomely proportioned. In the raised basement are community meeting rooms. The vivid **mural** on the neighboring building, one of the finest ever done in the Haight, was painted by Selma Brown and Ruby Newman in 1975–76. Dancers, masks, and musicians are set against an idyllic California landscape with a rainbow. All races, ages, and cultures blend in the design. Inscribed in the corner of the mural is a most San Franciscan motto: "Come together each in your own perceiving of your self."

⓬ *Page and Shrader Streets*

1900–02 Page Street

**1890 Page/
426 Shrader Street**

1901 Page Street

510 Shrader Street

1779–83 Haight

At the northwest corner of Page and Shrader streets stands **1900–02 Page Street**, a nine-unit building with both flats and apartments. This three-story building has a corner tower and turret. The first-floor windows and the two side entrances and side bay are distinguished by semicircular designs. The rusticated clapboard siding, so called because of the narrow, accentuated grooves, sets off the fancy millwork. The cornice has a band of wreaths and swags. It is, all in all, a very San Francisco Victorian painted an appropriate off white. The facing Salfield flats at **1890 Page/426 Shrader Street**, on the northeast corner of Page, now painted, were designed in the Shingle style by Samuel Newsom in 1889. There is fine ornament between the second and third floors, intricate shinglework, and swallow's nest stuccowork. The corner turrets and mid-roof gables are quite fine. This is a now-rare architectural style in San Francisco; the building deserves landmark status and careful restoration.

On the southwest corner of Page and Shrader is **1901 Page Street**, a fine Queen Anne/Colonial Revival house designed by Edward J. Vogel in 1896. It is unusual in being set off by small front and side yards and still has its original iron fence. Pink roses bloom here. Note the odd placement of the porthole windows on the side wall. Author Kathleen Thompson Norris lived here in the 1920s before moving to New York, where she wrote her best-selling novels. Later a workshop here made embroidered church vestments.

Just up Shrader Street, at **510 Shrader Street**, tucked between two larger neighbors, is an elaborate Eastlake cottage on a raised basement built as late as 1891. Its transoms have very fine stained-glass windows.

Continuation:
Some Haight Street Landmarks, or Golden Gate Park

From here you might either walk up Page Street into Golden Gate Park and McLaren Lodge (*Tour 13*), where you can obtain a map of the vast park, or return to Haight Street, backtracking to browse in its shops and restaurants and to check out the funky street scene.

Number **1779–83 Haight**, near Shrader, consists of a small ground-floor shop and two flats upstairs. It was built in 1893 by the Brooklyn Planning Mill and is the oldest intact building on the strip.

The former Masonic Lodge at **1748 Haight Street**, with shops on its ground floor, is a large, plain three-story building with a cavernous space upstairs. Masonic Lodge No. 449 was organized in 1914 and had its peak membership right before the stock market's Crash of 1929. After a second boom in the post–World War II period, the lodge withered and sold off its building.

Neda's Flowers
1677–81 Haight Street;
552-2920

1736 Haight Street

1701–05 Haight Street at Cole

1635 Haight Street

Neda's Flowers is at Parisian-style **1677–81 Haight**. The two blocks bounded by Haight, Waller, Cole, and Clayton streets were the site of The Chutes amusement park. There a three-hundred-foot inclined plane descended from a seventy-foot height to a small artificial lake. Gondolas were released from the top to rush down the incline and splash in the lake. The Chutes also had a merry-go-round, shooting gallery, bandstand, and a circular "Darwinian Temple" where evolution was popularized. The park closed and the blocks were developed after 1902.

Number **1775 Haight Street** was once the Diggers' free crash pad. At **1736 Haight Street** was the I-Thou Coffee Shop. This block also once housed the Mouse Studios/Pacific Ocean Trading Company, where many psychedelic posters were created. The corner commercial-residential building at **1701–05 Haight Street at Cole** was designed by Charles J. Rousseau for Maurice Rosenthal. The initials MR are worked into the pediment of the corner bay window. On the Cole Street side of the building is Joana Zegri's mural of 1969, *Evolution Rainbow*, restored in 1981 and 1983.

On the southwest corner of Haight and Belvedere at **1635 Haight Street** is the First Interstate Bank, built for the German Savings Bank. It is a neoclassical temple with fine marble counters and wainscotting in a warm, brown-veined marble.

Across the street at **1600 Haight Street** is the façade of the old Superba Theater, built as a nickelodeon in 1911 for J. Van Husen. It has a richly ornamented Beaux Arts façade like a proscenium arch. After serving as a food market, it has been adapted as **Wasteland**, a vintage clothing store.

The Victorian Conservatory of Flowers
in Golden Gate Park was erected in 1878
and stands in an artistically graded garden designed by William Bond Prichard

𝒲hat 𝒯his 𝒯our 𝒞overs
𝒫reliminaries
𝒥ntroduction: 𝒻rom the 𝒞ity to the 𝒮ea

TOUR 13:
GOLDEN GATE PARK
TO
LANDS END

① McLaren Lodge/Park Headquarters

② Fuchsia Garden

③ The Conservatory of Flowers

④ Fern Dell

⑤ John McLaren Memorial Rhododendron Dell

⑥ Music Concourse and Pavilion/California Academy of Sciences/M. H. de Young Memorial Museum/Asian Art Museum/View of Sutro Television Tower

⑦ Japanese Tea Garden

⑧ Strybing Arboretum and Botanical Gardens

⑨ Stow Lake and Strawberry Hill

⑩ Rainbow Falls/Prayerbook Cross

⑪ Lloyd Lake/The Portals of the Past

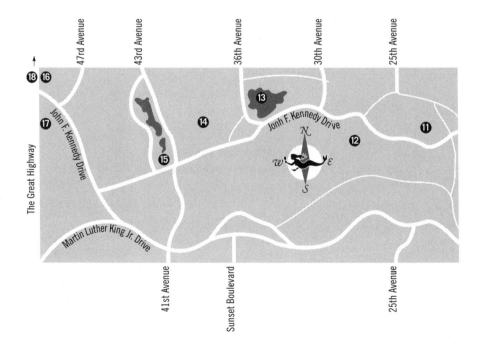

12 Old Speedway/Lindley Meadow

13 Spreckels Lake

14 Buffalo Paddock

15 The Chain of Lakes

16 The Dutch Windmill/Wilhelmina Tulip Garden

17 Beach Chalet Visitor's Center/Lucien Labaudt Murals

18 The Great Highway/Ocean Beach

19 The Cliff House/Seal Rocks (off map; *see Tour 14*)

20 Sutro Heights Park (off map; *see Tour 14*)

21 Land's End/The Golden Gate (off map; *see Tour 14*)

Continuation:

To Lincoln Park and the California Palace of the Legion of Honor,

or back Downtown

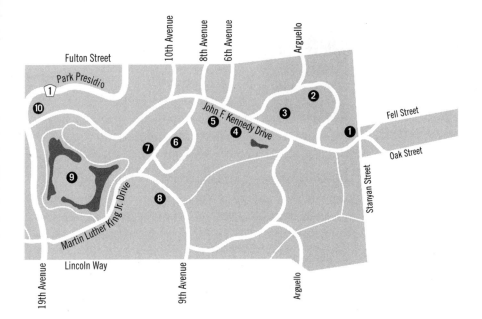

Preliminaries

Friends of Recreation and Parks
McLaren Lodge,
Golden Gate Park,
San Francisco 94117;
Phone 750-5105 for
walks and meeting places

Park Cyclery (Rentals)
1749 Waller Street
Open daily 10 A.M.
to 6 P.M.; 952-8383

Cliff House Restaurant
1090 Point Lobos;
386-3330

BEST TIMES TO DO THIS TOUR

The eastern end of the park fills up on weekends; weekdays are best. **John F. Kennedy Drive** is closed to cars on Sundays from Stanyan Street to Cross Over Drive from 8 A.M. to 6 P.M. The park is sunniest from about 10 A.M. to 3 P.M.; it chills quickly when the fog rolls in. But the fog transforms the park into a landscape of smokelike trees and meadows peopled with only occasional figures. It is also quite special by car on a lightly rainy day when it becomes your vast, private, seemingly tropical garden. The park is relatively safe at night and is quite different viewed in the moonlight. The soothing quality of this romantic landscape awaits the explorer unconventional enough to savor it when others don't.

The volunteer **Friends of Recreation and Parks** conducts free **guided walks** in the park on Saturdays and Sundays at 11 A.M. from May to October, rain or shine. Phone for walks and meeting places.

HOW TO TOUR GOLDEN GATE PARK

The best way to see Golden Gate Park is by bicycle. Bikes and helmets can be rented at **Park Cyclery** for five dollars per hour. Please stay on the designated bike paths and pedal slowly. Those who wish to just sample the park and Ocean Beach should see the Conservatory and the eastern end of the park, and perhaps the de Young Museum and the adjoining Asian Art Museum (there is a café here), and the Japanese Tea Garden next door. (Both museums are free on the first Wednesday of every month.) Then walk north out of the park to Fulton Street and catch the **5 Fulton trolley bus**, which passes along the northern edge of the park to La Playa, the street one short block from Ocean Beach (there is a supermarket here for refreshments). The **18 Forty-sixth Avenue bus** travels north on La Playa up to the **Cliff House Restaurant** then to Sutro Heights and Land's End. At the end of your tour at Forty-eighth Avenue and Geary is the terminus of the **38 Geary bus**, which brings you directly back to Union Square downtown. You can also alight from the 38 Geary at about Twentieth Avenue and walk one block north to Clement Street with its many inexpensive restaurants, including many good Asian places; try **Yet Wah.**

Yet Wah
2140 Clement Street, at Twenty-third
387-8040

Cala supermarket
On Stanyan Street at Haight

Transportation

The quickest way to the park by public transit is to take the **38 Geary bus** to Sixth Avenue and transfer to the southbound **44 O'Shaughnessy bus**, which passes through the Music Concourse. The **21 Hayes trolley bus** turns north at Hayes and Stanyan, one block from McLaren Lodge where this tour begins. The **7 Haight** and the **71 Haight-Noriega** pass up Haight Street to Stanyan at the east end of the park.

Maps

McLaren Lodge and the bookshops of the **de Young Museum**, the **Academy of Sciences**, and the **Strybing Arboretum** sell maps of Golden Gate Park. The free GGNRA map is useful for Land's End and is available at the Visitor Center underneath and behind the **Cliff House**, and also at the **Maritime Store** at the Hyde Street Pier near Fisherman's Wharf, and at **Fort Mason's Visitor Center.**

RESTAURANTS, CAFÉS, AND BARS

The few concessions in the park are fortunately minimal. There is a good café in the **de Young Museum**. It's best to bring your own picnic. There is a **Cala supermarket** at the east end of the park.

Introduction: From the City to the Sea

> The real, the only reason why a great park should be made, is to
> bring the country into the town, and make it possible for the
> inhabitants of crowded cities to enjoy the calm and restfulness
> which only the rural landscape and rural surroundings can give
> .... all other objects must, in a great park, be subordinated to the
> one central, controlling idea of rural repose, which space alone
> can give.
>
> —Charles Sprague Sargent, 1888

Golden Gate Park is a 1,017-acre eden, one of the premier works of Victorian landscape design in North America. In the 1860s this rectangle stretching from the edge of the city to the Pacific was described as "a mass of white, trackless, moving sands, without vegetation, and not pleasing to the senses." What few trees grew here were described as "stunted growths, seemingly ashamed to claim membership in the tree family."

The land transformed into this verdant oasis was originally a fraction of the Outside Lands. Squatters, some in the pay of well-connected land speculators, threw up fences and shacks claiming the city fringes. In 1864, 89.71 percent of the land was deeded to the squatters in exchange for the 10.29 percent reserved for public use, out of which Golden Gate Park was eventually carved.

The early prognosis for Golden Gate Park was not encouraging. The public's tenth had the most sand and the least water: the press dubbed it "The Great Sand Park." When Frederick Law Olmsted, America's foremost landscape architect and the designer with Calvert Vaux of New York City's Central Park, was asked his opinion in 1866, he declared it impossible to create a park. "It would not be wise nor safe to undertake to form a park upon any plan which assumed as a certainty that trees which would delight the eye can be made to grow [in] San Francisco," he said.

Nonetheless, Mayor Frank McCoppin and Governor Haight persisted. (Some claim that McCoppin, the principal stockholder in San Francisco Grading Company, which was then engaged in carting fill from Lone Mountain to the Mission District's swamps, pushed the "impossible" park project in expectation of securing the lucrative contract to grade it dead level.) On April 4, 1870 the California legislature passed AN ACT TO PROVIDE FOR THE IMPROVEMENT OF PUBLIC PARKS IN THE CITY OF SAN FRANCISCO. The governor appointed the first Park Commission and the project was launched. The commission put the topographical survey out to bid and awarded it to twenty-four-year-old surveyor **William Hammond Hall**, who came in with the lowest bid, $4,860. Hall produced a detailed topographic survey and a preliminary park plan in only six months. The commissioners were so pleased that they appointed him the first superintendent of Golden Gate Park in 1871.

William Hammond Hall is the man chiefly responsible for the park's superb landscape design, something he had never done before. He was born in Maryland in 1846 and raised in Stockton, California. He studied surveying and in 1865 joined the Board of Military Engineers. Later, with City Surveyor William P.

Humphreys, he worked on the Outside Lands survey and tramped over the entire western fringe of the city. He served as park superintendent from 1871 to 1876. Through a "leak" to influential General Alexander, Hall frustrated McCoppin's plan to flatten the site. McCoppin never forgot. In 1876 Hall resigned after being wrongly accused by a legislative investigating committee of appropriating park property. Hall went on to a brilliant career as an engineer and worked in central California, Nevada, England, South Africa, the Russian Transcaucasus, Panama, and Turkey. He became California's first State Engineer and sold for a handsome profit land he had bought when he foresaw it would be needed for San Francisco's Hetch-Hetchy water system. He was roasted in the press for this. He died at eighty-eight in 1934.

Hall's immediate problem was holding down the shifting sand in "The Great Sand Park." U.S. Army General Barton S. Alexander had gathered information on European dune reclamation techniques. The first beach grass, *Ammophila arenaria*, was imported from Paris in 1873 and planted on the shifting beach dunes. For most of the park, barley and lupine were sown together on the sand. The quick-sprouting barley held the sand down while the lupine took root.

In 1874 a now-lost casino with a dining hall and private rooms upstairs was built near what is today **Conservatory Drive West**. Operated by a concessionaire, it became a notorious rendezvous. The *San Francisco News Letter* complained in 1886

> [Private concessions have] desecrated the park by providing fast men and women with an enlarged edition of Marchand's. French dinners, high-priced wines, private bedrooms, fast scenes and night orgies are not the aesthetic influences expected to be cultivated by an institution maintained at the public expense, and which, instead of catering to the low, the vulgar and degrading, was expected to, and is well capable of administering to all that is purifying, elevating and ennobling in man's nature.

In 1873 Hall completed the Main—now **Kennedy**—Drive all the way to Ocean Beach. But after Hall's resignation the park was neglected, and between 1876 and 1886 money and greenery dried up. In 1886 Governor Stoneman fired all the park commissioners and called Hall back as consulting engineer. Hall agreed, but only for a year and only in order to hand-pick his successor. He chose a Scottish-born gardener, **John McLaren**, whose fame eventually overshadowed Hall's critical original role.

John McLaren was born in Scotland in 1846 and worked on estates there and at the Royal Botanical Gardens in Edinburgh. He came to America and by 1872 was employed as a gardener on several San Mateo County estates. McLaren dedicated his life to filling out the park plan, planting trees, and outfoxing politicians. In so doing he earned the undying affection of San Franciscans. In 1917, when "Uncle John" reached the city's mandatory retirement age of seventy, an ordinance was passed exempting the superintendent of parks from this rule. His pension was canceled and his salary doubled.

McLaren continued as ruler of the city's expanding park system for twenty-six more cycles of the seasons. He died in 1943, at ninety-six, in the Lodge inside the park he loved so well, and he was laid in state in the City Hall Rotunda for two days of official mourning. He nurtured his beloved park for fifty-six years, defying all the canons of modern "managerial science." He was autocratic, swore at his men (who swore right back), liked his nip of Scotch, lived where he worked, loved what he did, and outlasted all political trends and fads. Stories about the cagey old man with the thick Scottish burr continue to grow like the trees he planted. Of him it can truly be said, "If you seek his monument, look about you."

Golden Gate Park has not stood still in time. The passive contemplation of pastoral scenery has been augmented by active recreational uses. Every special interest wants its own piece of the park. Baseball, polo, tennis, golf, archery, soccer, model yachts, flycasting, professional sports, lawn bowling, kite flying, roller skating, skateboarding, off-road bicycles, model airplanes with noisy motors, and massive rock concerts have invaded the park. The municipality itself is another despoiler: the park has a former police academy and present-day police stables, a senior center, a large stadium with parking, and an odiferous sewage treatment plant inside it. In the 1950s, the State Department of Highways wanted the entire Panhandle and chunks of the rest of the park for a "landscaped" freeway. (The infamous Trafficways Plan of 1951 helped spark the famous "Freeway Revolt" in San Francisco, the first time any American city thwarted the bulldozing of a superhighway through its mature districts.) Museums, fine as they are in themselves, are another invasion, as blockbuster art exhibits flood the fragile park with thousands of automobiles. Every ethnic group wants a highly visible statue to its hero. Every historical interest wants just one more commemorative plaque. Every assassinated president must have a depressing memorial. Today, many (some say hundreds of) homeless people camp in the park, threatening its future.

Hall's plan for a "natural" park involved massive, but undulating, grading of virtually the entire site, section by section. He devised a plan that eventually turned the moving dunes into a stable honeycomb of valleys and low hills to create meadows walled in by windbreaking stands of trees. Each meadow acquired a different designated use, from baseball to polo. Like a grand hotel with many rooms, Golden Gate Park accommodates many, many different activities. But since each is screened by bands of trees, a visually restful landscape is the result.

Golden Gate Park slopes gently from east to west. It can be divided into two parts, with Stow Lake and Strawberry Hill at the center. The eastern end of the park is the oldest and houses the more exotic plants, and also cultural institutions. The western half of the park has more open space, a relaxed landscape, simpler horticulture, and facilities for physical activities that need space, like horseback riding and archery.

Once the land was graded and planted with lupine, trees were set out. Some hundred species of conifers were planted, ranging from the hardy Monterey pine and cypress to Torrey pines and pines from New Zealand. Evergreen conifers were selected because they absorb the moisture in the foggy winds. Many varieties of

Australian eucalyptus were also planted. Flowering and deciduous trees were only infrequently used. Carrying on a worldwide correspondence with botanical gardens, McLaren oversaw a steady exchange of information, seeds, cuttings, and plants. Specimens came from the Mediterranean, South Africa, China, Japan, and in particular Australia and New Zealand.

Golden Gate Park has had a complex history of which most San Franciscans are blissfully unaware. There have been four phases in the history of this park. First was the plutocratic decade from 1871 to 1882 when only those wealthy enough to own horses and carriages had access to the park. The plantings were simple in this period as the young trees were just taking root. The *beau monde* of San Francisco thronged The Avenue in the Panhandle to display their fine horses and fancy carriages and to socialize. The Main Drive to the ocean was a brisk ride and the park was studded with rustic shelters made of logs and branches. The elite park was managed like a rich man's estate and the Park Commission was then a State of California agency.

The second era in the park's evolution opened in 1883 when the Haight Street cable car line (and later other transit lines) made the park accessible to the middle class of the Victorian city. This phase lasted until about 1920. The Park and Ocean Railway along Lincoln Boulevard gave access to the Ocean Beach. The park then was a walker's domain. The east end of the park became an elaborate horticultural wonderland of exotic plants. The transit companies funded the Park Band at the **Music Shell** to draw patrons to their lines during weekends. The **Children's Playground** made the park a magnet for families. Early baseball diamonds and a track served athletes. The park was well funded by the city and well policed.

The third phase is vaguer in its outlines but important in its changes; it lasted from about 1920 to perhaps 1960. During this important era more and more recreational facilities both large and small were constructed in the park and it became less of a sylvan retreat and more the backdrop for active sports. All the classes from the rich to the working class enjoyed the city's principal park. Automobiles became more important than streetcars, and Masonic Avenue and Cross-Over Drive cut the park into segments. The park was still well maintained and actively policed. Even during the hardest days of the Great Depression shantytowns would have been unthinkable in the city's most important park. Abuses, however, did invade the park, the most obnoxious being a sewage plant in the western end of the reservation.

The present phase of the park probably began in the 1960s. By this time large recreational facilities and major museums had reached a critical mass, creating a little "city" in the "natural" park. Institutional expansion became an issue in the fragile landscape. Automobiles can overwhelm the ambiance of the park. Commuters use the park as a short-cut and the east end of the park is functionally now a set of large traffic islands. The University of California medical complex on Sutro Heights has grown enormously and its workers now use the park as an all-day parking lot. A general decline in civility that began in the hippie period saw vandalism increase in this once-sacrosanct eden. People began stealing plants and doing things that would have been unthinkable to previous generations of San Franciscans. Budget

McLaren Lodge/
Park Headquarters
Fell and Stanyan streets

cut-backs hit the park just as its landscape was aging. Slowly but surely the city began to abandon the less-seen sections of the huge park. The critical understory of plants was let go; only the things seen from the automobile were kept up. San Franciscans still love their park and in 1992 passed a $76 million bond issue to update its irrigation system and to plant new trees. But capital budgets are only half the story: gardening and maintenance are the key, and here the city has allowed fatal erosion. The number of gardeners has plummeted from a recent peak of 120 to 79 in 1993, just as the public has become more abusive. Those who know park gardens as more than a tangle of let-go plants will see that parts of the park are becoming a horticultural ruin. There is a loss of vision as well. Scattering red-painted dumpsters in the green landscape is unforgivable. When facilities are rebuilt too much concrete shows. Signage is haphazard, inappropriate, and proliferating. The will to police the park has collapsed. *Today squatters are allowed to make camps in the park's underbrush, something completely new in the city's long history!* A significant number of derelicts now *live* in the fragile man-made park. By default, parks and sidewalks have become the city's homeless "shelters." Public space is the canary in the coal mine, and public space is dying as America becomes a much harsher society.

There are a few hopeful developments as well. Beyond the **Lily Pond** behind the **Fern Dell**, and across **Middle Drive East,** is the former de Laveaga Dell, a fifteen-acre glen originally landscaped by John McLaren in 1921 with a lake and a small stream. It was abandoned as park budgets shrank. In 1992 a plan was approved to bring back this neglected spot and to make it the city's **AIDS Memorial Grove.** This mostly volunteer effort, with individual donations of time and funds, is San Francisco's way of remembering all those lost in the epidemic by bringing back this peaceful, pastoral spot.

There *is* much to enjoy in Golden Gate Park. If you have limited time, the best way to sample Golden Gate Park is to follow Kennedy Drive. As you travel along the wide, winding drive, the romantic theater of nineteenth-century landscaping unfolds. The sequence of views is as thought out as an extended piece of music. Each passage has its mood: from the exotic to the "natural," from the complex to the simple, from the cultural to the recreational, from the dense to the spacious, from the city to the sea.

If you can only do part of the park, walk north to Fulton Street along the park's northern border and catch the 5 Fulton trolley bus headed east back to Market Street downtown, or west to the Ocean Beach.

❶ McLaren Lodge/Park Headquarters, *1896, Edward R. Swain*

At Fell and Stanyan streets, immediately inside the park, is the handsome sandstone, red-tile-roofed headquarters of the **San Francisco Recreation and Park Commission** built in 1896 to designs by Edward R. Swain. It is considered one of the earliest Mission-style buildings. Originally built to house John McLaren and his family to the left and the Park Commission to the right, the Lodge is notable for its restful horizontal lines, porch, loggia, and fine interior.

Enter through the handsome oak door to the counter in the foyer; you can obtain a map of the park here. Ask if you may see the Park Commission's meeting room, a handsome Craftsman interior lined with pigskin and presided over by a large oil portrait of John McLaren. The chairs around the large oak table are especially fine. In 1949 the Playground Commission was merged with the Park Commission to form the Recreation and Park Commission. In 1950 **McLaren Lodge Annex** was built behind the old Lodge. From here San Francisco's superb system of over 215 parks and playgrounds is administered. In front of the Lodge is a lofty Monterey cypress affectionately known as "Uncle John McLaren's Christmas Tree." It is strung with colored lights every December. In 1943, as McLaren lay dying, he requested that despite the war-time blackout the tree be decorated. It was, and he saw it lit for one last time.

McLaren Lodge Annex

Fuchsia Garden

Conservatory of Flowers
Open seven days a week from 9 A.M. to 5 P.M.; there is a small fee; the first and last half-hour of every day is free; 641-7978

Across John F. Kennedy Drive (originally Main Drive) at the intersection of Kezar Drive is a glimpse down a long meadow framed by tall trees. Here is your introduction to the completely artificial, English-style landscape designed by William Hammond Hall. As you proceed west down Kennedy Drive, an artfully planned sequence of such long vistas opens before you and closes as you move on. The great success of this consummate work of landscape art is that most people think all this just happened.

❷ *Fuchsia Garden*

Just beyond the Lodge to the right is Conservatory Drive East. Take the pedestrian path on the left-hand side of Conservatory Drive East to the sign that says "Fuchsia Gardens." The trail to the left into the gardens forks immediately; take the right-hard fork and follow this path through the **Fuchsia Gardens** to the Conservatory of Flowers. The Fuchsia Gardens, begun about 1940; shelter more than 350 varieties under the shade of a tall canopy of trees. The vivid fuchsias bloom from July to August and continue blossoming until October. They are a plant particularly well adapted to San Francisco's cool climate. Gnarled, old fuchsia bushes can be found in the back yards of all the Victorian districts of the city. Their pendant, lanternlike buds explode to display wildly clashing colors: red, pink, white, purple—even fuchsia. This corner of the park was one of the first sections to be landscaped. Rustic picnic shelters built out of tree trunks and twisted branches originally graced this part of the park. The trail can get a little tricky; just keep heading west looking for the great white glasshouse. Just before the Conservatory of Flowers is the Succulent Garden which has recently been restored.

❸ **The Conservatory of Flowers**, *1876, William Bond Prichard, grading plan; 1878, conservatory probably designed by J. P. Gaynor; 1883, John Gash, central dome*

Golden Gate Park's Conservatory of Flowers is the crown jewel of Victorian architecture in Victoriana-rich San Francisco. This white bauble floats behind large flower

Fern Dell

beds laid out before it like oriental carpets. The trees around the Conservatory create perhaps the best arboreal composition in the park. A fascinating view of the glass house can be had from the beautifully designed pedestrian tunnel under Kennedy Drive. Approached from there, the Conservatory appears suddenly like a mirage.

The Conservatory was ordered in 1875 by California real estate magnate **James Lick**, probably from the Hammersmith works in Dublin, Ireland. Lick owned property all over the city and the state, and left bequests to many cultural and educational institutions. He died in 1876 before he could erect the great glass house on his San Jose estate as he had planned. A consortium of wealthy men headed by Leland Stanford (who at the time was seeking permission to build the Park and Ocean Railroad through the southeast corner of the park) donated the prefabricated glass house to the new park. A fire in 1883 destroyed the central dome and its exotic plants; a new, higher dome with insets of colored glass was designed by John Gash. The wood-frame structure rode out the earthquake of 1906 unscathed.

Enter the grand building trying your best to ignore the cacophony of trinkets and souvenir junk that now mars the once-elegant vestibule, formerly graced not with a cash register but with a large carved jardiniere from the Italian cloister of the Panama-Pacific International Exposition. The great central dome protects enormous palm trees and other tropical plants. A band of brilliant flash glass lends just a touch of color, the way a flower brightens a plant. There is an orchid collection here. Walk to the right. The east wing houses fantastic greenery; the pavilion at its far end contains the water lily pond, now unfortunately without the *Victoriana regia* water lily. In the murky pond, fat Japanese carp glitter in the half-light.

Walk back to the central dome and toward the west wing and its end pavilion, where seasonal flowers are displayed at the peak of their bloom. The cycle includes cyclamen, cinerarias, Easter lilies, calceolaria, schizanthus, begonias, chrysanthemums, and poinsettias. An unfortunate "restoration" in the 1970s tore out the intimate, old concrete paths here and installed modern interlocking pavers, an act akin to flooring a landmark Victorian with Astroturf. Some day this too should be removed and the appropriate pavement reinstalled.

Behind the Conservatory are greenhouses and forcing beds off limits to the casual visitor. In front of the Conservatory, great flower beds and the city's floral "welcome mat" display small colored plants arranged to make pictures, a most Victorian custom.

❹ *Fern Dell*

Across Kennedy Drive from the Conservatory is a small, seemingly primeval glade of prehistoric-looking tree ferns, acanthus, and banana trees. It is a delightful Amazonian-looking minijungle; you almost expect to see dinosaurs foraging here. Some of these rare trees probably came from the Panama-Pacific International Exposition of 1915. The best way to get there is to walk straight down the grand staircase of the Conservatory and through the pedestrian tunnel under John F. Kennedy Drive. On the other side of the tunnel take a sharp right; where the paved path forks, take the left fork onto the dirt path which takes you through the heart of the **Fern Dell**.

5 *John McLaren Memorial Rhododendron Dell*

John McLaren Memorial Rhododendron Dell

Music Concourse

Music Pavilion of 1899

Further west on Kennedy Drive is the **John McLaren Memorial Rhododendron Dell**, twenty acres devoted to the Scottish plantsman's favorite flower. McLaren hated statues and spent most of his life fighting the introduction of "stookies," as he called them. His method was to accept them under duress and then to plant low shrubs around them that would eventually envelop them. So, when he died, a statue was erected in his memory. It is a very fine piece of work by M. Earl Cummings and dates from 1911. (The statue was made by Cummings, a park commissioner and sculptor, during McLaren's lifetime, but McLaren had hidden it in a storage shed where it was found after his death.) The stocky Scotsman stands in his tweed, vested suit, with bow tie and goatee. Behind him is the stump of a tree fern that touches the back of the figure; in his hand he holds a pine cone, which he contemplates. As a concession to the subject's well-known hatred of statuary, the green bronze statue stands directly on the ground, not on a pedestal.

Up the drive, nearly hidden in its McLaren-designed setting, is a statue of the Scottish poet **Robert Burns** atop an eight-foot high pedestal. It is also by M. Earl Cummings, a gift of the Scots of San Francisco, and was placed here in 1908. Another well-hidden statue lurks in the bushes at the corner leading to the Music Concourse. It was modeled by Daniel Chester French in 1892 and memorializes **Thomas Starr King**, who lived from 1824 to 1864, a Unitarian minister from Boston who vigorously championed the Union cause and who was the first San Franciscan clergyman to open his pulpit to all faiths. The eight-foot-high, heroic-sized bronze stands atop a pink granite base with one hand on a fasces, symbolic of the Union, and the other holding a bible.

6 Music Concourse and Pavilion

The formally landscaped low depression that is today the **Music Concourse** was designed by engineer Michael M. O'Shaughnessy for the California Midwinter Fair of 1894, held to stimulate the city's economy in the wake of the Depression of 1893. Several large, eclectic pavilions were built around the concourse and a tall steel tower was erected in the center. Two relics survive from the fair on the north side of the Music Concourse: the bronze *Apple Press monument* of 1892, from the French exhibit, and Guillaume Geefs' "pompier" *Roman Gladiator*, dressed in a cloak and helmet and brandishing an upraised sword, cast in 1881. The pair of concrete sphinxes across the road replaced the bronze sphinxes sculpted in 1903 by Arthur Putnam. They once stood before the Egyptian-style art museum inherited from the Midwinter Fair that sat behind the palm grove here.

The oldest structure here is the classically styled **Music Pavilion of 1899** at the western end of the central space, built of Colusa sandstone and designed by the Reid Brothers, with trumpet blowing nudes by Robert I. Aitken. It was the gift of sugar magnate Claus Spreckels. Music is often presented here on Sunday afternoons at 2 P.M. At the opposite end of the concourse is a memorial to **Francis Scott Key**, the lyricist—if that's the word—of our national anthem. It was originally erected in 1887 as part of the James Lick bequest.

California Academy of Sciences, *Open daily, 10 A.M. to 5 P.M.; fee; Phone 750-7145 for current exhibitions*

M. H. de Young Memorial Museum *Open Tuesday to Sunday, 10 A.M. to 5 P.M.; fee; the de Young and the Asian Art Museum are free on the first Wednesday of each month.; Phone 750-3600 for information*

Asian Art Museum *Open Tuesday to Sunday, 10 A.M. to 5 P.M., Wednesday until 8:45 P.M.; fee; Free on the first Wednesday of each month; Phone 668-8921 for information*

The Music Concourse, with its polarded English plane trees, three fountains, and gravel floor, contains the only noticed deciduous trees in evergreen Golden Gate Park. Its formal French axial design is completely different in spirit from the (equally man-made) "natural" English, or romantic, landscaped park in which it is embedded. It gives the park a center, a destination of music, art, and science.

• California Academy of Sciences
The oldest scientific institution on the West Coast, founded in 1853, the **Academy of Sciences** includes a natural history museum, the **Steinhart Aquarium**, the **Morrison Planetarium**, a library, and a research institute. The **Whale Fountain** in the courtyard is by Robert B. Howard and was made for the 1939 Fair on Treasure Island. Many treasures are housed here, including an excellent exhibit on Native Americans with a fine collection of baskets.

• M. H. de Young Memorial Museum
The **M. H. de Young Museum** opened in 1919 (with wings added in 1925) to designs by Louis Christian Mullgardt, replicating his Court of the Ages at the Panama-Pacific International Exposition of 1915. Its elaborate terra-cotta ornament was later stripped off. **Michael Harry de Young** joined his older brother **Charles** to edit the *Daily Dramatic Chronicle*, founded in 1865 as a four-page theater program with a news supplement. In 1868, it became the *Daily Morning and Evening Chronicle*, the ancestor of today's *San Francisco Chronicle*. The de Young brothers' newspaper vigorously promoted the Midwinter Fair, and the profits from the fair created a permanent art museum for the city. In front of the museum is the 1917 **Pool of Enchantment** by M. Earl Cummings, depicting a Native American boy on an island piping to two listening mountain lions. Recently great steel braces have been erected on the exterior of the museum to strengthen it in case of an earthquake. Eventually this humdrum building should be replaced with a modern building, but one not disruptive of the character of the park.

The de Young has many treasures. Pictures from the Kress collection, in particular an El Greco picture of *St. Francis in Ecstasy*, and Mr. and Mrs. Laurence Rockefeller's collection of American painting from the colonial period to about 1900 are outstanding.

• Asian Art Museum
The **Asian Art Museum** of San Francisco is located in a wing of the de Young Museum designed by Gardner A. Dailey and Associates in 1965. Built around the core collection of Chicago insurance man Avery Brundage, this is San Francisco's Asian treasure house. Nearly half of Brundage's collection was of Chinese origin; the Chinese scroll paintings displayed are always very fine. The Magnin Jade Room is extraordinary.

• *View of the Sutro Television Tower*

Japanese Tea Garden
*Open daily from 9 A.M.
to 6:30 P.M.; fee; Free on
the first Wednesday of
each month; 752-1171*

Visible to the south of the Concourse is the nine-hundred-foot-tall
Sutro Television Tower, the tallest structure in San Francisco, erected
in 1973 by a consortium of television stations. Called a candelabra
configuration, the twelve million dollar steel tripod was designed by Albert C. Martin
and Associates in Los Angeles and fabricated in Columbia, South Carolina. On a clear
day it is visible for fifty miles. While a generally unloved structure, its Empire-waisted
design is a fine piece of engineering much more pleasing than the pseudo-Seattle space
needle that the City Planning Commission actually approved.

7 Japanese Tea Garden, *1894, George Turner Marsh*
Beyond the de Young Museum is the famous **Japanese Tea Garden**, begun by Australian-
born George Turner Marsh during the 1894 Midwinter Fair. Marsh spent his teenage
years in Japan and came to San Francisco in 1875, becoming a dealer in Asian art. He
was also an important real estate dealer in property north of the park and built his
house in the wild sand dunes at Twelfth Avenue and Clement Street. He named it after
his birthplace, Richmond, a suburb of Melbourne, hence the name of today's polyglot
Richmond District north of Golden Gate Park. When the Midwinter Fair closed, Marsh
sold his concession to the Park Commission and the popular Japanese garden was
retained. In 1895 Makoto Hagiwara received the concession to operate the teahouse
and the garden, which he did until 1925—with a brief *hiatus* between 1900 and 1908
when anti-Japanese sentiment was rampant in San Francisco.

The five-acre garden has a surprisingly complex horticultural and
architectural history, which this guide can only outline. The eastern half of the garden
dates from the 1894 fair, and the western section was completed in 1916. The two-story
Main Gate (closest to the museum) is called a *roman* and was part of Marsh's Japanese
Village. It was originally built by a Japanese carpenter for Marsh's summer house in
Mill Valley, Marin County. The simpler South Gate was part of the Japanese exhibit
at the Panama-Pacific International Exposition of 1915. The lake in front of the teahouse survives from the 1894 Village. At the teahouse, Jasmine and green teas are
served by kimono-clad women. The ten-and-a-half-foot bronze Buddha with the halo
was cast in Tajima, Japan in 1790 and was the gift of S. & G. Gump & Company in
1949. It represents the *Amazarashi-No-Hotoke*, "The Buddha who sits through sunny
and rainy weather without shelter."

The plants make the Japanese Tea Garden special. Most are from
Japan and some are native to China, though the Monterey pines overhead are
California natives pruned to blend with the Japanese garden. In the garden are Japanese
maples; Chinese magnolia and wisteria; deodar cedars; flowering cherry; Japanese
black, white, and red pine; Japanese flowering quince; Japanese wisteria; timber bamboo; redwood; gincko trees; Korean pines; mock orange; and many other rare exotics,
along with several California natives. From March to May the azaleas are in bloom;
the garden is at its peak in March and April, when the cherry blossoms float over it
like small white-pink clouds. Crowds spoil the garden's mood; in fact, one of the best
times to visit is during the fog or rain when the garden is empty and its borders seem
to vanish in the mist.

Strybing Arboretum and Botanical Gardens

Open 8 A.M. to 4:30 P.M. weekdays; 10 A.M. to 5 P.M. on weekends and holidays; free tour daily at 1:30 P.M.; Phone 661-1316 for information.
• *The information Kiosk sells a complete guide to this living library of plants and also has maps of Golden Gate Park.*

Stow Lake

Strawberry Hill

⑧ Strybing Arboretum and Botanical Gardens

The main entrance to the seventy-acre **Strybing Arboretum and Botanical Gardens** is off South Drive near the Ninth Avenue entrance to the park. However, if you are leaving the Japanese Tea Garden, you can enter the Arboretum through the Friend's Gate across the road from the Tea Garden where Hagiwara Tea Garden Drive meets Martin Luther King, Jr. Drive. After enjoying the Arboretum, exit through the Friend's Gate to continue your tour. The Arboretum was begun with the bequest of Helen Strybing and built in 1937 with WPA funds. The current landscape was designed by Robert Tetlow of the University of California Department of Landscape Architecture between 1959 and 1966. Other landscape architects have designed subsections within the Arboretum. Among the special gardens here are the garden of fragrance with labels in Braille (the mellow weathered limestone walls were built with stones from a medieval Spanish monastery bought by William Randolph Hearst but never assembled), a collection of California native plants, a redwood trail, a fine succulent garden, a Biblical garden, and demonstration gardens, among others. Also located here is the Hall of Flowers, an exhibit hall and the scene of San Francisco's annual August flower show. The congenial Helen Crocker Russell Library of Horticulture was designed by Gardner A. Dailey and Associates in 1967. The gazebo of the demonstration gardens was designed by Thomas D. Church using naturally weathered redwood.

⑨ *Stow Lake and Strawberry Hill*

Stow Lake, built in 1895, is at the center of the park and serves as its principal reservoir. A scenic drive circles the lake and leads to the boathouse, where small boats can be rented and refreshments secured. W. W. Stow was a lawyer and president of the Park Commission and persuaded Collis P. Huntington, one of the Big Four, to donate the funds to construct this fifteen-million-gallon reservoir. (Golden Gate Park requires over four million gallons of water every day to stay green.) In the middle of the lake is **Strawberry Hill**, a natural formation 428 feet high formed by the centuries-long piling-up of sand against an outcrop of ancient chert. The bridge garnished with cyclopean boulders on the south side of the lake was designed by Ernest Coxhead in the 1890s. A gentle dirt roadway corkscrews its way to the top of Strawberry Hill. On the east side of the hill is Huntington Falls, which cascades from a smaller reservoir atop the hill into the lake, one of two artificial waterfalls in Golden Gate Park. Strawberry Hill is thickly wooded with cypress, eucalyptus, and long-leafed acacia. Through the trees are tantalizing glimpses of the white city spread all around the verdant park. To the northwest you can glimpse the twin red piers of the Golden Gate Bridge with Mt. Tamalpais in the distance. Descending Strawberry Hill, you get a distant view of the golden onion domes of Russian Orthodox Cathedral of the Holy Virgin on Geary Boulevard in the Richmond District.

⑩ Rainbow Falls/ Prayerbook Cross

Rainbow Falls

Celtic cross

Lloyd Lake

Portals of the Past

Old Speedway Meadow

On Kennedy Drive north of Stow Lake is **Rainbow Falls**, an artificial waterfall built in the 1930s. John McLaren once noted that he often went on walks in the countryside, and when he found a striking effect in nature such as a "bonnie brook," he would attempt to duplicate it in the park. Atop the bluff behind the falls is a fifty-seven-foot tall **Celtic cross** carved from Colusa sandstone and designed by Ernest Coxhead. It was dedicated at the opening of the Midwinter Fair of 1894 and commemorates the first Anglican service held in California by Sir Francis Drake's chaplain, Francis Fletcher in June 1579, perhaps at Drake's Bay north of San Francisco.

⑪ Lloyd Lake/The Portals of the Past

Cross-Over Drive, built in 1936, cuts the park in half. On its other side, on the north side of Kennedy Drive, is **Lloyd Lake**, named for an executive of the Southern Pacific Railroad and a former park commissioner. Reflected on its tranquil surface are the six Ionic columns known as the **Portals of the Past**. They once framed the entrance to the A. N. Towne residence atop Nob Hill (*see Tour 7*). That elegant house was consumed in the flames after the earthquake of 1906. A photographer took a picture of the city's ruins through the surviving columns and entitled it "The Portals of the Past." In 1909 the portico was reerected here to create this dreamy and romantic set piece. It is San Francisco's only architectural monument to the catastrophe of 1906.

⑫ Old Speedway/Lindley Meadow

The large meadow across Kennedy Drive from Lloyd lake is called **Old Speedway Meadow**, surely an oxymoron. The bicycle path that runs through it follows the alignment of the old Speedway, a racetrack built for horses and carriages that was immensely popular with speed demons in the Victorian period. The Speedway was the first instance of a private interest group—the owners of racehorses—securing a piece of the park for their exclusive use. It leads to the Golden Gate Park Stadium, originally the Polo Field, another aristocratic usurpation. The Polo Field was carved out of the park in 1906. There, in 1911, President William Howard Taft ceremoniously broke ground for the Panama-Pacific International Exposition. After vigorous protests, the great Exposition was built on bayfill in the Marina District rather than inside fragile Golden Gate Park. The Human Be-In/Gathering of the Tribes was held in Golden Gate Park Stadium on January 14, 1967, the first event to attract massive media attention to the Haight-Ashbury hippies.

Lindley Meadow

Spreckels Lake

Model Yacht Club House

Buffalo Paddock

Next up Kennedy Drive is **Lindley Meadow**. The curving, flowing drive and the relaxed, informal placement of the stands of sheltering eucalyptus and cypress trees knit the park's sections into a harmonious whole. A casual traveler through the vast park might think it nothing but trees and lawns, so well hidden are its many and varied uses. Across Lindley Meadow rises a totemic sculpture, *The Goddess of the Forest*, carved in 1939 for the Treasure Island fair by Dudley C. Carter. It was carved out of a single redwood log as an example of art-in-action. The goddess is represented as a crouching nude female figure supporting a bear (California's emblem) in her lap, and holding an owl in her hands; an eagle protects the back of her head. The unvarnished redwood has achieved the soft, grayish-green patina characteristic of the way wood weathers in Northern California's climate. Like some enormous fetish, the goddess is accumulating the paired initials of lovers all around her base. She seems contented with the view.

13 Spreckels Lake

Further west along Kennedy Drive is **Spreckels Lake**, the model-yacht pond, completed in 1904 and named after Park Commissioner Adolph Bernard Spreckels, who later with his wife donated the Palace of the Legion of Honor in Lincoln Park. The lake is held up like a shimmering, reflecting platter with views of the stuccoed Richmond District visible through a thin screen of cypress trees. At the intersection with Thirty-sixth Avenue is the **Model Yacht Club House** erected by the WPA in 1938, an agreeable period piece.

Not visible from here, facing Fulton Street at the head of Thirty-seventh Avenue, is the Senior Center, originally the San Francisco Police Academy, an elegant little jewel of a building designed by John Reid, Jr. in the Beaux Arts manner favored under Mayor James Rolph's nineteen-year-long administration. Would that all civic buildings were as fine. John McLaren, who resisted putting nonpark buildings in his preserve, put the building here to keep the city from cutting a road across the park.

14 Buffalo Paddock

Next to Spreckels Lake and to the right is the **Buffalo Paddock**. Here stands a small herd of buffalo, an institution in the park since 1892. The buffalo are large, shaggy, unwieldy-looking creatures that stand motionless. The sudden apparition of them, especially if you come across them in the fog, is altogether surreal. Before the opening of the Fleischhacker Zoo in the 1930s, Golden Gate Park was something of a menagerie with an aviary, goats, moose, elk, deer, kangaroos, bears, seals, elephants, and sheep. Only the nearly catatonic buffalo remain. As the park's forests have mutated, however, skunks, raccoons, and other small mammals have moved in and now flourish here.

15 The Chain of Lakes

Beyond the Buffalo Paddock and just past the cross street on your right is the entrance to the **Chain of Lakes** trail. If you walk this pleasant loop trail you will come back to where you started on John F. Kennedy Drice. The Chain of Lakes, three artistically landscaped reservoirs, was completed in 1909 to John McLaren's designs. The six islands in the North Lake were originally each differently landscaped. The tiny islets are disposed with all the art of a few rocks in a Japanese garden. Swamp cypress indigenous to Florida's Everglades grow here in the water. Beyond North Lake the trees are planted along Kennedy Drive in straight rows, the only reminder that all of this is the work of human hands. To the north is the pitch-and-putt golf course. At the intersection with South Drive turn right, passing the large Soccer Field, which attracts an international gathering on weekends. Before the development of the park, there was a large tidal lake where the Soccer Field is today.

Chain of Lakes

Dutch Windmill

Queen Wilhelmina Tulip Garden

Beach Chalet Visitor's Center/Lucien Labaudt Murals
Visitor's Center in the downstairs portion; Phone the Friends of Recreation and Parks at 221-1311 for hours and information

16 The Dutch Windmill/Wilhelmina Tulip Garden

Continue west along John F. Kennedy Drive and follow it as it turns right, taking you to the windmill. At the northwestern corner of the park stands the **Dutch Windmill** designed by Alpheus Bull and erected in 1902. Because the park consumes large amounts of water, and because the monopolistic Spring Valley Water Company charged high rates, the park commissioners sought their own water supply. As it happens, an underground river runs under parts of the park; in 1902 the Dutch Windmill was constructed to tap this source. It was designed as a utilitarian yet picturesque addition to the park. It was one of the largest sail windmills in the world, with sails 114 feet across; it pumped thirty thousand gallons of water an hour. It was so successful that a second windmill was donated to the park by Samuel G. Murphy and built in 1905. After the city bought the water company in 1930, the mills fell into disuse and eventually lost their blades. In 1981 the Dutch Windmill was restored, though alas, it is strictly decorative and no longer pumps water. (The Murphy Windmill at the southwest corner of the park remains bladeless.) The Dutch Bulb Growers Association sends hundreds of tulip bulbs each year to plant the **Queen Wilhelmina Tulip Garden**, which is at its peak in April.

17 Beach Chalet Visitor's Center/Lucien Labaudt Murals

Facing the Great Highway, at the west end of Golden Gate Park, is the Beach Chalet, designed by Willis Polk in 1921. Inside this two-story, red-tile-roofed, white pillared structure is some of the finest public art in the city, a series of frescoes executed by Lucien Labaudt in 1936–37. They cover all four walls of the ground floor bar and make a complete tour of the city. Their theme is play and recreation and they complement the Coit Tower frescoes devoted to the working life of California (*see Tour 4A*).

Great Highway

Ocean Beach

Over the inside of the front door is a phrase from a poem of Bret Harte's, "Serene, indifferent of fate thou sittest at the Golden Gate." The scene surrounding the front entrance shows a man feeding pigeons and a woman knitting a sweater in Union Square. Step to the left. The next figure, an architect standing between the two windows, shows Arthur Brown, Jr., San Francisco's master builder. He holds the plans for Coit Tower, another public embellishment of the 1930s. Behind him rises the Beaux Arts Civic Center and his magnificent City Hall, fittingly the finest building in the city. A Corinthian capital is at his feet and steelwork rises behind him.

Next, in the southwest corner, are boaters at the St. Francis Yacht Harbor. The quotation here, from Joaquin Miller, reads, "Sails are furled from furthest corners of the world." To the left are sightseers at Land's End looking out at the Golden Gate. A ship lies wrecked on the rocks below. On the headlands rises the Moderne, vaguely Mayan Veterans' Hospital built in 1933. Also visible are Baker Beach and the Presidio.

On the wall over the right-hand side of the bar is a large fresco depicting recreation in Golden Gate Park. From left to right in the background are visible the Portals of the Past, the Conservatory, the de Young Museum, and the Japanese Tea Garden. In the foreground, among all the users of the park, is a man in a green plaid tweed suit who appears to be blessing and accepting a new seedling. It is "Uncle John" McLaren. In the center of this wall, over the bar, is a quote from Ina Coolbrith, "Fair city of my love and my desire." At bar level is a small painted-in plaque that reads, "Federal Art Project 1936–1937, Lucien Labaudt." The left side of the bar represents picnickers at Land's End with the Marin hills in the distance and a single pier of the unfinished Art Deco Golden Gate Bridge, completed in 1937. In the corner of the north wall is a scene showing the catching and selling of crabs at Fisherman's Wharf. The quotation is from George Sterling and reads, "At the end of our streets, the stars." In the corner to the left is a waterfront scene at Pier 26 with docks, sailors, and fishermen. The man pushing the car was the then-controversial head of the Longshoremen's Union, leftist, Australian-born Harry Bridges (later a port commissioner). Completing the cycle is a view with Chinatown in the background and a policeman and a florist in the foreground. It is a thought-provoking pairing, which represents perhaps the tough and the gentle, the full spectrum of life in the big city.

18 The Great Highway/Ocean Beach

The 18 Forty-sixth Avenue bus runs along the **Great Highway** from the western edge of Golden Gate Park up to the Cliff House, and then down Point Lobos Avenue to the Legion of Honor art museum in Lincoln Park. Or you can walk the approximately four blocks to the Cliff House and Seal Rocks.

Tawny **Ocean Beach** is a favorite place of release and relaxation for San Franciscans. Many bus lines end near it, bringing people of all ages to this, the edge of the continent. The water is cold and the undertow here very dangerous, but the air is brisk and clean and the waves soothing, their rhythm relaxing. Brown pelicans can be spotted diving for fish. Dogs romp in the surf. Lovers walk by the edge of the sea.

The city reserved the Ocean Beach in 1868 as public land and fought private encroachments. When the Park and Ocean Railroad that ran along Lincoln Way was completed in December of 1883, the beach suddenly became accessible for ten cents. Previous to that, expensive carriage rides were the only way out here—many poor people lived and died in San Francisco without ever having seen the Pacific. The Great Highway was named in 1874 and stretches from the Cliff House to the north and to the San Francisco Zoo to the south.

Cliff House

Camera Obscura

Seal Rocks

Farallones

⑲ *The Cliff House/Seal Rocks*

The current **Cliff House** is, unfortunately, a drab building. It is the fifth building on this site; the first was erected in 1858. Alas, it is nothing like the bold French-château-on-a-rock that Adolph Sutro erected here in 1896 and that burned in a spectacular fire in 1907. That confection, designed by C. J. Colley and F. S. Lemme, is the one lost architectural work that lives on in the city's collective memory and in countless postcards that still sell well. A seven-story gingerbread pile perched improbably on its high rock, it summed up the daring act of building on the barren, isolated, arid San Francisco peninsula. The late Victorians knew flamboyance, and *this* was flamboyant. It was hallucinatory by day and glittered like a beacon at night. Would that some philanthropist would give it back to San Francisco just the way it was! The GGNRA operates a Visitor Center tucked away in the base of the building, near the **Camera Obscura**, where you can get the fine GGNRA map and other informative brochures on the wildlife offshore here.

The splendid site remains as dramatic as ever. The surf boils amid the jagged rocks below. Local "surf rats" can often be seen surfing in Kelly's Cove just south of the Cliff House. Ryan Ragan, a surfer from Noe Valley, describes it as "thick, grinding, hollow, fast, hard-core. Maybe the gnarliest beach break in the world." Some intrepid local surfers even surf in the Four Fathom Shoal, also known as the Potato Patch, the choppy waters *outside* the Golden Gate. The beach far down across from the end of Sloat Boulevard is another favorite spot with "soul surfers."

Four hundred feet offshore are the **Seal Rocks**, a favorite rendezvous for Stellar sea lions and marine birds. The lusty barking of the gregarious, polygamous seals is a happy sound; like the cable cars and the fog horns, they provide passages in San Francisco's unique music. The Seal Rocks were the apple of Adolph Sutro's eye and he kept people from hunting the fur-bearing sea lions. Deeded by Congress to the city in 1887, the rocks were placed under the protection of the Park Commission.

Visible to the north is the magnificent sweep of the mountainous, untouched shore of Marin County, all part of the GGNRA. On clear days the **Farallones**, seven small rocky islands thirty-two miles offshore, can be spied on the horizon. A U.S. Light Station was established atop Beacon Peak there in 1855. Murre eggs were gathered on the Farallones until the federal government banned all egg gathering in 1897. President Theodore Roosevelt made a Federal Bird Reserve in 1907. Today some 250,000 sea birds nest on the rocks.

Point Lobos

Sutro Baths

Sutro Heights Park

Immediately north of the Cliff House, between it and rocky **Point Lobos**, lie the concrete ruins of the pools of **Sutro Baths**. Also built by Adolph Sutro and opened in 1896, the baths covered three acres and boasted the world's largest indoor pools of both fresh and salt water. Inside the baths were terraces with parterres planted with rare flowers and shrubs. This resort closed in 1952 and burned in 1966. An artistic, ultramodern, glass-enclosed swimming pool should be built here. The location is incomparable.

20 *Sutro Heights Park*

Across the Great Highway from the Cliff House is a parking lot and bus shelter and, beyond them, a path into **Sutro Heights Park**, today another unit of the GGNRA. On the grounds are a delightful Victorian kiosk and a terraced overlook on the summit. On the wind-sheltered south side of the peak is a rock garden filled with blooming plants.

Adolph Sutro was one of the most remarkable men of nineteenth-century San Francisco, a man of vision, determination, achievement, and lasting good works. Born to a wealthy Jewish textile manufacturer in Aix-la-Chapelle (Aachen, Prussia) in 1830, he studied mineralogy in his native city. In the reactionary wake of the revolutions of 1848, the entire Sutro family migrated to Baltimore, then a great German magnet. Adolph moved further west to San Francisco, arriving in 1850. He ran a tobacco store, something of a German specialty, and then went to Nevada when the Comstock silver bonanza was discovered. There he saw the chronic flooding and the foul air of the early mines and set about to devise the better system. He conceived of a tunnel that would run under the separate mines to drain and ventilate them and formed The Tunnel Company, incorporated in Nevada in 1865. After many reversals and battles, the great engineering feat was completed in 1869 and a ten-foot-high, twelve-foot-wide, three-mile-long tunnel (with two miles of lateral branches) was installed, improving conditions for the miners. The Tunnel Company exacted a royalty of from $1 to $2 per ton of ore mined, and made Sutro rich.

In 1879 Sutro sold his shares in the Sutro Tunnel and invested his "colossal fortune" in San Francisco real estate. He bought undeveloped, sandy wastes that he spent the rest of his life developing and planting with trees. From the French Bank he bought extensive property around San Francisco's Point Lobos, where potatoes had been cultivated in the 1840s. Sutro eventually owned one-twelfth of all the land in San Francisco, including the great San Miguel Rancho that encompassed Twin Peaks and all the city's central hills.

Here at Sutro Heights, in the remote northwest corner of the city, he engineered a waterworks, built a now-lost mansion, planted gardens (crowded with atrocious statuary), assembled a great scientific library (parts of which survive as the Sutro Library near San Francisco State University) and art collection, and then threw the lavish grounds open to the public. He served as a reform Populist mayor from 1894 to 1896. In 1898, sadly, he was declared incompetent, and he died at sixty-

eight. Sutro was a freethinker, a voracious reader, a man with a sci-   **Land's End**
entific bent, a creative businessman, and a great philanthropist. He
was the child of an age that believed in Progress.

㉑ *Land's End/The Golden Gate*

Off the Great Highway, north of the Cliff House and Sutro Heights Park, is Merrie
Way, now a paved parking lot with a spectacular view that offers a good place to watch
the sunset and afterglow. Paths beyond the parking lot lead to the disused roadbed of
the Ferries & Cliff House Railway, which circumnavigated these precipitous cliffs.
Point Lobos, the westernmost tip of the San Francisco peninsula, was named by the
Spanish for the sea lions, mistaken for seals (*lobos marinos*) that once thrived here.

    Land's End, today part of the GGNRA, is a wild and broken shore,
especially interesting in the winters when the rains cause the tiny wild flowers that
grow here to blossom. This scenic corner of the city has a fine view of the Golden Gate
and the Marin shore. Steep paths lead down to the water where great rocks break the
pounding surf. Many ships have foundered here; at low tide, the periscope of an
unlucky submarine can be spotted. The trails lead to Lincoln Park with its public golf
course and the **Legion of Honor Museum** (*see Tour 14*).

**California Palace of the
Legion of Honor**

Continuation:
*To Lincoln Park and the California Palace
of the Legion of Honor, or back Downtown*

From the Cliff House the 18 Forty-sixth Avenue bus heads east and north to Lincoln Park, ending in front of the **California Palace of the Legion of Honor**. You can also walk up Point Lobos Avenue, turn right at Forty-eighth Avenue (at the Seal Rock Inn) to the end of Geary Boulevard and the 38 Geary bus which takes you straight east to Union Square or Market Street.

Fort Point, built in 1853–61 to designs by the U.S. Army Corps of Engineers, was originally surmounted by 149 cannon in four tiers. Joseph B. Strauss, the chief engineer of the Art Deco Golden Gate Bridge, built in 1933–37, designed a great steel arch to preserve the landmark fort.

396   *San Francisco—The Ultimate Guide*

What This Tour Covers
Preliminaries

TOUR 14:
THE PRESIDIO
AND
ALONG THE
GOLDEN GATE

1. Marina Boulevard/Marina Green
2. The Palace of Fine Arts/Memories of the 1915 Fair/ The Exploratorium
3. The Presidio of San Francisco: Red, White, and Green/ Lombard Street Gate and Trophies
4. U.S. Army Presidio Museum/Refugee Cottages
5. Funston Avenue Victorian Officers' Quarters: American Architectural Benchmarks
6. Pershing Hall
7. Old Protestant Chapel/Roman Catholic Chapel of Our Lady/Site of the Spanish and Mexican Presidio
8. Officers' Open Mess/Old Comandancia
9. Pershing Square: Flag and Focal Point
10. Montgomery Street Enlisted Men's Barracks: Brick Row
11. Parade Ground/Centennial and Bicentennial Trees
12. Post Chapel and WPA Murals
13. San Francisco National Military Cemetery
14. Fort Point/The Seawall
15. The Golden Gate Bridge: Art Deco Masterpiece/ Golden Gate Bridge Vista Points
16. Lincoln Boulevard to Baker Beach/ Battery Chamberlin Disappearing Gun
17. El Camino Del Mar/Sea Cliff/China Beach
18. Lincoln Park/California Palace of the Legion of Honor

Continuation

The Bus Downtown, or a Nature Walk

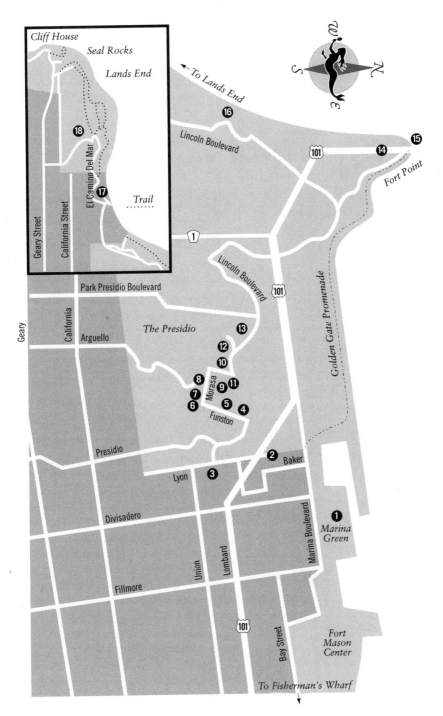

The Presidio and Along the Golden Gate

U.S. Army Presidio Museum
*Tuesday to Sunday,
10 A.M. to 4 P.M.*

Preliminaries

BEST TIMES TO DO THIS TOUR

The days when the **U.S. Army Presidio Museum** are open, are the best times to visit the Presidio. Veterans' Day on November 11 is the most moving day to visit. Each of the graves in the National Cemetery is decorated with a small flag on that day and commemorative ceremonies are held there.

Parking

There is usually ample parking available at the Presidio.

Transportation: By Public Transit

The heart of the Presidio can be seen by foot and reached by public transit. Take the **45 Greenwich electric trolley bus** on Sutter Street a block north of Union Square to its terminus at Lyon and Greenwich; from there transfer to the **45 shuttle bus** and ask the driver to let you off at Lincoln Boulevard and Funston Avenue across the street from the U.S. Army Museum. The **29 Sunset bus** also stops at Lincoln Boulevard and Funston Avenue, and it proceeds to the Golden Gate Bridge Toll Plaza, where you can alight near the view area. The bus continues along Lincoln Boulevard on the scenic bluffs on the Pacific coast side of the huge post, then passes across the Richmond District along Twenty-fifth Avenue and into the middle of Golden Gate Park near Stow Lake.

By Car

A leisurely automotive exploration with a good map along the winding scenic roads and past the many buildings and fortifications is the best way to see the spacious Presidio. Allow frequent stops to inspect sites and enjoy panoramas. Virtually all the grounds are open to the public twenty-four hours a day. Enter through the **Lombard Street Gate** with its sandstone carvings of Liberty and Victory, flanked by antique Spanish bronze cannons. Pass the modern Letterman Army Medical Center and continue to the white clapboard Army Museum at Lincoln Boulevard and Funston

Avenue. Park here at the museum. Ask the museum guard where you can secure a map of the post. Then walk up Funston Avenue to the intersection with Presidio Boulevard to examine the two exemplary groups of Victorian officers' quarters that line the landscaped street. Return to your car to continue up Funston to the original site of the Mexican presidio. See Fort Point, and then drive along scenic Lincoln Boulevard. There is a fine view point along the road's shoulder near Battery Dynamite.

Marina Boulevard

Marina Green

**The Palace of Fine Arts/
Memories of the 1915 Fair**
Baker and Beach streets

❶ *Marina Boulevard/Marina Green*

Marina Boulevard passes through a vast tract of tidal marsh filled in for the 1915 Panama-Pacific International Exposition, part of which became **Marina Green**, a favorite sunbathing spot popular on sunny weekends. That great one-year-long fair, the most elaborate San Francisco ever saw or ever will see, officially celebrated the opening of the Panama Canal but actually celebrated the rapid and booming rebuilding of the city between 1906 and 1915.

For the exposition, vast wood-and-plaster palaces were built, classically decorated on the outside, plain timber sheds on the inside. These were the Palace of Fine Arts, of which a replica survives, the Palace of Horticulture, the Great Palace of Machinery, the Palace of Education and Social Economy, the Palace of Liberal Arts, the Palace of Manufacture and Varied Industries, the Palace of Transportation, the Palace of Agriculture, and the Palace of Mines and Metallurgy. Extensive landscaped courts and colonnades linked the huge palaces. The fair was a dream of Inevitable Progress, a dream that had died the year before with the outbreak of World War I.

Along Marina Boulevard, with its lots looking over the Marina Green to the Bay, grand houses and flats have been built from the 1920s to the present, many in stucco. In the Marina District, stucco predominates as the exterior building material. It is less expensive than wood and is easily patched and maintained. Painted light colors, stucco reflects the light and the skies.

❷ The Palace of Fine Arts/Memories of the 1915 Fair, *1915, Bernard Maybeck, original building and landscaping; 1962–75, William G. Merchant and others, replication in concrete*

Floating like a dream across a pond dotted with exotic ducks is the huge, freestanding rotunda and colonnade of Bernard Maybeck's **Palace of Fine Arts of 1915**. This Beaux Arts hallucination was built for the Panama-Pacific International Exposition and outlasted the temporary materials it was originally made of. It was replicated—and simplified—in reinforced concrete between 1962 and 1975. It took a philanthropist, Walter S. Johnson, who lived across the street and loved the building, plus a 1959 city bond issue and matching funds from the State of California to raise the money to preserve this architectural extravagance for San Francisco.

Exploratorium
3601 Lyon Street at
Bay, behind the Palace
of Fine Arts; Phone
561-0360 for hours

The Presidio of San
Francisco

Park and walk along the giant colonnade to the lofty, open rotunda. Imagine an endless-seeming series of such triumphal spaces from here to Fort Mason. That was the Panama-Pacific International Exposition of 1915. The elevated planter boxes with the draped female figures looking downcast were sculpted by Ulric Ellerhusen and represent "the melancholy of life without art." The boxes were intended to hold trees and vines, enfolding the Palace in plants. Around the exterior of the dome are rectangular panels showing a nude woman, representing Art, being defended by nude men (Idealists) battling centaurs (Materialists). The Panama-Pacific International Exposition provided an endless stream of such didactic art; guidebooks explained their recondite and intricate symbolism to the public. As relief from all this uplift, The Zone, an amusement park of "a necessary garishness," as the fair directors put it, was carefully designed at the east end of the fairgrounds. The Zone had six thousand feet of commercial footage along a Midway lined with attractions.

• **Exploratorium**

Behind the rotunda and colonnade is the great semicircular, shedlike pavilion originally used to display academic paintings and sculpture. Today it houses the **Exploratorium**, a science museum organized around the theme of human perception. It is especially enjoyable for families with children.

❸ *The Presidio of San Francisco: Red, White, and Green*

The Presidio of San Francisco, a spacious 1,480-acre reserve with seventy miles of scenic roads set on the heights commanding the Golden Gate, is a garden city set in its own buffering forest. The Army created a model installation on this enormous reserve at the most scenic spot of the Bay Area. The Presidio embodies the power of the state and prominence of the military in the creation and sustenance of San Francisco. The Presidio of San Francisco is a great treasure for the student of American history, landscape design, architecture, and military industrial technology. Every period of American building from the 1850s on is preserved somewhere here.

Once principally a fortification, the Presidio evolved into an administrative headquarters and a medical center with an important hospital and adjoining scientific research institute. Today it is the headquarters of the Sixth Army and has a commissary, Officers' Club, and golf course for active and retired military. It employs about seven hundred military and civilian personnel.

On September 17, 1776, **José Joaquín Moraga** established a *presidio,* or fort, here; it was the third of four in Alta California (the San Diego fort was established in 1769; Monterey in 1770; San Francisco in 1776; and Santa Barbara in 1782). Presidios were frontier outposts of the Spanish Empire centered in Madrid. The Presidio was placed here in a global imperial chess game: Spain garrisoned this distant peninsula to keep Russia or Britain from gaining a foothold on San Francisco Bay. From here four missions, two *pueblos* (towns with their own government), a rancho, and an *asistencia* (outlying branch of a mission but without a resident priest) were founded.

The presidio garrisons forced wandering Native   **Fort Point**
American bands into mission *rancherías,* or settlements, next to
the missions. There Franciscan priests Christianized them and
taught them subsistence agriculture and herding. The adobe quadrangle at the presidio
of San Francisco had its own chapel separate from that of Mission Dolores at approximately the site of today's Roman Catholic chapel on Moraga Avenue near the head
of Funston Avenue.

In 1822, by accession, this fort became the northernmost outpost
of the new Mexican Republic. Spanish imperial regulations required that ships visiting San Francisco Bay anchor near the Presidio, in an area of what is now landfill near
today's Beach and Divisadero streets, in the Marina District. In December of 1824
strong ebb tides resulting from unusually heavy freshets made this anchorage dangerous. Visiting ships, mostly British and Yankee whalers, shifted to Richardson Bay off
Sausalito or Yerba Buena Cove (today's Financial District). Mexico became more con-
cerned with routes of overland migration than seaports when Yankee pioneer wagon
trains suddenly began to appear on this side of the Sierra. In 1835 Mexico abandoned
the Presidio in San Francisco and shifted its frontier garrison northward to Sonoma
(now Sonoma State Historic Park). The unmaintained adobe cluster at the Presidio of
San Francisco washed into ruins.

In March 1847, during the war with Mexico, two companies of the
U.S. Army's New York Volunteers occupied the derelict Presidio and rebuilt its adobe
buildings, adding cleaner roofs with wood shakes, better windows, and wood floors.
But by August 1848 the Presidio lay abandoned again, not to be reoccupied for sev-
eral years. On November 6, 1850, President Fillmore set aside for harbor defenses a
vast tract of the northwest tip of the San Francisco peninsula, from what is now
Aquatic Park to approximately the ocean end of Golden Gate Park—plus Alcatraz,
Angel, and Yerba Buena islands in the Bay. San Franciscans protested the tremendous
size of the new military reserve and on December 15, 1851 Fillmore cut back the
Presidio and Fort Mason to their present boundaries.

The Army built a few frame buildings for a new post in the late
1850s, replacing the inherited adobes (the last fell in the 1906 earthquake). Most of
the budget of the 1850s, however, went into constructing massive red-brick, granite,
and iron **Fort Point**, a French-style fort. Little was done at the Presidio itself until
1862–63 when Army engineers, using the old Mexican quadrangle as a southeast corner, laid out a parade ground oriented from the southwest to the northeast, looking
down the sheltered valley to San Francisco Bay. That vast rectangle of space is one of
the Bay Area's most magnificent pieces of landscape design and remains the core of
the Army post. To the east of the parade ground, a row of plain frame or Greek Revival
duplex Officers' Quarters was built in 1862. The officers' quarters on the east side of
the parade ground, commodious barracks on the west side, and ceremonial buildings
and a flagpole at the head of the parade ground completed the expansion.

Immediately after the Civil War in 1865, the Army turned its attention to Indian subjugation in the West. During the Indian Wars, conducted from 1865
to 1890, the Army's Department of the Pacific moved its headquarters from down-

Julius Kahn Playground

San Francisco National Military Cemetery

Presidio Army General Hospital

town San Francisco to the Presidio. Troops billeted at the Presidio for the Modoc War in 1870 and the campaigns against the Apaches in the Southwest. In the 1870s, the Army opened the Presidio grounds to the public and it soon functioned as an unofficial auxiliary to the city's parks, in particular for wealthy neighboring Pacific and Presidio heights. (The city's **Julius Kahn Playground** at Pacific Avenue and Spruce Street, inside the Presidio wall, still serves as the playground for the city's wealthiest neighborhood.)

In March of 1883, Major W. A. Jones of the Army Corps of Engineers initiated a massive program of forestation with his landscape plan for the treeless, wind-swept, sandy Presidio. As a work of landscape design—here truly "environmental design"—Major Jones' plan ranks with that of Golden Gate Park for beauty and utility. Jones' plan called for planting the ridges of the hills with pine, cypress, acacia, and euca-lyptus to create the illusion of a continuous forest larger than it is—and it is large. His dark forests provided the yin for the yang of the open parade ground. The headlands were threaded with view drives, today's scenic Lincoln Boulevard with its panoramic view of the Golden Gate.

In 1884, the Army designated the Presidio burial ground on the hill overlooking the parade ground a National Military Cemetery. Originally ten acres, the **San Francisco National Military Cemetery** now covers 28.3 acres within its precise rectan-gular encampment.

Between 1890 and 1914, the Presidio was rebuilt and improved. Many frame buildings gave way to permanent brick, stone, and concrete structures. The outstanding row of red-brick barracks with white trim on Montgomery Street along the western edge of the Parade Ground was built between 1895 and 1897. In the mid-1890s, the Army began the construction of modern reinforced concrete and earthwork batter-ies, mounting giant guns to replace obsolete Fort Point. Experimental Battery Dynamite, which shot charges of explosives, was constructed in 1894–95. The Presidio's batteries were only a part of a much larger system of seacoast and harbor fortifications armed with breech-loading rifled artillery. These defenses preempted vast tracts of land and expanded greatly in the 1890s. Without their guns, the batteries—the third wave of for-tification of San Francisco Bay—are historical sites today and have been incorporated into the GGNRA.

In 1899 the **Presidio Army General Hospital** was established for sick and wounded American soldiers infected during the subjugation of the U.S. colony in the Philippines, which America took from Spain. That early hospital, designed by San Francisco architect W. H. Wilcox and built between 1899 and 1902, was a model of mod-ern hospital design with natural ventilation, sunlight, and gardens woven into its pavil-ion design. Most of it was thoughtlessly demolished in 1975. A fragment of the hospital with its agreeable lowrise wings and courts survives along General Kennedy Avenue west of the new midrise Letterman hospital built in 1969. Adjoining Letterman Army Medical Center is the 1979 concrete bunker of the Letterman Army Institute of Research.

An eighteen–hole golf course lies between the scattered Officers' Quarters in the eastern portions of the post and the clustered Enlisted Family Housing at the far west end of the reservation. Entered from Arguello Street in Presidio Heights,

this scenic golf course was established by the civilian San Francisco   **Fort Winfield Scott**
Golf Club in 1895 with nine holes. Not until 1956 did the military
take over complete management of the course, permitting the civil-
ian club members to continue using the course. Over time it has been irrigated, and in
the 1930s the WPA planted fifteen thousand young trees here.

In 1907 Major William W. Harts created a master plan for the post.
In 1908 **Fort Winfield Scott**, functionally almost a separate fort, was built on the high ridge
west of the old post to man the great new earthwork batteries. It has its own central
parade ground ringed by enlisted men's barracks. These new buildings are built of modern concrete and stucco and were styled in a Spanish or Mission style with curvilinear
gables and red tile roofs. This rare, well-preserved Mission Revival cluster was the first
step in "Hispanicizing" the Presidio, a design process that is being continued after a brief
and disastrous hiatus in the 1960s and 1970s. The Spanish or Mission color scheme of
white walls and red tile roofs unified virtually all the post's buildings, from commandant's quarters to barracks, from warehouses to guard shacks. In the 1930s Georgian
Revival duplex brick officers' quarters were constructed in strings along the ridges in the
Presidio. Their East Coast "Colonial Revival" façades meld with the buildings in Mission
style, also called Spanish Colonial Revival.

The Presidio is important for its well-preserved array of utilitarian
buildings. The red brick stables of 1913–14 west of the National Cemetery and also the
1917–19 "temporary" frame warehouses with their great shed roofs, glimpsed from the
entrance to the road to the Golden Gate Bridge, are outstanding examples of American
industrial design. The cluster of maintenance shops near the Coast Guard Station preserves the rare Crissy Army Airfield hangars of the early 1920s. Utilitarian buildings like
these, lost everywhere else because of the pressures of real estate taxes and the need to
continually reuse all the building sites in the cramped city, are a rare barometer of
American building and technological history. The "least important," that is, the everyday
structures are the most important here in this outdoor museum of American architecture.

During World War II, the Presidio's dormant harbor defenses were
reactivated and the post was closed to the public. A new underground control point for
the harbor's defenses was built at Fort Winfield Scott, while nearby Fort Mason became
the Pacific Port of Embarcation for the war with Japan between 1942 and 1945. After
World War II, the Army expanded housing on the post when its role as a fortification
ceased, but its administrative and medical functions continued. The Presidio saw its last
arming in the 1950s when a Nike missile group was stationed here as part of the network
of Bay Area missile defenses. Today, it is a favored last post for Army brass about to retire.

The Presidio was designated a National Historic Landmark in 1960.
In 1965 its choice Funston Avenue Victorians were given new concrete foundations. In
the mid–1970s there were several large demolition projects at the Presidio, like a delayed-
action urban renewal campaign. The historic hospital was mostly demolished, leaving
only a fragment. A series of disruptive—not white and red—new buildings erupted
including the Letterman Army Medical Center and Institute of Research and the yellowish Enlisted Women's Barracks on the site of the old hospital. Just as in the city as a
whole, context was ignored—or fought—in new designs, so the Presidio lost sight of its
architectural tradition.

Lombard Street Gate and
Trophies

U.S. Army Presidio
Museum/
Refugee Cottages
*Lincoln Boulevard and
Funston Avenue; .
Tuesday to Sunday,
10 A.M. to 4 P.M.; free;
561-2211*

In 1972 the **Golden Gate National Recreation Area** was formed under the National Park Service. Massive Fort Point, the historic earthwork batteries, and the beaches and shoreline were turned over to the new national park. The horticultural riches of the reservation include 210,000 pine, cypress, and eucalyptus trees, 70,000 of which were planted in the 1880s by post commander Irwin McDowell. The buildings at the post number over 1,100, many of great historical and architectural significance. The Army continues to occupy the heart of the historic post, but has decided to close it. The Army has an agreement with the National Park Service to turn the post over to the Golden Gate National Recreation Area as it phases out its operations. The problem is money. In 1989, the Army spent nearly $7.8 million to maintain the Presidio's buildings and grounds. In contrast, the entire budget for the existing GGNRA was $9.5 million. The National Park Service will need even more money than the Army to run the post as a park since the Army has deferred maintenance on the buildings and forests for many years. Currently, plans are being formulated for the conversion of the post into a National Park. The vibrant model is highly successful Fort Mason, which is now nicknamed "Fort Culture." But the Presidio is vast, virtually a city within the city. The general idea is to convert the post into a "global center" for environmental issues, bringing together educators, environmentalists, scientists, governments, nonprofit groups, and business. Already the old Coast Guard station has been leased to the Gorbachev Foundation. The future is exciting indeed for this magnificent swath of public land.

- **Lombard Street Gate and Trophies**, *1894, J. B. Whittlemore*
The Presidio and Ferries Railroad opened in 1880 with a combination of cable, as far west as Steiner Street, and a steam railroad connector into the post; cable was extended into the Presidio in 1892. In 1894 architect J. B. Whittlemore designed the stone Presidio boundary wall, which was erected over the next three years. The pylons at the Main Entrance, near Lombard Street, include figures of **Liberty** and **Victory** and the castlelike emblem of the Army Corps of Engineers, with its motto: "Essayons." The two bronze Spanish cannons were cast in Seville, Spain in 1783 and are engraved with the monogram of Charles III. Lombard Street's extension into the Presidio, Lincoln Boulevard, curves gently into the government reservation, disconnecting the post from the city's relentless and differently oriented grid.

❹ U.S. Army Presidio Museum/Refugee Cottages
This handsome two-story white clapboard and brick hospital was built in 1864 and originally faced west to the parade ground. In 1878 it and the row of officers' quarters on Funston Avenue were reoriented toward the east. In 1897, as medicine became more scientific, a separate, two-story octagonal wing was added to the north side of the building for a laboratory. It is a conservative building, and its open porches with their square white timber columns give a hint of what post–Gold Rush San Francisco downtown hotels looked like in the late 1850s. It is the only example of this once-important type

of architecture left in San Francisco. Over time the third-floor porch   **Funston Avenue**
was glassed in, the fate of almost all open porches and balconies in
bright but windy San Francisco.

The museum inside is most interesting; there are layers of history
here, and the exhibits clearly separate and explain them. Several models and dioramas
from the Golden Gate International Exposition of 1939 held on Treasure Island are on
view, including a model of the Presidio in 1806 and a model of Mission Dolores' U-
shaped compound. A diorama of the summit of Nob Hill depicts the great Victorian
mansions and the new Fairmont Hotel on April 18, 1906 as the flames of the great fire
consume the downtown. Another elaborate diorama shows the great Panama-Pacific
International Exposition of 1915 in today's Marina District. Behind the museum are two
earthquake-refugee cottages designed by General Adolphus Greeley that were moved
here and restored in 1986. Photos in one cottage show the refugee camps that were established in the city parks. The cottages were rented out to homeless families at $2 per
month in a lease/purchase agreement. The last camp was cleared from the parks in June
1908. Cottages to the number of 5,343 were removed from the camps, all but a few to
be used as dwellings. The second cottage is furnished as it might have been in 1906.

 Funston Avenue Victorian Officers' Quarters:
American Architectural Benchmarks

Funston Avenue is named after **General Frederick Funston**, the man who captured
Aguinaldo, the Philippine independence leader, and who was in command at the
Presidio in 1906. He made the decision to dynamite firebreaks at Van Ness Avenue
and along other streets to prevent the entire city from being consumed in the three days
of fire that followed the earthquake.

To the student of American architecture, the **Funston Avenue** row of
some dozen Victorian frame houses is a prize specimen, a historical model of the evolution of the basic American frame house and its utilities from 1862 to the present.
These freestanding buildings on large lots—without the obscuring fences and walls
that exist between individual privately–owned properties—can be seen from all sides.
They were built for officers of the 9th Infantry Regiment in 1862. The split columns
of the front porches and the porches' simple railings are classic examples of American
carpentry. Here, continually maintained and uninterruptedly lived in, is a row of classic, all-American frame houses. Plumbing was added in 1883–84, electricity in 1912;
around 1947 the single-family houses were unobtrusively converted into duplexes; and
carports were added in 1951. In 1965, new reinforced concrete foundations were
inconspicuously built under the antique houses to preserve them.

At Presidio Boulevard and Funston Avenue is another cluster of
four two-story-with-attic houses, built in 1885. Very conservative for 1885, they were
designed by Captain Daniel D. Wheeler of the Presidio Quartermaster's Office. They
are strikingly handsome, straightforward Stick-style houses with hospitable, old-fashioned porches. They, too, are classically American.

Pershing Hall
Moraga Avenue at
Funston Avenue

Old Protestant Chapel/
Roman Catholic Chapel of
Our Lady/Site of Spanish
and Mexican Presidio

Officers' Open Mess/
Old Comandancia
Moraga Avenue

Pershing Square

6 Pershing Hall, *1903, James Campbell*

At the head of Funston Avenue is three-story, red brick **Pershing Hall** with its fine white porches looking down the Victorian officers' row. It, too, is a most American design. Built in 1903 as a Bachelor Officers' Quarters, it was constructed by James Campbell. The symmetrical T-plan building is a classic American congregate housing type seen most often in schools and colleges.

7 Old Protestant Chapel/Roman Catholic Chapel of Our Lady/ Site of the Spanish and Mexican Presidio, *1864, architect unknown; 1952, remodeled by Hewlitt Wells*

Up Moraga Avenue, named for José Joaquín Moraga, who founded the Presidio in 1776, is the **old post chapel**. This is approximately the site of the long-lost Mexican adobe presidio. The 1864 frame chapel was a simple single-story, New England-style gabled building with a square bell tower. By 1902 vines planted around it had engulfed the façade, leaving the bell tower peeping through a clipped mound of greenery. In 1952 the chapel was thoroughly reworked by Hewlitt Wells keeping only parts of the old building. The result is an interesting "California" frame building that has opened itself to a walled garden linking inside and out. The wall behind the altar was opened up as clear windows, with a screen of conifers planted behind the chapel and a view of the tall forest beyond.

8 Officers' Open Mess/Old Comandancia, *1821–30, architect unknown; 1934, Barney Meeden; 1973, Robert B. Wong*

Beyond the old chapel and a small Victorian building is the entrance to the **Officers' Open Mess** with its canvas canopy and antique green bronze cannons. The twin cannons were cast in Peru in the seventeenth century and were part of the armaments of the *Castillo de San Joaquin* that overlooked the Golden Gate. Fremont's men spiked them in 1846. The adobe Mexican-era **comandancia** of 1821–30 was located here. In 1847 occupying U.S. Army troops rebuilt the crumbling adobe and built a two-story plaster and wood addition. In 1934, to the designs of Quartermaster Barney Meeden, the entire complex was expanded, coated in lath and plaster, and roofed with red tiles to create a Spanish Colonial Revival building. This was a WPA project. In 1973 Robert B. Wong designed a large addition with a square tower and terraces carefully placed behind the old relic. The new building has slots in its red tile roof to allow light onto its view terraces. It is a model of the respectful integration of much larger new structures in historic landscapes by carefully respecting sightlines.

9 Pershing Square: Flag and Focal Point

The post's standard and the cannon fired at 6 A.M. and 5 P.M. stand in **Pershing Square**, the center of the post. The loud BOOM punctuates the day in San Francisco. Historic artillery is mounted here; some are war trophies. There is a fine view down the parade ground. A stone marker with a bronze tablet near the flagpole marks the northwest corner of the original Presidio of 1776. To the east 250 yards, at the edge of the parking lot, is a marker at the site of the original post's northeast corner. The squat stone structure with the pyramidal red tile roof at the corner of Sheridan and Anza avenues to the north is the old **U.S. Army magazine** built of local stone in 1863; the red tile roof was added in 1940.

⑩ Montgomery Street Enlisted Men's Barracks: Brick Row, *1895–97, U.S. Army Corps of Engineers*
One of the finest architectural formations on the post is the solid row of red brick barracks with white porches that marches down Montgomery Street. These five two-story-with-attic barracks fronting the parade ground were constructed between 1895 and 1897 and have recently been upgraded and restored. This, too, is a most American group. An old Native American burial ground was located in this general area.

⑪ Parade Ground/Centennial and Bicentennial Trees
On the east side of the main parade ground is the **centennial eucalyptus** planted in 1876, now tall and stately, and the **bicentennial cypress** planted in 1976. These two trees are living benchmarks of American history.
 The large white buildings along the east side of the parade ground are the headquarters of the Sixth U.S. Army. After seeing the heart of the post, drive to and walk through the San Francisco National Military Cemetery on the forested hill to the west. At the foot of the parade ground across Lincoln Boulevard is the bus stop for the 29 Sunset bus.

⑫ Post Chapel and WPA Murals, *1932, U.S. Army Corps of Engineers; murals by Victor Arnautoff*
During the 1930s, federal programs like the Works Progress Administration worked on improving the Presidio, building a new movie theater and a new post chapel. The 1932 **hilltop chapel** on Fisher Loop near the National Cemetery is in Spanish Colonial Revival style and has 1934 **murals** on the "Peacetime Activities of the Army" by Victor Arnautoff.

⑬ San Francisco National Military Cemetery, *1884, U.S. Army Corps of Engineers*
The San Francisco National Military Cemetery is today enfolded in an evergreen curtain of forests. This orderly rectangle of the dead with its occasional obelisks and Victorian monuments is set on the bluff above the parade ground. It is instructive to walk through this beautiful cemetery, with its commanding panorama of the Bay, and to read the names and dates of the soldiers, the names of the places where they fell, and the dates of wars they fought. America's reach west across a continent, and further west across the Pacific Ocean to Asia, is recorded in these markers. Beginning with the Indian Wars in the wild West, and reaching out to Alaska, Hawaii, the Philippines, Guam, China, Japan, Korea, and Vietnam, the pulses of American expansion are solemnly recorded here.

U.S. Army magazine

Montgomery Street
Enlisted Men's Barracks:
Brick Row
Montgomery Street

Parade Ground/Centennial
and Bicentennial Trees

Post Chapel and
WPA Murals
Fisher Loop, near cemetery; If driving, turn left at Montgomery and Sheridan, cross Taylor and Infantry roads, then drive up Fisher Loop to Post Chapel on the hill.

San Francisco National
Military Cemetery
Sheridan Avenue and Lincoln Boulevard

Fort Point/The Seawall

At head of Marine Drive
Open daily, 10 A.M. to
5 P.M.; free.

The Golden Gate Bridge

🄴 **Fort Point/The Seawall**

Fort Point, constructed between 1853 and 1861, is operated by the National Park Service. It is the first and only brick coast artillery fortress built west of the Mississippi River and is similar in plan to Fort Sumter, outside Charleston, South Carolina. The massive fort is built of locally manufactured red brick, granite, and iron. Its accurately restored courtyard has elegant cast-iron balconies along one side. Antique artillery is displayed and the fort is well labeled. The view from the top of the fort directly under the bridge, looking across the Golden Gate between the X-braces of the two piers, is memorable. Joseph Strauss admired the solidity of Fort Point. The elevated approach to the Golden Gate Bridge makes a great steel arch over the fort, preserving it. The fort was technologically obsolete within a year of its completion because shells and rifled cannons developed during the Civil War achieved the ability to pierce brick fortifications.

When the waters are rough, great waves splash up against the granite seawall and leap high into the air. The wall, with its interlocking granite blocks, is an impressive piece of solid construction and dates from the early 1850s. San Francisco began at this commanding site, the rock-bound portal to the Golden State.

🄵 **The Golden Gate Bridge: Art Deco Masterpiece**, *1937, Joseph P. Strauss, chief engineer; Irving F. Morrow, consulting architect*
The Golden Gate Bridge is one of the few things in life that does not disappoint. It is a magnificent, impressive, artistic structure spanning a submerged cleft in the Coastal Mountain Range, the Golden Gate. Through this rocky gate the waters of California have carved a channel to the sea. The name Golden Gate was given to this strait by Captain John C. Frémont in 1848.

The great "international orange" (more of a terra-cotta red) bridge is the joint work of chief engineer Joseph P. Strauss and consulting architect Irving F. Morrow. (There is some controversy on the role played by engineer Charles A. Ellis, who, some claim, had a larger role in the actual design than Strauss admitted.) The bridge was locally planned and financed by San Francisco and the five coastal counties to the north. It took only fifty-two months to design and construct the Golden Gate Bridge, which opened in 1937.

The Golden Gate Bridge is as much architecture as engineering. Irving F. Morrow's assertive use of Art Deco decoration makes the bridge what it is, an elegant, faceted, soaring design. The bridge's "arches" as you drive across it toward San Francisco look like the proscenium arch in a theater with the city like a painted backdrop. Morrow wanted no X-braces marring the top of the bridge (they do exist, underneath the roadbed, bracing the bases of the two piers). In the resulting design the telescoped piers, which become thinner as they rise, and the horizontal struts create a "ladder" with four differently sized openings.

The concrete abutments and anchorings of the bridge are the most artistic concrete construction in the region and were the first use of more durable high-silica cement. The span between the two towers is 4,200 feet and was the longest in the world until 1959. The clearance between the roadbed and mean low water is 220 feet, a height set by the military. The two towers are 746 feet tall. The cables are 7,650 feet long from anchorage to anchorage. The maximum side sway of the roadway in high winds at center span is 27.7 feet. As handsome as the bridge is, even more memorable is the way the fog pours in and out of the gate, dissolving this massive bridge in white mist.

San Francisco Vista Point

Marin Vista Point

Conzelman Road

The new toll booths were designed by Donald MacDonald in 1980–82 after an architectural competition and relate well to the landmark bridge while still being designs of our own time.

• *Golden Gate Bridge Vista Points*

Two major vista points offer free parking lots, one on the San Francisco side and one in Marin County. Enter the south-end **San Francisco vista point** from Lincoln Boulevard, right before the toll plaza underpass, or from the extreme right-hand lane of Highway 101 just before the toll booths. There is a statue of engineer and promoter Joseph P. Strauss. Near the pedestrian entrance to the bridge is a fine low, circular, stucco and glass pavilion designed in 1937 by Irving F. Morrow. A visitor center with maps and a souvenir shop are in the pavilion. Enter the **Marin vista point** from the right lane of Highway 101 north, at the bridge's north end. There are restrooms here and an overlook of San Francisco like that from a choice box seat. This is a beautiful view on a clear night. The spacious Bay is ever changing colors. There are sidewalks on both sides of the bridge, but the constant roar of the traffic right beside you makes the walk unpleasant.

There is another spectacular viewpoint from the ridge of the Marin hills along **Conzelman Road**. From there sparkling San Francisco is seen framed by the red steel harp of the bridge. Take the Alexander Avenue exit immediately north of the Marin vista point, turn left at the first intersection onto Battery Road, and pass through the tunnel. Beyond a small patch of military housing, turn left and travel south on McCullough Road; at the first intersection turn left onto Conzelman Road, which here is one-way. Who can say which is the best view of San Francisco? Certainly a contender for the prize is this vista on a clear moonlit night, with silvery fog gliding through the Golden Gate and suspending the bridge and eventually dissolving the glittering lighted city—all to the musical accompaniment of foghorns with their melancholy warnings. The panorama changes at times so quickly that real time seems a time-lapse film.

The underside of the bridge is best seen from the San Francisco side from the seawall in front of red brick Fort Point.

Lincoln Boulevard to Baker Beach/Battery Chamberlin Disappearing Gun
Beach open 7 A.M. to dusk; park rangers man the disappearing gun on the first weekend of each month. Phone For information, 922-0192

El Camino Del Mar

Sea Cliff

330 Seacliff Avenue

16 *Lincoln Boulevard to Baker Beach/ Battery Chamberlin Disappearing Gun*

Lincoln Boulevard passes along the crest of the bluff at the western edge of the Presidio and enjoys commanding views of the Pacific. A string of great fortifications was built here at the turn of the century and today is preserved as historic sites. There is parking and a vista point near Battery Dynamite. Further south is the turnoff to **Baker Beach** and Battery Chamberlin. This sandy beach enjoys a splendid view of the Golden Gate and the bridge. North of the parking lot, behind the ice-plant-covered sand dunes, is **Battery Chamberlin** with its disappearing gun carriage. This 1904, 95,000-pound cannon from the Smithsonian's collection can still be raised from behind the battery to its firing position. At the opposite, or south, end of the beach is a good view of the Mediterranean-style houses that stood on the edge of the rocky cliff along Seacliff Avenue, a picturesque assemblage of pale stucco cubes capped by red tile roofs. The steep cliff beyond, capped by evergreens, is Land's End. Point Bonita across the Golden Gate has a white lighthouse at its tip. Beyond the red brick building at the south end of the beach is a short trail up a bluff to the foot of Twenty-fifth Avenue North (with a gate that is locked at 10 P.M.). This *cul de sac* is a corner of Sea Cliff Gardens, a luxurious subdivision begun in 1904. Views from the top floors of the houses here have resulted in elaborate sun porches, viewing areas, and view-focused windows.

17 *El Camino Del Mar/Sea Cliff/China Beach*

Lincoln Boulevard leads to **El Camino Del Mar** and **Sea Cliff**, an immaculate residential district with well-tended gardens. To see Sea Cliff it is best to drive directly to China Beach and its parking area and then walk along Seacliff Avenue. Walk on the high or southern sidewalk. Visible between the freestanding houses built in the 1920s are slices of the dramatic panorama of the Golden Gate with the red Marin headlands across the water. Sea Cliff is the only San Francisco neighborhood that touches the ocean; all the rest of the ocean shoreline is public parks. The northeast corner of the district, the east end of Seacliff Avenue and the area near Twenty-fifth Avenue North, was laid out in 1904 by the John Brickell Company, which organized a homeowner association here and named the tract Sea Cliff Gardens. In 1916 a larger parcel to the west bounded approximately by California Street to the south, Twenty-eighth Avenue to the east, and Thirtieth Avenue to the west was developed by H. B. and Lawrence D. Allen and called Sea Cliff. Most of the houses here were built between 1920 and the Crash of 1929 in the then-popular Mediterranean style. The gardens here are lush and boast meticulously pruned vivid green shrubbery, some displaying fantastic forms. Where the road descends to China Beach stands **330 Seacliff Avenue**, a Mediterranean-style, L-shaped house with a red tile roof designed by Farr & Ward in 1930. This very Californian house is much enhanced by a picturesque, wind-swept pine tree.

China Beach, named after the Chinese fishermen's shacks that once huddled here, is a pocket beach set in a dramatic cove. Above the cove, in a bowllike amphitheater, are ranged terraces of large stucco houses whose windows face the Golden Gate. This beach is also known as Phelan Beach after James Duval Phelan, a banker who served as a reform mayor in San Francisco between 1897 and 1901 and who emphasized urban beautification and the expansion of the city's park system. He urged the preservation of this scenic cove. The concrete beach house here was built in the early 1950s and is a typical, if overlooked, piece of California public beach architecture of the period. Lifeguards are on duty here in the summer months from 10 A.M. to 5 P.M. for those hardy enough to brave these chilly waters. The rocky cliffs of Land's End visible from China Beach are colored gray, green, and maroon. The waves dash against the offshore rocks. On clear days the white cliffs of Point Reyes appear on the horizon to the north. The highest point visible is Mt. Tamalpais. At the east end of the beach is a submerged mass of rectangular granite paving stones dumped here after the earthquake and fire of 1906 and now polished smooth by the ceaseless sea. The rumbling stones make a death-rattle clatter as they roll back down the slope when the waves move out.

China Beach

Lincoln Park

California Palace of the Legion of Honor

Lincoln Park

⑱ *Lincoln Park*

Around the shoulder of the rocky peninsula is **Lincoln Park**, originally reserved in 1868 as part of the Outside Lands for the Golden Gate Cemetery, the city's paupers' cemetery. The first burials here occurred in 1870 when pioneer remains were disinterred from Yerba Buena Cemetery so that it could be used for the new city hall (today the site of the Civic Center Public Library). Many Chinese were buried here before their bones were disinterred for shipment back to their native villages. Nearby landowners objected to the unkempt, depressing potter's field—indeed to all the cemeteries within the city. After a long and bitter fight with the Catholic Church and some cemetery plot owners, the city prohibited burials within the city limits after 1901. A chain of new cemeteries was opened in Colma, over the line in San Mateo County. This commanding site was relandscaped by John McLaren as Lincoln Park, and a golf course was opened here in 1909. A Victorian Chinese funerary monument survives today in the middle of the Lincoln Park golf course.

- **California Palace of the Legion of Honor**, *1920, George Applegarth;*
1994, underground expansion, Edward Larrabee Barnes/ John M. Y. Lee &
Partners, and Barnes and Cavagnero
In 1920 the splendid **California Palace of the Legion of Honor** was completed to plans by George Applegarth, modeled on the Legion of Honor in Paris. It was the gift of Adolph Bernard and Alma de Bretteville Spreckels in memory of California's World War I dead. Few art museums have as beautiful a situation as this one. Inside the limestone palace are a collection of French art, opulent period rooms, and a sizable col-

Achenbach Foundation   lection of Rodin sculptures assembled by the Spreckels. The superb **Achenbach Foundation** here holds an outstanding collection of prints. In 1992–94, an expansion to the museum designed by Edward Larrabee Barnes inserted a circular lightwell in the entrance court for six new underground galleries. One of the finest Rodin bronzes, *The Shades*, stands across the parking lot from the museum. The view of the park-laced city from the balustrade is very fine.

Continuation: The Bus Downtown, or a Nature Walk

At Geary and Forty-eighth Avenue is the terminus of the 38 Geary bus, which can take you directly back to Union Square, or you can take the hiking trail to Land's End and the Cliff House. El Camino Del Mar dead ends just north of the California Palace of the Legion of Honor next to the Lincoln Park Golf Course. There is parking here and the head of the trail that skirts the rocky edge of Land's End and leads to Merrie Way, a parking lot near the Cliff House and the Sutro Baths ruins *(Tour 13)*. This was once the roadbed of the Ferries & Cliff House Railway, a narrow-gauge steam railroad that ran out California Street and operated here from 1888 to 1906. This scenic trail offers splendid views of the Golden Gate and forests of twisted cypress trees. The wild, broken shore, the booming surf, and the sense of remoteness from the city makes this one of the best nature walks in San Francisco. Stay on the trails, for the cliffs here are unstable and dangerous. The Park Service has planted California poppies along part of the trail, which becomes a shining, golden road in the spring. The 18 Forty-sixth Avenue bus terminates at the Legion of Honor near the head of the trail. The 38 Geary bus has its terminus at Geary and Forty-eighth Avenue, about two blocks from the other end of the trail, and can take you back to Union Square downtown *(Tour 1)*.

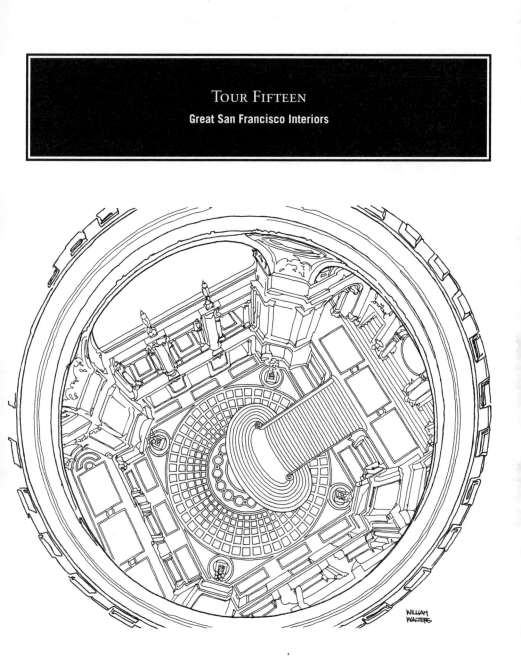

The great rotunda of San Francisco's Beaux Arts City Hall, designed by Bakewell & Brown and completed in 1915, is the grandest public space in San Francisco. The oval staircase landing is the city's most important public stage.

Great San Francisco Interiors
Preliminaries
Introduction

**TOUR 15:
GREAT
SAN FRANCISCO
INTERIORS**

1. Old Hibernia Bank/San Francisco District Police Station
2. Church of the New Jerusalem (Swedenborgian)
3. Sheraton Palace Hotel
4. City Hall
5. Temple Emanu-El
6. V. C. Morris Store/Circle Gallery
7. St. Mary's Roman Catholic Cathedral of the Assumption
8. San Francisco Museum of Modern Art
9. San Francisco Main Public Library

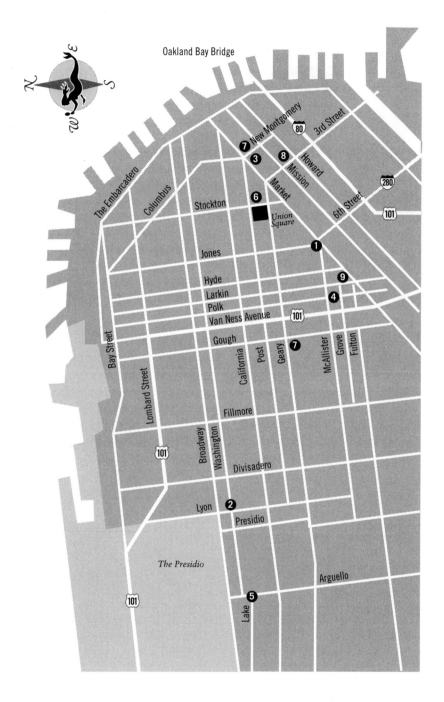

Great San Francisco Interiors

℘reliminaries

BEST TIMES TO DO THIS TOUR

The nine architectural gems presented here are scattered through out the city and can't be visited in a single walking tour. Perhaps the best thing to do is to select the periods that most interest you and visit the interiors that exemplify them. The best times to visit are noted, and directions are given for reaching each site by public transit. Or you can take a taxi.

ℐntroduction

Buildings are like shoes. The way the inside feels turns out to be more important than the way the outside looks. These publicly accessible San Francisco interiors present a chronological selection of the best of each surviving period of post-1906 San Francisco building. Most are great in size; all are great in idea, intention, design, and effect. Each of these interiors speaks for a locally important era of design.

① **Old Hibernia Bank/San Francisco District Police Station**, *Beaux Arts, 1892, 1905, 1907, Albert Pissis*

Today this architectural gem stands stranded on Skid Row. Completed in 1892 on a prominent corner site just off Market Street, this steel-frame, granite-clad monument was designed by Albert Pissis, the leading Beaux Arts–trained San Francisco architect of his day, and was widely considered to be among the most beautiful buildings in San Francisco. Originally built as a narrow structure along Jones Street, the bank was enlarged in 1905. The **Hibernia Bank** was one of the oldest financial institutions in the city and was founded in 1859 by John Sullivan and incorporated in 1864. The Irish Catholic Tobin family historically had a strong interest in the Hibernia Bank. The bank as a financial institution disappeared in a merger in the 1980s.

Old Hibernia Bank/ San Francisco District Police Station
1 Jones Street, at McAllister, off Market Street near the Civic Center

Getting there by public transit:
Take any line on Market Street and alight at Jones Street

This elegant Corinthian-columned bank utilizes its corner site dramatically, with a colonnade and dome sheltering the bronze doors of the corner entrance. It is a freestanding building; the granite façades on all four sides were originally white but have now weathered to gray. The well-built structure withstood the earthquake but was gutted by the fire in 1906. It was then carefully reconstructed and added onto and has been well maintained and preserved ever since. In 1993, the bank was converted into a District Police Station serving the Tenderloin. Walking into the high-ceilinged, opulently detailed banking hall with its extravagant plasterwork (the best in San Francisco) and beautiful stained-glass skylights is like walking into San Francisco's fabled past. Few spaces in the entire city are as handsome as this one. It is one of San Francisco's hidden treasures, waiting to be discovered in one of the city's least explored areas. The old Hibernia Bank epitomizes the pride of San Francisco–based banks.

The great banking hall is painted a pleasing tan, gold, and pale mauve, which delicately accentuates the richly molded plasterwork. A frieze of shields and torches encircles the hall. The twin steel doors to the vaults on the north wall are framed in red and green marble. Above them, in the frieze, is a splendid clock with a sunburst design. The two skylights, one round and the other oval, glow with soft, pearly colors.

When everything burned down around this sturdy bank, the two triangular lots flanking the bank were rebuilt with two sympathetic buildings, the Hotel Shaw and 1072–98 Market Street, which frame the view of the bank from Market Street. The hotel was designed by H. A. Minton in 1926 and is a five-story addition and complete remodel of the two-story, prefire Callaghan Building. The Shaw Hotel's green copper cornice echoes the Hibernia Bank's richly detailed dome. The building at 1072-98 Market Street, on the northeast corner of Jones, was built for the Anglo California Trust Company and designed by H. H. Winner in 1911. It has strikingly proportioned, tripartite Chicago windows on its two upper floors. This cluster of three buildings shows why San Francisco was fortunate to have the fire and rebuilding when she did; this kind of sympathetic, neighborly building design was what was best about early-twentieth-century city-building.

On the northeast corner of McAllister and Jones is one of San Francisco's most delightful sidewalk flower stands, shaped like a miniature Market Street trolley bus.

**Church of the
New Jerusalem
(Swedenborgian)**
*2107 Lyon Street at
Washington, in Presidio
Heights; Open daily 9-5,
Sunday worship at 11 A.M.;
Closed during weddings;
346-6466*

**Getting there by
public transit:**
*From downtown,
take the 3 Jackson trolley
bus on Sutter Street and
alight at Lyon Street. Walk
one block downhill to the
inconspicuous church*

❷ Church of the New Jerusalem (Swedenborgian),
Tuscan Revival façade, 1894, A. Page Brown

The simple stucco and brick exterior of this small neighborhood church gives no hint of the delights within. The arched facade is modeled on that of a village church near Verona, Italy. Half the lot consists of a pleasant garden with an olive tree, a cedar of Lebanon, and a redwood *(Sequoia sempervirens)*. In one corner is an old wrought iron Franciscan cross from Mission San Miguel in the Salinas Valley.

Enter the church through its modest portal. The interior, and its message, is the work of architect A. Page Brown and his patron, Reverend Joseph Worcester, a Swedenborgian minister from Massachusetts who had a love for California nature. A. C. Schweinfurth did the drawings for the building. Inside the church there is the mystical power of the forest. Madrone-trunk roof beams from Santa Cruz brace the ceiling. Large oil paintings of California forests by William Keith line one wall. The scent of the wood burned in the fireplace lightly perfumes the air. There are a few green plants, and, over the altar, part of a bristlecone pine from the White Mountains, earth's longest-lived tree. The two softly glowing stained-glass windows by Bruce Porter depict water. The round window in the gable shows a dove perched on a fountain. The blurry, beautifully colored mystical window on the side wall shows St. Christopher carrying a glowing child across a blue river.

The fine chairs, perhaps designed by young Bernard Maybeck, son of a woodcarver, combine the sense of solidity sought in the 1890s with the Arts and Crafts aesthetic. Made of hard, satin-finished maple held together by pegs, and woven rushes for the seats, they are comfortable (always of utmost importance in a chair!) and beautiful. Sturdy, and with low backs, the chairs are a lesson in the enduring virtues. And, like a religious congregation, they are more as a group than they are as individuals. The chairs are designed to fit together in compact rows, pewlike. Still, they retain their Protestant individuality. Gustav Stickley credited these chairs as the inspiration for his Craftsman, or Mission, furniture.

This church, with its warm, intimate, lodgelike feeling, is San Francisco's favorite wedding chapel. Nature is where most Californians worship: the seacoast, forests, mountains, and deserts of this magnificent state. The Reverend Joseph Worcester brought the power and beauty of the forest into this city church, using the best talents of turn-of-the-century San Francisco. This church and its furnishings are the single most important shrine of the Arts and Crafts Movement in the San Francisco Bay Area. What is best about Northern California design, and the values that animate it, suffuse this modest yet great church.

❸ **Sheraton Palace Hotel**, *Beaux Arts, 1909, Trowbridge and Livingston; 1991, restoration and addition, Skidmore, Owings & Merrill and Page & Turnbull*
The original **Palace Hotel** that stood on this site from 1873 to the conflagration of 1906 was *the* hotel in San Francisco and the Victorian West. It claimed to be the biggest in the world when it opened with 755 rooms (in a city of 250,000 people). It was a seven-story hollow brick rectangle with a glass-roofed Grand Court. The Crystal Roof Garden, just beneath the glass skylight, was alive with flowers and permitted a view down into the central court where carriages entered to deposit guests.

Sheraton Palace Hotel
633–65 Market Street, at New Montgomery Street; Always open; Sunday buffet brunch

Getting there by public transit:
Any Market Street line will take you to the Palace Hotel

Del Coronado Hotel

William Ralston, the head of the Bank of California, was the splashy investor behind this grand hotel. He had his chief architect, John P. Gaynor, travel to see other great hotels before designing the bay-windowed extravaganza that became the biggest building in San Francisco. Unhappily, Ralston drowned five weeks before the Palace opened in 1875. His rival, William Sharon, took over the hotel.

The great hotel was part of a larger real-estate scheme of this enterprising buccaneer banker. Ralston watched the Financial District shift south down Montgomery Street toward Market Street and formed a syndicate that secretly purchased lots south of Market, across from the foot of Montgomery Street. The syndicate had their own street, New Montgomery, cut from Market to Mission and put the front door of their grand Palace Hotel not on Market but on their own New Montgomery Street. The plan did not work out, however. The big hotel blocked the movement of prestige uses down New Montgomery and became the hard edge of the downtown district, not the generator of an expansion of the Financial District across the Market Street frontier.

One wit wrote in 1878 that "If you wish to hide from an enemy who dwells at the Palace, the safest thing to do is to board there yourself. There is slight chance of your ever meeting him .... It is annexing a state to get a bedroom." California's and the West's magnates all gravitated to the Palace, especially during the winter social season. From May to September, San Francisco high society moved *en bloc* to the great resort hotels, particularly the now-lost Del Monte Hotel built by the Southern Pacific Railroad on the Monterey peninsula, and vacationing Easterners filled the Palace. (Today the **Del Coronado Hotel** of 1886 in Coronado, near San Diego, is the last great Victorian seaside resort hotel that survives in California.)

In the 1890s the two top floors of the Palace housed millionaire regular residents. Dinners at the Palace were lavish and endless, featuring Pacific oysters, salmon, bass, shrimp, mountain quail, duck, venison, even grizzly-bear steaks. State banquets were served on the splendid Palace solid gold service. The Palace Grill was one of the city's most famous institutions. As one newspaper noted, "Here hobnob the European nobleman or celebrated scientist, the great stars of the stage and the world of music." Enrico Caruso, for example, was a guest at the Palace the morning of the earthquake of 1906. The panic-stricken Caruso ran out of the hotel in a towel, carrying an autographed picture of President Theodore Roosevelt and vowing never to return. He never did.

The fire gutted the grand hotel, though its iron-reinforced brick walls survived. The old walls were razed and a new structure was built atop the old hotel's brick water reservoir under the basement. A new ten million dollar grand hotel with a stunning, glass-roofed interior court and a sober, light Milwaukee brick exterior was designed by Trowbridge and Livingston of New York City. Young George Kelham, an architect who was to leave his signature in San Francisco with landmarks such as the Russ Building on Montgomery Street, was sent out West to supervise the construction.

At 1:00 P.M. Thursday, December 17, 1909, the doors of the new Palace Hotel were unlocked for the first time; the key was attached to four balloons, which carried it away. It was a declaration that the doors to the great hostelry would "remain open for all time." Every corridor was converted into a dining room to accommodate the 1,469 diners on opening night; the hotel's loyal clientele filled it to overflowing. Once the new Palace was open, there was an agreed-upon feeling that the city was back from the ashes. (The Fairmont had reopened on April 19, 1907, and the St. Francis on Union Square reopened that November.)

The new hotel replaced the traditional Grand Court with the glass-roofed Garden Court (originally the Palm Court), sometimes called the most elegant room in San Francisco. The room is 120 feet long, 85 feet wide, and 45 feet high. Its pillars are covered with *scagliola*, plaster painted in imitation of marble, and the ceiling is hung with crystal chandeliers. The best way to experience this great room is to attend its lavish Sunday buffet brunch served from 10:30 A.M. to 2:30 P.M.

The most historic event in the Garden Court was Woodrow Wilson's famous, if ill-fated, League of Nations speech. On August 2, 1923 President Warren G. Harding died of apoplexy at the Palace while still in office. (Was it the bill?) The last king of Hawaii also died at the luxurious Palace.

The other famous room in the Palace is now called Maxfield's, a bar with a large Maxfield Parrish mural of the **Pied Piper of Hamelin** and his doomed entourage. (Parrish had previously painted the famous mural of Old King Cole in New York's Knickerbocker Hotel, now in the St. Regis.) The bar became an ice-cream parlor during Prohibition.

In 1937 there was a famous eighty-seven-day strike at all of San Francisco's best hotels in an attempt to unionize this important San Francisco industry. The strike failed, but during World War II the Palace, Fairmont, Mark Hopkins, and St. Francis Hotels were declared essential war industries and unionization and the five-day work week were introduced.

In 1973 the Palace was purchased by Kokusai Kogyo of Japan, and it is now managed by Sheraton Hotels. A complete restoration and modernization was executed by Skidmore, Owings & Merrill, and Page & Turnbull, in 1991. This brought the monumental hotel back to its original splendor. Interesting historical memorabilia are displayed in vitrines along the hotel's principal corridor, which parallels New Montgomery Street.

4 **City Hall**, *Beaux Arts, 1915, Bakewell & Brown*

The great domed **City Hall**, completed in 1915, is the centerpiece of San Francisco's Beaux Arts Civic Center of municipal, state, and federal office buildings along with the new and old Main Public Libraries, the War Memorial Opera House, and the Veterans Building. The 1906 earthquake reduced the old City Hall (which stood where the old Main Library is today) to picturesque ruins. Shortly thereafter, a strong wave of civic reform ousted the corrupt, boss-ridden municipal administration and the city began with a clean slate.

City Hall
Polk Street between McAllister and Grove Streets, in the Civic Center; Open Monday to Friday, 8 A.M. to 5 P.M.

Getting there by public transit:
The 5 McAllister trolley bus on Market Street passes City Hall; alight at Polk Street. Both Muni Metro and BART stop at Civic Center

Great plans were made for a monumental municipal complex, and in January 1912 an $8.8 million bond issue was approved by the voters at the urging of the new reform Republican mayor, James Rolph, Jr., known to everyone as "Sunny Jim." Rolph was to continue as mayor from 1911 to 1930, when he was elected governor of California. Under his long administration a vast number of public buildings were built: schools, hospitals, libraries, fire and police stations, and many other civic facilities. All were characterized by excellent design and honest construction. The City Hall, the most important symbol of the new city, was the finest of all. In 1916 *The Architect*, a journal published in San Francisco, called it "the greatest architectural triumph of the greatest building period San Francisco has ever seen, a period not merely of rebuilding but of better building." When Rolph died, in 1934, he lay in state under the dome he built.

City Hall's design is the result of a competition with a $25,000 first prize, which was limited to San Francisco architects. Bakewell & Brown's design was chosen over seventy-two other entries. Arthur Brown, Jr. had trained at the Ecole des Beaux-Arts in Paris; his design is usually described as French Renaissance in style, but it could just as well be called American Renaissance. It was the acme of the City Beautiful movement in San Francisco. Christopher H. Snyder was the engineer, and John Galen Howard, Frederick H. Meyer, and John Reid, Jr., were the consulting architects. Jean Louis Bourgeois designed most of the interiors and the sculptures in the pediments were carved by Henri Crenier, both also trained at the Ecole des Beaux-Arts.

The City Hall is a rectangle 400 feet long and 300 feet wide, consisting of two office wings with central light courts joined by a 301-foot-5 ½-inch-high lead-clad copper dome, capping a 186-foot-6-inch-high ceremonial rotunda within. There are actually three domes—the exterior one, the coffered one with the central "eye" seen from inside the rotunda, and an inner dome between these two with the cartouche depicting a ship visible through the "eye." The building has a steel frame under its luxurious exterior of gray granite from Raymond, California. The lofty dome, which rises higher than that of the national capital, rests on four 50-ton and four 20-ton girders. The dome proper begins 191 feet above ground level, and its diameter at that point is 86 feet. A ring of freestanding Doric columns surmounted by tall urns surrounds the drum of the dome on the exterior. A slender steeple crowned with a torch caps the dome. When the city council is in night session, the light in the lantern is lit.

The Ecole des Beaux-Arts, while often thought of as merely training its students in correct Classical- or Renaissance-inspired ornament, actually provided an education in spatial planning much more than styles. Arthur Brown arranged the building's functions to tell a story. As originally laid out, once inside the building the citizens were flanked by their responsibilities: to the south was the Tax Collector, and to the north was the Register of Voters. Above this ground-floor material and electoral base are the three branches of the municipal government: Straight ahead, up the grand staircase that rises from the center of the rotunda, is the chamber of the Board of Supervisors, the eleven-member city council. The windows of the supervisors' chamber face the neighborhoods to the west. Paired with this great room is the mayor's office on the east, or downtown, side of the building's second floor. Above the legislative and executive branches, on the third floor, are the municipal courts and the law library. Brown's arrangement gives pride of place to the legislative branch but also clearly expresses the role of the executive and judicial branches. This is not just architecture; it is a civics lesson. Surrounding the organs of government is the city bureaucracy. And at the center of everything is the great public rotunda. The first landing of the grand staircase serves as the city's municipal stage for inaugurations, ceremonial occasions, and, on election night, as the place where vote tallies are officially announced.

In contrast to the sober Doric columns of the exterior, the rotunda is ornamented in leafy exuberance with elaborate Corinthian capitals. The interior of the rotunda is faced with light-colored Indiana sandstone and is paved with light-pink Tennessee marble. The splendid branched electric torchères and florid railings were executed in iron and bronze by Leo J. Myberg and are the finest Beaux Arts metalwork in the city. Over the sunburst clock on the east wall is a figure of Father Time facing a torch-bearing youth and the inscription, "San Francisco, O Glorious City of our Hearts that hast been tried and not found wanting, Go thou with like spirit to make the future thine." This is a building that exhorts!

The ceremonial entrance to City Hall is on the Polk Street, or downtown, side. The mayor's office opens onto a second-floor balcony overlooking the two-block square Civic Center Plaza. The pediment on this side is ornamented with an allegorical group carved by Henri Crenier showing San Francisco flanked by the riches and resources of California to one side and Commerce and Navigation on the other. The pediment on the Van Ness Avenue side, which faces the setting sun, depicts Wisdom flanked by Arts, Learning, and Truth on one side and Industry and Labor on the other. At the building's dedication one speaker urged the municipal government "to try to rise to its surroundings," a lofty ideal indeed. More than any other building, City Hall embodies the pride of San Francisco.

⑤ Temple Emanu-El, *Byzantine Revival, 1926, Bakewell & Brown, with Sylvain Schnaittacher*

The history of the Jews in San Francisco is an important and happy one. They came to San Francisco with the first steamers of the Gold Rush era and have flourished with the city's growth, which they in no small measure stimulated. Migrants came from the Eastern seaboard and the interior and from Bavaria, France, Alsace, Poland, England, and Russia. They came to a growing city that, though by no means free from prejudice, was relatively open. Here various congregations were organized, as with Roman Catholic parishes, often along national lines. The first synangogue, **Temple Emanu-El** ("God is with us"), was formed in 1850 by Bavarian-born German-speaking Jewish merchants. These men were sons of the liberal tradition of progressive nineteenth-century German Judaism, and Temple Emanu-El pursued the reform of Jewish ritual. With prosperity came a strong and continuing tradition of philanthropy, first to specifically Jewish institutions (such as a burial society, orphanage, schools, and hospitals) and then, by the second generation, as important supporters of the city's civic causes and cultural institutions. The history of the Jews in San Francisco is one of responsibility and generosity toward the city as a community.

Temple Emanu-El
Lake Street and Arguello Boulevard, in Presidio Heights; Open Monday to Friday, 9 A.M. to 5 P.M.; Friday Shabbat services at 5:30 P.M.; 951-2535

Getting there by public transit:
From downtown take the 1 California trolley bus and alight at Arguello Boulevard

The stately temple with the great red-tile-covered dome at Lake and Arguello streets was built in 1924–26 to replace the onion-domed synagogue at 450 Sutter Street, downtown, that burned in 1906. (Miller and Pfleuger's Mayan-Deco, bay-windowed medical-dental skyscraper of 1929 now occupies that site.) The congregation moved from the downtown Union Square area to Presidio Heights, near Pacific Heights and not too far from Sea Cliff, the city's wealthiest neighborhoods.

Having selected a lot and with defined needs (for a great worship space, classrooms, offices, a rabbi's study, and an auditorium), and a desire for a sumptuous building, the trustees of the congregation turned to Bakewell & Brown, with Sylvain Schnaittacher as associated architect; the hand of Arthur Brown, Jr. was the important one. He designed the splendid City Hall, the Opera House, Coit Tower, and many of San Francisco's other important buildings built between 1912 and the 1930s. Bruce Porter collaborated on the interior decoration. Bernard Maybeck, G. Albert Lansburgh, and Edgar Walter served as consultants.

Brown's inspiration for Temple Emanu-El was the dome and sublime massing of Justinian's Hagia Sophia in Constantinople. The Arguello Boulevard elevation best conveys this historic recall. Another important influence in the design of the temple was the memory of the courtyards and cloisters that linked together the massive buildings of the Panama-Pacific International Exhibition of 1915. Temple Emanu-El is like a single "cell" (cloister and great domed building) from that world's fair megastructure. (Of the Panama-Pacific International Exposition, the only remnant is a concrete replica of Bernard Maybeck's Palace of Fine Arts *[see Tour 14]* with its massive freestanding colonnade and rotunda.)

The desire for a grand building within a $1.2 million budget ruled out granite or marble, which were preferred, and mandated the use of steel frame and reinforced concrete with cement stucco—the best building materials for large structures in earthquake country. The red terra-cotta-tile roof harmonizes well with this material. To Brown, the dome surpassed all other architectural forms in impressive nobility and beauty. "It is," he wrote, "most appropriately used when men wish to give material form to their most exalted sentiments." Once the dome was decided on, the cloistered court followed, since it gave Brown the opportunity for a powerful contrast and play of masses. The dome is imposing; the temple has a volume larger than the Paris Opera and seats more than seventeen hundred people in a column-free and elevating space.

The cloistered court and its fountain set the House of God apart from the outside world, and yet link the two. In the courtyard is a mosaic Star of David with symbols of the twelve tribes of Israel, and olive, fig, date, and cypress trees. From the court the front of the temple with its nichelike portal rises majestically to create a truly powerful architectural effect. A bronze lamp hangs in the niche above the doors. It is the *Ner Tamid*, which burns continually as a symbol of God's eternal presence in the midst of His people. The play of light and shade across this entrance was carefully studied by Brown.

Passing through the great portal, one enters the low, vaulted vestibule painted like a starry sky. This transitional social space both links and separates the sky-covered court outside from the soaring dome within.

Entering the sanctuary, the worshipper has his attention immediately focused on the gilt-bronze and cloisonné enamel Ark that contains the scrolls of the Torah, the first five books of the Bible. A soaring canopy with green marble columns shelters and frames the Ark. As Brown expressed it, "The austerity of the surrounding walls and vaults, depending on their form and proportion alone to give them beauty, serves as a contrasting foil to the splendors of the Ark itself." Flanking the Ark are two seven-branch candelabra, the menorahs, symbolizing the six days of creation and the Sabbath. There are two pulpits, the lower one for preaching and the higher one for reading from the Torah. Behind the pulpits are a Skinner organ and a choir loft that accommodates up to fifty singers.

The balanced motifs of the circle in the square, of the dome, and of the apse govern the design and create exaltation, unity, harmony, and rhythm; a work of a distinctly religious character. To the south is the great portal with its lamp, to the north is the Ark with its holy book, and to the east and west are two titled, contemporary stained-glass windows by California artist Mark Adams installed in 1973. To the east, where the Bay is, is *Water*; to the west, where the sun sets, is *Fire*.

6 **V. C. Morris Store/Circle Gallery**, *1949, Frank Lloyd Wright*
Tucked into this narrow alley lined with small luxury shops is Frank
Lloyd Wright's only work in San Francisco, the complete transformation of a 1911 structure. Seen from the narrow side street of
Maiden Lane (once an infamous nest of brothels), the 46-foot-wide,
32-foot-high facade of tawny Roman brick invites the passerby to
enter its one emphatic, semicircular-arched entrance. A short glass-
walled tunnel lets one look inside even when the shop is closed. No
longer the **V. C. Morris** shop, it now houses the **Circle Gallery.**
　　　　　The brickwork of the arch is set in concentric
bands that make the entrance seem like an aura, the same effect
achieved by cathedral portals. But the beautifully detailed facade is
modern in spirit and method. Wright incorporated electric lights
judiciously in the facade: in a row with square white plastic covers
along the bottom with a Greek key design, hidden behind the latticelike brickwork
along the edge of the facade, and in a (now cemented over) three-quarter circle set under
glass in the sidewalk at the entrance. This careful use of light made the facade attractive at night to strollers. Wright's signature appears in a square red tile set in the lower
left-hand corner of the facade.
　　　　　This facade, even if it stood all alone in this architecturally creative
nation, would rank as an important architectural design. Its broad unadorned expanse,
so artistically treated at entrance and edges, is one of Wright's most direct references
to the great Louis Sullivan, Wright's teacher, whom he always referred to as *"lieber
meister."* The facade recalls the fine handful of small-town banks that Sullivan designed
in the last years of his tragic career. The use of simple planes and controlled ornament
testifies as well to the important influence of the Viennese Secession. The semicircular
arched entry with its impost return is also a recall of the strong-looking designs of
Henry Hobson Richardson, Sullivan's teacher. Here is a facade rich with important
references to American architectural history, yet at the same time wholly new.
　　　　　But the real surprise waits inside. Within this small, roughly cubic
shop Wright's genius created unexpected grandeur—a masterpiece of American design,
and one of the best works from the often-uninspired late 1940s. Inside the two-story-
high space Wright set a gently curving ramp that seems to rise weightlessly toward the
translucent white ceiling of its own accord. The motif of the circle anticipated by the
entrance is repeated everywhere, in round portholes, semicircular tables and low round
benches, in the circular designs in the ceiling, and in a large round suspended planter.
The V. C. Morris Store was designed to showcase china and crystal, round and glob-
ular shapes, many of them translucent. When filled with what it was so ingeniously
designed to display, it seemed a room full of bubbles, light, and sparkle. The customer
was smoothly led past all the stock in the store, and, from the top of the ramp, could
look down on table settings to get an overall impression. Today it is an art gallery. The
walnut furniture is Wright's.

**V. C. Morris Store/
Circle Gallery**
*140 Maiden Lane, off
Stockton Street and
Union Square;
Open retail hours;*
989-2100

**Getting there by
public transit:**
*It's off Stockton Street
a half block east of
Union Square, which is
a nexus of transit routes
from all directions*

St. Mary's Roman Catholic Cathedral of the Assumption
Geary Boulevard at Gough Street, on Cathedral Heights; Open every day

Getting there by public transit:
From Union Square take the 38 Geary bus and alight at Gough Street

The V. C. Morris Store has often been cited as a precursor of Wright's Guggenheim Museum in New York City, completed in 1959. But the museum plans were published in 1946, before the construction of this shop. Wright also designed a house for Mr. Morris that was never built. In 1949, Wright unveiled a grand design for a concrete "butterfly" bay bridge at the San Francisco Museum of Modern Art. Wright's other completed works in the Bay Area include a hexagonal-modular house near Stanford University, built in 1937, and his last major work, the futuristic Marin County Civic Center, constructed in San Rafael in stages beginning in 1962 after the master architect's death.

7 St. Mary's Roman Catholic Cathedral of the Assumption, *1971, Pietro Belluschi; Pier Luigi Nervi; McSweeney, Ryan & Lee*
St. Mary's Cathedral's interior is no doubt the grandest contemporary great space in San Francisco. Built in 1971, the prestressed-concreted hyperbolic paraboloid arches of its great 190-foot-high, Greek-cross-shaped cupola are a steel-and-concrete masterpiece.

The previous St. Mary's, built on Van Ness Avenue in 1887–91, burned down during the heyday of massive urban renewal—the complete demolition of old districts and radical changes in their use. Geary Street, which had always had the main streetcar line from the downtown straight west, was widened and made into a major automobile expressway. On the southwest corner of Geary and Gough, the crest of the hill, the Redevelopment Agency built a new supermarket. Archbishop McGucken knew he wanted the new cathedral on a hilltop, so the new market was relocated to Eddy and Laguna streets and the commanding site was sold to the church. The city also permitted a block of O'Farrell Street to be vacated to make the cathedral more visible from downtown.

The huge two-block parcel is cleverly designed. Most people think only the cathedral occupies the site, but in reality a large courtyarded high school, a rectory, and a convent, along with a large auditorium beneath the cathedral, are tucked underneath and behind this twelve million dollar complex. Its construction took five years.

The cathedral is credited to a local firm, McSweeney, Ryan & Lee, but two other designers were really responsible for this fine design. Pietro Belluschi of Boston, Italian by birth and an engineer by training, formed the concept of a Greek cross within a square capped by a great cupola that became the design for the new cathedral. Belluschi's bold design called for an engineer of genius, and Pier Luigi Nervi of Rome, one of the master designers of the twentieth century, was called in as a consultant and visited the site twice. Nervi, also by training an engineer, fused the mathematical and the aesthetic in reinforced-concrete structures he called "stone in motion." The lightness and grace with which this cupola leaps from its four 15-by-24-foot sculpted piers proclaims Nervi's genius. A mathematical model made possible a computer analysis of the whole structure. Looking up into this flowing, cross-shaped vault persuades the viewer of the elegant logic of its construction. It is a consummate expression of the modern age and the beauty of the age's technological prowess. Asked at the cathedral's unveiling what Michelangelo would have thought of this building, Nervi answered, "He could not have thought of it. This design comes from geometric theories not then proven."

The interior arrangement of the cathedral was also new. The Second Vatican Council in 1962, as part of its sweeping liturgical reforms, turned the altar around and made the priest face the congregation. This new cathedral expresses those reforms. The austerely simple stone altar is raised up on a platform and is surrounded by pews on three sides. Except for a cross and a *baldacchino* of hanging aluminum rods, there is no decoration in the sanctuary. Richard Lippold's *baldacchino* is like a rain of light falling on the altar. The stained-glass windows are by Hungarian-born Gyorgy Kepes and were made in Philadelphia. The four narrow windows in the cupola represent *fire* (west), *sky* (north), *water* (east), and *earth* (south).

Certainly, after the *baldacchino*, the most splendid sculpture in the clean, modern interior is the glorious organ on its freestanding, sculpted pedestal. Even when silent this instrument is a visual song. Ruffati Fratelli, an old family firm in Padua, Italy built the instrument. Mr. Ruffati and his three sons came here to install it.

The Second Vatican Council also encouraged an outward-looking attitude; in the design of the cathedral this is expressed by the large clear glass windows in the building's four corners. They give views of the city and make the city part of the cathedral. The view toward the slope of Twin Peaks to the southwest is particularly picturesque.

Tucked into the south end of the site is a high school with three courtyards. Underneath the cathedral itself are a large auditorium and many meeting rooms. A square marble-paved corridor links together the ground-floor meeting rooms. The corridor itself is beautifully handled; the high quality of the building is evidenced in places such as these.

Leave the cathedral through the western door behind the great organ. From the terrace on the west is a fine view of the city to the southwest. The old skyline of small, pale-colored cubes stepping up the many hills survives here.

From the terrace on the east (downtown) side of the cathedral plaza there is an interesting view of towers all around. The red-brick church was built in 1880 for St. Mark's Lutheran congregation and is a typical example of the use of Romanesque forms for American city churches in the late nineteenth century. Also visible is the green copper dome of the City Hall, the finest ornament on San Francisco's skyline. Farther to the right are the Gothic spires of St. Paul's Lutheran Church, designed by A. J. Craft and built in 1894. Its lacy spires are among the most beautiful in the city.

A few summary observations on the cathedral can be made: Its plan, structure, and technology are better than its ornamentation. The interior is better than the exterior—and it looked even better before the installation of the first of the side altars in the handsome skylighted bays embarrassingly revealed the mediocrity of this kind of contemporary religious art. Only Lippold's *baldacchino* saves the situation.

San Francisco Museum of Modern Art
151 Third Street between Mission and Howard, in the South of Market
Phone for hours and fee, 357-4000

Getting there by public transit: *From Union Square, take the 30 Stockton trolley bus south across Market Street to Mission and Fourth Streets. Transfer to a 14 Mission trolley bus one block east to Mission and Third Streets*

It is very much a building of its day—not only in its design, but in the fact that the sunken parking lot is far superior to the "plaza" and terrace (which should be open all the way around the cathedral). This is, in fact, probably the best parking lot in San Francisco. The plain, square coffers of the poured-concrete roofs over part of the parking area directly and elegantly display the character of *the* contemporary building material. When free of automobiles these are handsome, abstract spaces, a purely Cartesian world of well-proportioned grids.

8 **San Francisco Museum of Modern Art**, *1995, Mario Botta, architect; Hellmuth, Obata & Kassabaum San Francisco, architects of record*

Swiss architect Mario Botta's new home for the **San Francisco Museum of Modern Art (SFMOMA)** replaces the museum's former Civic Center location and promises to be the finest piece of contemporary architecture in San Francisco. Born in Mendrisio, Switzerland in 1943, he apprenticed with a Lugano architectural firm when he was fifteen. He received his professional degree from the University Institute of Architecture in Venice. He established his own practice in 1970 in Lugano and gained international notice in the early 1980s for a series of small private houses that project a powerful monumentality. His goal as an architect is both clear and lofty: "There must exist in the city large, ample spaces in which history, memory, dreams, imagination, and poetry can be linked and which are not dedicated to strictly functional uses .... Building, for me, is a way of bearing witness to the past, to the greatness of the past, by means of atavistic powers, the mysterious images, the magical symbols which put man back in touch with the deepest memories of his culture."

In this superb $62 million building Botta has achieved a sense of power and clarity of form that are the essence of great architecture. To this strong geometry he has applied textured panels of burnt-sienna brick that give delicacy to the exterior. The stepped-back, five-story museum is capped by a black-and-white-striped cylinder cut at an angle. A slot appears in the center of the windowless facade and cuts straight through the middle of the composition. Seen from across Third Street, the massive bulk of the building is softened by the set-backs and the central slot. The pattern in the brick panels is highly effective and gives texture and interest to what in actuality are quite massive walls. The ground-floor front offers a long glazed horizontal to the street, announcing the main entrance.

Inside, the great cylinder-atrium rises through the center of the museum and opens to the sky. A grand staircase makes the act of walking through space pleasurable. The five floors of galleries are laid out in a traditional manner that makes walking from each to the next a passage through the evolution of modern art.

The museum was opened in 1935 as a private institution, the San Francisco Museum of Art. Long inadequately housed in the Beaux Arts Veterans Memorial Building in the Civic Center, it added the word "Modern" to its name in 1975. Under director Harry Hopkins SFMOMA began to improve dramatically. In 1976, the museum received Clyfford Still's munificent gift of twenty-eight large paintings. SFMOMA's collection includes Matisse's Fauve masterpiece *Femme au chapeau* of 1905, Frida Kahlo's *Self Portrait with Rivera* of 1931, and Jackson Pollock's *Guardians of the Secret* of 1943. The museum also has an exceptional collection of over 9,000 photographs, over 4,700 paintings and sculptures, over 1,500 architecture and design objects, and a growing collection of media arts works. This is a great building showcasing great art.

San Francisco Main Public Library
Larkin Street between Fulton and Grove Streets, in the Civic Center; Phone for hours 557-4000

Getting there by public transit:
Both Muni Metro and BART stop at Civic Center; Muni buses 5, 6, 7, 8, 19, 21, 27, and 71 all stop near the main library

9 **San Francisco Main Public Library**, *Postmodern-Deconstructionist, 1995, Pei Cobb Freed & Partners, architects; Simon Martin-Vegue Winkelstein & Moris, associated architects*

San Francisco is a bookish place. Its having one of the most highly-educated populations of any U.S. city is evidenced by the great many specialized bookstores sprinkled all over the city and its neighborhoods. In 1988 San Francisco voters approved a $109.4 million bond issue for a new main library and symbolic branch library renovations. The interior furnishings for the new main library were paid for by $30 million in private donations raised by the Library Foundation of San Francisco, making this the largest public/private partnership in the history of the city.

The principal designer of the new main was James I. Freed of Pei Cobb Freed & Partners of New York City; Simon Martin-Vegue Winkelstein & Moris was the associated San Francisco firm. This monumental public building represents the culminating stage in a wave of grand arts and cultural monuments funded in the prosperous late 1980s and constructed in the early 1990s. The new main library attempts to look in two directions simultaneously: respectfully back to Bakewell & Brown's Beaux Arts Civic Center, and boldly into the present on its back Grove and Hyde Street facades. The result is a building with formal, postmodern–Beaux Arts Larkin and Fulton Streets facades, and 1990s deconstructed Grove and Hyde Street facades. This is either an imaginative fusion or architectural schizophrenia, depending on your point of view. (The unrelieved wall at the sidewalk level of the Grove and Hyde Streets corner facing Market Street is one of the building's most controversial features.)

Inside, the library is organized around a great five-story, skylit atrium sixty feet in diameter. A grand staircase ascends the periphery of the central space. The new main was under construction as this guide went to press, and so any comments on the interior would be speculative. The main branch of the San Francisco Public Library has many treasures, among them an outstanding collection of books printed in San Francisco, long a center for fine printing. The new main also has a path-breaking Gay and Lesbian Center, which houses the Barbara Grier and Donna McBride Collection of gay and lesbian literature, among many other holdings. Of particular interest to both San Franciscans and visitors is the San Francisco History Room, the city's official archive. Here you can see changing exhibits on the city and also browse through a unique collection of books and photographs on San Francisco.

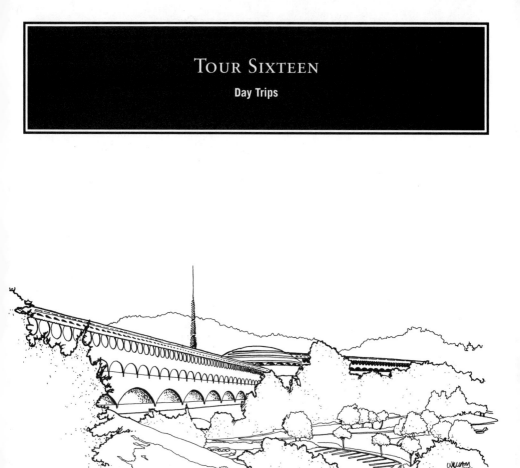

Marin County Civic Center,
**north of the Golden Gate Bridge, off Highway 101,
was designed in 1957 by Frank Lloyd Wright and built in stages.
The boomerang-shaped building bridges two valleys and is
a classic of 1950s futuristic design.**

Tour Sixteen: Day Trips

Preliminaries
San Francisco Bay Islands

- Alcatraz: The Rock
- Angel Island State Park: Ellis Island of the West
- Treasure Island: Memories of the 1939 Fair

Marin County

- Sausalito
- Mill Valley
- Muir Woods National Monument: Primeval Redwood Grove
- Marin County Civic Center: Frank Lloyd Wright Masterpiece
- Coastal Highway 1
- Point Reyes National Seashore

Napa Valley: Wine's Gentle Landscape
Introduction: Islands on the Land
A Brief History: Wine Making in California
- The City of Napa
  Domaine Carneros
  The Hess Collection (winery and art museum)
  Trefethen Vineyards
- Yountville
  Domaine Chandon
  Robert Mondavi Winery
  Louis M. Martini Winery
- Rutherford
- St. Helena: Main Street Jewel
  Beringer Vineyards
  Greystone Cellars/Culinary Institute of America
  Bothe-Napa Valley State Park
  Clos Pegase
- Calistoga and the Silverado Trail
- Mt. St. Helena/Robert Louis Stevenson State Park

The East Bay

- The Oakland Museum : The Museum of California
- Two Great Movie Palaces Near the Oakland Museum
- The University of California, Berkeley:
  The Athens of the West
- Off Campus in Berkeley
- John Muir National Historic Site
- Tao House/Eugene O'Neill National Historic Site
- Blackhawk: Gated Community and Postmodern
  Luxury Mall and Museums

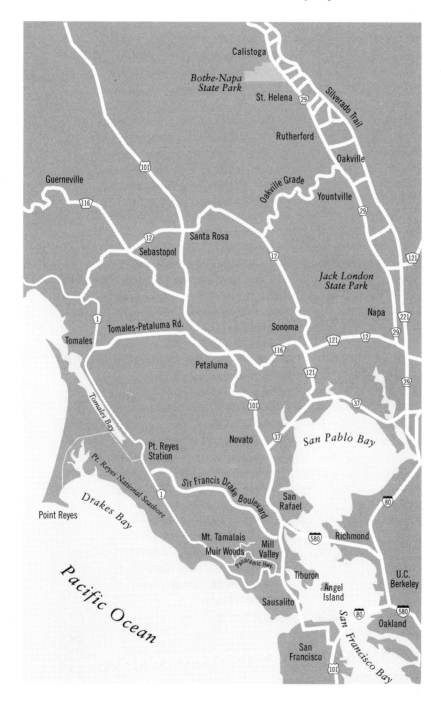

San Francisco Bay Islands, Marin County, Napa Valley, and The East Bay

San Mateo Peninsula

- Stanford University: A Pinnacle of Regional Environmental Design
- Filoli: Great Estate and Garden

Santa Cruz and the Monterey Bay Peninsula

- Santa Cruz: Turn-of-the-Century Seaside Resort / University of California at Santa Cruz
- The City of Monterey: California's First Capital
  Monterey Peninsula Museum of Art and La Mirada
  G. T. Marsh & Company
  San Carlos de Borromeo de Monterey Cathedral/Royal Presidio Chapel
  Larkin House
  Monterey Peninsula Museum of Art
  Colton Hall Museum and Old Monterey Jail
  Casa Amesti
  Robert Louis Stevenson (Gonzales) House
  Alvarado Street: Old Main Stem
  Custom House Plaza/Mexican Custom House
  Maritime Museum of Monterey/Stanton Center
  Annual Adobe House Tour
  Fisherman's Wharf
  Bicycle Trail/Monterey Sports Center
  Cannery Row
  Monterey Bay Aquarium
- The City of Pacific Grove: Victorian Chautauqua
  Del Monte Forest/The Seventeen-Mile Drive
  Pebble Beach
  The Lodge at Pebble Beach
- Carmel-by-the-Sea
  Ocean Avenue Shops
  Mission San Carlos Borromeo del Rio Carmelo/ Father Junipero Serra's Tomb
  Robinson Jeffers' Tor House
  Monastery Beach
  Point Lobos State Reserve

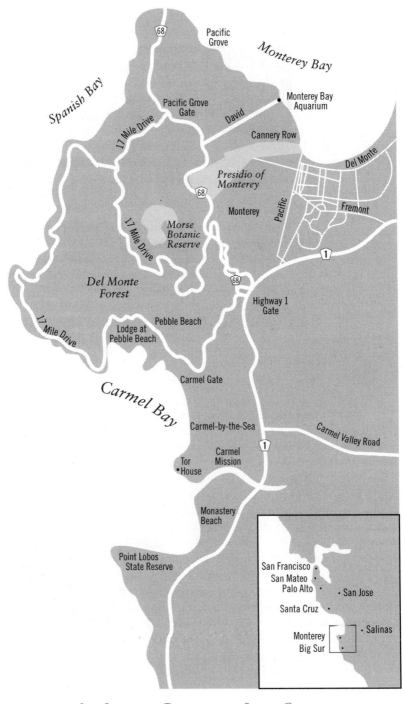

San Mateo Peninsula, Santa Cruz and the Monterey Bay Peninsula

Preliminaries

Greyhound buses
558-6789

BART
788-BART

Alcatraz: The Rock
Red & White Fleet
Pier 41, near the foot
of Powell; Round trip
prices start at $5.75 for
adults; $4.75 for seniors;
$3.25 for children;
Charge by phone
546-2700; Schedules:
546-2628

BEST TIMES
TO DO
THIS TOUR

It cannot be emphasized too strongly that weekdays are the best times for sightseeing outside the city. Saturdays and Sundays, when city people rush to the beaches and clog the back roads, are often overcrowded and congested. Sausalito, Muir Woods, the Napa Valley, and the Monterey Bay Aquarium are at capacity on weekends, especially in the summer. Try to make your visit bridge a weekend and some weekdays to see both the city and its richly rewarding surroundings.

Transportation

It is not always easy, or possible, to get to the region's attractions without an automobile. Transit cutbacks have left important places like Muir Woods National Monument without public transit access. Once you are outside San Francisco you are in modern automotive-dependent California. Monterey, once you arrive, is an exception: it has a clean and well-run transit system. **Greyhound buses** link San Francisco's Transbay Terminal with Monterey. Oakland and UC Berkeley are easily accessible via the **BART** subway.

San Francisco Bay Islands

• **Alcatraz: The Rock,** *Red & White Fleet*

Tickets are limited and are best bought in advance during the summer season at Pier 41, or you can charge by phone. Schedules vary with the seasons. You may stay on the island as long as you wish; however, be sure to note the time of the last return trip. The **Golden Gate National Park Association** publishes an excellent Official Map and Guide to Alcatraz. Park Rangers offer hourly tours of the island. *Dress warmly.*

Located in San Francisco Bay, rocky, fog-shrouded **Alcatraz** has been successively a roost for pelicans, hence its Spanish name; a harbor fortification; a military prison; from 1934 to 1963 a federal penitentiary for incorrigibles; and since 1972 a part of the Golden Gate National Recreation Area. A lighthouse has functioned here since 1854, when it was the first on the West Coast. Alcatraz was reserved by the U.S. Army in 1850 and a brick fort was constructed here in the early 1850s. In the 1860s the island was used to hold Confederate sympathizers, and from 1870 to 1890, Native American Indian prisoners. The Cellhouse of 1911, built by convicts, was one of the largest reinforced concrete structures in the world at its completion.

Since 1972 the island has been a national park and is preserved as a bleak, peeling, stabilized ruin. Visitors may see the prison's ruinous interior: "Broadway," "Times Square," the solitary confinement cells, and the walled Recreation Yard familiar from Hollywood gangster movies. There is no glamour here. Alcatraz is a monument to crime and the inhumanity with which criminals are treated. They lived in unheated concrete cells with one thin blanket; pneumonia was the silent executioner here. (Today in California we have modern, high-tech Pelican Bay prison in the far north of the state. There isolation is used to punish the state's most violent inmates.) Among the prisoners incarcerated on "The Rock" were Al Capone and "Machine Gun" Kelly. Robert Stroud, the "Birdman of Alcatraz," was never allowed to keep birds here, when he was transferred for killing a guard at Fort Leavenworth Prison. A small part of the island is closed from February through March during breeding season for night herons and sea gulls. While the island is ugly architecturally, the views back to San Francisco are splendid.

Alcatraz is extremely popular with tourists; children especially seem to like it. An automatic hush comes over chatting sightseers as the boat reaches the island's dock. But visitors with only a couple of days in San Francisco can do much better things with their time than spend half a day visiting a depressing ruined prison. The ferry to Sausalito passes quite near Alcatraz and gives a good enough view of it. A day trip to see the towering redwoods in Muir Woods National Monument north of San Francisco makes a much better outing.

Angel Island State Park: Ellis Island of the West
Red & White Fleet
Pier 43½ at Fisherman's Wharf near the foot of Powell; Round trip, $9 for adults; $8 for juniors (12–18); $4.50 for children.
• *In the summer there is ferry service from 21 Main Street in Tiburon, Marin County; 435-2131. Schedules vary with the seasons; phone 546-2628 for times. You can charge by phone at 546-2700*

Angel Island is a California state park and camp sites are available; Phone (800) 444-7275 for information and reservations. For the park's visitor center at Ayala Cove, phone 435-3522

• **Angel Island State Park: Ellis Island of the West,** *Red & White Fleet*
Forested **Angel Island** is one of San Francisco Bay's least crowded, most pleasurable "secrets." The mile-wide, triangular island is threaded with hiking trails and bicycle paths. No automobiles are permitted. From the 776-foot summit of Mt. Livermore there is a stunning panorama of the north Bay and gleaming San Francisco. It is a wonderful place to camp to see the glittering lights all around the bay from the unlighted island at night.

The island was discovered in 1765 by Gaspar de Portola; in 1775 Lieutenant Juan de Ayala anchored here while charting San Francisco Bay. The island became part of the harbor fortifications in 1863 with the establishment of Camp Reynolds. From 1910 to 1940 part of the island served as an Immigration Station; some 175,000 Chinese immigrants passed through here. While being held in the two-story detention barracks, some of these immigrants carved poems on the wall recording their anguish and their hope. Once scheduled for demolition, the barracks has been preserved as a museum and the poems found on its walls have been published by the Chinese Culture Foundation. The island with its historic military post and old immigration station became a California state park in 1956.

Treasure Island:
Memories of the 1939 Fair
Treasure Island Museum,
Treasure Island,
Building 1; Daily,
10 A.M. to 3:30 P.M.
Navy, Marine Corps,
Coast Guard museum;
free; 395-5067

•   **Treasure Island: Memories of the 1939 Fair**

Treasure Island is a flat man-made island linked to rocky Yerba Buena Island by a causeway. An exit from the San Francisco–Oakland Bay Bridge gives access to Treasure Island. Most of the island is off limits to civilians, for it is a U.S. Navy facility. But in the Administration Building there is a small museum devoted to the U.S. Navy, Marine Corps, and Coast Guard and to the **1939 Golden Gate International Exposition** for which the island was cr ?ated. The island was intended to become the city's airport and the terminus of the Manila Clippers, early pontoon-equipped aircraft. The surviving Streamline Moderne Administration Building was to be the airport's terminal. Only a few statues and a fountain survive as relics from the 1939 fair. What's most special about the island is the view back to San Francisco's Financial District. From this vantage point, especially at Christmastime when the Transamerica Pyramid is left lighted in the evening, the tight cluster of highrises makes an impressive sight.

Marin County

**Buck Center for
Research in Aging**

Marin County has a hard time of it from critical intellectuals. It *does* seem to be lotus land, where the sun always shines and everyone drifts by in a laid-back, tranquilized mood in shiny expensive automobiles talking mellowspeak on their cellular phones. An affluent suburban area with beautiful and varied geography, Mellow Marin harbors a beautiful and mostly monochromatic white-collar population famous for its vague state of mind. If all the world were a bookstore, Marin County would be the Self-help section, right between Ecology and Astrology. The clean environment, the modern houses with generous gardens, the tidy, high-style, lowrise office complexes full of financial analysts, the twee shopping centers stocked with upscale goods, and the almost litter-free roadsides give the driver motoring through Marin for the first time the feeling that he or she is passing through a life-sized scale model of Modern America.

Marin County was once mostly dairy country. Portuguese American cowboys worked their herds on these high coastal hills. Later ferries from San Francisco and electric railroads running inland up the picturesque valleys led to development of summer colonies for middle-class San Franciscans. San Rafael, the county seat, became the largest town. Sausalito and Tiburon served as railheads linking the railroads to the northern timber country with the ferries to San Francisco. The Golden Gate Bridge broke the county's isolation in 1937 and the county suburbanized in the booming 1950s.

Along with the suburban boom, Marin became an automotive Utopia. Only those who could afford a car and a new home came to Marin, creating a well-educated, well-paid population of professionals who demanded strict building controls. No highrise construction was permitted in Marin and high land values have justified high-style, state-of-the-art designs in houses, condominiums, and lowrise office and shopping center construction. In addition to all this good fortune, about half of Marin County is protected watershed or park land. Virtually the entire ocean side of the scenic, mountainous county is forever green and open.

Marin is changing, however; nothing doesn't. The population is aging; the children of Marinites cannot afford to buy in their parents' county; and the once-dynamic mix of impecunious creative people and upper-middle–class professionals is losing out to a flat social sameness of uniform wealth. "Equity exiles" have been selling their Marin houses at high prices and using the windfall to migrate to Oregon or Washington State, thereby expanding the *latté* belt but taking the variety out of the population mix. Nor is the school population holding its own; those who can afford to live here are having fewer and fewer children. And just to show that even paradise has its troubles there is the local saga of the Buck Trust. When philanthropist Beryl Buck died leaving behind shares in an obscure oil company, she wanted her bequest to go to the poor and the old in the county. When the little oil company was bought out by one of the oil giants, the Trust was suddenly awash with cash. But the county has an acute shortage of poor people. The result was to commission superstar architect I. M. Pei to design the campus-like **Buck Center for Research in Aging** on 488 acres north of Novato. The rich get richer while the poor get studied.

Buckeye Roadhouse
15 Shoreline Highway,
Mill Valley
331-2600

Lark Creek Inn
234 Magnolia Avenue,
Larkspur
924-7766

Golden Gate Transit
(415) 332-6600

Golden Gate Ferry
Phone (415) 332-6600
for schedule and fees; be
careful to inquire when
the last ferry back leaves
(usually about 8 P.M.)

Two Restaurants

The Buckeye Roadhouse, right off Highway 101 near the Mill Valley/Stinson Beach exit, in a 1937 roadhouse; a fine contemporary California restaurant. The **Lark Creek Inn,** located in a Victorian inn in a stand of redwoods right in Larkspur, is chef Bradley Ogden's rustic delight; some outdoor seating; reservations advised.

• *Sausalito*

BEST DAYS AND TIMES

The climate is pleasant, if windy, all year round. Summer weekends are very crowded and parking is impossible. Weekdays are always more relaxed and rewarding.

Transportation

Golden Gate Transit's clean buses provide excellent service from San Francisco to Marin County. Sit opposite the driver's side for a memorable view when crossing the Golden Gate Bridge.

Unless you are driving further north, it is not advisable to drive to Sausalito on weekends, since the town is small and trying to park is frustrating. The town of Sausalito collects more from parking fees and fines than from property taxes. Take the ferry. If you drive, take the Alexander Avenue exit off Highway 101 immediately after crossing the Golden Gate Bridge and enter Sausalito from the south. From the road you will see houses clinging to the steep cliffs, with parking atop the buildings.

The **Golden Gate Ferry** speeds passengers (no cars) from the Ferry Building at the foot of Market Street in San Francisco to the foot of El Portal in Sausalito. It is a bracing ride and on the way there are views of Alcatraz and through the Golden Gate. The view back to San Francisco is also splendid and displays the port city as it is best seen, from the water.

What is now the posh, cliff-clinging town of **Sausalito** was part of the Rancho Saucelito, 19,571 acres granted to London-born William A. Richardson in 1838 by Mexican governor José Figueroa. Legend has it that the name *Saucelito* means willow grove and refers to a bank of willows that grew near this steep shore. Richardson, who had converted to Catholicism three years earlier and married the daughter of the presidio *comandante,* had been named captain of the port at Yerba Buena, where he was expected to collect duties and enforce Mexico's trade bans. British and Yankee captains gravitated to Whaler's Cove because the quality of the water allowed it to be stored and firewood could be cut at nearby Angel Island. Richardson sought to lock up San Francisco

Bridgeway

New Town

Viña del Mar Plaza

Sausalito City Hall
At Caledonia and Litho streets; Historical museum open Monday, Wednesday, and Saturday from 10 A.M. to 4 P.M.; 289-4100

Bay by administering the Mexican customs at the legal port at Yerba Buena Cove and conducting smuggling operations at Whaler's Cove, now Richardson Bay, off his Rancho Saucelito.

　　Modern Sausalito began when twenty San Francisco businessmen organized the Sausalito Land & Ferry company in 1869. They bought three miles of waterfront property, the southern portion of Captain Richardson's old Rancho Saucelito, and subdivided it for San Franciscans seeking "a quiet rural home in a lovely place." By 1880 there was a small town here with two yacht clubs. Each lot buyer was given a pass for the company-run ferry to San Francisco. By 1885 Sausalito had about 1,500 residents and eight hotels. Eventually rail lines—at first steam, but electrified by 1905—reached up from Sausalito into bucolic Marin County. Wealthy San Franciscans began the colonization of the scenic county. In 1920 a frustrated San Francisco commuter, Harry E. Speas, incorporated Golden Gate Ferry Company to provide modern auto ferries to the city. The Art Deco span of the Golden Gate Bridge ended that era and Speas' fleet was dispersed, some ships going north to Puget Sound and one going as far as the Río de la Plata in Argentina.

　　Commercial Sausalito has evolved into two sections. South of the ferry slip at El Portal, **Bridgeway**, the scenic street along the water's edge with fine views of San Francisco, has become a tourist strip with generally upscale restaurants and shops. North of the ferry slip, beyond the yacht harbor and across Bridgeway, is a small grid centered on Caledonia Street. This is **New Town**—its shops and restaurants serve the local residents. El Portal is a one-block-long street flanked by **Viña del Mar Plaza**, a small park named after Sausalito's sister city in Chile. The fine fountain and improbable elephant light standards were designed by local architect W. A. Faville and are relics from San Francisco's famous Panama-Pacific International Exposition of 1915. Viña del Mar Plaza, with its lordly palms, is a landscape jewel. It has had to be closed to foot traffic and converted into a viewing-only oasis. On the corner of El Portal and Bridgeway, facing the park, is a delightful piece of naïve California Mission design with its red-tile-capped bay windows and impossible curvilinear Mission-style parapet with cutouts. Built in 1915, its exaggerated parapets look like a child's paper crown. The **Sausalito City Hall** in off-the-beaten-track New Town has a small historical museum.

Yacht Harbor

First Presbyterian Church
100 Bulkley Avenue

Golden Gate Transit
332-6600

Most visitors turn left at the fountain and spend their visit exploring Bridgeway and its shops. A more interesting alternative is to turn right at the fountain, cross the public parking lots, and wander up and down the wooden piers among the immaculate white sailboats that fill the spacious Sausalito **Yacht Harbor**. The best indication of the wealth in Marin is this bobbing, tinkling, sparkling flotilla of white hulls and blue canvas coverings. At the end of one pier is a hallucinatory pleasure barge that looks like a white gingerbread Taj Mahal.

Leave the yacht harbor and follow the asphalt bike path heading north. During World War II this area boomed as the Kaiser shipyards, with 17,500 workers who built ninety-three ships. When the war ended, squatters moved in and built houseboats here out of salvaged materials. Near Gate 5, just outside the Sausalito city limits, is a funky assortment of occupier-built houseboats, constructed atop everything from abandoned ferries slowly sinking into the mud to old barges and small ships. Marin County has waged a running war with this tenacious bohemian colony, mainly over sewage and sanitation problems.

As is so often the case, the bohemian pioneers have been followed by more conventional (and legal) imitators. At Gate B, further to the north of Richardson's Bay, is a neater, more orderly, and less romantic houseboat colony looking much like a floating suburb of shingled, skylighted, architect-designed houseboats all carefully arranged.

Even if you follow the usual path down Bridgeway, you can taste the residents' Sausalito by climbing up one of the steep staircases on the west side of the street. Just a few yards up, even on the busiest weekend, the paths and streets here are quiet and serene. When originally ferry-centered Sausalito was laid out, public easements were reserved for staircases that cascade down the slope, making pedestrian connectors between the terraced streets. One or two flights up any Sausalito staircase brings you to a quiet, tree-embowered world of patrolling house cats and residential serenity. The best architectural designs in Sausalito are these contemporary houses with sweeping views of the Bay and distant San Francisco. They do not show much of themselves from the twisting hillside streets, however, as they turn their faces out to the view. At 100 Bulkley Avenue is the shingle-clad **First Presbyterian Church**, designed by Ernest Coxhead in 1905—a fine example of the rustic imagery so dear to Northern Californians. There is also a good view down the hill to Viña del Mar Plaza.

- ## *Mill Valley*

Perhaps the most characteristic town in Marin County worth exploring is nontourist **Mill Valley**. The **Golden Gate Transit District**'s clean buses serve the town from both San Francisco and Sausalito. This narrow valley was once also a part of the Rancho Saucelito; a sawmill was built here on Cascade Creek in 1834 by Juan Read, an Irish-born sailor. The area was bought by a group of developers in 1887, subdivided in 1891, and a town founded. Built at the head of a narrow, redwood-filled valley, the town began developing when the electric interurban rail line opened in 1903 linking this sheltered, sunny valley with Sausalito and the San Francisco ferries. The depot at the head of the valley was the single node around which the town grew. San Franciscans began building small, uninsulated, rustic cottages under the trees within climbing distance of the depot. Immediately after the earthquake of 1906, many city people came to live here year round, insulating and expanding their summer cottages.

Today Mill Valley is a favorite residence for San Francisco architects, who appreciate the unpretentiousness of the local houses. Weathered, shingled houses stand nestled among the whispering trees along one-lane roads. Timber-reinforced stair paths lead up many of the steep slopes. The settlement has accommodated growth without spoiling its rustic charms. The downtown is still highly walkable and has a few shops featuring the works of local artists and artisans—prints and glass in particular.

Architect Bernard Maybeck's **Mill Valley Outdoor Art Club**, a few paces away from the old depot at the corner of Buena Vista and Blythedale Avenue, sums up the architectural tradition of early Marin and North Side Berkeley. This ingratiating clubhouse, set in a simple garden with redwoods and oaks, was built in 1905 and has been perfectly preserved. The club was founded with the express purpose of preserving the natural qualities of the town. The building's unusual roof-truss system pops through the roof. The **Mill Valley Public Library** was designed in 1969 by Wurster, Bernardi & Emmons and is a delightful piece of modern regional design, set by a creek.

When you have finished your exploration you can retire to the 1903 **depot**, now a café and bookstore. A new, small, brick-paved plaza in front of the depot occupies the area where tracks once were. Here the town's life comes to a public focal point. Sitting here you get an accurate picture of the valley's youth, old folks, and middle-aged inhabitants. It is a very California spot. Many musicians and rock stars live in secluded Marin County where the locals don't bother them. Mill Valley's **Sweetwater Tavern** and the **2 A.M. Club** often present well-known entertainers in a relaxed, intimate setting.

Mill Valley Outdoor Art Club
1 West Blithedale, Mill Valley; 382-2582

Mill Valley Public Library
at Throckmorton and Elma streets

Depot
87 Throckmorton Avenue, Mill Valley; 383-2665

Sweetwater Tavern
53 Throckmorton Avenue, Mill Valley; 388-2820

2 A.M. Club
380 Miller Avenue, Mill Valley; 388-6036

Muir Woods National Monument
West of Mill Valley, by back roads; No public transit goes directly to Muir Woods; Visitor Center with pamphlets, books, and refreshments; no picnicking or camping permitted.
• Open from 8 A.M. to sunset. The park has six miles of trails; the main path is wheelchair accessible. It is cool in these dense, shady groves; a warm jacket is good to have along; 388-2595

• **Muir Woods National Monument: Primeval Redwood Grove**

This majestic grove, the closest virgin stand of redwoods to San Francisco, is named after California's most famous conservationist, Scotland-born **John Muir**, one of the founders of the Sierra Club in 1892 and a tireless writer and campaigner for natural preservation in the United States. But the people who actually saved this lordly grove were Marin Congressman William Kent and his wife Elizabeth Thatcher Kent. Alarmed by a water company's proposal to flood Redwood Canyon for a reservoir, Kent bought the central 295 acres of the present park and then donated them to the federal government.

Marin County Civic Center
North of San Rafael,
off Highway 101;
For information about
hours and free docent
tours, phone 499-6104;
Golden Gate Transit
offers direct bus service
from San Francisco;
Phone 332-6600

President Theodore Roosevelt used the Antiquities Act of 1906, written to protect the Southwest's ancient sites, to proclaim the grove a national monument.

Today **Muir Woods** embraces 550 acres of towering redwoods, some of which reach 240 feet into the sky. The *Sequoia semper-virens* grow only in a coastal belt reaching from south of Monterey to the southwestern corner of Oregon. Their usual life span is from four hundred to eight hundred years, though a few are upward of two thousand years old. The redwoods depend on the constant mist from coastal fogs for moisture. Their thick bark helps protect them from forest fires. Walking among these trees, you learn the meaning of the word awesome. Their straight trunks seem to reach up to heaven itself. Their cool shade creates open forest floors carpeted with lacy swordferns.

Muir Woods is a popular place, and its main trail is sometimes congested on weekends. But if you secure a map at the Visitor Center you can explore less-crowded paths deeper in the park. Please stay on the marked trails, since trampling the earth here compacts the soil and damages the plants.

- **Marin County Civic Center: Frank Lloyd Wright Masterpiece**

On this undulating site of grassy, oak-dotted hills, so typical of all that is most beautiful in the California landscape, Frank Lloyd Wright designed one of California's great buildings, a work of visionary art. It is a futuristic vision curiously both dated and timeless. "Big Pink," as county workers call it, is one of Wright's last works. It was designed in 1957 and built in phases beginning in 1960. Wright and the Taliesin Associated Architects, with Aaron Green, associate architect, created a master plan calling for a low-lying boomerang-shaped building spanning the crowns of three hills. Roads pass under the bridgelike buildings leading to the front gates and escalators. Inside, long skylights cut through all the levels of the Administration Building, resulting in hallway balconies that look down on a linear garden. The building's great metal roof is painted blue like the sky. A small, freestanding Post Office east of the main building is the only U.S. government commission Wright ever received.

After Wright's death in 1959, William Wesley Peters and Taliesin Associated Architects completed the landscape plan with its fairgrounds and lagoon and designed the circular Main Veterans Memorial Auditorium of 1972 and an Exhibit Hall. The 160-acre site is most festive on the Fourth of July, when Marin County holds its annual county fair and fireworks burst over Wright's great building. Wright's theme here is the one he adopted in his last works, the circle. The circle, the globe, the dome, and the arch are all embroidered into the site's and the building's design in decorative grilles, finials, pavements, and furnishings. Wright's courtrooms in the Hall of Justice are round, with spectators sitting in curved rows. The gold, needlelike, triangular spire (actually an antenna) serves as a counterpoint to all the curved forms. The small, sheltered terrace garden near the spire is the complex's hidden oasis.

• *Coastal Highway 1*

The California Coastal Commission's *California Coastal Resource Guide* is the indispensable guide for those who want to know the coast. For weather conditions on the north coast, in particular to find out if the fog is in, phone the **Stinson Beach** weather report.

Stinson Beach
weather report 868-1922

Audubon Canyon Ranch Bird Sanctuary
(707)433-4400

The only practical way to see the coast is with an automobile. Public transportation to the coastal highway north of San Francisco is scarce. One **Golden Gate Transit** bus leaves San Francisco for Point Reyes at 8 A.M. on weekends and holidays. On the south coast, **SamTrans** (San Mateo County Transit) runs buses on the coastal highway; the problem is getting from the city to those bus lines. Those driving the coastal highway for the first time will want to be off it and back on Highway 101 before dark; though well marked with white reflectors along the center of the road, it is a difficult road to drive in the dark.

The Park Service map of the GGNRA shows parking areas and trails in coastal Marin. Walk to the top of some hill or bluff to look down on the coast spread out before you. Even overcast days have their own moody beauty on the north coast. The sea turns shades of slate gray, with burnished-silver patches where the sun breaks through the close cloud cover.

The California coast immediately north and south of San Francisco is unpeopled, unspoiled, rocky, wild, tonic. Both Marin County and Point Reyes to the north and the Monterey Peninsula and Bay to the south are among the great scenic treasures of North America. Most of the coast is protected in county or state shoreline parks and has been made accessible through very well designed roads, view spots, parking lots, and picnic spots. Highway 1, which winds along the coast, is designed for pleasure driving only—no trucks travel it. Many wide shoulders along the view side of the road offer travelers the opportunity to stop briefly to survey the panorama.

To the north is open, rocky coast, redwood forests, and the **Audubon Canyon Ranch Bird Sanctuary** at Bolinas Lagoon. Point Reyes, a little further north, is a vast, windswept, moorlike landscape. To the south of San Francisco, off Point Lobos State Park near Monterey and Carmel, is one of the richest undersea biological zones on the 1,264-mile California coast. Off this verdant, rocky point, great beds of giant kelp grow and sea life flourishes. The delicate red seaweeds strewn on the gravel beach at Lovers' Point in Pacific Grove are as impressive in their miniaturized delicacy as the redwoods are in their great size.

• *Point Reyes National Seashore*

Point Reyes National Seashore can be reached by **Golden Gate Transit** only on Saturday, Sunday, and holidays via the **80 bus**, which leaves Seventh and Market streets in downtown San Francisco at 8:06 A.M., with pickups along Van Ness Avenue at Geary, Sutter, Clay, and Union streets. At Fourth and Hetherton streets in San Rafael, underneath the elevated freeway, transfer to the **65 bus** to Point Reyes. Inquire about the bus back for your return. For weather conditions on the north coast, phone the Stinson Beach weather report. Because of the size of the park, a car is best.

Point Reyes National Seashore
In coastal West Marin is the Bear Valley Visitors Information Center; A map of the park is available at park headquarters; 663-1092

Beyond the Bolinas Lagoon, Highway 1 travels right over the San Andreas Fault to the small hamlet of Olema and the Point Reyes National Seashore Headquarters beyond. The San Andreas Fault, some 650 miles long and extending from Mendocino County's Point Arena in the north to Baja California in the south, is the great "strike-slip" fracture between the Pacific plate and the North American plate, two of the six great pieces of the earth's crust. It is California's longest and best-known earthquake zone, where the two plates grind past each other at the rate of about three inches a year. The sudden movement of about sixteen-and-one-half feet here in 1906 caused the devastating San Francisco earthquake. Point Reyes was, in fact, once a part of the Sierra Nevada, but as the Pacific plate slid past and under the North American plate, Point Reyes drifted north.

Point Reyes was named by the explorer Sebastián Vizcaíno in 1603 after the Feast of the Three Kings, or Epiphany. An estuary here is named Drake's Bay and is presumed by many to be the place where the English adventurer Francis Drake beached his ship, the *Golden Hind*, in 1579 while on a privateering expedition that took him around the globe. While on the Northern California coast, either here or in some other protected spot, he was crowned by the local (probably coast Miwok) Native Americans, claimed the land for Queen Elizabeth I, and named it Nova Albion. He then sailed westward across the Pacific, returning to London where he was knighted by the Queen.

Point Reyes is the foggiest spot on the California coast. A lighthouse was built here to guide coastal shipping. The surf and tides here are treacherous and not recommended for swimming. Heavy fogs and its remoteness kept the peninsula from development until the American era, when dairy and cattle ranches were eventually established. In 1962 the unspoiled peninsula was made a National Seashore with an added agreement that existing ranching could continue. In 1972 Point Reyes became part of the Golden Gate National Recreation Area, which extends from here to the southern edge of San Francisco. North of Point Reyes Station is the long slit of Tomales Bay, also a part of the San Andreas Fault. The local specialty is giant Pacific oysters grown in the bay from Japanese stock. Oyster beds can be seen near Millerton Point and other spots. The southern end of Tomales Bay is a refuge for countless migrating waterfowl. Point Reyes is famous as a whale-watching spot. On New Year's Day, avid fans of the California gray whale jam the roads and bluffs seeking glimpses of these huge creatures on their southern migration.

Napa Valley: Wine's Gentle Landscape

BEST DAYS AND TIMES

September and October are harvest time, and the wineries are in full operation then. See Mondavi in the winery listing for a summer concert series.

Transportation

The best way to see the wine country is by car. Cross the Golden Gate Bridge and travel north on Highway 101 to Highway 37. Follow Highway 37 east to Highway 12/121. Highway 12/121 continues east through beautiful rolling country to Highway 29, the Mt. St. Helena Highway, which passes straight up the Napa Valley and past many wineries. The select list of wineries in this chapter generally follows this south-to-north pattern. Choose perhaps three wineries to visit and then return down the east side of the valley, on the beautiful Silverado Trail. The town of Calistoga makes a good place to stay overnight, though the valley can be sampled in a long day trip from San Francisco.

Greyhound runs buses about six times daily from San Francisco, Vallejo, and Napa and then up the valley to Yountville, Oakville, Rutherford, St. Helena, and Calistoga. St. Helena is probably the best place to get off. There is no convenient bus service in the valley itself. You will have to hike, but the valley floor is flat.

Many tour companies offer one-day bus excursions from San Francisco's Union Square area to Napa Valley. They are far less agreeable than being on your own, however. Shop around for the best prices and tours.

Picnics

The Oakville Grocery is a gourmet's delight, a temple of food and wine.

Information

The **Napa Chamber of Commerce** can provide a list of lodgings and coming events. Antonia Allegra's *Napa Valley: The Ultimate Winery Guide*, is a beautiful and useful book.

The Oakville Grocery
7856 St. Helena Highway, Oakville 94562
(707) 944-8802

Napa Chamber of Commerce
1556 First Street, Napa 94559; (707) 226-7455

Note: *Many wineries are closed on major legal and religious holidays. Phone ahead to be certain the one you want to visit is open. Be aware that the California Highway Patrol is vigilant here: designate a nondrinking driver for safety's sake. Already-opened wine bottles can be legally transported in the trunk but not in the passenger area of the car*

Introduction: Islands on the Land

Napa Valley, an hour north of San Francisco, is the most famous wine-producing region in the United States. This gentle valley is only about thirty-five miles long and from one to five miles wide. It trends north-south and is drained by the Napa River, a short tidal stream that empties into San Pablo Bay, which in turn opens onto San Francisco Bay. State Highway 29, "the wine road," passes up the valley framed by rolling hills. Along this road are many of the state's best-known wineries. The valley is defined by the Mayacamas Range on the west, with Sonoma County on the other side, and the lower Howell Range to the east. These low mountains form barriers against the cool ocean fogs to one side and the summer heat of the interior valley on the other. At the northern end of Napa Valley are 4,343-foot-high Mt. St. Helena and the sulfurous spas clustered around **Calistoga**, the source of California's best-known bottled mineral water.

Both soil and climate in the Napa Valley are perfect for grape growing. Orderly rows of pruned vines staked out on wire trellises blanket the flat valley bottom and billow over the lower foothills. As with all California agricultural landscapes, there is an underlying mathematical rigor to the marching rows. The colors of the valley change with the seasons: in the winter months the landscape is a deep emerald green; in the spring the new growth on the vines is light green or yellow; in the summer the vines are dark green; and in the fall, at harvest time, the vines turn gold and scarlet and are hung with purple or green clusters of ripe fruit.

While the valley enjoys a moderate climate, with a yearly mean temperature of 57.7°F, occasional frosts do descend and can decimate the vineyards. Hence the mysterious propellers connected to warming devices that dot the landscape. In mid-April, when chills fall, they serve as giant fans to temper the air. In the newest vineyards, sprinkler systems spray a fine mist that freezes in a thin glazing of ice over the tender leaves and buds. This protective shield insulates the vines from lower, destructive temperatures.

The central part of the valley north of the fog-blocking Yountville Hills is the heart of the great wine region. The climate, soil structure, and varied exposures to sunlight here are most congenial to the prized Chardonnay and the rich, complex Cabernet Sauvignon grapes. Many of the most famous wineries in America cluster here and, in good years, produce world-class vintages. The clear skies, moderately warm temperatures, and gravelly soils of the Napa River flood plain nurture privileged vines and produce noble wines. **The Rutherford Bench**, the gravelly benchlands west of Highway 29 between Yountville and St. Helena, boasts many famous American wineries, including Robert Mondavi, Beaulieu, Heitz, and Oakville.

Traditionally, wineries were set in dense islands of shade trees and palms. Often a pair or row of palms, or some other tall windbreak, announced the entrance to each ranch. Some wineries sit on the floor of the valley nestled in sun-shading trees; others are set back on the low foothills. Wire trellises begin abruptly at right angles to the roadside and stretch back to the hills in taut rows.

The completion of the railroad led to a boom in vineyards and winery construction. The valley is studded with fine old Victorian houses, wineries, warehouses, and excavated hillside caves from the first era of expansion. San Francisco architects of note designed many of these buildings.

A Brief History: Wine Making in California

The Franciscan missionaries were the first to make wine in California. They imported the black grapes now known as "Mission grapes," which produced a heavy wine. In Carpinteria, south of Santa Barbara, *la viña grande,* a mammoth vine planted in mission days, still stands. In the post-Gold Rush period European immigrants from many lands planted vines and produced homemade wines. The key figure, however, in the history of commercial wine making in the state was a Hungarian, Agoston Haraszthy, who persuaded the governor of California to commission him to scour Europe for vines and information in 1861. When Haraszthy returned from his expedition, he brought back with him 150,000 cuttings and the latest French and German technology. His official report launched scientific viticulture in California. These experimental vines were planted in Sonoma County at Haraszthy's **Buena Vista** winery.

It took time for Californians to discover the best areas for grape growing. Robert Louis Stevenson noted in 1883 that wine making in California was still in the experimental stage. "The beginning of vine planting is like the beginning of mining for precious metals, he observed. The wine-grower also 'prospects.' One corner of land after another is tried with one kind of grape after another. This is a failure; that is better; a third is best. So, bit by bit, they grope about for their Clos Vougeot and Lafitte." In due time viticulture flourished, and when the phylloxera root louse devastated the vineyards of Europe in the 1870s and 1880s, cuttings of the pest-resistant American roots were shipped there to be grafted onto European vines.

A different kind of blight attacked California's vineyards fifty years later: the Volstead Act of 1919, which ushered in thirteen years of Prohibition in the United States. This remains one of the strangest chapters in the puritanical history of American manners and morals. Only "medicinal" and sacramental wines could be sold during this time. Many of Napa Valley's vineyards were converted to orchards or cattle ranches. The vital thread of continuity in wine making was snapped. The vineyards that survived grafted over to grapes suitable for shipment to home wine makers. In those years an average of 50,000 carloads of wine grapes were shipped from California, mostly to Italian American communities in the big Eastern cities. Interestingly, this was enough to produce 375 million bottles of wine, more than the amount produced by the 700 wineries that existed in 1920.

It took about a generation for the art of wine making to revive after the repeal of Prohibition. When it did, it did so with a new technology, including stainless-steel fermentation tanks and many other innovations. The **University of California at Davis** became the disseminating center for the reborn industry. Today—in everything from planting to tending to picking to crushing—the wine making process is highly automated.

Napa Valley Conference and Visitor's Bureau
1310 Napa Town Center, Napa 94558; Open Monday to Friday, 9 A.M. to 5 P.M., and Saturday and Sunday, 10 A.M. to 5 P.M.; (707) 226-7455

Napa County Historical Society
219 First Street, Napa; Open Tuesday and Thursday from noon to 4 P.M.; Phone for information about changing exhibits, (707) 224-1739

Victorian Gothic First Presbyterian Church of 1874

By 1960 the contemporary wine boom was on, and prices for choice land in the valley echoed the boom. In 1970 an acre of prime Napa soil cost $1,000; by 1980—if you could find it—an acre here cost $25,000. In 1971 there were fewer than thirty wineries in the valley; by 1988 there were 240 federally bonded wineries. So-called "boutique wineries" proliferated; Californians who made their fortunes in other places came to Napa Valley to be gentlemen wine makers. Individuals were followed by corporations such as Getty Oil, Atlantic Richfield Oil, Superior Oil, R. J. Reynolds tobacco, the Tejon Ranch, Coca-Cola, Pepsi-Cola, and even a division of the Hughes Corporation went into the grape-growing business. Some of these corporations have left the risky wine business. New buyers are often Europeans aware of the long-term value of vineyards, and willing to invest heavily in land and up-to-date facilities. By 1986, California produced about 366 million gallons of wine, about 86 percent of the national wine market.

Since 1980, the phylloxera root louse has reemerged in the valley. The aphidlike insect kills grapevines by infesting their roots, preventing the plants from absorbing water and nutrients. The wine industry and NASA scientists working out of the Ames Research Center in Silicon Valley's Mountain View have launched a high-tech approach to the menace. Using remote sensing devices and the ER-2, an updated version of the U-2 spy plane, scientists are photographing and mapping the phylloxera spread patterns. Infected grapevines must then be uprooted and the vineyards replanted with new rootstocks thought to have a greater resistance to the pest. It takes the new vines about five years to come into significant production. This is an expensive proposition, costing about twenty thousand dollars per acre. Grape growing and wine making continue to be on the frontiers of science and art.

• *The City of Napa*

Of the first, wooden, Napa River–oriented city nothing remains. However, many solid brick-and-stone railroad-era buildings survive downtown. With the automobile, Napa's commercial activity shifted to large modern shopping centers built north and west of the city near Highway 29, which is a full-scale California freeway with three interchanges west of the city of Napa. The city has always been the county seat for prosperous Napa County.

Downtown Napa today is a Victorian sampler of California nineteenth-century architecture and twentieth-century urban planning. The **Napa County Historical Society** has its research library and changing exhibits in the native stone 1902 Goodman Library, a gift from banker George E. Goodman and designed by architect L. M. Turton. Napa's close-in, tree-lined, leafy residential streets are rarely visited and are rich in perfectly preserved Victorian houses. The blocks south of Division Street and the **Victorian Gothic First Presbyterian Church of 1874** are well worth careful exploration.

- **Domaine Carneros**

On Route 121/12, 4 miles southwest of the city of Napa. Tastings and tours. Rising in splendor atop its knoll is this recent addition to the Carneros district of the valley. Designed after the Tattinger's Chateau de la Marquetterie in Champagne, France, this opulent winery masks up-to-date sparkling wine making operations behind what looks like an eighteenth-century chateau.

- **The Hess Collection Winery**

From Highway 29 south of the city of Napa, turn left onto Redwood Road at its intersection with Trancas. The winery is about six miles up the scenic, winding, hilly road on Mount Veeder. Tastings and self-guided tours; excellent slide show on the cycle of the seasons and wine making; contemporary art museum.

        Swiss entrepreneur Donald Hess built this fine old-new winery and housed part of his important collection of large-scale contemporary art works in an adjoining thirteen-thousand-square-foot art gallery. Two simple stone buildings from 1903 have been linked by a modern building designed by Swiss architect Beat A. H. Jordi. The international contemporary art collection is outstanding, with works by Stella, Motherwell, Bacon, Gilbert and George, and other modern masters (catalog available). **The Hess Collection** and **Clos Pegase** are the two wineries of most interest to lovers of modern art and architecture.

- **Trefethen Vineyards**

Three miles north of Napa. Tasting room open daily, tours of vineyards and production facilities can be seen. The 1886 winery barn is a classic utilitarian California farm building.

Domaine Carneros
1248 Duhig Road,
Napa 94558;
(707) 257-0101

The Hess Collection Winery
4411 Redwood Road,
Napa 94558;
(707) 255-1144

Trefethen Vineyards
1160 Oak Knoll Avenue,
Napa 94558;
(707) 255-7700

Vintage 1870
(closed Monday)

Mustards Grill
7399 St. Helena
Highway, between
Yountville and Oakville;
(707) 944-2424

Ristorante Piatte
6480 Washington Street
in Yountville;
(707) 944-2070

Napa Valley Balloons
P.O. Box 2860,
Yountville 94599;
(707) 944-0228
or (800) 253-2224

- *Yountville*

Tiny **Yountville** takes its name from **George Calvert Yount**, a North Carolina–born trapper who entered California in 1831, became a naturalized Mexican citizen, and obtained a land grant to 11,000-acre Rancho Caymus here in the Napa Valley. The town is canted slightly off the highway. The old brick Groezinger winery built in the 1870s has been converted into a tourist boutique complex called **Vintage 1870**. The town gem is **Mustards Grill**. Mustards serves lunch and dinner daily and has an excellent, moderately priced seasonal menu of "new American" dishes. It boasts a mesquite grill, woodburning oven, and stylish modern interior. **Ristorante Piatte** has gourmet pizzas and Italian fare in a somewhat Southwestern setting.

        Napa Valley Balloons offers one-hour ascents over the scenic valley in colorful hot-air balloons early each morning, weather permitting. Write or phone for costs and meeting place. Reservations must be made in advance.

Domaine Chandon
1 California Drive in
Yountville, off Highway
29, Veterans Home exit;
P.O. Box 2470,
Yountville 94599
(707) 944-2280

Robert Mondavi Winery
7801 St. Helena
Highway (Highway 29);
P.O. Box 106,
Oakville 94562;
(707) 226-1335

Louis M. Martini Winery
254 South St. Helena
Highway (Highway 29),
St. Helena 94574;
(707) 963-2736

Auberge du Soleil
180 Rutherford Hill
Road, Rutherford 94573;
(707) 963-1211

St. Helena Chamber of Commerce
1080 Main Street
(Highway 29);
P.O. Box 124, St. Helena
94574; (707) 963-4456

Richie Building
1331 Main Street

Odd Fellows Building

• **Domaine Chandon**

Tours; tastings; retail sales; call for information and restaurant reservations. The fine French-classic and nouvelle-cuisine restaurant serves lunch and dinner; reservations advised two weeks ahead of time. Sparkling wine, never called "champagne" here, is produced at this modern winery by the traditional *méthode champenoise.* Begun in 1973 by France's Moët-Hennessy, the contemporary winery was designed by San Francisco architects ROMA. The informative tour explains the making of sparkling wine.

• **Robert Mondavi Winery**

Tours; tastings; retail sales. The **Robert Mondavi Summer Festival** presents Saturday-evening jazz concerts in July. Robert Mondavi established this winery in 1966. A great arch and tower distinguish this contemporary California Mission-style stucco building designed by Cliff May. Mondavi and Château Mouton-Rothschild have begun making a Bordeaux-style wine from the Napa Valley's Cabernet Sauvignon and Cabernet Franc grapes called Opus One.

• **Louis M. Martini Winery**

Tours and tastings. This simple building is home to some great wines. The tastings offered are extensive.

• *Rutherford*

The small town of Rutherford grew up around the railroad station located here. The acclaimed, and expensive, **Auberge du Soleil** prepares French cuisine with a California touch. This restaurant-hotel serves lunch and a *prix fixe* dinner daily. A terraced dining room has views of the valley. Call for reservations.

• *St. Helena: Main Street Jewel*

The **St. Helena Chamber of Commerce** is located in an inconspicuous building on the right-hand side of the road on the way north from San Francisco. Good selection of brochures and information.

The jewel of St. Helena's main street is the brick and timber **Richie Building** designed by the Corlett Brothers of Napa in 1892 and highly ornamented with spindlework and fancy trimmings. Shops occupy the ground floor; the Masons met in the auditorium upstairs. Across the street is the less elaborate but still fine pressed-brick **Odd Fellows Building** of 1885. It was a common pattern in small California agricultural towns for the town merchants' Masonic hall to be paired with the less fancy Odd Fellows' hall in the center of town. The farmers' simpler Grange Hall was usually on a cheaper plot on a county road outside the towns.

Prosperity, as evidenced in the high-quality shops that pepper Main Street, has permitted St. Helena to preserve her small-town form. No large shopping center on the edge of town turns this nineteenth-century main street into a retail desert. Picnickers will want to stop at **The Model Bakery** to buy bread with herbs; some is baked with fragrant rosemary. The best art gallery in town is **The Evans Studio**. Evans' botanical prints of California flora are contemporary classics and make artistic and evocative reminders of your trip. Literary buffs may want to see the **Silverado Museum**. Housed in its own wing of the St. Helena Public Library Center built in 1979, this specialized museum is devoted to the works of Robert Louis Stevenson. **Tra Vigne Restaurant**, just south of downtown, has outside as well as indoor lunch and dinner daily. It serves superb Northern Italian cuisine and memorable house-baked bread in an airy setting designed by Guthrie Friedlander Architects; phone for reservations.

The Model Bakery
1357 Main Street,
St. Helena;
(707) 963-8192

The Evans Studio
1124 Pine Street;
P.O. Box 640;
St. Helena 94574;
(707) 963-2126

Silverado Museum
1490 Library Lane;
P.O. Box 409,
St. Helena 94574;
(707) 963-3757

Tra Vigne Restaurant
1050 Charter Oak Avenue,
immediately off Highway
29, St. Helena;
(707) 963-4444

- **Beringer Vineyards**

The **Beringer** winery, which dates from 1876, has its wine tasting and retail in the old Beringer house built in 1883 and designed by William Mooser. This "Rhine castle" is built of stone with half-timbering and set in a beautiful, mature garden landscape. A tour includes cool caverns where wines are stored. Chinese American laborers excavated the first of these caves a century ago.

Beringer Vineyards
2000 Main Street;
P.O. Box 111,
St. Helena 94574;
(707) 963-7115

- **Greystone Cellars/Culinary Institute of America**

Built for William Bowers Bourn in 1888 and designed by Percy & Hamilton, this imposing stone winery is the largest masonry structure erected in the Napa Valley. The Christian Brothers, a teaching order of the Roman Catholic Church, once produced both table and sacramental wines here. Since 1994 it has housed the West Coast branch of the Hyde Park, New York, **Culinary Institute of America** with continuing education for professional chefs.

Greystone Cellars/Culinary Institute of America
2555 Main Street,
St. Helena 94574;
(707) 967-1100

- **Bothe–Napa Valley State Park**

This nearly two-thousand-acre state park features a water-powered gristmill with a large overshot wheel built in 1846 and restored by the State of California. It is a picturesque monument to early agricultural technology. The only public campground in the Napa Valley, this state park is booked solid in the summertime; make reservations in advance. This rugged volcanic park has elevations ranging from three hundred to two thousand feet. Hiking trails thread through forests of coastal redwoods, douglas fir, tanoak, and madrone. It can get hot here in the summer with temperatures sometimes reaching 105 F, but the nights are usually cool. Winter is the rainy season; spring and fall are delightful.

Bothe-Napa Valley State Park, *Four miles north of St. Helena;*
3801 St. Helena Highway North(Highway 29);
For campsite reservations between April and October write to Mistix at P.O. Box 85705, San Diego, 92138-5705; Phone (800) 444-7275 in California; Entry is $5 per car; picnicking; fee for campsites; swimming pool open mid-June through Labor Day; (707) 942-4575

Clos Pegase
1060 Dunaweal Lane,
one mile south of
Calistoga (look for the
Stonegate Winery sign
south of Calistoga);
P.O. Box 305,
Calistoga 94515
(707) 942-4981

Sharpsteen Museum
1311 Washington Street,
Calistoga 94515;
(707) 942-5911

Indian Springs
1712 Lincoln Avenue,
Calistoga 94515;
(707) 942-4913

Calistoga Bookstore
1343 Lincoln Avenue,
Calistoga;
(707) 942-4123

• **Clos Pegase**

Opened in 1987, Jan Shrem's winery is the result of an architectural competition to design "a temple to wine" juried at the San Francisco Museum of Modern Art and won by Michael Graves Architects, with painter Edward Schmidt. In Greek mythology, Pegasus, the winged horse from heaven, touched his hoof on Mt. Helikon and broke open the spring of the Muses. Here Michael Graves, a professor of architecture at Princeton, has set an "archaic," almost Minoan orange monument against a green, oak-clad volcanic knoll that juts out of the narrow valley floor here. The winery sits on the valley floor while Shrem's house (not open to the public) crowns the knoll behind it. Extensive aging caves have been excavated under the abrupt hill. The grounds around the winery are dotted with contemporary sculpture. The views all around are superb. This is a great work of postmodern architecture, worthy of the valley it crowns.

If you are not continuing on to Calistoga, this is a good place to pick up the scenic **Silverado Trail**, at the end of Dunaweal Lane. You cut back across the valley to return to Highway 29, at Trancas Road just north of the city of Napa.

• *Calistoga and the Silverado Trail*

Underground at the head of the Napa Valley is a superheated pool of 250-degree mineral water that erupts in hot springs and can be tapped by wells. These medicinal hot springs were frequented by the Wappo tribe. The Spanish called the place Agua Caliente. In 1859, San Francisco's Sam Brannan bought the springs and built the state's first resort, which he named "Calistoga" by fusing "California" with "Saratoga," for New York State's elite Victorian resort. The **Sharpsteen Museum** has restored one of Brannan's fanciful gingerbread cottages. Calistoga's simple motels and low-key spas offer mud baths, hot mineral water Jacuzzis, saunas, massages, and blanket wraps. The mud baths are in small, square, tile tubs filled with dark, bubbling goo made of Canadian peat and Calistoga volcanic ash infused with hot mineral water. When submerged to your neck, you feel a sense of weightlessness. Most spas have separate baths for men and women; prices range from about $40 to $130, depending on treatments, massages, and such extras as facials. A delightful spot is **Indian Springs**. This small resort has cottages, tennis courts, mud baths, massages, and an immaculate old-fashioned 1913 swimming pool of local mineral water. The Calistoga Gliderport is adjacent. The **Calistoga Bookstore** is good for local maps, guides, and books on wine. Otherwise the shopping and restaurants here are not noteworthy. French-owned Source Perrier today owns the bottling plant for Calistoga's best-known mineral water. It is just outside the town near the head of the Silverado Trail (no tours).

Just outside Calistoga, at the east end of Lincoln Avenue, is the beginning of the **Silverado Trail**, a scenic, less-traveled road that skirts the base of the hills on the east side of Napa Valley and ends at Trancas Street, just north of Napa. It and Highway 29, together with several cross roads, form a ladderlike pattern in the valley.

Silverado Trail

Robert Louis Stevenson State Park
(707) 942-4575

The Oakland Museum: The Museum of California
10th and Oak Street, Oakland 94607, one block east of the Lake Merritt BART station; Open Wednesday to Saturday 10 A.M. to 5 P.M.; Sunday, noon to 7 P.M. Inexpensive parking under the museum; (510) 273-3401

• **Mt. St. Helena/Robert Louis Stevenson State Park**

Mt. St. Helena rises 4,343 feet and dominates the Napa Valley. Russian explorers named it in the early nineteenth century in honor of their empress. Silver and quicksilver were mined here in the mid-nineteenth century. Robert Louis Stevenson honeymooned in an abandoned silver mine seven miles north of Calistoga in what is now **Robert Louis Stevenson State Park**; he modeled Spyglass Hill in *Treasure Island* after it. The five-mile Robert Louis Stevenson Memorial Trail climbs to the summit of Mt. St. Helena; the state park embraces 3,670 acres. On a clear day the view stretches from the formidable Sierra Nevada to distant San Francisco. The verdant Napa Valley spreads out at your feet and in the fall the vines are tinged with scarlet.

The East Bay

• **The Oakland Museum: The Museum of California**

The Oakland Museum's second name, "the Museum of California," is more accurate than its formal name. This is the outstanding regional museum, presenting all California in microcosm in three sections devoted to the art, history, and ecology of the state. Opened in 1969 and designed by Kevin Roche, John Dinkeloo and Associates, with Dan Kiley, landscape architect, much of the building is underground, tucked into its gently sloping four-block site, with lavish plantings atop it. The Art Gallery presents select California works, from the earliest artist-explorers to the latest trendsetters, with an important display of early-twentieth-century paintings and some Craftsman artifacts. There is a fine selection of major works by Bay Area figurative painters of the 1950s and 1960s. The History Gallery displays pieces from the largest collection of Californiana in existence—everything from Indian pictographs to the recent past presented in chronological sequence. The Natural History section is arranged to take you on an imaginary walk across the different environmental zones of the state, from the Pacific shore to the Sierra crest and the Great Basin. This last section is particularly handsome, with meticulous models showing the geology, botany, and animal life of California. The museum's bookshop is good for California art books and natural history guides.

Sun Hong Kong Restaurant
389 Eighth Street, near Franklin, Oakland;
(510) 465-1940

Holmes Book Company
274 Fourteenth Street, between Harrison and Alice, Oakland;
(510) 893-6860

Oakland Paramount Theater
2025 Broadway, at Twenty-first Street, Oakland; Tours of the landmark interior are offered on the first and third Saturdays of the month at 10 A.M.; small fee; (510) 465-6400

I. Magnin & Company
Broadway and Twentieth Street, Oakland

Fox Oakland Theater
1900 Telegraph Avenue, at Nineteenth

The University of California Visitor Center
in the lobby of the Student Union, near Telegraph Avenue and Bancroft Way;
(510) 642-4636

City of Berkeley Convention and Visitors Bureau, *1834 University Avenue, Berkeley 94703;*
(800) 847-4823

College Avenue

• *Near the Oakland Museum: Two Great Movie Palaces*

A short walk from the Oakland Museum is the **Sun Hong Kong Restaurant**, in Oakland's bustling Chinatown; excellent and popular; avoid the peak lunch hour. **Holmes Book Company,** in downtown Oakland, is a large old-fashioned shop not far from the museum. The California Room upstairs has new and used books on the state. Oakland was building in the 1930s when the Art Deco style was supreme. One of the major Art Deco monuments in the nation is the **Oakland Paramount Theater**. Designed in 1931 by Miller and Pfleuger, and restored in 1976 by Skidmore, Owings & Merrill, this fantastic interior uses sheet metal and light in innovative ways. Artists Ralph Stackpole and Robert Howard did the relief sculptures. The Paramount was as lavish as the Depression-era celluloid fantasies it was built to screen. This is a must for Art Deco and movie palace buffs.

Downtown Oakland has other important Art Deco and Zigzag Moderne commercial buildings in its downtown. The elegant green-tiled **I. Magnin & Company** was designed by Weeks & Day in 1931. On Telegraph Avenue at Nineteenth is the now-closed hallucinatory Moorish fantasy of the old **Fox Oakland Theater** and office building, concocted in 1928 by M. I. Diggs, Weeks & Day. Hollywood has nothing as amazing as Oakland's two old movie palaces.

• *The University of California, Berkeley: The Athens of the West*

The **Visitor Center** in the lobby of the Student Union can provide you with a campus map and walking-tour booklet. The information desk in the lobby can also tell you about the day's events.

For information on the City of Berkeley, write to the **Berkeley Convention and Visitors Bureau.** The **College Avenue** retail strip is the most interesting shopping area. The **Judah L. Magnes Museum**, Western Jewish History Center, is in the Claremont district; see the list of museums in the front of this guide.

BART links San Francisco's Market Street with downtown Berkeley; the campus is a few blocks east of the Berkeley BART stop. A more scenic return to San Francisco is offered by the **AC Transit F bus**, which passes south down Shattuck Avenue in downtown Berkeley, across the San Francisco–Oakland Bay Bridge, and to the TransBay Terminal in downtown San Francisco.

California included a state university in its first state constitution and, along with Michigan and Wisconsin, was among the first states to realize the tremendous economic and cultural benefits a great public university could bring. The **University of California at Berkeley**, familiarly known as Cal, has its origins in the Contra Costa Academy, founded in Oakland in 1853 and directed by Congregationalist minister Henry Durant. This high school became the College of California in 1855. In 1860 a new site was dedicated at what is now Founders' Rock in Berkeley. Absorbed and chartered by the state in 1868, the college moved to Berkeley in 1873, the same year that it graduated its first class of twelve men. Today Berkeley is the flagship campus of the nine-branch University of California system. Embracing 1,232 acres, the campus has more than 320 buildings.

University House

Low Library

Women's Gymnasium

Greek Theater

Zellerbach Auditorium

The University of California at Berkeley is situated directly east of the Golden Gate. Frederick Law Olmsted and Calvert Vaux produced the first campus plan in 1865, with an axis (now Campanile Way) pointed toward this dramatic feature. But the most important moment in the campus' history occurred when Mrs. Phoebe Apperson Hearst decided to found a school of mining here in memory of her mine-owning husband, Senator George Hearst. Guided by Bernard Maybeck, she was induced to sponsor an international competition for a new campus plan that was juried in 1899. A Paris architect, Emile Henri Bénard, won with a grand, if not grandiose, plan reflecting the monumental ideals of the Ecole des Beaux-Arts. But Bénard refused to leave Paris to execute the plan and the university Regents selected Ecole des Beaux-Arts–trained New York architect John Galen Howard, a member of the fourth-place team, to adapt the Bénard plan to reality and to carry out the building of the new campus.

Howard became University Architect, revised the plan, designed many of the university's best buildings, and founded the Department of Architecture. He set his formal "Athens of the West" between the tree-lined banks of the north and south branches of Strawberry Creek. **University House**, the president's house, is a Renaissance villa in a walled garden; **Low Library** could house the pope; and the **Women's Gymnasium** of 1925 is a Hollywood Roman Empire hallucination. Also notable is the Howard-designed **Greek Theater** of 1903, modeled on the theater at Epidaurus and donated by William Randolph Hearst. Around this monumental white-granite core, Howard also designed many less-costly but equally artistic brown-shingled frame buildings, a few of which survive. Unfortunately the explosive growth of the campus after World War II ignored Howard's fine plan and crowded the campus with indifferent if not positively unsightly structures that you cannot fail to notice. The lush campus landscaping distracts the eye from some, though not all, of these later behemoths.

The open spaces surrounding the Student Union, Sproul Hall, and, one level down, **Zellerbach Auditorium** exemplify the best of mid-1960s design. Designed in 1965 by DeMars & Reayl/Hardison, with Lawrence Halprin & Associates as landscape designers, this is one of the few California "plazas" that actually functions like a plaza. Here is the social center of the campus, the best spot to sit in and watch the ebb and flow of the backpack-toting students and the activities of the expositors of the social, political, or religious movements of the moment.

Sather Gate

Sather Tower
Observation loggia at the top, open daily from 10 A.M. to 3 P.M. except university holidays; small fee

Hearst Mining Building

University Art Museum
2626 Bancroft Way, Berkeley; Open Wednesday to Sunday from 11 A.M. to 5 P.M., Thursday to 9 P.M.; small fee; (510) 642-0808

Pacific Film Archive
Phone for information (510)642-1124

Phoebe Apperson Hearst Museum of Anthropology
in Kroeber Hall Open weekdays, 10 A.M. to 4:30 P.M.; Saturday and Sunday, noon to 4:30 P.M.; small fee

Lawrence Hall of Science
One Centennial Drive, near Grizzly Peak Boulevard; Open 10 A.M. to 5 P.M. daily; small fee; (510)643-5132

Botanical Garden
Open from 9 A.M. to 4:45 P.M. daily; free; (510)642-0849

Beyond Sproul Plaza is John Galen Howard's beautiful **Sather Gate**, the ceremonial entrance to the campus, completed in 1910. The bronzework of this gateless gate is especially handsome. The pedestrian bridge here spans Strawberry Creek, the chief natural feature of the central campus. Beyond the gate are the academic buildings. Walk straight ahead between Wheeler and Durant halls, both by Howard, to Campanile Way and then up this handsome axis to the lofty campanile.

The symbolic center of the campus is the 307-foot-high, steel-frame, white-granite-clad campanile, **Sather Tower**, modeled on the bell tower of St. Mark in Venice and dedicated in 1914. An elevator takes you to the observation loggia at the top. A twelve-bell carillon is played here three times a day. The soaring tower is John Galen Howard's masterpiece and is one of the most beautiful architectural embellishments in California. It is capped by a bronze light that makes real the university's motto, "Fiat Lux"—let there be light.

From the Campanile Esplanade there is a superb view down Campanile Way, across the Bay, to the Golden Gate and its great bridge. The white building to the right houses the Bancroft Library, with its famous collection of Western Americana, and the Doe Library. The red brick Victorian structure to the left is South Hall, built in 1878 (the oldest building on the campus). Beyond the looming concrete bulk of Evans Hall is Mining Circle and the handsome granite-clad **Hearst Mining Building**, completed by Howard in 1907. The Memorial Vestibule, with its steel-lattice trusses and tile vaults with skylit domes, is reminiscent of Labrouste's Reading Room at the Bibliothèque Nationale in Paris.

Across Bancroft Way is the modernistic **University Art Museum**. Designed by Mario Ciampi and opened in 1970, this concrete ziggurat encloses a great space and a series of cantilevered ramps and galleries with both permanent and changing exhibits. The art displayed here tends toward the unconventional and large scale. A permanent collection of Hans Hofmann works occupies the uppermost gallery. On the ground floor is the outstanding **Pacific Film Archive**; its intimate theater screens both historic and avant-garde works. There is a small café here as well. The **Phoebe Apperson Hearst Museum of Anthropology** mounts small but select changing exhibits from one of the finest anthropological collections. **Lawrence Hall of Science**, a science museum and planetarium, sits on the ridge above the campus; phone for planetarium schedule. The **Botanical Garden** is nearby, located in Strawberry Canyon. Among many other features, it boasts a fine cactus collection.

• *Off Campus in Berkeley*

Berkeley might have the best collection of bookstores in the nation. **University Press Books**, across the street from the campus, is a unique resource for serious books in all fields; a cutting-edge bookshop in every scholarly discipline; has a café next door; a scholar's paradise. **Cody's Books** is a superb general bookstore, one of the best in the nation. Several other interesting bookshops are clustered nearby along Telegraph Avenue. **Black Oak Books** is a literary landmark and presents a fine program of readings. Athletic clothing is the other Berkeley shopping specialty; there are many shops serving students strung out along raffish **Telegraph Avenue.**

Not far from Telegraph Avenue is one of California's major architectural monuments, architect Bernard Maybeck's **First Church of Christ, Scientist.** Built between 1910 and 1912, it has a 1927 Sunday school addition by Henry Gutterson. In this eclectic building Maybeck fused elements of Gothic, Japanese, Romanesque, and Craftsman design—along with modern materials such as poured concrete, asbestos shingles, and industrial sash windows—in a throughly original concept. The main body of the church is in the shape of a Greek cross. In the spring, when the wisteria vines that drape the building bloom, the result is the perfect marriage of architecture and landscaping. It is like a Japanese pagoda in a Gothic forest. Across the street from the famous church is the notorious **Peoples Park,** born in idealism but now the scruffy resort of derelicts old and young.

If you have a special interest in Northern California's distinctive regional architectural flowering of the early twentieth century, you should explore the north-side Berkeley hills beyond the campus' North Gate at Hearst and Euclid. The tangle of streets and paths east of Euclid Avenue and north of Cedar Street—including Rose Walk, Buena Vista Way, La Loma Avenue, and several *cul-de-sacs* in this hilly terrain—contains a concentration of deliberately rustic, brown-shingled houses designed by Bernard Maybeck, John Galen Howard, and many other gifted architectural designers on the University of California School of Architecture faculty. Those influenced by the Arts and Crafts Movement sought "honest" houses simply furnished and integrated with their settings.

Under the influence of the Hillside Club, the originally grass-covered hills, with their fine view of the Bay far below, were laid out with contoured streets threaded together by pedestrian paths. Over time the houses here have been overgrown by a jungle of trees and vines, making the architecture somewhat hard to see and fufilling, perhaps all too well, the original intention of blending with nature. The intellectual and stylistic roots of Northern California's environmentalist mentality are here in this bosky enclave. If you are driving, you should park and explore the area on foot, since that is the only way fully to experience this unique neighborhood. Individual houses are not as important as the total effect achieved by this seemingly unplanned, planned environment.

University Press Books
*2340 Bancroft Way,
near Telegraph;
(510) 548-0585*

Cody's Books
*2454 Telegraph Avenue,
at Haste; (510) 845-7852*

Black Oak Books
*1491 Shattuck Avenue,
off Vine; (510) 486-0698*

Telegraph Avenue

First Church of Christ, Scientist
*1910 Dwight Way,
corner of Bowditch;
Sunday morning services
at 11 A.M.; Public tours on
the first Sunday of each
month at 12:15 P.M.;
(510) 845-7199*

Peoples Park

Chez Panisse
1517 Shattuck Avenue,
between Cedar and Vine;
(510) 548-5525

Berkeley's and the Bay Area's gastronomic monument to contemporary California cuisine is Alice Waters's **Chez Panisse**. Worth the trip, as the French would say. Reservations are essential; closed Sunday; expensive but memorable.

John Muir National Historic Site
4202 Alhambra Valley Road, Martinez 94553; Open daily, 10 A.M. to 4:30 P.M., except Thanksgiving, Christmas, and New Year's Day; small fee.
• *Highway 4 to Martinez and the Alhambra Avenue exit, turn left under the freeway, and park in the John Muir National Historic Site lot.*
• *By public transit, take BART's Concord line to Pleasant Hill; transfer to the 116 County Connection bus, which stops at the Muir House; the bus runs Monday to Saturday between 10:30 A.M. and 3:30 P.M.; (510) 228-8860*

• **John Muir National Historic Site**

John Muir, the author of some of America's finest nature writing, the great champion of wilderness and its conservation, and the first president of the Sierra Club, was born in Scotland in 1838, studied geology and botany at the University of Wisconsin, and explored on foot the Midwest, Gulf Coast, Alaska, and the Sierra. In his forties he married Louise Strentzel, the daughter of an Alhambra Valley fruit rancher. Here between 1881 and 1891 he managed his and his father-in-law's fruit ranches. When his father-in-law died, Muir and his wife moved into this great square 1881 Italianate house. (The Martinez adobe of 1849 is also on the property.) From here Muir wrote and conducted his campaigns to save wilderness areas from destruction. He agitated for the preservation of Yosemite, which was made a National Park in 1890. He also persuaded the Cleveland and Theodore Roosevelt administrations to create the first federal forest reservations. The National Park Service has furnished the house in period; Muir's own desk is in the recreated study upstairs. A fine brief film on Muir's life is shown and a shop here carries some of Muir's undying books. *The Wilderness World of John Muir*, edited by Edwin Way Teale, is the best compendium and makes a fine companion to Yosemite and California's great natural wonders. Maps can be secured here for Muir's grave, which lies about a mile to the south in a small private burial ground that can be glimpsed in the fields behind 5031 Alhambra Valley Road.

Tao House/Eugene O'Neill National Historic Site
P.O. Box 280, Danville 94526; (510) 838-0249; reservations required.
• *The two-hour tour and van ride to Tao House are free. Van departs Wednesday through Sunday at 10 A.M. and 12:30 P.M. from Danville's City parking lot on Hartz Avenue.*
• *By public transit, take BART's Concord line to the Walnut Creek station, transfer to the 121 County Connection bus, which runs to Danville approximately every thirty minutes except Sunday and holidays*

• **Tao House/Eugene O'Neill National Historic Site**

When playwright **Eugene O'Neill** won the Nobel prize, he used the money to build this spacious house on fifteen acres on Las Trampas Ridge in Contra Costa's scenic San Ramon Valley for himself and his wife, actress Carlotta Monterey. The house enjoys a sweeping view of the Bay Area's tallest peak, 3,849-foot Mt. Diablo. O'Neill named his dwelling Tao House after the Chinese philosophy he practiced. The house blends California's white-walled Mission style with a black-glazed Chinese-looking tile roof. Inside, two carved teak Foo dogs guard the stairs to the study. In this study between 1937 and 1944, behind three closed doors, O'Neill wrote his last five plays, including *The Ice Man Cometh* and *Long Day's Journey into Night*. O'Neill gave his manuscripts and books to Yale University, but a National Park Service exhibit here recounts his life from his birth in New York City in 1888 to his death in Boston in 1953.

• Blackhawk: Gated Community and Postmodern Luxury Mall and Museums

Blackhawk Plaza

The Museums at Blackhawk:
Open Tuesday to Sunday, 10 A.M. to 5 P.M.; closed Monday and major holidays; (510) 736-2277
• The University of California Museum of Art, Science and Culture *and* Behring Auto Museum

Visitors with an interest in excess should make the journey to see **Blackhawk Plaza** near Danville, about thirty-five miles east of San Francisco. Here in the arid, rolling hills of Contra Costa County is a social and cultural monument to contemporary California: a gated community of luxury houses built around two golf courses you cannot see, and a *luxe* postmodern shopping mall with two interesting museums you can see. Blackhawk was developed by Kenneth Behring and Kenneth H. Hofmann and takes suburban paranoia to new levels. Seven guarded gates and a private police force make this the ultimate suburban fortress. The large, architecturally confused houses sit on relatively small plots of land with very little space between them. Two eighteen-hole golf courses create irrigated oases around which many of the houses are built.

    Blackhawk Plaza is an ambitious development of some fifty shops set around an artificial stream. At the head of the mall sit **The Museums at Blackhawk**, comprised of the University of California Museum of Art, Science and Culture and the Behring Auto Museum. **The University of California Museum of Art, Science and Culture**, designed by The Dahlin Group, with fine interiors by Formations, Inc., of Portland, is one of the most successful small museum designs of the present day. The artful displays are the state of the museum art. The shiny **Behring Auto Museum** is also impressive and highly appropriate in the auto-centered environment. There sparkling vintage automobiles glisten in a granite and glass corporate palace. The mall itself is in an Italian Renaissance Revival mode with colonnades, fountains, and a sea of red tile roofs. It has an almost papal grandeur and is one of the great monuments to Consumption. An inviting outdoor café lets you soak up the ambiance. The Blackhawk Market is the most upscale of upscale supermarkets. But there is a disconcerting stillness to the place; you wonder how these shops pay the rent. Blackhawk Plaza is a trend-setting fusion of commerce and culture and one of the great statements of contemporary California. Gated communities are, however, alarming. The physical pulling apart of American society has its culmination in this *apartheid* for the newly rich. And putting a public university collection in a private mall not practically accessible by public transit is not right.

San Mateo Peninsula

Kepler's Books & Magazines
1010 El Camino Real, Menlo Park 94025;
324-4321

Café Borrone
1010 El Camino Real, Menlo Park; 327-0830

Stanford University Bookstore

Originally cattle country, the fine climate on the **San Mateo Peninsula** attracted fruit orchards, especially apricot orchards, by the turn of the century. Today it is California's premier high-technology industrial zone, known as Silicon Valley, where smokestackless laboratories and factories produce microchips, the fingernail-sized silicon wafers that govern computers, word processors, modern weapons, and electronic games. This is one of the places that puts California in the forefront of the modern world. The suburbscape here consists of pale, one-story industrial park buildings that are set back from the road behind landscaped parking lots and sport tasteful, low-to-the-ground signs bearing utterly uncommunicative high-tech names or inscrutable initials.

Professor Frederick Terman of Stanford University is generally credited with being the father of Silicon Valley. In 1937 he persuaded two of his brightest students, William Hewlett and David Packard, to found their own company locally rather than go east in search of employment. With $500 and a rented garage in Palo Alto, the two young engineers founded Hewlett-Packard, which by 1976 had passed $1 billion per year in sales of computers and electronic instruments. With the invention of the transistor by Schockley, Bardeen, and Brattain in 1957 and of the microelectronic integrated circuit by Noyce and Kilby, also in 1957, the groundwork was laid for the development of the modern computer.

A great place to see the Silicon Valley denizens is **Kepler's Books & Magazines**. It has a large stock of books, hosts readings, and is, of course, good on high-tech and computer magazines. Next door is **Café Borrone**, a good place to soak up the local ambiance. The **Stanford University Bookstore**, on the campus, is another welcome oasis of high civilization.

• *Stanford University: A Pinnacle of Regional Environmental Design*
New York-born **Leland Stanford** amassed one of the largest fortunes in the West as one of the four founders of the Central (later Southern) Pacific Railroad, the first transcontinental railroad and the utility that made the United States a continental market. The railroad was built with generous federal subsidies and given a baron's portion of the public lands in California. Stanford and his wife, Jane, had one child, Leland Stanford, Jr., who was raised like the crown prince of California in his parents' Nob Hill mansion. But in 1884 the boy died of typhoid fever at fifteen while on a trip to Italy with his parents. The Stanfords were disconsolate. The Episcopalian minister who traveled back home with the Stanfords and their son's casket introduced the couple to spiritualism. Through séances they felt they achieved contact with the lost Leland, Jr. The Stanfords determined to preserve the memory of their son by founding a university and naming it after him.

The Stanfords gave the new institution, founded in 1885, 83,000 acres of what were described at the time as "the most valuable estates in California," consisting of three great ranches. **The Palo Alto Farm** became the university campus; hence Stanford's nickname: The Farm. It consisted of 7,200 choice, sunny acres—the finest horse country in California and a classic stretch of California landscape. Today the campus embraces 8,200 acres. Part is leased to the **Stanford Shopping Center**, and other sections are leased to the **Stanford Industrial Park**.

In 1888 Leland Stanford engaged Frederick Law Olmsted to do the landscape plan, and Shepley, Rutan and Coolidge to design the original buildings. All were Boston-area designers. The strong hand of the client ruled in both landscape and architecture. The result is one of the most forceful, coherent, and successful late-1880s architectural and landscape designs in the nation. Charles Allerton Coolidge was a *protégé* of the great Henry Hobson Richardson, and in Stanford's Old Quad he fused Richardsonian massing, arches, and decorative detail with Mission-style red tile roofs and "Southwestern" landscaping to create one of the region's earliest and best Mission-style designs. Emphatic yellow sandstone arches link the old campus buildings into a whole around a central court with islands of semitropical landscaping.

Stanford had clear political purposes in mind when he formulated his grant of endowment. Fundamental principles of American government were to be taught so that "agrarianism and communism can have only an ephemeral existence." Another purpose of the new university was to provide "complete protection against monopoly of the rich"—a curious end for a fortune extracted by a railroad commonly known as "the Octopus."

Two features of Stanford's donation were novel and progressive. The first was the prohibition of "sectarian teaching" and the desire for an ecumenical atmosphere—basically Protestant, but with a consistent interest in Far Eastern religious thought. The second progressive feature was the specific inclusion of women students.

Stanford has become one of the great American universities. Its buildings and grounds are the finest extensive architectural and landscape monuments of the booming 1880s in the West. The visitor who lingers even briefly in its arcaded quadrangles will immediately know why this institution commands such fierce loyalty among its sons and daughters. The bright blue skies, the warm, yellow sandstone cloisters, the vast and immaculate grounds, and the serene air of this unhurried, insulated world leave an unforgettable impression. You can't help thinking that this is how God would have done it if he had had the money.

Stanford University

Guide and Visitor Service
*Stanford University,
Stanford 94305;
Tours, daily events;
Excellent map available
in Hoover Tower lobby;
723-2560*

From San Francisco:
•*By Car: A half-hour
drive south, on I-280
or Highway 101 to
Palo Alto.*

• *By Bus: SamTrans 7F
from TransBay Terminal.
Also, express bus service
early in the morning and
late in the afternoon;
(800)660-4287*

• *By train: CalTrain/
Southern Pacific Depot,
4th and Townsend streets;
stops at Palo Alto
railroad station;
(800)660-4287*

Campus Transit
*Free shuttle bus,
the "Marguerite," on
weekdays from the
Stanford Shopping
Center, 11:30 A.M.
to 1:30 P.M.*

Palm Drive

Oval

Outer Quad

Hoover Tower

Inner Quad

Memorial Church

The approach to Stanford University up **Palm Drive** provides a sense of space, power, wealth, and ease. Traveling almost due south you pass through a large, unbuilt reserve that separates the university from the outside world.

At the head of Palm Drive is the sunken **Oval** and the north face of the **Outer Quad**. There is visitor parking here. (There is also visitor parking in front of the University Museum where this walk ends.) The best procedure is to park here and walk to the lobby of Hoover Tower and secure the excellent bird's-eye-view map of the campus, then return to the broad stairs and the front terrace.

Hoover Tower, designed by Bakewell & Brown, looms over the campus in a vaguely Moderne style. A thirty-five-bell Belgian carillon, cast for the New York World's Fair of 1939, was installed in the tower at its completion in 1941. The carillon is played at noon and 5 P.M.

Take the elevator to the observation platform atop the 285-foot-tall tower; from here there is a fine view of the ordered sea of red tile roofs of the old buildings and the surrounding later ones. South of the Quads are the untouched, oak-dotted hills that billow back to the Coast Range.

To the east, on the flat industrial bayshore, is the enormous gray Moffett Field dirigible Hanger No. 1, built by the Navy in 1933. Today the Ames Research Center occupies part of this base. There, it has been reported, is Illiac 4, a system of sixty-four massive computers connected to hydroplanes planted in the world's seabed. They monitor the ocean for the sounds of Russian submarines. Beyond Moffett Field is the flat, blue sheet of San Francisco Bay and across the Bay the Contra Costa range. Leaving the Tower, you can visit paired rooms in its base with mementos of both Herbert and Lou Henry Hoover.

A triple-arched gate at the far end of Memorial Court leads to the **Inner Quad**, the heart of the university. This rectangular quadrangle runs east-west and creates a minor axis crossing the major north-south axis of Palm Drive. This change of direction makes the three-acre Inner Quad the crossroads, or center, of the campus. It is completely surrounded by arcades with semicircular arches. Behind these arcades are twelve one-story buildings.

Integrated into the center of the far side of the quad is the façade of the **Memorial Church**, originally constructed in 1903 and then rebuilt with a steel skeleton in 1913, after the earthquake. The base of the opulent church has the most exuberant stone carving of any Stanford building. San Francisco architect Clinton Day modeled the original design on Richardson's famous Trinity Church in Boston. But in 1906, when the eighty-foot-high central tower fell, the church was rebuilt and provided with a humdrum dome in place of the daring tower. The interior has some fine mosaic work and beautiful stained glass windows.

Beginning at the front door of the church and running west under the arcade are numbered plaques, underneath which each senior class has deposited memorabilia. Note the seemingly infinite regression of the arches ahead and the strong patterns of the window frames with their sunken windows. Continue around the Inner Quad, passing Memorial Court where you entered, and turn right at the corner to the east entrance gate. Leave the Quad and walk toward the round fountain.

Beyond the fountain is the **Green Library** of 1919, designed by San Francisco architects Bakewell & Brown. Nearby is the Thomas Welton Stanford Art Gallery with changing exhibits. From the fountain walk under the row of oaks toward the antlerlike fountain by Aristides Demetrios in White Plaza. The Stanford University Bookstore is near the fountain and is a good place for books and souvenirs. Beyond and to the right is **Tresidder Memorial Union**, where you can buy something to eat and sit on the terrace under the trees among the students.

Walk to the Oval and down its center. One block down Palm Drive to the left is Museum Way, which leads to the **Leland Stanford Junior Museum**, an amalgam of fine art and Stanford-family memorabilia. Though architecturally dull, it was designed by Ernest Ransome in 1892 using a then-revolutionary material: reinforced concrete. The Asian art and the Rodin collection are particularly notable. The famous gold spike driven by Stanford in 1869 to mark the completion of the transcontinental railroad is here, along with photographs by Eadweard Muybridge of horses in motion that were forerunners of the motion picture. (The museum might still be closed for repairs from the earthquake of 1989; phone ahead to avoid disappointment.) Next to the museum is the B. Gerald Cantor **Rodin Sculpture Garden** with a large collection of the French master's work.

An appropriate conclusion to your visit is the gray-granite, temple-like **Stanford Mausoleum**, set in the spacious **University Arboretum**. Four marble sphinxes guard the tomb—two males sphinxes in front and two female sphinxes to the rear. Here lie father, mother, and son. Near the Mausoleum is a smaller circular path that contains the fascinating living ruins of the Stanfords' cactus garden. It is a quiet, abandoned spot where the century-old plants have gone wild, creating a botanical tangle with its own curious charm. Cactus gardens were very popular in Victorian California, and this was once one of the most extensive.

To see the exterior of the **Hanna House**, designed by Frank Lloyd Wright in 1937, walk up Mayfield Avenue and turn right at Frenchman's Road. At number 737 is one of Wright's first hexagonal grid houses. Even its beds were originally hexagonal. Not surprisingly, this turned out to be impractical. The red brick and stained-wood horizontal house is set between old oaks in perfect harmony with its hilltop site. All along Mayfield Avenue you will see a varied array of modern California houses built for Stanford's faculty.

The **Lou Henry Hoover House** was built in 1919 on Cabrillo Avenue at the head of Santa Ynez Street. (A closer view of the back of the house is possible from Mirada Avenue.) This fascinating stucco-covered, concrete-and-hollow tile house was designed by Mrs. Hoover, who had unconventional ideas. Its flat roofs were used for terraces connected by outside stairways. In style it is almost pueblolike, or cubist. While its exterior is fresh and innovative, its interior is finished with Tudor-style woodwork. It was here that Herbert Hoover received news in 1928 that he had been elected president. Today the house serves Stanford's presidents.

Green Library

Tresidder Memorial Union

Leland Stanford
Junior Museum
Phone 723-4177 to see if the museum has reopened

Rodin Sculpture Garden

Stanford Mausoleum

University Arboretum

Hanna House
737 Mayfield Avenue

Lou Henry Hoover House
on Cabrillo Avenue at the head of Santa Ynez Street

Linear Accelerator
Tours available; free;
Phone 926-3300
for hours

In the hills behind the Old Quad, and extending underneath Interstate 280, is the two-mile long **Linear Accelerator** operated by Stanford for the U.S. Department of Energy. Used in particle physics research, this is the most powerful electron accelerator yet built.

Filoli
Advance reservations
must be made; write to
Garden Tours, Filoli
Center, Cañada Road,
Woodside 94062;
or phone 364-2880 from
Monday through Friday
between 9 A.M. and
3 P.M. The house and
garden are open for tours
from mid-February until
mid-November, Tuesday
through Friday and on
Saturday morning; fee

• On Cañada Road,
twenty-five miles south
of San Francisco, near
the Edgewood Road exit
off scenic I-280.

• **Filoli: Great Estate and Garden**

This great Georgian Revival estate designed by Willis Polk, built between 1915 and 1917 for utility baron William Bowers Bourn, has some of the finest publicly accessible gardens in America. Bourn was the heir to a Gold Rush mining fortune (*see Tour 8*) and was himself a utility magnate who headed the San Francisco Gas Company and San Francisco's Spring Valley Water Company. On the choicest part of the huge, ancient-oak-dotted Spring Valley watershed, Bourn built this mansion and began its extensive gardens. The name *Filoli* is derived from his motto: "Fight, Love, Live." The original gardens were designed by Bruce Porter and Isabella Worn and lavishly loved by Mrs. William P. Roth, the subsequent owner of the estate, who donated it to the National Trust for Historic Preservation. The sixteen acres of gardens are laid out as a succession of distinct areas, leading from the formal Walled Garden to Yew Alley. April and May are the peak months for floral displays.

$\mathcal{S}anta$ $\mathcal{C}ruz$ and the $\mathcal{M}onterey$ $\mathcal{B}ay$ $\mathcal{P}eninsula$

BEST DAYS AND TIMES

The Santa Cruz Boardwalk is open from Memorial Day to Labor Day and on weekends the rest of the year. The town offers varied accommodations, including motels and hotels.

$\mathcal{I}nformation$

The **Santa Cruz County Conference and Visitors Council** provides walking-tour maps of Victorian neighborhoods.

$\mathcal{S}anta$ $\mathcal{C}ruz$: $\mathcal{T}urn\text{-}of\text{-}the\text{-}\mathcal{C}entury$ $\mathcal{S}easide$ $\mathcal{R}esort$

Santa Cruz sits on the northern edge of Monterey Bay, opposite the city of Monterey. The coastal mountains, with redwoods in their canyons, rise behind it. A mission was founded here on August 28, 1791 near the San Lorenzo River, and named **Mision de la Exaltacion de la Santa Cruz,** the mission of the Exaltation of the Sacred Cross. This mission was abandoned and vanished. The present building, just north of the downtown, is a replica and is not noteworthy.

Modern Santa Cruz began when a public bathhouse was built near the beach in 1865. Redwood logging and some manufacturing gave economic life to the city. In 1904 a huge casino-dance hall was built and day-trippers from San Francisco were lured to the town. A boardwalk (now paved with asphalt) was begun in 1903 by the Santa Cruz Beach, Cottage, and Tent City Corporation. It became the democratic resort for the northern half of the state. While nearly all of California's turn-of-the-century seaside resorts have sadly been demolished—San Diego's Belmont Park, the Long Beach Pike, and San Francisco's Playland—Santa Cruz's **Boardwalk** is still going strong. The 1907 Moorish-style Casino has gone through many simplifying alterations but is still here. The wonderful 1910 **carousel,** with its fine horses carved by Charles I. D. Looff, has been restored. The **Giant Dipper** roller coaster, designed by Arthur Looff and built in 1924, dominates the Boardwalk like some huge sculpture and is especially beautiful at night when illuminated by its 3,150 light bulbs. Painted white with a red track, the huge timber roller coaster is one of the last and the best of its kind. It and the carousel are both on the National Register of Historic Places. There is an agreeable, nostalgic quality to an afternoon in this fun zone where you can walk about eating french-fried artichokes and looking at the rides and their riders, a tangy blend of innocence and sleaze and un-self-consciousness lacking in the overproduced and too-expensive "theme parks" of the present. Second and Third streets on **Beach Hill** behind the north end of the Boardwalk have many fine Victorian houses, including some impressive examples of the Shingle style of the 1890s.

Santa Cruz County Conference and Visitors Council
701 Front Street,
Santa Cruz 95060;
(408) 425-1234 or
(800) 833-3494

Mision de la Exaltacion de la Santa Cruz

Boardwalk
(408) 426-7433

carousel

Giant Dipper

Beach Hill

El Palomar Hotel

**University of California
at Santa Cruz**
*At the entrance to the
campus in the cluster of
old ranch buildings is the
red-painted, wood-and-
stone Cook House where
you can secure a guide
map, and also inquire
about student-led tours;
(408) 459-0111*

The local population of the town of Santa Cruz are zealous guardians of the town's appearance. Many fine Victorian, Craftsman, and even a few Moderne stucco buildings in Santa Cruz make a day of random exploration of side streets a delight. The welcoming, courtyarded, Monterey Revival-style Santa Cruz City Hall that was designed by C. J. Ryan in 1937–38 and built by the WPA says a lot about the city's self-respect. The tactful wing added in 1967 and designed by Robert Stevens Associates says even more. Jose's Parrula y Cantina in the grand space of the 1920s **El Palomar Hotel** evokes memories of California in the palmy 1920s when Hollywood Spanish was the reigning style.

- **University of California at Santa Cruz**

Located in the hills northwest of town, the campus of the **University of California at Santa Cruz** consists of two thousand acres of rolling meadows and redwood forests overlooking Monterey Bay. It was once the Henry Cowell Ranch, site of a lime quarry and cement factory and later of a cattle ranch. In 1961 the Regents of the University of California purchased the handsome site and engaged John Carl Warnecke and Thomas D. Church to prepare the campus plan. Their idea was to keep the rolling meadows open and to build the college buildings in small clusters beneath the hillside redwoods. While the recent buildings on other major UC campuses are banal, the aim here from the first was to produce an architectural showplace, and in this the Regents have succeeded. Taken together these structures, designed by a variety of outstanding architects, are the best collection of designs from the 1960s and 1970s in California.

At the entrance to the campus, several of the old ranch and lime-processing structures have been carefully preserved. This is one of the very few places in the state where you can see preserved examples of typical vernacular structures from a century ago. Included in this grouping are a granary, a cooperage, lime kilns, a blacksmith's shop, a bull barn, a slaughterhouse, a powder house, a cookhouse, workers' cabins, and a horse barn. Most have been converted to new uses, though a few are maintained as stabilized ruins.

Once seen as a refuge for throwbacks from the 1960s, UC Santa Cruz has emerged as a respected center for creative scholarship. You also have to admire a student body with the imagination to campaign to make the local banana slug, a yellowish snaillike creature found in these damp forests, the school's athletic mascot.

The City of Monterey: California's First Historic Capital

BEST TIMES TO VISIT

Summer can be very congested, especially in quaint Carmel. The summer is also the foggiest time of year. Plan your visit for early autumn through late May, if you can. The famous three-day **Monterey Jazz Festival** is held each September at the Monterey County Fairgrounds; for dates and information write to them or phone. The **Adobe Tour**, held by the Monterey History and Art Association on the last Saturday in April, is the single best day to visit Monterey. Write or phone for information.

Information

The **Visitor Center for Monterey State Historic Park** is at the Maritime Museum of Monterey at the Stanton Center. The Stanton Center's bookstore here sells an excellent and beautifully illustrated booklet, *Historic Monterey: Path of History Walking Tour*; a good map is available of state historic sites. The **Monterey Peninsula Chamber of Commerce and Visitors & Convention Bureau** can provide its *Hotel and Motel Guide* and its *Restaurant Guide*. The best map is the AAA Tour Map of Monterey, which has a detailed map of downtown Monterey.

Monterey is two-and-a-half hours south of San Francisco via San Jose and the coastal towns of Santa Cruz, Watsonville, and Castroville (the artichoke capital). It is a special place in this special state and has some of the most beautiful rocky coastal scenery anywhere. It was California's colonial capital in the Spanish and Mexican eras and retains many important landmarks (much restored, of course) now incorporated into the **Monterey State Historic Park**. It is also the gateway to the spectacular Big Sur coast, a piece of this planet that defies description for its dramatic beauty. This area has attracted a very wealthy population, including many retirees, and they and tourism support many restaurants and upscale shops. It is a famous place for magnificent golf courses, and golf is the reigning established religion. There is a lot to see and do on the Monterey Peninsula; it is worth a whole vacation by itself.

Monterey Jazz Festival
P.O. Box JAZZ,
Monterey 93942;
(408) 373-3366

Adobe Tour
Monterey History and Art Association
5 Custom House Plaza,
Monterey 93940;
(408) 372-2608

Visitor Center for Monterey State Historic Park
At Maritime Museum of Monterey, at the Stanton Center, 5 Custom House Plaza, Monterey 93940

Monterey Peninsula Chamber of Commerce and Visitors & Convention Bureau
380 Alvarado Street,
P.O. Box 1770,
Monterey 93940;
(408) 649-1770

Note: *Motorists traveling from San Francisco should enter Monterey via Fremont Street.*

Monterey is a somewhat open harbor sheltered to the south by a rocky, forested peninsula. The Bay of Monterey was discovered in 1542 by the Spanish explorer **Juan Rodríguez Cabrillo**, who named it **La Bahia de los Piños** (the Bay of the Pines). In 1602 Sebastián Vizcaíno, sailing under orders from the Viceroy of Mexico, Gaspar de Zúniga, landed near the mouth of the Carmel River. Vizcaíno named the best anchorage he discovered on his exploration—he missed San Francisco Bay—after Viceroy Zúniga, the Count of Monterrey. A settlement was established here in June 1770, and in 1775 it was made the capital of Alta California. The bay provided the chief reason for settling here.

On June 3, 1770, an expedition led by **Gaspar de Portolá** and accompanied by **Father Junípero Serra** established a presidio, or fort, here (today the U.S. Army Presidio outside town) and soon thereafter a mission at nearby Carmel. Under Spanish rule between 1770 and 1820, Monterey consisted of a walled stockade within which the inhabitants lived. The British explorer Vancouver visited the place in 1792, and in 1796 the first American ship, the *Otter* from Boston, dropped anchor in the open bay. In 1822 the remote outpost became part of the new Mexican Republic after its break with Spain. During this period adobe houses sprang up outside the walled stockade and the fort evolved into a town. By the 1830s traders from Boston and other U.S. ports began frequenting it.

Some Americans stayed, converted to Catholicism, and married into the local Mexican elite. This brief cultural fusion had a marked influence on the architecture of the town. Yankee house builders took Mexican adobe construction and married it with Yankee woodwork in the form of doors, windows, hipped roofs, and especially second-floor balconies. Thus was born the Monterey style, California's first local architectural creation. **The Larkin House** museum is a fine example of the type.

Property and influence were in the hands of the Californios during the early period, but that quickly changed. With the United States' occupation on July 7, 1846—and United States law—political power, land, and influence passed to the Protestant Yankees. Yankee-imposed county taxes required cash from Californio landowners who had little hard money. When their land was auctioned off for failure to pay these taxes, wealthy Yankee investors and partnerships snapped it up.

Monterey's early American period was marked by a classic example of barely legal land grabbing. **The City of Monterey,** as the successor to the Mexican pueblo, held thousands of acres of surrounding property. Delos Ashley, a young lawyer, secured the job of investigating the title of these lands for the city and presented the town with a bill for $991.50. The city treasury was empty, and at Ashley's prompting the city's politicians quietly passed an act to sell the municipal lands to pay the city debt. An obscure notice was published in an out-of-town paper, and a public auction was held on the steps of Colton Hall on February 19, 1859. The only bid was made by Ashley's partner, Scotland-born David Jacks, who offered $1002.50 for thirty thousand acres of choice Monterey Peninsula land. Ashley billed they city $11 for drawing up the transfer papers; thus the city ended up with precisely nothing from the auction. Eventually Jacks bought out Ashley for $500 and ended as the largest landowner on the peninsula.

By the late nineteenth century, San Franciscans in particular had discovered the charms of the sleepy fishing village. When the railroad made the scenic peninsula easily accessible, small hotels opened, and the third phase of Monterey's history began. Because one of the first things the Americans did upon taking California in 1846 was to move the capital out of Monterey, some of the old Monterey-style buildings in the town survived unchanged when it lapsed into a stagnant backwater. Poverty preserved these early examples of specifically Californian design. Some of the very earliest efforts at architectural preservation in the West were here in the old colonial capital. Individuals, patriotic organizations, the City of Monterey, and finally the State of California all contributed to rescuing and preserving this unique historic town in its spectacular natural setting.

Monterey Peninsula Museum of Art *at La Mirada Off Fremont Street, at the eastern entrance to the city, across from El Estero Park; 720 Via Mirada, Monterey 93940; Tuesday through Saturday, 10 A.M. to 4 P.M.; Sunday, 1 to 4 P.M. La Mirada tours, Tuesday through Sunday at 2 and 4 P.M.; (408) 372-3689*

In 1882 Father Angelo Cassanova, the resident priest in Monterey, had the roofless sanctuary of the ruined Carmel mission cleaned in order to examine the tomb of Father Junípero Serra, which was found to be intact. In 1884, he raised the funds to put a roof over the decayed church to mark the centenary of Serra's death. In 1900 the Native Sons of the Golden West leased the adobe **Custom House** from the Treasury Department and three years later persuaded the State of California to take the lease and promise its restoration (the building did not open to the public until 1929). In 1938 the Custom House became part of the State of California park system. Today the beautifully designed Monterey State Historic Park consists of two loose clusters of about two dozen adobes and other historic buildings.

- **Monterey Peninsula Museum of Art and La Mirada**

On a hill overlooking El Estero Park, this branch of the **Monterey Peninsula Museum of Art** consists of a much-expanded 1790s adobe house known as **La Mirada** and a new Charles Moore-designed art museum, which contains the Jane and Justin Dart Collection of works by Armin Carl Hansen. Hansen (1886-1957) painted vibrantly colorful pictures of the sea and the waters of Monterey Bay and of the fishermen who wrested their livelihoods from them. There are also collections of *netsuke* and early Chinese ceramics and bronzes.

The new museum is attached to the much-expanded Jose Castro adobe built in the 1790s. Bought by Hollywood scriptwriter Groveneur Morris in 1919, the originally two-room adobe had various wings added. The complex has a charming and very Californian Spanish-style entrance court with colorful tilework. In the 1940s Mr. and Mrs. Frank Work acquired the house and redecorated it. They commissioned a series of interesting murals of Old Monterey from B. de Pezthuis for the dining room in the old adobe. They also decorated the rest of the house in a style perhaps best described as High Decorator; it is a period piece of 1940sand 1950s taste. There is also a garden shop here.

G. T. Marsh & Company

At Fremont and Camino el Estero, across the street from the lagoon of El Estero Park; Open Monday to Saturday, 9:30 A.M. to 5 P.M.; 699 Fremont, Monterey 93940; (408) 372-3547

San Carlos de Borromeo de Monterey Cathedral/ Royal Presidio Chapel

Church Street, opposite Figueroa; Open daily; masses at 8:30 A.M. and 5 P.M. daily; (408) 378-2628

• **G. T. Marsh & Company**

Marsh's is the oldest Asian art importer and antique dealer in California and was originally, in 1876, located in San Francisco's Palace Hotel. This elaborate, concrete, Chinese-style building was designed by Orrin Jenkins and constructed in 1927-28. It has an airy interior with Asian art goods and antiques, enclosed gardens, and a suite of Japanese rooms. The rear, or Church Street, side of the building is quite unusual. Just behind it, on Church Street, is the San Carlos de Borromeo de Monterey Cathedral.

• **San Carlos de Borromeo de Monterey Cathedral/ Royal Presidio Chapel,** *1795, master mason Manuel Ruiz; 1858, expansion; 1942, restoration by Harry Downie*

The church built on this site in 1775 was damaged by a fire in 1789. In 1795 the present stone and adobe building was dedicated. The design for it was drawn by the Academy of San Carlos in Mexico and the original drawings survive in the National Archives in Mexico City. It has a severe neoclassical façade surmounted by a scalloped gable and a square bell tower with a pyramidal roof, and it is built of sandstone quarried near Carmel. The Native American laborers worked under Mexican master mason Manuel Ruiz. Ruiz probably carved the chalkrock Virgin of Guadalupe over the front door, the oldest piece of "European" art in California. In 1850, the chapel became the first cathedral in California; in 1858 the interior of the church was enlarged, leaving the original façade intact. Probably at that time the fine exterior transept door frames on the side of the church were added. Some experts think the stone portals were originally side altars at Carmel Mission, transferred here in 1858. The interior of the chapel was provided with a wood floor and a carved *reredos* behind the altar in the Victorian period. In 1942 Harry Downie "restored" the chapel, reinstalling a tile floor and simplifying the interior. The large crucifix installed behind the altar is from Barcelona and dates from 1880. The statue of Mary of the Immaculate Conception in the niche to the left of the crucifix dates from the eighteenth century and may have been brought from Mexico by Father Serra.

Drive next to the Larkin House, sign up for a house tour, and secure a Monterey State Historic Park map. (If it is a weekend between 2 and 4 P.M. you may want to see the interior of the **Casa Amesti**, a block away. It does not appear on the state park's map.) If there is time before the tours, walk all around the block on which the Larkin House sits: Calle Principal, Madison, Pacific, and Jefferson. This is the heart of the most important of the two surviving clusters of Monterey-style adobes. It is a unique environment of antique buildings and colonial street patterns.

• Larkin House

The brightest jewel in Monterey is the interior of the **Larkin House**, the first two-story house built in Monterey. This 1835 Monterey-style adobe originally housed American Consul Thomas O. Larkin's store and merchandise on the ground floor and living quarters for his family upstairs. The historic house was bought in 1922 by Alice Larkin Toulmin, Larkin's granddaughter. She filled both floors of the house with her collection of antique furniture, including a few original Larkin items such as his Boston-made desk, and commissioned interior decorator Frances Elkins to brighten up the interior with well-chosen colors. In 1957 Alice Larkin Toulman gave the Larkin House, its furnishings, and an endowment for its maintenance to the State of California. This is one of the finest house museums in California. With an outstanding collection of antique English, American, and some Chinese furniture and furnishings, it is put together in a way that makes a most comfortable home, so rarely the feeling house museums give. The State of California guides here give a superior tour.

Larkin House
510 Calle Principal, at Jefferson Street; Tours daily (closed Tuesday and Thursday); Phone for tour times (408)649-7118

Monterey Peninsula Museum of Art
559 Pacific Street, Monterey 93940 (408)372-5477 Open Tuesday to Saturday, 10 A.M. to 4 P.M.; Sunday, 1 to 4 P.M.; closed major holidays; free

Colton Hall Museum and Old Monterey Jail
West side of Pacific Street, between Jefferson and Madison; Seasonal hours, call ahead; (408)646-5640

• Monterey Peninsula Museum of Art

Housed in an attractive 1920s Spanish-style building, this museum focuses on American art with an emphasis on California and Monterey Peninsula art. Since the coming of the railroad in 1875, the scenic Monterey Peninsula has attracted many painters and photographers. The fine collection here includes paintings by Albert Bierstadt, Euphemia Charlton Fortune, Percy Gray, William Keith, and William Ritschel, and photographs by Ansel Adams and Edward Weston. Ritschel's portrait of Irving R. Wiles of circa 1913 is striking. There are also bronzes by Frederick Remington, contemporary graphics, Asian art, and tribal art. It is a more rewarding museum than the new branch at La Mirada.

• Colton Hall Museum and Old Monterey Jail, *1847–49, Walter Colton; 1872, portico; 1949, restoration*

Colton Hall was erected in 1847–49 by Monterey's first U.S. mayor, the Rev. Walter Colton, who came to California as chaplain on one of Commodore Sloat's frigates. It is the oldest surviving U.S. building in California and was patterned after New England academy buildings. The ground floor of the two-story structure housed schoolrooms, and the upstairs served as the town hall. The building is a taut and sober New England design built of an easily worked, light yellowish-white local limestone. The building probably had a second-story wooden porch along its principal façade instead of the small porch and two exterior staircases that were added in 1872. From September to November 1849, forty-eight delegates elected from ten districts met in the second floor hall to write California's first constitution. That charter was written in both English and Spanish, though it was modeled on those of New York and Iowa. After serving the county and then the city of Monterey for many years in many capacities (the ground floor still houses city offices), the unique building was restored in 1949 and the second-floor assembly hall made into a museum maintained by the City of Monterey.

Casa Amesti
516 Polk Street, between Hartnell and Alvarado streets; Open Saturday and Sunday, except Christmas, from 2 P.M. to 4 P.M.; tours conducted by Monterey History and Art Association; small fee; (408) 372-2608

Robert Louis Stevenson (Gonzales) House
530 Houston Street; Open daily; small fee; Part of Monterey State Historic Park; Phone for tour information, (408)626-5300

Adjoining Colton Hall is the **Old Jail,** built of hard Monterey granite in 1854 and with ironwork from San Francisco foundries. It contained six cells, a debtors' room, and a large room for the jailer, and it served as a jail until 1959. Each cell is "themed" to tell about a phase of Monterey history.

• **Casa Amesti**, *1833–50s; 1918, Frances Elkins, restoration and gardens*
The curiously pruned and sculpted cypress trees in front of **Casa Amesti** look surreal. This lot was granted to José Amesti, a Spanish Basque immigrant, in 1833. He began the construction of a one-story adobe house, which he later added on to in the 1850s. This is a classic Monterey-style adobe with a wood porch and slightly pitched shingle roof. José Amesti became *alcalde,* or mayor, of Monterey. He gave his large house to his daughter Carmen when she married James (Santiago) McKinley, a Scottish sailor who became a Mexican citizen. In the late nineteenth century the big adobe became a boardinghouse. Some credit a French woman who ran the boardinghouse with planting flowers in front of her building and forcing Polk Street to bend around her garden.

In 1918, Frances Elkins, a noted interior decorator, bought the historic house and decorated and furnished it. She planted a formal Italian boxwood garden in the back that is now at its splendid maturity. Frances Elkins left the house to the National Trust for Historic Preservation upon her death in 1953. The Old Capital Club, established in 1955, leases and maintains the house and opens it to the public on Saturday and Sunday afternoons. A functioning city club, the house is not a house museum. The second-floor gallery, or living room, best retains the Elkins atmosphere. In that room Chinese pieces meld with European furniture in a worldly whole. Be sure to walk through the boxwood garden behind the house after the tour.

• **Robert Louis Stevenson (Gonzales) House**
This two-story adobe was begun in the 1830s by **Rafael Gonzales,** a customs official. A Swiss-born merchant, Jean Girardin, bought it in 1856 and added to the house on the Houston Street side. (This street was known as Merchants' Row in the early days.) Later it became the French Hotel. **Robert Louis Stevenson** stayed here in the fall and winter of 1879 while pursuing Fanny Van de Grift Osbourne, who was summering at the Bonifacio Adobe. He wrote "The Old Pacific Capital," a sketch of Monterey in the 1870s, while lodging here. At Christmas the penniless Stevenson moved to San Francisco. The historic adobe with its literary associations was bought in 1937 by Edith C. van Antwerp and Mrs. C. Tobin Clark, who saved it from destruction. They gave it to the State of California, which has installed a small museum of Stevensoniana in the house. A children's room displays period clothing and fancy antique toys. Behind the house is a large garden.

• **Alvarado Street: Old Main Stem**
Though adobes and gardens attract people to Monterey, the rest of
the tidy town is also worth examining. Alvarado Street is a classy version of the typical California main street with interesting vintage buildings studding it. The **Old Monterey Book Company**'s interior is the
downtown's hidden treasure. Old and rare books, first editions, and
prints fill this nostalgic bookshop. An artful mural on one wall depicts
characters emerging from books. The **Monterey Hotel** of 1904, recently
restored, has a splendid façade with fine bays and elaborate windows.

• **Custom House Plaza/Mexican Custom House**
At the end of Alvarado Street, across Del Monte Avenue, is the new
Monterey shaped by urban renewal. Historically, this beach zone was
devoted to maritime and railroad uses. In 1964 a forty-five acre redevelopment area was cleared here. A few historic buildings were left,
including the Mexican **Custom House** of 1827-46 and the **Pacific House**
adobe of 1847. The master plan was by Harold Wise, with architects
Wurster, Bernardi & Emmons and Milton Schwartz and Associates,
with Lawrence Halprin, landscape architect. Lighthouse Avenue was
tunneled under **Custom House Plaza**, a walled-in, arenalike space with
an attractive modern Mission-style central fountain. The walled
Memory Garden behind Pacific House (where the **State Park
Information Center** is), begun in 1927, is the most appealing part of the
new Custom House Plaza design. The new Monterey Convention
Center nearby is comfortable but forgettable architecture.

**Old Monterey
Book Company**
*136 Bonifacio Place,
off Alvarado;
(408) 372-3111*

Monterey Hotel
*406 Alvarado Street,
Monterey 93940;
(408) 375-3184*

Custom House

Pacific House

Custom House Plaza

**State Park Information
Center**

**Maritime Museum of
Monterey/Stanton Center**
*5 Custom House Plaza,
Monterey 93940; Open
daily, 10 A.M. to 5 P.M.;
(408) 373-2469*

**Monterey History and Art
Association**
(408) 372-2608

• **Maritime Museum of Monterey/Stanton Center**
This new museum is a shrine to the ship and to mariners. It houses a collection of models and nautical mementos begun by Allan Knight, a former mayor of Carmel. Included
is a scale model of the U.S. Navy sailing frigate *Savannah,* Commodore John Drake Sloat's
flagship when he took Monterey in 1846. The centerpiece of the exhibit is an impressive
Fresnel lighthouse lens made by Barbier & Fenestre in Paris in 1887. Between 1889 and
1978 it crowned the lighthouse at Point Sur. Its light could be seen over twenty-four miles
at sea. A romantic "historical" film in the museum's theater presents a politically correct
and insipid version of Monterey's history.

• **Annual Adobe House Tour**
Headquartered in the same building as the Maritime Museum is the **Monterey History and
Art Association,** founded in 1931. It is one of the key institutions in the conservation of
Monterey and the preservation of its significant gardens, buildings, and artifacts from
Spanish, Mexican, and early American California. The informative, old-fashioned historic
markers on metal poles in front of many historic buildings are some of the History and
Art Association's work. Each year, on the last Saturday in April, the association holds its
fund-raising Adobe Tour. This is the single best day to visit Monterey. Write for information and reservations.

Fisherman's Wharf

Rappa's Restaurant
at the end of the wharf;
(408)372-7562

Municipal Wharf No. 2

Bay Bike Rentals
640 Wave Street;
(408) 646-9090

Adventures by the Sea
299 Cannery Row;
(408) 372-1807

Monterey Sports Center
301 East Franklin Street,
at Washington;
(408) 646-3700

Cannery Row

• **Fisherman's Wharf**

Monterey's Fisherman's Wharf, a pier that juts out into Monterey Bay, is solidly and cozily lined with small seafood restaurants, outdoor food vendors, and gift shops. It is a perfect tourist mecca, more fun than brand-new, ersatz Cannery Row, and has the happy air of an old-fashioned California amusement pier. The French-fried squid here are tempting and tasty. This agreeable mini-honky-tonk has escaped the deadening hand of the taste police. **Rappa's Restaurant** at the end of the wharf has splendid views of the harbor with its bobbing boats and visiting wildlife.

To the east of the marina, beyond the parking lots, is **Municipal Wharf No. 2**, built in 1926 and today a working fish pier as well as home to a flock of sparkling white pleasure boats. The wholesale fish warehouses at its end specialize in squid that is shipped worldwide.

• **Bicycle Trail/Monterey Sports Center**

A flat and scenic six-mile bicycle trail runs along the shore of Monterey Bay from the city of Seaside to the city of Pacific Grove. Bicycles can be rented at **Bay Bike Rentals** or **Adventures by the Sea**. An outstanding amenity here is the new **Monterey Sports Center**, near the bay front and Municipal Wharf No. 2. Consisting of an attractive modern building that has two large indoor pools with a water slide, a gym, weight rooms, sun deck, tot activity room, and an array of exercise programs, it provides Monterey with a Scandinavian level of public recreation. This is probably the finest new public recreation facility in California, and it must be one of the best in the nation. In an era of drastic cuts in municipal sports and recreation budgets in all California localities, it is highly instructive to see how the citizens of Monterey view their responsibility to the physical health of their people.

• **Cannery Row**

Just outside the center of Monterey, northwest of Fisherman's Wharf, is the transformed **Cannery Row** that was integral to Monterey when it was an important fishing port. Monterey once harvested the silvery sardines that teemed along the California coast. F. E. Booth opened the first large fish cannery here in 1895 with vast outdoor drying racks, giving off a pungent odor. In 1906, the ramshackle Chinese fishing village clinging to the rocks on China Point burned to the ground. The site was redeveloped with a string of large sardine canneries. New Monterey, the streets up the hill from Cannery Row, then called Ocean View Avenue, filled up with fisherfolk and cannery workers. Honky-tonks, restaurants, cheap hotels, and whorehouses sat across the street from the bustling canneries. By the 1940s thirty sardine and fish canneries worked around the clock along this strip fed by a fleet of one hundred fishing boats. It was in this milieu that John Steinbeck created the characters for his novels *Cannery Row* and *Sweet Thursday*. With its "tin and iron and rust and splintered wood, chipped pavement and weedy lots and junk heaps," Cannery Row for him became "a poem, a stink, a grating noise, a quality of light, a tone, a habit, a nostalgia, a dream."

In the 1940s the sardines inexplicably vanished from California's coastal waters and the canneries fell silent. The last one held on until 1973. The derelict, oil-soaked canneries burned in spectacular fires, or were torn down leaving a bleak no-man's land. But the power of the name Cannery Row that Steinbeck had made famous, and the strong expansion of the tourism industry here, led to the rebuilding and marketing of the former industrial zone with new hotels, large complexes of tourist shops, restaurants, bars, and clubs. All of this has sprouted since the mid-1970s; Steinbeck wouldn't recognize the place.

Monterey Bay Aquarium
886 Cannery Row; Open 10 A.M. to 6 P.M. daily; closed Christmas; fee. Fine bookshop with local guides and nature books; (408) 375-3333

• **Monterey Bay Aquarium**, *1977–84, Esherick, Homsey, Dodge & Davis*
The most popular attraction on redeveloped Cannery Row is the **Monterey Bay Aquarium,** dedicated to the interpretation of the marine riches of the Monterey Bay. It is least crowded early in the morning and on weekdays. Focusing on Monterey Bay, with its rich abundance of sea life both plant and animal, this modern educational institution brings the hidden ocean depths up to the land. Terraces face the bay and step down to the water to embrace tidal pools. This outstanding aquarium was designed by Esherick, Homsey, Dodge & Davis between 1977 and 1984. It is the munificent gift of industrialist David Packard, one of the founders of Silicon Valley's Hewlett-Packard, and undertakes serious research on the marine environment as well as presenting its public exhibits. The aquarium is built on the site of the Hovden Cannery and portions of the old cannery have been incorporated in the new building. This is one of the best new museum buildings in California, a building that understands the history of its site and that is a stimulating place to learn about the biological riches of the California coast.

The City of Pacific Grove: Victorian Chautauqua

The City of Pacific Grove
For information on sites and lodgings write or visit the Pacific Grove Chamber of Commerce, Forest and Central streets; P.O. Box 167, Pacific Grove 93950; (408) 373-3304

Hopkins Marine Laboratory of Stanford University

Marine Gardens Park

The Pacific Grove Museum of Natural History
300 Forest, at Central; (408) 648-3116

The Seventeen-Mile Drive

Del Monte Forest

S.F.B. Morse Botanical Reserve

The city of Pacific Grove, located at the northern tip of the Monterey peninsula, is a complex quilt of grids, parks, and subdivisions. The city's shoreline from Lovers' Point around Point Piños and south to Asilomar State Beach and Conference Grounds is all part of a public park of intricate beauty. Tiny iridescent abalone shells and miniature seaweed bejewel the shore (collecting is not permitted). **Pacific Grove** was founded as a dry Methodist summer tent city and chautauqua. The first chautauqua in the West was held here in 1879. (Chautauquas were camp meetings or summer family vacations of sermons, psalm-singing, uplifting lectures, and simple living.) The small-scale grid of streets between Lighthouse Avenue and Ocean View Boulevard, lined with miniature Victorian cottages that have elaborate and lovingly cared-for landscapes of plants in containers set out in front of them, is a national treasure. This is probably the finest modest seaside Victorian cottage cluster on the West Coast.

Post-Darwinian science came to this Methodist Eden in 1892 when **Timothy Hopkins,** the adopted son of Mark Hopkins, endowed the **Hopkins Marine Laboratory of Stanford University** in Pacific Grove. It studies the rich offshore marine life here. Off the coast at Pacific Grove is the undersea **Marine Gardens Park,** a protected sanctuary for the abundant plants and sea life that thrive here.

The Pacific Grove Museum of Natural History, in town, features local natural history, with displays on the Monarch butterfly migrations and local seaweed.

- **Del Monte Forest/The Seventeen-Mile Drive**

The scenic **Seventeen-Mile Drive** is a private toll road through **Del Monte Forest.** Enter at the Pacific Grove Gate at Sunset Drive, pay the five-dollar fee, and secure the map. Most travelers simply follow the red line along the coast and out the Carmel Gate. You may, however, wander about all the roads in this vast, privately policed forest. Smoking and fires are prohibited. The map has well-marked major sites, and it is highly recommended that you stop at several, get out of the car, and experience this dramatic landscape. Scattered throughout the forest are many private homes in a variety of architectural styles. Off Congress Road near the center of the reservation, and not on the map provided at the gate, is the **S.F.B. Morse Botanical Reserve,** hidden in the heart of the forest.

This superb landscape was originally the Rancho el Pescadero, which sold for $500 in 1846. David Jacks, a Scotsman, purchased it for 12¢ an acre in 1858 and then made a handsome profit when he sold it to railroad baron Charles Crocker's Pacific Improvement Company for $5 an acre. On part of his 7,000-acre barony Crocker erected the ornate Del Monte Hotel, in 1880 (burned in 1924), which became *the* resort for San Francisco society. A private scenic drive circled out from the grand hotel and back.

In 1915 **Samuel F. B. Morse**, grandnephew of the inventor of the telegraph and the 1906 captain of the Yale football team, became the manager of the Pacific Improvement Company. At that point the sand mine on the property was its most profitable asset. Morse began major improvements, building **The Lodge at Pebble Beach** and laying out what became the world-famous **Pebble Beach Golf Course** in 1916. During the opulent 1920s, **Seventeen-Mile Drive** was paved, bridle paths were threaded through the pine and cypress forests, and lots were sold to the wealthy for the construction of palatial seaside mansions. The style imposed on all construction was Spanish or Mediterranean, and Morse engaged the well-known Santa Barbara architect George Washington Smith to design the **Cypress Point Clubhouse**. Smith also designed the most prominent building visible as you enter the Carmel gate, the **Crocker Marble Palace**, begun in 1926. Built for Mrs. Templeton Crocker of the railroad and banking fortune, this mansion is encrusted with Italian marble. Such was its opulence that its private beach was heated with underground pipes! Today many of the luxurious establishments here are owned by large corporations that use them for executive seminars and meetings.

> **Pebble Beach Golf Course**
>
> **Cypress Point Clubhouse**
>
> **Crocker Marble Palace**
>
> **Crocker Grove**
>
> **Lone Cypress**
>
> **Pebble Beach Resort Reservations**
> *(408) 624-6611 or*
> *(800)654-9300*
>
> **AT&T Pebble Beach National ProAm Golf Tournament**
> *P.O. Box 869,*
> *Monterey 93942-0869*

The Monterey cypress and Monterey pine occur naturally only in this small region. The cypress is a rare survivor from the Pleistocene era. **Crocker Grove** preserves the largest stand of these trees. Beyond Cypress Point is the much-photographed **Lone Cypress,** sculpted by the constant winds.

• Pebble Beach

This wealthy residential enclave is surrounded by three of the finest golf courses anywhere. The golf courses skirt the sea and are of an unbelievably brilliant emerald green. The California coast is especially beautiful and pristine here. The low rocky shore is a filigree of eroded granite with scattered pockets of pure white sand. Unique Monterey pines and wind-sculpted Monterey cypresses cling to the rocks and blanket many slopes in great evergreen forests laced with quiet private roads.

The three golf courses that frame Pebble Beach are the **Pebble Beach Golf Links**, the **Spyglass Hill Golf Club**, and the **Cypress Point Club**. In 1990, Tokyo developer Minoru Isutani's Cosmo World Company bought the Pebble Beach Company for $841 million in what unfolded as a highly controversial deal. Critics claimed that Isutani planned to sell $1 billion worth of club memberships in golf-crazy Japan. But the California Coastal Commission, which must rule on changes of use in its jurisdiction, scotched the plan. In 1992, Isutani was forced to sell Pebble Beach for $500 million to a new partnership called Lone Cypress Company backed by Sumitomo Bank and a Japanese golfing company.

Pebble Beach Resort Reservations handles reservations for Spyglass Hill, Spanish Bay, and for Pebble Beach. Reservations for the old Del Monte course are handled by the course office. Master sheets show what days groups are booked; try to avoid groups unless you can be placed well ahead of the field. Remember to reconfirm your tee time twenty-four hours before play. Write for information on the **AT&T Pebble Beach National ProAm Golf Tournament**.

The Lodge at Pebble Beach
Pebble Beach 93953
(408) 624-3811

Harrison Memorial Library
at Ocean and Lincoln

Carmel Art Association
on Lincoln Avenue

- **The Lodge at Pebble Beach**

The Lodge at Pebble Beach was at first a rustic pine log lodge built in 1908 on the vast parklike property of the great Del Monte Hotel. The Del Monte Hotel in the city of Monterey opened in 1880 and, with its companion seven-thousand-acre **Del Monte Forest**, was developed by Charles Crocker's Pacific Improvement Company and linked to San Francisco by the Southern Pacific Railroad. The great gingerbread pile of the "Del" became *the* high society hotel for San Francisco's elite until it burned down, in 1924. To this great railroad-accessible resort wealthy families transported mountains of luggage, their servants, and horses and carriages for the season.

In 1919, when golf first became popular among the elite, the Pebble Beach Golf Links opened here. The Pebble Beach course at the lodge was designed by Jack Neville and Douglas Grant (players, not golf course architects) for Samuel Finley Breeze Morse, the manager of the Pacific Improvement Company.

On the third Sunday of August, the **Concours d'Elegance** is staged here. The velvet lawns are then briefly invaded by green and white striped tents and a string of long, low, luxurious Duesenbergs, Bugattis, Rolls Royces, and other Great Gatsby-style conveyances.

If you leave the Del Monte Forest by the Carmel Gate you will emerge in (almost too) picturesque Carmel, near Ocean Avenue's string of posh shops.

- *Carmel-by-the-Sea*

Carmel is a unique community in California. It began as a seaside colony for professors from Stanford and Berkeley and for writers, artists, musicians, and others seeking peace, quiet, and natural beauty. In 1916, C. W. Johnston described it as "the home of a few artists and literary people, most possibly being cranks." Today it is a decidedly wealthy enclave and the mile-square village is chiefly known for its setting and for what it does *not* have. Restrictive zoning that was passed in the 1920s preserves the residential character of the village of five thousand and strictly controls all commercial development. There are no neon signs, no tall buildings, and no paved sidewalks or streetlights in the residential areas. Houses here have no numbers; mail is picked up at the Post Office, which serves as the nerve center of the village. So zealous is the village about preserving its character that a few years ago it passed an ordinance forbidding outdoor plastic plants. What abides are quaint, flower-bordered cottages nestled under the twisted pines. Many are what the English call "twee." Today Carmel is too expensive for most writers, but in the past it was the occasional home of Jack London, Sinclair Lewis, Upton Sinclair, and poet Robinson Jeffers. The **Harrison Memorial Library** of 1927, designed by Bernard Maybeck, testifies to the strong literary interests of the inhabitants. The **Carmel Art Association** sometimes exhibits local art work, almost all of a soothing, if not soporific, disposition.

- **Ocean Avenue Shops**

Carmel has attracted one of the greatest concentrations of upscale boutiques in the nation. All along Ocean Avenue and overflowing into the side streets of the quaint, one-story town are posh shops selling luxury goods. On weekends the congestion approaches pedestrian gridlock; weekdays are the best time to visit. Carmel's stringent controls prohibit walk-away food, including ice cream cones. The most interesting shop might be **Talbot Ties**, with two shops on Ocean Avenue. At the foot of Ocean Avenue is **Carmel Beach**, one of the prettiest in California. Its white sand makes a perfect spot to sunbathe or picnic, but swimming isn't safe here.

- **Mission San Carlos Borromeo Del Rio Carmelo/ Father Junípero Serra's Tomb**

A few blocks from Ocean Avenue's shopping frenzy is the quadrangle at the **Mission San Carlos Borromeo del Rio Carmelo**. This stone mission, built between 1793 and 1797, is one of California's chief beauty spots. The sunshine, space, and flowers within the quadrangle etch themselves onto the visitor's memory. The yellow stone chapel is the quintessential California mission building. This was Father Serra's favorite mission of the nine he himself founded, and he made it the headquarters of the mission chain.

Born in 1713 on the island of Majorca, **Father Serra** became a Franciscan priest and studied at the Lullian University in Palma de Majorca. There he taught philosophy for fifteen years before becoming the religious leader of the Sacred Expedition sent from Spanish Imperial Mexico City to colonize and evangelize Alta California. In California he was a commissioner of the Inquisition and was known for his fiery preaching and mortification of the flesh through self-flagellation. When he died at Carmel on August 28, 1784 he was buried at the foot of the main altar. The campaign to have Junipero Serra declared a saint continues before the Congregation for the Causes of Saints at the Vatican.

The present stone church was begun in 1793 under Father Lasuen and dedicated in 1797. The church is one of the most romantic buildings in California. It has a Baroque façade with a star-shaped central window and a bell tower capped by a Moorish dome. The church formed part of an irregular, arcaded quadrangle with the priests' quarters, a kitchen, soldiers' quarters, a smithy, a carpenter shop, and girls' quarters arranged around a fountained court. Indian families lived in a village nearby. Under Father Lasuen, the mission reached a peak population of 927 in 1794. In 1833 the mission was closed down by the Mexican government, and by the 1850s nothing remained but ruins.

Talbot Ties
On Ocean Avenue, at Dolores; also on Ocean Avenue at Monte Verde

Carmel Beach
At the foot of Ocean Avenue

Mission San Carlos Borromeo Del Rio Carmelo/ Father Junípero Serra's Tomb
3080 Rio Road at Lasuan, on the south edge of Carmel; Open Monday to Saturday, 9:30 A.M. to 4:30 P.M.; Sunday, 10:30 A.M. to 4:30 P.M. Daily masses posted

Robinson Jeffers'
Tor House
26304 Ocean Avenue
and Stewart Way.
• *At Ocean Avenue turn*
left onto Scenic Road and
continue south to Stewart
Way. There turn left, go
one block, and turn left
again onto Ocean View
Road. Watch for the
granite boulder tower a
little down the road

Open from 10 A.M. to
4 P.M. on Friday and
Saturday; All visitors
must be twelve years of
age or older; Phone
(408) 624-1813 to be
sure the house is open

Restoration began in 1882 when Father Angelo Cassanova, the parish priest at Monterey, had the site cleared and the tombs of Serra, Crespi, and Lasuen identified and examined. In 1884, the mission was inexpertly "restored" with an incongruous peaked roof replacing the original catenary arches. In 1924, Father Ramón Mestres began an accurate restoration of the mission church. In that year a Mortuary Chapel was built next to the old church to house an elaborate California marble sarcophagus by sculptor Jo Mora with bronze figures of Father Serra and Crespi. Also in this chapel is a statue of the Virgin that Father Serra brought with him to the founding of Mission San Diego, the first mission, and then later to Monterey. In a glassed- in altar niche is an extensive collection of the original mission silver ritual objects. Another room houses part of the mission's original library of religious books. In the long process of restoration and rebuilding, the church's peaked roof was replaced with an appropriate arched roof. Excavations in the surrounding bean fields uncovered the outline of the mission's adobe quadrangle. The extensive compound as it appears today is the result of a systematic reconstruction that began in 1931. Harry Downie, the curator of the mission, oversaw the rebuilding, which lasted until about 1937. A new *reredos* was made for the church in 1957, adapted from the antique *reredos* at Mission Dolores in San Francisco. Father Serra's spare cell was also reconstructed. There are historical exhibits in two museums that flank the entrance to the church. In one of them the process of rebuilding is explained. Harry Downie, who created most of what is seen today and who died in 1980, lies buried in the walled mission cemetery to the right of the church. Some of the most romantic gardens in the state surround the old church.

• **Robinson Jeffers' Tor House**

One of California's greatest, and darkest, poets was **Robinson Jeffers**, who came to Carmel in 1914 seeking isolation from the world's madness. Here he communed with this granite coast and its people and wrote poems decrying the folly of mankind and proclaiming the eternal solace of the earth and sea. On a cliff overlooking the ocean he built, with his own hands, a granite house for himself and his wife Una, which he named **Tor House** after the rocky eminence it crowns. From Hawk Tower he scanned the horizon for the swift birds he loved. A copy of Jeffers' *Selected Poems* remains the best companion to this elemental coast.

• **Monastery Beach**

Monastery Beach, or San Jose Creek Beach, is the southern end of the Carmel River State Beach Park. The coarse-grained decomposed granite beach descends steeply from here to the Carmel Submarine Canyon, an underwater canyon more than ten thousand feet deep. Upwelling water here brings the nutrients that feed the exceptionally rich marine life of Carmel Bay. The brown "seaweed" visible just offshore is the top of a stand of kelp. Off this beach is the **Carmel Bay Ecological Reserve** established in 1960, the nation's first underwater marine wilderness reserve. Though divers may explore here, they may not disturb the rich marine life.

This blustery, windy beach has its own glory. The sea here is a vivid aquamarine color that shades off to deep blue edged with white breakers crashing on granite shores.

• **Point Lobos State Reserve**

Point Lobos State Reserve, one of the jewels of the California State Park System, consists of both the 554-acre peninsular reserve south of Carmel Bay and the adjoining 750-acre underwater Ecological Reserve. This dramatic wave-dashed rocky headland is crowned by a great grove of Monterey cypress and fringed by scattered off-shore rocks. The point derives its name, La Punta de los Lobos Marinos (the point of the sea-wolves), from the California and Stellar sea lions whose lusty barking echoes among these rocks. Sea lions, sea otters, pelicans, migrating birds, and gray whales also flourish here. The jagged rocks like frozen waves, the startling color of the aquamarine water in the pocket coves, the churning surf, the complex plant life including wind-sculpted trees and microscopic wild flowers, and the sense that the place is teeming with sleek seals, frolicking sea otters, and wheeling sea birds makes this an unforgettable spot. Children especially love to see the seals and the otters, but adults need the refreshment of nature as well.

In 1933 the Save-the-Redwoods League acquired this almost primeval area and gave it to the State of California for a state park. It and Pebble Beach on the other side of Carmel Bay, are the only places in the world where Monterey cypress occur naturally. The park is laid out with a minimum of roads and the best way to experience its scenic splendor is on foot. The park closes at night to leave its wild denizens free to feed.

Monastery Beach
Immediately off Highway 1, south of Carmel and just north of Point Lobos State Reserve; Free parking along the road

Carmel Bay Ecological Reserve

Point Lobos State Reserve
Immediately off Highway 1, south of Carmel; Open daily from 9 A.M. closing time varies with the season; $6 per car; Free guided nature walks; No smoking, dogs, fishing, specimen collecting, or feeding the animals; picnicking in designated areas only, diving by permit only. Information station and pamphlet-and-book stall at the main parking lot inside the reserve; (408) 624-4909

Some Key Books and Sources

This guide owes much to many other diligent investigations. My general view of American urban development owes much to Jon C. Teaford's **The Unheralded Triumph: City Government in America, 1870–1900** (1985) and to Olivier Zunz's **The Changing Face on Inequality: Urbanization, Industrial Development, and Immigrations in Detroit, 1880–1920** (1982). The journals I have found especially useful have been the **Architect and Engineer** (1890–1930), **San Francisco Municipal Reports** (1861–1917), **San Francisco News Letter** (1856–1928), **San Francisco Real Estate Circular** (1866–1921), and the contemporary reportage of Mr. Gerald D. Adams in the **San Francisco Examiner**. Peter R. Decker's revealing and statistically grounded **Fortunes and Failures: White-Collar Mobility in Nineteenth-Century San Francisco** (1978), and Terrence F. McDonald's almost unreadable **The Parameters of Urban Fiscal Policy: Socioeconomic Change and Political Culture in San Francisco, 1860–1906** (1986) are modern historical scholarship's two gifts to San Francisco's self-understanding. William Issel and Robert W. Cherney's **San Francisco, 1865–1932: Politics, Power, and Urban Development** (1986) is a good political history but stops short of the San Francisco we know today. Unfortunately, the narrow vision of contemporary historians has precluded a general history as wide-ranging as John P. Young's **San Francisco: A History of the Pacific Coast Metropolis** (1912). Today each reader must forge his or her own synthesis from many fine, but specialized, studies. We need fewer studies of ethnic and sexual groups seen in artificial isolation and more synthetic works on the city's social classes, their interrelationships, and the evolution of San Francisco's tolerant common culture. For there is a common culture that is distinctively San Franciscan, and it is this culture that has permitted so many minority groups their dignity and their place in this civilized city. Not since Howard S. Becker edited **Culture and Civility in San Francisco** (1971) has the definition of this culture been attempted.

Index

O

Oakland Museum, 53, 455–56
Oak Street (1700 block), 366
Ocean Beach, 390–91
Octagon House, 55, 223. *See
also* Feusier Octagon House
Octavia Street (2400 block), 277
Old Bank of America
Headquarters, 122
Old Bush Street Synagogue, 296
Old Chinese Telephone
Exchange, 159
Old Federal Reserve Bank, 127
Old Hale Brothers, 80
Old Hibernia Bank, 417
Old Notre Dame School, 319–20
Old St. John's Lutheran Church,
327
Old St. Mary's Roman Catholic
Church, 154
Old Speedway Meadow, 387
Old Telegraph Hill Dwellers
Association Clinic, 185–86
Old Transamerica Building,
104–5
Old United States Mint, 55, 89
Olympic Club, 81
O'Neill (Eugene) National
Historic Site, 460
Open Studio/SF, 310

P

Pacific Avenue
500 block, 107–8
2000 block, 276–77
Pacific Coast Stock Exchange,
129
Pacific Film Archive, 54
Pacific Grove, 478–80

Pacific Heights, eastern, 261–65
best time to tour, 260
map, 259
parking, 260
restaurants, cafés, and bars,
260
tour of, 265–81
transportation to, 260
Pacific Heritage Museum, 55,
113–14, 156
Pacific Telephone and Telegraph
Company Headquarters,
100, 102, 137
Pacific Telesis Tower, 101,
134–35
Pacific–Union Club, 244–45
Page Street
1500 block, 365
1700 block, 367–68
1800 block, 369
1900 block, 369
Palace Hotel, 136
Palace of Fine Arts, 281,
399–400
Panhandle, 356, 366
Pan Pacific Hotel, 81
Park Branch Public Library, 368
Park Hyatt Hotel, 127
Parking, 25–26. *See also
individual neighborhoods*
Park Lane Apartments, 247
Pershing Hall, 406
Pershing Square, 406
Phelan, James D., 266–67
Phoenix Theater, 68
Pier 39, 205
Pier 45, 204–5
Pine Street (900 block), 243
Point Lobos, 392
Point Reyes National Seashore,
445–46

Polk Street, 254
Pony Express, 113
Population, 10–11
Portals of the Past, 387
Portsmouth Square, 151, 157
Post offices
Chinatown, 150, 168
Philatelic Unit, 73
Precita Eyes Mural Arts Center,
313
Presidio
best time to tour, 398
map, 397
parking, 398
tour of, 400–408
transportation to, 398–99
Presidio Army General Hospital,
402
Presidio Museum, 56, 240, 398,
404–5
Public transit, 26–27. *See also*
Cable cars *and individual
neighborhoods*
Purple Onion, 180

Q

Queen Wilhelmina Tulip Garden,
389
Quong Sang Chong & Company,
159

R

Rainbow Falls, 387
Randall (Joseph D.) Junior
Museum, 55
Recreational vehicle parks, 48
Redwood Park, 111
Refugee Cottages, 404–5
Reservations, 16
Residence clubs. *See* Lodgings

About the Author

Randolph Delehanty was born in 1944 in Memphis, Tennessee, and raised in Englewood and Tenafly, New Jersey. He grew up in a bilingual family and speaks English and Spanish. He holds degrees in history from Georgetown University, the University of Chicago, and Harvard University, where he was a University Prize Fellow. In 1970 he moved to Berkeley and began researching California history at the Bancroft Library on the University of California campus. From 1973 to 1978 he was the first historian for The Foundation for San Francisco's Architectural Heritage. In 1983 he returned to Harvard for two years to study American history and to complete his doctorate. For many years he taught in the Humanities Department at San Francisco State University. Randolph Delehanty has also written *California: A Guidebook*. With photographer E. Andrew McKinney he wrote *Preserving the West*, a survey of the state of landscape and architectural preservation in the seven far western states for the National Trust for Historic Preservation. He and photographer Richard Sexton co-authored *In the Victorian Style*, on San Francisco's fanciful domestic architecture, and *New Orleans: Elegance and Decadence*, an interpretation of the unique culture and lifestyle of the Crescent City, both published by Chronicle Books. He lives in the Faubourg Marigny in New Orleans and is the curator of the Roger Houston Ogden Collection of Southern art in New Orleans. He is working on a major book on visual art in the American South drawn from The Ogden Collection, with photographer Van Jones Martin, on *Classic Natchez*, and on a guide to New Orleans to be published by Chronicle Books. He can be contacted through Chronicle Books or at The Ogden Collection, 460 Broadway Street, New Orleans, LA 70118.

About the Artists

William Walters was born in 1953 in Gainesville, Florida. He studied architecture at the University of Florida and graduated in 1974. In that year he moved to San Francisco. He is the principal in Walters Architects in San Francisco. He lives on Potrero Hill with his wife and young daughter. He can be contacted at Walters Architects, 1246 Eighteenth Street, San Francisco, CA 94107.

John Tomlinson is an illustrator and geodetic surveyor and lives in Portland, Oregon. He was born in 1946 in Portland and studied geography at Portland State University, where he graduated in 1972. His bird's-eye views begin with postage-stamp size sketches of each building and block as seen by the walker. He then assembles, manipulates, and redrafts these sketches as a single view. He can be contacted at P.O. Box 8714, Portland, OR 97207.